D1193159

AMERICAN MEDICINAL PLANTS

AN ILLUSTRATED AND DESCRIPTIVE GUIDE TO PLANTS
INDIGENOUS TO AND NATURALIZED IN THE UNITED STATES
WHICH ARE USED IN MEDICINE

Charles F. Millspaugh

WITH
A NEW TABLE OF REVISED CLASSIFICATION
AND NOMENCLATURE BY

E. S. HARRAR

James B. Duke Emeritus Professor of Wood Science,
Duke University

DOVER PUBLICATIONS, INC.
NEW YORK

Copyright © 1974 by Dover Publications, Inc.
All rights reserved under Pan American and International Copyright Conventions.

Published in Canada by General Publishing Company, Ltd., 30 Lesmill Road, Don Mills, Toronto, Ontario.
Published in the United Kingdom by Constable and Company, Ltd..

This Dover edition, first published in 1974, is a one-volume, unabridged republication of the work as published by John C. Yorston & Company, Philadelphia, in two volumes in 1892 under the title *Medicinal Plants*.
This edition also contains a new table of revised classification and nomenclature prepared by E. S. Harrar.
See Publisher's Note to the Dover Edition, page viii, for further bibliographical details.

International Standard Book Number: 0-486-23034-1
Library of Congress Catalog Card Number: 73-91487

Manufactured in the United States of America
Dover Publications, Inc.
180 Varick Street
New York, N.Y. 10014

TO

JOHN HILL MILLSPAUGH, Artist

MY BELOVED FATHER

TO WHOM I AM INDEBTED FOR WHATEVER I MAY POSSESS
OF ART IN DRAWING AND COLORING

THE PLATES

ARE GRATEFULLY DEDICATED

TO

TIMOTHY F. ALLEN, A. M., M. D.

MY HONORED PROFESSOR AND PRECEPTOR

THE TEXT OF THIS WORK

IS RESPECTFULLY INSCRIBED

CONTENTS

FULL–PAGE PLATES WITH DESCRIPTIVE TEXT

APPENDIX

PUBLISHER'S NOTE
TO THE DOVER EDITION

In preparing this inexpensive reprint edition, it has, of course, been necessary to modify somewhat the handsome but extremely costly format of the original work. The most drastic alteration is perhaps the conversion of all of the full-page colored plates to black-and-white halftones. However, thanks to the present high quality of offset lithographic photography, the minute but essential detail in the plates has been preserved. Thus, if the reader will refer to the plates in conjunction with Dr. Millspaugh's full textual descriptions of the natural coloring of the plants, very little if any of the essential information contained in the originals will be lost. We have attempted to facilitate this process by placing the illustrations opposite either the caption or the text description wherever possible.

When examining the plates in this edition, the reader should keep in mind that all the illustrations are approximately 18 per cent smaller than those in the original work, whereas all indications of scale are those of the original edition.

This edition contains, in addition to the original serial pagination, a new consecutive pagination.

The reader's attention is directed to the new table (page xvii) prepared by Dr. E. S. Harrar, which reflects changes in the classification and nomenclature of the plants that have been made since the original publication.

PREFACE

In preparing for the use of students of *materia medica* this systematic account of Medicinal Plants in the order of their botanical classification, the Publishers desire to call attention to its important features, and explanation of arrangement, which they believe will show it to be one of the best works of the kind ever prepared, and offered for the use and benefit of the profession.

The work occupied over five years of continuous labor, in addition to many years of preparatory work, on the part of the careful and talented author, who, besides being a physician, is well known as an accomplished botanist, and artist, and the fact that the coloring and drawings are by his own hand is a sufficient guarantee of their accuracy.

The study of botany for medical remedies, or any other purpose, *without colored plates* would be like the study of osteology without bones, or the study of geography without maps. However comprehensive or practical a text-book may be, its verbal description cannot compare in value with a sight of the thing described, or what is next best, its faithful representation.

The following are some of the features and arrangement referred to, viz.:

1°. The 180 beautifully COLORED FULL-PAGE plates, embodying over 1000 minor drawings, illustrating the root, stem, leaves, calyx, flower, corolla, stamen, filament, anther, ovary, fruit, seed, etc., are all made to a mechanical scale, and drawn from the plants as they stood in the soil, by the author, the coloring is *natural*, without regard to artistic beauty or pleasing fancy, executed from fresh living individual plants, selected with especial reference to typical features, propitious soil, and natural localities, in which he was aided, by experienced botanists.

2°. The plants are arranged in the work in their NATURAL ORDER, given in prominent type, and under the first plant of each order *the order* itself being described, and the properties of most of the medicinal plants of other countries of the world coming under such order mentioned, thereby giving information upon over ONE THOUSAND MEDICINAL PLANTS.

3°. Then follows the TRIBE,—should the order be a large one, to give a correct idea of its place.

4°. Then the GENUS is mentioned in black-faced type, with foot-notes, showing, wherever possible, the derivation of the name.

5°. Then the name of the Botanist who classified it, and lastly, in this department is given the old, or sexual, arrangement according to Linnæus.

6°. All of this is considered essential, as it is conceded that plants of like
botanical, and therefore chemical nature, have a similar action, giving
a class of what we may term *generic* symptoms, though each has its
special (*specific*) symptoms that characterize it. It is for this reason
that the plants here treated of are arranged as above; for, if alpha-
betically arranged, the work would have lost at least one-half its value.

7°. Then follows the Botanical and common names.

8°. Then the Synonymy which follows has become necessary, as most species,
unfortunately, have received more than one name, resulting mostly
from two causes: first, that of different views held concerning the limits
of the genera and species; and, second, from an unavoidable ignorance
in the discoverer, in a given locality, of the previous discovery of the
plant in another. The descriptive binominal system, invented by Linnæus
in 1753, is the earliest date any such names can have, though many
plants had been quite fully described before that time. It becomes,
therefore, quite a necessity in all botanical works that full mention of
aliases should be made, to render reference to earlier writers satisfactory.
The Common Names in the English, French and German languages,
under which the plant is known in different localities and countries.

9°. Then follows a Description of the plant, which is condensed even at a
sacrifice of grammatical construction, using botanical terms freely, but
not unreservedly; where several species of a genus occur in sequence,
the genus is separately described to avoid repetition, and under the
first genus of any order the natural order itself is described in brief.

10°. Then the origin of the plant, its geographical distribution throughout the
United States, its favorite locations and time of flowering; this is followed by a concise history of the species, and fully describes the uses
of the plant for Medicinal purposes, from the earliest known period,
according to the Aborigines, and *all schools* of practice in Medicine.

11°. Then follows a mention of the part used, and the various preparations
in use in *general* pharmacopœias, which are, chiefly according to the
text of the last revision (6th) of the "United States Pharmacopœia,"
and the "American Homœopathic Pharmacopœia." The description of
the physical properties is, however, *original* and of great value.

12°. Then the Chemical Constituents or nature of the plants.

13°. The Physiological action of the plants is described symptomatically,
cases of *actual toxic effects* are duly noted, and its scope is also very
full in pharmacology.

14°. It contains a GLOSSARY of botanical names.

15°. A Bibliography, and Bibliographical Index to the works consulted in general, amongst which the following are only a few of those consulted, viz.: Drs. Robert Bentley, F. L. S., and Henry Trimen, M. B., F. L. S., "*Medicinal Plants*," London. Dr. Wm. P. C. Barton, "*Vegetable Materia Medica of the United States*." Dr. Jacob Bigelow's "*American Medical Botany*." Drs. Friedrich A. Flückiger and David Hambury, F. L. S., "*Pharmacographia*,"—a history of drugs of vegetable origin met with in Great Britain and India. Dr. William Woodville, "*Medical Botany*," London. The "*American Homœopathic Pharmacopœia*." The "*Pharmacopœia of the United States*." Dr. G. Spratt's "*Medicinal Plants*," admitted into the London, Edinburgh and Dublin Pharmacopœias. "*New Homœopathic Pharmacopœia*" of Buchner and Gruner. Dr. Asa Gray's "*Flora of North America*," and "*Genera of the Plants of the United States*." John Lindley's, Ph. D., F. R. S., "*Flora Medica*," London.

16°. A carefully prepared GENERAL INDEX is given in order to render it easy of consultation, whereby any plate, reference or subject matter thereto can be quickly found.

17°. Also a THERAPEUTIC INDEX showing the use of remedies for the cure of disease, a very practical and valuable feature of the work, and one that will be found of great assistance to physicians, pharmacists and chemists.

18°. And INDEXES OF COMMON NAMES of the Plants in both the French and German languages, whereby they can be easily found in the work, by the names they are known in those countries.

19°. In conclusion, THE AUTHOR says:—I offer my thanks to many who have kindly contributed to whatever success this work may attain. To the many authors from whose books, pamphlets, and articles I have drawn, I must generalize my obligation, hoping that personal references in the text will in all cases be found satisfactory. To the late Professor Asa Gray, who, in disinterested kindness, allowed me the unreserved use of his many most valuable works on our American Flora, my special consideration is due. To the following botanists who willingly lent their aid in procuring many species not growing near my locations, I can but generally acknowledge: Mr. J. H. Sears, Salem, Mass.; Dr. T. F. Lucy, Elmira, N. Y.; Mr. F. V. Coville, Ithaca, N. Y.; Mr. C. H. Gross, Landisville, N. J.; Mr. J. A. Shafer, Pittsburgh, Pa.; Miss Mary C. Cuthbert, Augusta, Ga.; Messrs. J. U. and C. G. Lloyd, Cincinnati, O.; Mr. James Galen, Rawlinsville, Pa.; Miss M. C. Reynolds, St. Augustine, Fla.; Dr. Thos. M. Wood, Wilmington, N. C.; Rev. E. V. Campbell, St. Cloud, Minn.; and Mr. A. B. Seymour, Champaign, Ill.

THE PUBLISHERS.

NATURAL ARRANGEMENT
OF THE PLANTS INCLUDED IN THIS WORK.

Dicotyledonous Phænogams.

RANUNCULACEÆ.

Anemoneæ.
Anemone patens, var Nuttal-
   liana, 1
Anemone triloba, 2
Ranunculeæ.
Ranunculus sceleratus, 3
                repens, 4
                bulbosus, 5
                acris, 6
Helleborineæ.
Caltha palustris, 7
Helleborus viridis, 8
Cimicifugeæ.
Hydrastis Canadensis, 9
Actæa alba, 10
Cimicifuga racemosa, 11

MAGNOLIACEÆ.

Magnolia glauca, 12

ANONACEÆ.

Asimina triloba, 13

MENISPERMACEÆ.

Menispermum Canadense, 14

BERBERIDACEÆ.

Berberis vulgaris, 15
Caulophyllum thalictroides, 16
Podophyllum peltatum, 17

NYMPHACEÆ.

Nymphæa odorata, 18

SARRACENIACEÆ.

Sarracenia purpurea, 19

PAPAVERACEÆ.

Argemone Mexicana, 20
Chelidonium majus, 21
Sanguinaria Canadensis, 22

CRUCIFERÆ.

Brassiceæ.
Brassica alba, 23
          nigra, 24
Lepidineæ.
Capsella Bursa-pastoris, 25
Raphaneæ.
Raphanus Raphanistrum, 26

VIOLACEÆ.

Viola tricolor, 27

CISTACEÆ.

Helianthemum Canadense, 28

DROSERACEÆ.

Drosera rotundifolia, 29

HYPERICACEÆ.

Hypericum perforatum, 30

CARYOPHYLLACEÆ.

Lychnis Githago, 31

GERANIACEÆ.

Geranium maculatum, 32

RUTACEÆ.

Xanthoxylum Americanum, 33
Ptelea trifoliata, 34

SIMARUBACEÆ.

Ailantus glandulosus, 35

ANACARDIACEÆ.

Rhus glabra, 36
      venenata, 37
      Toxicodendron, 38
      aromatica, 39

VITACEÆ.

Ampelopsis quinquefolia, 40

RHAMNACEÆ.

Rhamnus catharticus, 41

CELASTRACEÆ.

Euonymus atropurpureus, 42

SAPINDACEÆ.

Æsculus Hippocastanum, 43
         glabra, 44

POLYGALACEÆ.

Polygala Senega, 45

LEGUMINOSÆ.

Genisteæ.
Genista tinctoria, 46
Trifolieæ.
Trifolium pratense, 47
          repens, 48
Melilotus officinalis, 49
          alba, 49
Galegeæ.
Robinia Pseudacacia, 50

Monocotyledonous Phænogams.

Acrogenous Cryptogams.

ADDITIONS AND CORRECTIONS.

As might be expected in a work issued in parts, and extending over a long period of time, many inequalities of treatment will be found. The following corrections are some of the more noticeable:

Page 14-2, line 15, for "*A. platyphyllus*," read *C. platyphyllus*.
"   15-2, "   2 from bottom, for "lava," read Clava.
"   23-2, " 21 for "Maritiima," read Maritima.
"   35-2, "   5, for "*Simarouba*," read *Simaruba*.
"   35-2, "   2 from bottom, the same correction.
"   41-3, foot-note, for "Rhamneitne," read Rhamnetine.
"   46-2, line 6, for "*Copiava*," read *Copaiva*.
"   46-2, " 20, for "*Cyticus*," read *Cytisus*.
"   46-3, " 19, for "*augustifolia*," read *angustifolia*.
"   46-3, " 28, for "*Psoralia*," read *Psoralea*.
"   49-2, " 16, for "*Dipterix*," read *Dipteryx*.
"   77,   "   9, for "reeping," read Creeping.
"   85-2, " 24, for "Etsupra," read Et supra.
"   110-2, " 13 from bottom, for "emale," read female.
"   128-2, " 12 from bottom, for "*chinensis*," read *Chinensis*.
"   129-2, " 14, for "Centuary," read Centaury.
"   133,   last foot-note is now unnecessary.
"   141,   line 3 from bottom, for "*moorcroftianum*," read *Moorcroftianum*.
"   134-3, Description of Plate, for "A cluster of Follicles," read A follicle; and add, 5. A section of the root.
"   147-2, line 17, for "*cyparissias*," read *Cyparissias*.
"   160-3, " 19, for "cerefera," read cerifera.
"   164-2, foot-note, for "*Ut supra*," read *Et supra*.

Plate 66 should be titled Thaspium aureum.
"   107, the spike of flowers is not broad enough; it should have been more fusiform. As it now is, the plate much more resembles *Plantago Rugelii* than *P. major*.
"   158, should be titled Castanea vesca, var. Americana.

TABLE OF REVISED CLASSIFICATION
AND NOMENCLATURE

THERE have been numerous revisions in the classification and technical nomenclature of American plants and plant groups since the publication of *American Medicinal Plants* in 1892. The following table, which parallels Dr. Millspaugh's "Natural Arrangement of the Plants Included in This Work" (pp. xiii-xv) reflects those changes and also includes the common name or names most frequently encountered in the botanical literature for each of the 180 described species.

RANUNCULACEAE, Crowfoot family

1. *Anemone patens* var. *wolfgangiana* (Bess.) Koch
   Spreading pasque-flower, Prairie-smoke

2. *Hepatica americana* (DC.) Ker
   Roundlobe hepatica, Hepatica, Liverleaf

3. *Ranunculus sceleratus* L.
   Cursed crowfoot, Blister buttercup

4. *Ranunculus repens* L.
   Creeping buttercup, Creeping spearwort

5. *Ranunculus bulbosus* L.
   Bulb or Bulbous buttercup

6. *Ranunculus acris* L.
   Tall or Common buttercup

7. *Caltha palustris* L.
   Cowslip, Marshmarigold, King-cup

8. *Helleborus viridis* L.
   Green hellebore, Winter-aconite

9. *Hydrastis canadensis* L.
   Goldenseal, Tumeric

10. *Actaea pachypoda* Ell.
    White baneberry, White cohosh, Doll's-eyes

11. *Cimicfuga racemosa* (L.) Nutt.
    Black snakeroot, Cohosh, Cohosh bugbane

MAGNOLIACEAE, Magnolia family

12. *Magnolia virginiana* L.
    Sweetbay, Swampbay

ANNONACEAE, Custard-apple family

13. *Asimina triloba* (L.) Dunal
    Common pawpaw

MENISPERMIACEAE, Moonseed family

14. *Menispermum canadense* L.
    Common moonseed, Yellow parilla

BERBERIDACEAE, Barberry family

15. *Berberis vulgaris* L.
    European barberry, Common barberry

16. *Caulophyllum thalictroides* (L.) Michx.
    Blue cohosh, Papooseroot

17. *Podophyllum peltatum* L.
    Common mayapple, Wild jalap

NYMPHAEACEAE, Waterlily family

18. *Nymphaea odorata* Ait.
    Fragrant waterlily, American waterlily

SARRACENIACEAE, Pitcherplant family

19. *Sarracenia purpurea* L.
    Common pitcherplant, Sidesaddle-flower

PAPAVERACEAE, Poppy family

20. *Argemone mexicana* L.
    Mexican pricklepoppy, Prickly poppy

21. *Chelidonium majus* L.
    Celandine

22. *Sanguinaria canadensis* L.
    Bloodroot, Red poccoon

CRUCIFERAE, Mustard family

23. *Brassica hirta* Moench
    White mustard

24. *Brassica nigra* (L.) Koch
    Black mustard

25. *Capsella bursa-patoris* (L.) Medic.
    Pickpocket, Shepherd's purse

60. *Oenothera biennis* L.
    Evening-primrose

CACTACEAE, Cactus family

61. *Opuntia humifusa* Raf.
    Prickly-pear

UMBELLIFERAE, Parsley family

62. *Eryngium yuccifolium* Michx.
    Button snakeroot, Rattlesnake-master

63. *Pastinaca sativa* L.
    Parsnip, Garden parsnip

64. *Angelica atropurpurea* L.
    Purple-stem angelica, Alexanders

65. *Aethusa cynapium* L.
    Fools parsley

66. *Thaspium trifoliatum* (L.) Gray
    Meadow-parsnip

67. *Cicuta maculata* L.
    Spotted cowbane, Spotted water-hemlock

68. *Conium maculatum* L.
    Poison-hemlock

ARALIACEAE, Ginseng family

69. *Aralia racemosa* L.
    Hercules-club, Devil's-walking stick, Spikenard

70. *Panax quinquifolius* L.
    Ginseng, Sang

CORNACEAE, Dogwood family

71. *Cornus florida* L.
    Flowering dogwood

72. *Cornus rugosa* Lam.
    Roundleaf dogwood

73. *Cornus amomum* Mill.
    Silky dogwood

CAPRIFOLIACEAE, Honeysuckle family

74. *Triosteum perfoliatum* L.
    Tinker's-weed, Wild-coffee, Horsegentian

75. *Sambucus canadensis* L.
    Common elderberry

RUBIACEAE, Madder family

76. *Cephalanthus occidentalis* L.
    Buttonbush

77. *Mitchella repens* L.
    Partridgeberry, Running-box

COMPOSITAE, Composite family

78. *Eupatorium purpureum* L.
    Sweet or Common Joe-Pye-weed, Blue-stem Joe-pye-weed

79. *Eupatorium perfoliatum* L.
    Thoroughwort, Boneset

80. *Erigeron canadensis* L.
    Horseweed, Horseweed fleabane

81. *Inula helenium* L.
    Elecampane

82. *Ambrosia artermisiaefolia* L.
    Common ragweed

83. *Helianthus annus* L.
    Common sunflower

84. *Anthemis nobilis* L.
    Garden chamomile, Roman chamomile

85. *Achillea millefolium* L.
    Common yarrow, Milfoil

86. *Tanacetum vulgare* L.
    Common tansy, Golden-buttons

87. *Artemisia vulgaris* L.
    Mugwort, Mugwort wormwood

88. *Artemisia absinthium* L.
    Common wormwood

89. *Gnaphalium obtusifolium* var. *praecox* Fer.
    Catfoot, Fragrant cudweed

90. *Erechthites hieracifolia* (L.) Raf.
    Pilwort, Fireweed, American burnweed

91. *Senecio aureus* L.
    Golden ragwort, Golden groundsel, Squaw-weed

92. *Arctium lappa* L.
    Great burdock

93. *Cichorium intybus* L.
    Common chicory, Blue sailors

94. *Prenanthes serpentaria* Pursh.
    Lion's foot

95. *Taraxacum officinale* Weber
    Common dandelion

96. *Lactuca canadensis* L.
    Lettuce, Canadian lettuce

CAMPANULACEAE

97. *Lobelia cardinalis* L.
    Cardinal-flower

98. *Lobelia syphilitica* L.
    Blue cardinal-flower, Bigblue lobelia

99. *Lobelia inflata* L.
    Indian tobacco

ERICACEAE, Heath family

100. *Arctostaphylos uva-ursi* (L.) Spreng
    Bearberry, Kinnikinick

101. *Epigaea repens* L.
    Trailing arbutus, Mayflower

102. *Gaultheria procumbens* L.
Teaberry, Checkerberry wintergreen

103. *Kalmia latifolia* L.
Mountain-laurel

PYROLACEAE, Wintergreen family

104. *Chimaphila umbellata* var. *cisatlantica* Blake
Pipsissewa, Prince's pine

105. *Monotropa uniflora* L.
Indianpipe

AQUIFOLIACEAE, Holly family

106. *Ilex verticillata* (L.) Gray
Winterberry, Black-alder

PLANTAGINACEAE, Plantain family

107. *Plantago major* L.
Common plantain, Rippleseed plantain

PRIMULACEAE, Primrose family

108. *Anagallis arvensis* L.
Common or Scarlet pimpernel

BIGNONIACEAE

109. *Catalpa bignonioides* Walt.
Southern catalpa

SCROPHULARIACEAE, Figwort Family

110. *Verbascum thapsus* L.
Common mullein, Flannel mullein

111. *Linaria vulgaris* Hill
Butter-and-eggs, Butter-and-eggs toad-flax

112. *Scrophularia nodosa* L.
Figwort, Wood figwort

113. *Chelone glabra* L.
Balmony, White turtlehead

114. *Veronicastrum virginicum* (L.) Farw.
Culver-root, Culverphysic

115. *Euphrasia officinalis* L.
Eyebright, Drug euphrasia

LABITAE, Mint family

116. *Mentha piperita* L.
Peppermint

117. *Lycopus virginicus* L.
Water-horehound, Buglewood

118. *Hedeoma pulegioides* (L.) Pers.
Pennyroyal, False-pennyroyal, Pudding-grass

119. *Collinsonia canadensis* L.
Richweed, Stonewort, Citronella horse-balm

120. *Scutellaria lateriflora* L.
Mad-dog skullcap, Sideflowering skullcap

121. *Lamium album* L.
Snowflake, White deadnettle

HYDROPHYLLACEAE, Waterleaf family

122. *Hydrophyllum virginicum* L.
John's-cabbage, Virginia waterleaf

CONVOLVULACEAE, Convolvulus family

123. *Convolvulus arvensis* L.
Field bindweed, European glorybind

SOLANACEAE, Nightshade family

124. *Solanum dulcamara* L.
Deadly nightshade, Bitter nightshade

125. *Solanum nigrum* L.
Black nightshade

126. *Hyoscyamus niger* L.
Black henbane

127. *Datura stamonium* L.
Jimsonweed

128. *Nicotiana tobacum* L.
Common tobacco

GENTIANACEAE, Gentian family

129. *Menyanthes trifoliata* L.
Buckbean, Common bogbean

LOGANIACEAE, Logania family

130. *Gelsemium sempervirens* (L.) Ait.
Carolina jessamine, Evergreen trumpet-flower

131. *Spiglea marilandica* L.
Indian-pink, Pinkroot spiglea

APOCYNACEAE, Dogbane family

132. *Apocynum androsaemifolium* L.
Spreading dogbane

133. *Apocynum cannabinum* L.
Indian hemp, Indian dogbane

ASCLEPIADACEAE, Milkweed family

134. *Asclepias syriaca* L.
Common milkweed

135. *Asclepias tuberosa* L.
Butterfly milkweed, Chigger-flower

OLEACEAE, Olive family

136. *Chionanthus virginicus* L.
Fringetree, Old-man's-beard

137. *Fraxinus americana* L.
White ash

ARISTOLOCHIACEAE Birthwort family

138. *Aristolochia serpentaria* L.
Virginia snakewood, Dutchman's pipe

PHYTOLACCACEAE, Pokeweed family

139. *Phytolacca americana* L.
Pokeweed, Pigeonberry

CHENOPODIACEAE, Goosefoot family

140. *Chenopodium ambrosioides* var. *anthelminticum* (L.) Gray
Wormseed, Drug wormseed goosefoot

POLYGONACEAE, Buckwheat family

141. *Polygonum punctatum* Ell.
Dotted smartweed, Water smartweed

142. *Fagopyrum sagittatum* Gilib.
Common buckwheat

143. *Rumex crispus* L.
Yellow dock, Curly dock

144. *Rumex obtusifolius* L.
Red-veined dock, Bitter dock

LAURACEAE, Laurel family

145. *Lindera benzoin* (L.) Blume
Spicebush

THYMELACEAE, Mezereum family

146. *Dirca palustris* L.
Leatherwood, Moosewood

EUPHORBIACEAE, Spurge family

147. *Euphorbia maculata* L.
Eyebane, Spotted eyebane

148. *Euphorbia corollata* L.
Flowering spurge, Tramp's spurge

149. *Euphorbia ipecacuanhae* L.
Wild ipecac, Carolina ipecac

150. *Euphorbia lathyris* L.
Caper spurge, Mole-plant

151. *Stillingia sylvatica* L.
Queen's-delight

ULMACEAE, Elm family

152. *Celtis occidentalis* L.
Common hackberry

URTICACEAE, Nettle family

153. *Urtica urens* L.
Burning nettle

CANNABINACEAE, Hemp family

154. *Cannabis sativa* L.
Hemp, Marijuana

155. *Humulus lupulus* L.
Common hop

JUGLANDACEAE, Walnut family

156. *Juglans cinerea* L.
Butternut

157. *Carya tomentosa* Nutt.
Mockernut hickory

FAGACEAE, Beech family

158. *Castanea dentata* (Marsh.) Borkh.
American chestnut

BETULACEAE

159. *Ostrya virginiana* (Mill.) K. Koch
Hophornbeam

MYRICACEAE, Wax-myrtle family

160. *Myrica cerifera* L.
Wax-myrtle

SALICACEAE, Willow family

161. *Salix purpurea* L.
Purple-osier, Basket willow

162. *Populus tremuloides* Michx.
Quaking aspen

PINACEAE, Pine family

163. *Picea mariana* (Mill.) B.S.P.
Black spruce

164. *Tsuga canadensis* (L.) Carr.
Eastern hemlock

CUPRESSACEAE, Cedar family

165. *Thuja occidentalis* L.
Eastern white-cedar, Arborvitae

166. *Juniperus virginiana* L.
Eastern redcedar

ARACEAE, Arum family

167. *Arisaema triphyllum* (L.) Schott
Small Jack-in-the-pulpit, Indian Jack-in-
the-pulpit

168. *Arisaema dracontium* (L.) Schott
Green-dragon, Dragon-root

169. *Symplocarpus foetidus* (L.) Nutt.
Skunk-cabbage

ORCHIDACEAE, Orchid family

170. *Cypripedium calceolus* var. *pubescens*
(Willd.) Correll
Large yellow lady's-slipper
Golden slipper, Moccasin-flower

HAEMORODACEAE, Bloodwort family

171. *Lachnanthes tinctoria* (Walt.) Ell.
     Redroot, Blood redroot

172. Transferred to the Liliaceae, q.v.

IRIDACEAE, Iris family

173. *Iris versicolor* L.
     Blue flag, Poison flag

DIOSCOREACEAE, Yam family

174. *Dioscorea villosa* L.
     Yam, Atlantic yam

LILIACEAE, Lily family

172. *Aletris farinosa* L.
     Stargrass, Watertube stargrass

175. *Trillium erectum* var. *album* (Michx.)
     Pursh.
     White-flowered trillium

176. *Veratrum viride* Ait.
     White hellebore, Itchweed, Falsehellebore

177. *Chamaelirium luteum* (L.) Gray
     Blazing-star, Fairywand

178. *Lilium superbum* L.
     Turk's-cap lily

EQUISETACEAE, Horsetail family

179. *Equisetum hyemale* L.
     Scouring-rush

LYCOPODIACEAE

180. *Lycopodium clavatum* L.
     Running-pine, Running club-moss

PLATES 1 TO 166.

SERIES

PHÆNOGAMIA.

Plants producing true flowers and seeds.

CLASS

DICOTYLEDONS.

Plants with stems composed of bark, wood, and pith; netted veined leaves; and a pair or more of opposite or whorled seed-leaves (cotyledons).

[To precede plate 1.]

GENUS.—**ANEMONE,*** LINN.

SEX. SYST.—POLYANDRIA POLYGNIA.

1

PULSATILLA NUTTALLIANA.

PASQUE FLOWER.

SYN.—ANEMONE PATENS, VAR. NUTTALLIANA, GRAY; ANEMONE NUTTALLIANA, D. C.; ANEMONE LUDOVICIANA, NUTT.; ANEMONE FLAVESCENS, ZUCC.; CLEMATIS HIRSUTISSIMA, POIR; PULSATILLA PATENS, GRAY; PULSATILLA PATENS VAR.; WOLFGANGIANA, TRAUVT; PULSATILLA NUTTALLIANA, GRAY.

COM. NAMES.—PASQUE FLOWER (CROCUS, MAY FLOWER, PRAIRIE FLOWER, AMERICAN PULSATILLA, HARTSHORN PLANT, GOSLINWEED).

A TINCTURE OF THE WHOLE FRESH PLANT, ANEMONE PATENS, VAR. NUTTALLIANA, GRAY.

Description.—This beautiful prairie flower grows to a height of from 4 to 10 inches, from a branched perennial *root.* *Stem* erect and hairy, encircled near the flower by a many-cleft, silky-haired *involucre*, composed of numerous linnear, acute lobes, which form the true stem-leaves. *Leaves* upon long hairy petioles, rising more or less erect from the rootstock; they are ternately divided, the lateral divisions sessile and deeply 2-cleft, the central stalked and 3-cleft; all the segments deeply incised into narrow, linnear, acute lobes, smooth above and hairy beneath. *Inflorescence* a conspicuous, terminal, villous, light purplish-blue flower, fully developed and fertilized before the appearance of the true leaves. *Sepals* generally 5, at first incumbent, then spreading, answering to petals in appearance; villous upon their outer surface. *Petals* wanting, or replaced by minute glandular bodies, resembling abortive stamens. *Stamens* innumerable, in a dense circlet surrounding the pistils; *filaments* slender; *anthers* extrose, 2-celled; *pollen* with three longitudinal, deep sulci. *Pistils* numerous, in a dense cluster, separate, hairy; *style* long and slender, with a somewhat recurved summit; *stigma* indefinate. *Fruit* a plumose head, similar to that of *Clematis;* *carpels* 1-seeded, with long feathery tails, composed of the lengthened, persistent, hairy styles. *Seeds* suspended.

Ranunculaceæ.—This natural order is composed of herbs and woody climbers.

---

* Ἄνεμος; *anemos*, the wind. So named upon the supposition that the flowers of this genus only opened when the wind was blowing.

Its genera are various, but easily distinguishable by the acrid juice prevailing to a greater or lesser extent in all species, and by the disconnection of the parts of its flowers. The tribes vary greatly in regard to the *sepals ;* in some they are want-ing, and replaced by petal-like organs ; in others, very fugacious ; while in one only, in this country, are they present in the mature flower. The stamens are numerous, furnished with short anthers. The fruit varies from a dry pod to a fleshy berry ; the *ovules* are anatropous, so distinguished by the dorsal rhaphe when suspended ; the *seeds* have a minute embryo, invested with fleshy albumen. The leaves are usually palmately, and generally ternately, divided, and are desti-tute of stipules. This family of plants, many of which are poisonous, contains, beside those treated of in this work, the following species of special interest to us : *Clematis erecta, Helleborus niger, Delphinium Staphisagria, Aconitum napel-lus, cammarum, ferox,* and *lycoctonum,* and *Paonia officinalis.*

History and Habitat.—The American pasque flower is found in abundance upon the prairies from Wisconsin northward, and westward to the Rocky Moun-tains, flowering from March to April. Lieberg says* that in Eastern Dakota this plant attains a luxuriance of growth never met with farther east, and that it wholly disappears west of the Missouri. Its habit of being in flower about Easter-tide gave it the principal distinguishing name, "Pasque flower ;" its peculiar effect upon the nose and eyes when crushed between the fingers gave it another, but local, appellation, " Hartshorn plant ;"† and the silky-hariness of the involucre and newly-appearing leaves caused the children in localities to term it " Goslin weed."

The U. S. Ph. allows the use of this species under the drug Pulsatilla, with or in place of *Herba Pulsatillæ nigricantis.*

PART USED AND PREPARATION.—The whole, fresh, flowering plant is chopped and pounded to a pulp and weighed. Then two parts by weight of alcohol are taken, the pulp mixed thoroughly with one-sixth part of it, and the rest of the alcohol added. After thorough mixture the whole is allowed to stand eight days in a well-stoppered bottle. The tincture thus prepared, after straining and filtering, should have a light seal-brown color by transmitted light, an acrid astringent taste, and a decidedly acid reaction.

CHEMICAL CONSTITUENTS.—I am unable to find any data upon this spe-cies. It is said to have been found similar to its European relative, *Anemone Pulsatilla,* which, together with *Anemone nemorosa* and *pratensis* (Eu.), contains :

Anemonin, $C_{15}H_{12}O_6$.—This body forms in colorless, klinorhombic prisms, from an aqueous distillate of the herb when the volatile oil is present. When dry it has a sharp and burning taste and neutral reaction. It softens at 150° (302.0° F.), and soon decomposes ; it dissolves in hot water and alcohol, slightly also in cold.

Anemonic Acid, $C_{15}H_{14}O_7$.—This amorphous, white powder separates from the aqueous distillate together with the above and under the same circumstances.

---

* *Bot. Gaz.,* 1884, p. 104. † *Ibid,* 1884, p. 77.

It is a tasteless acid, insoluble in water, alcohol, ether, oils, and dilute acids, but enters into combination with alkalies. (Wittstein.)

Oil of Anemone.—This acrid yellow oil separates from the aqueous infusion of the plant, and, owing to the presence of the water, soon breaks down into the bodies mentioned above.

PHYSIOLOGICAL ACTION.—The following represents the general action of the tincture when taken in moderate doses, as reported by Drs. Burk, Duncan, and Wesselhoeft: Profuse lacrymation, with smarting and burning of the eyes, mouth, and throat, followed by mucoid discharges; sharp pains about the stomach and bowels, with rumbling of flatus; pressure in the region of the stomach as from a weight; frequent urging to urinate, with an increased secretion; a tickling in the throat and constant inclination to cough; rheumatic pains, especially in the thighs, with erysipeloid eruptions, especially about the limbs; heat and feverishness, with great debility.

The action of this drug will be seen to be very like that of *Herba Pulsatillæ nigricantis*, differing mostly in a less intense action.

DESCRIPTION OF PLATE I.

1. Whole plant, from St. Cloud, Minn.,* April 24th, 1884.
2. Full-grown leaf in outline.
3. Sexual organs.
4. Receptacle.
5. Pistil (enlarged).
6. Stamen (enlarged).
7. Pollen x 380.
8. Ripe carpel.
9. Fruit.

* One of a number of typical living plants, sent me, with their natural soil intact, by Rev. E. V. Campbell, through whose kindness I also procured the full-grown leaf and ripe fruit.

1.

CĒm.ad nat.del.et pinxt.   ANEMÒNE PÀTENS, ᴠᴀʀ. NUTTALLIÀNA, Gray.

Tribe.—ANEMONEÆ.

GENUS.—**ANEMONE**, LINN.

SEX. SYST.—POLYANDRIA POLYGYNIA.

2

HEPATICA.

LIVER-LEAF.

SYN.—ANEMONE HEPATICA, LINN.; HEPATICA TRILOBA, CHAIX.; HEPATICA TRILOBA, VAR. AMERICANA, D. C.; HEPATICA TRI-LOBA, VAR. OBTUSA, PURSH.; HEPATICA AMERICANA, KER.

COM. NAMES.—LIVER-LEAF, HEPATICA,* ROUND-LOBED HEPATICA, LIVER-WORT,† LIVER-WEED, TREFOIL, HERB TRINITY, KIDNEY-WORT; (FR.) HÉPATIQUE; (GER.), EDELLEBERE.

A TINCTURE OF THE FRESH LEAVES OF ANEMONE HEPATICA, LINN.

Description.—This dwarf herb, so eagerly sought after as one of our earliest spring flowers, grows from radical scaly buds amid the thick, leathery leaves of the previous year's growth. *Root* fibrous, perennial. *Stem* none. *Leaves* ever-green, all radical on long, slender petioles; light green and hairy when young; dark olive-green above and purplish beneath, when old, and while the plant is in blossom; they are cordate in general outline, 3-lobed, the lobes ovate, obtuse. *Inflorescence* solitary, terminal, on long, hairy scapes, circinate, then erect. *Involucre* simple, composed of three entire, obtuse, hairy, persistent leaves, somewhat resembling a calyx, from its close proximity to the flower. *Calyx* composed of from 6 to 9 ovate, obtuse, petaloid *sepals*, varying in color from pure white to a deep purplish-blue with white borders; these latter, I have noticed, are always destitute of stamens. ‡ *Stamens* numerous, hypogynous; *filaments* long, slender, and smooth; *anthers* short, 2-celled. *Pistils* 12 to 20, hairy; *ovary* 1-celled; *ovules* one in each cell, suspended, anatropous; *style* single, short, pointed; *stigma* a stigmatose marginal line, extending down the inner side of the style. *Achenia* loosely aggregated in a globose head, ovate-oblong, hairy, tipped with the short persistent style; *seed* filling the whole cell to which it conforms.

History and Habitat.—Hepatica is a native of the colder portions of the North Temperate Zone, growing in rich, open woods as far as the limit of trees. In North America it grows from Minnesota, Iowa and Missouri, east and north-east to the Atlantic; flowering, in some seasons, as early as March, and continuing in flower until May. This plant was placed in the genus Anemone by

---

* Επατικὸς, *epatikos*, affecting the liver; or, 'ηπαρ, *epar*, the liver, from a fancied resemblance of the leaves to that organ, or their action upon it.

† The proper liverwort is *Marchantia polymorpha*, a cryptogamous plant (*Muscales*) of the order *Hepaticeæ*.

‡ Author in *Bull. Torr. Club*, 1884, p. 55.

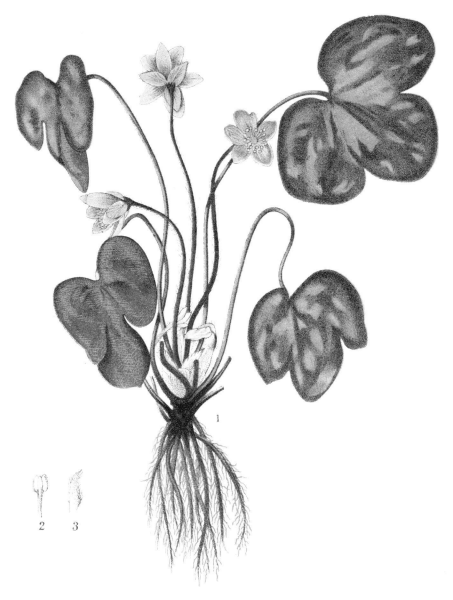

E.m. ad nat del. et pinxt.

ANEMÒNE HEPÁTICA, Linn.

Linnæus, from whence it has received several removals, until finally it has been returned to its original place among its congeners. The Liver-leaf has held a place among medicinal plants from ancient times until the present. It is now falling into disuse on account of its mild properties, forming as it does simply a slightly astringent, mucilaginous infusion. It was used in hæmoptysis, coughs, and other lung affections, as well as in all diseases of the liver, and in hemorrhoids; in the latter troubles its exhibition must have met with no very flattering success. As a pectoral it may be taken in the form of an infusion, hot or cold, in almost any amount, as its virtues are not of a powerful or disturbing nature.

Hepatica has been dismissed from the U. S. Ph., and is simply mentioned in the Eclectic Materia Medica.

PART USED AND PREPARATION.—The full-grown leaves of the year are chopped and pounded to a pulp and weighed. Then two parts by weight of alcohol are taken, the pulp thoroughly mixed with one-sixth part of it, and the rest of the alcohol added. After stirring the whole well it is poured into a well-stoppered bottle and allowed to stand eight days in a dark, cool place. The tincture, separated by straining and filtering, should have a very light greenish-orange color by transmitted light, a slightly astringent taste, and an acid reaction.

CHEMICAL CONSTITUENTS.—The only bodies found in this plant are *tannin*, in small amount, sugar, and mucilage. No special analysis has been made to determine an active principle.

PHYSIOLOGICAL ACTION.—As far as known, Hepatica has very little action upon the system. A farther proving may develop some symptoms in the direction of a slight irritative cough with expectoration.

DESCRIPTION OF PLATE 2.

1. Whole plant, Binghamton, N. Y., April 27th, 1884.
2. Stamen (enlarged).
3. Pistil (enlarged).

3

RANUNCULUS SCELERATUS.

CURSED CROWFOOT.

SYN.—RANUNCULUS SCELERATUS, LINN.
COM. NAMES.—CURSED CROWFOOT, CELERY-LEAVED CROWFOOT, MARSH CROWFOOT; (FR.) RANONCULE; (GER.) SCHARF HAHNEN-FUSS.

A TINCTURE OF THE WHOLE PLANT RANUNCULUS SCELERATUS, LINN.

Description.—This smooth perennial herb grows to a height of about 1 foot. *Stem* erect, glabrous, thick, succulent, hollow, and branching; *juice* acrid and blistering. *Leaves* thickish, the upper sessile or nearly so, the lobes oblong-linear and nearly entire; *stem-leaves* 3-lobed, rounded; *root-leaves* 3-parted, but not to the base, the lobes obtusely cut and toothed; *petioles* of the lower leaves long, and sheathing at their dilated bases. *Flowers* small, pale-yellow; *sepals* reflexed; *petals* scarcely exceeding the sepals. *Fruit* an oblong, cylindrical head; *carpels* numerous, barely mucronate.

Ranunculus.—This large genus contains, in North America, 53 species and 33 varieties, characterized as follows: *Root* annual or perennial. *Leaves* mostly radical, those of the stems alternate and situated at the base of the branches, variously lobed, cut, or dissected, seldom entire. *Inflorescence* solitary or sometimes corymbed; *flowers* yellow, rarely white. *Sepals* 5, rarely only 3, not appendaged, deciduous, and imbricated in the bud. *Petals* 5, or often more, flat, with a little pit, pore, gland, or nectariferous scale at the base inside. *Stamens* numerous; *filaments* filiform. *Style* short, subulate. *Fruit* a cylindrical or rounded head, composed of numerous carpels; *achenia* mostly flattened and pointed by the remains of the style; *seeds* solitary, erect, rarely suspended.

History and Habitat.—The Cursed Crowfoot is indigenous to Europe and North America; with us it appears as if introduced. It grows in marshy tracts and wet ditches, and blossoms from June to August.

The general and medical history of the species is generic, they having been used indiscriminately, *R. sceleratus*, however, being considered the most poisonous, its juice possessing remarkable caustic power, quickly raising a blister wherever

---

* Latin for a little frog, referring to its habitat.

applied, and a dose of two drops sometimes exciting fatal inflammation along the whole alimentary tract.

This genus was known to the ancient physicians as Βρατραχιον (*Bratrachion*). Hippocrates, Paulus Ægineta, and Dioscorides spoke of various species, the latter using them as external applications for the removal of psora, leprous nails, steotomatous and other tumors, as well as fomentations to chilblains, and in toothache. Galen, Paulus, and the physicians of Arabia, all speak highly of the plants as powerful escharotics; and the Bedouins use them as rubefacients.

Gerarde says: "There be divers sorts or kinds of these pernitious herbes comprehended under the name of Ranunculus or Crowfoote, whereof most are very dangerous to be taken into the body, and therefore they require a very exquisite moderation, with a most exact and due manner of tempering; not any of them are to be taken alone by themselves, because they are of a most violent force, and therefore have the great nede of correction. The knowledge of these plants is as necessarie to the phisition as of other herbes, to the end they may shun the same, as Scribonius Largus saith, and not take them ignorantly, or also if necessitie at any time require that they may use them, and that with some deliberation and special choice and with their proper correctives. For these dangerous simples are likewise many times of themselves beneficial and oftentimes profitable; for some of them are not so dangerous but that they may in some sort and oftentimes in fit and due season profit and do good." In regard to the acrid properties of the plants, he further says: "Cunning beggars do use to stampe the leaves and lay it unto their legs and armes, which causeth such filthy ulcers as we daily see (among such wicked vagabondes), to moove the people the more to pittie."

Van Swieten, Tissot, and others mention a curious practice, formerly prevailing in several countries of Europe, of applying Ranunculus to the wrists and fingers for the cure of intermittent fevers. This practice we noted only a few days since, when called to see a child of a new-settled German family in our city; the little one's wrists were bound up in the leaves and branches of *R. acris;* it was suffering with an attack of lobar pneumonia.

In former practice the plants were used, in view of external stimulation, in rheumatism (especially sciatic), hip disease, hemicrania, and in local spasmodic and fixed pains; in asthma, icterus, dysuria, and pneumonia. Withering, in speaking of *R. flammula*, says: "It is an instantaneous emetic, as if Nature had furnished an antidote to poisons from among poisons of its own tribe; and it is to be preferred to almost any other vomit in promoting the instantaneous expulsion of deleterious substances from the stomach."

Many species of this genus are used as pot-herbs, as the process of boiling throws off the volatile acrid principle and renders them inert, though some cases are reported where this happy result failed, and serious symptoms supervened. In Northern Persia the young tubers, leaves, stems, and blossoms of *R. edulis*, Boiss, are brought into market and sold as a pot-herb; the Swedish peasantry use *R. ficaria*, Linn.; and the shepherds of Wallachia, *R. sceleratus*, Linn.*

---

* Lewis Sturtevant, M.D., in *Bot. Gaz.*, vii, 316.

Ranunculus is among the articles dropped from the U. S. Ph. at the last revision.

PART USED AND PREPARATION.—The fresh herb, gathered when in fruit, but still green and untouched by frost, is chopped and pounded to a pulp and weighed. Then two parts by weight of alcohol are taken, the pulp thoroughly mixed with one-sixth part of it, and the rest of the alcohol added. After having stirred the whole well, it is poured into a well-stoppered bottle, and allowed to stand eight days in a dark, cool place. The tincture is then separated by straining and filtering. Thus prepared it has a clear reddish-orange color by transmitted light; an acrid odor and taste; and an acid reaction.

CHEMICAL CONSTITUENTS.—We consider here the genus as a whole, taking this species as a chemical type.

Anemonol, or *Oil of Ranunculus.*—Mr. O. L. Erdmann* found this to be the acrid principle of this species, and extracted it as a golden-yellow volatile body, decomposing by age into *anemonin* and *anemonic acid*, both of which are as described on pages 1–2 and 1–3, and

Anemoninic Acid.—When boiled with an excess of baryta water, anemonin decomposes, forming, among other bodies, red flakes of anemoninate of barium (Löwig and Weidman). Prof. Frehling, who afterward examined into the subject, says, "this acid cannot be formed from anemonin by simply assumption with water."†

PHYSIOLOGICAL ACTION.—According to Basiner,‡ the oil of Ranunculus acts, in warm-blooded animals, as an acrid narcotic, producing, in small doses, stupor and slow respiration; in larger doses, also, paralysis of the posterior and anterior extremities, and, before death, convulsions of the whole body. The acrid action is shown by a corrosive gastritis and by hyperæmia of the kidneys, more particularly their cortical substance. Anemonin causes similar symptoms, but is followed by no convulsions, nor does it irritate sufficiently to corrode the organs, as in the oil.

Krapf states§ that a small portion of a leaf or flower of *R. sceleratus*, or two drops of the juice, excited acute pain in the stomach, and a sense of inflammation of the throat; when he chewed the most succulent leaves, the salivary glands were strongly stimulated; his tongue was excoriated and cracked; his teeth smarted, and his cornea became tender and bloody.||

A man, at Bevay, France, swallowed a glassful of the juice, which had been kept for some time; he was seized in four hours with violent colic and vomiting, and died the second day.¶

---

* *Am. Jour. Phar.*, 1859, p. 440.
† *Drugs and Med. of N. A.*, i, 68.
‡ *Die Vergift mit Ranunkelöl, Anemonin*, etc., in *Am. Jour. Phar.*, 1882, 130.
§ *Exp. de Nonnull. Ranun. Ven. Qual.*
|| *Orfila, Tox. Gen.*, i, 754.
¶ *Jour. de Chim. Méd.*, 1836, 273.

Krapf (*op. cit.*) relates a case in which the plant was used internally, giving the following serious symptoms and result: Contortion of the eyes; convulsions of the facial muscles, outer parts of the abdomen, and the limbs; pain, swelling, redness, and bleeding of the gums; peeling off of the cuticle and cracking of the tongue; ptyalism; hiccough; complete inactivity of the stomach, with horrid pains and fits of anxiety; slight fainting turns; all followed by cold sweat and death.

The symptoms caused by this drug, as detailed in *Allen's Encyclopedia of Pure Materia Medica,** as well as the cases reported above, show this drug to be an acrid irritant poison, both to the mucous membranes with which it comes in contact, and to the nerves themselves.

DESCRIPTION OF PLATE 3.

1. Whole plant (a small specimen), Salem, Mass., July 20th, 1885.
2. Sepal.
3. Petal.
4. Carpel.
5. Section of same.
(2–5 enlarged.)

---

* Vol. viii, 270–77.

ad nat del.et pinxt

RANÚNCULUS SCELERÀTUS, Linn.

4

RANUNCULUS REPENS.

CREEPING BUTTERCUPS.

SYN.—RANUNCULUS REPENS, LINN.; R. PROSTRATUS, TOMENTOSUS, AND LANUGINOSUS, VAR. γ, POIR.; R. INTERMEDIUS, EATON; R. CLINTONII, BECK.

COM. NAMES.—CREEPING BUTTERCUPS OR CROWFOOT; (FR.) RANONCULE; (GER.) HAHNENFUSS.

A TINCTURE OF THE WHOLE PLANT RANUNCULUS REPENS, LINN.

Description.—This extremely variable, low, hairy or glabrous herb, extends to from 1 to 4 feet. *Stems* at first upright then ascending, some forming long runners in summer. *Leaves* 3-divided to the base: *leaflets* all petiolulate, or at least the terminal one, broadly cuneate or ovate, usually 3-cleft or parted and variously cut. *Peduncles* furrowed. *Calyx* spreading. *Petals* obovate, bright yellow, much longer than the sepals. *Fruit* a globular head of numerous carpels; *achenia* flat, strongly margined, and furnished with a stout, straight beak.

History and Habitat.—The Creeping Buttercups are indigenous to North America, where they habit moist or shady places, ditches and wet meadows, from Georgia northward and westward; flowering from May to August.

In woods that tend to dryness the plant is erect and shows no tendency to spread much by runners; but in low, wet ditches along swamp lands its growth is often prodigious.

This species is one of the lesser in acridity, and its medical uses have been simply generical, it being generally used only when the more powerful species could not be procured; its history, therefore, will be covered by *R. sceleratus, 3.*

PART USED AND PREPARATION.—The whole fresh herb, gathered at its fullest growth in October, is chopped and pounded to a pulp, enclosed in a piece of new linen and pressed. The juice is then mingled, by brisk agitation, with an equal part by weight of alcohol, and allowed to stand eight days in a dark, cool place. The tincture formed by filtration should have a brownish-green color by transmitted light, a slightly acrid taste, and an acid reaction.

4.

RANÚNCULUS REPENS, Linn.

ℭ𝔪.ad nat.del.et pinxt.

PHYSIOLOGICAL ACTION.—The provings of this species are not yet sufficiently developed to distinguish its action from that of the preceding.

DESCRIPTION OF PLATE 4.

1. End of a flowering stem, Ithaca, N. Y., June 24th, 1885.
   2, 3 and 4. Leaf forms.
   5. Carpel.
   6. Section of a carpel.
   (5 and 6 enlarged.)

5

RANUNCULUS BULBOSUS.

BULBOUS BUTTERCUPS.

SYN.—RANUNCULUS BULBOSUS, LINN.

COM. NAMES.—BULBOUS CROWFOOT OR BUTTERCUPS, BUTTER-FLOW-
ER, KING'S CUPS, GOLD CUPS, ST. ANTHONY'S TURNIP OR RAPE;
(GER.) KNOLLINGER HAHNENFUSS.

A TINCTURE OF THE WHOLE FRESH PLANT RANUNCULUS BULBOSUS, LINN.

Description.—This erect, hairy herb grows to a height of about 1 foot. *Stems* many, volute, villous, from a bulbous, onion-like base. *Leaves* all ternately divided to the very base, especially noticeable in the radical ones, all appearing more or less pinnate; *leaflets* short, cuneate, cleft and toothed, the lateral sessile, the terminal stalked, all 3-parted. *Peduncles* furrowed. *Petals* 5 or more, round, cuneate at the base, bright glossy yellow, much longer than the calyx. *Calyx* reflexed. *Fruit* in a globular head; *achenia* ovoid, flattish, and tipped with a very short beak. Read description of Ranunculus, under *R. sceleratus, 3.*

History and Habitat.—Bulbous Crowfoot is an immigrant from Europe, now pretty thoroughly established along the Atlantic coast, in some places being an actual pest in meadows and pastures; it has not extended far inward, but seems decidedly prone so to do. It blossoms northward from May to July.

This species, being one of the more acrid of the genus, and of frequent occurrence in the East, has been used, like *R. sceleratus,* as a local irritant where vesication seemed necessary; its use was often prolonged to ulceration, from which severe cases of gangrene sometimes resulted.*

This was the official species of the U. S. Ph., now dismissed.

PART USED AND PREPARATION.—The whole fresh plant while in flower in the month of June, is treated as in the preceding species. The resulting tincture has a clear, light yellow color by transmitted light, a slightly sweetish then acrid taste, and a strongly acid reaction.

CHEMICAL CONSTITUENTS.—So far no analysis has been made of this species to determine (should such exist) a specific principle that might differ from the general constituents of the acrid Ranunculi as given under *R. sceleratus, 3.*

---

* The general uses of the Ranunculi will be found under R. sceleratus, 3, where special mention is made of the various species.

PHYSIOLOGICAL ACTION.—R. bulbosus has a peculiarly powerful irritant action upon the skin, whether applied locally or internally. Murray states* that a slice of the fresh root (bulb?) placed in contact with the palmar surface of a finger brought on pain in two minutes; when taken off, the skin was found without signs of extra circulation or irritation, and the itching and heat passed away; in two hours it nevertheless returned again, and in ten hours a serous blister had formed, followed by a bad ulcer, which proved very difficult to heal.

Early English practitioners used the bulb to produce vesication when a "lasting blister" was judged necessary, but were very chary of prescribing the drug internally, so great was their dread of its properties.

Four persons who partook of the bulbs, boiled in a chicken-broth, suffered from violent burning in the hypogastric region, great anxiety about the region of the heart, pressure at the pit of the stomach, with painful soreness of that organ when pressed.

A lady who applied the bruised plant to the chest as a counter-irritant, became ill-humored, fretful, cross and disposed to quarrel, and suffered from soreness and smarting of the eyelashes some time before its action was felt at the region nearest the application.

Violent attacks of epilepsy are recorded as having been induced by this plant; a sailor who inhaled the fumes of the burning plant was attacked with this disease for the first time in his life; it returned again in two weeks, passed into cachexia, nodous gout, headache, and terminated in death.†

The specific symptoms caused by this drug, so carefully collated by Prof. Allen,‡ show a decided irritant action upon the brain and spinal cord, as well as the mucous membranes generally.

DESCRIPTION OF PLATE 5.

1. Whole plant, Salem, Mass., June 25th, 1885.
   2. Petal.
   3. Anther.
   4. Fruit.
   5. Achenium.
   6. Longitudinal section of achenium.
      (3, 5 and 6 enlarged.)

* *App. Med.*, iii, 87.
† Stapf, *Add. to Mat. Med. Pura, l. c.*
‡ *Encyc. Pure Mat. Med.*, viii, 257–269.

5

2 3 6 1 4 5

Œm.ad nat.del.et pinxt.   RANÚNCULUS BULBÒSUS, Linn.

N. ORD.—RANUNCULACEÆ.
GENUS.—**RANUNCULUS**, LINN.
SEX. SYST.—POLYANDRIA POLYGYNIA.

6

RANUNCULUS ACRIS.

TALL BUTTERCUPS.

SYN.—RANUNCULUS ACRIS, LINN.; RANUNCULUS PRATENSIS ERECTUS
ACRIS, GERARDE.
COM. NAMES.—TALL BUTTERCUPS OR CROWFOOT, UPRIGHT BUTTER-
CUPS OR CROWFOOT, ACRID BUTTERCUPS, BLISTERWEED, YEL-
LOW PILE-WEED, BUR-WORT, MEADOWBLOOM; (FR.) RENONCULE
ACRE; (GER.) SCHARFHAHENFUSS.

A TINCTURE OF THE WHOLE FRESH PLANT, RANUNCULUS ACRIS, LINN.

Description.—This erect, perennial herb attains a height of from 2 to 3 feet.
Root fibrous, from a slightly tuber-like crown. *Stem* subcylindrical, hollow, hairy,
and branching above. *Leaves* 3-divided, the divisions all sessile, 3-parted, and
clothed with more or less rigid hairs ; *segments* of the lower leaves cut into lanceolate, closely-crowded lobes ; of the upper linear, and sometimes entire ; *petioles*
of the radicle and lower stem leaves long and hairy, upper cauline leaves sometimes sessile. *Inflorescence* axillary and terminal ; *flowers* nearly as large as those
of R. bulbosus (5), but not so deep a yellow. *Calyx* spreading, villous, much
shorter than the corolla. *Petals* obovate, bright yellow. *Filaments* short ; *anthers*
incurved. *Fruit* a globular head ; *carpels* numerous, lenticular and smooth ; *beak*
short and recurved. Read description of the genus, under Ranunculus sclera-
tus, 3 ; and the natural order, under Pulsatilla Nuttalliana, 1.

History and Habitat.—This species of the genus has become quite widely
distributed in this country since its introduction from Europe. It flowers from
June until August. This plant, when past its flowering season, is often mistaken
for Geranium maculatum, 32,* both on account of its vulgar name, crowfoot, and
from a similarity in the foliage.
The medical and general history, and the chemistry and action, of the different species of Ranunculus are generic rather than specific. I give a digest under
R. sceleratus, 3.

PART USED AND PREPARATION.—The whole fresh herb, gathered in
October, should be chopped and pounded to a pulp and pressed out in a piece

---

* Williams and Partridge, *Bost. Med. and Surg. Jour.*, March, 1838.

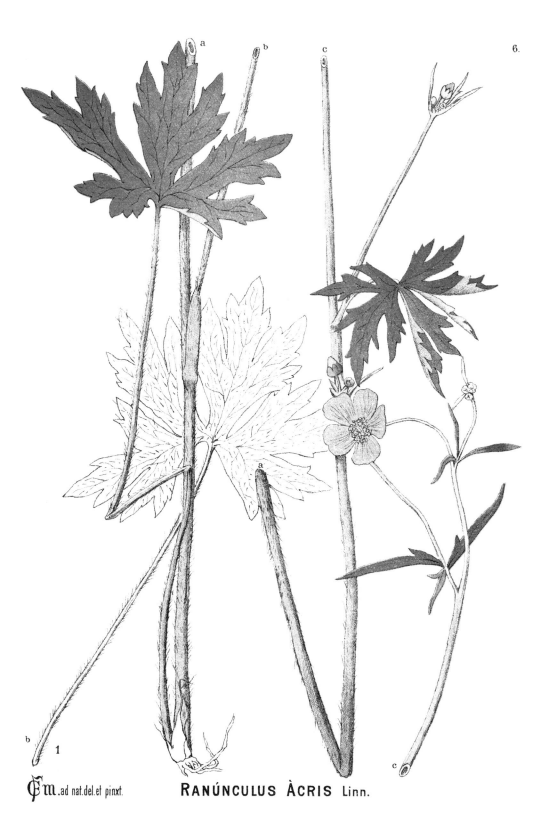

a
b
c
6.

a

b
1

ℭℳ.ad nat.del.et pinxt.

RANÚNCULUS ÀCRIS Linn.

c

of new linen. The juice is then, by rapid succussion, mixed with an equal part by weight of alcohol, and allowed to stand eight days, in a well-stoppered bottle, in a dark, cool place.

The tincture, separated by filtration, has a brownish-orange color by transmitted light, a biting, then astringent taste, and an acid reaction.

DESCRIPTION OF PLATE 6.

1. a, b, and c. Whole plant, Ithaca, N. Y., June 2d, 1880.

GENUS.—**CALTHA**,* LINN.

SEX. SYST.—POLYANDRIA POLYGYNIA.

7

CALTHA.

MARSH MARIGOLD.

SYN.—CALTHA PALUSTRIS,† LINN.; CALTHA ARTICA, R. BR.

COM. NAMES.—MARSH MARIGOLD,‡ COWSLIPS,§ COW'S LIPS, MEADOW-BOUTS, WATERBOUTS, COLT'S FOOT,|| MARE-BLEBS OR -BLOBS,¶ AMERICAN COWSLIPS,** PALSY-WORT, WATER DRAGON; (GER.) SUMPF RINGELBLUME.

A TINCTURE OF THE WHOLE FLOWERING PLANT CALTHA PALUSTRIS, LINN.

Description.—This glabrous, perennial herb, grows to a height of from 6 to 12 inches. *Root* a bundle of coarse and closely fasciculated fibers. *Stem* erect, somewhat quadrilateral, furrowed, hollow, thick, and juicy, branched above. *Leaves* alternate, large, orbicular, cordate, or reniform, finely crenate or entire; *petioles* of the radical leaves long, those of the cauline about equal in length to the width of the leaf; *stipules* quite large, withering after the expansion of the leaf, which they cover in the bud. *Inflorescence* corymbose; *flowers* large and regular. *Sepals* 5-6, petaloid, broadly ovate, imbricate in æstivation. *Petals* wanting. *Stamens* numerous; *filaments* about the length of the anthers; *anthers* large, innate, and extrorse. *Pistils* 5-10; *styles* nearly or quite absent; *stigmas* forming blunt, recurved, mucro-nations to the ovaries. *Fruit* a spreading whorl; *follicles* latterly compressed; *seeds* numerous, oblong, purplish, furnished with a prominent raphe, and arranged in a double series. Read description of the Order under Pulsatilla Nuttalliana, 1.

History and Habitat.—The marsh-marigold is indigenous to the northern portions of Europe, Asia, and America; growing on low, wet meadows, bogs, and the banks of spring-fed rivulets; flowering in the United States from April to May.

---

* Κάλαθος, *kalathos*, a chalice, the golden calyx resembling that utensil.

† Care should be taken not to confound this plant with *Calla palustris, Linn*, on account of the similarity in the names; it bears no resemblance whatever to Calla; the habitats are the same.

‡ I have known American physicians who claimed that they made their tincture of *Calendula* from flowers gathered in their own neighborhoods (*Caltha*); this error arose from the common name of calendula being marigold. *Calendula officinalis, Linn.*, belongs to the Compositæ, and does not grow wild in this country. The corn-marigold belongs to the genus *Chrysanthemum* (Compositæ); the fig-marigold to *Mesembryanthemum* (Mesembryanthemeæ); the French and African marigolds to *Tagetes* (Compositæ), and the bur-marigold to *Bidens* (Compositæ).

§ Cowslips are properly species of the primrose family (Primulaceæ).

|| Colt's foot is only applicable to *Tussilago Farfara, Linn.* (Compositæ).

¶ *Mare*, marsh; *blebs*, bladders, more properly blisters.

** The true American cowslip is *Dodecatheon Meadia, Linn.* (Primulaceæ).

The plant is extensively gathered in early spring, and cooked for "greens," making one of our most excellent pot-herbs; the pickled flower-buds are mentioned as a fine substitute for capers. The fresh plant is very acrid, so much so that cattle will not eat of it. Rafinesque asserts that cattle browsing upon it die in consequence of an inflammation of the stomach.

The medical history of this herb is very sparse, and of no consequence; it has been used in cough syrups, which would, without doubt, have been fully as efficacious without it.

PART USED AND PREPARATION.—The fresh herb, gathered when flowering, is chopped and pounded to a pulp, enclosed in a piece of new linen, and pressed. The expressed juice is then, by brisk succussion, mingled with an equal part by weight of alcohol. This mixture is allowed to stand eight days in a dark, cool place.

The tincture, separated from the above mass by filtration, has a clear, orange-brown color by transmitted light, a sweet, then somewhat acrid taste, and a neutral reaction.

CHEMICAL CONSTITUENTS.—The acridity so noticeable in the fresh herb entirely disappears on the application of heat; this property is considered by Lloyd to resemble, or be identical with, acrid oil of ranunculus,* though his attempt to extract this oil and anemonin, from a distillate of the fresh plant, was unsuccessful.

Tannin is present in appreciable quantity, the tincture responding quickly to the tests with acetate of lead and chloride of iron.

PHYSIOLOGICAL ACTION.—We have a scanty proving of this drug detailed in the Encyclopedia of Pure Materia Medica; insufficient, however, to afford an insight to its real action.

DESCRIPTION OF PLATE 7.

1. End of branch, from Binghamton, N. Y., May 11th, 1884.
2. Section of flower.
3. Stamen (enlarged).
4. Achenium (enlarged).
5. Section of ovary (enlarged).
6. Section of stem.

* See under Ranunculus sceleratus, 3.

2   3   4   5   6   1

Cm.ad nat.del.et pinxt.   CÁLTHA PALÚSTRIS, Linn.

8

HELLEBORUS VIRIDIS.

GREEN HELLEBORE.

SYN.—HELLEBORUS VIRIDIS, LINN.
COM. NAMES.—GREEN HELLEBORE; (FR.) ELLÉBORE VERT; (GER.) GRÜNE NIESSWURZ.

A TINCTURE OF THE ROOT OF HELLEBORUS VIRIDIS, LINN.

Description.—This perennial herb usually attains a growth of from 1 to 2 feet. *Rhizome* thick and woody. *Stem* smooth, usually a little inclined to branch above. *Leaves* alternate, compound, the leaflets sharply serrate; those of the stem nearly sessile and palmately parted; those of the root glabrous, long petioled and pedately divided into from 7 to 15 lanceolate, acute lobes. *Inflorescence* on axillary, solitary, nodding, sometimes geminate peduncles; *flowers* regular, an inch or more in diameter. *Calyx* persistent; *sepals* 5, roundish-ovate, veiny, petaloid, imbricated in the bud. *Petals* 8 to 10, very small, cyathiform, irregularly 2-lipped, all shorter than the stamens. *Stamens* indefinite. *Pistils* 3 to 10, sessile; *stigmas* orbicular. *Fruit* a cluster of sessile, coriaceous pods, all cohering at their bases; *seeds* numerous.

History and Habitat.—This European immigrant is now pretty thoroughly naturalized on Long Island and in a few counties of Eastern Pennsylvania, where it grows in the opens, and flowers in April.

On account of its general rarity, this species has had but little use in medicine, its place being supplied by either *H. niger* or *H. fetidus;* it is, however, much more active than either of these species, and ranks next in energy to *H. orientalis,* which is considered the most highly poisonous species of the genus. Green Hellebore has, however, been somewhat used as a drastic and hydragogue cathartic in dropsies; an emmenagogue in amenorrhœa; a vermifuge in children afflicted with lumbricoids; as a nervine in mania and melancholia; and an anti-spasmodic in epilepsy. Its principal field, however, has been in veterinary medication, for animals afflicted with lice or lumbrici. For the reason given above, the root is no longer officinal in the pharmacopœias.

Ἑλεῖν, *helein,* to injure; βορά, *bora,* food.

PART USED AND PREPARATION.—The fresh root, gathered when the leaves are about to fall, but before the first frost, is treated as directed under Hydrastis.* The resulting tincture has a deep brownish-orange color by transmitted light; an odor somewhat resembling that of Bourbon whisky; an acrid, bitter taste, prickling the tongue and causing salivation; and an acid reaction.

CHEMICAL CONSTITUENTS.—The chemistry of the Hellebores is generic rather than specific, the species differing, so far as known, only in the quantity of the principles contained.

Helleborin,† $C_{36}H_{42}O_6$.—This glucoside was isolated by Marmé and A. Husemann (1864) from the green, fatty matter extracted by boiling alcohol from an aqueous extract of the root. It resulted as shining, colorless, concentric needles, tasteless when dry, but acrid and burning in alcoholic solution. Helleborin proves a highly narcotic, powerful poison, more abundant in *viridis* than in *niger;* it is insoluble in water, soluble in hot alcohol, and fuses and carbonizes above 250° (482° F.). When boiled with zinc chloride, Helleborin breaks down into sugar and *Helleboresin* as follows:

Helleborin.   Water.   Glucose.   Helleboresin.
$$C_{36}H_{42}O_6 + (H_2O)_4 = C_6H_{12}O_6 + C_{30}H_{38}O_4.$$

Helleboreïn, $C_{26}H_{44}O_{15}$. — This slightly acid glucoside was also isolated by Marmé and Husemann, as translucent, warty masses of microscopic needles, which quickly defloresce and are very hygroscopic; they are of a sweetish taste, and are readily soluble in water, less so in alcohol, and insoluble in ether. Helleboreïn is a narcotic poison, more abundant in *niger* than *viridis;* its aqueous solution dries to a yellowish resin, which becomes straw-color at 160° (320° F.), and conglutinates; at 220°–230° (428°–446° F.) it becomes brown and pasty; and at 280° (536° F.) it chars.

When boiled with a dilute mineral acid, it breaks down into sugar and *Helleboretin,* as follows:

Helleboreïn.   Glucose.   Helleboretin.
$$C_{26}H_{44}O_{15} = (C_6H_{12}O_6)_2 + C_{14}H_{20}O_3.$$

Helleboretin, $C_{14}H_{20}O_3$, is strangely wanting in physiological effect, considering its source; it has a violet color and no crystalline form.

Helleboric Acid.—This body is so far considered, if not identical, at least isomeric with *aconitic* and *equisetic acids.*

PHYSIOLOGICAL ACTION.—According to the experiments of Von Schroff, with from 2 to 4 grains of the alcoholic extract of the root, this species causes: roaring in the ears; violent sneezing; burning in the mouth, and profuse salivation; gurgling in the abdomen; profuse liquid stools, accompanied by violent

---

* Page 9–2.

† Bastic (1352) discovered a bitter, crystalline body in the roots of Hellebore, to which he gave this name. It proved, however, to be chemically indifferent.

colic, great tenesmus, nausea, and inclination to vomit; frequent passages of pale urine; decreased heart's action; soporific condition; and a sensation of heat over the whole body.

The action of the Hellebores in general should be consulted in connection with this species.

DESCRIPTION OF PLATE 8.

1. Top of plant, from Sellersville, Pa., April 20th, 1884.
2. A mature lower leaf.
3. Petal.
4. Stamen.
5. Pistil.
6. Fruiting carpel.
    (4–6 enlarged.)

Ĉ.m.. ad nat del.et pinxt.

HELLEBORUS VIRIDIS, Linn.

Tribe.—CIMICIFUGEÆ.

GENUS.—**HYDRASTIS,*** LINN.

SEX. SYST.—POLYANDRIA POLYGYNIA.

9

HYDRASTIS.

GOLDEN-SEAL.

SYN.—HYDRASTIS CANADENSIS, LINN.; WARNERIA CANADENSIS, MILL.

COM. NAMES.—GOLDEN-SEAL, ORANGE-ROOT, YELLOW-ROOT, YELLOW-PUCCOON, GROUND-RASPBERRY, WILD CURCUMA, TURMERIC-ROOT, INDIAN DYE, INDIAN TURMERIC; (FR.) HYDRASTIS; (GER.) CANADISCHE, GELBWURZEL.

A TINCTURE OF THE FRESH ROOT OF HYDRASTIS CANADENSIS, LINN.

Description.—This low perennial herb, now becoming quite rare in this State (N. Y.), grows from 6 to 10 inches high, its leaves and fruit much resembling those of the raspberry. *Rhizome* thick, sarcous, oblong, irregular, and knotted, having a yellowish-brown, thin bark, and a bright-yellow interior; *rootlets* numerous, scattered, coriaceous fibres. *Stem* simple, subcylindrical, thick, erect, and very hairy, surrounded, at its point of issuance from the rootstalk, by several oblong, sheathing, scaphoid, greenish yellow, leafy bracts. *Leaves* 2, alternate, near the summit of the plant, orbicular-cordate at the base, palmately five- to seven-lobed, the lobes doubly serrate, acute, veiny; attaining, when full grown during the fruiting season, a width of from 4 to 10 inches. The root sometimes puts off an accessory or root-leaf which answers to the characteristics of the stem-leaves, with the one exception, that it is petiolate while they are sessile. *Peduncle* about 1 inch long; *inflorescence*—when fully expanded—a single, greenish-white, apetalous, asepalous flower. *Sepals* 3, pale-rose color, caducous. *Petals* none. *Stamens* numerous; *filaments* linear or linear-spatulate; *anthers* oval, innate. *Pistils* numerous, twelve or more in a dense head; *ovary* 1-celled, one- to two-ovuled; *styles* short; *stigma* flattened and dilated, one- to two-lipped. *Fruit* a succulent, globose berry, compounded of many miniature one- to two-seeded drupes; appearing like an enlarged red-raspberry. *Seeds* inversely egg-shaped, nearly black and glossy; *embryo* basal, very small; *albumen* sarcoid and oily. A description of the natural order may be found under Pulsatilla Nuttalliana, 1.

---

* Derivation not positive, (?) ὕδωρ, *water;* δράω, *to act;* its juice being very active.

History and Habitat.—Hydrastis is indigenous to Canada and the United States, east of the Mississippi, and but quite rare east of the Alleghany Mountains; in the southeastern portion of the country it grows only upon the mountains. It seeks the rich soil of shady woods, and moist places at the edge of wooded lands, flowering from April to May, and fruiting in July. The American aborigines valued the root highly as a tonic, stomachic, and application to sore eyes and general ulcerations, as well as a yellow dye for their clothing and implements of warfare.

The officinal preparations in the U.S. Ph. are: *Extractum Hydrastis Fluidum*, and *Tinctura Hydrastis*. The Eclectic: *Decoctum Hydrastis, Extractum Hydrastis Hydro-alcoholicum, Tinctura Hydrastis Composita, Lotio Hydrastis Composita, Tinctura Hydrastis*, and *Vinum Hydrastis Compositum*.

PARTS USED AND PREPARATION.—The fresh root, gathered as the plant is budding to blossom, or in the fall, is chopped and pounded to a pulp and weighed. Then two parts by weight of alcohol are taken, the pulp thoroughly mixed with one-sixth part of it, and the rest of the alcohol added. After stirring the whole well, it is poured into a well-stoppered bottle, and allowed to remain eight days in a dark, cool place. The tincture is then poured off, strained and filtered, and presents the following physical properties: a reddish-orange color, by transmitted light, staining everything with which it comes in contact, a deep yellow color; a persistent bitter, then burning taste; no distinguishing odor, and a slightly acid reaction.

Berberinum.—The pure alkaloid Berberina, one part to ten, or ninety-nine sugar of milk, and triturated.

CHEMICAL CONSTITUENTS.—Berberina (*vide* Berberis, 15). Dr. Mahla of Chicago proved this alkaloid identical with that obtained from Berberis (Am. Jour. Phar., Vol. xxxv., p. 433).

Hydrastia, $C_{22}H_{23}NO_6$, an alkaloid discovered by A. B. Durand (Am. Jour. Phar., Vol. xxiii., p. 13), has been referred to by many writers upon Phyto-chemistry, as pure-white crystals, but J. U. Lloyd (Am. Jour. Phar., Vol. li., p. 16) determines that it cannot be extracted pure, but is always so intimately associated with a yellow substance that when viewed in quantity it shows easily the impurity. He decides that this yellowishness is not due to berberina. The crystals when viewed separately are in the form of brilliant, yellowish-white, glossy, quadrangular prisms, becoming opaque when dry. Hydrastia fuses at 135° (275° F.), and decomposes at higher temperatures; it is slightly soluble in cold alcohol, readily in hot, from which it is deposited on cooling in the crystalline form above described; the taste is not bitter, but somewhat nauseous and acrid.

Xanthopuccina, a third alkaloid, was determined by Herm. Lerchen (Am. Jour. Phar., Vol. l., p. 470) in the menstruum, after the extraction of berberina and hydrastia; a yellow color is the only property given.

Hydrastis contains, beside the above-mentioned bodies, a green fixed oil of a disagreeable odor and taste; a little volatile oil, to which the odor of the root is due; a black, resinous substance (Lloyd); albumen, sugar, starch, a fatty resin and 10 per cent. of mineral matters (Herm. Lerchen).

PHYSIOLOGICAL ACTION.—When taken in large doses hydrastis causes a train of symptoms due to a hyper-secretion of the mucous membranes. If persisted in, it causes severe ulceration of any surface it may touch; and a catarrhal inflammation of mucous surfaces, followed by extreme dryness and fission. It causes also a catarrhal inflammation of the mucous linings of the hepatic ducts and gall-bladder—showing in an icteric hue of the skin—and a similar condition of the bladder catarrhal cystitis.

DESCRIPTION OF PLATE 9.

1. Sepal (somewhat enlarged).
2. Stamen   "   "
3. Fruit.
4. Pistil (somewhat enlarged).
5–6. Seed.
7. Whole plant from Newfield, N. Y., May 20, 1880.

9.

2

1

4

3

5 6

7

Ĉ.m. ad nat del. et pinxt.　　　HYDRÁSTIS CANADÉNSIS, Linn.

Tribe.—CIMICIFUGEÆ.

GENUS.—**ACTÆA**,* LINN.

SEX. SYST.—POLYANDRIA MONOGYNIA.

10
ACTÆA ALBA.

WHITE BANEBERRY.

SYN.—ACTÆA ALBA, BIGEL; ACTÆA SPICATA, VAR. ALBA, MICHX.;
ACTÆA PACHYPODA, ELL.; ACTÆA AMERICANA, VAR. α, PURSH.;
ACTÆA BRACHYPETALA, VAR. α, DC.

COM. NAMES.—WHITE BANEBERRY, WHITE COHOSH, AMERICAN HERB
CHRISTOPHER, TOAD ROOT; (FR.) HERBE DE STE. CHRISTOPHE
BLANC; (GER.) WEISSES CHRISTOPHSKRAUT.

A TINCTURE OF THE FRESH ROOT OF ACTÆA ALBA, BIGEL.

Description.—This delicate-flowered perennial grows to a height of 2 feet
and sometimes slightly over. *Root* somewhat similar to that of cimicifuga, but
neither as odorous, dark in color, nor as large. *Stem* erect, nearly smooth. *Leaves*
large, 2-3-ternately decompound; *leaflets* ovate, acutely cleft, and dentate or incisely serrate. *Inflorescence* a short, terminal ovate-oblong, simple raceme; *flowers*
creamy-white, sometimes by abortion declinous; *pedicles* becoming pink, and thickened in fruit, until they are equal in size to the common peduncle. *Sepals* 4 to 5
petaloid, early deciduous. *Petals* 3 to 9, small, slender and spatulate, their tips either
truncate or emarginate, their bases converted into short claws. The petals of this
species appear like metamorphosed stamens (*staminidia*). *Stamens* numerous;
filaments white, slender; *anthers* innate, introrse. *Pistil* simple, solitary, with a
sulcus at the insertion of the parietal placenta; *stigma* sessile, 2-lobed. *Fruit* a
cluster of bluish-white, many-seeded berries or carpels; *seeds* smooth, compressed,
and horizontal.

History and Habitat.—The white cohosh is a common herb in our rocky
woods, especially southward and westward. It flowers in May and ripens its
pretty china-like fruit in October. This species, together with *Actæa rubra* (red
cohosh), has received the attention of many writers upon medical botany. The
two species vary principally in the color of the berries and thickness of the
pedicles; probably slightly only in their properties and action. They are, however, widely different from *Actæa racemosa*, our *Cimicifuga*, and should under no
circumstances be confounded with that drug. Just how much our species of Actæa
differ from the European *Actæa spicata*, Linn., still remains to be proven. This
much we know, that the American species are much milder in their properties.

---

* Ἀκτῆ, *akte*, elder, from a resemblance in the foliage.

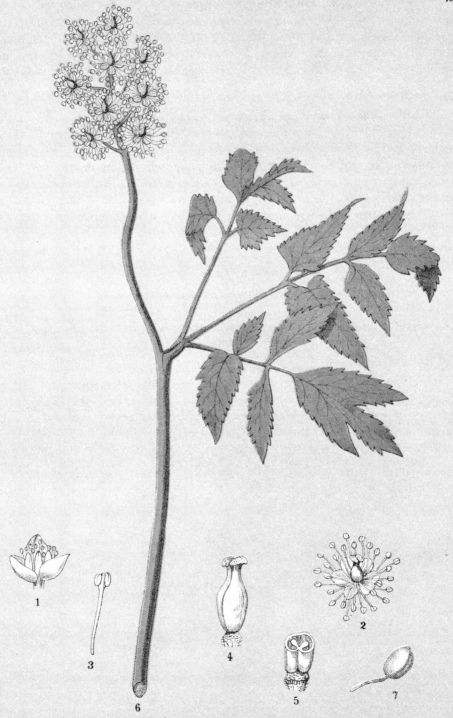

1

3

6

4

5

2

7

ℭℳ.ad nat.del.et pinxt.

ACTÆA SPICÀTA Linn.

The white cohosh hardly deserves a place here, as the European baneberry will without doubt cover its entire action and more beside; it will, however, often be found useful in many forms of reflex uterine headache, some types of chronic fleeting rheumatism, congestion, in the female especially, and reflex uterine gastralgia. Rafinesque says the roots are repellant, nervine, and used for debility in Canada.

PART USED AND PREPARATION.—The whole fresh plant, while the fruit is ripening, should be chopped and pounded to a pulp and weighed. Then two parts by weight of alcohol are to be taken, the pulp thoroughly mixed with one-sixth part of it, and the rest of the alcohol added. After mixing well, pour the whole into a well-stoppered bottle, and allow it to stand eight days in a dark, cool place.

The tincture is then separated by decanting, straining and filtering.

DESCRIPTION OF PLATE 10.

ACTÆA SPICATA, var. ALBA.*

1. Flower, showing calyx.
2. Expanded flower of *Actæa rubra*.
3. Stamen (enlarged).
4. Pistil (enlarged).
5. Horizontal section of ovary (enlarged).
6. Top of plant, Ithaca, N. Y., May 10th, 1880.

* The Plate is wrongly titled *Actæa spicata*.

Tribe.—CIMICIFUGEÆ.

GENUS.— **CIMICIFUGA**,* LINN.

SEX. SYST.—POLYANDRIA MONOGYNIA.

11

CIMICIFUGA.

BLACK COHOSH.

SYN.—CIMICIFUGA RACEMOSA, ELL.; C. SERPENTARIA, PURSH.; AC-
TÆA RACEMOSA, LINN.; A. ORTHOSTACHYA, AND GYROSTACHYA,
WEND.; A. MONOGYNIA, WALT.; MACROTRYS ACTÆOIDES, RAF.;
M. SERPENTARIA, AND RACEMOSA, EATON; BOTROPHIS SERPEN-
TARIA, RAF.; B. ACTÆOIDES, FISCH AND MEY.; CHRYSTOPHOR-
IANA CANADENSE RACEMOSA, PLUCK.

COM. NAMES.—BLACK COHOSH, BLACK SNAKE-ROOT,† RICH WEED,‡
SQUAW-ROOT,§ RATTLE-WEED, RATTLE-ROOT, RATTLESNAKE
ROOT,‖ BUGBANE; (FR.) ACTEE À GRAPPÉ; (GER.) SWARZE COHOSCH,
TRAUBENFÖRMIGES CHRISTOPHSKRAUT.

A TINCTURE OF THE FRESH ROOT OF CIMICIFUGA RACEMOSA, LINN.

Description.—This tall, graceful, and showy perennial grows to a height of
from 3 to 8 feet. *Rootstock* thick, blackish, successively knotted and fringe-ringed,
whitish-yellow internally, with a ring of cuneiform wood-bundles pointing inward;
rootlets long, simple, and uniform, a section under a lens shows the cuneiform-
bundles arranged like a cross. *Stem* smooth, angular, or furrowed. *Leaves* alternate, tri-ternately divided, the lowermost almost radical, very large and ample, the
petiole at its base almost as large as the stem; *leaflets* various on the same petiole,
simple, bifid, and trifid, all ovate-oblong, cut serrate. *Inflorescence* of very long,
simple, or compound, virgate, inclined, upper-axillary or terminal racemes; flowers
scattered, fœtid, creamy-white. *Sepals* 4-5, petal-like, scaphoid, early deciduous.
Petals (*Staminodia*) 1-8, very small, long clawed, and 2-horned or forked; apices
antherose. *Stamens* numerous; *filaments* slender, club-shaped, creamy-white;
anthers innate, introrse, yellow. *Pistil* solitary, simple; *ovary* ovoid, sessile; *style*
short; *stigma* simple, inclined to be lateral, the centre somewhat cylindrically depressed. *Fruit* numerous, dry, ovoid or globose, dehiscent carpels, arranged upon
a raceme from 1 to 3 feet in length, and retaining each its stigma in the form of
an oblique beak; *seeds* semi-discoid, smooth, horizontal, and compressed.

History and Habitat.—This indigenous plant is comparatively common all

---

* *Cimex,* a bug, *fugo,* I drive away. A Siberian species being used as a vermifuge.

† The black snake-root is *Sanicula Canadensis* (Umbelliferæ). If written black-snake root the name might be
applied, but does not apply.

‡ Two other plants are known by this name, viz.: *Collinsonia Canadensis* (Labiatæ), and *Pilea pumila* (Urticaceæ).

§ The true squaw root is *Conopholis* (*Orobanche*) *Americana* (Orobanchaceæ).

‖ This name properly belongs to many species of *Nabalus* (Compositæ).

over the eastern half of the United States and in Canada, growing in rich, open woods, and along the edges of fields, but especially noticeable on newly cleared hill-sides. When woods in its favorite localities are at all dense, the plant will be found only in the borders. Black cohosh was a favorite remedy among all tribes of the aborigines, being largely used by them in rheumatism, disorders of menstruation, and slow parturition. It was also used as a remedy against the bites of venomous snakes, with what success history does not relate, but we can easily judge.

The plant was first made known by Pluckenet in 1696; Colden recommended its use in 1743, and Dr. S. Garden in 1823. In England its use began in 1860.* Its uses at this time were confined to chorea, rheumatism, dropsy, hysteria, and affections of the lungs. In regard to chorea, Dr. G. B. Wood states† that he administered the drug in a case, which rapidly recovered under its use after the failure of purgatives and metallic tonics. In convulsions occurring periodically, connected with uterine disorder, Dr. Wood also derived the happiest effects from its use. In inflammatory rheumatism Dr. N. F. Johnson used the remedy with "the best results, the disease disappearing in from 2 to 10 days"; he says, "the more acute the disease the more prompt and decided will be the action of the drug."‡ Dr. A. Clapp§ used the drug in "chronic facial erysipelas, with satisfactory results." Dr. Williams says :‖ "Indians and quacks recommend its use in rheumatism," etc.; he then recommends it himself! The statement of Dr. Wheeler¶ that some eminent physicians thought it to be a good substitute for Secale cornutum in parturition, relaxing the parts and thereby rendering labor short and easy, is one that should have received much attention.

In all the above uses except mayhap those concerning the lungs, we have *proven* its application trustworthy. Its usefulness in phthisis when given in proper dosage is simply to palliate the cough through its action upon the nerve centres. It will be found in most cases to act with far more constant success in females than in males, as its action upon the female economy is marked and distinctive.

The officinal preparations in the U. S. Ph. are: *Extractum Cimicifugæ Fluidum*, and *Tinctura Cimicifugæ*. In the Eclectic Materia Medica: *Decoctum Cimicifugæ; Extractum Cimicifugæ Alcoholicum* and *Fluidum; Resina Cimicifugæ; Tinctura Cimicifugæ; Tinctura Cimicifugæ Composita ;** Tinctura Colchici Composita,†† and Enema Cimicifugæ Composita.‡‡*

PART USED AND PREPARATION.—The fresh root should be treated as in the preceding species. The resulting tincture is almost opaque; in thin layers it has a deep olive-green color by transmitted light; it retains the peculiar odor of the root; its taste is at first peculiar, soon becoming very acrid and bitter, and its reaction acid.

CHEMICAL CONSTITUENTS.—*Cimicifugin* or *Macrotin*, the so-called resinoid,

* Fluck. & Han., *Pharmacographia*, p. 16.
‡ Clapp, *Cat., Am. Med. Ass'n*, 1852, p. 725.
‖ *Rept. Indig. Med. Bot. Mass., Am. Med. Ass'n*, 1849, p. 914.
** Cimicifuga, Sanguinaria, and Phytolacca.
‡‡ Cimicifuga and Geranium maculatum.
† Dunglison's *New Rem.*, p. 145.
§ *Op. et loc. cit.*
¶ *Bost. Med. and Surg. Jour.*, Sept., 1839, p. 65
†† Colchicum and Cimicifuga.

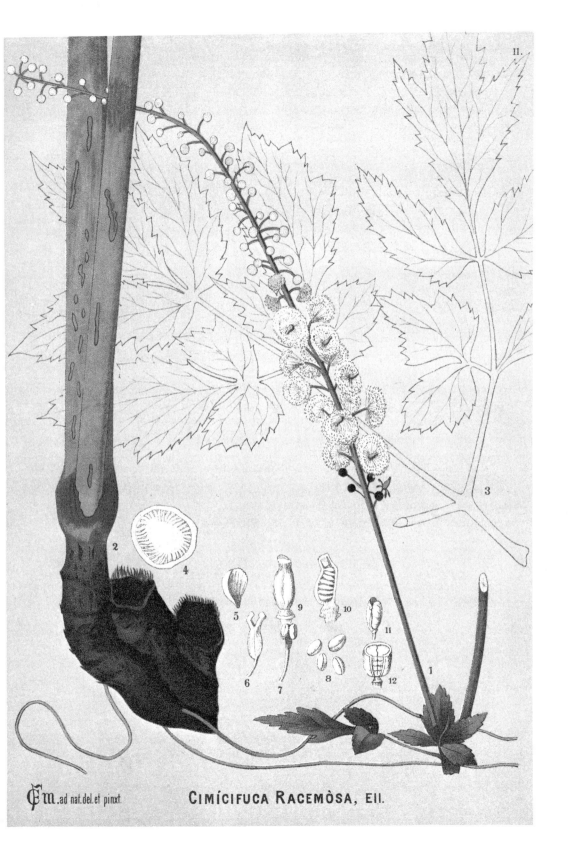

ℭℳ.ad nat.del.et pinxt.

CIMÍCIFUCA RACEMÒSA, Ell.

is not strictly speaking a chemical derivative, being simply a precipitate of whatever principles in the root are not soluble in water. An alkaloid has, however, been determined by T. E. Conard,* and corroborated by M. S. Falck,† to which the above name might be, but has not been, applied. This alkaloid is a neutral crystalline body, having an intensely acrid taste, and is soluble in alcohol, chloroform, and ether, slightly also in water. It has been determined also in the "resinoid."

A resin soluble in alcohol and ether, another soluble in alcohol only; fatty and waxy matters, volatile oil having the odor of the root, green and brown coloring matters, gum, uncrystallizable sugar, tannic acid, extractive, and other plant constituents have also been determined.‡

PHYSIOLOGICAL ACTION.—Cimicifuga acts as a severe irritant to the nerve centres in general, and causes through its action upon the vaso-motor system cerebral, cerebro-spinal and pelvic congestion, followed by inflammatory action, especially upon the nerves themselves. The chorea-like spasmodic action following the exhibition of the drug is of two types, one having apparently a rheumatic basis, the other uterine; the latter is most common, as the choreas curable by this drug will be found aggravated or originating at the age of puberty or during menstruation. It causes rheumatic pains resembling those of torticollis, lumbago, and especially pleurodynia, sympathetic angina pectoris, and rheumatoid gout. The drug seems also to cause irritation of the uterus directly, especially when this irritation is rheumatoid in its character, and in consequence the individual under the effects of the drug will present symptoms of epileptiform or hysterical spasms, restlessness and jactitation of muscles, dysmenorrhœa or amenorrhœa, cephalalgia, infra-mammary pain, etc., as the case may be. In pregnancy it often causes abortion, and in labor will stimulate the uterus and cause rapid, painless expansion of the parts. According to Dr. Chapman it produces free nausea, with abundant expectoration, followed by nervous trembling, vertigo, and remarkable slowness of the pulse.

DESCRIPTION OF PLATE 11.

1. Part of the summit of a plant showing one of the smaller racemes, Binghamton, N.Y., July 10th, 1884.
2. Lower portion of stem, with a part of the root showing the remains of the growth of the two previous seasons.
3. Portion of one of the smaller leaves.
4. Section of the root.
5. A sepal (somewhat enlarged).
6. A staminodium (enlarged).
7. Stamen (enlarged).
8. Pollen x 300.
9. Pistil (enlarged).
10. Section of pistil (enlarged).
11. Fruit.
12. Section of capsule showing seeds.

* *Am. Jour. Phar.*, 1871, p. 151. † *Period. cit.*, 1884, p. 459.
‡ Tilghman, *Jour. Phil. Coll. Phar.*, 1834, p. 20; J. S. Jones, *Am. Jour. Phar.*, 1843, p. 1; G. H. Davis, *period. cit.*, 1861, p. 391; E. C. Jones, *Proc. Am. Phar. Ass'n*, 1865, p. 186; T. E. Conard, *art. cit. sup.*; M. S. Falck, *art. cit. sup.*

GENUS.—**MAGNOLIA**,* LINN.

SEX. SYST.—POLYANDRIA POLYGYNIA.

12
MAGNOLIA GLAUCA.

SWEET BAY.

SYN.—MAGNOLIA GLAUCA, LINN; M. VIRGINICA, *a* GLAUCA, LINN.; M. FRAGRANS, SALISB.; M. LONGIFOLIA, SWEET.

COM. NAMES.—SMALL, LAUREL, OR SWEET MAGNOLIA; SWEET, OR WHITE BAY; CASTOR, OR BEAVER WOOD; ELK OR INDIAN BARK; SWAMP SASSAFRAS, OR LAUREL; BEAVER TREE, BREWSTER; (FR.) LE MAGNOLIER GLAUQUE; (GER.) MAGNOLIE.

A TINCTURE OF THE FRESH FLOWERS OF MAGNOLIA GLAUCA, LINN.

Description.—This beautiful swamp shrub usually grows to a height of from 4 to 20 feet.† *Bark* smooth, whitish. *Buds* conical, silky; *leaves* all scattered, oblong, oval, or ovate-lanceolate, obtuse, thickish, shining green above and bluish-white beneath, evergreen southward, deciduous northward. *Inflorescence* solitary and terminal; *flowers* globular, white, very fragrant. *Sepals* 3, oblong, scaphoid. *Petals* 6 to 9, erect, broadly ovate, and narrowed at the base. *Stamens* numerous, imbricated; *filaments* short; *anthers* long, adnate, introrse. *Pistils* coherent in a mass aggregated upon the elongated torus. *Fruit* oblong, conical, small, and rather ligneous; *carpels* many, dehiscing by a longitudinal dorsal suture; *seeds* 1 to 2 in each carpel, baccate, vermilion, hanging from the bursted carpels by an extenuate thread composed of spiral vessels; *endocarp* bony.

Magnoliaceæ.—This small but magnificent family of trees and shrubs, represented in North America by 4 genera and 11 species, is characterized by having: the *buds* covered by membranous stipules; *leaves* alternate, coriaceous, pinnately veined, entire, and punctate with minute pellucid dots. *Flowers* single, large, polypetalous, the calyx and corolla colored alike, in æstivation generally imbricate in 3 or more rows of 3, all deciduous. *Stamens* numerous, hypogynous; *filaments* short; *anthers* long, adnate, introrse. *Pistils* many, coherent, generally closely packed together over the prolonged receptacle; *styles* short or none; *stigmas* simple. *Fruit* a fleshy, or dry cone, composed of many coherent carpels. *Seeds* 1 to 2 in each carpel, anatropous; *albumen* fleshy; *embryo* minute, basal.

---

* In honor of Professor Magnol, a botanist of the 17th century, at Montpellier.

† Mr. Britton observed, in Manahawken Swamp, Ocean Co., N. J., an individual with a diameter of trunk of 32.25 inches, whose rings showed a growth of 150 years.

The only other proven drug of this order is the Asiatic Star-anise (*Illicium anisatum*, Linn.), an aromatic and carminative, often substituted in general practice for the true Aniseed, the fruit of an umbelliferous plant. The South American Winter's Bark, from *Wintera aromatica*, Murr., is used in Brazil as an aromatic tonic, especially though in colic. The North American *Illicium floridanum*, Ellis, is reputed to have an action similar to that of aromatic tonics in general; and the Tulip Tree (*Liriodendron Tulipifera*, Linn.) yields a bark that is at once bitter and aromatic, much valued as a stimulating tonic and diaphoretic in intermittents and chronic rheumatism; it should be proven. The Javanese *Aromadendron elegans* has a native reputation as a carminative, stomachic, and antihysteric; and the wood of *Manglietia glauca* is supposed to be antiputrefactive, therefore it is used by the inhabitants of the island for the manufacture of coffins. Several other genera furnish aromatic and bitter tonic barks, many of which are used by the natives of the countries in which they grow.

History and Habitat.—The Sweet Magnolia is indigenous to North America, from Cape Ann and Long Island southward. At first it keeps to the seaboard, but gradually extends inland the farther south it is found. It grows in swamps, and expands its fragrant flowers from May (southward) to June and August.

The use of the fresh bark, cones, and seeds of this species, together with those of M. grandiflora, acuminata, tripetala, and macrophylla, has descended to the laity and general practitioner from the Aborigines, who employed a warm decoction of the bark and cones extensively against rheumatism, and a cold infusion as an antiperiodic. The fresh bark has long been considered as a bitter, aromatic tonic, febrifuge, diaphoretic, antiperiodic and gentle laxative, in acute coryzas, bronchial catarrhs, chronic rheumatism, dyspepsia, remittent and intermittent fevers and typhoid states, being deemed contraindicated, however, if inflammation be present. The odor of the cut flowers, especially at night in a close room, is very penetrating, unpleasant, and to some insupportable, causing, in susceptible persons, a great oppression of the chest and vertigo. Dr. Wm. Barton "imputed to the odor the power of increasing the pain of inflammatory gout, and occasioning an exacerbation of a diurnal fever."* It is thoroughly believed in the South that a growth of magnolias in stagnant waters renders them pure and prevents the generation of malarial poisons.

The bark is still official in the U. S. Ph.

PART USED AND PREPARATION.—The fresh flowers are chopped and pounded to a pulp and weighed. Then two parts by weight of alcohol are taken, the pulp thoroughly mixed with one-sixth part of it, and the rest of the alcohol added. After stirring the whole well, it is poured into a well-stoppered vial and allowed to stand eight days in a dark, cool place. The tincture thus prepared should, after filtration, have a deep brownish-red color by transmitted light, a perfume much like the wilted flowers, an acrid and bitter taste, and an acid reaction.

* W. P. C. Barton, *Med. Bot. loc. cit.*

1

2   3

4

€.m. ad nat del.et pinxt.

MAGNÒLIA GLAÙCA, Linn.

CHEMICAL CONSTITUENTS.—The flowers have not been examined; they probably, however, contain a volatile oil at least. The bark of *M. grandiflora* was examined by Dr. Procter,* who found a volatile oil, resin, and a crystalline principle resembling *liriodendrine*.

Magnolin.—This bitter principle was extracted from the fruit of *M. umbrella* by Wallace Procter, 1872, as acicular crystals, having a bitter taste. They are insoluble in water, soluble in alcohol and chloroform, melt at 80°-82° (176°-179.6° F.), and emit white vapors at 125° (257° F.), which condense in oily drops, consisting partly of the original principle and of resin. (Wittstein.)

PHYSIOLOGICAL ACTION.—The effects of the odor of the flowers, as reported by Drs. Barton. S. A. Jones,† and T. F. Allen,‡ are: Great uneasiness and oppression of the chest, with an inability to expand the lungs, a feeling as if having swallowed a large bolus of unmasticated food which distressed the stomach, and a tendency to fainting. Showing thus a dilation of the vascular system so commonly following the insufflation of strongly odorous flowers in susceptible persons. Magnolia certainly deserves a careful proving of the fresh bark and flowers; the *flowers alone* can hardly add to our medicamentæ while we have Cactus grandiflorus.

DESCRIPTION OF PLATE 12.

1. End of a flowering branch, Landisville, N. J., July 3d, 1885.
2. Stamen.
3. Section of a carpel.
4. Fruit.
(2 and 3 enlarged.)

---

* *Am. Jour. Phar.*, 1842, p. 89.   † *Am. Hom. Obs.*, June, 1875.   ‡ *Encyc. Pure Mat. Med.*, vi., 142.

GENUS.—**ASIMINA**,* ADANS.

SEX. SYST.—POLYANDRIA POLYGYNIA.

13

ASIMINA TRILOBA.

PAWPAW.

SYN.—ASIMINA TRILOBA, DUNAL.; ASIMINA CAMPANIFLORA, SPACH.; ANNONA TRILOBA, LINN.; ORCHIDOCARPUM ARIETINUM, MICHX.; PORCELIA TRILOBA, PERS.; UVARIA TRILOBA, TORR. AND GRAY.
COM. NAMES.—PAWPAW, PAPAW,† AMERICAN CUSTARD-APPLE; (FR.) ASIMINIER; (GER.) DREILAPPIGE ASIMINE.

A TINCTURE OF THE RIPE SEEDS OF ASIMINA TRILOBA, DUNAL.

Description.—This curious-fruited tree attains a height of from 10 to 30 feet, with about the same diameter of foliage. *Bark* smooth, grayish. *Leaves* long, thin, and membraneous, entire, oblong-lanceolate, acute or acuminate, and are covered with a rusty-hairiness upon the nether surface when first expanding, but soon become entirely glabrous. *Inflorescence* solitary in the axils of the previous year's leaves; *flowers* dull purple, appearing with, or just before, the leaves. *Sepals* 3, ovate, much shorter than the petals. *Petals* 6, spreading, veiny, rounded-ovate, their upper third more or less recurved; they are arranged in two rows, the outer larger, all enlarging after anthesis. *Stamens* indefinite, arranged in a globular head, thus concealing the ovaries and styles. *Pistils* few, their stigmas projecting beyond the stamens than which they are longer. *Fruits* 1-4, developed from each flower, they are oblong, rounded, pulpy, several-seeded, and resemble in shape the shorter red bananas. *Seeds* oval, horizontal, flattish-compressed, and surrounded by a fleshy aril.

Anonaceæ.—This chiefly tropical order consists of *trees* or *shrubs* having naked buds and aromatic or fetid bark. *Leaves* alternate, entire, pinnate-veined, and usually punctate; stipules wanting. *Æstivation* valvular; *flowers* large, dull colored. *Sepals* 3, often connected at the base. *Petals* 6, thick, arranged in two rows. *Torus* rounded, hypogynous; *stamens* numerous or indefinite; *filaments* very short, sometimes just perceptible; *anthers* adnate, extrorse; *connectivum* fleshy, somewhat quadrangular, often nectariferous. *Pistils* numerous, crowded, and sometimes coherent, especially in fruit; *styles* short or wanting; *stigmas* simple, capitellate. *Fruit* fleshy or pulpy; *seeds* anatropous, one or more in each ovary; *testa* brittle; *embryo* basal, minute; *albumen* hard, ruminated.

---

* Asiminier, the name applied by the French Colonists.
† This name more properly applies to the West Indian *Carica Papaya* (Papayaceæ).

The plants of this family are not generally considered medicinal, but Blume states that many species of the genera Uvaria, Unona, and Zylopia are employed in Java, but require caution, as they often cause vertigo, hemorrhage, and sometimes abortion in pregnant states.* The South American *Frutta de Burro* (*Xylopia longifolia*) is termed by Humboldt a valuable fruit, for use as a febrifuge, along the river Orinoco. *Piper Æthiopicum* is the seed of *Habzelia Æthiopica;* another species of the same genus (*H. aromatica*) being used by the natives of Guiana as a spice. The Jamaica nutmeg (*Monodora myristica*) is said to be similar to, but not so pungent as, the nutmeg of commerce (*Myristica moschata*). Jamaica bitterwood (*Xylopia glabra*) is considered tonic and stimulant.† To the arts this order furnishes Jamaica Lancewood (*Guatteria virgata*), useful on account of its lightness and elasticity, in the manufacture of coaches, fishing-rods, and bows. Succulent fruits are yielded by *Anncna Cherimolia* (Cherimoyer), and *Anona squamosa* (Custard-apple).

History and Habitat.—The common pawpaw is indigenous to the central belt of the United States from Western New York to the Mississippi and southward. It locates along streams where the soil is rich and frosts late. This small tree is a native, especially of the Ohio valley, where it flowers from March to May, according to the season. It is grown in a protected place in Central Park, New York City, but is not hardy north of Cincinnati. The fruit, when ripe, is soft, sweet, and insipid, having a taste somewhat between that of the May-apple and the banana, tending to the former. It was greatly prized by the aborigines,—who eagerly sought anything edible in the vegetable world—and now is occasionally exposed for sale in city markets. When green they have a very unpleasant odor, and are only fit to eat after having been touched by frost, when they turn from yellowish-green to black, and become internally of the color and consistence of custard.‡ It is claimed that they improve greatly in size, taste, and succulency upon cultivation. Three other species: *A. grandiflora*, *A. parviflora*, and *A. pygmæa* complete the genus north of Mexico.

The former uses of this plant in medicine are of little or no importance. A tincture of the seed proves emetic; the bark being bitter has been considered tonic and stimulant. The chemical properties and physiological action have never been—to my knowledge—determined.

PART USED AND PREPARATION.—The coarsely powdered, fresh, ripe seeds are covered with five parts by weight of alcohol, and allowed to remain eight days in a well-stoppered bottle in a dark, cool place.

The tincture thus prepared is filtered off. It has a clear, pale, canary color by transmitted light; an astringent straw-like taste; an odor somewhat like that of the red raspberry, and a slight acidity.

All that is known of the medicinal power of this drug is a proving by Dr.

---

* Lindley, *Flor. Med.*, p. 29.   † *Idem*, pp. 27–8.   ‡ Whence the name "American Custard-apple."

5

1

4   3

2

6

Ɛm .ad nat del et pinxt.   ASÍMINA TRÍLOBA, Dunal.

Eisenboeg.* A preparation from the seeds, bark, and green fruit might prove of more utility, and possess greater power of action.

DESCRIPTION OF PLATE 13.

1. End of a flowering branch (several blossoms missing) from North Bend, Ohio, May 15th, 1884.
2. Calyx and torus, after removal of the stamens.
3. A stamen (enlarged).
4. Pollen x 250.
5. Fruit and full-grown leaf.
6. Seed and opened aril.

Drawn from living specimens received from Ohio through the kindness of Mr. R. H. Warder, son of the late Dr. John A. Warder, President of the American Forestry Association, 1881.

---

* Allen, *Ency. Pure Mat. Med.*, Vol. 1, p. 498-9.

14

MENISPERMUM.

YELLOW PARILLA.

SYN.—MENISPERMUM CANADENSE, LINN.; M. ANGULATUM, MŒN.; M. SMILACINUM, D. C.; CISSAMPELOS SMILACINA, LINN.
COM. NAMES.—YELLOW PARILLA, CANADIAN MOONSEED, TEXAS OR YELLOW SARSAPARILLA, MAPLE VINE.

A TINCTURE OF THE FRESH ROOT OF MENISPERMUM CANADENSE, L.

Description.—This perennial climber reaches a length of from 8 to 15 feet. *Root* cylindrical, long, yellow; *stem* slender. *Leaves* ample, peltate, with the insertion of the petiole near the base, 3 to 7 lobed or angled; *lobes* obtuse or more or less acute; *venation* palmate, the veins pubescent below; *petioles* about the length of the leaves. *Inflorescence* in long, supra-axillary compound racemes or panicles. *Sepals* 4 to 8, obovate-oblong, arranged in a double series. *Petals* 6 to 8, small, somewhat cuneate, fleshy, with a thickened free margin. *Stamens* 12 to 20 (in the sterile flowers), as long as the petals; *filaments* hardly thickened at the summit; *anthers* innate, 4-celled. *Pistils* 2 to 4 (in the fertile flowers), raised upon a short, common torus, usually perfecting but two drupes; *stigmas* flattened. *Fruit* a globose-reniform, black, and stipitate drupe, furnished with a bloom, and retaining the mark of the stigma; *nutlet* more or less lunate, wrinkled and grooved, laterally flattened; *embryo* slender, horseshoe-shaped; *cotyledons* filiform.

Menispermaceæ.—This goodly-sized family of tropical or sub-tropical, woody climbers, is represented in North America by but 3 genera and 6 species. *Leaves* alternate, palmate or peltate; *stipules* none. *Inflorescence* in axillary racemes or panicles; *flowers* small, monœcious, diœcious or polygamous; *æstivation* imbricate. *Sepals* arranged in two or more rows, deciduous. *Petals* usually equal in number to the sepals, hypogynous. *Stamens* monadelphous or separate, equal in number to the petals and opposite them, or from 2 to 4 times as many, adnate or innate, composed of 4 horizontal ovoid lobes arranged tip to base, and opening longitudinally (apparently horizontal. See Fig. 6). *Pistils* 3 to 6; *ovaries* several, united or separate, nearly straight; *stigmas* apical, but looking downward in fruit on account of the incurving of the ripening ovaries. *Fruit* a 1-celled drupe; *seeds* 1 in each cell; *embryo* large, long and curved, surrounded by the albumen; *albumen* scanty.
  Our only proven plant of this order, beside Menispermum, is the Indian Cocculus Indicus (*Anamirta paniculata*, Cole), a narcotico-poison, used by the

---

* Μήνη, *mene*, moon; σπέρμα, *sperma*, seed; the seed being lunate in shape.

natives to stupefy fish, and supposedly in this country and Europe to give bitterness to malt liquors.

Many other species are used in medicine, of which the following hold a more or less permanent place: The Brazilian Pareira brava, the roots of *Chonodrodendron tomentosum*, R. et P., a tonic and diuretic, considered almost specific in its action upon the mucous membranes of the genito-urinary tract; the Indian Gulancha (*Tinospora cordifolia*, Miers.), a valuable tonic, antiperiodic and diuretic; the African Columbo (*Jateorhiza Columba*, Miers.), a bitter stomachic and mild tonic, often used with good effect in vomiting of pregnancy and atonic dyspepsia; the West-Indian False Pareira brava (*Cissampelos Pareira*, Linn.), more often used than the true article for the purposes mentioned. The root of the Crayor and Senegal *Cocculus Bakis*, Guill., is used by the natives in the treatment of their intermittents and in urethral discharges; the root of the Cochin-China *C. fibraurea*, D. C., is used like the former, and also in various liver affections; *C. cinerascens* and *A. platyphyllus*, St. Hil., command the same attention by the Brazilians; while the Javanese use *C. crispus*, D. C, which is powerfully bitter, in like troubles. *Cocculus acuminatus*, D. C., is considered alexiteric in Brazil. The Malabar and Ceylon *Clypea Burmanni*, W. and A., is employed, according to Lindley, in intermittents and hepatic disturbances, as well as a remedy against dysentery and hemorrhoids. *Cissampelos ovalifolia*, D. C., in Brazil, and *Abuta rufescens*, Aubl., in Guayana are used, like most of the members of this order, as a remedy in intermittents and obstruction of the liver.

History and Habitat.—The Canadian Moonseed is indigenous to North America, where it is quite common on the banks of streams from Canada southward to the Carolinas and westward to the Mississippi.

Our first knowledge of this plant as a remedy was undoubtedly handed down from the Aborigines, who are said by Rafinesque to have used the root in scrofulosis; the early settlers also found it useful as a diuretic in strangury in horses. Its employment generally by early practitioners has been very similar to that of Sarsaparilla, *i. e.*, in mercurial, syphilitic, scrofulous and rheumatic diatheses; also as a laxative and tonic in general debility, atonic dyspepsia and kindred disorders; and as a remedy in pleural adhesions and inflammation of the alimentative mucous membranes.

Menispermum was admitted to the U. S. Ph. at the last revision, the rhizome and rootlets being now officinal. In the Eclectic Materia Medica its preparations are: *Decoctum Menispermi, Menispermin*, and as a component of *Syrupus Rumecis Compositus.**

PART USED AND PREPARATION.—The fresh root is chopped and pounded to a pulp and weighed. Then two parts by weight of alcohol are taken, the pulp thoroughly mixed with one sixth part of it and the rest of the alcohol added. After stirring the whole well, pour it into a well-stoppered bottle and let it stand eight days in a dark, cool place.

---

* Yellowdock root; False-bittersweet, root bark; American ivy bark; Figwort; and Moonseed root.

14.

9

8

4

1

2

5

3

6

7

Cm. ad nat. del. et pinxt. MENISPÉRMUM CANADÉNSE, Linn.

The tincture, separated from this mass by filtration, is opaque; in thin layers it has a deep madder-lake color by transmitted light; a bitterish odor; an acid, bitter and astringent taste; and acid reaction.

CHEMICAL CONSTITUENTS.—Berberina. Prof. J. M. Maisch, who first investigated this root,* found a small quantity of this alkaloid, the nature of which is detailed in the next drug, page 15–2. He also found a second alkaloid, which was afterward named

Menispermine.†—A white, amorphous, tasteless alkaloid, insoluble in water, slightly soluble in alcohol, ether and chloroform.

Menispine.‡—This second specific alkaloid, determined by Barber in his analysis, differs in solubility and tests from both *oxycanthine*§ and *menispermine*. It resulted as a whitish, amorphous, very bitter powder, slightly soluble in water, ether and chloroform, and very soluble in absolute alcohol. Tincture of iodine gives a dark-red precipitate with this body, and with *menispermine*, a yellow precipitate.

Menispermo-tannic Acid.‖—This specific tannin gives a dark-green color with ferric chloride.

Two yellowish resins, one soluble in ether, and the general constituents of plants, were also determined.

PHYSIOLOGICAL ACTION.—Prof. E. M. Hale's experiments with from 35 drops upward of a tincture of the root, and various doses of the "resinoid" *menispermine*, resulted as follows: Temporal and occipital headache, with stretching and yawning, and fullness of the head; swollen tongue; salivation; dryness of the buccal mucous membranes and of the throat; nausea; thirst; colic; rectal tenesmus; scanty, high-colored urine; aching of the extremities; itching of the skin; restlessness and troubled sleep.

Excessive doses cause an increase in the rate and volume of the pulse, and excessive vomiting and purging. The action of the drug is that of an irritant to the nerves governing the alimentary tract, resulting in increased secretions from the mucous membranes.

DESCRIPTION OF PLATE 14.

1. Part of male flowering stem, Ithaca, N. Y., June 24th, 1885.
2. End of stem.
3. Staminate flower.
4. Sepal.
5. Petal.
6. Stamen.
7. Female flower.
8. Carpel.
9. Outline of a leaf.
   (3–8 enlarged.)

---

* *Am. Jour. Phar.*, 1863, 303.
‡ Name proposed by Prof. Maisch, *Ibid.*
† H. L. Barber, *Am. Jour. Phar.*, 1884, 401.
§ See page 15–2.   ‖ Barber, *Ibid.*

GENUS.—**BERBERIS**,* LINN.

SEX. SYST.—HEXANDRIA MONOGYNIA.

15

BERBERIS.

BARBERRY.

SYN.—BERBERIS VULGARIS, LINN.; BERBERIS VULGARIS, VAR. CAN-
ADENSIS, TORR., SPINA ACIDA; BERBERIS DUMETORUM, RAII.
COM. NAMES.—COMMON BARBERRY, BERBERRY; (FR.) EPINE-VINETTE;
(GER.) SAURDORN.

A TINCTURE OF THE FRESH ROOT BARK OF BERBERIS VULGARIS, LINN.

Description.—This attractive, bushy shrub grows to a height of from 3 to 8 feet; the stem-wood, inner-bark and pith are yellow. *Leaves* inversely egg-shaped, short-petioled, closely serrate, and bristly-toothed. Occurring either singly or in a dense fascicle above the spines, they are of a cold-green color and very acid; *spines* triple, branched or sometimes simple, minutely maculate and surrounded by the rosette of leaves. *Inflorescence* long, drooping, many-flowered racemes, of pale yellow flowers. *Bractlets* 2 to 6, situate about the base of the calyx. *Sepals* 6, deciduous, rounded, the outer three smaller. *Petals* 6, entire, obovate, concave, with two minute, oblong, deeper-colored glandular spots at the base, inside and above the short claw. *Stamens* 6, their *filaments* ligulate, blunt, opposite the petals, but shorter and attached to their bases; *anthers* adnate. *Pistil* about the length of the stamens; *ovary* more or less inflated-cylindrical; *style* rarely present, very short; *stigma* short, flattened, sessile or nearly so. *Fruit* a one- to nine-seeded, oblong, scarlet, sour berry, evenly depressed in the median diameter; *seeds* erect on a short stalk rising from the base of the cell, oblong, with a crust-like integument.

Berberidaceæ.—Shrubs or herbs with alternate leaves and perfect flowers. *Sepals* 3 to 9, deciduous, often colored and furnished with a calyculus of petal-like scales, all together with the petals imbricate in two or more rows in æstivation (Jeffersonia with a single row). *Petals* as many as the sepals. *Stamens* hypogynous, equal in number to the petals and opposite them (Podophyllum) twice as many); *filaments* short; *anther* sextrorse, opening (except Podophyllum) by two valves or hinged lids at the top. *Pistil* only one, *ovary* simple, solitary; *style* short or wanting; *stigma* flattened. *Fruit* a capsule or berry with either a few *seeds* at the top or bottom of the cell, or many, situated along the whole extent of the ventral ridge; all anatropous, and furnished with albumen; *embryo* small (Berberis excepted).

---

* From Amyrberis, Arabic for the fruit.

History and Habitat.—Berberis was well known to the ancients as a medicine, a dietetic for the sick, and a dye. As a drug it was steeped in beer and given to patients suffering from jaundice, as well as to check hemorrhages; as a food preparation for the sick, the berries were made into a confection, and used as a refrigerant in fevers and burning gastric ailments; those not sick used the bruised leaves in a manner similar to sorrel as a sauce for meats; as a dye, the roots were steeped with strong ash-lye, and used to give the hair a yellow color. The same preparation is now sometimes used to dye wool, while by using alum, in place of the ash-lye, it makes a good as well as a beautiful dye for linen fabrics. A jelly made of the berries is still used in lieu of tamarinds as a pleasant refrigerant, as so also is a confection. Its popular use as a remedy—barberry bark and cider —was held in all forms of abdominal inflammation, but especially those accompanied with hepatic derangement and jaundice.

Berberis vulgaris is indigenous to Great Britain and other parts of Europe, and is becoming quite thoroughly naturalized here, especially in the Eastern States, blossoming from May to June. It is cultivated in many parts of the country as an ornamental bush, on account of its beautiful berries. Our own species, B. Canadensis, Pursh., is a shrub about *three feet high*, with *less bristly* teeth to the leaves, a few-flowered raceme, *petals notched* at the apex, and *oval berries*. In Berberis proper, upon the summer shoots may be seen a perfect instance of gradation, in all forms, from the leaf as described above, to a fully-developed spine, a fine instance of vegetable morphology. The leaves of the barberry are at times, especially in Europe, infested with a peculiar blight; Æcidium Berberidis (Microspheria Berberidis; Lysiphe Berberides) a member of the coniomycetous fungi; order, uredinei. It consists in its full-grown condition of little cups filled with a reddish or brownish powder (spores), formed by a bulging upward and bursting of the epidermis of the leaf, by the parasite developed within. This blight caused much fear at one time in Europe, upon the supposition that it was communicated to grain, which however was very probably false.

Berberis, like many other excellent remedies, has been dismissed this year (1882) from the U. S. Ph. In the Eclectic Materia Medica it is still retained, though not in an officinal preparation.

PART USED AND PREPARATION.—The fresh bark of the root. This is coarsely powdered and weighed. Then after adding two parts by weight of alcohol the whole is put into a well-stoppered bottle and allowed to stand eight days in a dark, cool place, shaking the contents twice a day; the tincture is then strained and filtered. Thus prepared, it has a deep orange-brown color by transmitted light; and stains the neck of the bottle yellow. It has an extremely bitter taste, and a slight acid reaction.

CHEMICAL CONSTITUENTS.—Berberin, $C_{20}H_{17}NO_4$. This alkaloid was first discovered in 1824, in the bark of Geoffroya inermis,[*] two years afterward in the bark of Xanthoxylum lava Herculis,[†] in 1851 in the root of Hydrastis Canadensis,[‡] and in 1835 in the bark of Berberis vulgaris;[§] yet, it is only lately

---

[*] Jamaicin.   [†] Xanthropicrit.   [‡] Hydrastin.   [§] Berberin.

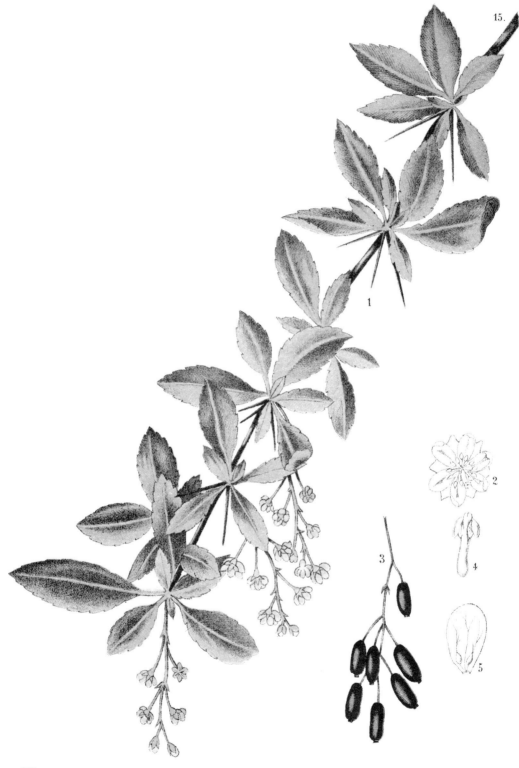

15.

1

2

3

4

5

Cm.ad nat.del.et pinxt.

BÉRBERIS VULGÀRIS , Linn.

that its true properties were recognized. It exists in a number of other plants, among which of particular interest to us are Coptis trifoliata, Caulophyllum, and Xanthorrhiza. Berberin crystallizes in fine yellow needles of a strong and persistent bitter taste, losing water at 100° (212° F.), and fusing at 120° (248° F.) to a reddish-brown resinoid, decomposing at higher heat. Berberin is soluble in water and alcohol.

Oxyacanthin,* $C_{32} H_{46} N_2 O_{11}$ (Berbina Vinetina). This bitter alkaloid exists together with the berberin in the root. It is a non-crystallizable, white, electric powder, but will form in needles upon the addition of ether or alcohol; it turns yellow by exposure in sunlight, has an alkaline reaction, loses 3.13 per cent. weight upon exposure to 100° (212° F.), fuses at 139° (282°.2 F.), and like berberin decomposes upon subjection to higher temperatures. It is soluble in both water and alcohol, though not freely. (*Et supra* Wittstein.)

The acidity of the leaves and fruit is due to the presence of oxalic acid.

PHYSIOLOGICAL ACTION.—Berberis in moderate doses produces feverishness, inflammation of the mucous membranes from the throat to the intestines, and dysentery. It causes also a high degree of inflammation of the kidneys with hematuria. It seems to act with much force upon the venous system, causing pelvic engorgements and hemorrhoids. Its use in early medicine was purely symptomatic. The action as above given refers to man; upon animals no such effects appear to follow, even though experiments were made with the alkaloid Berberin.

DESCRIPTION OF PLATE 15.

1. End of branch in flower, with old leaves, Salem, Mass., June 4, 1880.
    2. Flower (enlarged).
    3. Fruit.
    4. Stamen (enlarged).
    5. Petal (enlarged, showing glands).

* *Crategus oxyacantha* contains an alkaloid by this name.

GENUS.—**CAULOPHYLLUM,*** MICHX.

SEX. SYST.—HEXANDRIA MONOGYNIA.

16
CAULOPHYLLUM.

BLUE COHOSH.

SYN.—CAULOPHYLLUM THALICTROIDES, MICHX.; LEONTICE THALICT-
ROIDES, LINN.; LEONTOPETALON THALICTROIDES, HILL.
COM. NAMES.—BLUE COHOSH, PAPPOOSE-ROOT, SQUAW-ROOT,† BLUE
BERRY,‡ BLUE GINSENG, YELLOW GINSENG; (FR.) COHOCHE BLEU;
(GER.) BLAU COHOSCH.

A TINCTURE OF THE FRESH ROOT OF CAULOPHYLLUM THALICTROIDES,
MICHX.

Description.—This erect, perennial herb, attains a growth of from 1 to 2½
feet. *Root* horizontal or contorted, wrinkled and branched, showing many upright nodules, bearing at their summits the scars of previous stems, and giving
off numerous cylindrical, branching rootlets from the older portions. *Stem* simple, glaucous when young, smooth when old, arising from several imbricate,
membraneous scales. *Leaves* large, triternately decompound, the upper much
smaller and biternate (pl. 16, fig. 1); *leaflets* 2 to 3 lobed, obtusely wedge-shape at
the base; *petioles* blending with the stem in such a manner as to render their
junction almost obscure. *Inflorescence* a loose raceme or panicle; *peduncle* arising from the base of the upper leaf; *flowers* purplish or yellowish-green. *Sepals*
6, oval-oblong, with 3 small bractlets at the base. *Petals* 6, gland-like, with a
short claw and a somewhat reniform or hooded body, the whole much smaller
than the sepals, at the base of which they are inserted. *Stamens* 6, overlaying,
and about the same length as the petals; *anthers* oblong, 2-celled, the cells opening by uplifting valves. *Pistils* gibbous; *ovary* resembling the anthers in form,
2-celled; *style* short, apical; *stigma* minute, unilateral. *Fruit* a 2-seeded pod;
epicarp thin, papyraceous, bursting and withering before fertilization is complete,
leaving the naked seeds to farther develop upon their erect, thick funiculi; *pericarp* fleshy, deep blue; *albumen* corneous; *embryo* minute, apical. Read description of the natural order, under Berberis, 15.

History and Habitat.—The Blue Cohosh is indigenous to the United States,
growing abundantly in moist, rich woods, from Canada southward to Kentucky

---

* Καυλός, *kaulos*, a stem; and φύλλον, *phyllon*, a leaf, the stem resembling the petiole of a large leaf.
† The true squaw-root is *Conopholis Americana, Wall.* (Orobanchaceæ).
‡ This vulgarism properly belongs to several species of *Vaccinium* (Ericaceæ).

and the Carolinas. It blossoms from April to May, before the full development of the leaves. The berries are mawkish, insipid, and without special flavor. The seeds are said to resemble coffee when roasted.

The aborigines found in Caulophyllum their most valuable parturient; an infusion of the root, drank as tea, for a week or two preceding confinement, rendering delivery rapid and comparatively painless. They also used the root as a remedy for rheumatism, dropsy, uterine inflammation, and colic (Raf.). These uses have been proven reliable by all methods of practice since.

The root is officinal in the U. S. Ph. The preparations in the Eclectic Materia Medica are: *Extractum Caulophylli Alcoholicum, Resina Caulophylli,* and *Tinctura Caulophylli Composita.**

PART USED AND PREPARATION.—The fresh root, gathered in early spring, should be chopped and pounded to a pulp and weighed. Then two parts by weight of alcohol are taken, the pulp mixed thoroughly with one-sixth part of it, and the rest of the alcohol added. After stirring the whole well, and pouring it into a well-stoppered bottle, allow it to stand at least eight days in a dark, cool place.

The tincture, obtained from the above mass by filtration, should have a deep orange-red color, by transmitted light, a taste at first sharp and penetrating, then sweetish, an acid reaction, and should foam largely on succussion.

CHEMICAL CONSTITUENTS.—*Saponin.* This body was discovered in the roots of Caulophyllum by Prof. Mayer. A. E. Ebert† corroborates the discovery, and adds the presence of two resins, one soluble in alcohol and ether, the other not soluble in ether.

Caulophyllin.—The mass sold under this name is a mixture of the resins, extracted by simply pouring the partly-evaporated alcoholic tincture into water.

Ebert determined also gum, starch, and a greenish-yellow coloring-matter, beside the general plant constituents.

PHYSIOLOGICAL ACTION.—The dust of the powdered root is extremely irritating to the mucous membranes with which it comes in contact, so much so that the Lloyds say,‡ "workmen dislike to handle it, some even preferring capsicum." This irritation follows the administration of the drug throughout the body, but especially upon the female generative organs. It also exhibits the power of causing contractions of both voluntary and involuntary muscular fibres, the latter showing in the gravid uterus especially; here it does not cause the long-lasting contractions of ergot, but intermittent and more successful ones. Its spasmodic action on general muscles is somewhat chorea-like. Caulophyllum also causes many forms of constant pains in the small joints, as well as fleeting rheumatic pains in the extremities. There is hardly an American remedy in our Materia

* Caulophyllum, Secale, Polygonum, and Oil of Sabina.
† *Am. Jour. Phar.,* 1864, p. 203.
‡ "*Berberidaceæ,*" C. G. and J. U. Lloyd, 1878.

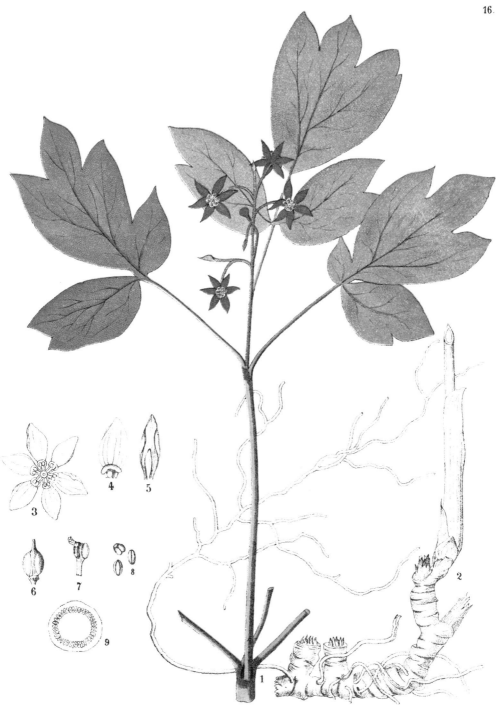

Œm.ad nat.del.et pinxt.   CAULOPHÝLLUM THALICTROÏDES, Michx.

Medica that needs, and probably merits, a more thorough proving, upon females especially, than Caulophyllum; and the sooner it is done, the better able will we be to cope with many of our most obstinate uterine cases.

DESCRIPTION OF PLATE 16.

1. Summit of flowering plant, Ithaca, N. Y., April 18th, 1880.
2. Root, rootlet, sheathing scales, and stem.
3. Flower (enlarged).
4. An enlarged sepal, showing the gland-like petal (enlarged).
5. Under surface of sepal, showing bract (enlarged).
6. Pistil (enlarged).
7. Stamen (enlarged), showing open anther-cell.
8. Pollen x 200 (3 views).
9. Section of the root.

GENUS.—**PODOPHYLLUM**,* LINN.

SEX. SYST.—POLYANDRIA MONOGYNIA.

17

PODOPHYLLUM.

MAY-APPLE.

SYN.—PODOPHYLLUM PELTATUM, LINN.; ANAPODOPHYLLUM CANA-DENSE, CATESBY; ACONITIFOLIUS HUMILIS, Etc., MENTZ.

COM. NAMES.—MAY-APPLE, INDIAN-APPLE, HOG-APPLE, WILD LEMON, DUCK'S FOOT, WILD JALAP, PECA, RACCOON-BERRY, MANDRAKE;† (FR.) PODOPHYLLE; (GER.) FUSSBLATT, SCHILDBLÄTTIGER ENTENFUSS.

A TINCTURE OF THE FRESH ROOT OF PODOPHYLLUM PELTATUM, LINN.

Description.—This well-known plant grows to a height of from 8 to 18 inches. *Root* perennial, horizontal, extending several feet; the annual growths are from 1 to 3 inches in length, distinguishable by the scars of previous stems; they are cylindrical, from ¼ to ½ inches in diameter, and give off a few, nearly simple, fibrous rootlets. *Stems* single, simple, erect, and rounded, the flowerless ones surmounted by a single 7 to 9 lobed leaf, round in its general outline, peltate in the centre, and somewhat resembling an umbrella; the flowering stems generally bifurcated at the summit, thus bearing two leaves, with a flower, at the bifurcation. *Leaves* of the flowering stems 2, somewhat one-sided and deeply lobed, the lobes variously incised and toothed; drooping at the edges, and strongly marked by the prominent roundish ribs below. *Inflorescence* a single, drooping, pedunculated flower, generally in the fork of the stem, but sometimes varying greatly in its location.‡ *Calyx* during the prefloral stage, with three fugacious green bractlets at its base; *sepals* 6, breaking off from the peduncle as the bud expands, never appearing upon the flower except when, by accident, one of them clings to and deforms a petal. *Petals* either 6 or 9, obovate, creamy-white, and fleshy. *Stamens* generally 12 to 18, twice as many as the petals; *filaments* short; *anthers* large, flattened, opening extrorsely by a single longitudinal line, thus forming what might be termed two lateral valves, hinged upon the inner surface; *pollen* shaped like grains of rice, and furnished with three comparatively deep sulci. *Pistil* simple; *ovary* more or less ovoid, 1-celled; *ovules* many, situated in many rows upon a broad, lateral placenta, extending the whole length of the cell; *style* not manifest; *stigma* more or less peltate-globose, composed of a number of fleshy lobes

---

* Πούς, *pous*, a foot; φύγγον, *phyllon*, a leaf. Probably from a supposed likeness of the leaf to the webbed foot of some aquatic bird.

† The true mandrake is *Atropa mandragora;* habitat, south of Europe.

‡ See article by Foerste, *Bull. Torr. Club,* 1884, p. 63.

closely set, each resembling a half meat of the hickory-nut. *Fruit* an egg-shaped, yellow edible berry, 1 to 2 inches long, irregularly blotched, and retaining the withered stigma, or is marked by its scar; *seeds* enclosed within a copious, pulpy arillus; *embryo* minute, situated at the base of the fleshy albumen.

History and Habitat.—The May-apple is indigenous throughout the United States, growing profusely upon wet meadows and in damp, open woods; it flowers in May, and fruits in August. The apples, when fully ripe, are gathered, especially by children, who seem to relish their sweet, mawkish taste. I have also seen them exposed for sale in markets, though catharsis often follows indulgence in them, and, to susceptible persons, it is often quite severe. The fruit tastes somewhat like that of the paw-paw (*Asimina triloba*), and is much esteemed by the aborigines. The odor of the flowers is nauseous; I am always forcibly reminded of a bad case of ozæna when inhaling their perfume (?). The foliage and stems, when appearing in spring, have been used for a potherb, and in some cases with fatal results. Only one species of Podophyllum is recognized in this country, although Rafinesque has mentioned two others, together with ten named varieties. There is, however, one other species of this genus growing in the mountains of Nepaul, the *Podophyllum hexandrum.*

This plant constitutes one of the principal remedies used by the American aborigines, by whom it is especially valued on account of its cathartic action. Their use of the drug as an anthelmintic seems to be successful only as far as purging is concerned; specifically, it has no anthelmintic power. The use of podophyllum as a component of cathartic pills is very general.

The officinal preparations of the U. S. Ph. are: *Abstractum Podophylli, Extractum Podophylli, Extractum Podophylli Fluidum,* and *Resina Podophylli;* the Eclectic: *Decoctum Podophylli, Tinctura Podophylli* and *Podophyllin,* and as a component of *Emplastrum Picis Compositum, Pilulæ Aloes Compositæ, Tinctura Corydalis Comp., Pilulæ Baptisiæ Compositæ, Pilulæ Copaibæ Compositæ, Pilulæ Ferri Compositæ, Pilulæ Leptandrini Compositæ, Pilulæ Podophyllini Compositæ, Pulvis Leptandrini Compositus,* and *Pulvis Podophyllini Compositus.*

PART USED AND PREPARATION.—The fresh root should be procured after the fruiting season, and chopped and pounded to a pulp and weighed. Then take two parts by weight of alcohol, mix the pulp thoroughly with one-sixth part of it, and add the rest. After stirring the whole well pour it into a well-stoppered bottle, and allow it to stand at least eight days in a dark, cool place. The tincture, separated by straining and filtering, should have a brownish-orange color by transmitted light, a bitter, acrid taste, and an acid reaction.

CHEMICAL CONSTITUENTS.—From many careful examinations and assays of the root of this plant, F. B. Power[*] and Prof. Maisch[†] claim the absence of any alkaloid, their observations in this respect being corroborated by Podwissotzki, whose exhaustive analyses of the resin[‡] are largely drawn from here.

---

[*] 1877.

[†] *Am. Jour. Phar.*, 1879, p. 580.

[‡] *Archiv. für experimentelle Pathologie und Pharmacognosie,* v. xiii, 1 and 2, 1880; and *Pharm. Zeitschrift für Russland,* Nos. 44–50. 1881. F. B. Power, in *Am. Jour. Phar.*, 1882, p. 102.

Podophyllin.—A resin mass, first observed and used by Prof. John King (1835). This resin is prepared substantially as follows: The root is exhausted with alcohol by percolation, and the alcohol evaporated from the percolate until it is of a syrupy consistence; this is warmed, and poured into many times its bulk of cold water constantly agitated, and allowed to stand for twenty-four hours, when the resin will be precipitated; this precipitate should be washed by decantation, straining and pressing, and dried at a temperature of about 80° F.; greater heat renders it darker, and the addition of alum to the water gives it a deep yellow color. Podophyllin prepared as above is of a blanched yellowish-gray color, slightly soluble in water, partly in ether, and boils at 124° (255° F.). The yield of the resin is about eighty-four pounds to the ton; highest in the month of April, lowest in July.*

Podophyllin contains, according to Podwissotzki:

Picropodophyllin, $C_{11}H_8O_2 + H_2O$.—This body purifies into colorless, silky, delicate crystals, soluble in strong alcohol, choloroform, and ether, insoluble in water, and low-per cent. alcohol, and melts at from 200 to 210° (392 to 410° F.). Picropodophyllin, when in solution, possesses a very bitter taste, and the action of podophyllin intensified.

Podophyllotoxin, $C_{11}H_{14}O_2$.—A bitter amorphous substance, soluble in dilute alcohol and hot water, precipitating from the latter, on cooling, in fine flakes. Its medical properties are very similar to picropodophyllin, and its availability greater, as it is more soluble.

Picropodophyllinic Acid.—This resinous acid is notable from the fact that it holds in solution the active principle of podophyllin, crystalline picropodophyllin. In its pure form, or as nearly pure as traces of picropodophyllin will allow, it is in the form of hornlike granules, readily soluble in alcohol, chloroform, and ether.

Podophylloquercetin, $C_{10}H_8O_4$.—This body, having none of the emetic or cathartic properties of podophyllin, is soluble in alcohol and ether; from the latter it crystallizes in short yellowish needles, having a metallic lustre. By exposure to air it takes on a greenish color. It melts at 247 to 250° (476.6 to 482° F.). It is to this body that the investigator claims is due the griping pains produced by podophyllin.

Podophyllinic Acid.—This principle results as a brown amorphous resinous body, soluble in alcohol and ether, insoluble in water, and having no action upon the animal organism.

Fatty oils and extractive matters were also determined. The claims as to the presence of *berberin* and *saponin* have been entirely refuted, as before mentioned.

PHYSIOLOGICAL ACTION.—The force of podophyllum seems to be almost entirely expended upon the lining membrane of the almentary canal. Whatever

* Biddle, *Am. Jour. Phar.*, 1879, p. 544.

action noted upon those organs, and the glands in connection with this tract, is, so far as known, reflex and sympathetic.

On Animals.—Among other experiments with this drug upon animals, those of Dr. Anstie seem to be the most characteristic. He found, resulting from his many applications of an alcoholic solution to the peritoneal cavity direct, that no local inflammation arose, although an intense hyperæmia occurred in the duodenum especially, and the whole of the small intestine, even going so far as to cause a breaking down of the tissues and resulting ulceration, causing discharges of glairy mucus streaked with blood; this hyperæmia ceased usually at the ileo-cæcal valve. *Post mortem* the mucous-membranes were found inflamed and covered with bloody mucus. Other observers noted that retching, salivation, and emesis, followed by purging, colic, and intense tenesmus, with low pulse, and rapid exhaustion followed the administration of the drug.

On Man.—Here the same action takes place, but extends to the rectum with sufficient intensity to cause prolapsus and hemhorrhoids. The first effect of the drug is an excitation of salivary and biliary secretions, followed by torpor and icterus. The symptoms of disturbance caused by the drug in doses varying from $\frac{1}{4}$ to $\frac{1}{2}$ grains of "podophyllin," and in persons working in the dust of the dried root, are substantially as follows: Inflammation of the eyes, soreness and pustulation of the nose; salivation and white-coated tongue; extreme nausea, followed by vomiting; severe pains in the transverse colon and abdomen, followed by an urgent call to stool; thin, offensive, copious stools; weak pulse, prostration, drowsiness, and cold extremities.

DESCRIPTION OF PLATE 17.

1. Whole plant, once reduced, Newfield, N. Y., May 20th, 1880.
    2. Flower.
    3. Bud, showing sepals.
    4. Pistil.
    5. Pistil in section (enlarged).
    6. Pistil in horizontal section (enlarged).
    7. One of the lobes of the stigma (enlarged).
    8. Anther (enlarged).
    9. Pollen; side and end views x 200.
    10. Fruit.

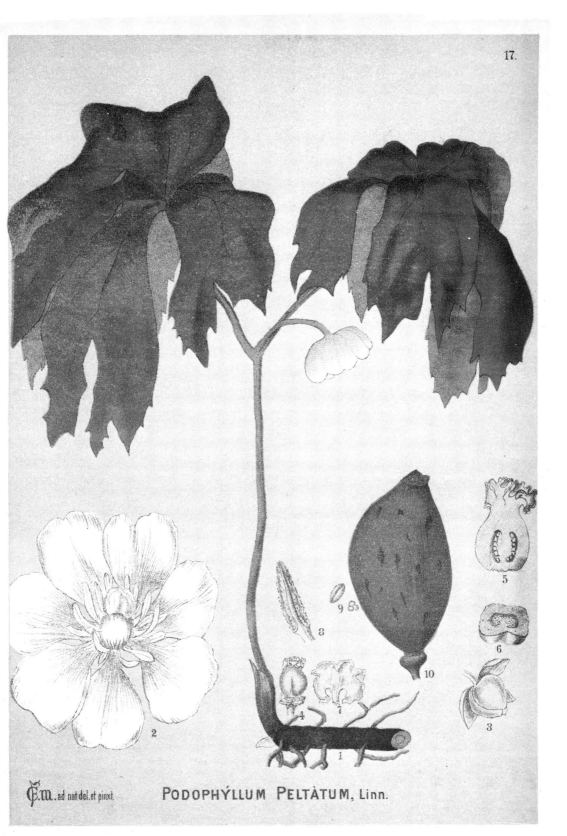

℃.m. ad nat del. et pinxt

PODOPHÝLLUM PELTÀTUM, Linn.

Tribe.—*NYMPHEÆ.*

GENUS.—**NYMPHÆA**,* TOURN.

SEX. SYST.—POLYANDRIA MONOGYNIA.

18

NYMPHÆA.

SWEET WATER LILY.

SYN.—NYMPHÆA ODORATA, AIT · NYMPHÆA ALBA, MICHX.; CAS-
TALIA PUDICA, SALISB.

COM. NAMES.—SWEET-SCENTED WATER LILY, WATER NYMPH, WATER
LILY, LARGE WHITE WATER LILY, WHITE POND LILY.

A TINCTURE OF THE FRESH ROOT OF NYMPHÆA ODORATA, AIT.

Description.—This beautiful perennial aquatic herb, grows to the surface
of the water from a thick submerged horizontal rootstock. The *stem* is absent,
the flowers growing on long peduncles, and the leaves on separate petioles, all
round, smooth, and furnished with four equal, central canals. *Stipules* deltoid or
nearly renniform, emarginate, closely appressed to the rootstalk at the base of
the petiole; *leaves* always floating, orbicular, with one deep cuneiform fissure
passing from the circumference to the centre at the juncture of the leaf with its
petiole, thus making it more or less heart-shaped; smooth and shining dark green
above, wine color beneath, plainly marked with the interlacing veins; margin
entire. *Inflorescence* solitary, axillary; flowers large, white, showy and fragrant,
often being nearly six inches in diameter when fully expanded. *Sepals* four, elliptical, scaphoid, nearly free, persistent, bright green on the outer surface, greenish-
white internally. *Petals* numerous, arranged imbricately upon the fleshy ovary,
the outer rows large, the inner smaller, all obtuse. *Stamens* indefinite, arranged
like the petals upon the surface of the ovary about the centre of the flower; *filaments* of the outer rows petaloid, the inner more or less ligulate; *anthers* with
adnate, introrse cells. *Ovary* large, globular, depressed, eighteen to twenty-four-
celled; *ovules* anatropous, borne upon the sides of the ovary, none being upon the
ventral suture; *style* none; *stigma* compound, peltate, marked by as many rays as
there are cells to the ovary, these rays projecting beyond the general surface, thus
forming a fringe of recurved, sterile, stigmatose appendages. *Fruit* a depressed,
globular, fleshy body, retaining the stigma and marked plainly by the scars of the
fallen petals and stamens, decaying; dehiscence none; *seeds* oblong, stipitate,
shorter than the enveloping sac-like false coat; *embryo* situated in the albumen,
close to the hilum; *radicle* very minute; *cotyledons* large and thick, enveloping a
well-formed plumule.

---

* The name is given on account of its situation being similar to the supposed habit of fabled water nymphs.

Nymphaceæ.—This beautiful family of aquatic plants, whose species have been themes for poets, and designs for ancient sculptors, is tropical or sub-tropical in its most general *habitat*. Its prominent species are: *Victoria regia*, a native of tropical South America, named in honor of Queen Victoria. Its magnificent flowers are rose-white, and often measure nearly two feet in diameter, while that of its leaves often reaches five feet. *Nymphæa lotus*, a native of Egypt and Nubia, with white flowers. The seeds of this plant are eaten by the natives, but do not form the lotus of the *lotus-eaters.** *Nymphæa alba*. This European species differs but slightly from our *N. odorata*. This order contains in the United States the following genera: *Brasenia, Cabomba, Neliumbium, Nuphar* and *Nymphæa*.

History and Habitat.—This, our most beautiful northern flower, frequents ponds and still-flowing streams in the Eastern United States, especially near the coast, flowering from June to August. There are many varieties, due mostly to color and mode of growth, some being blue, others pink or rose-color; but the true N. odorata is pure white or creamy. The stems of the flowers and leaves vary in length according to the depth of the water. The flowers form one of the most typical illustrations of plant metamorphosis; the petals are but colored sepals, the stamens but anther-tipped petals, the stigmas but changed stamens, and all gradually merging into each other in easily distinguishable stages. After ripening, the fruits, now becoming spongy and water-soaked, sink to the mud, where they decay and allow the escape of the seeds.

The flowers open as the sun rises, and are usually fully expanded at about eight o'clock; after that time they again gradually close, being entirely shut during the heat of the afternoon and at night.

In the very centre of the disk-like compound stigma, is a small, glutinous protuberance, called by many botanists a nectary or honey-gland. I am inclined to term this the true stigma, on account of the well-known fact that pollen grains need moisture to enable them to burst their outer coat and allow the escape of the fertilizing tubes. This glandular body is always moist, while the stigmatose disk is dry, and rejects water as freely as does the upper surface of the leaves.

Our species are often said to be much inferior to the European in beauty; but, as their purity of color and exquisite fragrance far excel that of *Nymphæa alba*, it fully deserves to rank as superior in all respects.

Rafinesque states that in Canada the fresh leaves are boiled and eaten as "greens," that the fresh roots are used as a part substitute for soap, and that the juice of the roots, mingled with that of lemons, is used to remove freckles and pimples from the face.

The roots, in decoction, were much esteemed by Indian squaws as an internal remedy, and injection or wash for the worst forms of leucorrhœa, its properties in this direction being due to its great astringency. The macerated root was also used as an application in the form of a poultice to suppurating glands; its styptic properties were also fully known and utilized.

* This plant is mentioned under *Genista tinctoria*, 46.

The roots have been used for dyeing fabrics deep brown, the goods thus dyed retaining their color admirably.

Nymphæa has no place in the U. S. Ph.; in the Eclectic Materia Medica it is officinal as *Cataplasma Nymphæ* and *Infusum Nymphæ*.

PART USED AND PREPARATION.—The fresh root, gathered in the fall, is chopped and pounded to a pulp and weighed. Then two parts by weight of alcohol are taken, the pulp thoroughly mixed with one-sixth part of it, and the rest of the alcohol added. After stirring the whole well, it is poured into a well-stoppered bottle and allowed to stand for eight days in a dark, cool place. The tincture, separated by straining and filtering, presents the following physical properties: A deep wine-red color by transmitted light, a sherry-like odor, a slightly bitter, astringent taste, and a very strong acid reaction.

CHEMICAL CONSTITUENTS.—The bitter acrid principle of Nymphæa odorata has not been isolated. According to Bigelow, the roots contain tannin, gallic acid, and mucilage. It is quite likely that the constituents are similar, if not the same, as those of the European species, *N. alba*, the roots of which, according to Grüning,* contain: *Tanno-nymphæin*, $C_{56}H_{52}O_{36}$; *Nymphæo-phlobaphene*, $C_{56}H_{48}O_{36}$; and *Nymphæa-tannic acid*, $C_{56}H_{53}O_{38}$, a brown, red, transparent mass, yielding easily a pale yellow powder. This is the true special tannin, to which the great astringency of the root is due.

PHYSIOLOGICAL ACTION.—I can find no accounts of poisonings with this plant, nor experiments in this direction. In the provers who took large doses of the tincture, a marked dryness of the fauces was experienced, followed by painful deglutition; pain in the hypogastric region, with loose evacuations; venereal excitement, and involuntary passage of the urine.

DESCRIPTION OF PLATE 18.

1. A small flower, from a pond near New Milford, Pa., July 17th, 1883.
    2. A medium-size leaf.
    3. Section of a peduncle, showing air cavities or canals.
    4. Root.

---

* *Arch. d. Thar.,* 3, xvii., p. 736; *Am. Jour. Phar.*, 1883, p. 96.

CMm.ad nat.del.et pinxt.   NYMPHÆA ODORÀTA, Ait.

19

SARRACENIA.

PITCHER-PLANT.

SYN.—SARRACENIA PURPUREA, LINN.; SARAZINA GIBBOSA, RAF.
COM. NAMES.—PITCHER-PLANT, HUNTSMAN'S CUP, WATER-CUP, EVE'S
CUPS, SIDE-SADDLE FLOWER, FLY-CATCHER.

A TINCTURE OF THE FRESH ROOT OF SARRACENIA PURPUREA, LINN.

Description.—This peculiar bog perennial is characterized as follows: *Root* somewhat ligneous, yellowish, furnished with numerous yellowish-brown fibrous rootlets; *stem* none; *leaves* (*ascidia*) all radical, pitcher-shaped, and composed of four parts: the *petiole* about one-third the whole length, slender, dilated at the base and somewhat equitant; *tube* ovate, narrowing to the petiole, and longitudinally marked with reddish veins; *hood* auriculate-cordate, wavy, covered in the throat with numerous stiff, sharp, curved bristles pointing downward; *wing* broad, laterally undulate, passing along the median line of the upper surface of the tube, from the base of the hood to the petiole. These ascidia, usually six in number, lie dorsally prostrate upon the sphagnum in which the plant usually grows, the open mouths of the tubes looking upward toward the nodding flower and forming about the scape a rosette of gaping wells half filled with water, and having a path represented by the free margin of the wings leading to each.[†] *Inflorescence* a single large reddish purple flower, terminal and nodding upon a long smooth and naked scape. *Sepals* 5, colored, persistent, 3-bracted at their base. *Petals* 5, obovate or somewhat fiddle-shaped, caducous, incurved over the style. *Stamens* numerous, hypogynous. *Ovary* globose, 5-celled; *style* greenish-yellow, composed of a short erect shaft, and an umbrella-like expanded extremity consisting of 5 petaloid segments rayed at their approximations, each ray ending in a short nipple-like projection, which constitutes the stigma. *Fruit* a granular 5-celled and valved capsule; *placentæ* axial, many seeded; *seeds* anatropous; *embryo* small, basal; *albumen* fleshy.

Sarraceniaceæ.—This family of bog plants is characterized as follows: *Root* perennial; *leaves* all radical, purplish or yellowish-green, more or less inflated tubular, the true blade represented by a hood or lamina surrounding the throat of the tube. *Flowers* single (*Exc. Heliamphora*) nodding at the summit of a long,

---

[*] In honor of Dr. Sarrazin of Quebec, who sent the plant to Tournefort.
[†] In the plate most of the leaves have been cut off, and those remaining have been constrained to take such positions as would best show their various characters within the small scope of the paper.

naked, (Exc. same) cylindrical scape; *floral envelope* consisting of from 4 to 10 leaflets, the external more or less sepaloid and bracted at the base. *Stamens* numerous hypogynous; *anthers* versatile, introse, 2-celled, opening by longitudinal fissures. *Style* single, truncate, with a minute stigma (or as above described), persistent. *Fruit* a 3 to 5-celled capsule, opening loculicidally; *placentæ* projecting from the axis into the cells. *Seeds* obovoid, numerous; *embryo* cylindrical; *albumen* copious. This limited family is represented by three genera, viz.: *Darlingtonia*, with one species, having two free honeyed wings projecting laterally from the inner edge of the small mouth of the tube; *Sarracenia*, with eight species and two varieties; and *Heliamphora*, of Guiana and Venezuela. The leaves of this family are all apparently formed with the intent of capturing insects and digesting their remains through the agency of the water they hold, which becomes acid and causes decomposition of the captured insects. It certainly seems intentional adaptation to the necessities of the plant that insects are caught and macerated, from the structure, for which no other reason would account. Mr. W. K. Higley, in his interesting paper on "The Northern Pitcher-Plant," * says: "Inside these pitchers are found hairs, which cover more or less of the inner surface. Those which cover the hood continue to or a little beyond the junction with the tube. Following this area is a smooth surface which extends to near the point where the leaf begins to contract, when a patch of less stiff hairs are met with. This time they extend into the narrow portion of the tube. All the hairs point downward.

"The position and form of these hairs, especially those on the hood and upper part of the tube, and in fact, any that may be above the fluid, in the lower part of the leaf, would show that their function, in part, at least, is to prevent the escape of any insect that may have entered the tube. The hairs in the lower part of the tube probably act, to some extent, as absorbents of the nitrogenous matter decaying within the leaf. Some acute observers claim that at the end of each hair there is a minute opening, thus allowing the nitrogenous fluid to pass directly into the apical cell of the hair. This does not seem to be the case, but instead, the wall surrounding the entire cell is very thin. These hairs are simple trichomes, that is, they are rather cells than organs. Unlike the tentacles of the sundew, in no case do the spiral bundles enter their tissue. I am inclined to believe that these cellular hairs serve more than one purpose in the economy of the plant.

"A study of the structure and physiology of the whole family shows that all the forms need a great deal of absorbing surface, for there seems to be a lack of stomata. The tissue of the leaf is almost constantly gorged with a large supply of nourishment, consisting, evidently, of absorbed nitrogenous matter, and needs a great extent of surface exposed to the air for the purpose of absorption in carrying on the functions of assimilation and metastasis. In support of this there is considerable evidence, the most important of which is the fact that many of these hairs, especially those on the hood, contain chlorophyl. From a study of marked leaves through the whole season I am led to believe that some of these hairs are

* *Bulletin Chicago Academy of Sciences*, Vol. I, No. 5, p. 41.

absorbed as the leaves grow old. This would indicate that as the functions of the leaf are lessened the extent of absorbing surface is reduced.

"When the leaf has apparently nearly stopped absorbing the moisture from the tube, it may still be an active insect trap. At this time an especially strong odor is given off from the decaying mass of insects. It would seem that the insects caught now could be of no use except as a fertilizer, when by the decay of the leaves, all this mass of decomposing nitrogenous matter is deposited around the roots of the plant, the decaying material, moreover, seems to hasten the decay of the leaf, as its vitality is lessened by the advance of the season."

The acidity of the water, after it has stood a time in the leaf, is found to be due to malic and citric acids.

History and Habitat.—The Northern Pitcher-plant grows in sphagnum swamps from Pennsylvania northward and westward, and southward east of the Alleghanies. It flowers northward in June, and ripens its fruit in August. The previous use of this plant by the Indians in small-pox, for which it has been held by them as specific, is corroborated by homœopathic practice, but has in almost all instances been an absolute failure in the hands of the "old school." They judged that the use of the root not only greatly shortened the run of the disease and checked maturation, but prevented deep pitting in convalescence. At the last meeting of the Epidemiological Society,* a communication was read from Mr. Herbert Miles, Assistant Surgeon to the Royal Artillery, respecting a plant that was stated to be a specific for small-pox. The remedy is given in the form of a strong infusion of the rhizome, and Mr. Miles had, after very considerable difficulty, succeeded in obtaining a small supply of the plant, which he forwarded to the Society. Mr. Miles is quartered in Canada, where an epidemic of small-pox having broken out among the Indians, the disease had proved virulent in the extreme among the unprotected, because unvaccinated, natives. However, the alarm had greatly diminished on an old squaw going amongst them, and treating the cases with the infusion. This treatment, it is said, was so successful as to cure every case. Dr. Hooker pronounced the specimens received to be Sarracenia purpurea. At a meeting of the Medical Society of Nova Scotia, held at Halifax, a resolution was passed—concerning the use of Sarracenia in Variola—that there was not "any reliable data upon which to ground any opinion in favor of its value as a remedial agent." †

Across the face of an article on the use of this drug in small-pox, appearing in the volume I have cited above, a former owner of the book has written: "This medicine was thoroughly tested by Mr. John Thomas Lane in the spring of 1864 at the Small-pox Hospital at Claremont, in Alexandria, Va., for the period of several weeks, in the presence of the medical officers of the Third Division Hospital; and proved to be without any curative powers in this disease, and Mr. Lane a humbug. He lost more than fifty per cent. of the cases of variola committed to him, more than were lost by any other treatment." Mr. F. H. Bignell says,‡

---

* *Lond. Pharm. Journ.*, Dec., 1861; *Jour. Mat. Med.*, IV, N. S., 37.   † *Med. and Surg. Reporter*, ibid., 507.

‡ A paper read before the *Quebec Geog. Soc'y.*

in regard to the use of the drug in this disease : " On the Mistassini side my attention was particularly attracted to the Sarracenia purpurea, of which the root furnishes the greatest remedy known for that dreadful scourge, small-pox. I may mention that, to my personal knowledge, this precious root not only saved my brother's life, but its use also appears to wholly obviate the unsightly pitting common to the disease ; if it is extracted and dried at the proper season. Indeed, I have known many cases which were considered hopeless by medical men, but were cured by the Sarracenia purpurea ; even Indians, with whom the dread malady so often proves fatal, finding it an absolute specific."

The root is also recommended in cases where there is a torpidity of the organs of the alimentary tract, and of the kidneys.

There are no officinal preparations outside of the Homœopathic tincture.

PART USED AND PREPARATION.—The fresh root gathered after the fruiting season, or the whole fresh plant when budding to blossom and before the leaves are fully expanded, should be chopped and pounded to a pulp and weighed. Then two parts by weight of alcohol taken, the mass mixed thoroughly with one-sixth part of it and the rest of the alcohol added. After thorough stirring, the whole should be poured into a well-stoppered bottle, and allowed to stand eight days in a dark, cool place.

The tincture separated from the above by filtration, has a deep reddish-brown color by transmitted light; its taste is at first somewhat sourish, then bitter and slightly astringent, and its reaction strongly acid.

CHEMICAL CONSTITUENTS.—*Sarracenin.* This bitter alkaloidal body was discovered by Martin. Hetet* isolated it as white handsome prisms and octahedra, soluble in water and alcohol. Its salts with acids are soluble, and that with sulphuric forms beautiful bitter needles. Hetet claims that this alkaloid is identical with *veratria*, both in its properties and reactions.

Acrylic Acid.—$C_3H_4O_2$. This volatile body was discovered in the plant by Björklund and Dragendorf. It is a limpid liquid, possessing a sour pungent smell and boiling at 142° (287°.6 F.). Its vapor is irritating, attacking the mucous membranes of the nose and eyes violently, and causing severe inflammation.

Sarracenic Acid.—This body constitutes the yellow coloring matter predominant in the older plants. Its characteristics are uninvestigated.

Besides these, the plant contains a pulverizable tanno resin, and a bitter, aromatic extractive, soluble in water and alcohol.

PHYSIOLOGICAL ACTION.—Dr. Porcher found in his experiments with 180 grains of the root, that it caused diuresis, moderate catharsis, and gastric excitation, as well as an increased and irregular heart's action, and congestion of the head; and remarks as follows: "These symptoms distinctly point to the parts of

---

* *Rep. de Phar.*, 879, p. 109.

the system influenced by the drug—the gastric filaments of the ganglionic or organic system of nerves. This produced an increased action of the circulating system, and drove the blood to the head; it also increased the peristaltic action of the whole alimentary canal, and promoted the renal and other glandular secretions, without any apparent effect upon the nerves of animal life." Dr. Cigliano,* in his experiments, says the drug produces "eruptions similar to *crusta lactea;* on the forehead and hands papular eruptions, changing to vesicular with the depression, as in small-pox, lasting from seven to eight days." This last again corroborates the aborigine's use of the drug, and adds one more proof to the many that are tending to reveal the fact that our American native practice was essentially correct.

DESCRIPTION OF PLATE 19.

1 and 2. Whole plant, with a number of the leaves removed, and those remaining brought into constrained positions to better show their characters within the limit of the sheet. From Spruce Pond, Smithsfields, N. Y., June 18th, 1884.

2. Scape and flower.
3. Pistil.
4. Stigma.
5. Stamens.
6. A portion of the hood, showing hairs.
7. Section of the root.
(4–6 enlarged.)

* *Il Dinamico,* 1871; translated in *Am. Observer,* 1871, p. 467, Dr. Lilienthal.

℃m.ad nat.del.et pinxt. SARRACÉNIA PURPÙREA, Linn.

N. ORD.—PAPAVERACEÆ.
GENUS.—**ARGEMONE,*** LINN.
SEX. SYST.—POLYANDRIA MONOGYNIA.

20

ARGEMONE.

PRICKLY POPPY.

SYN.—ARGEMONE MEXICANA, LINN.
COM. NAMES.—PRICKLY POPPY, DEVIL'S FIG, MEXICAN POPPY, THORN
APPLE,† YELLOW THISTLE,‡ THORN POPPY; (MEX.) CHICALOTE; (FR.)
ARGÉMONE; (GER.) STACHELMOHN.

A TINCTURE OF THE WHOLE PLANT ARGEMONE MEXICANA, L.

Description.—This annual weedy herb, grows to a height of from 1 to 3 feet. *Root* long, subcylindrical; *stem* erect, branching, prickly-bristled, and furnished, as the rest of the plant, with a gamboge-yellow milky juice. *Leaves* sessile, broadly lanceolate in general outline, sinuate lobed, spiny toothed, and blotched or striped with white along the principal veins. *Inflorescence* solitary in the axils of the upper leaves, and terminal; *buds* erect, pedunculate; *flowers* large, yellow, or rarely white. *Sepals* 2 to 3, roundish, acuminate, often prickly, very fugacious. *Petals* 4 to 6, *i. e.*, twice as many as the sepals, roundish, more or less crumpled in the bud. *Stamens* indefinitely numerous; *filaments* filiform, greatly attenuated at the apex; *anthers* large, innate. *Ovary* strictly 1-celled; *style* almost none; *stigmas* 3 to 6, stellate-radiate, purple, velvety on the receptive surface; *lobes* reflexed. *Fruit* an oblong-ovate, prickly pod, opening by 3 to 6 valves at the apex, leaving a skeleton of from 3 to 6 filiform placentæ in the shape of the original pod; *seeds* globular, crested, and pitted.

Papaveraceæ.—This principally European family of herbs, noted for their milky, and generally colored, narcotic or acrid juice, is represented in North America by 15 genera, 23 species, and 7 recognized varieties. The order is further characterized as follows: *Leaves* alternate, exstipulate. *Peduncles* 1-flowered; *flowers* regular, the parts in twos or muliples of two. *Sepals* 2, very rarely 3, fugacious *Petals* 4 to 12, early deciduous, rarely absent, imbricated in the bud. *Stamens* numerous, rarely as few as 16, distinct, hypogynous; *anthers* 2-celled, innate, introrse. *Ovary* 1-celled, with two or more parietal placentæ. *Fruit* a dry, 1- rarely few or many-celled pod. *Seeds* numerous, anatropous; *embryo* minute, basal; *albumen* fleshy or oily.

---

* 'Αργέμα, *argema*, cataract; as the juice was supposed to cure that disease.
† Applicable only to *Datura Stramonium* (Solanaceæ.)
‡ The true Yellow Thistle is *Cirsium horridulum* (Compositæ.)

The only remedy in our Materia Medica derived from this order, beside the three here represented, is Opium, the inspissated juice obtained by incising the unripe capsules of the South European and Asiatic White Poppy (*Papaver somniferum*, Linn.) ; our other remedies, Papaverinum and Morphinum, being also derived from the same substance ; the only other remedy used in general medicine being the petals of the Red Poppy (*Papaver Rhœas*, Linn.) ; they have a slightly narcotic action, but are as yet principally used as a coloring-matter for pharmaceutical preparations.

History and Habitat.—The Prickly Poppy is indigenous to tropical and subtropical America, from whence it has become scattered even as far north as Virginia, and escaped from cultivation in many places still further north. It grows with us in waste places and blossoms from April to July.

The use of the oil of the seeds, the leaves, and the petals of this species has been quite prominent among the natives of all tropical countries in which the plant grows. Among the ancient Greeks the juice was supposed curative of cataract and of opacities of the cornea. The oil of the seeds is spoken of as being as active as that of Croton tiglium.* Lindley says that in India the juice is employed in chronic ophthalmia and in primary syphilis ; and the infusion in strangury from blisters (of cantharis ?) ; he also states that the seeds are narcotic, and are smoked with tobacco. In Mexico the plant is still held in the pharmacopœia, the juice being recommended, mixed with water, for skin diseases, and for incipient opacities, the flowers as a pectoral and narcotic.† In Java the juice is said to be employed as a caustic in chancres. In the West Indies the plant is administered as a substitute for Ipecacuanha. The juice when inspissated resembles, in its physical properties, gamboge. As a whole the plant has generally been conceded to be anodyne, detersive, resolutive, hypnotic, diuretic, diaphoretic, ophthalmic, anti-icteric, and a hydragogue cathartic ; and, according to Rafinesque, appearing to unite the properties of Opium, Gamboge, and Celandine.

PART USED AND PREPARATION.—The whole fresh plant, gathered while in blossom, is chopped and pounded to a pulp and weighed. Then two parts by weight of alcohol are taken, the pulp thoroughly mixed with one-sixth part of it and the rest of the alcohol added. After stirring the whole well, it is poured into a well-stoppered bottle, and allowed to stand eight days in a dark, cool place.

The tincture, separated from the above mass by pressure and filtration, has a brownish yellow color by transmitted light, no distinguishing odor or taste, and an acid reaction.

The plant, from its history, deserves at our hands a most thorough proving, and should by all means receive it ; for a new proving the tincture should be made while the plant is in fruit, and just before the capsules are ripe.

CHEMICAL CONSTITUENTS.—Morphia, $C_{17}H_{19}NO_3$.—There is considerable doubt that this alkaloid exists in this species, although Charbonnier‡ reports its presence from his analysis of the carpels and leaves.

---

* *Jour. de Pharm.*, xiv, 73.   † Maisch, in *Am. Jour. Pharm.*, 1885, 506.   ‡ *Jour. de Pharm.*, 1868.

Oil of Argemone.—This fat oil, obtained by pressure from the seeds, is reported by Wittstein, but upon whose authority we are unable to ascertain. He describes it as, light yellow, still liquid at 5° (41° F.), of a slightly nauseous odor and raw taste, drying, dissolves in 5 to 6 times its volume of alcohol, and is easily saponified.

PHYSIOLOGICAL ACTION.—This is as yet unknown, but certainly deserves prolonged experimentation.

DESCRIPTION OF PLATE 20.

1. Upper part of plant, Salem, Mass., July 31, 1885.
2. Root.
3. Stamens.
4. Pistil.
5. Horizontal section of ovary.
6. Fruit.

(3–5 enlarged.)

C.m. ad nat del. et pinxt.

ARGEMÒNE MEXICÀNA, Linn.

GENUS.—**CHELIDONIUM,*** LINN.

SEX. SYST.—POLYANDRIA MONOGYNIA.

21

CHELIDONIUM.

CELANDINE.

SYN.—CHELIDONIUM MAJUS, LINN.

COM. NAMES.—COMMON CELANDINE, TETTERWORT; (FR.) HERBE À L'HIRONDELLE; (GER.) SCHÖLLKRAUT.

A TINCTURE OF THE FRESH PLANT CHELIDONIUM MAJUS, LINN.

Description.—This upright, widely branching, perennial herb, grows to a height of from 1 to 2 feet from a fusiform root. *Stem* upright, cylindrical and branching, somewhat hairy and very brittle. *Leaves* alternate, petiolate, large, pale-green and glaucous, lyrate pinnatifid, with a crenately cut or lobed border, the terminal lobe obovate-cuneate. *Inflorescence*, pedunculated, somewhat umbel-late, axillary clusters, with nodding buds and medium-sized flowers, the sepals, petals and stamens of which are early deciduous. *Peduncles* 2 to 4 inches long, bearing from 3 to 8 *pedicels* 1 inch in length, and involucrate at their base. *Sepals* 2. *Corolla* cruciform; *petals* 4. *Stamens* 16 to 24. *Style* merely present; *stigma* 2-lobed. *Fruit* a linear, slender pod, about 1 inch in length, somewhat swelled at intervals, the two valves opening upward from the base to the apex; *seeds* rounded, reniform, with a glandular ridge at the hilum, and a crustaceous, blackish-brown testa, marked with more or less regular, hexagonal reticulations. A description of the Papaveraceæ will be found under Argemone Mexicana, 20.

History and Habitat.—Celandine grows all over Germany and France, in waste places, on old walls, along roadways, and about dwellings; it is pretty well naturalized in the United States, but so far it is not found at any great distance from dwellings, flowering from early in May until October. A fine gamboge-yel-low, acrid juice, pervades the plant, root, stem and leaves; this fact led those who practised upon the doctrine of signatures, to employ the drug in hepatic disorders, from its resemblance to bile in color. It proved one of the hits of that practice. The U. S. Ph. still mentions Chelidonium, but not officinally; it will probably be thrown aside at the next revision as worthless, *totidem verbis*. In the Eclectic Materia Medica it is official as *Decoctum Chelidonii*.

PART USED AND PREPARATION.—The fresh plant, gathered in Spring, is chopped and pounded to a pulp, enclosed in a piece of new linen and subjected

---

* χελιδών, *swallow*. Its flowers appearing with the arrival of that bird; or, it was said that when the eyes of young swallows became, through injury or otherwise, affected with a white film, the parents gathered and applied the juice of this plant, rapidly curing the trouble.

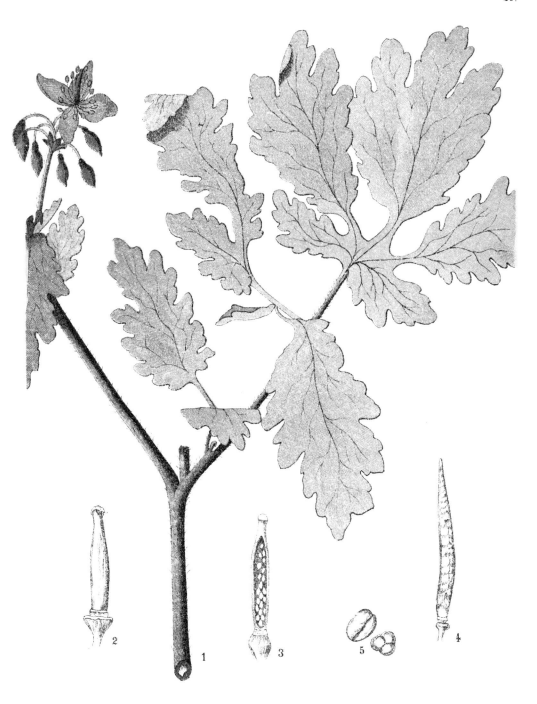

CHELIDÒNIUM MÀJUS, Linn.

to pressure, the fresh juice is then by brisk succussion mingled with an equal part by weight of alcohol. This mixture is allowed to stand eight days in a dark, cool place, then filtered. The tincture thus formed is of a brownish-orange color by transmitted light, having an odor quite like that of tincture of apis mellifica, an acrid, bitter taste, and strong acid reaction.

CHEMICAL CONSTITUENTS.—*Chelerythrin,* $C_{19}H_{17}NO_4$. This alkaloid is identical with Sanguinarina, *vide* 22.

Chelidonin, $C_{19}H_{17}N_3O_3 + Aq.$ This alkaloid exists particularly in the root. When pure it has the following properties: colorless, glassy, tabular, bitter crystals, losing water at 100° (212° F.), fusing at 130° (266° F.), and decomposing at higher heats; it is insoluble in water, slowly soluble in alcohol, and forms colorless salts.

Chelidoxanthin. A bitter principle existing in all parts of the plant, crystallizing in short, friable, yellow needles, which are very slowly soluble in both water and alcohol.

Chelidonic Acid.—$C_4H(CO, OH)_3$. A tribasic acid occurring together with the other acids in all parts of the plant. It crystallizes in small colorless needles, which carbonize by heat, and are soluble both in water and alcohol.

Malic Acid.—Is also present in the plant, *vide* Pyrus Americana, 56.

Citric Acid.—Herr Haitinger determines (Monatsch., Ch. ii., p. 485) that notable quantities are contained in this plant. *Vide ut supra.*

PHYSIOLOGICAL ACTION.—The principal action of Chelidonium seems to be that of causing congestion of the lungs and liver, especially the latter; it is also an excessive irritant, and has a narcotic action upon the nervous system. The lungs of animals poisoned by this drug have been found, post-mortem, to be highly engorged, and in some cases hepatized. The liver under its action becomes the seat of much pain, soreness and tenderness; the bowels move rapidly and freely, with thin, bright-yellow, pasty evacuations; the urine becomes bright-yellow, and even stains the linen dark-yellow. It irritates the respiratory nerves, causing a tickling, like dust, in the trachea and bronchi, with violent spasmodic coughing, followed by dyspnœa and oppression of the chest. Sensations of indolence, sleepiness and languor are persistent. Its action upon the skin is that of vesication.

DESCRIPTION OF PLATE 21.

1. A portion of the upper part of a blossoming plant from Ithaca, N. Y., May 10th, 1880.
2. Pistil (enlarged).
3. Section of the ovary (enlarged).
4. Fruit.
5. Pollen x 380

GENUS.—**SANGUINARIA**,* DILL.

SEX. SYST.—POLYANDRIA MONOGYNIA.

22

SANGUINARIA.

BLOODROOT.

SYN.—SANGUINARIA CANADENSIS, L. SANGUINARIA MINOR, DILL.

COM. NAMES.—BLOODROOT, RED PUCCOON, PUCCOON, TETTERWORT, REDROOT, PAUSON, TURMERIC, INDIAN PAINT, (FR.) SANGUIN-AIRE, (GER.) BLUTWURZEL.

TINCTURE OF THE FRESH ROOT OF SANGUINARIA CANADENSIS, L.

Description.—This low, erect, perennial plant, dots with its creamy white flowers our open woods and bottom lands in early spring, the most beautiful harbinger of its season. It arises by a naked scape enveloped by its leaf, to a height of from 3 to 6 inches. *Root* horizontal, extending from 2 to 4 inches, with a diameter of from one-quarter to three-quarters of an inch, slightly branched, cylindrical, giving off, especially from the under side, numerous tender rootlets, and somewhat annulate by the scars of previous membraneous sheathing scales which enveloped the scape and petiole. When fresh it is brownish-red externally, and, upon breaking or cutting, it shows minute points of bright red juice, which rapidly coalesce and cover the entire wounded surface. When dry similar red dots appear upon the fracture, the root becomes longitudinally wrinkled, the section showing a bark of about one-twelfth the whole diameter, a very slight cambium line and a granular white centre. The *stem* is a simple, smooth, naked scape, terminated by a single flower, from one to one and a half inches in diameter. The *leaf*, which does not reach its full expansion until the flower has fallen, is palmately seven- to nine-lobed, with an equal number of reddish ribs, from which (especially noticeable upon the under surface) extend a perfect network of veins; it has a heart-shaped base, and obtuse lobes; the upper surface is light green, the under whitish, glaucous. *Sepals* 2, caducous, forming the ephemeral *calyx*. *Petals* 8-12, spatulate, not crumpled. The *stamens*, generally 24, unequal and about one-half the length of the petals, arranged more or less distinctly in two rows. *Anthers* innate, introrse, dehiscent. *Pollen* grains globular, more or less six-sided by compression, of a beautiful golden-yellow color. *Ovary* 1-celled, with 2 parietal placentæ. *Style* short, thick, rounded. *Stigma* thick, glandularly pubescent, 2-grooved. *Pod* oblong, sharp-pointed, turgid, opening by two uplifting valves, allowing the escape of the numerous anatropous, sometimes crested seeds. *Embryo* minute, situated at the base of the sarcous, oily albumen.

---

* *Sanguis*, blood. From the color of the juice.

History and Habitat.—This is the only species of the genus, although Rafinesque has described six varieties. It is found, as the specific name denotes, in Canada, and in all parts of the United States except southward to Florida, and westward to Mexico and Oregon, the sea-coasts, and high mountains. It grows in rich open woods, or on bottom lands along shaded streams, flowering from March, in early springs, until May, fruiting in June.

For many years it has been used by the aborigines of this country for painting their faces, clothing and implements of warfare, and by the laity as a domestic remedy in gastric troubles, compounded with podophyllum and kali tartaricum. Applied to a denuded surface it is quite a powerful escharotic.

The root is still officinal in the U. S. Ph. as *Acetum Sanguinariæ, Tinctura Sanguinariæ, Radix Sanguinariæ,* and *Extractum Sanguinariæ.* In the Eclectic Materia Medica this drug and its derivatives have a prominent place, especially in compounds with Lobelia; sanguinaria not having emetic properties. It takes a part in the following preparations: *Pilulæ Taraxaci Compositæ; Pulvis Ipecacuanhæ Compositus; Pulvis Lobeliæ Compositus; Pulvis Myricæ Compositus; Tinctura Lobeliæ Composita; Tinctura Viburnii Composita;* and *Sanguinarin,* a so-called alka-resinoid principle, which is often confused by both prescriber and pharmacist with the true alkaloid sanguinarina.

PART USED, AND PREPARATION.—The fresh root, gathered when the seeds are ripe, is chopped and pounded to a pulp and weighed. Then two parts by weight of alcohol are taken, and after thoroughly mixing the pulp with one-sixth part of it the rest of the alcohol is added. After having stirred the whole, pour it into a well-stoppered bottle and let it stand eight days in a dark, cool place. The tincture is then separated by decanting, straining, and filtering.

Thus prepared it is, by transmitted light, of a deep orange-red color, slightly bitter and acid, and has a strong acid reaction to litmus.

CHEMICAL CONSTITUENTS.—Sanguinarina,* $C_{19} H_{17} NO_4$. This alkaloid crystallizes from alcohol in warty or needle-like masses, very acrid to the taste, toxic, and when pulverized and insufflated causes violent sneezing; these masses are soluble in ether or alcohol, insoluble or nearly so in water. The various salts of this body are of a red color, and give orange-colored aqueous solutions.

Puccina has been claimed to be another alkaloid principle of this plant, remaining in the menstruum after the precipitation of sanguinarina by sulphuric acid; but Hopp determined this body to be a sulphatic salt of sanguinarina.

Porphyroxin has been determined as a third alkaloid, so named from its supposed identity with Merck's opium principle porphyroxin, a mixture which owes its color reaction to Hesse's rhœadine. (Maisch.) It exists as tabular or linear, white and tasteless crystals.

Acid.—The acid of sanguinaria is not fully determined, though it would prove doubtless to be chelidonic acid (*vide* Chelidonium).

---

* This alkaloid is identical with *Chelerythrine,* from Chelidonium majus, *vide,* 21.

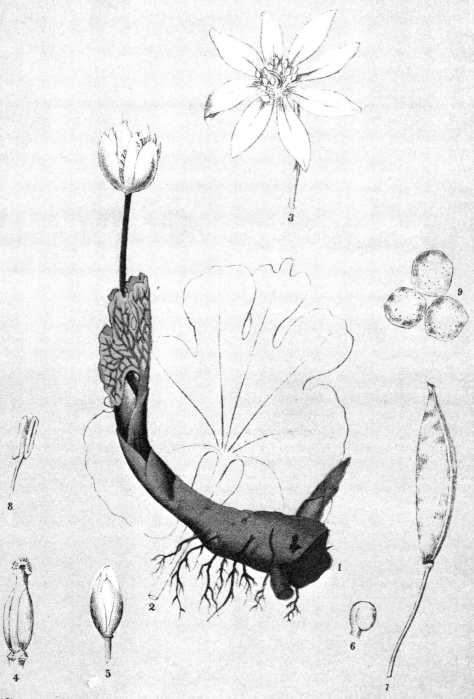

℃M. ad nat.del.et pinxt. SANGUINARIA CANADENSIS, Linn.

Gum, Lignin, an Orange-colored Resin, Albumen, and a Saccharine matter have also been determined.

PHYSIOLOGICAL ACTION.—Sanguinaria in toxic doses causes a train of symptoms showing it to be an irritant; it causes nausea, vomiting, sensations of burning in the mucous membranes whenever it comes in contact with them, faintness, vertigo, and insensibility. It reduces the heart's action and muscular strength, and depresses the nerve force, central and peripheral. Death has occurred from overdoses, after the following sequence of symptoms; violent vomiting, followed by terrible thirst and great burning in the stomach and intestines, accompanied by soreness over the region of those organs; heaviness of the upper chest with difficult breathing; dilation of the pupils; great muscular prostration; faintness and coldness of the surface, showing that death follows from cardiac paralysis. (Allen, Ency. Pure Mat. Med., viii., p. 481, *et seq.*)

DESCRIPTION OF PLATE 22.

1. Whole plant, Chemung, N. Y., May 3d, 1880.
2. Expanded leaf.
3. Expanded flower.
4. Pistil (enlarged).
5. Bud, showing sepals.
6. Seed (enlarged).
7. Pod.
8. Stamen (enlarged).
9. Pollen grains x 380.

N. ORD.—CRUCIFERÆ.

Tribe.—BRASSICEÆ.

GENUS.—**SINAPIS**, TOURN.

SEX. SYST.—TETRADYNAMIA SILIQUOSA.

23

SINAPIS ALBA.

WHITE MUSTARD.

SYN.—BRASSICA ALBA, HOOK, f.; SINAPIS ALBA, LINN.; LEUCOSINAPIS ALBA, SPACH.

COM. NAMES.—WHITE OR YELLOW MUSTARD;* (FR.) MOUTARDE BLANC; (GER.) WEISSER SENF.

A TINCTURE OF THE RIPE SEEDS OF SINAPIS ALBA, LINN.

Description.—This coarse, hairy annual, usually grows to a height of about 2 feet. *Stem* erect; *branches* few, ascending, all parts covered with bristling re-flexed hairs. *Leaves* all petioled and pinnatifid, the lowest having a large termi-nal lobe and the divisions cutting down to the midrib. *Flowers* about twice as large as those of *S. nigra; sepals* 4, narrowly oblong, spreading; *petals* 4, spread-ing, alternate with the sepals, and consisting of a narrow claw and an orbiculate blade. *Stamens* 6, hypogynous, tetradynamous, the two having shorter filaments being lateral and inserted lower down than the others, the four with longer fila-ments situated in pairs from before backward and accompanied by a quite large gland to each pair. *Pistil* slightly exceeding the stamens; *ovary* hairy; *style* nearly terete, persistent; *stigma* bi-labiate. *Fruit* a linear, bristly, ascending silique; *valves* short, furnished with 3 prominent veins; *pedicels* spreading; *beak* sword-shaped, 1-seeded, about half the length of the pod. *Seeds* globular, pale-yellowish, 1 to 6 in each pod; *cotyledons* incumbent, conduplicate, narrow, and plane.

Cruciferæ.—This large family of pungent and often acrid herbs is represented in North America by 42 genera, containing in all 275 species and 50 recognized varieties. The order is characterized as follows: *Leaves* alternate; *stipules* none. *Inflorescence* in terminal racemes or corymbs; *flowers* cruciform, tetradynamous. *Sepals* 4, deciduous; *petals* 4, hypogynous, regular, placed opposite each other in pairs. *Stamens* 6, rarely 4 or 2, when 6, then two are inserted lower down than the rest and furnished with shorter filaments. *Fruit* a 2-celled silicle, loment, silique or necument. *Seeds* campylotropous; *embryo* large; *albumen* none; *coty-ledons* incumbent o ||, acumbent o =, or conduplicate o)), being straight in one genus only.

---

* The name mustard is modernized from *mustum ardens,* hot must; as wine-must is often mixed with the seed-meal in the manufacture of table mustard.

Only three other plants of this order are proven and find place in our Materia Medica, viz.: The seeds of the European bitter Candytuft (*Iberis amara*, Linn.), extolled as a remedy for cardiac hypertrophy, but needing further corroborative proving; the Buenos Ayres Pepperwort (*Lepidium Bonariense*, D. C.), used in Brazil much as arnica is among the laity here; and the British Rape or Cole Seed (*Brassica napus*, Linn.).

Many species, however, find a place in domestic practice, principal among which are: The South European Scurvy Grass (*Cochlearia officinalis*, Linn.), long known and used as an anti-scorbutic; *C. armoracia*, Linn., our common horse-radish, is much used as a counter-irritant, diuretic, diaphoretic, and stimulant; the dried flowers of the Cuckoo Flower (*Cardamine pratensis*, Linn.) have been recommended for the cure of epilepsy in children; and the seeds of the Oriental *Arabis Chinensis* are considered by the natives stomachic, and are said to cause abortion in pregnant women.

Many species afford vegetables of value as foods, or, more properly, relishes, notably the Cresses, of which the following European species are most used: The Common Water Cress (*Nasturtium officinale*, R. Br.); Winter Cress (*Barbarea vulgaris*, R. Br.); Belleisle Cress (*B. præcox*, R. Br.); and the Common Cress (*Lepidium sativum*, Linn.). The edible Pepperwort of New Zealand (*L. olera-ceum*) is greatly valued, as also are the Chinese Mustard (*Sinapis Chinensis*, Linn.), and the British Sea Kale (*Crambe maritiima*, Linn.). The most useful species, however, for relishes, and nourishment as well, are the Turnip (*Brassica Rapa*, Linn.), and the Cabbage (*B. oleracea*, Linn.), with its numerous varieties by culti-vation, prominent among which stands the Cauliflower as *var. Botrytis*, Dec.

History and Habitat.—White Mustard has as yet hardly become naturalized in this country from its European and Oriental haunts, but has escaped from cul-tivation here in many places, and grows the life of what is commonly known as a roadside weed.

The previous uses of the seeds of this plant are intimately connected with those of *S. nigra*, as they are usually mixed in the preparation of *Sinapis* or mustard flour, which is used as an emetic, diuretic, stomachic, and gastro-intestinal stimu-lant; and externally applied, wet with vinegar, as a rubefacient and vesicant. The power of vesication resides in the oil to a high degree. The unground seeds of this species have held a high place in former practice as a remedy in atonic dys-pepsia, and various kindred complaints where there appeared to be a torpid state of the alimentary tract, as they were known to increase peristaltic activity; but the exhibition of the seeds proved dangerous, as they are liable to become im-pacted in the bowel and set up a fatal inflammation.

The seeds, though mentioned, have no officinal preparation in the U. S. Ph.; in the Eclectic Materia Medica their use is as *Cataplasma Sinapis*.

PART USED AND PREPARATION.—The ripe seeds, prepared as noted under the next (Sinapis Nigra, p. 24-2), yield a tincture having a light, clear orange color by transmitted light; a sinapic odor and taste, biting and burning the tongue; and an acid reaction.

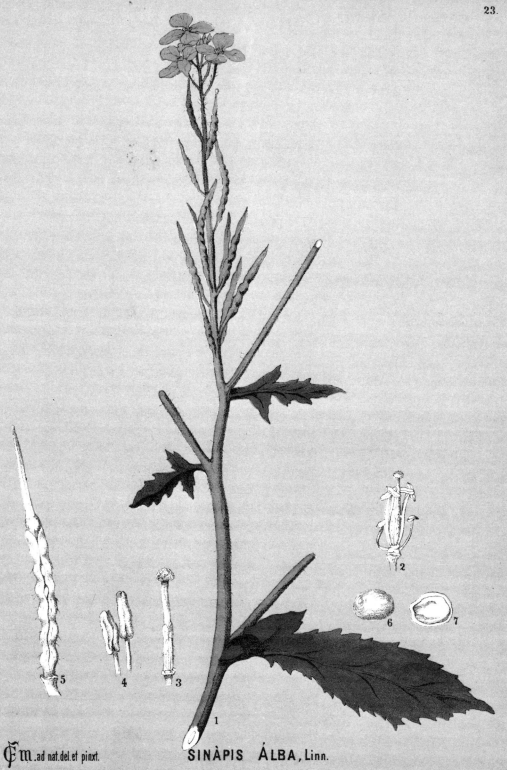

C.M. .ad nat. del. et pinxt.

SINÀPIS ÁLBA, Linn.

CHEMICAL CONSTITUENTS.—*Sinalbin*, $C_{30}H_{44}N_2S_2O_{16}$, or *Sulpho-sinapisin*. This peculiar compound body, determined by Hill, may be obtained from the seed-cake, after removal of the fat oil, by boiling the cake in alcohol. Sinalbin results as clear, colorless, united, acicular crystals, fusing at 130° (266° F.), soluble in water and slightly in alcohol. In the presence of water and myrosin, this body breaks down into its components as follows:

Sinalbin = Sulpho-cyanate Acrinol + Sulphate of Sinapine + Sugar.
$$C_{30}H_{44}N_2S_2O_{16} = C_8H_7NSO + C_{16}H_{25}NSO_9 + C_6H_{12}O_6.$$

The first of these resultants is proven to be the vesicating principle of the seed, though it does not pre-exist in them while dry.

Sinapine, $C_{16}H_{23}NO_5$.—This volatile alkaloid too readily decomposes to be isolated except as a sulpho-cyanide; when heated with baryta water it breaks down as follows:

Sinapine.　　Water.　　Sinapic Acid　　Choline.*
$$C_{16}H_{23}NO_5 + (H_2O)_2 = C_{11}H_{12}O_5 + C_5H_{15}NO_2.$$

Oil of Mustard (mixed).— This yellow, fixed, fat oil, obtainable by pressure from the seed-meal, has a sp. gr. of .917–.920, thickens at –12° (10.4° F.), is not drying, and contains glyceroles of Erucic,† Sinapoleic,‡ and Behenic Acids.§ This oil is used largely to adulterate olive oil, as it has a great power of resisting rancidity.

Myrosin.—This emulsion-like body is obtained from the seeds of this species by treating them with water, evaporating the menstruum at 40° (104° F.) to a syrup, and precipitating with alcohol. The precipitate, dried by gentle heat, results as impure myrosin, which has not yet been isolated from the albumen that is intimately mixed with it.

PHYSIOLOGICAL ACTION.—The essential oil of mustard (Sinalbin?) is a virulent, irritant poison, causing, when ingested, severe burning, followed by increased heart's action, and, if pushed to extremes, loss of sensibility, paralysis, stupor, rigors, and death. When applied to the skin it causes almost immediate vesication, followed by deep ulceration hard to heal. The symptoms caused by small repeated doses of the ground seeds are, in abstract: Salivation, with yellow-coated tongue; burning and scraping in the throat, followed by a sense of constriction; thirst; nausea and vomiting; painful flatulence; burning and crawling in the rectum; copious pasty stools; dark-colored urine; creeping chills, and inclination to sweat.

DESCRIPTION OF PLATE 23.

1. End of flowering branch, Salem, Mass., July 28th, 1885.
2. Essential organs.
3. Pistil.
4. Anthers.
5. Silique.
6. Seed.
7. Longitudinal section of seed.
(2–7 enlarged.)

---

* *Am. Jour. Phar.*, 1883, 551.　　† Or Brassic ($C_{22}H_{42}O_2$).　　‡ $C_{20}H_{38}O_2$.　　§ $C_{22}H_{44}O_2$.

24
SINAPIS NIGRA.

BLACK MUSTARD.

SYN.—SINAPIS NIGRA, LINN.; BRASSICA NIGRA, BOISS.; BRASSICA SINAPIOIDES, ROTH.

COM. NAMES.—BLACK MUSTARD, BROWN OR RED MUSTARD; (FR.) MOUTARDE NOIRE; (GER.) SCHWARZ SENF.

A TINCTURE OF THE RIPE SEEDS OF SINAPIS NIGRA, LINN.

Description.—This useful plant has become a troublesome weed in many parts of North America, growing from 3 to 6 feet high. The *root* is fusiform, thin and branching. The *stem* generally erect, smooth and numerously branched; the lower *leaves* are either lyrate or lobed, the terminal lobe large, rough, and harsh to the touch, with two or more small lateral divisions or lobes at its base, the stem leaves are entire, lanceolate and smooth. The *inflorescence* is a dense head at first, extending as the fruits form into an elongated raceme, which continues flowering at its top until frost checks the growth. The *pods* are smooth, about one-quarter inch long, upon appressed pedicels, and closely set to the elongated axis of the inflorescence, they are 4-angled, erect, and surmounted by the 4-angled, stout, persistent style. *Valves* 2, each 1-nerved. *Seeds* 4 to 6 in each cell, they are spherical, or somewhat oval, of a dark, reddish-brown color, 25 of them in line would about equal an inch, and 50 would generally weigh 1 grain. The pitted reticulation of the outer coat is coarser, while the seeds themselves are smaller and more pungent than S. alba.

A description of the order and genus is incorporated in the description of Sinapis alba, 23.

History and Habitat.—Black Mustard is found wild over the whole extent of Europe, excepting its most northern latitudes, as well as the central part of Asia and in Northern Africa. It is quite extensively cultivated in Italy, Germany, and England, and fully naturalized in both North and South America, flowering in temperate regions from June to September. It was well known to the ancients as a medicinal agent, but not as a condiment until somewhat more modern times. The seeds, when ground, form a greenish-yellow powder, inodorous when dry,

---

* Σιναπι, *sinapi*, turnip. *Brassica* or *Sinapis campestris.*

penetrating when moist, with at first a bitter, then extremely pungent taste, blistering the tongue. The seeds should be of a bright reddish-brown color, free from gray coating, this ashy film being the effect of dampness, during the ripening, and a great detriment to the value and properties of the seed.

The fresh plants, soon after their appearance, while the leaves are yet young and tender, are used by the laity in many parts of this country as a pot-herb ("greens"). This relish is termed at that stage of its growth, *scurvy-grass*, though the true Scurvy-grass is *Sinapis arvensis (Brassica Sinapistrum)*. The use of Sinapis nigra in the U. S. Ph. is simply as *Charta Sinapis*. In the Eclectic Materia Medica the use is the same, and both employ the volatile oil in *Linimentum Sinapis Compositum*.

PART USED AND PREPARATION.—The ripe seeds are coarsely powdered and covered with five parts by weight of alcohol, poured into a well-stoppered bottle, and allowed to stand eight days in a dark, cool place, being shaken twice a day. The tincture is separated by decanting, straining and filtering.

Thus prepared, it has a clear, greenish-yellow color by transmitted or reflected light, a sweetish, biting taste, afterward somewhat burning, and is neutral to litmus paper.

CHEMICAL CONSTITUENTS.—Sinapisin; this body exists (Simon) as an unsaponifiable fat, in the seeds of black mustard, from which it may be obtained by percolating the powdered seeds with alcohol of 94 per cent., evaporating the percolate, treating the residue with ether, again evaporating, treating with alcohol of 90 per cent. and filtering through animal charcoal. The impure crystals thus gained are to be dissolved in ether, from which they deposit on evaporation as snowy scales, soluble in alcohol, ether and oils. (Wittstein).

Sinigrin,—$C_{10} H_{18} KNS_2 O_{10}$, or *potasso-myronic acid*, is the principle peculiar to this species, from which it may be obtained as silky, needle-like crystals, soluble in alcohol and water. When acted upon by *myrosin* it breaks down, forming mustard oil, glucose, and $KHSO_4$.

An analysis of three samples of black mustard farina, made by A. R. Leeds and E. Everhart, reported in the Journal of the American Chemical Society, 1881, p. 130, gave the following averages, each sample differing but very slightly from the others:

Moisture,	6.833
Myronate of potash (sinigrin),	.646
Sulphocyanide of sinapine (sinalbin),	11.123
Myrosin,	28.483
Mustard oil,	29.208
Ash,	3.757
Cellulose (by difference),	19.950
	100.

For a full description of *erucic acid, sinapoleic acid, myrosin*, and *fat-oil*, which exist alike in both S. alba and S. nigra, see 23.

Ⅎ𝔪. ad nat. del. et pinxt.

SINÀPIS NÌGRA, Linn.

PHYSIOLOGICAL ACTION.—So far as I can determine, no specific toxic symptoms have been noted; under S. alba I have given the general action of mustard without differentiation.

DESCRIPTION OF PLATE 24.

1. End of a branch in fruit and flower, Binghamton, N. Y., July 5, 1883.
   2. Outline of one of the lower leaves.
   3. Fruit (enlarged).
   4. Pollen grains x 380.

25
BURSA-PASTORIS.†

SHEPHERD'S PURSE.

SYN.—CAPSELLA BURSA-PASTORIS, MŒN.; THLASPI BURSA-PASTORIS, LINN.

COM. NAMES.—SHEPHERD'S PURSE; (FR.) BOURSE DE PASTEUR; (GER.) HIRTENTÄSCHLEIN.

A TINCTURE OF THE WHOLE PLANT CAPSELLA BURSA-PASTORIS, MŒN.

Description.—This intrusive little annual grows to a height of from 6 to 18 inches. *Root* tap-shaped. *Stem* erect, simple, or branching at the summit, smooth or sometimes pubescent. *Leaves* mostly rosulate at the root, pinnatifid or pinnatifidly toothed; *stem leaves* sessile and partly clasping, more or less sagittate, toothed or in some cases entire, especially those at the base of the racemes. *Inflorescence* apparently a dense cluster at the summit of the stem, but as fruiting advances showing a racemose arrangement; *flowers* minute, white; *pedicels* long, especially in fruit. *Sepals* ovate, long-pointed, and having inserted about their middle a filamentous appendage. *Petals* spatulate. *Anthers* sagittate. *Style* short; *stigma* capitate. *Silicle* obcordate-triangular, flattened contrary to the septum; *valves* 2, scaphoid, wingless. *Seeds* numerous; *cotyledons* plane, incumbent. Read description of Cruciferæ under Sinapis alba, 23.

History and Habitat.—This European immigrant has become too thoroughly a nuisance as a weed about the cultivated lands of this country from Florida northward and westward, where it flowers from earliest spring to September.

This plant was formerly classed with the genus Thlaspi, from which it was removed on account of its wingless valves.

The Shepherd's Purse has been used in English domestic practice from early times, as an astringent in diarrhœa; it was much used in decoction with milk to check active purgings in calves. Later its value here was much doubted, and other properties accorded it, especially those of a stimulating astringent and diuretic. It has been employed in fresh decoction in hematuria, hemorrhoids, diarrhœa and dysentery, and locally as a vulnerary in ecchymosis and as an application in rheumatic affections. The juice on cotton, inserted in the nostrils, was often used to check hemorrhage in epistaxis.

---

* From *capsula*, a pod.

† I use the specific name, which should always distinguish this plant in medicine, to avoid confusion in synonyms.

PART USED AND PREPARATION.—The fresh plant, gathered when the flowering season is about half completed and the fruits rapidly forming, is chopped and pounded to a pulp and weighed. Then two-thirds by weight of alcohol is taken, the pulp thoroughly mixed with the spirit and the whole pressed out in a piece of new linen. The tincture thus prepared has, after filtration, an orange-brown color by transmitted light, a peculiar odor, resembling decayed vegetation, a pungent taste, too like its odor, and an acid reaction.

CHEMICAL CONSTITUENTS.—Several partial analyses have been made of this plant, but none have resulted in the separation and determination of a peculiar principle. The general constituents of plants, and a volatile oil said to be identical with oil of mustard, as well as a fixed oil, have been determined.

Clinical Uses.—In the absence of provings of this drug, it has been found curative in various uterine hemorrhages, especially those with which uterine cramp and colic are associated; also in various passive hemorrhages from mucous surfaces.* A thorough proving is greatly to be desired.

DESCRIPTION OF PLATE 25.

1. Whole of young plant above the radicle leaves, Binghamton, N. Y., May 24th, 1885.
    2, 3, 4. Forms of radicle leaves.
    5. Flower.
    6. Petal.
    7. Pistil.
    8. Stamen.
    9. Silicle.
    10. Open silicle, showing seeds.

* See Hale, *New Rem.*, p. 625.

€m. ad nat del et pinxt.

CAPSÉLLA BURSA-PASTÓRIS , Moench.

Tribe.—RAPHANEÆ.

GENUS.—**RAPHANUS,*** LINN.

SEX. SYST.—TETRADYNAMIA SILIQUOSA.

26

RAPHANUS.

RADISH.

SYN.—RAPHANUS RAPHANISTRUM, LINN.
COM. NAMES.—WILD RADISH, JOINTED CHARLOCK, CHARLOCK; (FR.)
RAÎFOOT, COMMUNE; (GER.) WILDE RETTIG.

A TINCTURE OF THE FRESH ROOT OF RAPHANUS RHAPHANISTRUM, LINN.

Description.—This rapid-growing annual or biennial herb usually attains a height of from 1 to 2 feet. *Root* tap-shaped; *stem* erect, glaucous, sparingly bristly, and much branched below. *Leaves* lyrate, petiolate or sessile, dentate, and rough, the terminal lobe oval or obovate. *Calyx* erect, somewhat 2-saccate at the base. *Petals* at first yellow and veiny, becoming purplish or whitish with age, obovate and unguiculate. *Stamens* distinct toothless. *Style* long; *stigma* capitate. *Pod* linear-oblong, terete upward, longer than the style, 2-jointed, indehiscent, and valveless; the upper joint markedly necklace-form by strong contractions between the seeds; the lower joint often seedless and stalk-like. *Seeds* 3 to 8, large and spherical; *cotyledons* conduplicate and incumbent.

History and Habitat.—The Wild Radish grows profusely over the fields of Great Britain and Europe, and has become a troublesome weed in New England, New York, New Jersey, and Pennsylvania, from whence it is spreading westward. It blossoms in July and fruits in September.

The cultivated forms, *R. sativus*, Linn., and its varieties, *niger* (Black Spanish), *oblongus* (Long Radish), and *rotundus* (Globose Radish), supposed to be of Chinese origin, are well-known salad roots; all of them have contributed more or less to our provings. Very little and unpronounced use has been made in medicine of these forms, or of the wild plant. The seeds have proved emetic, and the root diuretic and laxative.

PART USED AND PREPARATION.—The fresh, perfect roots, gathered when full formed, at about the time of flowering, are chopped and pounded to a pulp and weighed. Then two parts by weight of alcohol are taken, the pulp thoroughly mixed with one sixth part of it, and the rest of the alcohol added.

---

* 'Ρά, *ra*, quickly; φαίνω, *phaino*, to appear; from its rapid germination.

ŒM.ad nat.del.et pinxt. RÁPHANUS RAPHANÍSTRUM, Linn.

1

2 3 4 5

After thoroughly stirring the whole, it is poured into a well-stoppered bottle, and allowed to stand eight days in a dark, cool place, shaking twice a day. The tincture, after straining and filtering, has a clear yellow-color by transmitted light; an offensive odor, something like that of boiling cabbage; a similar miserable taste; and an acid reaction.

PHYSIOLOGICAL ACTION.—The effects noted in people who have eaten too freely of radishes, and in others who took large quantities of the tincture, were substantially as follows: Mental excitement, followed by depression and anxiety; confusion and vertigo with cephallagia; stuffiness of the nostrils; paleness of the face; bitter taste in the mouth; constriction of the œsophagus; violent thirst; nausea with violent pressure in the stomach; great distention of the abdomen, which became hard and tense, though painless, and no flatulence escaped; numerous liquid diarrhœic stools; great desire to urinate, with greatly augmented quantity; great sexual excitement in women, coming on in paroxysms of great violence; lancinating pains in the chest; violent palpitation of the heart; attacks of hysteria; emaciation; itching of the skin; restlessness; and chilliness followed by inclination to sweat.

DESCRIPTION OF PLATE 26.

1. Whole plant, Jamaica, L. I., July 29th, 1886.
   2. A sepal and stamen.
   3. Petal.
   4. Pistil.
   5. A ripe pod.
   6. A section of a pod.
   (2–4 and 6 enlarged.)

GENUS.—**V I O L A**,* LINN.

SEX. SYST.—PENTANDRIA MONOGYNIA.

27

VIOLA TRICOLOR (JACEA†).

WILD PANSY.

SYN.—VIOLA TRICOLOR, LINN.; VIOLA BICOLOR, PURSH; VIOLA TEN-
ELLA, MUHL.; VIOLA ARVENSIS, ELL.; JACEA TRICOLOR, SIVE
TRINITATIS, ETC., J. BAUH.

COM. NAMES.—PANSY, PANSIE, PANSEY, HEART'S-EASE, THREE COL-
ORED VIOLET, TRINITY VIOLET, FIELD PANSY, WILD PANSY;
(FR.) PENSÉE; (GER.) STIEFMÜTTERCHEN-KRAUT, FREISAMKRAUT.

A TINCTURE OF THE WHOLE FRESH PLANT VIOLA TRICOLOR, LINN.

Description.—This beautiful little plant, belonging to the leafy-stemmed violets,
springs from an annual, biennial, or short-lived perennial, fusiform root. *Stem* 3 to 8
inches high, angled, at first creeping, then erect, simple or branched, and leafy
throughout; *stipules* very large, herbaceous, lyrate-pinnatifid. *Inflorescence* several
smallish flowers on a terminal and axillary peduncle. *Calyx* with short auricles.
Corolla with an obtuse, thick spur; *petals* short clawed. *Ovary* partly concealed
in the concave receptacle; *style* somewhat conical, narrowing toward the ovary;
stigma cup-shaped. *Capsule* smooth; *seeds* oblong.

Description.—Violaceæ and Viola.—The plants under this natural order and
genus are low, caulescent or acaulescent, those with stems springing from annual or
perennial roots, those without stems from scaly root-stocks. The *leaves* are alternate and petiolate, with leaf-like persistent *stipules*. In the stemless violets the
scapes are axillary, solitary, and furnished with two bracts at the base. *Inflorescence*
a single, more or less irregular flower upon the incurved summit of the scape or
peduncle; many species having also radical apetalous or cryptopetalous, fertile
summer flowers. *Calyx* herbaceous, persistent; *sepals* 5, often auriculate at the
base, the odd one superior. *Corolla* irregular; *petals* 5, somewhat unequal,
hypogynous, alternate with the sepals, the superior one—which becomes inferior
by the inversion of the scape—is saccate or spurred at the base, the two lower
petals with an appendage at the base concealed in the spur. *Stamens* 5, hypogynous upon a ring-like or concave torus, alternate with the petals, closely surrounding the ovary, and are sometimes slightly coherent into a ring or tube; *filaments*
very short and broad, projecting beyond the anther into a little persistent wing or
tip, or sometimes obsolete. The two lower filaments, when present, are furnished

---

* Derivation Latin, obscure.   † Herring's Condensed Materia Medica.

each with a little projection, concealed in the sac or spur of the lower petal; *anthers* adnate, 2-celled, the cells somewhat separated at the base, opening by a longitudinal introrse slit. *Ovary* sessile, ovoid, one-celled, with three parietal placentæ; *style* terminal, various, usually declined; *stigma* various. *Fruit* an ovoid, crustaceous or papyraceous, 3 valved, loculicidal capsule; *seeds* many, horizontal, and furnished with a distinct wart-like excrescence at the hilum, raphe apparent; *albumen* fleshy; *embryo* straight, situated in the axis.

This description essentially includes the two genera *Ionidum* (*solea*) and *Viola* of the northern United States; in the tropics many plants of this order are shrubby. The genus *Ionidum* contains the Brazilian Poaya da Praja (*Ionidum Ipecacuanha*, A. de St. H.; *I. Itubu*, H B K.; *Viola Itubu*, Aubl.; *Pombalia Itubu*, D C.); the Poaya do campo (*Ionidum Poaya*.); the Chimborazian Cuichunchulli (*Ionidum microphyllum*, H B K.) noted as a supposed specific for the "mal de San Lazaro" or Elephantiasis tuberculata; and the Chilian purgative Maytensillo (*Ionidum parviflorum*, Linn.), the roots of which are stated by Lindley to bear in appearance and properties a great similarity to Ipecacuanha.

History and Habitat.—The wild pansy has become naturalized in this country from Europe, growing here in dry, sandy soils, from New York westward to Illinois and southward, blossoming northward from April until the summer months. The varieties of this plant in cultivation are innumerable, affording some of the most beautiful of our garden-plants; the principal changes in cultivation are in the size and colors of the flowers, varying, as they now do, from pure white to silver, gold, bronze, and jet-black, with admixtures in immense variety. The use of the pansy in medicine dates far back in ancient medication, the first real experimentation with the plant is that of Starck in 1776, who wrote "*De crusta lactea infantum ejusdemque remedis dissertatio, etc.*," in that year; the provings substantiate this use of the plant and show it to be useful in other forms of impetigo. Its use in some forms of burrowing ulcers, tinea capitis and scabies is also sanctioned by the provings.

The plant is mentioned in the U. S. Ph. and the Eclectic Materia Medica.

Part Used and Preparation.—The whole plant, gathered while in flower, should be chopped and pounded to a pulp and weighed; then two parts by weight of alcohol taken, the pulp thoroughly mixed with one-sixth part of it, and the rest of the alcohol added. The whole should be well mixed, poured into a well-stoppered bottle, and allowed to stand at least eight days in a dark, cool place.

The tincture, separated by filtering, should have an orange-brown color by transmitted light, a cucumber-like odor, rich, sweet taste, and strong acid reaction.

CHEMICAL CONSTITUENTS.—*Violin;** this acrid, bitter principle, bearing in its properties a close resemblance to *emetia*,† was extracted by Boullay from *Viola adorata*; it is found also in *Viola tricolor* and *var. arvensis* as well as in

---

* *Violia, Violine.*   † Alkaloid of *Cephælis Ipecacuanha.*

ad nat.del.et pinxt.

VÌOLA TRÍCOLOR , Linn.

Viola pedata. According to Wittstein it is a pale yellow, bitter powder, fusible, and inflammable at greater heat; it dissolves slightly in water and alcohol, and is insoluble in ether.

Violaqueritrin, $C_{42}H_{42}O_{24}$. This coloring-matter was discovered by Karl Mandelin* in *viola tricolor var. arvensis;* it forms a yellow crystalline mass, easily soluble in alkalies, and hot water, crystallizing from the latter on cooling.

Salicylic Acid, $C_6H_4 \begin{cases} OH \\ CO_2H. \end{cases}$ This acid, so far in its history, has been but rarely extracted under its own form from plants; the flowers of *Spirea ulmaria* alone yielding it.† Karl Mandelin, however, who has made careful analyses of viola tricolor, extracts the acid pure. He reports in his " Inaugural Dissertation" (Dorpat, 1881) a proportion of from .043 per cent. in cultivated plants, to .107 per cent. in *var. arvensis.* He finds it in all parts of the fresh plant, and principally in the roots, stems and leaves.

Pectin, or *vegetable jelly,* $C_{23}H_{40}O_{28}$ $(H_2O)_4$. From the fact that a mixture of one part of the juice of this plant with ten parts water, will form a jelly-like mass, the presence of the above body or a very strong mucilage seems proven. This property has given various uses to *Viola* as an expectorant, emollient, and infusion for coughs and bronchial affections.

Sugar, both crystallizable and uncrystallizable, salts of potassium, tartrate of magnesium, and other general constituents of plants have been determined.

PHYSIOLOGICAL ACTION.—The emetic effect of some of the violets, due to the presence of *violin,* has been noted to some extent in this species. The most characteristic symptom of its action is an offensive odor of the urine, like that of the cat. The pains caused by this drug are of a stitching character, while its action seems spent almost entirely upon the skin, and the male sexual organs. On the skin it causes burning, stinging, and itching, followed by breaking down of the tissues into either squamous spots, or any grade of incrusted eruptions; the eruption pours out a thin yellow fluid. Boils, impetigo, especially crustea lactea, ichorous and burrowing ulcers, and zoster followed the exhibition of generous doses of this drug. On the genital organs of the male the prepuce becomes swollen, with stitching and burning pains in the glans and scrotum, the testicle becomes indurated, and venereal ulcers form ; stitchings are frequent in the urethra, followed by urging to urinate with profuse discharge.

DESCRIPTION OF PLATE 27.

1. Whole plant from Binghamton, N. Y., May 13, 1884.
    2. Bud showing sepals.
    3. Pistil (enlarged).
    4. Discharged anther (enlarged).
    5. Pollen x 380.

* *Phar. Zeit. für Russland,* 1883, pp. 329–334. *Am. Jour. Phar.,* 1883, p. 470.   † Lowig.

N. ORD.—CISTACEÆ.

GENUS.—**HELIANTHEMUM**,* TOURN.

SEX. SYST.—POLYANDRIA MONOGYNIA.

28

CISTUS.

ROCK ROSE.

SYN.—HELIANTHEMUM CANADENSE, MICHX.; H. RAMULIFLORUM, MICHX.; H. ROSMARINIFOLIUM, PURSH.; H. CORYMBOSUM, PURSH.; CISTUS CANADENSIS, LINN.; C. RAMULIFLORUM, POIR.; LECHEA MAJOR, LINN; HETERAMERIS CANADENSIS, SPACH.; H. MICHAUXII, SPACH.

COM. NAMES.—ROCK ROSE,† FROST-WORT, FROST-PLANT. FROST-WEED, HOLLY ROSE; (FR.) HELIANTHEME DU CANADA; (GER.) CANADISCHES SONNENRÖSCHEN.

A TINCTURE OF THE WHOLE PLANT HELIANTHEMUM CANADENSE, MICHX.

Description.—This peculiar plant grows to a height of from 6 to 12 inches. *Stem* at first simple, erect or ascending, somewhat hairy; *pubescence* stellate and fasciculate. *Leaves* sessile or nearly so, oblong lanceolate. *Flowers* of two sorts, both diurnal; *Primary form:* few or solitary, large, pedunculate; *calyx* hairy pubescent; *petals* 5, obovate, fugacious, crumpled in the bud, erosely marginate; *stamens* indefinitely numerous; *pod* ovate, shining, many-seeded; *Secondary form:* numerous, small, sessile, axillary, solitary or few-clustered upon short leafy branches; *sepals* 5, the outer pair sometimes wanting; *petals* very small or absent; *stamens* 3 to 10; *pod* minute, hoary, 3- few-seeded. *Style* columnar or absent; *stigma* capitate, 3-lobed, fimbriolate. *Fruit* a 1-celled, 3-valved capsule. *Seed* somewhat triangular; *testa* rough; *embryo* incurved in the form of a hook or ring.

There are two very distinct forms of this species, differentiable as follows:

EARLY FLOWERING FORM (FIG. 1).	LATER FLOWERING FORM (FIG. 2).
Stems upright, branching, bright crimson, nearly glaucous.	Stem upright, less branched, purplish, covered with a downy pubescence.
Leaves ovate-lanceolate, light green.	Leaves dark green.
Primary flowers axillary solitary.	Primary flowers terminal clustered.
Secondary flower-buds minute.	Secondary flowers numerous, larger.
Capsule of primary flowers nearly twice as large as the later form.	Capsule of primary flowers smaller.

Cistaceæ.—This small family of low shrubs or herbs is represented in North America by 3 genera and 17 species; its members are characterized as follows:

---

* Ἥλιος, *helios*, the sun; ἄνθεμον, *anthemon*, a flower.

† The true Rock Rose is *C. Creticus*, Linn., a native of Syria.

Leaves simple, mostly entire, the lower often opposite, the upper alternate ; *stipules* absent. *Flowers* regular. *Calyx* persistent ; *sepals* 5, the two outer often smaller, bract-like, or absent, the three inner twisted in the bud. *Petals* 3 to 5, twisted in an opposite direction to the sepals, fugacious. *Stamens* distinct, mostly indefinite, hypogynous ; *filaments* slender ; *anthers* short, innate. *Ovules* few or many, stipitate, and furnished with an apical orifice ; *style* small or wanting. *Fruit* a 1-celled capsule ; *valves* 3 to 5, each with a dissepiment attached to its median line and placental at the axis. *Seeds* mostly orthotropous ; *embryo* long and slender, straightish or curved ; *albumen* mealy.

The only other plant of this order used in medicine is the European Rock Rose (*Cistus Creticus*, Linn.), from which the natural exudation, a gum resin called Ladanum, has been much esteemed as a stimulant, especially to mucous membranes, and as an emmenagogue. *C. Ladaniferous*, Linn., *C. Ledon*, Lam., and *C. Laurifolius*, Linn., are said to yield the same substance.

History and Habitat.—Frost-wort is indigenous to North America, where it ranges from Maine to Wisconsin and thence southward ; it habits sandy soils, and flowers from April to August. In early winter the bark near the root fissures, and spicules of ice project from the rents ; this fact gave the plant its vulgarisms, Frost-wort, etc.

This plant has been long held in repute as a remedy for scrofula and for many disorders arising in persons of strumous diatheses, especially, however, those diseases in such persons which have seemed to need an astringent, tonic, or alterative, such as diarrhœa, aphthous ulcerations, ulcers, ophthalmia, syphilis, and the like.

The preparation of the Eclectic Materia Medica is *Decoctum Helianthemi.*

PART USED AND PREPARATION.—The whole fresh flowering plant is chopped and pounded to a pulp and weighed. Then two parts by weight of alcohol are taken, the pulp thoroughly mixed with one-sixth part of it, and the rest of the alcohol added. After stirring the whole well, it is poured into a well-stoppered bottle, and allowed to stand eight days in a dark, cool place.

The tincture, separated from the mass by pressing and filtering, has a beautiful crimson color by transmitted light ; an odor resembling that of damp clover hay ; a sourish, bitterish, and astringent taste, and an acid reaction.

CHEMICAL CONSTITUENTS.—No analysis of this species has, to our knowledge, been made ; the tincture, however, would indicate a bitter principle, and probably tannin.

PHYSIOLOGICAL ACTION.—When taken in large doses the decoction causes nausea and vomiting. Small doses persisted in cause the following train of symptoms : Headache ; pressure and stitches in the eyes ; swelling and discharge in the internal ear, and of the salivary and cervical glands ; swelling of the inner nose, and sneezing ; soreness, dryness, and rawness of the tongue, mouth,

℃m.ad nat.del.et pinxt.

HELIÁNTHEMUM CANADÉNSE, Michx.

and throat; abdominal flatulence; diarrhœa; swelling and hardness of the mammæ; pains in the chest; articular drawing and tearing pains; itching vesicular eruption; chilliness, heat and restlessness, with thirst and trembling during the fever.

DESCRIPTION OF PLATE 28.

1. Early flowering form, with primary flower, June 15th, 1885.
2. Late flowering form, August 1st, 1885, Salem, Mass.
   3. Primary flower-bud.
   4. Pistil and stamen.
   5. Horizontal section of ovary.
   6. Ovule.
   7. Open fruit.
   8. Seeds.
   9. Section of seed.
   10. Secondary bud.
      (3–6 and 8–10 enlarged.)

GENUS.—**DROSERA,**[*] LINN.

SEX. SYST.—PENTANDRIA PENTAGYNIA.

29

DROSERA.

SUNDEW.

SYN.—DROSERA ROTUNDIFOLIA, L.; RORELLA ROTUNDIFOLIA, AND ROS SOLIS FOL. ROTUND. RAII.

COM. NAMES.—ROUND-LEAVED SUNDEW, RED-ROT, MOOR GRASS, YOUTH ROOT; (FR.) DROSÉRE À FEUILLES RONDES, ROSEÉ DU SOLEIL; (GER.) RUNDBLATTRIGER SONNENTHAU.

A TINCTURE OF THE WHOLE FRESH PLANT, DROSERA ROTUNDIFOLIA, L.

Description.—This low, stemless, perennial herb is characterized as follows: *Leaves* orbicular, tufted, the upper surface covered with red, glandular, setose hairs, each bearing a pellucid globule of glutinous fluid at its apex; *petioles* long, hairy, and spreading; *stipules* replaced by a fringy tuft of hairs. *Scapes* naked, 1 to 3 from each root; *inflorescence* a terminal, unilateral, at first circinate then nodding raceme which becomes gradually erect as the buds expand and fruits ripen; thus each flower as it opens appears terminal. *Flowers* 5 to 10, white, diurnal, opening only in sunshine, the parts sometimes in sixes. *Petals* oblong, *styles* generally 3, deeply forked; *stigmas* 6, situated upon the inner face of the club shaped apex of each fork. *Pod* globular, 3–valved; *seeds* numerous, fusiform, arranged in 2 to 5 rows along the placentiferous median line of each valve, *testa* loose, arilliform and chaffy.

Droseraceæ.—The members of this small family of bog plants are known mainly by their being mostly clothed with gland-bearing hairs. *Leaves* clustered at the base of the scape, or alternate, petiolate, circinate in the bud. *Flowers* hypogynous; *calyx* composed of 5 equal and persistent sepals; *corolla* of 5 equal and regular, marcescent petals, convolute in the bud. *Stamens* equaling in number the petals and alternate with them; *anthers* innate, extrorse. *Styles* 3 to 5 generally distinct, undivided, bifurcated or two-lobed, at the apex. *Fruit* a 1-celled 3 to 5-valved, loculicidal capsule; *placenta* thick at the base of the pod, or merely a line on each valve; *seeds* numerous, anatropous; *albumen* sarcous or cartilaginous; *embryo* basal, minute.

The species under consideration is the only one used in medicine. The North Carolinian fly-trap (*Dionea muscipula*, Ellis) has furnished material for the study of carnivority in plants; the sundew has also been experimented upon in this

---

[*] Δροσερός, *droseros,* dewy; in allusion to the appearance of the leaves.

regard, but as yet the results are far from proving it carnivorous *per se*, though the plants allowed insects as "food" appear to flourish better and ripen more seeds than those deprived of that nourishment.*

History and Habitat.—The sundew grows in dense sphagnum or sandy swamps in England and America. Its range here extends from Florida northward, most common north, where it blossoms in June and July.

The previous uses of this plant in medicine have been but slight; it was supposed in the sixteenth century to be curative of consumption; of this quality, however, Gerarde says: "The later physitians have thought this herbe to be a rare and singular remedie for all those that be in a consumption of the lungs, and especially the distilled water thereof; for, as the best doth keep and hold fast the moisture and the dew, and so fast that the extreme heate of the sun cannot consume and waste away the same; so, likewise, men thought that herewith the naturale and heate in men's bodies is preserved and cherished. But the use thereof doth otherwise teach, and reason showeth the contrarie; for, seeing it is an extreme biting herbe, and that the distilled water is not altogether without this biting qualitie, it cannot be taken with safetie: for it hath also been observed that they have sooner perished that used the distilled water hereof, than those that abstained from it and have followed the right and ordinary course of diet." Geoffroi asserts† that its infusion is a valuable pectoral, useful in pulmonary ulceration and in asthma. Rafinesque says‡ the juice is used "to destroy warts and corns; with milk, for freckles and sunburns. It makes milk solid, but sour like bonyclabber, liked in Sweden. Deemed pectoral in South America, a sirup used in asthma." Many medical writers, among them Schenck and Valentin, recommend its use in "different kinds" of coughs, arising from bronchial attacks, phthisis, and other diseases of the lungs. A fit summary of all this practice may be found in Hahnemann's observations. "Drosera is one of the most powerful medicinal agents in our country. It was formerly used externally, but without success, in cutaneous affections, and it seems to have been taken with greater advantage internally. Modern practitioners who, according to custom, have tried only large doses, have not ventured upon giving it internally, fearing to kill their patients, and have therefore rejected it."

No preparations of Drosera are official either in the U. S. Ph. or Eclectic Materia Medica.

PART USED AND PREPARATION.—The entire fresh plant gathered in July should be chopped and pounded to a pulp, enclosed in a piece of new linen and pressed out. The juice should then be added to an equal part by weight of alcohol, thoroughly mixed and allowed to stand eight days in a well-stoppered bottle in a dark, cool place. The tincture separated from the above mass by

---

* Büsgen, *Jour. Chem. Soc.*, 1884, p. 917. A more extended discussion of this subject will be found under Sarracenia, 19.

† *Mer. et de L. Dict. de M. Med.*, II., p. 699.

‡ *Med. Flora*, II., p. 217.

ad nat del. et pinxt.

DRÓSERA ROTUNDIFÒLIA, Linn.

29.

filtration should be opaque, and present in thin layers a reddish-brown color, have an acrid, astringent taste, and an acid reaction.

CHEMICAL CONSTITUENTS.—*Alizarin*, $C_{14}H_8O_4$* ($C_{10}H_6O_3 + H_2O$ or $C_{14}H_{10}O_4$).† This dioxyanthroquinone coloring matter was first discovered in Madder root (*Rubia tinctoria*), as a glucoside ‡ It crystallizes from its solution in alcohol in long, lustrous, translucent, yellowish-red, neutral and bitter prisms, containing three molecules of water, which it loses at 100°–120° (212°–248° F.). It sublimes at 215° (419° F.), in brilliant red needles that are only slightly soluble in water, but fully in alcohol and ether. (Wittstein.)

The plant is acrid and corrosive, but the principle to which this property is due has not, as far as I can determine, been investigated. Rafinesque states that the glutinous secretion of the leaf hairs is acid; this may be a similar body to that which renders the water in the leaves of the pitcher-plant acid.§

PHYSIOLOGICAL ACTION.—Drosera has long been deemed poisonous to animals, especially sheep; in the latter its action was mostly supposed to be upon the mucous membrane of the intestinal tract. Dr. Curie slowly poisoned three cats with daily doses of the drug;‖ the post-mortem examination with the microscope revealed the pleural surface of both lungs studded with true tubercle. In one cat the mesenteric glands were much enlarged; in another the submaxillary glands, with the solitary glands of the colon and Peyer's patches. Burdach states that in man the juice produces shuddering, sense of constriction at the chest, rawness in the throat, cough, hæmoptysis, pain in the bowels, diarrhœa, sweat, and diminished secretion of urine. The cough caused by this drug arises from a tickling in the larynx; it is spasmodic in its nature and causes vomiting if the stomach contains food.

Drosera asserts altogether a peculiar action upon the lungs and, in fact, the whole respiratory tract, thus leading us to value it deservingly in pertussis, bronchial irritation and even phthisis, where in fact it gives many a patient a restful night and more peaceful day when the disease is too far advanced for still greater benefit.

DESCRIPTION OF PLATE 29.

1. Whole plant from Spruce Pond, N. Y., July 21st, 1884.
    2. Stamen.
    3. Pistil.
    4. Leaf hair.
    (2–4 enlarged.)

---

* Grieb et Lieb. † Schunck. ‡ Rubianic acid. § Sarracenia purpurea, 19.
‖ French Acad. Sci., *British Jour. Hom.*, xx., 39.

GENUS.—**HYPERICUM**,* LINN.

SEX. SYST.—POLYADELPHIA POLYANDRIA.

30

HYPERICUM.

ST. JOHN'S WORT.

SYN.—HYPERICUM PERFORATUM, LINN.; H. VULGARE, BAUH.; H. PSEUDOPERFORATUM, BERTOL.

COM. NAMES.—ST. JOHN'S WORT, GOD'S WONDER PLANT, DEVIL'S SCOURGE, WITCHES' HERB; (FR.) HERBE ST. JEAN, CHASSE DIABLE, MILLE-PERTUIS; (GER.) JOHANNISKRAUT, HARTHEU, HEXEN-KRAUT.

A TINCTURE OF THE WHOLE PLANT HYPERICUM PERFORATUM, LINN.

Description.—This rapidly-spreading perennial grows to a height of a foot or more. *Stem* erect, somewhat two-edged, much branched at the summit and producing many long runners from its base. *Leaves* elliptical to linear oblong, obtuse, and punctate with numerous scattered pellucid dots. *Inflorescence* in a dense, terminal, leafy cyme; *flowers* numerous, deep yellow. *Calyx* erect; *sepals* lanceolate, acute. *Petals* twice as long as the sepals, black-dotted along the edges, margins unequal. *Stamens* numerous, in 3 to 5 clusters; *filaments* filiform; *anthers* black-dotted. *Styles* 3-divergent. *Fruit* a globose-ovoid capsule, 3-celled by the meeting of the placentæ in the axis; *seeds* pitted.

Hypericaceæ.—This family of herbs or shrubs is represented in North America by 3 genera, containing in all 39 species and 6 varieties. *Leaves* opposite, entire, dotted; *stipules* none. *Inflorescence* cymose; *flowers* regular, hypogynous. *Sepals* 5, nearly equal, sometimes united at the base, persistent, and imbricated in the bud. *Petals* 5, alternate with the sepals, deciduous, oblique, convolute or imbricated in the bud. *Stamens* mostly numerous, united or clustered, and not furnished with interposed glands; *anthers* introrse, fixed by the middle. *Ovules* anatropous; *styles* 2 to 5, persistent; *stigmas* hardly evident, capitate. *Fruit* a 1- to 5-celled pod; *dehiscence* septicidal; *valves* 2 to 5. *Seeds* numerous, usually cylindrical; *embryo* straight; *albumen* none; *tegmen* fleshy.

The only plants of this order used in general medicine are: The Isle of France *Hypericum lanceolatum*, which is considered specific for syphilis by the natives; the Brazilian *H. connatum*, used as an astringent in sore throat; *H. laxiusculum*, considered alexiteric; and some Russian species, which are vaunted as cures for hydrophobia. The European *Androsæmum officinale*, All., is vulnerary; and the Guiana *Visnia Guianensis*, Pers., yields a purgative juice, greatly resembling gamboge.

---

* The ancient name, of unknown derivation.

History and Habitat.—This European immigrant has become so thoroughly naturalized with us as to become a very troublesome weed upon our farm-lands, where its rapid and rank growth render it difficult to exterminate and very exhausting to the soil. It flowers in July and August, and fruits a little later.

Hypericum is mentioned by some of the earliest writers upon Materia Medica as a febrifuge and anthelmintic. Paul of Ægina speaks of it as an emmenagogue, and as being desiccative and diuretic; also as a vulnerary. Galen, Dioscorides and others recommend its use as above. Gerarde says, in his *Herball:* "S. John's Wort, with his flowers and seed boyled and drunken, provoketh urine, and is right good against stone in the bladder, and stoppeth the laske. The leaves, flowers, and seeds stamped, and put into a glass with oyle olive, and set in the hot sunne for certain weeks together, and then strained from these herbes, and the like quantity of new put in, and sunned in like manner, doth make an oyle of the colour of blood, which is a most precious remedy for deep wounds and those that are thorow the body, for sinews that are pricked, or any wound with a venomed weapon." The popular and empirical uses of this plant were various, depending in great part upon its balsamic odor and property. Among the more superstitious peasantry of Middle Europe the most astonishing virtues were assigned to the herb; it became in fact with them a *fuga dæmonum,* and was gathered under this idea, especially on St. John's Day. It was also supposed to be useful in mania, hysteria, and hypochondriasis. Later on, especially in Eclectic practice, it became noted as a diuretic, astringent, nervine, and anti-hemorrhagic, but is thrown aside by the so-called "regulars," whose latest author (our contemporary, Dr. Johnson) says:* "In scientific medicine it has become obsolete long ago. One author of comparatively recent date considers 'the saturated tincture nearly as valuable as that of arnica for bruises, etc.' As tincture of arnica, however, apart from the alcohol which it contains, is of doubtful efficacy in these cases, the above statement does not tend to inspire faith in St. John's Wort." This, my reader, is one of the deductions of "scientific medicine."

The great use of Hypericum in wounds where the nerves are involved to any extent is the rightful discovery of the true science of medicine. Dr. Franklin, who had ample field to test it during the war, says: "Lacerated wounds of parts rich in nerves yield nicely to this drug." Many cases of injury to the cranium and spinal column are reported benefited by its use; and every homœopathic physician of at least three months' practice can attest to its merits. It is to the nervous system what arnica is to the muscular.

Hypericum is no longer officinal in the pharmacopœias. In the Eclectic Materia Medica its preparation is *Infusum Hyperici.*

PART USED AND PREPARATION.—The fresh blossoming plant is chopped and pounded to a pulp and weighed. Then two parts by weight of alcohol are taken, the pulp mixed thoroughly with one-sixth part of it, and the rest of the alcohol added. After having stirred the whole well, pour it into a closely-stoppered bottle, and let it stand eight days in a dark, cool place.

---

* *Med. Bot. of North America,* Wood's Library, Dec., 1884.

ℭ.ᴍ.ad nat.del.et pinxt.

HYPÉRICUM PERFORÀTUM, Linn.

The tincture, separated from this mass by filtration, should have a deep crimson color, almost opaque; an odor resembling that of port wine; a slightly astringent vinous taste; and an acid reaction.

CHEMICAL CONSITUENTS. —*Oleum Hyperici.* This body is a product of the apparently black dots upon the petals and fruits. It gives a beautiful red color to alcohol and essential oils. This oil is doubtless one of the active principles of the plant. A resin, acrid and slightly bitter, however, is one of the most active, if not the active, principle. The Tilden analysis* yields a "Bitter principle," which does not appear as a result in the analyses of Blair† or Buchner.

Tannin, and the usual plant constituents, have also been determined.

PHYSIOLOGICAL ACTION.—The compiled results of the ingestion of this drug are in substance as follows: Mental depression and exhaustion; vertigo and confusion of the head with pain, heat, and throbbing; dilation of the pupils; nausea; profuse urination; dry, hacking cough; increased heart's action; numbness, weakness, and trembling of the legs; tearing pains in the upper extremities; great weakness and prostration; fuzzy feeling of the hands; restless sleep; shiverings and coldness of the body followed by dry heat.

DESCRIPTION OF PLATE 30.

1 and 2. Whole plant, Binghamton, N. Y., July 7th, 1885.
3 and 4. Stamens.
5. Pistil.
6. Section of ovary.
7. Leaf.
8. Petal.
(3–6 enlarged.)

* *Jour. Mat. Med.*, N. S., i, 232.   † *Am. Jour. Phar.*, xi, 23.

Tribe.—SILENEÆ.

GENUS —**LYCHNIS,*** TOURN.

SEX. SYST.—DECANDRIA PENTAGYNIA.

31
AGROSTEMMA GITHAGO.

CORN COCKLE.

SYN.—LYCHNIS GITHAGO, LAM.; AGROSTEMMA GITHAGO,† LINN.

COM. NAMES.—CORN COCKLE, COCKLE OR COCKEL, ROSE CAMPION; (FR.) LA NIELLE DES BLÉS, L'IVRAIE; (GER.) GEMEINE RADE, KORN RADE.

A TINCTURE OF THE RIPE SEEDS OF LYCHNIS GITHAGO, LAM.

Description.—This softly pubescent annual, a pernicious emigrant, grows to a height of from 1 to 3 feet. *Stem* erect, dichotomous; *leaves* linear-lanceolate, acute, covered with a whitish cottony down; *stipules* none; *pubescence* consisting of long appressed cilia. *Inflorescence* solitary, axillary and terminal, long-peduncled flowers. *Calyx* cylindrical-campanulate, pubescent, and naked as regards bracts; *lobes* 5, linear-lanceolate, foliaceous, deciduous. *Petals* obovate, emarginate, crownless, slender-clawed, shorter than the lobes of the calyx. *Stamens* 10. *Ovary* stipeless; *styles* 5, or rarely 4. *Fruit* a 1-celled coriacious capsule, opening by 8 or 10 teeth; *seeds* numerous, velvety black, reniform, muricately roughened in longitudinal concentric curved lines from the hilum.

Caryophyllaceæ.—*Stems* usually enlarged at the nodes; *leaves* opposite, entire, often united at the base, the upper sometimes alternate. *Flowers* symmetrical, 4- to 5-merous; *sepals* 4 to 5, distinct or cohering, persistent, continuous with the peduncle; *petals* 4 to 5 or none, hypogynous or perigynous, the latter clawless, the former unguiculate, inserted upon the peduncle of the ovary, they are sometimes deeply notched, sometimes simply emarginate, and in a few species split through their whole length. *Stamens* not more than twice the number of the petals, in many species equal in number with the sepals and opposite them; *filaments* subulate, sometimes monadelphous at the base, inserted with the petals upon the peduncle of the ovary; *anthers* versatile or innate, introrse, 2-celled, opening longitudinally. *Ovary* generally gynophorous, composed of from 2 to 5 confluent carpels; *styles* 2 to 5, rarely one by cohesion, filiform, stigmatic down the inner

---

* Λύχνος, *lychnos*, a lamp; from the use of the cottony substance on the leaves of some spices in lieu of wicks.

† *Git* or *gith*, the name of certain black aromatic grains, which were employed by the Romans in cookery. These grains are the seeds of the European fennel flower (*Nigella sativa*, Linn.); and bear little resemblance to those of the cockle except in size and color.

face. *Fruit* a coriaceous capsule, 2- to 5-valved and -celled, or more commonly 1-celled by the wasting away of the dissepiments; *placenta* central and generally free; *dehiscence* loculicidal, or more commonly terminal by the splitting of the apex into twice as many teeth as there are styles. *Seeds* generally indefinite, inserted upon, and clustered about, the base of the central placenta, amphitropous or campylotropous; *embryo* external to the albumen and generally coiled around it, or in *Dianthus* nearly straight; *albumen* farinaceous.

The usefulness of this family of more or less mild plants lies mostly in the principle *saponin* found in many of its species, but especially prominent in two, viz.: the European soapwort (*Saponaria officinalis*, Linn.), and the Spanish fleshy-leaved Gypsophila (*Gypsophila Struthium*, Linn.). This substance is detergent and often used alone and in the composition of soap. The plants in which this principle exists are deemed nearly equal to Sarsaparilla as cleansers of the blood in syphilis and similar affections when the skin is involved; *parillin*, the active principle of sarsaparilla, being similar in its properties to *saponin*. Several species of the genus *Silene* are considered to be anthelmintics, some measure of success having followed the use of the Fire pink (*Silene Virginiaca*, Linn.).* Many species of pinks (*Dianthus*) were formerly used and esteemed as astringents and sudorifics, and one species, *Dianthus plumarius*, useful in epilepsy, but all have fallen into disuse, their petals now only being utilized as a coloring matter for ointments and perfumes.

History and Habitat.—The cockle was introduced into this country with grain from Europe, and is very seldom to be found growing elsewhere than in a field of wheat. It blossoms and ripens its seed in good season for the harvest, thus mixing well with the grain. The seeds are so small that they are only with difficulty separated, and when left and ground with the wheat render the resulting flour dark-colored, unwholesome, bitter, and in some cases poisonous, as will be noted hereafter.

PART USED AND PREPARATION.—The ripe, dried seeds are broken into a coarse powder and weighed. Then five parts by weight of alcohol are poured upon the powder, and the whole allowed to stand eight days in a well-stoppered bottle, in a dark, cool place, shaking thoroughly twice a day. The tincture separated from this mass by filtration should be of a clear, light bistre color by transmitted light; its odor is strangely similar to the taste of the sweet acorn; its taste like its odor, and also somewhat acrid; and its reaction strongly acid.

CHEMICAL CONSTITUENTS.—*Agrostemmin.*—I am unable to find the authority for this body, which Wittstein says is an "alkaloid alleged to exist in the seeds of Lychnis Githago. It is obtained by extracting with alcohol of 40 per cent. containing acetic acid, and by precipitating with calcined magnesia. The precipitate to be treated with alcohol and left to crystallize. It results as yellowish-white,

---

* Barton *Collections*, vol. i, p. 39.

31.

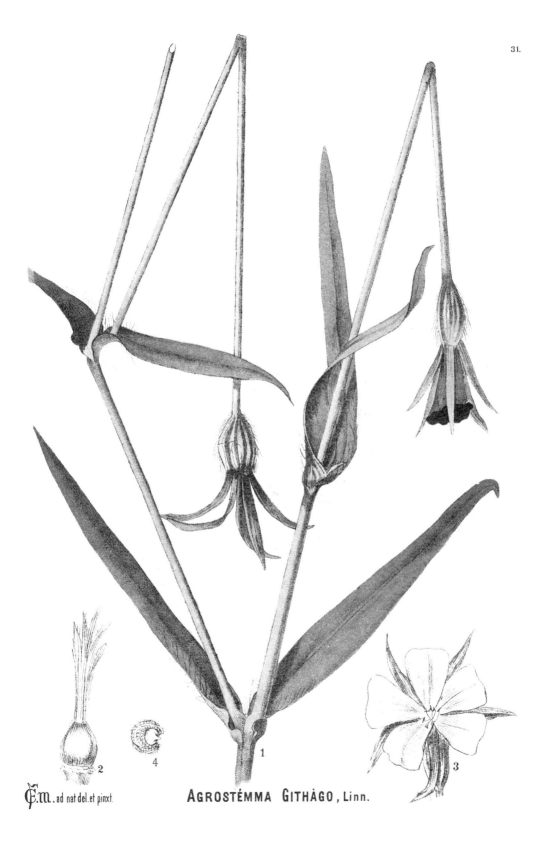

1   2   4   3

Ŧ.m. . ad nat del. et pinxt.   AGROSTÉMMA GITHÀGO, Linn.

minute scales, fusible by heat and slowly soluble in water. It has a perceptibly alkaline reaction and yields crystallizable salts with acids."

Githagin. — Specific *saponin*, described under Aesculus Hippocastanum, page 43–4.

PHYSIOLOGICAL ACTION.—The seeds of the cockle are said to be frequently allowed to adulterate the cheaper grades of flour in France, being intentionally ground with the wheat. Two 500 gram. (14½ oz.) lots of wheat flour, containing respectively 30 and 45 per cent. of these seeds, administered to two calves, caused severe cramps in the stomach within an hour, followed by diarrhœa, and finally death. Ducks and geese will eat of the seeds, but suffer death as above, and show post-mortem severe inflammation of the bowels.* In feeding my chickens " wheat screenings " I have often noted that they always carefully avoid the cockle seeds ; not even the young chicks will pick up a single seed.

The following symptoms are noted by Dr. Allen ;† they were observed from eating bread made of flour contaminated by cockle seed : Coma, in some cases ; vertigo ; headache with a sensation of heat and burning rising into the vertex ; mouth hot and dry ; nausea, sour and bitter vomiting ; burning, extending along the œsophagus, from the stomach into the throat ; cutting pains in the stomach ; diarrhœa, with tenesmus and burning in the bowels and rectum ; pulse at first small and rapid, then tense, hard, and slower ; hot skin ; tearing along the spine with impaired locomotion, and difficulty in maintaining an erect position. These symptoms class the seeds among the cerebro-spinal irritants.

DESCRIPTION OF PLATE 31.

1. End of a flowering branch, Ithaca, N. Y., June 13th, 1880.
2. Pistil.
3. Flower.
4. Seed, x 25.

(2 and 3 enlarged.)

---

* *Am. Jour. Phar,*, 1879, p. 129; from *Arch. d. Pharm.*, 1879, p. 87.
† *Ency. Pure Mat. Med.*, vol. i, p. 132.

32

GERANIUM MACULATUM.

WILD GERANIUM.

SYN.—GERANIUM MACULATUM, LINN.
COM. NAMES.—WILD GERANIUM OR CRANESBILL, SPOTTED GERANIUM
OR CRANESBILL, CROWFOOT,† ALUM-ROOT, TORMENTIL, STORK-
BILL; (FR.) BEC DE GRUE; (GER.) GEFLECKTER STORCHSNABEL.

A TINCTURE OF THE FRESH AUTUMNAL ROOT OF GERANIUM MACULATUM,
LINN.

Description.—This erect perennial, hairy herb, grows to a height of from one
to one and a half feet. *Root* somewhat woody. *Stem* erect, hairy, forking. *Leaves*
of two kinds; those from the root, long petioled, those of the stem, opposite; all
generally 5-parted, the cuneate divisions lobed and cut at the end, hairy. The
leaves when old become somewhat blotched with whitish-green, whence the specific
name. *Stipules* lanceolate. *Inflorescence* a terminal open panicle; *pedicels* about
one inch long, from one to two sometimes three flowered; *flowers* large and
showy. *Sepals* equal, cuspidate, persistent, villous. *Petals* equal, entire, bearded
upon the claw. *Stamens* 10, unequal, the longer 5 alternate with the petals, and
furnished each with a basal gland; *filaments* slightly hairy at the base; *anthers* perfect on all the filaments. *Style* terminal, persistent, smooth inside. (This is noticeable in the fruit after their cleavage from the axis.) *Seeds* minutely reticulate.

GERANIACEÆ.—This order, having a position between *Zygophyllaceæ* and
Rutaceæ, is characterized by generally strong-scented herbs or shrubs, having astringent roots; *leaves* palmately veined and usually lobed; *flowers* symmetrical.
(Exc. *Impatiens* and *Tropæolum.*)   *Calyx* of 5 persistent sepals, imbricated in the
bud; *corolla* of 5 petals, furnished with claws, mostly convolute in the bud; *stamens* 10, in two rows, the outer often sterile; *filaments* broad and united at the
base; *styles* 5, connected about an axis; *stigmas* 5, separate; *ovary* 5-carpeled,
each carpel containing from 1 to 2 seeds, the carpels opening by the curling back
of the drying persistent styles; *seeds* destitute of albumen. (Exc. *Oxalis.*)   *Cotyledons* convolute, and plicate with each other.

This is one of those orders that are often broken up into smaller ones then
recombined, in botanical history.   It contains in the more northern United States
the following genera: *Erodium, Flærkea, Geranium, Impatiens, Limnanthes,* and
Oxalis.   There are two particularly interesting genera besides the above, viz.,
Pelargonium, to which belong our cultivated geraniums, introduced from the Cape

---

* Γέρανος, *geranos,* a crane; the styles bearing resemblance to a crane's bill.
† More applicable from usage to the *Ranunculæ.*

of Good Hope, and *Tropæolum*, containing the garden nasturtium. Of this order our only proven plants are the one under consideration and *Oxalis stricta*, Linn.*

History and Habitat.—The wild geranium grows luxuriantly in our open woods and new clearings, flowering from April to July.

The American Aborigines value the root of this plant as an astringent in looseness of the bowels, and exhaustive discharges of all kinds; it was thus brought forward by Colden, Coellen, and Shoepf, and recommended as a remedy in the second stages of dysentery and cholera infantum, cynanche tonsillaris, oral aphthæ, passive hemorrhage, leucorrhœa, etc., in fact the uses of a decoction of the root have been great wherever an astringent or styptic seemed to be required.

Geranium root is officinal in the U. S. Ph. as *Extractum Geranii Fluidum*, and in the Eclectic Materia Medica as *Extractum Geranii*.

PART USED AND PREPARATION.—The fresh root, gathered in autumn, is chopped and pounded to a pulp and weighed. Then two parts by weight of alcohol are taken, the pulp mixed thoroughly with one-sixth part of it, and the rest of the alcohol added. After having stirred the whole well, it should be poured into a well-stoppered bottle, and allowed to stand eight days in a dark, cool place.

The tincture prepared from this mass by filtration, should have a deep reddish-brown color by transmitted light, a sweet and astringent taste, and a strong acid reaction. This tincture becomes muddy on long standing, but does not deposit; at least mine has not yet done so, although it has been made over three years.†

CHEMICAL CONSTITUENTS.—An analysis by Dr. Bigelow in 1833 corroborated Staples' determination of *tannin* in quite large percentage, and *gallic acid*. The gallic acid in his hands differed somewhat from that body as extracted from galls.

Messrs. Tilden (1863)‡ determined beside the above: *two resins*, one soluble in alcohol, the other in ether; an *oleo-resin* soluble in ether; gum, pectin, starch, sugar, and the usual plant constituents.

Dr. Staples (1829)§ detected, beside the above, a "peculiar crystalline principle," which does not seem, so far, to have been analysed or even corroborated.

PHYSIOLOGICAL ACTION.—In moderate doses Geranium causes constipation, attended with but fruitless attempts at evacuation; some pain in the stomach and bowels, and tenesmus when a stool is gained; stool odorless. Its action will be seen to so far differ but slightly, if at all, from that of *Acidum Tannicum*, which should be studied in this connection.

DESCRIPTION OF PLATE 32.

1. Whole plant (once reduced), with a portion of the stem removed: Pamrapo, N. J., May 21st, 1879.
      2. Flower.
      3. Pistil and calyx.
      4. Ovary.
      5. Fruit (once reduced).

* Author's proving. See *Trans. Hom. Med. Soc. State N. Y.*, Vol. XIX, 1884, p. 136.
† A better method of preparing the tincture, should be by using *dilute* alcohol.
‡ *Am. Jour. Phar.*, 1863, p. 22.   § *Jour. Phil. Col. Phar.*, i, p. 171.

32.

ℰ.m. ad nat del.et pinxt.   GERÀNIUM MACULÀTUM Linn.

GENUS.—**XANTHOXYLUM**,* COLDEN.

SEX. SYST.—DIOECIA PENTANDRIA.

33
XANTHOXYLUM.

PRICKLY ASH.

SYN.—XANTHOXYLUM AMERICANUM, MILL.; X. CLAVA-HERCULIS, LAM. (Not LINN.); X. FRAXINEUM, AND MITE, WILLD.; X. FRAXINIFOLIUM, MARSH. (Not WALT.); X. RAMIFLORUM, MICHX.; X. TRICARPUM, HOOK. (Not MICHX.); THYLAX FRAXINEUM, RAF.

COM. NAMES.—NORTHERN PRICKLY ASH,† TOOTHACHE TREE, PELLITORY,‡ YELLOW WOOD,§ SUTERBERRY, ANGELICA TREE;‖ (FR.) FRÊNE ÉPINEAUX; (GER.) ZAHNWEHOLZ.

A TINCTURE OF THE FRESH BARK OF XANTHOXYLUM AMERICANUM, MILL.

Description.—This well-known shrub grows to a height of from 3 to 8 feet, with a like spread of banches. *Bark* grayish, smooth, white maculate, and slightly warty; *branches* alternate, beset with short, triangular, sharp prickles, similar to those of the rose bush, and generally arranged in pairs beneath the axils of the younger branches; *leaves* alternate, pinnately compound; *leaflets* 4 to 5 pairs and an odd one, ovate-oblong, acute, entire or glandularly serrate, nearly sessile, the under surface downy when young; *petiole* often prickly on the upper side. *Inflorescence* sessile umbellate clusters axillary to the yet undeveloped branchlets; *flowers* yellowish-green, polygamo-dioecious, appearing before the leaves; *perfect flowers* with 3 pistils, *sterile flowers* with rudimentary, abortive, gland-like ovaries, *fertile flowers* with 5 fruiting pistils. *Calyx* none. *Petals* 5, oblong, blunt, with a glandularly fibrillate border and somewhat inflated base. *Stamens* 5, exserted, alternate with the petals and inserted upon the torus; *anthers* innate, sagittate, 4-celled. *Pistils* 3 or 5; *styles* exserted, slender, somewhat intertwined, connivant, or sometimes united at the apex; *stigmas* capitate or obtuse. *Ovaries* distinct 1-celled. *Fruit* reddish-green, short-stalked, fleshy, pitted, 2-valved pods; *seeds* oval, blackish, one to each pod, suspended.

Rutaceæ.—A large family of herbs, shrubs and trees inhabiting chiefly the Southern hemisphere. *Leaves* simple or compund, pellucid-dotted and rich in a pungent or bitter and aromatic oil; *stipules* none. *Flowers* by abortion diœcious

---

* Ξανθός, *xanthos*, yellow; ξύλον, *xylon*, wood.

† The Southern Prickly Ash is *X Carolinianum*, Lam.

‡ The true Pellitories are the African *Anacyclus pyrethrum*, D. C. (Compositæ), and various European and the American species of the genus *Parietaria* (Urticaceæ).

§ The true yellow-wood with us is *Cladrastris tinctoria*, Raf. (Leguminosæ).

‖ The true Angelica tree, so often confounded with the prickly ash from its slightly similar effects, is *Aralia spinosa*, Linn. (Araliaceæ).

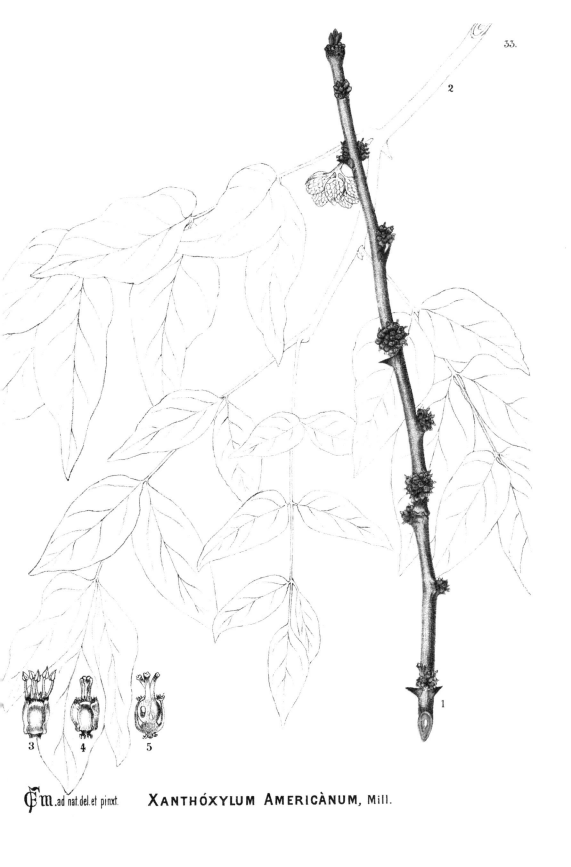

33.

2

1

3   4   5

℃m. ad nat. del. et pinxt.   XANTHÓXYLUM AMERICÀNUM, Mill.

or polygamous, usually regular and hypogynous; *calyx* of 3 to 5 sepals, or wanting; *petals* 3 to 5, convolutely inbricated in the bud. *Stamens* as many as the sepals and alternate with them, twice as many, or rarely numerous; *filaments* arising from the base of the gynophore. *Pistils* 2 to 5, separate or combined into a compound ovary of as many cells, gynophorus or raised on a glandular torus; *styles* generally united or cohering, even when the ovaries are separate. *Fruit* mostly capsular, sometimes drupaceous, and baccate; *seeds* few, anatropous and pendulus; *testa* smooth, shiny, or crustaceous; *embryo* large, curved or straight; *albumen* sarcous, generally enclosing the embryo; *cotyledons* oval, flat.

This large order now contains, beside the typical Rutaceæ, the formerly separate families Xanthoxylaceæ and Aurantiaceæ, including thus many valuable medicinal plants and pleasant fruits, among them are the following more or less prominent: The Central American Carony or Angustura bark (*Galipea Cusparea*, St. Hil., *Angustura vera*), of which we have an excellent proving; the European Rue (*Ruta graveolens*, Linn.), also prominent in our Materia Medica; the famed Buchu of the Cape of Good Hope (*Barosma crenulata*, Hook.), and the lesser species *B. betulina*, B. & W., and *B. serratifolia*, Willd., of the same country; the powerful diaphoretic Jaborandi (*Pilocarpus pennatifolius*, Lam.; the following febrifuges: the Brazilian *Evodia febrifuga*, *Ticorea jasminifolia*, and *T. febrifuga*, all of St. Hil.; and the European Bastard Dittany (*Dictamnus fraxinella*, Linn.). Next our attention is brought to the *Auranticeæ*, the latest addition to the order, where we find the following well-known fruits: the Bitter or Saville Orange (*Citrus Vulgaris*, Risso.), supposed to be the original of the Sweet or China Orange (*Citrus Aurantium*, Linn.), which cannot be said to be ever found in a really wild state; the source of the Oil of Bergamot (*Citrus Bergamina*, Risso.), supposed to be either a variety of the orange, or lemon, or a hybrid; the Citron (*Citrus Medica*, Risso.), its wild state growing in the mountainous northern district of India; the Limes (*Citrus acida*, Roxb., *C. Lumina*, and *C. Limetta*, Risso.); and finally the Indian astringent Bael (*Aegle Marmelos*, Correa, *Cratæva Marmelos*, Linn.) the ripe fruit of which is known as the Bengal Quince, and said to be made into a laxative preserve, or a pleasant refrigerant drink. Lastly, the former *Xanthoxylaceæ* yield us beside *Ptelea* and *Xanthoxylum* treated of here, the following stimulants: the Chinese *Xanthoxylum Avicenne*, D. C., supposed to be a general antidote for all poisons by the natives; the West Indian *X. Clava-Herculis*, Linn.; the Bengalese *X. Alatum*, Roxb.; and the Japanese *X. piperita*, D. C.; the astringent tonics *Brucea Sumatrana*, Roxb., and the Abyssinian *B. antidysenterica*, Mill., the Indian *Toddalia aculeata*, Pers., and the African sub-astringent Lopez-root *T. lanceolata*, Lam.).

History and Habitat.—The northern prickly ash is common in localities only, throughout the northern portion of the Eastern United States, where it flowers in April and May, before the appearance of the leaves. Three other species are found in the South United States, viz.: *X. Clava-Herculis*, Linn. (*X. Carolinianum*, Lam.); *X. Caribæum*, Lam. (*X. Floridanum*, Nutt.); and *X. Pterota*, H.B.K.

Xanthoxylum was an article of American aboriginal medicine called *Hantola;*

the Western tribes used principally the bark of the root in decoction, for colics, gonorrhœa, and rheumatism; chewed for aching teeth; and made into a poultice with bears grease and applied to ulcers and sores.* From personal experience one day in the woods while botanizing, I found that, upon chewing the bark for relief of toothache, speedy mitigation of the pain followed, though the sensation of the acrid bark was nearly or fully as unpleasant as the ache, and so painful finally in itself that I abandoned its use, only to have the toothache return when the irritation of the bark had left the mucous membranes. A decoction of the bark is diaphoretic and excites secretion generally. Its action upon the salivary glands causes in time almost as full ptyalism as mercury. Its speedy relief of rheumatism is said to occur only when it causes free perspiration; for this disease a pint a day is taken of a decoction of one ounce of the bark boiled in a quart of water. It is a powerful stimulant to healing wounds or indolent ulcerations. Dr. King, who introduced the use of this drug in Cincinnati in 1849, both in the treatment of tympanitis, distention of the bowels during peritonitis, and in Asiatic cholera, says:† "In tympanitis one half to one drachm of the tincture may be given *per oris*, in a little sweetened water, and repeated hourly, and the same amount used as an enema. The action is usually prompt and permanent. In Asiatic cholera, during 1849 and 1850, it was much employed by our (Eclectic) physicians in Cincinnati, and with great success; it acted like electricity, so sudden and diffusive was its influence over the system. In typhus fever, typhoid pneumonia, and typhoid conditions generally, I am compelled to say that I consider the tincture of prickly-ash berries superior to any other form of medication. I have known cases of typhoid pneumonia in which the patients were so low that all prospect of recovery was despaired of, to be so immediately benefited that the patients who, a few minutes before, were unable to notice anything around them, would reply to questions, and manifest considerable attention, and ultimately recover."

Prickly ash is official in the U. S. Ph., as *Extractum Xanthoxyli Fluidum;* and in the Eclectic Materia Medica its preparations are: *Enema Xanthoxyli; Extractum Xanthoxyli Fluidum; Oleoresina Xanthoxyli; Tinctura Xanthoxyli; Tinctura Laricis Composita.*‡

PART USED AND PREPARATION.—The fresh bark, together with that of the root, is ground to a pulp, covered in a well-stoppered bottle with two parts by weight of alcohol, and allowed to stand eight days in a dark, cool place, being shaken twice a day.

The tincture separated from this mass by filtration has a clear, yellowish-green color by transmitted light; it retains the peculiar odor and taste of the bark, and exhibits an acid reaction.

CHEMICAL CONSTITUENTS.—*Xanthoxylin.* This body, extracted by Dr. Staples from the bark, and so named, has been determined to be *berberin.*§

* Rafinesque, *Med. Flora.* 2, p. 115.
† *College Jour.*, March, 1856; quoted by Miller in *The Jour. of Mat. Med.*, Vol. III, N. S., 1861, 9.
‡ Tamarac bark, Juniper berries, Prickly Ash bark, Wild Cherry bark, Seneca Snake-root, Tansy, Whiskey, Molasses, and Hydro-alcoholic Extract of Podophyllum.   § See under Berberis, p. 16-2.

Oil of Xanthoxylum—probably also containing resin and extractive—is a dark brown, aromatic, warm, pungent, turbid body, found in about 25 per cent. in the berries by W. S. Merrell.   An etherial oil of the bark is obtainable, answering to the above ; it is, though, simply an extract containing all the principles in the bark.   Volatile oil and resin have also been determined.

This plant has not been carefully analyzed.   Some idea of its probable constituents other than the above might be gained from those of *Xanthoxylum piperitum*, which contains :

Xanthoxylen or *Xanthoxylene*, $C_{10}H_{16}$, is the colorless watery liquid part of the volatile oil.   It has a pleasant aromatic odor, and great refracting power ; it boils at 162° (324° F.).

Xanthoxylin, $C_{20}H_{24}O_8$.   This crystallizable product of the volatile oil which may be extracted after the oil is freed from Xanthoxylene by distillation at 130° (266° F.).   It crystallizes in large, colorless, silky, neutral, aromatic, klinorhombic forms, soluble in alcohol and ether.   The crystals fuse at 80° (176° F.), and volatilize at higher temperatures undecomposed (*et supra, Wittstein.*)

PHYSIOLOGICAL ACTION.—Although we have a quite full proving of this drug by Dr. C. Cullis,* it is hardly sufficient to determine its physiological sphere of action.   The drug proves, however, at least a stimulant of mucous surfaces and attendant secretory glands by an irritant action upon the nerves.   Its action, taken all in all, appears quite like that of Mezereum.

DESCRIPTION OF PLATE 33.

1. End of a flowering branch, Binghamton, N. Y., May 8th, 1884.
    2. End of fruiting branch.
    3. Sterile flower.
4-5. Fertile flowers.
    5. Longitudinal section of a tri-pistillate flower.
        (2-5 enlarged.)

---

* Allen, *Ency. Pure. Mat. Med.*, X, p. 169.

34

PTELEA.

WAFER ASH.

SYN.—PTELEA TRIFOLIATA, LINN.; P. VITICIFOLIA, SALISB.; AMYRIS
ELEMIFOLIA, LINN.
COM. NAMES.—WAFER ASH, SHRUBBY TREFOIL, TREE TREFOIL, HOP
TREE, STINKING ASH, WINGSEED, SWAMP DOGWOOD, PICKAWAY.
(FR.) ORME DE SAMAIRE À TROIS FEUILLES; (GER.) DRIBLÄTTRIGE
LEDERBAUM.

A TINCTURE OF THE BARK OF PTELEA TRIFOLIATA, LINN.

Description.—This peculiar shrub attains a growth of from 6 to 8 feet. *Leaves* trifoliate, long petioled; *leaflets* sessile or very slightly petiolulate, ovate, pointed, dark shining green above, pale and somewhat downy beneath, the terminal more or less wedge-shaped and contracted at the base, all more or less crenulate. *Inflorescence* in compound lateral and terminal cymes; *flowers* numerous, greenish-white, polygamous, their odor disagreeable. *Sepals* 3 to 5, usually 4, somewhat deltoid, much shorter than the petals. *Petals* 3 to 5, usually 4, spreading, imbricated in the bud. *Stamens* as many as the petals and alternate with them; *filaments* in the sterile flowers long, dilated, and hairy at the base; shorter than the ovary in the fertile; *anthers* larger, present in both kinds of flowers, but sterile in the female. *Ovary* 2-celled; *style* short or wanting; *stigma* capitate, 2-lobed. *Fruit* a large, dense, globular cluster of nearly orbicular, 2-seeded, membranaceous, reticulate-veined samaras; *seed* somewhat triangularly compressed.

History and Habitat.—The Wafer Ash is indigenous to North America, ranging from Pennsylvania westward to Wisconsin and southward to Florida and Texas. It grows in moist, shady places, on the borders of woods, and among rocks, flowering in June at the northern range. The plant was sent to England for cultivation in 1704 by Bannister, but, being lost there, Catesby reinforced their gardens from Carolina twenty years later.

Rafinesque first introduced the plant in American medical literature in his work on *Medical Botany*, 1830, speaking of the leaves as vulnerary and vermifuge. Schoepf gives the same in substance; and Mérat and De Lens speak of the fruit as aromatic and bitter, and an affirmed substitute for hops. Howard speaks of the bark of the root as an excellent stimulant, expectorant tonic; especially useful

---

* Πτεω, *ptao*, to fly: the Greek name of the elm, alluding to the winged fruits.

in agues. Jones* speaks of the plant as "a pure unirritating tonic" in cold infusion, especially adapted to convalescence after debilitating fevers. Following these, its use became general, especially in Eclectic practice, for a variety of troubles, especially asthma, phthisis, glandular degeneration in general, syphilis, scrofula, chronic diarrhœa, epilepsy, dyspepsia, intermittent fever, and chronic rheumatism.

The Eclectic preparations are: *Extractum Pteleæ Hydro-alcoholicum ; Infusum Pteleæ; and Pteleæ Oleo-resineæ.*

PART USED AND PREPARATION.—The fresh bark, gathered after the fruit is ripe, but before the leaves begin to fade, is treated as in the preceding drug. The tincture, separated by pressure and filtration, has a brownish orange color by transmitted light ; a bitter odor ; an extremely bitter taste ; and an acid reaction.

CHEMICAL CONSTITUENTS.—The analysis of G. M. Smyser† resulted in the determination of albumen, bitter extractive, tannic and gallic acids, a brittle, tasteless resin, and a soft acrid resin. According to Justin Speer,‡ the root-bark contains a crystalline yellow coloring-matter, oleo-resin, and *berberina*,§ but no tannin.

PHYSIOLOGICAL ACTION.—In Dr. E. M. Hale's provings of this drug upon a number of observers, who took from 30 to 500 drops of the tincture, and from 1 grain to a scruple of "Ptelein," the following disturbances occurred : Mental depression and confusion ; frontal headache, vertigo ; contraction of the pupil ; aural pains with swelling of the lymphatics ; tongue sore, yellow-coated ; ptyalism ; voracious appetite ; nausea, with pressure in the stomach as of a stone ; griping colic ; great urging followed by copious diarrhœic stools ; urine increased ; heart's action increased ; general restlessness and prostration, followed by chilliness and fever.

DESCRIPTION OF PLATE 34.

1. Female flower.
2. Male flower.
3. Stamen.
4. Anther.
5. Fruiting branch.
6. Samara.
7. Section of fruit.
8. Seed.
(1–4 and 7–8 enlarged.)

---

* *Eclectic Practice.*   † *Am. Jour. Phar.*, 1862.   ‡ *Ibid.*, 1867.   § See p. 15–2.

ₔm.ad nat.del.et pinxt.   PTÈLEA TRIFOLIÀTA , Linn.

Tribe.—SIMARUBEÆ.

GENUS.—**AILANTHUS**,* DESF.

SEX. SYST.—MONŒCIA POLYGAMIA.

35

AILANTUS.

TREE OF HEAVEN.

SYN.—AILANTHUS GLANDULOSUS, DESF.

COM. NAMES.—TREE OF HEAVEN, CHINESE AILANTHUS, TILLOW TREE, CHINESE SUMACH; (FR.) AILÁNTE, VERNIS DES JAPON;† (GER.) GÖTTERBAUM.

A TINCTURE OF THE FRESH BARK AND FLOWERS OF AILANTHUS GLANDULOSUS, DESF.

Description.—This beautiful tree, which so much resembles an overgrown staghorn sumach, grows in this country to a height of from 30 to 60 feet. *Stem* erect, columnar, much branched; *wood* hard, heavy and glossy, like satin. *Leaves* long, odd-pinnately compound; *petioles* 1 to 2 feet long; *leaflets* oblong, pointed, with two blunt teeth at the base, rendering them somewhat hastate; *teeth* glandular upon the under surface. *Inflorescence* in large terminal thyrsoid panicles; *flowers* greenish, diœciously-polygamous. *Calyx* 5-toothed. *Petals* 5, inserted under an hypogynous disk. *Stamens* 10; *filaments* inflated and hairy at the base; *anthers* 2-celled. *Ovary* 5-lobed; *style* columnar; *stigma* capitate, radiately 5-lobed. *Fruit* composed of from 2 to 5 long, thin, somewhat twisted, linear-oblong, veiny, 1-celled, 1-seeded samaras.

Simarubaceæ.—This small family of mostly tropical trees and shrubs, is represented in North America by 7 genera of 1 species each. The characteristics of the order are as follows: *Bark* bitter. *Leaves* alternate, pinnately-compound; *stipules* none. *Flowers* hermaphrodite or unisexual. *Calyx* persistent; *sepals* 4 to 5. *Corolla* deciduous, twisted in æstivation; *petals* 4 to 5, hypogynous. *Stamens* as many or twice as many as the petals; *filaments* inserted upon an hypogynous disk. *Ovary* composed of 4 to 5 lobes; *ovules* suspended, 1 in each cell; *style* various. *Carpels* 2-valved, as many as the petals, capsular or keyed; *seeds* pendulous; *albumen* none; *cotyledons* thick; *radicle* short, superior.

The only proven plants of this order, excepting the one under consideration, are: the tropical-American Cedron (*Simaba Cedron*, Planch), and the South-American Quassia or Dysentery-bark (*Simarouba amara*, Aubl.), the bark of which was once a noted remedy in dysentery.

---

* The name should be spelled, *Ailantus*, being derived from a Moluccian species called *Ailanto*.

† Also used to designate *Rhus vernix*.

The other more or less prominent medical plants are: the West-Indian Jamaica Quassia or Bitter Ash (*Picræna excelsa*, Lindl.), noted for its extreme and lasting bitter wood, so largely used in commerce for the manufacture of Quassia-cups, the water from which is useful as a stomachic tonic, anthelmintic, and antiperiodic; the Brazilian *Simarouba versicolor*, St. Hil., noted as being so bitter that insects will not attack the wood; and the Indian *Nima quassioides*, Hamilt., employed as a bitter tonic in the North of India.

History and Habitat.—This large tree, that has caused more newspaper comment than any other now planted in this country, is a native of China, and is included in this work as an American remedy because it is from the naturalized tree that our provings were made.

The Ailanthus tree was introduced into England in the year 1751, and thrived well; about the year 1800 it was brought to this country, and soon grew in public favor as an ornamental tree for lawns, walks and streets; later on it became in greater demand on account of its supposed property of absorbing from the atmosphere malarial poisons; under this new idea the tree became a great favorite in cities and large towns, especially as its growth was rapid and its beautiful foliage pleasing. The occurrence, however, of several severe epidemics, especially in the larger cities, set people thinking—might not this tree, which so fully absorbs poison, also throw off toxic effluvia? may it not store up the noxious gases and again set them forth in the flowering season? Certainly the staminate flowers smell bad enough to lay any disease to their emanations. A war upon the trees followed, both wordy and actual, which almost banished them from the country. The feeling, however, died a natural death, and to-day many fine trees abound, especially in the larger eastern cities.

Another vote for its preservation lay in the fact that the tree afforded material for a silkworm (*Attacus Cynthia*, Drury), which has been successfully acclimated in this country by Dr. Stewardson and Mr. Morris. The cost of production of silk from their culture is said to be about one-fourth that of mulberry silk, beside, the product is tough and stronger than any other fabric made; it is said that the Chinese wear garments of this material through several generations of constant use.

The bark of the tree was experimented with in France about the year 1859, and found to be emetic, cathartic and anthelmintic. The bark has been employed by Roberts and others, both dried and fresh, as a remedy for dysentery and diarrhœa, and as an injection in gonorrhœa and leucorrhœa; an alcoholic extract was found by Prof. Hetet* efficacious in the removal of tapeworm, though the prostrating nausea caused by the draught renders it disagreeable. The tincture has been used in doses of from five to sixty drops in palpitation of the heart, asthma and epilepsy.

PART USED AND PREPARATION.—Equal parts of the fresh shoots, leaves and blossoms, and the young bark, are chopped and pounded to a pulp and weighed. Then two parts by weight of alcohol are taken, the pulp mixed thor-

* *Jour. de Chine Med.*, Dec., 1859.

oughly with one-sixth part of it, and the rest of the alcohol added. After stirring the whole well, and pouring it into a well-stoppered bottle, it is allowed to stand eight days in a dark, cool place. The tincture is then separated by decanting, straining and filtering; it has a deep orange-brown color by transmitted light; a strongly vinous odor; a mawkish taste; and an acid reaction.

CHEMICAL CONSTITUENTS.—Several analyses of the bark have been made, all of which agree with the latest one by Mr. F. H. Davis.* He determined the presence of fixed and volatile oil, resin, wax, sugar, tannin, gum, starch, and oxalic acid; but failed, as had the others, to detect the presence of alkaloids or glucosides.

PHYSIOLOGICAL ACTION.—Ailanthus causes nausea, vomiting, great relaxation of the muscles, and death-like sickness, very similar to that produced by tobacco-smoking in beginners. According to M. Hetet, the purgative property resides in the resin, while the volatile oil gives rise to the prostrating and other ill effects produced in some persons by the emanations from the flowers. The characteristic symptoms produced by Ailanthus are: vertigo and dizziness, severe headache, purulent discharges from the mucous membranes of the nose and eyes, dilated pupils with photophobia, pale, sickly, bilious countenance, irritation of the throat, loss of appetite, tenderness in the stomach and abdomen, looseness of the bowels, suppressed urine, oppression of breathing, languor and lassitude.

DESCRIPTION OF PLATE 35.

1. End of a flowering branch, several leaves and thyrsi removed, Binghamton, N. Y., June 30th, 1885.
2. Flower.
3. Calyx and pistil.
4. Petal and stamen.
5. Stigma.
6. Stamens.
7. Section of ovary.
8. A leaflet.
9. Fruit.
10. Full leaf in outline.
    (2–7 enlarged.)

* *Am. Jour. Phar.*, 1885, 600.

35.

8

2 3 4 5 7 6 9 1 10

Ⓒ.m. ad nat del.et pinxt.

AILÁNTHUS GLANDULÒSUS, Desf.

Section.—*SUMAC*,* D. C.

GENUS.—**RHUS**, LINN.

SEX. SYST.—PENTANDRIA TRIGYNIA.

36
RHUS GLABRA.

SMOOTH SUMACH.

SYN.—RHUS GLABRA, LINN.; R. ELEGANS, AIT.; R. VIRGINICUM, CATESB.;
R. CAROLINIANUM, MILL.

COM. NAMES.—SMOOTH SUMACH OR SUMAC; SHUMAKE; (FR.) SUMAC;
(GER.) SUMACH.

A TINCTURE OF THE FRESH BARK OF RHUS GLABRA, LINN.

Description.—This smooth shrub usually attains a growth of from 5 to 15 feet in height. *Branches* somewhat straggling. *Leaves* odd-pinnate; *petioles* crimson, 12 to 18 inches long; *leaflets* 12 to 30, lanceolate-oblong, acutely serrate, pointed, and whitened beneath. *Inflorescence* dense, terminal, thyrsoid panicles; *flowers* perfect, polygamous. *Sepals* lanceolate, or more or less triangular, very acute, nearly as long as the petals. *Petals* incurved at the apex. *Hypogynous disk* almost entire, its lobes, however, separating when a sepal is detached from the calyx. bringing away with it a stamen and petal; *lobe* somewhat reniform. *Fruit* globular, clothed with acid, velvety, crimson hairs; *stone* smooth.

Rhus.—This genus is widely distributed, and contains numerous species characterized in general as follows: *Leaves* usually compound. *Flowers* polygamous or dioecious, greenish-white or yellowish-green; *sepals* 5, small, united at the base, generally persistent; *petals* 5, ovate, spreading, slightly hairy within. *Stamens* 5, alternate with the petals; *filaments* inserted with the petals underneath the lobes of a chrome-yellow hypogynous disk, situated at the base of the sepals. *Styles* 3, short, generally united into one, sometimes distinct; *stigmas* 3, capitate. *Fruit* consisting of many small, indehiscent, dry, drupes; *stone* or *nutlet* osseous; *seed* suspended from the apex of a funiculus that arises from the base, and extends to the apex of the cell; *cotyledons* foliaceous.

Many other species of *Rhus* are used beside those embodied in this work; among which are the following: The Japanese *R. vernix* affords the finest of the black lacquers, so extensively used in China and Japan for coating household articles, etc. This species in its toxic action is said to greatly simulate *R. venenata*, of this country. The South European *R. coriaria*, and *R. cotinus*, are extensively used in tanning the finer grades of morocco leather; the seeds of the former

---

* An alteration of the Arabic *simaq* (Forsk.).
† The ancient Greek and Latin name (Celtic *Rhudd.*, red).

1   2   3   4   5

ℭ.𝔪. . ad nat del. et pinxt.

RHÚS GLÀBRA, Linn.

species are said to be used at Aleppo to provoke an appetite, and in Turkey generally, in the manufacture of vinegar. Inferior grades of the inimitable black lacquer, made from *R. vernix*, are furnished by *R. Javanica, R. Sinense*, and *R. succedaneum*. Our southern *R. pumila*, Michx., has been variously considered; some writers claiming it to be entirely innocuous, others judge it to be the most poisonous of the North American species, claiming that it will show its effects upon those who are not susceptible to the influences of *R. toxicodendron*. The Floridian and West Indian *R. metopium* produces a substance called Doctor's Gum, which is said to be emetis and purgative; and the Chinese *R. Buchi-amela*, Roxb., certain galls used in Germany for the manufacture of tannic and gallic acids, and pyrogallol.

Anacardiaceæ.—This large, chiefly tropical family, consists of mostly poisonous trees or shrubs, having a resinous or milky, acrid juice, which turns black or blackish in drying. *Leaves* alternate, usually compound, and devoid of dots; *stipules* none. *Inflorescence* usually in axillary or terminal, erect panicles; *flowers* small, regular, often polygamous; *æstivation* imbricate, rarely valvate. *Sepals* 3, or 5, usually distinct, but sometimes more or less united at the base, and persistent. *Petals* as many as the sepals, and inserted beneath an hypogynous disk, lining the base of the calyx. *Stamens* as many as the petals and alternate with them; *filaments* distinct. *Ovary* ovoid; *styles* 3, distinct or combined; *stigmas* 3, decidedly distinct. *Fruit* drupaceous, indehiscent, 1-celled; *seed* borne upon a curved stalk arising from the base of the cell; *testa* membranaceous; *embryo* more or less curved; *albumen* none.

The following plants of this family figure more or less prominently in our Materia Medica: The Indian Cashew-nut (*Anacardium orientale, Semecarpus Anacardium*, Linn.); the fruit of this tree is also called the marking-nut, and is almost universally used for stamping linen. The Cuban *guao* (*Comocladia dentata*, Jacq.), which is said by the natives (and corroborated by others) to cause the death of any who sleep beneath its shades; this is especially true of individuals of plethoric habit. The New Zealand *Karaka* or *Kopi-tree* (*Coryno-carpus lævigatus*, Foster); and the Mexican and Peruvian Schinus, a product of *Schinus molle*, Linn., used by the natives for healing tumors and reducing inflammation, especially of the eye.

Other members used in medicine and the arts are: The Brazilian *Schinus arœira*, Linn., which is said to exude an effluvia that causes swellings to appear in those who remain for a few hours beneath it. (Note *S. molle* above.) The Tropic American *Anacardium occidentale*, Linn., is used as a vermifuge, and the juice is said to be efficient in the removal of warts, corns, and vegetative growths; the nuts, however, are edible, either raw or boiled. The Mediterranean *Lentisk* or Mastic Tree (*Pistacia Lentiscus*, Linn.) yields Gum Mastich, a concretion highly valued by the Turks as a masticatory for sweetening the breath and hardening the gums. This product is useful also, for a temporary filling in carious teeth, easing the pain therein. *Pistacia terebinthus*, Linn., yields the famous Chian Turpentine; while the European *P. vera* furnishes the Pistachio nuts of the confectioner; the Cochin China *P. oleosa*, a valuable oil; and the African *P. Atlantica*, an Arabian article of food.

The Indian Mango (*Mangifera Indica*, Linn.) yields a luscious fruit which holds the place in that country, that the peach does in this. The Malabar *Holigarna longifolia*, Roxb., and *Stagmaria verniciflua*, Jack., of the Indian archipelago, furnish to the Chinese two of their famous black lacquers. It is said that the resin of the last named species is noxious and acrid, and that it is unsafe to remain long under the branches of the tree.

History and Habitat.—Rhus glabra is one of our least nocuous species. It grows in rocky or barren soil, common throughout North America, flowering northward in June and July.

An infusion of the berries of this species is said to furnish an unequalled black dye for wool. The berries, when dried, form an article of trade in Canada, known as *sacacomi*, this, when smoked as a substitute for tobacco, is said to antidote the habit; the Western Indians make a preparation of equal parts of the roots, leaves, and of tobacco, which they smoke under the name of *Kinikah*.*

A cold infusion of the berries is often used as a cooling drink in fevers; it is also claimed to be of benefit in diabetes and strangury. The bark of the root is claimed to form an antiseptic dressing for ulcers and open wounds; while an infusion of the same is considered an excellent astringent for use in aphthous and mercurial sore mouths, diarrhœa, dysentery, gonorrhœa, and leucorrhœa, and to be anti-syphilitic. I have known the juice of the root to remove warts, I have also known these strange growths to disappear from the use of various innocuous "charms," such as a neighbor's potato surreptitiously obtained, rubbed upon the growths and cast over the left shoulder without noting its fall, etc., etc.

Smooth Sumac is official in the U. S. Ph., as: *Extractum Rhois Glabra*. In the Eclectic Materia Medica the preparations are: *Decoctum Rhus Glabri*, and *Extractum Rhus Fluidum*.

PART USED AND PREPARATION.—The fresh bark, including that of the root, gathered when the plant is mature, should be chopped and pounded to a pulp and weighed. Then two parts by weight of alcohol are taken, the pulp well mixed with one-sixth part of it, and the rest of the alcohol added. After stirring the whole well, it should be poured into a well-stoppered bottle, and allowed to stand for eight days in a dark, cool place.

The tincture, separated from the mass by filtration, should exhibit a beautiful, very deep crimson color by transmitted light. Its taste should be at first sour, then astringent, leaving a sensation upon the tongue very like that of alum; its odor sour-vinous; and its reaction strongly acid.

CHEMICAL CONSTITUENTS.—*Gallotannic acid*, $C_{14}H_{10}O_9$. This pure tannin of nut-galls also exists in the leaves and bark of the plant. It is an amorphous, porous, resinous, friable mass, freely soluble in water, less so in alcohol, and insoluble in pure ether.

---

* Rafinesque, *Med. Flor.*, ii., 257.

Calcium Bimalate.—This salt is found clinging to the hairs of the fruit as a concretion exuded from them; when soaked off the fruits are no longer sour.

Oil of Rhus.—This waxy oil may be extracted from the seeds of this and other species of the genus. It will acquire a tallow-like consistence on standing, and can be made into candles, which burn brilliantly, but emit a very annoying pungent smoke.

Resin, oleo-resin, sugar, starch, coloring matter, and gum, have also been determined.*

PHYSIOLOGICAL ACTION.—Rhus glabra caused in one individual, in doses of from 30 to 120 drops of the tincture, headache, dryness and heat of the nostrils, with hemorrhage, ulceration of the mouth, loss of appetite, with painful distress in the stomach and bowels, followed by diarrhœa, scanty secretion of urine, great weariness and fatigue, loss of flesh, heat and dryness of the skin, followed by copious sweat during sleep.† One symptom was also developed in this case that I desire to comment upon, viz.: "Dreams of flying through the air." During the summer of 1879, while botanizing near Bergen Point, N. J., I came into a swarm of furious mosquitoes; quickly cutting a large branch from a sumach bush at hand, I used it vigorously to fight off the pests. Several fine specimens of Baptisia tinctoria grew at hand, and while studying them I kept the sumach branch in constant motion, perspiring freely during the time. On leaving the spot I cut a cane from the same shrub, and also ate of the refreshing berries. For three successive nights following this occurrence I flew (!) over the city of New York with a graceful and delicious motion that I would give several years of my life to experience in reality. Query: Did I absorb from my perspiring hands sufficient juice of the bark to produce the effect of the drug, or was it from the berries I held in my mouth? I noticed no other symptoms, and never before or since enjoyed a like dream.

DESCRIPTION OF PLATE 36.

1. End of flowering branch, Waverly, N. Y., July 4th, 1884.
2. Flower.
3. Petal.
4. Pistil.
5. Stamen, lobe of disk, and sepal.
(2–5 enlarged.)

* *Am. Jour. Phar.*, N. S., i., 56; *ibid.*, XXV., 193; Tilden, *Jour. Mat. Med.*, N. S., i., 195; *Proc. Royal Society*, 1862, 402. † Dr. Marshall in Hale's *New Rem.*, 2d ed., 872.

37

RHUS VENENATA.

POISON SUMACH.

SYN.—RHUS VENENATA, D. C.
COM. NAMES.—POISON OR SWAMP SUMACH, POISON ELDER, POISON OR
SWAMP DOGWOOD, POISON ASH, POISON TREE, POISON WOOD.

A TINCTURE OF THE BARK OF RHUS VENENATA, D. C.

Description.—This too common swamp shrub grows to a height of from 6 to 30 feet. *Stem* erect, branching at the top; *branches* smooth or nearly so, sometimes verrucose. *Leaves* odd-pinnately compound; *petiole* brilliant red or purplish; *leaflets* 7 to 13, smooth, ovate-lanceolate, acute, entire. *Inflorescence* loose, slender, erect panicles, in the axils of the uppermost leaves; *flowers* polygamous, greenish-white; *pedicels* pubescent. *Calyx* persistent. *Fruit* a persistent, drooping, thyrsoid receme of globular, smooth, grayish-white berries, about the size of a small pea; *testa* thin, papyraceous, loose and shining; *nutlet* oblong, flattened, longitudinally striate by deep sulci; *inner coat* soft, membranaceous, incised; *cotyledons* somewhat thick and fleshy.

History and Habitat.—The Poison Sumach is indigenous to North America, ranging from Florida to Mississippi and northward to Canada. It habits swampy ground, and blossoms in June at the north.

This most poisonous of our northern species has at times been confounded and considered identical with the Japanese *R. vernix*, L.; how near the resemblance may be I have had no opportunity to judge; however, we, as Homœopathists, should not confound them, as climatic difference may cause varying properties, and *R. vernix* may yet be proven.

The poisonous nature of this species has precluded its use in domestic and previous practices; the principal effort concerning it has been attempts by farmers and others toward its extermination; very few persons, however, who understand the plant will even approach its vicinity unless compelled by circumstances to do so.

Like the *R. vernix* of Japan, the wounded bark in spring and autumn exudes a thick, whitish, opaque and viscid fluid, having a penetrating smell, which on exposure soon changes to a deep black. On boiling the juice in water long enough to evaporate the volatile oil, and applying the resulting fluid to any substance, it forms a glossy-black permanent coating; thus making a varnish of value which might be used in lieu of the famous Japanese varnish which they utilize so extensively upon their fans, boxes, and household utensils and furniture.

It is a well-known fact that this species will prove poisonous to many persons who are unaffected by *R. toxicodendron*, and, like it, even the emanations of the shrub are virulent to many, while others may handle, and even chew it, with impunity.

PART USED AND PREPARATION.—The fresh bark, stemlets and leaves are treated as in the preceding species. The resulting tincture is opaque in even small quantity; in thin layers it has a deep red color; its taste is bitter and astringent; and its reaction acid.

CHEMICAL CONSTITUENTS.—An examination of the juice by Dr. Bigelow* is the only analysis so far made; this shows no active principle. An examination of the chemistry of *R. toxicodendron*, page 38-3, would not be out of place here.

PHYSIOLOGICAL ACTION.—Many opportunities are offered for study under this rubric, on account of the numerous cases of poisoning, both on record and often occurring in country practice. The general effects are usually ushered in within a day of the exposure, commencing with a general flush of the skin, accompanied by intolerable itching and more or less tumefaction, especially at first of the hands and face; this continues until an erysipelatous condition apparently ensues. A more livid appearance follows, with great burning, followed by groupings of watery vesicles, which soon coalesce; this is followed by pustules forming of the watery vesicles, which finally discharge and form yellow crusts, which later on become brown and disgusting in appearance. Great heat and swelling have meantime progressed until the face is often unrecognizable; this condition is about four or five days at its height before resolution commences. Marks are often left, and sometimes the crusts remain chronic on some portion of the exposed parts for long periods. One case in my practice had resisted all the efforts of physicians for over thirty years; then yielded in about thirty days to a high potency of the drug itself at my hands.

Several cases of poisoning came under my observation here some four years ago in several young men employed in a boot factory as finishers. Their duty was to dress the new boots with a black varnish applied with a sponge by the right hand, while the left hand and arm was thrust into the boot. All suffered from a scabby eruption about the left biceps and right hand and wrist, while the fingers of the right were cracked, sore, inflamed and painful. Upon first observing the cases I judged some poison must be used in the varnish, and so informed them; to me Rhus seemed to be that substance. While on a train, a month or so later, I overheard two manufacturers of boots, who sat before me, talking of their trade; when, on passing a swampy spot, one pointed out of the car window at some *R. venenata*, and exclaimed, "That is the stuff we use." These cases all yielded finely to *idem* high.

The specific action of the drug, collated from various cases, is as follows: Sadness and gloomy forebodings; vertigo; dull, heavy headache; smarting and burning of the eyes, with dimness of vision; redness and swelling of the face;

* *Am. Med. Bot.*, 1, 4c2.

37.

6

7

8

2

3

4

5

1

℄.ad nat.del.et pinxt.   RHÚS VENENÀTA, DC.

tongue red, especially at the tip, swollen and cracked; difficult deglutition; profuse watery stools; burning of the urethra; hoarseness and dryness of the larnyx; increased heart's action; trembling of the limbs; bruised and paralyzed feeling in the legs, with aching and weakness; tired, weak, and prostrated generally; almost all forms of skin trouble, from simple redness and burning to vesicles, cracks, pustules and complete destruction; restlessness, chilliness and heat, with great dryness but no subsequent sweat;—all of which show the poison to be of a highly irritative nature.

DESCRIPTION OF PLATE 37.

1. End of flowering branch, Ithaca, N. Y., June 24th, 1885.
2. Flower.
3. Pistil.
4. Stamen.
5. Fruiting thyrsus.
6. Fruit.
7. Fruit, with outer coat removed.
8. Nutlet.
   (2–4 and 6–8 enlarged.)

38

RHUS TOXICODENDRON.

POISON IVY.

SYN.—RHUS TOXICODENDRON, LINN.; R. TOXICODENDRON, VAR. QUER-
CIFOLIUM, MICHX.; R. VERRUCOSA, SCHEELE; R. TOXICARIUM, AND
HUMILE, SALISB.; R. RADICANS, VAR. TOXICODENDRON, PERS.;
TOXICODENDRON PUBESCENS, MILL.

COM. NAMES.—POISON IVY, THREE-LEAVED IVY, POISON OAK, POISON
VINE, MERCURY; (FR.) SUMAC VÉNÉNEUX, ARBRE À POISON; (GER.)
GIFTSUMACH.

A TINCTURE OF THE FRESH LEAVES OF RHUS TOXICODENDRON, LINN.

Description.—This decumbent or more or less erect shrub, grows to a height
of from 2 to 4 feet, or more, according to whether *Rhus radicans* is distinct from
this species or not. *Root* reddish, branching. *Leaves* 3-foliate, thin; *leaflets* rhombic-ovate, acute, rather downy beneath; they are entire when young (see plate),
but when full grown become variously dentate, crenate, sinuate, or cut-lobed.
The lateral leaflets are unequal at the base, and sessile, the terminal one larger
and situated at the end of a prolongation of the common petiole. *Inflorescence*
loose, slender, axillary, racemose panicles. *Flowers* polygamous. *Fruit* glabrous,
globose, pale brown; *nutlet* somewhat gibbous, striate, and tuberculate.

History and Habitat.—The Poison Ivy grows in thickets and low grounds,
quite common in North America, flowering in June.

Rhus toxicodendron was introduced into England as a plant in 1640; but was
not used as a medicine until 1798, when Du Fresnoy, a physician at Valenciennes,
had brought to his notice a young man who had been cured of an herpetic eruption (*dartre*) on his wrist, of six years' standing, on being accidentally poisoned
by this plant. He thereupon commenced the use of this plant in the treatment of
obstinate herpetic eruptions, and in palsy; many cases of each yielding nicely to
the drug.* Since Du Fresnoy's success, the plant has rapidly gained a place in
general practice, meeting some success in the treatment of paralysis, rheumatism,
amaurosis, and various forms of chronic and obstinate eruptive diseases.

The milky juice of this species is used as an indelible ink for marking linen,
and as an ingredient of liquid dressings or varnishes for finishing boots and shoes.

---

* *Des caractères, du traitement, et de la cure des datres, etc., par l'usage du Rhus radicans.*

I an certain, however, that *Rhus venenata* is more extensively used for the latter purpose, as will be seen from my experiences detailed under that drug.

The fresh leaves are officinal in the U. S. Ph.; in the Eclectic Materia Medicas the preparation advised is *Tinctura Rhus Toxicodendron*.

PART USED AND PREPARATION.—On account of the care necessary in the preparation of our medicamentæ, it is an absolute necessity that we should know, without a chance for doubt, the exact plant that we use, after proving. I have therefore, especially in this case, carefully examined into the relationship existing between *R. Toxicodendron* and its so-called variety *radicans*. The only differences acknowledged by authors are as follows:

R. toxicodendron, L.	*R. radicans*, L.*
Stem erect.	Stem more or less tortuous.
Height of growth 2 to 4 feet.	Height 4 to 30 feet or more.
Stem devoid of rootlets.	Stem profusely studded with dark-colored rootlets, by which it clings to its chosen support.
Leaves trifoliate.	Same.
Leaflets variously toothed or crenate, smooth above and slightly pubescent underneath.	Leaflets entire, or slightly dentate, smooth both sides.

During the present season I have carefully examined a great number of individuals in this and adjoining counties, and conclude, as the result of my observations, that an individual commencing its growth as *toxicodendron* may become *radicans* if proper support is reached. I found in several places along the Chenango River, both forms growing from the same root. At the entrance of a ravine near Glenwood Cemetery, upon the outskirts of this city, is the plant from which the accompanying plate was made; this individual is *radicans* in its mode of growth (climbing about 9 feet into a young elm tree), but it bore no rootlets, being supported merely by the shoots of the elm; its foliage answers exactly to *toxicodendron*. One large plant, on the bank of the Susquehanna River, below the usual high-water mark, has all the characters of *radicans* except the rootlets, and grows in a trailing manner along the bank; passing in its growth four excellent supports: *i. e.*, two sturdy elms, one sycamore, and a large stump surrounded by bushes. It is said that the two forms differ in their place of growth, *toxicodendron* choosing open places and *radicans* shady spots; it however follows as a necessity that if *toxicodendron* is *radicans* when it climbs, *radicans* is in the shade because of its support.

Many other far more competent observers than myself, have doubted the verity of the distinctions in these forms: among them are Michaux and Pursh, who considered them merely localisms, and Bigelow states: " among the plants which grow around Boston, I have frequently observed individual shoots from the same stock, having the characters of both varieties. I have also observed that young plants of *R. radicans* frequently do not put out rooting fibers until they are

---

* *Rhus Toxicodendron, var. radicans*, Torrey; *Toxicodendron vulgare*, Mill.; *Rhus Toxicodendron, var. a vulgare*, Michx.; *Rhus scandens*, Salisbury.

several years old, and that they seem, in this respect, to be considerably influenced by the contiguity of supporting objects."

My tinctures of both forms are exactly alike in physical properties; portions of each yielded the same amount of solid extract per ounce, after evaporation; and as far as I can determine, they are identical.

The bulk of our guiding symptoms are compiled from cases of poisoning, where the form causing the effect is not identified. I then, in the light of all this, would suggest that our tincture be made as follows:

Take equal parts by weight of fresh leaves of each form, gathered on a cloudy, sultry day, just before the flowers are developed, chop and pound them to a pulp, and weigh, treating the resulting mass as in the preceding species. The resulting tincture should have a dark brown color by transmitted light, and will give off no characteristic odor; it will have a biting and astringent taste, and a strong acid reaction.

CHEMICAL CONSTITUENTS.—*Rhoitannic Acid,* $C_{18}H_{28}O_{13}$. This specific tannin of Rhus is a yellowish-green, gummy mass, having a slightly bitter and astringent taste and an acid reaction (Wittstein).

Toxicodendric Acid.—This peculiar, poisonous, volatile principle, was isolated from this plant by Prof. Maisch.* He describes it as resembling both formic and acetic acids in some of its reactions, but distinguishable in its failure to produce a red color with neutral ferric salts.

PHYSIOLOGICAL ACTION.—The toxic action of this species is one difficult to explain. The first noticeable peculiarity is its choice of victims, many persons being entirely devoid of response to its influences, many others peculiarly susceptible. Out of ten men employed to " clear out a twelve-acre lot that was completely filled with poison vine, cat briers, and brambles, the poison vine greatly predominating," four only escaped poisoning. "At first there was a lively fight between the poison vine and the men, and it looked as if the former would get the better of it; for most of the men soon began to show signs of being tired, and at the end of the fourth day six of the men were flat on their backs, too sick for anything." † I remember one illustration. When a lad, while in bathing with five others, we all ran a race, stark naked, through the underbrush near by, passing in and out through a clump of what was afterward found to be poison ivy; two of the party were taken ill the next day and soon developed quite serious symptoms of poisoning; all the others, including myself, escaped.

Another peculiarity is that in many cases it is not necessary to even touch the plant to be severely poisoned. While playing croquet one sultry day in June, with a young lady cousin, she struck her ball with sufficient force to cause it to roll underneath a clump of poison ivy that grew at a short distance from the edge of the lawn. She, knowing her susceptibility to the poison, carefully reached under the vine and extracted the ball without touching even a leaf. During the evening

---

* *Proc. Am. Phar. Assoc.,* 1865, 166.   † *Rural New Yorker,* quoted in daily press, original not accessible.

of the same day, her face began to itch and burn, and in the night it swelled to such extent that the eyes were not only closed, but the lashes even were lost to view in the swollen countenance. Nearly two weeks elapsed before the symptoms caused by this exposure entirely subsided.

A third peculiarity is that the plant is more poisonous during the night, or at any time in June and July when the sun is not shining upon it. Absence of sunlight, together with dampness, seems to favor the exhalation of the volatile principle (*Toxicodendric Acid*) contained in the leaves. Of this Porcher says:* "An acrimonious vapor, combined with carburetted hydrogen, exhales from a growing plant of the poison oak during the night. It can be collected in a jar, and is capable of inflaming and blistering the skin of persons of excitable constitution, who plunge their arms into it."

The symptoms caused by this plant are: First, redness and swelling of the affected part, with intolerable itching and burning, followed by vertigo, weariness, and a sort of intoxication. Infiltration of the face and eyes, and agglutination of the lids after sleep; great restlessness, pain, thirst, and fever. The surface of the skin, after a time, becomes studded with confluent bullæ where the cellular tissue is loose, then a dermatitis follows resembling erysipelas; this may spread rapidly and finally communicate to the mucous membranes. This is followed by swelling of the mouth and throat, cough, nausea, and vomiting. Rheumatoid pains develop about the joints, and a painful stiffness asserts itself in the lumbar region, while the legs and arms become numb. Confusion of mind and delirium may then set in, during which the patient may become so ill-humored, restless, and anxious, that he will jump out of bed. The concomitant symptoms are inflammation of the eyes, dilation of the pupil, weakness of vision, and sometimes dilopia; frequent epistaxis; brown coated tongue, with a triangular red tip; swelling of the parotid glands, with difficult deglutition; griping in the abdomen; diarrhœa; profuse urination; oppression of the chest; rapid pulse; great weakness, weariness, and prostration; soreness of the muscles, worse while at rest, and passing off when exercising; sleepiness; and chilliness, followed by fever and copious sweat.

There are almost as many antidotes recommended for Rhus tox. poisoning as for the bite of the rattlesnake. Prominent, however, among the applications are: alkaline lotions, especially carbolate of soda, alum-curd, and hyposulphite of soda, keeping the skin constantly moist with the agent in solution; meanwhile administering Bryonia, Belladonna, Apis, Grindelia robusta, or Verbena urticifolia.

DESCRIPTION OF PLATE 38.

1. End of flowering branch, Binghamton, N. Y., June 27th, 1884.
2. Outline of leaf.
3. Flower.
4. Calyx and pistil.
(3 and 4 enlarged.)

---

* *Resorc. South. Fields and Forests,* 202.

38

3 Œm.ad nat.del.et pinxt   Rhus Toxicodéndron, Linn.

39

RHUS AROMATICA.

FRAGRANT SUMACH.

SYN.—RHUS AROMATICA, AIT.; RHUS CANADENSIS, MARSH.; RHUS SUAVEOLENS, AIT.; BETULA TRIPHYLLA, THUN.; TURPINIA PUBESCENS, AND GLABRA, AND LOBADIUM AROMATICUM, RAF.

COM. NAMES.—FRAGRANT, OR SWEET-SCENTED SUMACH, STINK BUSH, SKUNK BUSH.

A TINCTURE OF THE FRESH ROOT BARK OF RHUS AROMATICA, AIT.

Description.—This straggling but very pretty bush usually grows to a height of about 4 feet. *Leaves* 3-foliate, slightly sweet-scented; *leaflets* rhombic-ovate, prominently ribbed, crenate or cut-toothed; the middle leaflet broadly cuneate at the base, and narrowing gradually to its insertion at the end of the common petiole; all sessile, and coriaceous when old. *Inflorescence* single or clustered, scaly bracted, catkin-like spikes; *scales* reddish, and furnished with copious hairs upon the border; *flowers* polygamo-diœcious, prefolial. *Hypogynous disk* 5-parted, large; *lobes* strongly reniform, the hilum of each almost entirely surrounding the base of the filament inserted under it. *Fruit* similar to that of *Rhus glabra*, but somewhat flattened; *nutlet* smooth, depressed.

History and Habitat.—This least poisonous of all our indigenous species of Rhus, is common in dry, rocky soils, where it flowers in April or May, before the appearance of the leaves. It is the finest species to cultivate, its dense foliage becoming still more so, and the leaves enlarging and varying beautifully. It was introduced into England as an ornamental shrub in 1759.

The previous medical uses of the berries were the same as those of *R. glabra*.

This fruit is termed the squaw-berry, because the Indian women gather large quantities, which are dried and used for food. The berries are excessively sour, but very much used while fresh during the summer months; when macerated they make a pleasant drink. The wood is very tough, far more so than the willow, and is used by the Indians in Utah, Arizona, Southern California, and New Mexico for making into baskets. This wood exhales a peculiar odor, which is always recognizable about the camps of these Indians, and never leaves articles made from it.*

---

* Dr. Edward Palmer in *Am. Nat.*, 1878, 597.

$\mathfrak{E.m.}$, ad nat.del.et pinxt.

RHÚS AROMÁTICA, Ait.

PART USED AND PREPARATION.—The fresh bark of the root is treated as in the preceding species. The tincture obtained is the most transparent and lightest in color of all the species of Rhus here mentioned. It has a beautiful, clear, crimson color by transmitted light; a decidedly terebinthic odor; very astringent taste, and strong acid reaction.

CHEMICAL CONSTITUENTS.—*Volatile Oil.* This body has, when first distilled, the disgusting odor of bed-bugs; but when treated with ether and evaporated, it acquires a pleasant aroma after having been exposed to the air for twenty-four hours.

Beside the above, Mr. H. W. Harper* determined the presence of gallotannin, resin, acid resin, fixed oil, and a red coloring matter.

DESCRIPTION OF PLATE 39.

1. A flowering branch, from Lowmansville, N. Y., May 14th, 1884.
2. End of late summer branch, showing the inflorescence preparing for the next season.
3. Flower.
4. Petal.
5. Stamen and lobe of disk.
6. Pistil and hypogynous disk.
7. Dormant inflorescence.
8. Scale of same, outer face.
9. Scale of same, inner face.
(3–9 enlarged.)

* *Am. Jour. Phar.*, 1881, 212.

N. ORD.—VITACEÆ.

GENUS.—**AMPELOPSIS,*** MICHX.

SEX. SYST.—PENTANDRIA MONOGYNIA.

40

AMPELOPSIS.

VIRGINIAN CREEPER.

SYN.—AMPELOPSIS QUINQUEFOLIA, MICHX., AMPELOPSIS HEDERA-
CEA, DC., VITIS QUINQUEFOLIA, LAM., VITIS HEDERACEA, WILLD.,
HEDERA QUINQUEFOLIA, LINN., CISSUS HEDERACEA, PERS.

COM. NAMES.—VIRGINIAN CREEPER, AMERICAN IVY, WOODBINE,
FIVE-LEAVES, FALSE GRAPE, WILD WOOD-VINE.

A TINCTURE OF THE FRESH SHOOTS AND BARK OF AMPELOPSIS QUINQUE-
FOLIA, MICHX.

Description.—This common vine is familiar to all residents of the Northern United States, being often planted as a porch screen on account of its rapid growth, its beautiful shade and the magnificence of its autumnal coloring. The *stem* is extensively climbing, reaching out in all directions, and fastening itself by the disk-like appendages of the tendrils to anything that will give it support, thus sometimes reaching a great height. *Leaves* long petioled, digitate, smooth, with five oblong-lanceolate coarsely serrate leaflets. *Flower clusters* cyme-like, the pedicels angularly jointed and somewhat umbellate. *Flowers* small, and perfect. *Calyx* entire, crenate, or slightly 5-toothed. *Petals* 5, at first seemingly united, then becoming distinct, concave and thick, expanding and reflexing before they fall. *Disk* none. *Stamens* 5; *filaments* slender; *anthers* large, oblong introrse. *Ovary* somewhat lobed at the base, conical, 5-angled, 2-celled; *style* short or wanting; *stigma* small and simple, or slightly 2-lobed. *Ovules* 2 in each cell of the ovary and erect, anatropous from its base. *Fruit* a dark purplish blue berry when ripe, about the size of a pea. *Seeds* bony, with a minute *embryo* at the base.

History and Habitat.—This woody climber haunts low, moist grounds, well supplied with trees or bushes, often making the bodies of elm trees grandly picturesque by its dense green covering of their trunks, or hanging in festoons from blasted trees, and covering rocks and stumps with its dense verdure, it renders beautiful everything it clings to, while after the first frosts its vividly brilliant coloring makes one of the most striking points in an ·autumn landscape. It opens its yellowish green flowers, few at a time, in July; the berries being ripe in October. The Virginian Creeper is dreaded by many, in its wild state, when

* ἄμπιλο, *a vine,* and ὄψις, *appearance.*

without support, from its often being taken for poison ivy, to which, however, it bears no resemblance, except perhaps in this mode of growth. This indigenous vine is being cultivated in Europe much as the European ivy is here, for adorning walls. Ampelopsis is not mentioned in the U. S. Ph.; in the Eclectic Materia Medica its preparations are *Decoctum ampelopsis*, and *Infusum ampelopsis*.

PART USED AND PREPARATION.—The fresh young shoots and bark are chopped and pounded to a pulp and weighed. Then two parts by weight of alcohol are taken, and having mixed the pulp well with one-sixth part of it, the rest of the alcohol is added. The whole is then stirred, poured into a well-stoppered bottle and allowed to stand eight days in a dark, cool place.

Having separated the tincture by decanting, straining and filtering, it presents by transmitted light a slightly brownish-red color; is of a decided sour, astringent taste and has a strong acid reaction.

CHEMICAL CONSTITUENTS.—*Pyrocatechin,*[*] $C_6 H_6 O_2$, determined by Gorup-Besanez in small quantity in the green leaves. This body crystallizes in square prisms readily soluble in water and alcohol.

Cisso-Tannic Acid, $C_{10} H_{12} O_8$, determined by Wittstein in the autumnal colored leaves as the pigment of the red coloration; it is liquid at ordinary temperatures, and has an astringent, bitter taste. In this acid as a sediment is another body termed by this author *insoluble* or *changed cisso-tannic acid* ($C_{26} H_{28} O_{13}$), insoluble in water, soluble in alcohol. It exists when dry as a dense dark-brown, brittle, shining mass, having a bitter, acrid taste.

The leaves when green contain also free tartaric acid and its salts, with sodium and potassium.

Glycollic Acid, $C_2 H_4 O_3$, and *Calcium glycollate* ($C_2 H_3 O_3)_2$ Ca, exist in the ripe berries. (Schorlemmer.)

PHYSIOLOGICAL ACTION.—Little or nothing is known of the action of this drug upon man. Mr. Bernay, however, in Pharm. Jour. and Trans., vol. vii., 1876, p. 80, reports that two children, aged respectively two and a half and five years, after chewing the leaves and swallowing the juice were quickly seized with vomiting and purging, with tenesmus; then collapse, sweating, and faint pulse; followed by deep sleep for two hours, from which a return of the vomiting and purging aroused them. The pupils were dilated and remained somewhat so four hours after the commencement of the attack.

DESCRIPTION OF PLATE 40.

1. Flowering spray, from Ithaca, N. Y., June 17, 1880.
2. Branch showing tendrils.
3. Flower (enlarged).
4. Berries.

---

[*] Oxyphenic Acid.

40.

Cm.ad nat.del.et pinxt. AMPE LÓPSIS QUINQUEFÒLIA, Michx.

41
RHAMNUS CATHARTICUS.

BUCKTHORN.

SYN.—RHAMNUS CATHARTICUS, LINN.; R. SOLUTIVUS, GER.; CERVIS-
PINA CATHARTICA, MŒNCH.
COM. NAMES.—PURGING BUCKTHORN; (FR.) NERPRUN, BOURQUÉPINE;
(GER.) WEGDORN, KREUZDORN.

A TINCTURE OF THE RIPE BERRIES OF RHAMNUS CATHARTICUS, LINN.

Description.—This dense-spreading shrub or small tree attains a growth of from 6 to 12 feet. *Stem* erect; *bark* grayish; *branchlets* numerous, tipped with a sharp spine. *Leaves* somewhat opposite or sometimes more or less tufted, oval, acuminate, and minutely denticulate-serrate; *veins* prominent beneath, and arched in a direction parallel to the margin. *Inflorescence* in axillary clusters; *flowers* minute, greenish-yellow, polygamous or diœcious, the sterile ones with ovate sepals and petals and an abortive ovary. *Calyx* urceolate, 4 to 5 cleft, persistent; *lobes* lanceolate; *torus* thin, lining the tube. *Petals* 4 to 5 small, linear-oblong; *claws* short. *Stamens* short, mostly 4, rudimentary in the fertile flowers; *filaments* surrounded by the corolla. *Ovary* free, 2 to 4 celled, not enclosed in the torus; *styles* 2 to 4 distinct or more or less united; *stigmas* 4, somewhat club-shaped or ligulate. *Fruit* an ovoid, berry-like drupe; *nutlets* 3 to 4, seed-like, cartilaginous; *seeds* grooved on the back and rounded at the sides, a horizontal section resembling the face of a horse's hoof; *cotyledons* leaf-like, the edges revolute.

Rhamnaceæ.—A small family of shrubs or small trees, often with thorny branchlets. *Leaves* mostly alternate, simple; *stipules* small or obsolete. *Inflorescence* various; *flowers* small and regular (sometimes apetalous, or, by abortion, diœcious or polygamous); in æstivation the sepals are valvate and the petals convolute. *Petals* clawed, concave, inserted into the edge of a fleshy disk lining the short tube of the calyx. *Stamens* 4 or 5, perigynous, as many as the sepals and alternate with them. *Ovary* 2 to 5 celled; *ovules* solitary, anatropous; *styles* more

---

* From the Celtic *ram*, branching.

41.

℄ m.ad nat.del.et pinxt.   RHÁMNUS CATHÁRTICUS, Linn.

or less united; *stigmas* 2 to 5, simple, and usually distinct. *Fruit* a capsule, drupe, or berry; *seeds* erect, one in each cell; *axil* none; *embryo* large; *cotyledons* broad; *albumen* sparing and fleshy.

This family furnishes us with only one other proven plant, viz.: the European Black Alder (*Rhamnus frangula*, Linn.), the bark of which is a mild but certain purgative, useful in habitual constipation.

Among the other plants of the order useful to medicine, we find the French Berry, a purgative fruit yielded by *Rhamnus infectorius*, Linn. The fruit of the Indian *Zizyphus œnophila*, Mill., is eaten by the natives, who consider the bark a fine vulnerary. The East Indian *Z. Jujuba*, Lam., and the Persian *Z. vulgaris* yield a mucilaginous juice from which is made the famous Jujube Paste, esteemed for the manufacture of a pleasant pectoral lozenge, called by the French *Pate´de Jujube;* the Arabian *Z. lotus* yields a berry known as the Lote; this is supposed to be the true Lotus of the Lotophagi. It is found on the eastern as well as the western extremity of the African desert, and is described by Mr. Park as small farinaceous berries, of a yellow color and delicious taste. The natives, he says, convert them into a sort of bread, by exposing them some days to the sun, and afterwards pounding them gently in a wooden mortar until the farinaceous part is separated from the stone. The meal is then mixed with a little water, and formed into cakes, which, when dried in the sun, resemble in color and taste the sweetest gingerbread. The roots of the North American *Berchemia volubilis*, De C., are claimed to be a useful remedy in cachexias and an antisyphilitic. The twigs of the New Jersey Tea (*Ceanothus Americanus*, Linn.) are very useful on account of their mild astringency as an injection in gonorrhœa, gleet, and leucorrhœa; this plant is now being proven for a place in our Materia Medica. The Mexican *Ceanothus azurea*, Desf., is considered a powerful febrifuge; while the Senegal *C. discolor* is a useful astringent in dysentery. *Hovenia dulcis*, Don., enlarges its peduncles in fruit to such extent, and they become so sweet and succulent, that the Japanese consider them a rare delicacy; they are said to greatly resemble in taste a Bergamot pear.

History and Habitat.—The Purging Buckthorn is indigenous to Europe and Northern Asia, from whence it was introduced into this country as a hedge-plant; it has escaped in many places in New York and New England, where it flowers from April to May, according to the season.

The medical history of this plant extends back to a period dating from before the Norman Conquest; it was then called Waythorn or Hartsthorn. In the 13th century Welsh physicians prescribed the juice in honey as a mild aperient drink. In Spain it is referred to as early as 1305; and it is then noted by all writers on medical plants during the 16th century. Buckthorn first appeared in the London Pharmacopœia in 1650; it has also held a place in the Pharmacopœia of the United States, but its space is now held by *R. frangula*. The Purging Buckthorn has now fallen into disuse on account of the violence of its action and the resulting severe irritation of the bowels.

The principal uses now are those of economy, the juice of the fresh berries giving a saffron-colored dye, and that of the bark a beautiful yellow. A fine green pigment for water-coloring is made by the French from the ripe berries mixed with alum; this color, called *Vert de Vessie*, or sap-green, has been used as the principle for most of the foliage of the plates in this work.

PART USED AND PREPARATION.—The fresh, ripe berries are pounded to a pulp, sufficient to separate them from the nutlets, and weighed. Then two parts by weight of alcohol are taken, the pulp thoroughly mixed with one-sixth part of it, and the rest of the alcohol added. The whole is then poured into a well-stoppered bottle, and allowed to stand eight days in a dark, cool place, being shaken twice a day.

The tincture, separated from this mass by pressing and filtering, is opaque; in thin layers it exhibits an orange-red color by transmitted light; and a taste at once acid and astringent.

CHEMICAL CONSTITUENTS.—*Rhamnocathartin.*[*] A bitter, brittle, yellowish, amorphous substance, soluble in water and alcohol, not soluble in ether; when fused it passes into a thick, yellow oil.

Rhamnin,[†] $C_{12}H_{12}O_5 + (H_2O)_2$.[‡]—This glucoside, discovered in the berries by a Pontoise pharmacist named Fleury, in 1840, was isolated, named, and further studied by Lefort.[§] Rhamnin, when pure, forms minute, yellow, translucent tables, scarcely soluble in cold water, soluble in hot alcohol, and breaks down as in the next body.

Rhamnegine, $C_{24}H_{32}O_{14}$.—This second glucoside of Lefort is in all respects, except solubility, identical in its physical and chemical properties with the preceding. When decomposed by heating with a dilute mineral acid, it breaks down into a crystallizable sugar, isomeric with mannite and *rhamnetin*, $C_{12}H_{10}O_5$.

Rhamnotannic Acid.—This tannin-like body, obtained in the separation of rhamnin, results as a greenish-yellowish, amorphous, friable, bitter mass, soluble in alcohol and insoluble in water.

PHYSIOLOGICAL ACTION.—The purgation following the ingestion of the ripe fruit of Rhamnus catharticus is, in almost every instance, accompanied by considerable thirst, dryness of the mouth and throat, and severe griping pains in the abdomen. A case is reported[||] of the effects of eating the berries by a lad; the symptoms were as follows: Eyes glistening and injected; lips trembling; a simulation of trismus; the abdomen became hard and distended; colic; diarrhœa; respiration short and anxious; pulse variable; the skin was at one time warm, at another cold; the boy was unable to rise, could not walk, and seemed to

---

[*] Cathartin.　　[†] Rhamneitne (Gallatly, 1858); Chrysorhamnine (Schutzeberger and Bertiche, 1865).
[‡] $C_{18}H_{22}O_{10}$ (Schutzenberger).　　[§] *Jour. de Phar.*, 1866, p. 420.　　[||] Leopold, *Casp. Woch.*, 1850.

endeavor to press the head against the wall. The symptoms all showed a high state of irritation of the alimentary tract.

DESCRIPTION OF PLATE 41.

1. End of a fruiting branch, Ithaca, N. Y., July 17th, 1885.
    2. Female flower.
    3. Section of ovary.
    4. Male flower.
    5. Petal.
    6. Stamen.
    7. The persistent calyx-tube.
    8. Nutlet.
    9. Horizontal section of the nutlet.
        (2–9 enlarged.)

N. ORD.—CELASTRACEÆ.
Tribe.—EUONYMEÆ.
GENUS.—**EUONYMUS**,* TOURN.
SEX. SYST.—PENTANDRIA MONOGYNIA.

42

EUONYMUS ATROPURPUREUS.

WA-A-HOO.

SYN.—EUONYMUS ATROPURPUREUS, JACQ.; E. CAROLINIENSIS, AND LATI-
FOLIUS, MARSH.
COM. NAMES.—WAHOO, WAHOON, BURNING BUSH, SPINDLE-TREE, INDIAN
ARROW-WOOD; (FR.) FUSAIN, OU BONNET DE PRETRE; (GER.) SPINDEL-
BAUM.

A TINCTURE OF THE FRESH BARK OF EUONYMUS ATROPURPUREUS, JACQ.

Description.—This low shrub seldom attains, out of cultivation, a height of over
10 feet, varying usually from 6 to 10. *Stem* erect; *branches* straight, appearing
more or less terete by having 4 double, white, linear ridges upon its surface, *bark*
blotched with white verrucose spots between the ridges. *Leaves* opposite, thin,
petioled; oval-oblong, acute at the base, and pointed; *margin* finely serrate; *midrib*
prominent. *Inflorescence* loose, few-flowered, divaricate cymes, terminating long,
lateral and axillary, drooping peduncles, ranged along the young shoots of the
season; *flowers* perfect, their parts in fours. *Calyx* short and flat; *sepals* orbicular,
spreading, united at the base. *Petals* broadly ovate, somewhat acute, spreading.
Stamens mounted upon the angles of a flat, somewhat quadrilateral disk, which is
more or less united with the ovary and covers its superior surface; *filaments* merely
mamma-like processes of the disk; *anthers* appearing sessile, 2-celled, opening by
a broad transverse chink upon their upper faces, and furnished with a broad dorsal
connective. *Style* simply a central projection of the disk; *stigma* hardly evident.
Fruit a smooth deeply four lobed and celled, loculicidal capsule; *cells* 2 to 3 seeded;
seeds elliptical, ashy, enveloped by a red aril.

Celastraceæ.—Shrubs with simple, opposite or alternate leaves; *stipules*
minute caducous. *Flowers* small and regular; *æstivation* imbricate. *Calyx* 4 to 5
lobed, persistent. *Petals* plane, as many as the sepals, and inserted by a broad
base underneath the disk. *Stamens* as many as the petals and alternate with
them, inserted upon a disk which fills the calyx cup and is sometimes more or less

---

* Ευονυμη, *Euonyme*, the mother of the Furies; or εὖ, *eu*, well; ὄνομα, *onoma*, named; alluding to the poisonous
effects of the plant upon cattle.

united with the ovary. *Ovary* free from the calyx; *ovules* anatropous, erect or pendulous; *styles* united into one. *Fruit* a 2 to 5 celled capsule; *seeds* arilled, one or few to each cell, *embyro* large, *cotyledons* faliaceous; *albumen* sarcous, thin, or sometimes absent.

The only proven plant of this order is the European Spindle Tree (*Euonymus Europæus*, Linn.), the properties of which are very similar to, if not identical with, the species under consideration. The following plants of the family are more or less useful, viz.: The common Bittersweet, or, better, Staff Vine (*Celastrus scandens*), so often confounded, by the laity, with Dulcamara, has orange-colored fruit; has been largely used in domestic practice, as an alterative, diuretic and cholagogue in various diseases where it seemed necessary to "cleanse the blood." It was considered without equal for the removal of hepatic obstruction. The Indian *C. paniculatus* is considered stimulant. The branches of the Chilian *Maytenus Chilensis* are used in decoction by the natives as a wash for the swellings produced in those who have rested in the shade of the Lithri Tree.* The root-bark of the Indian *Elæodendron Roxburghii* is used by the natives, in decoction, for the reduction of almost any kind of swelling; and the African *Catha edulis* is claimed to be used by the Arabs as an anti-somnolent and intoxicant. Almost all the species of this small order are used in their native countries to subdue inflammation.

History and Habitat.—The Wahoo grows in moist, open woods, or along rivers from Western New York to Wisconsin, and southward. It flowers at the north in June and ripens its beautiful fruit in October. It is the fiery appearence of the fruiting bush after the leaves have fallen, and the capsules bursted, and especially when contrasted with a snow background, that gives it an appearance eminently fitting the name often applied, the Burning Bush.

Especially of late Wahoo has attracted much attention in medical circles as a laxative tonic, alterative, and depurant in torpidity of the liver; also as a remedy for derangement of the stomach and in secondary syphilis, and an expectorant in colds, coughs and asthma. It needs, however, more thorough proving to determine its sphere of usefulness. Mr. Hardyman, of Cardiff, states† that he has used *Euonymin* in 2 grain doses at bedtime, and finds it of much value in hepatic obstruction, needing, however, a saline purge to complete its usefulness. When used in this way I should much prefer the seeds of the plant to salts to procure the cathartic action. The oil of the seeds has been used both in this country and Europe to destroy lice (*Pediculus Capitis, Vestimenti,* and *Pubis*).

The officinal preparation in the U. S. Ph. is *Extractum Euonymi.*

PART USED AND PREPARATION.—The fresh bark of the twigs and root, of the wild plant, is chopped and pounded to a pulp and weighed. Then two parts by weight of alcohol are taken, and after thoroughly mixing the pulp with one-sixth part of it, the rest of the alcohol is added. After having stirred the whole well, pour it into a well-stoppered bottle, and let it stand eight days in a dark, cool place.

---

* *Lithrea caustica* (*Laurus caustica*), Lauraceæ.   † The practitioner in New Rem., 1880, 80.

42.

1

2

3   4   5   6   7   8

€.m. ad nat del. et pinxt.   **EUÓNYMUS ATROPURPÙREUS, Jacq**

The tincture separated from the mass by pressing and filtering, has a clear lemon-yellow color by transmitted light. It has an acrid and bitter taste, no specific odor, and an acid reaction.

CHEMICAL CONSTITUENTS.—*Euonymin.* On treating the tincture with chloroform, a dark substance is obtained which partly dissolves in ether as a beautiful yellow resin. The insoluble portion dissolved in alcohol, and the resin precipitated by plumbic acetate, the menstruum after filtration and evaporation yields a neutral, amorphous, bitter body soluble in alcohol and sparingly in water.*

Euonic Acid.—This acid crystallizes in acicular forms, and is precipitable from its solutions by plumbic subacetate (Wenzel).

Resins, gum, sugar, a crystallizable bitter principle, asparagin, tartaric, citric, and malic acids were also extracted.

PHYSIOLOGICAL ACTION.—In large doses the Wahoo acts as a drastic purge attended by griping and followed by prostration ; the discharges being sero-mucoid with an admixture of bile. It promotes the biliary functions and intestinal secretions, increasing capillary circulation generally.

The symptoms noted are: deathly nausea ; vertigo ; excessive tormina ; prostration and cold sweat. Profuse and violent evacuation of the bowels, accompanied by much flatulence and colic.†

DESCRIPTION OF PLATE 42.

1. Portion of a flowering branch, Cincinnati, O., June 17th, 1885.
2. End of branch.
3. Flower showing calyx.
4. Face of flower.
5. Section of flower.
6. Stamen.
7. Fruit.
8 Horizontal section of ovary.
(3–8 enlarged.)

---

* Wenzel in *Am. Jour. Phar.*, 1862, 312.   † Hale, *New Remedies*, 293.

43

AESCULUS HIPPO-CASTANUM.

HORSE CHESTNUT.

SYN.—AESCULUS HIPPOCASTANUM, LINN.; CASTANEA FOLIO MULTI-FIDO, BAUH.; CASTANEA EQUINA, GER.; CASTANEA PAVINA.
COM. NAMES.—COMMON HORSE CHESTNUT,† ASIATIC HORSE CHEST-NUT, BUCKEYE;‡ (FR.) MARRONNIER D'INDE; (GER.) ROSSKAS-TANIE.

A TINCTURE OF THE FRESH, RIPE, HULLED NUT OF AESCULUS HIPPOCASTA-NUM, LINN.

Description.—This stately, umbrageous tree usually attains a growth of about 60 feet in height, and 50 feet in diameter of foliage. *Trunk* erect; ovate, and smooth-barked when young; oval, tending to quadrilateral, when old; *bark* of the full grown tree greyish, rough, and fissured; *inner bark* smooth, greenish-white, tough, fibrous, astringent, and bitter; *wood* light, not durable. *Leaves* op-posite, digitately 7-lobed; *leaflets* 7, obovate, with a cuneate base, acute tip, and doubly-serrate margin; straight-feather-veined, early deciduous. *Inflorescence* dense, pyramidal, upright, hyacinthine thyrsi, terminal upon the shoots of the season; *flowers* many, often polygamous, the greater proportion of them sterile; *pedicels* articulated. *Calyx* tubular or bell-shaped, oblique or inflated at the base; *limb* 5-lobed. *Corolla* spreading, white, spotted with purple and yellow; *petals* 4-5, usually 5, more or less unequal, nearly hypogynous, clawed and undulate margined. *Stamens* 6-8, usually 7, declined; *filaments* unequal, awl-shaped, long and slender; *anthers* oval, 2-celled. *Ovary* ovate, stipitate, 3-celled; *style* 1, fili-form; *stigma* acute; *ovules* 2 in each cell. *Fruit* a roundish, echinate, 3-celled, 3-valved capsule, splitting into 3 dissepiments, disclosing 1-2 full formed, some-what hemispherical nuts, and sometimes an aborted third; *seed* a large amyla-ceous nut, having a dense shining *testa* marked with a large roundish hilum; *coty-ledons* thick, sarcous, cohering; *radicle* conical, curved.

Sapindaceæ.—This large and variable order is chiefly tropical, especially the

---

* An ancient Latin name. The Aesculus of the Romans was a kind of oak.

† Horses are said to eat greedily of the fruit, and the Arabs to use the powdered nuts in the food of their horses when affected with pulmonary disorders; hence the vulgarism.

‡ From a resemblance of the nut to the eye of that animal. This name is more applicable to the American species.

43.

C.M. ad nat del. et pinxt.

ÆSCULUS HIPPOCASTÀNUM, Linn.

typical suborder, of which the genus under consideration is the only North American representative. The family is composed of trees, shrubs, or tendril-bearing climbers, showing widely different characters of leaf, flower, and fruit; and includes the soap-berries, bladder-nuts, and maples. The *leaves* are usually alternate (Exc. Aesculus), simple or compound. *Flowers* mostly irregular and unsymmetrical; *sepals* 4-5, imbricate in æstivation; *petals* 4-5, alternate with the sepals, and sometimes wanting. *Disk* sarcous, regular, expanded, or glandular, protruding between the petals and stamens. *Stamens* 5-10, perigynous or hypogynous; *filaments* free or cohering at their bases; *anthers* introrse. *Ovary* 2-3 celled and lobed; *ovules* 1-2 in each cell; *style* simple, or 2-3 cleft. *Fruit* a capsule, samara, or fleshy indehiscent drupe; *embryo* curved or convolute (Exc. Staphylea); *albumen* wanting.

The plants that are of particular interest to us in this family, beside the two under consideration here, are: *Guarana* or Brazilian Cocoa (*Paullinia sorbilis*, Mart.), and the Brazilian *timbo-sipo* (*Paullinia pinnata*, D. C). Economically the berries of *Sapindus saponaria* and the bark and roots of other species are used in lieu of soap in cleansing woollens. The genus Paullinia contains many species in which a deleterious narcotic constituent is developed in the juice or seeds; the native Brazilians prepare a slow but potent and certain poison from *Paullinia pinnata*; *P. australis* is supposed to be the origin of a venomous honey found in the Brazilian woods; and *P. curruru* yields an arrow poison to the natives of Guiana, who also prepare a narcotic intoxicating drink from *P. cu'ana*. The products of most species of this order are to be regarded with suspicion, yet the Chinese *Lee-chee* (*Nephelium Lichti*) and *Longan* (*Nephelium Longan*) are delicious fruits; the Brazilian *Fruta de Pavao* (*Schmidelia edulis*) is sweet and palatable; and the Jamaica wing-leaved honey-berry (*Melicocca bijugis*) edible, sub-acid, and pleasant. The berries of many species of the genus *Sapindus* are edible, though the seeds, used by the natives of the country of their growth to poison fish, are active narcotic toxicants.

History and Habitat.—The horse chestnut is a native of Asia; it was introduced into Europe about the middle of the sixteenth century by seed, and first cultivated in England by Tradescant in 1633;* after this its growth became quite general, as the tree accommodates itself quickly to all temperate regions. It is one of our first trees to bud in the spring, and flowers in April and May, its fruit being fully ripe at the first autumn frost. Being one of our most dense shade trees, dark, cool, and clean, it is extensively planted in the yards and along the streets of almost every American city and village. The nuts are eaten greedily by horses, sheep, goats, cows, and pigs, and form an excellent fattening food for those animals when prepared in such a manner as to drive off the acrimony. This is best accomplished by boiling them in potash and washing them with water. Germination, however, renders them pleasant food through change of the bitter principles to saccharine, a result similar to that produced in malting barley. The

---

* Woodville.

nuts are said to yield a starch of finer quality than that of any cereal (Parmentier) ; paste made of the powdered nuts is claimed to be very tenacious and not attacked by moths and vermin ; the saponaceous property of the seeds, when used in lieu of soap, is highly esteemed in cleaning and fulling woollens, especially in France and Switzerland (Marcandier). The nuts of *Aesculus Californica* are largely used by the natives of that State for making into bread, after removing the bitterness by freely washing the powdered cotyledons. The fruit of *Ae. pavia* is used by the Aborigines for stupefying fish ; this species is so common in Ohio that it has become an emblem, and given rise to the sobriquet " Buckeye State."

The use of *Cortex hippocastani* dates from the writings of Matthiolus.* In Europe it was put forward, especially by Zannichelli, as an efficient remedy for intermittent fevers of various types ; this use has been upheld by many able medical writers, from whose works it would appear equal if not superior at that time to Peruvian bark. The usual dose given was from one to four scruples of the powder, repeated from two to six times in twenty-four hours ; this use seems never to have extended to England or America. The bark and nuts were introduced into the Edinburgh College with a view to their errhine power ; it being known that insufflation of the powder caused violent sneezing, it was recommended for the purpose of producing or promoting nasal discharge.

In this country, especially among the laity, the nuts have been greatly esteemed as a remedy for hemorrhoids and rheumatism, used either as a decoction or as a salve prepared with lard. So great is the faith of many people afflicted with either of these diseased conditions, that they carry a few nuts in their pockets from season to season, fully confident that the disorder is warded off by this means.† In Europe the oil procured by means of ether is used largely in neuralgia and rheumatism. An infusion of the bark or nuts is said to act favorably in the healing of indolent and gangrenous ulcers. The testa of the nuts is narcotic ; according to Dr. McDowell 10 grains are equal to 3 grains of opium.

Aesculus is not officinal in the U. S. Ph., nor has it an officinal preparation in the Eclectic Materia Medica, though used—especially as an extract—under the name *Aesculin*.

PART USED AND PREPARATION.—The fresh, ripe, hulled nut is pounded to a pulp and weighed. Then two parts by weight of alcohol are taken, the pulp mixed thoroughly with one-sixth part of it, and the rest of the alcohol added. After stirring the whole well, and pouring it into a well-stoppered bottle, it is allowed to stand at least eight days in a dark, cool place.

The tincture, separated from the mass by filtration, has a clear brownish-orange color by transmitted light ; no characteristic odor ; an extremely bitter, acrid, and astringent taste, and an acid reaction. An amylaceous deposit takes place on standing, which, being of no value to the preparation, may be filtered off.

---

* Epist. Medicinal. op. omn. p. 101, 125.

† I know at present many who indulge in this practice who have been sufferers, and they are really free from the disease while carrying the nuts. This should not seem a fallacy, to us as homœopathists, in cases where Aesculus is indicated.

CHEMICAL CONSTITUENTS.—*Aesculin*, $C_{21} H_{24} O_{13} + H_2O$. This aromatic glucoside exists in the bark of many trees of the genera Pavia and Aesculus. It crystallizes in fine, snowy needles and globules, which lose their water of crystallization and fuse at 160° (320° F.), decomposing at higher temperatures. They are soluble in both hot and cold water and in alcohol, their solutions exhibiting a fine light-blue fluorescence. Boiling with dilute mineral acids decomposes this body into glucose and

Aesculetin, $C_9 H_6 O_4$, another glucoside, which also exists in a free state in the bark. This body is only sparingly soluble in water, and crystallizes in bitter needles, which break down under the action of boiling potash into formic, oxalic, and protocatechinic acids.

Paviin, $C_{32} H_{36} O_{20}$. This glucoside is considered identical with *fraxin*, and will be found described under Fraxinus Americana, 137.

Oil of Aesculus. This oil is readily obtained from the nuts of this species by etherial extraction. It results as a beautiful yellow liquid, congealing at 1° (33.8° F.), and becoming solid at −5° (23° F.).

Quercitrin, $C_{33} H_{30} O_7$. This coloring matter of quercitron, occurs in the testa of the nut,* and in the flowers.

Aesculetinic acid is one of the resultants of a still farther decomposition taking place in glucose and aesculetin when they are decomposition products of the action of baryta water upon aesculin.

*Aescinic acid.** This amorphous body is a decomposition product of aphrodaescin when boiled with liquor potassa.

Argyraescin. This acrid, amorphous glucoside was discovered by Rochelder in 1862 as a constituent of the seed. It is soluble in alcohol and water ; a watery solution forming a soapy foam on agitation. This body together with

*Aphrodaescin,** another acrid, amorphous principle, having the same properties of solubility and saponification, and breaking down under the action of a concentrated mineral acid into sugar and *aescigenin,** so markedly resemble saponin that a question arises as to whether they are specific principles, or are to be considered together as

Saponin, $C_{32} H_{54} O_{18}$. This peculiar glucoside, existing in the roots of *Saponaria officinalis*, many species of *Lychnis*,† *Polygala Senega*,‡ *Gypsophila Struthium*,§ *Lucuma glycyphlœa*,‖ *Monninia polystachya*,¶ *Quillaja Saponaria*** and many other plants, including ferns ; has, before the observation of Rochelder, been accounted a principle of the nuts of this plant. It is a white, amorphous, sternutatory powder, having at first a sweetish, then a pungent and lastingly acrid taste. It is readily soluble in water, the solution frothing like that of soap on agitation, and is resolved under the action of concentrated hydrochloric acid into an amorphous sugar and *sapogenin*.

Although our tincture is made of the nuclei of the nuts only, still it would seem as if the bitterness, astringency, and acrimony present, were due to all or nearly all of the above constituents found in the bark.

---

* Rochelder.　† Githagin.　‡ Senegin, Polygalin.　§ Struthiin.　‖ Monesin.　¶ Monninin.　** Quillajin

PHYSIOLOGICAL ACTION.—We have no accessible accounts of poisonings by this drug, still the provings, being made with goodly sized doses of the tincture, are sufficient to give us an insight into the physiological action. Aesculus hippocastanum causes inflammation of the mucous membranes of the respiratory and digestive tracts, and especially of the rectum ; this is shown in the following list of symptoms: Dryness, heat, burning and swelling of the mucous membranes of the nose, larynx, and trachea, with a subsequent copious catarrhal discharge ; the same symptoms prevail in the mouth and œsophagus, followed by profuse ptyalism and mucous discharge ; the tongue becomes coated with a thick white or yellow fur, and feels as if scalded ; the throat becomes congested, raw, and burning, followed by a sense of constriction, and renders deglutition painful and difficult. Constant burning in the stomach and epigastrium, followed by nausea, retching, and violent vomiting, with great tenderness and colic throughout the abdomen, are markedly present. Severe dryness, burning, and soreness of the rectum, with prolapse, and sufficient inflammation of the hemorrhoidal veins to result in purple tumors, indicate the severity of the action of the drug in this locality. Ineffectual efforts at stool, with great urging, and constant severe pain in the lumbar region, extending to the hips and sacrum, are constant symptoms of the drug. Its action upon the liver and portal system is marked by severe congestion, and attendant burning, constrictive pains and deep soreness. The provings, however, fail to substantiate its previous use in intermittent fever and neuralgia ; its febrile symptoms being only slight, and its pains, other than those referable to the alimentary tract, slight and not characteristic of nerve irritation.

DESCRIPTION OF PLATE 43.

1. End of flowering branch from Ithaca, N. Y., June 4, 1880.
2. A medium-size leaf.
3. Flower.
4. Stamen.
5. Nut.

(3 and 4 slightly enlarged.)

44

ÆSCULUS GLABRA.

BUCKEYE.

SYN.—ÆSCULUS GLABRA AND PALLIDA, WILLD.; Æ. ECHINATA, MUHL.;
Æ. OHIOENSIS AND MACROSTACHYA, MICHX.; PAVIA GLABRA AND
PALLIDA, SPACH.; P. ALBA, POIR.; P. MACROSTACHYA, LOIS.; MAC-
ROTHYRSUS DISCOLOR, SPACH.

COM. NAMES.—OHIO BUCKEYE, FETID BUCKEYE, SMOOTH HORSE-
CHESTNUT.

A TINCTURE OF THE FRESH NUT OF ÆSCULUS GLABRA, WILLD.

Description.—This species differs from the preceding in the following par-
ticulars: *Bark* exhaling a very unpleasant odor, similar to that of the flowers of
the preceding. *Leaf* small, smooth; *leaflets* 5, ovate-lanceolate, acute, and finely
serrate. *Inflorescence* smaller and more cymose; *flowers* small, pale yellow, narrowly tubular-campanulate, polygamous. *Petals* only 4, upright, not reflexed.
Stamens curved, not declined; *filaments* filiform, long-hairy. *Fruit* echinulate
with very short pyramidal points.

History and Habitat.—The Buckeye is indigenous to the United States, where
it ranges from Western Pennsylvania and Virginia to Michigan, Indiana, and Kentucky; it habits the rich alluvial soil along the bottom-lands of the Ohio River and
the streams feeding it, and blossoms in June.

The previous uses of this species are almost identical with those of Æ. Hippocastanum, though not so extensive, as its qualities are more toxic, and were, on
that account, dreaded.

PART USED AND PREPARATION.—The fresh-hulled nut is treated as in
the preceding species. The resulting tincture has a clear amber color by transmitted light; a honey-like odor; a slightly bitter and pungent taste; and an acid
reaction.

Æsculus glabra should be more thoroughly proven, as its symptoms cover a
larger therapeutic field than its congener. The tincture for this further proving
should include the nut-shells and bark as well as the kernels; a larger scope
would undoubtedly be covered by such a preparation.

CHEMICAL CONSTITUENTS.—So far as we are able to ascertain, no special analysis of this species has been made that determines its individuality; we can therefore do no better than refer to the preceding species.

PHYSIOLOGICAL ACTION.—The principal proving of this remedy is that recorded by Prof. E. M. Hale,* who claims its sphere of action to be an irritant of the cerebro-spinal system and the alimentary tract. The symptoms prominent in his record are: Confusion of mind, vertigo, stupefaction and coma; dimness of vision; thickness of speech; nausea and vomiting; eyes fixed and expressionless; paresis of the tongue; tympanitic distension of the stomach with cramp-like pains; constipation, with hard knotty stools; lameness and weakness of the lumbar region; and spasms and convulsions, followed by wryneck, episthotonos and paralysis.

DESCRIPTION OF PLATE 44.†

1. A leaf.
2. Flower.
3. Stamen.
4. Anther.
5. Fruit.
(2–4 enlarged.)

---

* *New Remedies*, 1877, p. 19 (Symptomatology).
† The fruits of Æ. Hippocastanum and flava are added for comparison.

44.

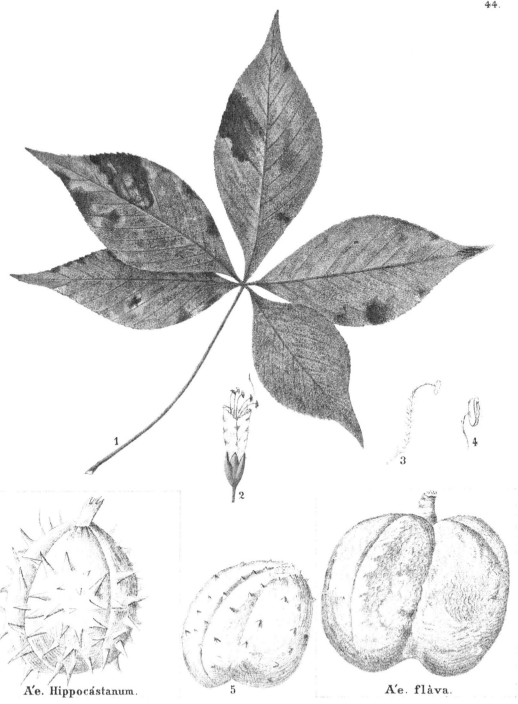

1

2

3

4

A'e. Hippocástanum.

5

A'e. flàva.

.ad nat del.et pinxt.

A'ESCULUS GLÀBRA, Willd.

GENUS.—**POLYGALA**,* TOURN.

SEX. SYST.—DIADELPHIA OCTANDRIA.

45

SENEGA.

SENECA SNAKEROOT.

SYN.—POLYGALA SENEGA, LINN.; P. VIRGINIANA, LEM.; PLANTULA
MARILANDICA, RAII.; SENEGA OFFICINALIS, SPACH.

COM. NAMES.—SENECA, SENEKA, OR SENEGA SNAKEROOT, MILK-
WORT, MOUNTAIN FLAX; (FR.) POLYGALE DE VIRGINIE; (GER.)
SENEGAWURZEL.

A TINCTURE OF THE DRIED ROOT OF POLYGALA SENEGA, LINN.

Description.—*Rootstock* thick, hard, knotty, and sometimes slightly branched.
Stems several, simple, tough and wiry, from 6 to 12 inches high. *Leaves* alternate,
sessile, lanceolate or oblong-lanceolate, acute at both ends; *margins* rough; *stipules*
none. *Inflorescence* a solitary, loose, terminal spike; *flowers* small, greenish-white,
almost sessile, and very irregular. *Calyx* persistent; *sepals* 5, arranged in two sets
as to form; the outer set, composed of 3, are small, acute, lanceolate, and greenish; the inner set, of 2, are large, broad, orbicular, concave, slightly veiny bodies,
called *alæ*, enclosing the petals. *Petals* 3, hypogynous, connected and united with
the stamen-tube; the middle or lower one keel-shaped, and short-crested along the
back; the two lateral oblong, blunt, and veiny. *Stamens* 8, enclosed by the lower
petal; *filaments* united below into two bundles of 4 each; *anthers* small, 1-celled,
and opening by a pore at the apex. *Ovary* laterally compressed, 2-celled by a
transverse partition; *ovules* anatropous, pendulous, one in each cell. *Style* large,
inflated, and curved above, greatly resembling in form a pipe thrust into the summit of the ovary; *stigma* a fringe-like appendage to the upper margin of the
bowl-like enlargement of the style. *Fruit* a small, 2-celled capsule, flattened
contrary to the partition, and partly enclosed by the persistent calyx; *dehiscence*
loculicidal. *Seeds* black, hairy, with a white caruncle extending the length of the
seed; *embryo* straight, axial; *albumen* scanty.

Polygaleæ.—This small family is represented in North America by 3 genera,
comprising 45 species, of which 40 belong to the typical genus Polygala. This
natural order is characterized as follows: Herbs or shrubby plants having *roots*
furnished with a bitter, milky juice. *Leaves* mostly alternate and entire; *stipules*
absent. *Flowers* very irregular, hypogynous, and pseudopapilionaceous; *calyx*
consisting of 5 very irregular sepals, the odd one superior (Exc. Krameria).

---

* Πολύς, *polus*, much; γάλα, *gala*, milk; as some species were supposed to increase this secretion.

2   3   4   5

6   7   8

10   9

11

12   13

℃m.ad nat.del.et pinxt.   POLÝGALA SÉNEGA, Linn.

1

Stamens 4 to 8, monadelphous or diadelphous; *anthers* innate, 1-celled, opening at the top by a pore or chink. *Style* curved and hooded. *Fruit* a 2-celled and 2-seeded capsule.

The only remedy furnished to our Materia Medica by this order, beside Senega, is the Peruvian or Red Ratanhia (*Krameria triandra*, R. et Pav.), for which many other species are often substituted in general medicine, viz.: the Mexican and Brazilian Savanilla or Violet Ratanhia (*K. Ixina*, Linn.); the Para or Brown Rhatany (*K. argentea*, Mart.); the North American *K. lanceolata*, Torr.; the Texan *K. secundiflora*, D. C; and the Chilian *K. cistoidea*, Hook. The genus Polygala furnishes many plants noted as tonics, alexiterics, cathartics, and diaphoretics, notable amongst them being the North American *P. sanquinea*, L.; the European *P. amara*, L., and *rubella*, Muhl.; the Austrian *P. chamæbuxus*, L.; the British *P. vulgaris*, L.; and the Nepaul *P. crotalarioides*, D. C. The Brazilian *P. Poaya*, L., is strongly emetic when fresh, and is considered scarcely inferior in its action to Ipecacuanha; while the Javanese *P. venenosa*, Juss., is so dreaded as a virulent poison that the natives refuse to touch it. The East Indian *Soulamea amara*, D. C., is a valuable febrifuge, used with marked success in pleurisy and Asiatic cholera; and *Bardiera diversifolia* is considered an energetic diuretic and sudorific. The Peruvian astringents, termed by the natives *Zallhoy*, derived from *Monninia polystachia*, *petrocarpa*, and *salicifolia*, R. et Pav., are excellent antidysenterics, and, on account of the saponin-like body, *monninin*, contained in them, are also used as detergents and dentifrices.

History and Habitat.—Senega Snakeroot is indigenous to North America, growing in rocky soils, from New England northwest to the Saskatchewan River and thence southward. It flowers in May and June.

About the year 1735, John Tennent, a Scotch physician, noted that the Seneca Indians obtained excellent effects from a certain plant, as a remedy for the bite of the rattlesnake; after considerable painstaking and much bribing, he was shown the roots and given to understand that what is now known to be Seneca Snakeroot was the agent used. Noting, then, that the symptoms of the bite were similar in some respects to those of pleurisy and the latter stages of peripneumonia, he conceived the idea of using this root also in those diseases. His success was such that he wrote to Dr. Mead, of London, the results of his experiments.* His epistle was printed at Edinburgh in 1738, and the new drug favorably received throughout Europe, and cultivated in England in 1739. The action of Seneka was claimed to be that of a stimulating expectorant, thus claiming usage in the latter stages of croup, pneumonia, humid asthma in the aged, etc.; also, when pushed to diuresis and diaphoresis, it was found valuable in rheumatism, anasarca from renal troubles, amenorrhœa, dysmenorrhœa, and kindred complaints. Among the German physicians Seneka received praise in the treatment of ophthalmia after the inflammatory period had passed; and was claimed by Dr. Ammon to prevent the formation of cataract, and promote the formation of pus in hypopyon. The use of Seneka against

---

* Tennent, *Epist. to Dr. Richard Mead concerning the Epidemical Diseases of Virginia*, etc.

the poisonous effects of rattlesnake bites, and those of rabid animals (Barton), is not warranted by the results so far gained, at least in civilized practice.

Seneka is officinal in the U. S. Phar. as: *Abstractum Senegæ, Extractum Senegæ Fluidum, Syrupus Senegæ,* and *Syrupus Scillæ Compositus.** In the Eclectic Materia Medica the preparations are: *Infusorum Senegæ* and *Tinctura Laricis Composita.†*

PART USED AND PREPARATION.—The dried root, gathered when the leaves are dead, and before the first frost, is coarsely powdered and covered with five parts by weight of alcohol, poured into a well-stoppered bottle, and allowed to stand eight days in a dark, moderately warm place, being shaken twice a day.

The tincture, separated from this mass by decanting and filtering, has a clear, slightly brownish, orange color by transmitted light, an odor greatly resembling sweet cider, at first an aromatic then bitterish and chokingly acrid taste, and an acid reaction. After tasting the tincture or chewing the rootlets, a very peculiar sensation of acridity and enlargement is felt at the root of the tongue, which, once recognized, will always mentally associate itself with this plant.

CHEMICAL CONSTITUENTS.—*Polygalic Acid.‡* $C_{22}H_{18}O_{11}$. This peculiar body, existing principally in the rootlets, was discovered by M. Peschier, and more thoroughly studied, fifteen years later, by Quevenne,§ who isolated it as a white, odorless, acrid, amorphous powder. This acid has not yet been proven to be characteristically different from the general characters of various specific forms of *saponin,* though it has been carefully studied by many organic chemists, among whom are Gehlin, Procter, Dulong, Bucholz, Bolley, Christophsohn, Schneider, Fentulle, Folchi and others. The stubbornness of this body in resisting the action of solvents and reagents without changing form completely renders it, like *trilline,* very difficult to comprehend. Polygalic acid, when superheated upon platinum foil, bursts into a bright flame and leaves no residue; it dissolves thoroughly in hot water, and remains in solution; it dissolves also in boiling absolute alcohol, but deposits again on cooling; on evaporating its watery solution without stirring, it is deposited in greenish scales. This acid forms a frothing, saponaceous solution in boiling water; breaks down under the action of dilute mineral acids into *sapogenin* and amorphous sugar; and has prominent acridity and sternutatory power; —all of which prompted Gehlin to give it the name of *Senegin.‖* Christophsohn, Bolley, Schneider, and Bucholz regard the acid as identical with *Saponin.* The physiological action of Senega would also tend to prove at least a similarity between this acid and Saponin.

Virgineic Acid.—This still doubtful body exists, according to Quevenne, in the fixed oil of the root.

---

* Squills, Seneka, Tartar Emetic, and Calcium Phosphate.
† Tamarac bark, Juniper berries, Prickly Ash bark, Wild Cherry bark, Seneca Snakeroot, Tansy, and Podophyllum.
‡ Senegin; Polygalin.
§ *Jour. de Phar.,* 1836, 449.
‖ Berlin *Jahrsbuch,* 1804, 112.

Polygalin.—The body termed thus by Peschier is now deemed to be simply the volatile oil of Dulong* and other analysts.

Isolusin.—A doubtful bitter principle isolated by Peschier ; and

Oil of Senega.†—A bitter, rancid, disagreeable, reddish-brown body, having the consistency of syrup, and an acid reaction.

PHYSIOLOGICAL ACTION.—In doses of from 10 minims of the tincture to a scruple of the powdered root, Seneka causes: anxiousness, with heaviness and dullness of the head and vertigo ; aching and weakness of the eyes, with lachrymation, pressure in the ball, flickerings, dazzling vision, and contracted pupils ; sneezing ; pytalism ; inflammation of the fauces and œsophagus, with constriction ; thirst and anorexia ; nausea ; mucous vomiting ; burning in the stomach ; cutting colic ; copious, thin, watery stools ; profuse urination, with burning, scalding, and sticking pains along the urethra, and frothing urine ; roughness and irritation of the larynx, with orgasm of blood to the chest, accompanied by constriction, aching, soreness, and oppression ; general debility ; restless sleep ; and profuse diaphoresis.

From these symptoms, it will be noted that Seneka acts quite similarly to *Saponin*, causing, like it, a paresis of the muscles of the respiratory tract, the terminal filaments of the vagus, inhibitory centres, accelerator nerves, and the vasomotor system in general, resulting in capillary congestions, followed by rapid exosmosis.

DESCRIPTION OF PLATE 45.

1. Whole plant, Ithaca, N. Y., June 7th, 1885.
2. The calyx from below.
3. The face of a flower.
4. Middle petal, showing the crest, hood, and stamens.
5. Petal and stamen.
6. Pistil.
7. Section of ovary.
8. Capsule.
9. Section of same.
10. Seed, showing caruncle.
11 and 12. Sections of same.
13. Plan of flower.

(2–13 enlarged.)

---

* *Jour. de Phar.*, 1837, 567.   † Not Seneca Oil.

Tribe.—GENISTEÆ.

GENUS.—**GENISTA,** * LINN.

SEX. SYST.—MONADELPHIA DECANDRIA.

46
GENISTA.

DYER'S BROOM.

SYN.—GENISTA TINCTORIA, LINN.
COM. NAMES.—DYER'S BROOM, GREENWOOD, DYER'S GREEN-WEED,
WOAD- OR WOOD-WAXEN, WHIN; (FR.) GENET DES TEINTUIERS;
(GER.) FÄRBEGINSTER.

A TINCTURE OF THE WHOLE FRESH PLANT GENISTA TINCTORIA, LINN.

Description.—This thornless, perennial, shrubby plant grows to a height of a foot or more. *Stem* erect; *branches* numerous, terete-angled, the younger ones erect. *Leaves* alternate, simple, lanceolate, nearly smooth, and sessile. *Inflorescence* a terminal spiked raceme; *flowers* yellow, nearly sessile, bracted. *Calyx* 2-lipped, the upper 2-parted, the lower 3-toothed; *lobes* 5, acute, pointed. *Corolla* perigynous, papilionaceous; *petals* 5, as follows: *vexillum* or *standard* straight, oblong-oval, spreading, superior to and partly enclosing the other petals; *alæ* or *wings* 2, oblique, spatulate with a straight claw, and exterior to the two lower petals; *carina* or *keel* oblong, straight, deflexed, claws curved, composed of two connivant petals coherent by their anterior edges and enclosing the essential organs; *æstivation* imbricate. *Stamens* 10, monadelphous; *filaments* inserted with the petals upon the base of the calyx; *sheath* entire; *anthers* of two forms, the alternate ones shorter. *Ovary* 1-celled. *Pod* flat, continuous, smooth. *Seeds* several; *cotyledons* large, sarcous; *radicle* incurved.

Leguminosæ.—This immense family of herbs, shrubs, and trees, growing in every part of the world, from the equator to the frigid zones, is represented in North America alone by 78 genera, having, in all, 791 species and 122 recognized varieties. The general features of this order are: *Leaves* alternate, usually compound, mostly entire; *stipules* present. *Flowers* papilionaceous or regular, hypogynous. *Sepals* 5, more or less combined, with the odd sepal inferior in its relation to the bract. *Petals* 5, the odd one superior, *i. e.,* next the axis of inflorescence. *Stamens* 5, 10, or many; *filaments* monadelphous, diadelphous, or in rare instances distinct. *Pistil* single, simple, and free; *ovary* solitary and simple, free from the calyx. *Fruit* a legume; *seeds* various; *albumen* mostly wanting.

To give the materia-medicist a better idea of phyto-grouping, I shall mention

---

* Celtic *gen*, a small bush.

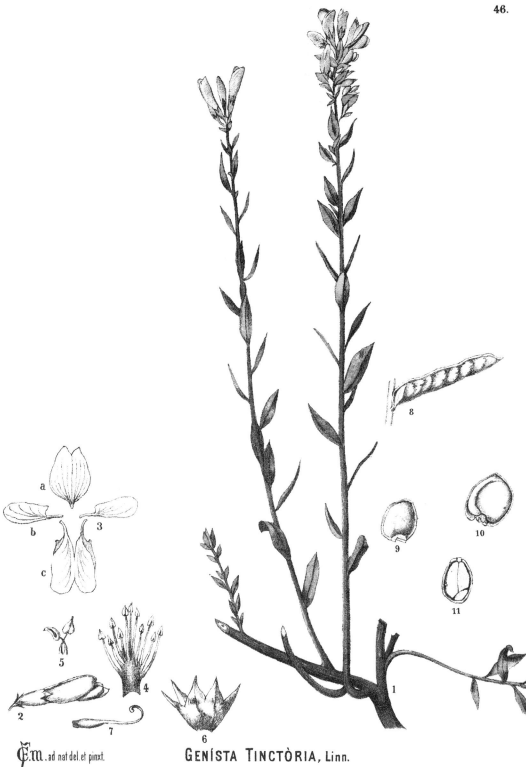

a
b
3
c

5
4
2
7
6

8
9
10
11

Œ.m. ad nat del.et pinxt.

GENÍSTA TINCTÒRIA, Linn.

somewhat extensively the numerous medical and œconomical products furnished by this magnificent family, though to specify all would fill a volume, extending as they do from some of our most esculent vegetables through almost all the necessities of man to many narcotico-acrid poisons. The species proven and established as curative agents in the Homœopathic Materia Medica, are, beside the eight represented in this work: *Copiava*, the oleoresin of *Copaifera multijuga*, Hayne, and many other South American species of the genus, prominent among which are: *C. officinalis*, Linn.; *C. bijuga*, Hayne; *C. Langsdorfii*, Desf.; *C. coriacea*, Mart.; and *C. Guianensis*, Desf.; the Cochin-China *Derris pinnata*, Linn.; the irritating Cowitch gathered from the pods of *Dolichos* (*Mucuna*) *puriens*, Linn., which grows in both the East and West Indies; the Central American Logwood, the heart of *Hæmatoxylon Campechianum*, Linn.; the Brazilian Barba de boi, called by Mure *Hedysarum ildefonsianum*, but more probably, from his description, the *H. lagocephalum* of Link.; Indigo or Indigotin, a blue coloring-matter extracted from different species of the genus *Indigofera*, growing in India, Africa, and South America, principally, however, from *Indigofera tinctoria*, Linn., *I. anil*, Linn., and *I. argentea*, Linn.; an inferior quality of this substance is also obtainable from *Isatis tinctoria* (Cruciferæ); *Polygonum tinctorium* (Polygonaceæ); *Nerium tinctorum* (Apocynaceæ); *Baptisia tinctoria; Tephrosia apollinea;* and several minor plants; Laburnum, a South European poisonous tree, *Cyticus Laburnum*, Linn.; Lathyrus, the European Chickling vetch, *Lathyrus sativus*, Linn.; Mim.; the Brazilian *Mimosa humilis*, Willd.; the powerful Calabar Bean, the state poison of Old Calabar, in Western Africa, *Physostigma venenosum*, Balf.; Jamaica Dogwood (*Piscidia erythrina*, Linn.), which produced in Mr. Hamilton such sudden and powerful sleep that the glass from which a drachm of the tincture had been taken remained for twelve hours in his hand;* the Alexandrian Senna, the well-known anthelmintic, consisting of the dried leaves of *Cassia obovata*, Coll., *C. acutifolia*, Del., and *C. lanceolata*, Lam.; Tongo, the Tonka Bean, the odorous fruit of the Guianian *Dipteryx* (*Coumarouna*) *odorata*, Willd.; the Californian *Astragalus Menziesii*, Gray; the Guianian *Erythrophlæum Guinense*, G. Don; and the Brazilian Cabbage Tree *Geoffroya* (*Andira*) *vermifuga*, Mart.

In the pharmacopœias of the United States, Great Britain, Germany, India, etc., and in general secondary lists we find more or less prominent the following members of this order: The European Broom (*Cytisus*, Genista, *scoparius*, Link), a renowned diuretic, emetic, and purgative, which has long enjoyed a popular reputation in dropsical affections, though contraindicated in all acute renal troubles; it contains a body of the tannic-acid group, termed *scoparin* ($C_{21}H_{22}O_{10}$) to which its diuretic qualities are due, and an oily, narcotico-poisonous, volatile alkaloid, *sparteine* ($C_{15}H_{13}N$), which resembles, chemically, nicotia and conia in having no oxygen. The Oriental Fenugreek (*Trigonella Fœnum-græcum*, Linn.), whose fatty seeds are largely used in veterinary practice, mostly as a vehicle for drugs. The common Liquorice, a product of several varieties of *Glycyrrhiza glabra*, Linn., growing along both shores of the Mediterranean and in Asia, can hardly be classed as a medicine, but rather as an adjunct to prescriptions. The Bengal Kino or Dhak,

---

* *Pharm. Jour.*, 1845, p. 76.

the inspissated juice of the Indian *Butea frondosa*, Kœnig, is considered to be a good substitute for the officinal Kino; the seeds form a Mohammedan vermifuge of considerable repute. Kino, noted as an astringent application to indolent ulcers, and internally as a remedy in diarrhœa and pyrosis, is the inspissated juice of two species of the genus *Pterocarpus*, as follows: Malabar Kino, from *P. marsupium*, D.C., African Kino, from *P. erinaceus*, Poir.; other kinos are used, produced by plants outside of this family. Balsam of Peru, a well-known astringent, used to check excessive discharges from mucous surfaces, as in leucorrhœa, gonorrhœa, and gleet, and internally in asthma and bronchitis as an expectorant, is the resinous exudation of the Central American *Toluifera Pereira*, Baill. Balsam of Tolu is the resinous exudation of the South American *Toluifera balsamum*, Linn.; it forms one of the most useful stimulant expectorants, and components of cough-candies, of the day; the tropical Bonduc Seeds, the fruit of *Cæsalpinia Bonducella*, Roxb., are used in India as a tonic and antiperiodic in general debility and intermittent fevers. The Cassias used, other than those previously mentioned, are: the Asiatic Indian Laburnum (*Cassia Fistula*, Linn.), a noted purgative or mild laxative, according as the dose is large or small; the American Wild Senna (*Cassia Marilandica*, Linn.), a cathartic, whose action often causes severe griping; and Tinnivelly Senna (*Cassia augustifolia*, Vahl.), which is considered a safe and brisk purgative. The active principle of the sennas (cathartic acid) seems to be eliminated by digestion, and to pass into mother's milk in an active state, as babes are often purposely or accidentally purged by the nurse's use of senna leaves. The well-known laxative refrigerants, East and West Indian and Egyptian Tamarinds, are the fruits of *Tamarindus Indica*, Linn. Cutch or Catechu, a product of the Indian *Acacia Catechu*, Willd., is used, like "pale catechu," as an astringent, useful in chronic dysentery and diarrhœa, as well as in speaker's aphonia and passive hemorrhages. The root of the Mediterranean *Anthyllis Hermanniæ*, Linn., is a powerful diuretic; and *A. vulneraria*, Linn., is an excellent styptic. The seeds of the Indian *Psoralia corylifolia*, Linn., are considered stomachic and deobstruent. The root of the East and West Indian *Clitoria ternatea*, Linn., is emetic; while that of the Circassian *Pueraria tuberosa*, D.C, is employed by the natives to reduce swellings of joints; and that of the New Zealand *Tephrosia purpurea*, Pers., is tonic and antidyspeptic. The bark of the Indian *Agati grandiflora*, Desv., is a powerfully bitter tonic. The leaves of the South European Bladder Senna (*Colutea arborescens*, Linn), are purgative, and used as an aᴸulteration of senna; while those of *Coronilla Emerus*, Linn., and *C. varia*, Linn., have a similar property, the latter being considered also diuretic and even poisonous. The leaves of the European *Arthrolobium scorpioides*, D.C., are vesicant; and the roots of the Indian *Ormocarpum sennoides*, D.C., tonic and stimulant. The leaves of the East Indian *Phaseolus trilobus*, Willd., are considered by Hindoo practitioners to be sedative, antibilious, and tonic. The Guadeloupe Dragon's Blood, an exudation of *Pterocarpus Draco*, Linn., was once used as a substitute for the true commercial article,* as an astringent in dysentery. Rumph states that the roots of the Molucca *Cæsalpinia Nuga*, Ait., are useful in

---

* Resina Draconis, from *Calamus Draco*, Willd. (Palmæ); another substitute for which was claimed in the exudation of the Canary Island *Dracæna Draco*, Linn. (Liliaceæ).

calculous and kidney complaints. The root of the East Indian Flower Fence (*Poinciana pulcherrima*, Linn.), is claimed by Schomburgh to be an acrid poison, and the leaves and flowers as having been used in decoction as a successful remedy against the fevers of Tortcola; while Macfadyen claims them to be a powerful emmenagogue, even to abortion. Jatahy, the resin of the Jamaica *Hymenæ Courbaril*, Linn., is employed, according to Martius, as a remedy for obstinate coughs and incipient phthisis with hematic sputa; while Gum Animi, from the same species, is employed like a pastile for fumigation in asthma. Lignalœs, a fragrant product of disease in the Cochin-China Eaglewood, *Alœxylon Agallochum*, Lour., is said by Loureiro to be an astringent useful in preventing vomiting and easing diarrhœa; its perfume is also claimed to be useful against paralysis and vertigo. Two astringents—the first acrid and the second diuretic—are found in the West Indian *Mimosa fragifolia*, Linn., and *M. Unguis*, Linn. The Javanese *Euchresta Horsfieldii* is esteemed by the natives as an antidote to poisons of any description. The roots of the North American Turkey pea (*Tephrosia Virginiana*, Pers.) are purgative, and were greatly esteemed by the Aborigines as an anthelmintic; and the roots of the Chinese *Robinia amara* are powerfully bitter and astringent; while *R. flava*, of the same country, is used as a febrifuge. This glance at a few of the medicinal plants of the order shows a general stimulant, tonic, and astringent line of action to prevail.

Many virulent poisons are found in this order, principal among which are: The seeds of the European Bitter Vetch (*Vicia ervilia*, Willd.) are said by M. Virey to be poisonous, and cause a weakness of the limbs when eaten mixed with flour, in bread, and to cause horses to become almost paralytic; Christison claims that flour containing the ground seeds of *Lathyrus Cicera*, Linn., is also poisonous. The roots of the East Indian *Phaseolus radiatus*, Linn., are said by Royle to be a narcotic-poison. The powdered bark of *Robinia maculata* is used in Campeachy as a poison for rodents. The violet seeds of the European *Anagyris fœtida*, Linn., are said to have poisonous properties similar to those of laburnum. The branchlets of the Jamaica *Tephrosia toxicaria*, Pers., are used by the natives to stupefy fish; this poison is said to act immediately, and to somewhat resemble digitalis in its effects. The blue flowers of the West Indian *Sabinea florida*, D.C., are considered poisonous—a property probably due to their indigo.

Many valuable gums are produced either as natural exudations, as a result of insect depredations, or are intimately held in the wood-cells of many species. Principal among them are: the Gum Arabics, derived as follows: Kordofan or White Sennaar Gum, as well as Senegal Gum, are produced by *Acacia Senegal*, Willd.; Suakin or Talha Gum, by *A. stenocarpa*, Hoch., and *A. Seyal*, var. *Fistula*; Morocco or Brown Barbary Gum, supposedly by *A. Arabica*, Willd.; Cape Gum, by *A. horrida*, Willd.; East India Gum, by *A. Arabica* and other species; Australian Gum, by various species, principally *A. pycantha*, Benth.; and Red Gum, by the Senegal *A. Adansonii*, Guill. Gum Sassa is a product of the Abyssinian *Acacia Sassa*, Willd. The Oriental Tragacanth, of varied utility, is produced by *Astragalus gummifer*, Labi.

Among the many food-products, our attention is first called to the beans and pease—the first of which will be found described under Phaseolus vulgaris, page

51, *et seq.;* our common garden pea is derived from *Pisum sativum*, Linn., whose native country is extremely doubtful. The Asiatic Lentil, the seed of *Lens esculenta*, Mœn., is well known as a food; and it was for an indigestible mess of these that Esau is said to have sold his birthright to his brother Jacob. It is the opinion of many writers on Egyptology that the Camel's Thorn (*Alhagi Maurorum*, Tourn), which exudes a sweet substance that may be gathered by merely shaking the branches, was the manna that is said to have nourished the children of Israel while in the wilderness. The unripe seeds of the common European *Lathyrus Aphaca*, while still young and tender, are claimed to be a useful substitute for our garden pease; yet, according to Lindley, they are narcotic when ripe, and if eaten then produce excessive headache; Dutch Mice, the tuberous roots of the same species, are amylaceous, and eaten in Holland. The fruit of the Caspian *Vicia Faba*, Linn., is eaten young, as in the last-mentioned species, but the roots are a narcotic poison. Johannisbrod, so greatly esteemed in Germany, is the pulp of the fruit of the Syrian *Ceratonia Siliqua*, Linn.* The tropical oil, ground, or peanut, the fruit of *Arachis hypogæa*, Linn.—which so strangely ripens under the ground after flowering at some distance above it—furnishes an oil not inferior to that from the olive, which is used largely to adulterate table oils. The fruits are too well known as an article of commerce to need description. The "cake," formed after pressing out the oil from the nuts, is very digestible, and should be more extensively used as a flesh-forming food for cattle.

Among the many food-products of the North American Indians derived from this order we find: the Prairie Potato or Bread-root (*Psoralea esculenta*), greatly esteemed by the Sioux, who use this root extensively under the name of *tip-sinnah*. It is of a sweetish, turnip-like taste, is often cut in thin slices and dried for winter use, and when pulverized forms a light, starchy flour; it is very palatable, however prepared.

Another so-called wild potato, or ground-nut of the Sioux—the true *pomme-de-terre* of the French—is afforded by *Apios tuberosa*, and is largely used as an article of diet.

Bur Clover (*Medicago lupulina*) produces an abundance of seed, much relished by the Indians. The Indian pop-pea, the fruit of several species of the genus *Astragalus*, is highly valued, when boiled, by the Indians of the Western Territories. The Screw bean (*Strombocarpus pubescens*), although insipid until quite dry, is no sooner ripe than it becomes very sweet and palatable, and is considered a superb article of diet by the Indians along the Colorado River, who collect with assiduity all they can store for winter use. When ground it is made into sun-baked bread, like the next. The fruit of the Mesquite (*Prosopsis juliflora*) is an important article of food for many Indian tribes; the pods, with their seeds, are pounded into a coarse meal, mixed into doughy cakes with water, and baked in the sun, after which they keep for long periods. This bread-cake is very sweet and nutritious.†

Many leguminose plants afford excellent dyes, principal among which are indigo and logwood, both of which have been mentioned; further than these we

---

* Johanniskraut is *Hypericum perforatum* (Hypericaceæ), and Johanniswurzel, *Filix Mas* (Filices).
† J. A. Dodge, in *U. S. Agric. Rept.*, 1870, pp. 404–428.

have: The Indian Red Saunders in the wood of *Pterocarpus santalinus*, Linn., valued in India as a red dye for silks and other fabrics; Brazil Wood (*Cæsalpina echinata*, Lam.) affords a red dye; Braziletto Wood, from *C. Braziliensis;* Sappan Wood, from *C. Sappan*, and Camwood, from *Baphia nitida*, are all well-known dyes.

The fibres of the Spanish Broom (*Spartium junceum*), whose seeds are emetic and purgative, are used in Southern Europe for cordage, and also for the manufacture of gunny-bags. The Prayer Bead, the seed of the Indian Liquorice (*Abrus precatorius*, Linn.) is a beautiful little scarlet oval with a black spot. These seeds are used by the Hindoos as a standard of weight called *Rati*, and are celebrated as having been used to determine the value of the great Koh-i-noor diamond; they are also used in the manufacture of rosaries. Valuable timbers, elegant perfumes, fine balsams, brilliant varnishes, and numerous articles of commerce, difficult to classify, are products of this most varied order.

History and Habitat.—Genista is indigenous to Northern Asia and Europe, but has become thoroughly naturalized in eastern New York and lower New England, especially, however, in Essex County, Massachusetts, where it has become an actual pest on dry, sandy hillsides, which it renders positively yellow, in June and July, with its profusion of flowers.

Though once vaunted in Russia as a prophylactic in hydrophobia, this plant has nearly dropped out of medical thought. Its leaves and seeds are mildly purgative, its seeds alone often emetic, and the whole plant sometimes diuretic. Ray says that after cows have browsed upon this plant their milk becomes bitter—a property communicated also to butter and cheese if made from such milk.

As its common names denote, Genista is one of the many leguminose plants yielding dyes. The flowers, and indeed the whole plant, yield a clear, greenish-yellow coloring-matter, that, in conjunction with Woad (*Isatis tinctoria*—Cruciferæ), gave fine results in the dyeing of wool green.

PART USED AND PREPARATION.—The whole plant, while in flower, is chopped and pounded to a pulp and weighed. Then two parts by weight of alcohol are taken, the pulp thoroughly mixed with one-sixth part of it, and the rest of the alcohol added. The whole is then placed in a bottle, tightly corked, and allowed to stand eight days in a dark, cool place.

The tincture, separated from this mass by filtration, has a deep reddish-orange color by transmitted light; a strong herbaceous odor; an astringent taste; and an acid reaction.

CHEMICAL CONSTITUENTS.—No analysis of this species has, so far, resulted in the isolation of its active principle, the general constituents of plants and a volatile oil only being separated.

PHYSIOLOGICAL ACTION.—Our provings of Genista by Dr. E. B. Cushing are the only data obtainable, so far, for the determination of its action. These experiments failed to prove the plant capable of acting as an emetic, purgative, or diuretic; still, they cannot be pronounced as conclusive.

DESCRIPTION OF PLATE 46.

1. A branch, with two flowering branchlets, Salem, Mass., June 25th, 1885.
2. Flower.
3. Elements of the corolla—*a*, standard; *b*, wings; *c*, keel, laid open.
4. Stamens.*
5. Anthers.
6. Calyx, opened.
7. Pistil.
8. Fruit.
9. Seed.
10. Longitudinal section of seed.
11. Horizontal section of same.

(2–7 and 9–11 enlarged.)

* By some inexplicable error, this figure contains 11 stamens, instead of 10, as should be.

Tribe.—*TRIFOLIEÆ.*

GENUS.—**T R I F O L I U M** ,* LINN.

SEX. SYST.—DIADELPHIA DECANDRIA.

47

T R I F O L I U M .

RED CLOVER.

SYN.—TRIFOLIUM PRATENSE, LINN.

COM. NAMES.—COMMON RED CLOVER; (FR.) TRÈFLE; (GER.) ACKER-KLEE.

A TINCTURE OF THE FLOWER-HEADS OF TRIFOLIUM PRATENSE, L.

Description.—This largely-cultivated biennial, or short-lived perennial plant, attains a height of from 1 to 3 feet. The *root* is large, diffusely branched, and gives rise to many stems. *Stems* ascending, stout and slightly hairy. *Stipules* broadly lanceolate, clasping at the base and surmounted by an awl-shaped tip; *leaves* three-foliate, on long petioles; *leaflets* oval or obovate, sometimes retuse or even emarginate, with a nearly entire edge, and marked with a whitish-green Λ-shaped spot on the central portion of the upper surface. *Inflorescence* a dense, ovoid head of bracted, sessile flowers. *Calyx* not distinctly hairy, but having a bearded zone in the throat; *teeth* setiform, the lowermost longer than the others, which are equal. *Corolla* extended-tubular, about twice the length of the calyx, withering soon after expansion; *petals* more or less coherent with one another. *Legumes* dry, scarious, containing each a single seed; *seed* somewhat kidney-shaped.

TRIFOLIUM.—This genus comprises leguminose herbs growing in tufts or diffusely spreading, and characterized as follows: *Leaves* palmately or sometimes pinnately three-foliate, rarely more; *leaflets* usually minutely toothed, rarely entire; *stipules* scarious, coherent with the petioles. *Inflorescence* dense heads or spikes, or sometimes, when the flowers are few, umbellike. *Calyx* persistent, tubular or somewhat bell-shaped, five-cleft or toothed; *teeth* awl shaped. *Corolla* five-cleft, withering or persistent, monopetalous at the base; *vexillum* longer than the alæ, and generally than the keel. *Stamens* rendered more or less diadelphous by the tenth filament, the tube usually free from the corolla; when united with it, it is through the mediumship of the claws of the alæ and keel. *Ovary* two- to six-seeded; *style* filiform. Fruit a small, scarious legume, containing from one to two or sometimes three to six seeds; *dehiscence* none, or, if present, it takes

---

* *Tres*, three; *folium*, a leaf.

place at the suture and extends through the calyx. A description of the natural order may be found under Genista tinctoria, 46.

History and Habitat.—Red clover has become extensively naturalized here since its introduction from Europe, escaping to unused fields, along roadsides, and even to open woods, beautifying all with its close, red, sweet-scented heads, which appear from May to August. As hay, clover is highly valuable, either alone or mixed with succulent grasses. Its nutritive ratio is lower by nearly one-half than that of timothy (*Phleum pratense*), yet ruminants seem to eat of it more greedily and with a fuller sign of satisfaction. Porcher says that, in Ireland, when food is scarce, the powdered flowers are mixed with bread, and esteemed wholesome and nutritious. As a green manure for field fertilization, and an element of importance in rotation of crops it is also greatly prized, on account of its large percentage of potash, lime, and phosphoric acid.

Its former use in medicine has been as a component of a salve, or extract, for all kinds of indolent sores and ulcers, to which it proves peculiarly soothing. A strong infusion is often used in half-ounce doses, to suspend the spasm of whooping-cough.

Trifolium is not officinal either in the U. S. Ph. or Eclectic Materia Medica.

PART USED AND PREPARATION.—The fresh blossoms are pounded to a pulp and weighed. Then two parts by weight of alcohol are taken, the pulp thoroughly mixed with one-sixth part of it and the rest of the alcohol added. After having stirred the whole well, allow it to stand at least eight days in a dark, cool place.

The tincture thus formed, after decanting, straining and filtering, should have a light, clear, orange-brown color by transmitted light, a slightly astringent, hay-like taste, and a decided acid reaction.

CHEMICAL CONSTITUENTS.—The only assay of the flower-heads that I have been able to find is one by Grazel, reported in the *Proceedings of the Cal. Phar. Soc.*, 1883, p, 49. He found, beside the usual constituents of vegetable matter, an acid, an extractive, tannin, and a resinoid principle soluble in ether, giving a green color when dissolved in liquor ammonia, and a yellow color in liquor potassa.

PHYSIOLOGICAL ACTION.—With the exception of the following effects, noted by Dr. T. C. Duncan, little or nothing is known of the action of this plant: Excessive dryness of the throat and fauces, causing a severe, hacking, irritative cough, a feeling of congestion of the lungs, dry, costive passages from the bowels, and a copious flow of pale yellow urine.

DESCRIPTION OF PLATE 47.

1. Upper part of stem, Bergen, N. J., June 13th, 1879.
2. Outline of root.
3. Flower (enlarged).
4. Fruiting-head.
5. Pollen, x 380.

ℭM. ad nat.del.et pinxt.

TRIFÒLIUM PRATÉNSE, Linn.

48

TRIFOLIUM REPENS.

WHITE CLOVER.

SYN.—TRIFOLIUM REPENS, LINN.

COM. NAMES.—WHITE CLOVER; (FR.) TRÈFLE BLANC; (GER.) WIESEN KLEE.

A TINCTURE OF THE FRESH BLOSSOMS OF TRIFOLIUM REPENS, LINN.

Description.—This prostrate perennial herb has no positive size, the *stem* is slender, spreading and creeping, pale and glabrous throughout. *Petioles* very long and slender; *leaflets* obovate, obovate-emarginate or obcordate, the edges very minutely toothed, the caret-shaped grayish spot upon the upper surface pale and indistinct; *stipules* nearly linear-lanceolate, scarious and pointed. *Peduncles* glabrous, longer than the petioles. *Inflorescence* axillary, consisting of small, open, more or less flattened globose heads. *Calyx* much shorter than the corolla; *teeth* shorter than the tube, awl-shaped and of unequal sizes. *Corolla* white, larger in proportion to the size of the head than the preceding. *Fruit* a 4-seeded legume. (Read also the generic description under T. pratense, 47.)

History and Habitat.—This species is doubtless indigenous, at least to the northern portion of America, from which it has spread southward and westward, over fields, roadsides and open woods, blossoming earlier than the preceding, and changing from a creamy-white to a dull-rose and finally a rusty-brown color. As hay the white clover is far inferior to the red, especially in the warmer climates where the cattle refuse to eat of it altogether, probably on account of its action upon the salivary glands.

This species is not mentioned in the U. S. Ph., nor is it spoken of in the Eclectic Materia Medica.

PART USED AND PREPARATION.—The fresh flower-heads prepared as in T. pratense, afford a tincture of a clear chestnut-brown color by transmitted light, of less astringency, greater acidity, and a more penetrating taste.

CHEMICAL CONSTITUENTS.—Although without doubt this species will prove of greater use in medicine than the preceding, I can find no data upon its specific chemistry.

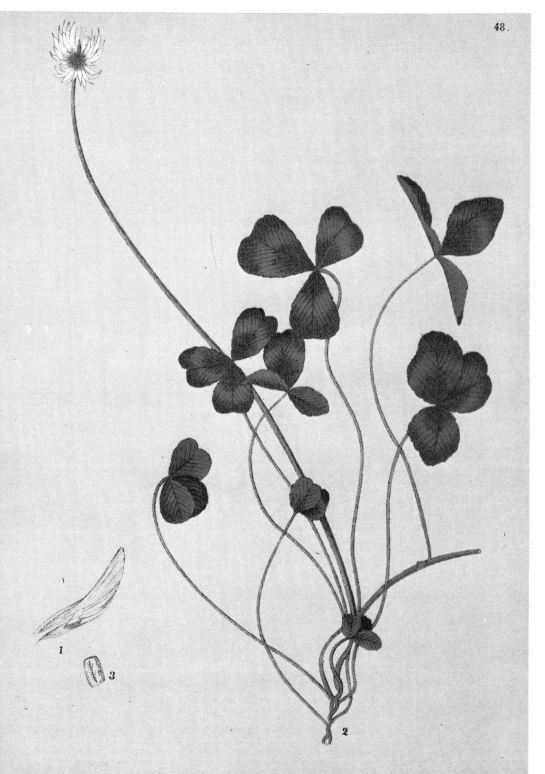

1

3

2

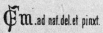

TRIFÒLIUM RÈPENS, Linn.

PHYSIOLOGICAL ACTION.—Dr. T. C. Duncan notes the following symptoms in seven persons who partook of the pounded fresh flower-heads: A sensation of fulness and congestion of the salivary glands, with pain, which in one individual amounted to mump-like pains in the parotids; this was quickly followed in all by a copious flow of saliva. A similar effect has been noted in the south upon all stock that ate of the plant. A further and critical examination into the chemistry and action of this species is greatly to be desired.

DESCRIPTION OF PLATE 48.

1. Flower (enlarged).
2. Whole plant from a stony pasture, Ithaca, N. Y., June 3d, 1880.
3. Pollen x 380.

N. ORD.—LEGUMINOSÆ.

Tribe.—TRIFOLIEÆ.

GENUS.—**MELILOTUS,*** TOURN.

SEX. SYST.—DIADELPHIA DECANDRIA.

49

MELILOTUS.

SWEET CLOVER.

MELILOTUS OFFICINALIS, WILLD.

    SYN.—MELILOTUS VULGARIS, EATON. TRIFOLIUM OFFICINALE, LINN.
    COM. NAMES.—SWEET CLOVER, YELLOW MELILOT, YELLOW SWEET
        CLOVER, MELILOT; (FR.) MELILOT; (GER.) STEINKLEE, MELILO-
        TENKLEE.

MELILOTUS ALBA, LAM.

    SYN.—MELILOTUS LEUCANTHA, KOCH, MELILOTUS OFFICINALIS,
        PURSH, MELILOTUS OFFICINALIS, VAR. ALBA., NUTT.
    COM. NAMES.—SWEET CLOVER, WHITE MELILOT, MELILOT.

A TINCTURE OF THE FRESH FLOWERS OF M. OFFICINALIS, AND M. ALBA.†

Description.—Melilotus officinalis.—This sweet-scented European plant has now become quite thoroughly naturalized here, growing either as an annual or perennial herb. *Stem* with its spreading branches 2 to 4 feet high. *Leaves* alternate, pinnately 3-divided. *Leaflets* obovate-oblong, obtuse, sharply and widely serrate, from one-half to one inch long. *Racemes* axillary, spiked, from 2 to 3 inches long while flowering. *Flowers* small, yellow, about one-quarter of an inch long when fully expanded. *Calyx* persistent, with 5 unequal pointed teeth. *Corolla* more than twice the length of the calyx, deciduous. *Petals: vexillum* ovate, acute, slightly longer than the wings: *alæ* induplicate; *carina* completely united, cohering to, and looking backward between, the alæ, entirely free from the stamen tube. *Stamens* 10, diadelphous, inserted with the corolla; *anthers* uniform; *pollen* grains more or less abruptly cylindrical, resembling Trifolium, but much smaller and more uniform. *Ovary* free, 1-celled, containing 1 or 2 amphitropous ovules; *style* filiform, terminal. *Pod* (legume) about one-sixth of an inch in length, pyriform in the cup of the withered calyx, inflated or gibbous, coriaceous, transversely wrinkled, scarcely dehiscent and tipped with the persistent style.

---

* μελ, *honey,* λωτός, *a leguminose plant, so called.*

† The "Amer. Hom. Phar." orders separate tinctures to be made. The provings were made of a tincture of both M. officinalis and M. alba combined. The German Pharmacopœia recognizes only M. officinalis (Yellow Melilot).

Ɛm. ad nat del. et pinxt.

MELILÒTUS   OFFICINÀLIS , Willd.

Melilotus alba.—This biennial species is taller and more widely branched than the preceding, the flowers are smaller, white, and more densely crowded, the vexillum is comparatively longer and the leaflets mucronate-truncate. For a full description of the Leguminosæ, vide Genista tinctoria, 46.

History and Habitat.—Melilot, especially the white species, is found in many places in the Eastern States and New York, flowering from June to August, and growing in stony, waste places, generally along river-banks, though sometimes in cultivated ground, where it has become naturalized from Europe. Its sweet-scented flowers have been variously used as flavoring for many products. notably Gruyère cheese, snuff and smoking tobacco. In Europe it has been often used in the food of cattle to whet their appetites; it is also claimed that when packed with furs and clothing it protects the articles from moths, besides giving them a pleasant odor before wearing. The odor of Melilot is due to an aromatic compound cumaric anhydride, which when first observed was supposed to be benzoic acid; its identity was proven some years after by Guillemette; it also occurs in faham-leaves, sweet bed-straw (*Gallium triflorum*), tonka-beans (*Dipterix odorata*), sweet woodruff (*Asperula odorata*), and sweet-scented vernal grass (*Anthoxanthum odoratum*).

The flowers of the Melilots have been extensively used by the laity, boiled with lard, as a salve for ulcers, open indolent sores and broken breasts with much success.

Melilotus is neither official in the U. S. Ph., nor the Eclectic Materia Medica.

PART USED AND PREPARATION.—The fresh flowers are pounded to a pulp and weighed. Then two parts by weight of alcohol are taken, the pulp mixed thoroughly with one-sixth part of it and the rest of the alcohol added. After having stirred the whole well and poured it into a well-stoppered bottle, it is allowed to stand eight days in a dark, cool place. The tincture separated by decanting, straining, and filtering, is by transmitted light of a clear, reddish brown color, it has a vanilla-like odor, a bitterish taste very similar to that imparted to the palate by chewing tea-leaves, and a decided acid reaction.

CHEMICAL CONSTITUENTS.—Cumarin, or Cumaric Anhydride, $C_9H_6O_2$, is found combined with either of the acids; it is sparingly soluble in cold water, more freely in alcohol and boiling water, and crystallizes in large transparent, fragrant prisms, melting at 67° (152.6° F.) and boiling at 291° (556.0° F.).

MeliloticAcid, or Hydrocumaric Acid.—$C_9H_{10}O_3$, crystallizes from water in large, pointed prisms, melting at 82° (179.6° F.). On fusing with potash it yields acetic and salicylic acids.

Hydrocumaric Acid.   Potash.   Acetic Acid.   Salicylic Acid.   Potash.

$$C_9H_{10}O_3 + 5HKO = C_2H_4O_2 + C_7H_6O_3 + HKO \; Aq.$$

Cumaric Acid.—$C_9H_8O_3$, occurs together with the preceding; it crystallizes from water in long needles, melting at 195° (383.0° F.). (Schorlemmer).

PHYSIOLOGICAL ACTION.—What slight action Melilotus has upon the system is without doubt due to the principle cumarin, which in quite large doses causes nausea, vomiting, vertigo, and great depression, with sleepiness, confusion, severe pain in the head, depression of the heart's action and cold extremities.

DESCRIPTION OF PLATE 49.

1. A branch from Binghamton, N. Y., July 25, 1882.
2. Flower (enlarged).
3. Pod (enlarged).
4. Seed (enlarged).
5. Pollen x 380.

Tribe.—*GALEGEÆ*.

GENUS.—**ROBINIA**,* LINN.

SEX. SYST.--DIADELPHIA DECANDRIA.

50

ROBINIA.

FALSE ACACIA.

SYN. — ROBINIA PSEUD - ACACIA, LINN.; PSEUDACACIA ODORATA, MOENCH.

COM. NAMES.—COMMON LOCUST, YELLOW LOCUST, TREENAIL, BLACK LOCUST; (FR.) ROBINIER; (GER.) FALSCHE ACACIEN.

A TINCTURE OF THE FRESH BARK OF YOUNG TWIGS, ROBINIA PSEUD-ACACIA.

Description.—This commonly cultivated, ornamental tree, grows to a height of from 50 to 80 feet, attaining its greatest height only in the southern parts of the United States. The *stem* is erect, straight, deliquescent, from 1 to 4 feet in diameter and covered with a dark, rough bark; *wood* yellow, much valued for its lightness, hardness and durability. *Branches* naked, spinous when young, the spines taking the place of stipules. *Leaves* odd-pinnate, the base of the stalks forming sheaths about the developing buds of the next season; *leaflets* in from 8 to 12 pairs of ovate or oblong, stipellate, nearly sessile, smooth blades. *Inflorescence* axillary; of showy, drooping, slender, loose racemes; of white or creamy, fragrant flowers. *Calyx* short, more or less campanulate, five-toothed or cut and slightly two-lipped by the coherence of the two upper teeth. *Corolla* papillionaceous; *standard* large, rounded and reflexed, slightly longer than the *wings*, and obtuse *keel*. *Stamens* diadelphous, nine-and-one. *Style* bearded along the inner side. *Fruit* a nearly sessile, smooth, linear, flat pod, from 2 to 3 inches long, one-celled and four- to eight-seeded, at length with two thin valves. *Seeds* small, dark brown, somewhat renniform, but the hilum is small and so near one end that their form is more like the body of a retort; *testa* smooth; *radicle* incurved; *cotyledons* leafy. For description of the N. Ord. Leguminosæ, *vide* Genista tinctoria, 46.

History and Habitat.—This tree is indigenous to the central and southern belts of the United States, and so fully cultivated in the northern parts, that it now grows there spontaneously, blossoming in May and June. The inner bark of the roots, stem, and inner coating of the pods is sweet and mucilaginous. The seeds, upon pressure, yield a large quantity of oil. They are quite acrid, but lose this quality upon boiling; they then furnish a pleasant, nutritious article of food, much esteemed by the aborigines. The yellow locust should take first rank among ornamental trees to be planted by settlers in the West, not only on

---

* John Robin, herbalist to Henry IV.

account of its beautiful foliage and fragrant flowers (points of great use for shade and honey), but also for its invaluable wood. Locust is well known for its great durability, even when thoroughly exposed, and is thus exceedingly valuable for fence-posts, railroad ties and supports for structures generally.

Robinia is not mentioned in the U. S. Ph. It has a place, but is not officinal, in the Eclectic Materia Medica.

PART USED AND PREPARATION.—The fresh bark of the young twigs is chopped and pounded to a pulp and weighed. Then two parts by weight of alcohol are taken, the pulp mixed thoroughly with one-sixth part of it and the rest of the alcohol added. After having stirred the whole well it is poured into a well-stoppered bottle and allowed to stand eight days in a dark, cool place. The tincture is then separated by straining and filtering. Thus prepared, it has a beautiful, clear, reddish-orange color by transmitted light, a dry, sweetish taste peculiar to the inner bark, and a decided acid reaction.

CHEMICAL CONSTITUENTS.—Robinin, $C_{25}H_{30}O_{16}+Aq.$ This aromatic glucoside bears great resemblance to *quercetin*, yielding as products of decomposition this body, and peculiar sugars. (Schorlemmer.) Robinin is found principally in the flowers; it forms fine, satiny, yellow needles, neutral and tasteless, losing water at 100° (212° F.), and fusing at 195° (383° F.). It is soluble in both water and alcohol.

Robinic acid. This body was discovered in the roots by Reinsch, but afterwards doubted. Prof. Hlasiwetz (*Chem. Gaz.*, Aug. 15, 1855), in his examination of the root, decided that the above body was *Asparagine;* he obtained some two and a half ounces of this substance from thirty pounds of the root. The body answers to the following properties: Large, hard, refractive, octohedral crystals, colorless and constant upon recrystallization, and having a mawkish taste; they fuse when heated, giving off an ammoniacal odor. *Tannin*, and the usual plant constituents, have also been determined.

PHYSIOLOGICAL ACTION.—Robinia causes extreme nausea, profuse acid vomitings, fluid eructations and purging. These symptoms followed eating of the bark. (Dr. A. R. Ball.)

Dr. Shaw (*Med. Times and Gazette*, vol. i., p. 570) gives the following effects noticed in a child who had eaten of the seeds: Inability to hold the head upright, nausea and attempts to vomit, with a tendency to syncope, when in an upright position; voice, respiration and heart's action feeble, as from exhaustion; a painful, paralytic condition of the extremities, which became shrunken on the fifth day. All the symptoms seemed like those produced by a long-continued diarrhœa, though in this case purging was not present.

DESCRIPTION OF PLATE 50.

1. Flower (somewhat enlarged).
2. Stamens.
3. Pistil.
4. Fruit.
5. End of young branch in flower, Ithaca, N. Y., May 24th, 1880.

C.m. ad nat del. et pinxt

ROBÍNIA PSEUDACÀCIA, Linn.

51
PHASEOLUS.

COMMON BEAN.

SYN.—PHASEOLUS VULGARIS, LINN.
COM. NAMES.—KIDNEY BEAN, WHITE BEAN, POLE BEAN, STRING BEAN;
(FR.) HARICOT; (GER.) SCHMINKBOHNE.

A TINCTURE OF THE DRIED SEEDS OF PHASEOLUS VULGARIS, LINN.

Description.—This common cultivated annual herb grows to various heights, according to its form and the method of cultivation. *Stem* twining and twisted, or short and erect in the bushy forms. *Leaves* pinnately trifoliate; *leaflets* large, ovate, pointed, entire. *Inflorescence* in solitary axillary racemes, the peduncle stout and shorter than the leaves. *Calyx* campanulate; *teeth* 5, unequal, the three lower ones larger, cuneate, acute, the two upper merely apparent. *Corolla* papilionaceous; *keel* circinate and somewhat spirally twisted; *vexillum* entire or nearly so, notched at the apex; *alæ* pear-shaped, each furnished with a long claw and short incurved appendage. *Stamens* diadelphous; *filaments* circinate, dilated at the base. *Ovary* stipitate, hairy; *style* long, circinate, with a hairy margin; *stigma* pointed, hairy. *Fruit* a continuous, pendent, compressed, loculicidal, more or less falcate pod, polyspermous, and with cellular partitions between the seeds; *seeds* more or less reniform, cylindrical, or compressed; *hilum* small, oval-oblong, naked; *cotyledons* thick; *radicle* incurved.

History and Habitat.—The Common Bean, so extensively cultivated as an esculent, was formerly supposed to have been introduced here from India, but Prof. Gray claims it a native plant, as the fruit and seeds were found in the tombs of ancient Peruvians at Ançon, along with other purely native vegetables; it is, however, probable that the plant is not indigenous north of Mexico. The Bean has been cultivated by the natives from remote aboriginal times, many varieties having become valuable to them then (as they are to us now) as a potage, both while green, legume and all, and the seeds alone when ripe and dried. No previous medical use is discoverable.

---

* From the Latin *phaselus*, a little boat, the pod being somewhat scaphoid.

PART USED AND PREPARATION.—The ripe dried seeds are pounded to a pulp and macerated for eight days in twice their weight of strong alcohol, being shaken twice a day, and kept in closely-stoppered bottles in a dark, cool place. The tincture, separated from this mass by filtration, has a disgusting fecal odor, a clear but slightly yellowish color, and a neutral reaction.

CHEMICAL CONSTITUENTS.—*Legumin*, or *Vegetable Casein*. This albuminoid, or proteid body, containing both N and S, is found in many seeds of the Leguminosæ, from which it may be separated by triturating them, after soaking in warm water and pressing the pulp through a sieve. The liquid deposits starch on standing, and the casein-like body may be precipitated from the liquor by acetic acid.

Phaseolin.—This peculiar amorphous body is obtained by extracting the seeds with alcohol, and treating the extract with ether to remove the sugar. Phaseolin produces a volatile oil, of very disgusting fecal odor, by decomposition.

Inosite,* or animal galactose, existing in the muscles of the heart and lungs, as well as in the parenchyma of the liver and kidneys, is also found in the seeds of this and other Leguminosæ.

The following analyses of Beans by Einhof† and Braconnot‡ show the general constituents :

	Einhof.	Braconnot.
Skins, ...	288	7.
Starchy fibrous matter, ...	425	
Starch, ...	1380	42.34
Animo-veg. matter and starch, ...	799	5.36
Extractive, ...	131	
Albumen and animo-veg. matter, ...	52	
Mucilage, ...	744	
Loss and water, ...	21	23.
Legumin, ...		18.20
Pectic acid, legumin and starch, ...		1.50
Fatty matter, ...		.70
Pulp skeleton, ...		.70
Uncrystallizable sugar, ...		.20
Earthy salts, ...		1.00
	3840	100.00

PHYSIOLOGICAL ACTION.—The only accounts of the ill effects produced by eating raw beans are those of Dr. Demeures§ and William Dale, Esq.;‖ the latter I exclude here, as the beans were mildewed, and the severity of the symptoms, together with their character, appear to me to be due to the fungus. The symptoms produced in the first case were : Severe frontal headache accompanied by pain, soreness, and itching of the eyeball ; eyeball painful to touch ; pain in the epigastrium when touched, and hernia-like pain at right inguinal ring. Beans,

---

* See p. 95–3.
† *Gehlen's Jour.*, vi, 545.
‡ *Ann. de Chim. et Phys.*, xxxiv, 85.

§ *Jour. de la Société Gall.*, 1 Ser., 4, 112.
‖ *Brit. Med. Jour.*, 1864, 471.

when cooked, produce a well-known flatulency, which symptom I have also noted from a dose of about five drops of the tincture. The seeds certainly deserve a thorough proving, especially so if the symptoms recorded by Dale could be verified.

DESCRIPTION OF PLATE 51.

1. Summit of plant, Binghamton, N. Y., July 27th, 1886.
2. Flower.
3. Calyx and standard.
4. Ala.
5. Keel and calyx.
6. Stamen.
7. Pistil.
8. Stigma.
   (3–8 enlarged.)

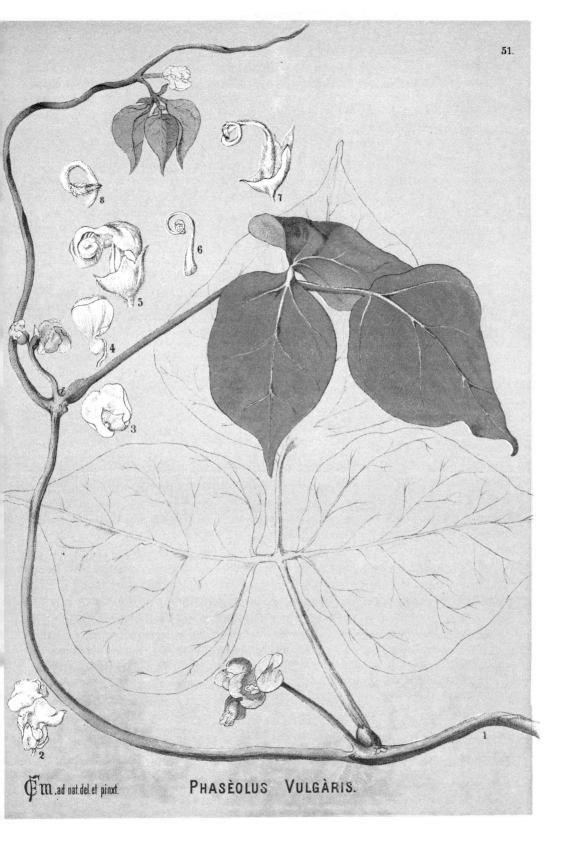

Œm.ad nat.del.et pinxt.

PHASÈOLUS VULGÀRIS.

52

BAPTISIA.

WILD INDIGO.

SYN.—BAPTISIA TINCTORIA, R. BR.; SOPHORA TINCTORIA, LINN.; POD-
ALYRIA TINCTORIA, MICHX.

COM. NAMES.—WILD INDIGO, FALSE INDIGO, INDIGO WEED, YELLOW
WILD INDIGO, DYER'S BAPTISIA, HORSEFLY WEED, RATTLE BUSH,
YELLOW BROOM, CLOVER BROOM; (FR.) INDIGO SAUVAGE, INDIGO
TREFLE; (GER.) BAPTISIE.

A TINCTURE OF THE FRESH ROOT OF BAPTISIA TINCTORIA, R.BR.

Description.—This slender, glaucous, perennial, bushy-branching herb, grows
to a height of from 2 to 3 feet. *Root* large, irregular, ligneous, light yellowish-
brown internally, blackish externally; *rootlets* numerous and lighter in color.
Leaves palmately 3-foliate, sessile or nearly so, becoming like all other portions of
the plant—even the yellow flowers—black, when dry; *leaflets* ½ to ¾ inch long,
rounded or cuneate-obovate, dark bluish-green with a light green stripe on the
midrib; *stipules* and *bracts* minute, caducous. *Inflorescence* short, loose, few-
flowered racemes, terminal upon the branches; *flowers* canary-yellow, about as
long as the leaflets. *Calyx* cup-shaped; *limb* 4-toothed, the upper tooth double,
therefore broader than the rest. *Corolla : standard* about the length of the wings,
or slightly shorter, emarginate, and reflexed laterally; *keel* somewhat incurved,
the two petals composing it nearly separate, straight; *wings* oblong, straight.
Stamens 10, distinct; *anthers* alike and uniform. *Ovary* stipitate; *style* curved,
dilated below; *stigma* minute. *Fruit* an oval, centrally inflated, mucronate legume,
stalked in the persistent cup of the calyx; *stipe* nearly twice the length of the
calyx-cup. *Seeds* many, ovoid, cinnamon-brown; *hilum* small, rounded; *embryo*
straight or incurved. Read description of Leguminosæ under Genista tinctoria,
46.

History and Habitat.—Wild Indigo is indigenous to the Canadas and the
United States. It grows as far south as Florida and west to the Mississippi,
plentifully however only near the coast, where it delights in the dry, sandy soils.

---

* βαπτίζω, *Baptizo*, I dye.   Some species yielding an inferior indigo dye.

52.

ℭℳ.ad nat.del.et pinxt.

BAPTÍSIA TINCTÒRIA, R.Br.

As regards New York State : I have noted in traveling upon the N. Y. & Erie R. R., that it ceased entirely at Narrowsburg, 122 miles from New York City.* I have not met with the plant in Chenango, Broome, Tioga nor Tompkins Counties, and Dr. Lucy fails to find it in Chemung ; this is probably due to the rich loam of these localities. Dr. Barton says:† "It promiscuously inhabits a variety of situations, though almost always in a dry soil, in every State of the Union." It flowers in the Northern States from June to August.

The young shoots of this plant resemble, in form and general appearance, those of asparagus, and are used, especially in New England, in lieu of that herb for a pottage. As a dye, it is no longer used, being far inferior to Indigofera and its employment unnecessary.

The most important previous use of the plant as a drug, was as an "antiseptic" dressing for gangrenous wounds, especially in such cases as were accompanied by a low form of fever ; and in decoction in putrid fevers generally. Dr. Thatcher says:‡ "its employment has been extended in a few instances to Typhus or putrid fever, with such good effect as to encourage further trials. In the form of fomentation or cataplasm it has proved eminently beneficial when applied to phagedenic and gangrenous ulcers ; *especially if the decoction be administered internally at the same time*" (italics ours). Dr. Comstock says :§ "I would observe that it is used in cases of mortification, in fevers supposed to be putrid, and inclining to putrescency, and in general where antiseptics are indicated." Our provings thoroughly corroborate, and our practice substantiates the above use of the drug. Any physician, of whatever school of practice, who fails to use this remedy in Typhoid alone where it is so often indicated, allows many an opportunity to save a life to escape him. The National Dispensatory|| contains under this drug the following, written, we feel compelled to say, in willful ignorance : "Nothing has recently been added to the knowledge possessed many years ago respecting this medicinal plant." The U. S. Pharmacopœia gives no officinal preparation ; this in the full light of our excellent success with the drug, and our vastly lower percentage of death in Typhoid.

The preparations of the Eclectic Materia Medica are : *Extractum Baptisiæ Alcoholicum ; Unguentum Baptisiæ, and Pilulæ Baptisiæ Compositæ.*¶

PART USED AND PREPARATION.—The fresh root with its bark is chopped and pounded to a pulp and weighed. Then two parts by weight of alcohol are taken, the pulp mixed thoroughly with one-sixth part of it and the rest of the alcohol added. After stirring the whole well, it is poured into a well-stoppered bottle and allowed to stand eight days in a dark, cool place.

The tincture separated from this mass by filtration is opaque, in thin layers it presents a deep brownish-red color by transmitted light ; it has no distinguishing

---

* Author in *Bull. Torrey Club*, vol. xi, 1884, p. 133.
† *Veg. Mat. Med.*, vol. ii, p. 56.
‡ *Thatcher's Dispensatory*, p. 361, quoted in Barton's *Veg. Mat. Med.*, pp. 58–59, vol. ii.
§ "Letter to Mr. Weems," in *Veg. Mat. Med.* Barton, vol. ii, p. 58.
|| 1879, p. 267.
¶ Leptandria, Podophyllin, Sanguinaria and Baptisia.

odor, a peculiar bitter and astringent taste, imparts to the tongue on first application a cold sensation quite similar to that of sulphate of soda (Glauber's Salt). and has an acid reaction.

CHEMICAL CONSTITUENTS.—An analysis of the root was made by Dr. Greene,* U. S. N., for the express purpose of obtaining the alkaloid, the previous analyses by Smedley,† and Warner,‡ resulting in alkaloidal salts only. Dr. Greene succeeded in obtaining pale yellow crystals of various forms, some being perfect octahedra. This purified alkaloid was found to be soluble in water, alcohol, and ether, other physical and chemical properties are as yet unknown. A whitish yellow resin was also determined in his analysis, whether or not it is the same as one isolated by Smedley is not stated.

PHYSIOLOGICAL ACTION.—The symptoms of disturbance in the system following the ingestion of doses varying from 1 to 200 drops of the tincture of the root, 30 grs. of the powder, and 4 to 14 grs. of "Baptisin" in different individuals are marked, and correspond to those of Typhoid or disintegrating forms of fever. They are substantially as follows:§ mentally gloomy, low-spirited, indisposed to think followed by inability, dullness, and stupidity. Vertigo. Dull, heavy headache with weakness and weariness of body, and tendency to delirium. Soreness and lameness of the eyeballs, with hot, flushed face. Tongue coated white, yellow or yellowish-brown. Loss of appetite, nausea, and burning in the stomach. Dull pains in the region of the liver, especially at the site of the gall-bladder. Face sallow, with burning cheeks. Constant pain and aching in the abdomen, followed by marked distention, and soreness on pressure. Soft, dark, mucous stools, followed by constipation. Urine dark red. Difficult breathing with oppression of the chest. Pulse at first accelerated and full, then low and faint. Aching, stiffness, and soreness of back and extremities. Chills general, followed by fever, restlessness, weakness and great prostration. No sweat.

Dr. Hughes says:‖ "Baptisia is capable of exciting true primary *pyrexia* in the human subject. This is no slight thing, for there are very few other drugs to which we can ascribe such power. And this pyrexia is exceedingly like that of the early stages of Typhoid. We have no evidence that Baptisia affects Peyer's patches as they are affected in Typhoid, nor even that it acts upon them at all as Arsenic and Iodine, and perhaps Mercury and Turpentine do. But it is certain that it produces congestion and catarrh of the intestinal mucous membrane with abdominal tenderness, distention, and diarrhœa." Still, as the specific condition of inflammation of the patches of Peyer does not appear until the second or perhaps third stage, our remedy properly used has done its work ere this and is not then required, nor will any other be, such condition not following, having been thwarted.

* *Am. Jour. Phar.*, 1879, p. 577.
† *Idem*, 1862, p. 310.
‡ *Idem*, 1871, p. 251.
§ Allen, *Ency. Pure Mat. Med.*, vol. ii, pp. 31–39.
‖ *Pharmacodynamics*, p. 162.

The only post-mortem examination that has come to my notice is that of a cat under Dr. Burt's experiments. In this animal the large and small intestines were found greatly congested, and filled with mucus and blood.

DESCRIPTION OF PLATE 52.

1. End of flowering branch, Pamrapo, N. J., July 6th, 1879.
2. Flower.
3. Pistil.
4. Stamen.
5. Pollen, x 250.
6. Pod.

(3 and 4 enlarged.)

S. ORD.—CÆSALPINIEÆ.
GENUS.—**GYMNOCLADUS,*** LAM.
SEX. SYST.—DIŒCIA DECANDRIA.

53
GYMNOCLADUS.

COFFEE TREE.

SYN.—GYMNOCLADUS CANADENSIS, LAM.; GUILANDICA DIOICA, LINN.
COM. NAMES.—KENTUCKY COFFEE TREE, AMERICAN COFFEE BEAN,
KENTUCKY MAHOGANY, NICKAR TREE, BONDUE, CHICOT.

A TINCTURE OF THE FRESH FRUIT PULP OF GYMNOCLADUS
CANADENSIS, LAM.

Description.—This peculiar tree, when mature, reaches a height of from 50 to 60 feet. *Trunk* erect; *bark* extremely rough, and curiously broken transversely; *branches* few, thornless, when young cane-like, and in winter so destitute of anything looking like a bud that the whole tree appears as if dead. *Leaves* bi-pinnate, 2 to 3 feet long, bearing a pair of opposite leaflets near the base, and from 4 to 7 larger, odd-pinnate accessory leaf-stalks, each of which (upon the younger branches) is composed of from 6 to 8 pairs of leaflets, so that each leaf may bear from forty-eight to one hundred and seventy-four leaflets. These leaves develop late and fall early. *Leaflets* alternate, vertical, ovate-lanceolate, taper-pointed and entire, the lower pair upon the base of the petiole almost cordate, larger and more pointed; *stipules* none. *Inflorescence* terminal compound racemes or thyrsi; *flowers* diœcious, pedicillate; *æstivation* imbricate. *Calyx* elongated-tubular below; *limb* 5-cleft; *lobes* lanceolate, equal. *Corolla* not papilionaceous; *petals* oblong, equal, inserted upon the summit of the calyx-tube. *Stamens* 10, included, inserted with the petals; *filaments* distinct, short, and bearded; *anthers* sagittate, versatile, introrse, 2-celled, opening longitudinally. *Style* single. *Ovules* anatropous. *Fruit* an oblong, flattened pod, 6 to 10 inches long and about 1 inch broad, pulpy inside; *seeds* 2 to 4, flattish, hard, somewhat ovoid, about one-half an inch broad, and of a dark olive color; *embryo* straight.

History and Habitat.—The Kentucky Coffee Tree grows in rich woods, along rivers and lakes, from Western New York and Pennsylvania, to Illinois and south-westward, where it flowers in June.

The previous uses of this plant in medicine are grounded upon its peculiar action on nerve-centres. A decoction of the leaves and fruit pulp has been found useful in locomotor ataxia, reflex troubles incident upon masturbation, laryngeal

---

* Γημνός, *gymnos*, naked; κλάδος, *klados*, branch, from the barren and dead appearance of the tree in winter.

coughs dependent upon a chronic irritation of the mucous membranes of the air-passages, puerperal peritonitis, erysipelas, and typhoid forms of fever. To the arts it furnishes a hard wood, something like mahogany, with a fine grain, suitable for cabinet-work; it weighs 40 lbs. 7 oz. per cubic foot, and has a sp. gr. of 647. The seeds are said to have been used by the early settlers of Central United States as a substitute for coffee, and the leaves as a purgative and insecticide. Concerning the use of Gymnocladus as a fly-poison, a Virginia correspondent of *The American Agriculturist* says: "Back of our house here, and overhanging the piazza, is a very large coffee-tree. Though this locality is infested, like Egypt, with a plague of flies, we have never suffered any serious annoyance from them. One year this tree was nearly stripped of its leaves by a cloud of potato-flies (the blistering fly), and we feared that the tree would die from the complete defoliation. In three days the ground beneath was black with a carpet of corpses, and the tree put out new leaves, and still flourishes. For ten years we have used the bruised leaves, sprinkled with molasses water, as a fly-poison. It attracts swarms of the noisome insects, and is sure death to them."

Gymnocladus is official in none of the Pharmacopœias.

PART USED AND PREPARATION.—The fresh, green pulp of the unripe seed-pods is to be crushed and prepared as in the preceding drug. The tincture, after filtering from the mass, has a clear orange color by transmitted light; is gummy upon the fingers; and of a familiarly characteristic odor, resembling that of the pulp.

CHEMICAL CONSTITUENTS.—*Cytisine*, $C_{24}H_{27}N_3O$. This alkaloid, found in the seeds of *Cytisus Laburnum*, is said to exist also in the leaves and fruit pulp of this tree. Extracted from Laburnum, it crystallizes in radiate, colorless, deliquescent forms, having a caustic and bitter taste, and an alkaline reaction, neutralizing acids completely. It sublimes without decomposition by the careful application of heat.

PHYSIOLOGICAL ACTION.—Gymnocladus causes vertigo with a sensation of fullness of the head; burning of the eyes; sneezing; salivation; nausea with burning of the stomach; desire to urinate; increased sexual desire; pains in the limbs, numbness of the body, sleepiness, and coldness.

DESCRIPTION OF PLATE 53.

1. End of a sterile branch, Ithaca, N. Y., June 17th, 1885.
   2. A small leaf, four times reduced.
   3 and 4. Sterile flowers.
   5. Sterile flower in section.
   6 and 7. Stamens, posterior and lateral views.
   (5, 6 and 7 enlarged.)

Em.ad nat.del.et pinxt.

GYMNÓCLADUS CANADÉNSIS, Lam.

GENUS.—**GEUM**,* LINN.

SEX. SYST.—ICOSANDRIA POLYGYNIA.

54
GEUM RIVALE.

WATER AVENS.

SYN.—GEUM RIVALE, LINN.

COM. NAMES.—PURPLE OR WATER AVENS, CHOCOLATE-ROOT; (FR.) BENOITE AQUATIQUE; (GER.) SUMPFNELKENWURZEL.

A TINCTURE OF THE WHOLE PLANT, GEUM RIVALE, LINN.

Description.—This beautiful perennial plant, distinguished on account of its hibiscus-like petals, grows to a height of from one to two feet. *Root* creeping, ligneous, giving off numerous fibrous rootlets. *Stem* simple or nearly so, hairy. *Leaves* of two kinds; those from the root on long deeply grooved petioles, lyrate and irregularly pinnate; those of the stem few, nearly sessile, more or less lyrate below and 3-lobed above, serrate, pointed; *stipules* ovate, incised. *Inflorescence* terminal on long, sometimes branched, peduncles; *flowers* few, large and handsome, nodding on bracted pedicels. *Calyx* erect, concave below, 5-lobed, with 5 alternating bractlets in the sinuses. *Petals* 5, erect, retuse, dilated obovate, contracted into a claw at the base. *Stamens* numerous, inserted into a stipitate disk in the cup of the calyx; *anthers* introrse, opening by a longitudinal slit or pore. *Pistils* many; *ovary* hairy; *styles* long, with flexed tips. *Fruit* a dense, hairy, conical head, situated upon an erect stalk arising from the cup of the calyx; *seeds* oval, bearded, the epicarp retaining the persistent style, which is now hispid below and plumose above the angular flexion of the style.

Rosaceæ.—This grand natural order is represented in North America by 35 genera, 213 species, and 92 varieties, aside from innumerable cultivated specimens. The general characters of the order are: Plants consisting of trees, shrubs and herbs, and furnishing our most valuable fruits. *Leaves* alternate; *stipules* generally present though sometimes early deciduous. *Flowers* regular, handsome. *Calyx* of 5 to 8 sepals united to form the calyx-tube; in some species with a second set as bractlets, outside of, and alternate with, the sepals. *Petals* as many as the sepals, and inserted with the stamens upon a thin disk that lines the calyx-tube. *Stamens* very numerous, perigynous; *filaments* slender. *Pistils* one or many,

---

* Γευω, *geuo ;* a pleasant flavor, one of the species having aromatic roots.

either distinct in or upon a receptacle, or combined in the calyx-tube. *Fruit* either an achenium, a follicle, a drupe, or a pome. *Seeds* single, or a few in each ovary; *albumen* wanting; *cotyledons* large and thick; *embryo* straight. Beside the useful and edible fruits—almonds, peaches, prunes, plums, and cherries (*Amygdaleæ*); crab-apples, apples, quinces, pears, etc. (*Pomeæ*); and strawberries, raspberries, thimble-berries, and blackberries (*Rosaceæ*);—we have many useful medicinal plants among the species in this order. Bitter almonds (*Amygdalus communis*, L., 1 *var. amara*, *DC.*); sweet almonds (*Amygdalus communis*, L., 2 *var. dulcis*, *DC.*); wild cherry bark (*Prunus Virginiana*, *Miller*); cherry-laurel (*Prunus Lauro-cerasus*, L.); kousso (*Brayera anthelmintica*, *Kunth.*); peaches (*Amygdalus Persica*, *Prunus Persica*); and the three mentioned in this work. The genera *Potentilla*, *Spirea*, and *Gillenia*, will in time also be proven to be of benefit in the treatment of disease.

History and Habitat.—This indigenous inhabitant of bogs and springy meadows, grows from the New England States and Pennsylvania westward to Wisconsin and northward, flowering in May. Geum at one time gained great renown as " Indian Chocolate;" it was given in decoction prepared with sugar and milk, for dysentery, chronic diarrhœa, colics, debility, dyspepsia, and most ailments of the digestive tract; it was also used as a styptic in uterine hemorrhage, leucorrhœa, and hemoptysis, and as a febrifuge. (Rafinesque.)

Though Geum has been dismissed from the U. S. Ph., it still retains a place in the Eclectic Materia Medica.

PART USED AND PREPARATION.—The whole plant, gathered before blossoming in the spring, is chopped and pounded to a pulp and weighed. Then two parts by weight of alcohol are taken, the pulp mixed thoroughly with one-sixth part of it, and the rest of the alcohol added. After having stirred the whole well, pour it into a well-stoppered bottle, and let it stand eight days in a dark, cool place. The tincture, separated by straining and filtering, should have a deep orange-brown color by transmitted light, a slightly astringent taste, and an acid reaction.

CHEMICAL CONSTITUENTS.—An analysis of Avens by Buchner, proves it to be very similar to the European *Geum urbanum;* which, botanically, differs but slightly from the species under consideration. All the qualities of both species are given up freely to both water and alcohol.

Volatile Oil of Geum.—A greenish-yellow, acid, butyraceous oil, having an odor like cloves. This body may be readily obtained by distillation of the roots in water. (Wittstein.)

The Water Avens contains also a resin, an acid, bitter extractive, tannin, gum, and other general plant constituents.

PHYSIOLOGICAL ACTION.—The action of this species has not yet been determined.   A short proving by the late Dr. Herring gave as symptoms : severe jerking, tearing pains, like electric shocks, shooting from deep within the abdomen to the end of the urethra, coming on after eating.

DESCRIPTION OF PLATE 54.

1. Part of flowering and fruiting plant, from Lowmansville, N. Y., May 30th, 1884.
    2. Root leaf.
    3. Sepal, showing bracts.
    4. Petal.
    5. Stamen (enlarged), outer view.
    6. Stamen (enlarged), inner view, with open cell.
    7. Achenium (enlarged).

54.

Cm. _ad nat. del. et pinxt.

GÈUM RIVÀLE, Linn.

55

FRAGARIA.

WILD STRAWBERRY.

SYN.—FRAGARIA VESCA, LINN.

COM. NAMES.—WILD, FIELD,† OR WOOD STRAWBERRY ; (FR.) LE FRAI-
SIER ; (GER.) ERDBEERE.

A TINCTURE OF THE FRESH RIPE FRUIT OF FRAGARIA VESCA, LINN.

Description.—*Root* perennial, horizontal, knotty ; *stolons* creeping along the
ground and rooting at the end, sending therefrom young plants, following in due
time the same process ; *stem* none. *Leaves* mostly radical, ternately compound,
hairy ; *stipules* adherent to the base of the petioles of the radical leaves ; *leaflets*
sessile or nearly so, cuneate-obovate, coarsely serrate, and so strongly veined as
to appear plicate ; *petioles* much longer than the leaves. *Inflorescence* loose leafy
cymes, upon long naked scapes ; *leaves* of the cymes small ; *stipules* lanceolate-
oblong, acute ; *pedicels* erect or drooping ; *flowers* white. *Calyx* concave at the
base and furnished with 5 intermediate bracteoles alternate with its lobes ; the
whole remaining spread or reflexed in fruit ; *lobes* acute. *Petals* 5, obtuse, somewhat crenate edged. *Stamens* small, indefinite. *Styles* deeply lateral. *Fruit* consisting of the greatly enlarged and now pulpy and scarlet globular receptacle ;
achenia dry, scattered upon the surface of the fruit, not sunk in pits.

History and Habitat.—The Wild Strawberry grows on dry and rocky banks,
where it is common throughout the North Temperate Zone in Europe, Asia, and
America. With us it is thoroughly indigenous North, flowering in May and June
and fruiting in July and August. This species, together with *F. Virginica*—which
is more common, grows in richer soil, and has the achenia sunk in pits upon the
surface of the receptacle—form our delicious wild strawberries. The other North
American species of Fragaria are *F. Virginica var. Illinœnsis*, Gray, supposed to
be the original of the "Boston Pine" and "Hovey's Seedling ;" and *var. glauca*,
Watson ; *F. Californica*, C.&S. ; *F. Chilensis*, Duch. ; and *var. Scouleri*, Hook ;
and *F. Indica*, Andr., an adventive form. The *F. Virginica*, Ehr., is supposed to

---

* From the Latin *fragrans*, odorous, on account of the aroma of the fruit.
† More properly applicable to the *F. Virginica.*

be the original of the beautiful scarlet Virginia strawberry. Rafinesque judged that about one hundred varieties existed, but contented himself with naming only seven of F. vesca, of which, however, none are recognized by botanists to-day.

The previous medical uses of Fragaria were few; the berries were ordered to be freely eaten of in various calcareous disorders. Many early writers considered the fruit as beneficial in gouty affections; Linnaeus extols their efficacy in preventing paroxysms of gout in his own case; and Rosseau claims that he was always relieved of a calcareous affliction by eating freely of them. The root in infusion has been used in England for dysuria and gonorrhœa. The dried leaves (Strawberry Tea) yield a slightly astringent infusion used in domestic practice as an excitant, and as an astringent in diarrhœa and dysentery.

PART USED AND PREPARATION.—The fresh, ripe berries, dealt with as in the preceding drug, yield an opaque tincture, having, when in thin layers, a deep brownish-carmine color by transmitted light. This tincture has a very astringent, somewhat vinous taste, the odor of the berries, and a strong acid reaction.

CHEMICAL CONSTITUENTS.—The fruit contains cisso-tanic,* malic, and citric acids; sugar, mucilage, and a peculiar volatile aromatic body uninvestigated.

PHYSIOLOGICAL ACTION.—It is a patent fact that many people with delicate stomach find it almost impossible to eat strawberries and cream—especially early in the season—without suffering from symptoms of disordered digestion; the symptoms often culminating in quite severe attacks. A case in my practice several years ago, while a small-pox scare was prevalent in this city, gave nearly all the symptoms of the toxic effect of the fruit. A young lady, closely veiled, called hastily upon me early one morning, and when seated, withdrew her veil, and in a frightened manner desired to know if she had small-pox. Her face was swollen, bluish-red, and covered with a fine petechial eruption, which she said covered her whole body, but especially her face and trunk. She complained of feeling at times somewhat faint, slightly nauseated, and generally swollen, but especially in the epigastric region and abdomen; her speech was somewhat difficult, and examination showed a swollen tongue. I laughingly ventured asking her—although it was winter—where she had found strawberries, whereupon she asked me, in astonishment, how I knew she had been eating the fruit, adding that a friend in Florida sent her about two quarts, among other fruit, and that she and a lady friend had eaten them all the night before, on retiring. As the symptoms had apparently reached their height, I told her the cause, and advised that she eat nothing for twenty-four hours, giving no remedy, that I might watch the pure symptoms. In the afternoon of the same day the skin was hot and swollen, the patient thirsty and restless, and little sleep was gained that night; the next day the eruption began to fade, the appetite returned, and restlessness ceased. On the third day exfoliation

---

* See under *Ampelopsis quinquefolia*, p. 40-2.

began and was very profuse, the skin appearing quite similar to the condition existing after a severe attack of scarlatina. The young lady who shared her fruit exhibited no symptoms whatever.

DESCRIPTION OF PLATE 55.

1. Whole plant, from Ithaca, N. Y., May 8th, 1880.
2. A flower.
3. Stamen.
(2 and 3 enlarged.)

Œm.ad nat.del.et pinxt.

FRAGÀRIA VÉSCA, Linn.

56

PIRUS.

AMERICAN MOUNTAIN ASH.

SYN.—PIRUS (PYRUS) AMERICANA, D. C.; P. ACUPARIA, MEYER; SORBUS
AMERICANA, WILLD.; S. ACUPARIA, VAR. AMERICANA, MICHX.; S.
HUMIFUSA, RAF.

COM. NAMES.—AMERICAN MOUNTAIN ASH, AMERICAN SERVICE TREE;
(FR.) SORBIS; (GER.) VOGELBEEREN.

A TINCTURE OF THE FRESH BARK OF PIRUS AMERICANA, D. C.

Description.—This nearly smooth tree grows to a height of from 10 to 35
feet. *Bark* somewhat resembling the cherry. *Leaf-buds* pointed, glabrous and
glutinous; *leaves* compound, odd-pinnate; *leaflets* 13 to 15, lanceolate, taper-
pointed, sharply serrate with pointed teeth, bright and shining green above, not
pale below; *teeth* mucronate. *Inflorescence* in large, flattish, compound, terminal
cymes. *Calyx* with an urn-shaped tube; *limb* 5-cleft. *Petals* roundish obovate.
Stamens numerous. *Styles* 3, separate. *Fruit* a bright-scarlet, globose, baccate
pome about the size of a pea; *seeds* two in each cell; *testa* cartilaginous.

History and Habitat.—This beautiful mountain tree is indigenous from Maine
to Pennsylvania, westward to Michigan, and southward along the Alleghany
Mountains. In the north it also habits swampy spots, and flowers in June. The
large clusters of brilliant red berries of this species and the *P. acuparia* of Europe,
which hang long after the leaves have fallen, make the trees fine lawn ornaments.

The close botanical and chemical relation of the American and European
species render them so closely allied that many botanists consider them identical,
and the chemistry of the bark, so far as distinguished, is so much like that of the
wild cherry (*Cerasus serotina*, D. C.) that its medical uses have been substitutive.

The previous use of the bark in medicine has been as a tonic in fevers of

---

* The classical name of the Pear tree.

supposed malarial types, where it was often substituted for cinchona. The berries were used as an antiscorbutic.

PART USED AND PREPARATION.—The fresh bark is chopped and pounded to a pulp and weighed. Then two parts by weight of alcohol are taken, the pulp thoroughly mixed with one-sixth part of it, and the rest of the alcohol added. After stirring the whole well, it is poured into a well-stoppered bottle and allowed to stand eight days in a dark, cool place.

The tincture, separated from the above mass by filtration, has a reddish-brown color by transmitted light, a bitter taste, and an acid reaction.

CHEMICAL CONSTITUENTS.—So far as I am able to ascertain, no analysis of the bark of this species has been made to determine its specific principles; a glance, however, at the chemistry of the European species may be of benefit.

Sorbus (Pirus) acuparia.

Amygdalin, $C_{20}H_{27}NO_{11}$.—This glucoside occurs in the bark, buds, flowers and kernels of many rosaceous plants; it separates as pearly scales, which crystallize from water as transparent prisms, having the formula $C_{20}H_{27}NO_{11}(H_2O)_3$. Amygdalin loses its water of crystallization at 120° (248° F.), liquefies at 200° (392° F.), and caramelizes and decomposes at higher temperatures; it is soluble in water and alcohol, but not in ether. Under the action of dilute acids it splits up as follows:

$$\underset{\text{Amygdalin.}}{C_{20}H_{27}NO_{11}} + \underset{\text{Water.}}{(H_2O)_2} = \underset{\substack{\text{Hydrocyanic}\\\text{Acid.}}}{CNH} + \underset{\substack{\text{Benzaldehyde}\\\text{or Oil of}\\\text{Bitter Almonds.}}}{C_7H_6O} + \underset{\text{Glucose.}}{(C_6H_{12}O_6)_2}.$$

Sorbin, $C_6H_{12}O_6$, is the glucose found in the berries; it forms in large, sweet crystals, which melt at 110° (230° F.).

Sorbic and Parasorbic Acid, $C_6H_8O_2$, two isomeric acids of the acrylic group, are also found in the berries of this species.

Citric Acid, $C_6H_8O_7$.—This widely-distributed body occurs, together with malic acid, in the fruits of both species. Citric acid crystallizes in rectorhombic, glassy forms, readily soluble in water, alcohol and ether, and having a pure and pleasant acid taste. These crystals become white when exposed to the air, lose two molecules of water at 100° (212° F.), fuse at 150° (302° F.), and decompose with a specific empyreumatic odor at higher temperatures.

Malic Acid, $C_4H_6O_5$.—This acid is found in the berries as they begin to ripen. It is obtained from its aqueous solution in small, colorless, deliquescent prisms, having a strong but pleasant acid taste.

PHYSIOLOGICAL ACTION.—The tincture produced, in Dr. Gatchell and others under his observation,* a set of symptoms showing an irritation of the

* *Am. Hom. Obs.*, 1878, p. 520.

alimentary mucous membranes, and reflex nervous irritation. It also caused arthritic disturbances and symptoms of chill, heat, and perspiration.

DESCRIPTION OF PLATE 56.

1. A portion of a cyme, Binghamton, May 28th, 1885.
2. A flower, showing perianth.
3. A pistil.
4. Stamens.
5. Two leaflets.
6. A branch in fruit.
7. Section of fruit.
(3, 4 and 7 enlarged.)

Cm.ad nat.del.et pinxt.

PÌRUS AMERICÀNA, DC.

GENUS.—**PENTHORUM**,* GRONOV.

SEX. SYST.—DECANDRIA PENTAGYNIA.

57
PENTHORUM.

DITCH STONE CROP.

SYN.—PENTHORUM SEDOIDES, LINN.
COM. NAMES.—DITCH OR VIRGINIA STONE CROP.

A TINCTURE OF THE WHOLE PLANT PENTHORUM SEDOIDES, LINN.

Description.—This homely perennial grows to a height of from 8 to 12 inches. *Stem* erect, somewhat angled, simple or somewhat branched; *leaves* scattered, nearly sessile, lanceolate, acute at both ends, and sharply serrate. *Inflorescence* a loose terminal cyme of revolute spikes; *flowers* yellowish-green, arranged along the upper surface of the branches of the cyme; *pedicels* glandularly pubescent. *Calyx* pubescent below; *sepals* 5, cuneate, acute. *Petals* rarely present. *Stamens* 10; *filaments* smooth; *anthers* 2-celled, opening longitudinally. *Pistils* 5, united below; *styles* short, forming beaks in fruit; *stigmas* small, capitate. *Fruit* a 5-angled, -horned, and -celled capsule, opening by the falling off of the beaks; *carpels* many seeded; *seeds* ellipitical, pointed.

Crassulaceæ.—This family of mostly succulent herbs is represented in North America by 6 genera, 47 species, and 2 varieties. *Leaves* mostly sessile; *stipules* none. *Inflorescence* cymose or racemose; *flowers* perfectly symmetrical. *Calyx* mostly monosepalous and free from the ovaries; *sepals* 3 to 20, persistent, and united at the base. *Corolla* sometimes monopetalous, sometimes wanting; *petals* if present imbricated in the bud and inserted with the stamens. *Stamens* distinct, equal to, or twice as many as, the sepals, inserted upon the base of the calyx. *Pistils* distinct (exc. Penthorum), minutely scaled at the base. *Fruit* a cluster of follicles opening along the inner suture (exc. Penthorum). *Seeds* numerous, anatropous; *embryo* straight; albumen thin.

This order yields but few medicinal plants, and those of little prominence. The common European Houseleek (*Sempervivum tectorum,* Linn.), whose leaves are cooling and astringent; the Orpine (*Sedum Telephium,* Linn.), whose leaves, boiled with milk, have been used by the laity as a remedy in diarrhœa; and the Stone Crop (*S. acre,* Linn.)—whose apparently dechlorophylled leaves make a fitting cover for the old ruins which afford the plant a habitat throughout Europe—is acrid, and has been recommended in cancerous troubles and epilepsy.—(*Doctrine of Signatures?*)

---

* Πέντε, *pente,* five; ὄρος, *oros,* a rule; from the floral symmetry.

Œ.m. . ad nat del. et pinxt.

PÉNTHORUM SEDOÌDES , Linn.

History and Habitat.—Penthorum is an indigenous ditch-weed, common in all localities in the United States, where it flowers from June to September.

It has always held a place in domestic practice as an astringent in diarrhœa and dysentery. Drs. Briggs* and Scudder brought it to the notice of practitioners as a remedy, both topic and internal, for irritation of the mucous membranes and various forms of subacute inflammation of the same, as in pharyngitis, vaginitis, tonsillitis, etc.

PART USED AND PREPARATION.—The whole fresh plant is to be chopped and pounded to a pulp and weighed. Then two parts by weight of alcohol are taken, the pulp mixed thoroughly with one-sixth part of it, and the rest of the alcohol added. After stirring the whole well, pour it into a well-stoppered bottle, and allow it to stand eight days in a dark, cool place, shaking often.

The tincture, separated from this mass by filtration, has a brilliant reddish-orange color by transmitted light; no special odor; an astringent taste; and an acid reaction.

CHEMICAL CONSTITUENTS.—An analysis by the Lloyd brothers failed to yield a peculiar principle, or even a volatile oil. A peculiar tannin was, however, determined, which first turns blue then precipitates black from its alcoholic solution with ferrous, and deep green with ferric sulphate.

PHYSIOLOGICAL ACTION.—Penthorum, according to Dr. Morrow's experiments, causes many symptoms simulating a coryza: rawness of throat and tongue; increased appetite followed by nausea; burning in the rectum; loose stools followed by constipation; increased urine; cough, and constriction of the chest.

DESCRIPTION OF PLATE 57.

1. Whole plant, Binghamton, N. Y., July 30th, 1885.
   2. Flower.
   3. View of calyx.
   4. Anther.
   5. Carpel.
   6. Fruit.
   (2–6 enlarged.)

* *Ec. Med. Jour.*, 1875, 479.

Tribe.—HAMAMELEÆ.

GENUS.—**HAMAMELIS**,* LINN.

SEX. SYST.—TETRANDRIA DIGYNIA.

58

HAMAMELIS.

WITCH HAZEL.

SYN.—HAMAMELIS VIRGINICA, LINN., HAMAMELIS MACROPHYLLA, PURSH, HAMAMELIS DIOICA, WALT., HAMAMELIS CORYLIFOLIA, MŒNCH.

COM. NAMES.—WITCH HAZEL, SNAPPING-HAZELNUT, WATER-SEEKER, WINTER-BLOOM, SPOTTED ALDER.

A TINCTURE OF THE FRESH TWIGS AND BARK OF HAMAMELIS VIRGINICA, LINN.

Description.—This strange shrub, whose flowers do not open until its leaves fall, grows to a height of from 5 to 15 feet. The *stem* is usually single, sometimes as large as 4 inches in diameter at the base. *Bark* smooth, brown. *Branches* numerous, long, flexuous and forking. *Leaves* 3 to 5 inches long, cordate-ovate or oval, with sinuate edges and straight veins, downy stellate-pubescent when young, but becoming smooth with age. *Petioles* about one-half an inch long. *Involucre* 3-leaved, scale-like, pubescent, on a short peduncle. *Flowers* many, axillary, several in a cluster or head. *Calyx* persistent, of 4 broadly-ovate, hairy, recurved divisions, with 2 or 3 little bracts at the base. *Corolla* of 4 long, strap-shaped, yellow petals, which soon wither and curl. *Stamens* 8, four are fertile, four sterile; *sterile stamens* scale-like, truncate, opposite the petals; *fertile stamens* shorter, curving inward toward the pistil; *filaments* short; *anther* adnate, introrse, 2-celled, the cells rather widely separated, opening laterally by uplifted valves. *Pollen*, grains ellipsoid, with 3 evenly separated deep sulci. *Ovaries* 2, united below. *Styles* 2, short. *Capsule* roundish ovoid, hard and leathery, the lower half with the persistent calyx and bracts, the upper smooth. *Dehiscence* loculicidal from the apex, during which the exocarp cleaves from the endocarp, which contains the seeds, and soon bursts, disclosing 2 cells, black and shining within, each with a single seed. *Nutlets* stony, oblong, narrow, deep glossy black, except the dull white tip. *Embryo* long, straight. *Albumen* little or none.

History and Habitat.—This plant, about which was formerly draped, by those versed in the occult arts, a veil of deep mystery, and whose forked branches were used as a divining-rod while searching for water and ores, grows profusely in the damp woods of Canada and the United States, flowering in October and ripening its fruit in the following summer.

---

* ἅμα, *like to,* μηλίς, *an apple tree.* Some plants bear a slight resemblance to small wild apple trees.

The many varied uses of a watery infusion of Witch-hazel bark were fully known to the aborigines, whose knowledge of our medicinal flora has been strangely correct as since proven. Its use in hæmorrhages, congestions, inflammations and hæmorrhoids is now generally known through the medium of an aqueous distillate of the bark.

The U. S. Ph. (1882) has wisely added Hamamelis to their medicaments, officinal as *Extractum Hamamelidis Fluidum.* In the Eclectic Materia Medica the officinal preparation is *Decoctum Hamamelis.*

PART USED AND PREPARATION.—The bark of the young twigs and roots is chopped and pounded to a pulp and weighed, then two parts by weight of alcohol are taken, the pulp mixed with one-sixth part of it, and the rest of the alcohol added ; after having stirred the whole well, pour it into a well-stoppered bottle, and let it stand eight days in a dark, cool place. The tincture, separated by decanting, straining and filtering is by transmitted light of a deep yellowish-brown color. It has a sweetish, slightly astringent taste, an acid reaction, and a peculiar odor, which, once noticed, will always distinguish it.

CHEMICAL CONSTITUENTS.—No analysis of this plant has been made to determine its principles except as far as tannin is concerned ; this body was found in small percentage. Water seems, nevertheless, to extract all or nearly all of its virtues. The active body, however, must be more or less volatile, as preparations of the plant, made without using proper care in regard to this feature, have not the action usually sought for. It is also a fact that the bark of the root alone is not sufficiently medicinal, and that the curative property of the tincture does not lie entirely in the tannin.

PHYSIOLOGICAL ACTION.—Hamamelis, according to Dr. H. C. Preston, who first attempted the study of its action, causes a determination of venous blood to the head, chest, abdomen and pelvis. Its action would seem to be, not upon the circulation itself, but upon the coats of the veins, causing a relaxation, with consequent engorgement and exosmosis, this action in many cases proceeding to actual rupture of the vessels. The symptoms pointing to the above conclusion are produced as follows : Vertigo, venous epistaxis, preceded by severe pressure both in the os frontis and superior nares, relieved by the hæmorrhage ; nausea and vomiting, pain and tenderness of the abdomen, with flatulence and diarrhœic passages from the bowels ; pulsations in the rectum synchronous with the pulse ; much lumbar pain, with weakness of the lower limbs and general lassitude. The action of hamamelis upon the heart and circulation in general is not marked in these experiments.

DESCRIPTION OF PLATE 58.

1. End of flowering branch, Binghamton, N. Y., October 23d, 1881.
2. Leaves added in June.
3. Flower (enlarged), the petals broken off.
4. Fruit.
5. Pollen grains, side and end view, x 380.
6. Nutlet.

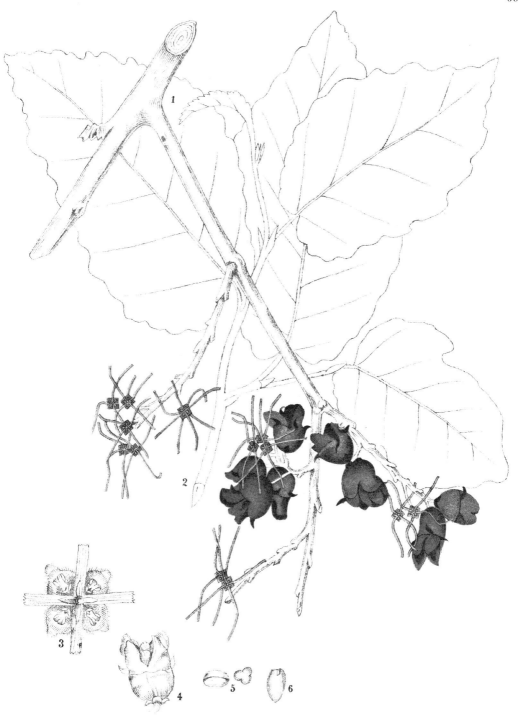

Ɠ.m ad nat del.et pinxt.

HAMAMÈLIS VIRGÍNICA, Linn.

GENUS.—**EPILOBIUM,**[*] LINN.

SEX. SYST.—OCTANDRIA MONOGYNIA.

59

EPILOBIUM.

WILLOW-HERB.

SYN.—EPILOBIUM PALUSTRE, VAR. LINEARE, GRAY; E. PALUSTRE, GRAY; E. ROSMARINIFOLIUM, PURSH.; E. LINEARE, MUHL.; E. PALUS- TRE, VAR. ALBESCENS, RICH.; E. PALUSTRE, VAR. ALBIFLORUM, LEHM.; E. OLIGANTHUM, MICHX., F.; E. TENELLUM DENSUM, LEPTO- PHYLLUM, AND CILIATUM, RAF.; E. ANGUSTISSIMUM, WILLD. (GREENLAND); E. PUBESCENS, PRESL.; E. SQUAMATUM, NUTT.

COM. NAMES.—SWAMP WILLOW-HERB, NARROW-LEAVED WILLOW- HERB, MARSH EPILOBIUM, SWAMP WILLOW, WICKOP; (FR.) HERBE DE ST. ANTOINE; (GER.) ANTONSKRAUT.

A TINCTURE OF THE WHOLE PLANT EPILOBIUM PALUSTRE, VAR. LINEARE, GRAY.

Description.—This slender, perennial herb usually attains a growth of from 6 inches to 2 feet. *Stem* erect, roundish, terete, minutely hoary, pubescent, and branchy above. *Leaves* nearly sessile, narrowly lanceolate or linear, acute, attenu- ate at the base, and with more or less revolute margins; the upper alternate; the lower opposite, entire, or denticulate. *Inflorescence* in a terminal corymb; *flower- buds* nodding; *flowers* minute, rose-colored. *Calyx-tube* not prolonged beyond the ovary; *limb* 4-cleft, deciduous. *Petals* 4, erect, mostly notched at the end, and about twice the length of the calyx. *Stamens* 8, erect; *anthers* short. *Style* erect, included; *stigma* clavate, nearly entire. *Fruit* an elongated, linear, hoary, some- what quadrangular, loculicidal pod; *seeds* numerous, bearing a tuft of long hairs upon the apex.

Onagraceæ.—This innocent order of mostly perennial herbs, represented in North America by 15 genera, 155 species, and numerous varieties, is characterized as follows: *Flowers* 4-merous (sometimes 2, 3, 5, or 6-merous), perfect, and sym- metrical. *Calyx* with its tube adhering to the ovary; *lobes* valvate in the bud or obsolete. *Petals* convolute in the bud, sometimes absent. *Stamens* as many, or twice as many, as the petals or calyx-lobes; *filaments* inserted at the summit of the calyx-tube; *pollen* with its grains often connected by cobwebby threads. *Style* single, slender; *stigma* 2- to 4-lobed or capitate. *Fruit* capsular or baccate; *seeds* small, anatropous; *albumen* wanting.

---

[*] Ἐπί, *epi*, upon; λόβος, *lobos*, a pod; as the flowers seem to be.

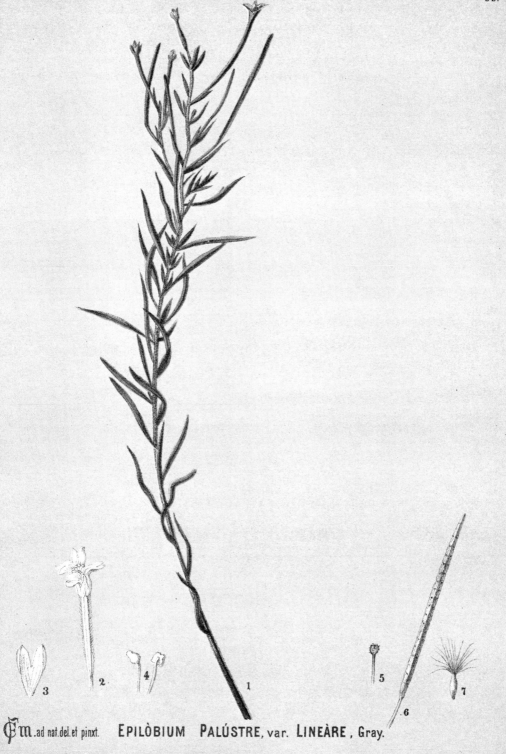

CM.ad nat.del.et pinxt. EPILÒBIUM PALÚSTRE, var. LINEÀRE, Gray.

History and Habitat.—The Swamp Willow-Herb is indigenous to North America, where it extends from the mountains of North Carolina, and from Southern Illinois, northward to the Arctic Circle. It habits high sphagnum swamps, and flowers in July and August.

Epilobium has proven itself a mild tonic and astringent, quite useful in slight types of diarrhœa and dysentery attended with colic, cramps in the stomach, and light typhoid abdominal symptoms. In irritation of the intestinal canal, followed by diarrhœa and some tympanitis, it has often proved quite beneficial in the hands of our Eclectic physicians.

PART USED AND PREPARATION.—The whole fresh plant, while in flower, should be chopped and pounded to a pulp and weighed; then two parts by weight of alcohol taken, the pulp thoroughly mixed with one-sixth part of it, and the rest of the alcohol added. Pour the whole into a well-stoppered bottle, and allow it to stand eight days in a dark, cool place, shaking twice a day. The tincture, prepared from this mass by decanting, pressing, and filtering, should have a light yellowish-brown color by transmitted light; a smooth, then astringent taste, and an acid reaction.

CHEMICAL CONSTITUENTS.—No analysis of this plant has so far been made. It contains, however, tannin and gallic acid, beside the usual plant constituents.

PHYSIOLOGICAL ACTION.—The experiments of Dr. Wright, who took from one-half to one ounce of the tincture, caused some symptoms that must have been due to so large a "drink." Outside of the symptoms that we are prone to lay to the alcohol, the following also occurred: Salivation; loose stools; red urine; and chills, followed by feverishness and general aching throughout the body.

A proving with the tincture prepared as here directed, should be made.

DESCRIPTION OF PLATE 59.

1. A small plant from Appalachin, N. Y., July 26th, 1886.
2. A flower.
3. Petal.
4. Stamens.
5. Pistil.
6. Pod.
7. Seed.
(2–5 and 7 enlarged.)

GENUS.—**ŒNOTHERA,*** LINN.

SEX. SYST.—OCTANDRIA MONOGYNIA.

60
OENOTHERA.

EVENING PRIMROSE.

SYN.—ŒNOTHERA BIENNIS, LINN.; ŒNOTHERA PARVIFLORA, LINN.; ŒNOTHERA GAUROIDES, HORNEM; ONAGRA BIENNIS, SCOP.; ONAGRA VULGARIS, AND CHRYSANTHA, SPACH.

COM. NAMES.—COMMON EVENING PRIMROSE, NIGHT WILLOW-HERB, SCABBISH, TREE PRIMROSE, CURE-ALL; (FR.) ONAGRE; (GER.) NACHTKERZ.

A TINCTURE OF THE WHOLE, FRESH, NEWLY BLOSSOMING PLANT, ŒNOTHERA BIENNIS, LINN.

Description.—This nocturnal annual, or biennial plant, attains a growth of from 2 to 4 feet. *Root* conical; *bark* thin, yellowish, or brownish. The roots of the first year are fleshy and succulent, in the second they become fibrous and woody. *Leaves* alternate, 2–6 inches long, ovate-lanceolate, acute, very minutely toothed, and pubescent; the cauline sessile, those near the root contracted into a petiole. *Inflorescence* a terminal, foliaceous spike, lengthening greatly as the flowers develop and the fruit matures; *flowers* odorous, light-yellow, ephemeral. *Calyx-tube* cylindrical, caducous, prolonged quite a distance beyond the ovary, being more than twice as long as its lobes; *limb* of 4 long, reflexed lobes. *Petals* 4, obcordate, not clawed, withering and becoming orange-brown after a night's expansion. *Stamens* 8, nearly equal, shorter than, and both opposite and alternate with, the petals; *filaments* slender, sometimes curved; *anthers* linear, versatile. *Ovary* ovate; *style* terminal, long, cylindrical, exserted; *stigmas* a group of 4 linear, diverging lobes. *Fruit* a 4-valved, many-seeded follicle; *follicle* oblong, sessile, tapering above; *seeds* naked. Read description of the order under Epilobium palustre, 59.

History and Habitat.—The Evening Primrose is common in the United States, growing in fields and waste places generally, and flowering from July to September. It varies greatly in its growth, affording at least 5 distinct varieties, *viz.*, *var. α grandiflora*, a large-flowered form; *var. β muricata*, with rough, bristly stem and pods; *var. γ canescens; var. δ hirsutissima*, a particularly hairy form;

---

* Theophrastus describes a plant whose dried root caught the odor of wine. Hence he called it οἶνος, *oinos*, wine; θήρα, *thera*, catch. (Barton.) Or taking θήρα to mean a hunt or chase, it is alleged that the meaning is applicable to the belief that it was the root of this plant, or one of its botanical relatives, that was eaten to provoke an appetite for wine.

This genus is a large and varied one, containing 57 species, and 33 varieties, in North America alone.

1

2

3

ad nat del. et pinxt.

ŒNOTHÈRA BIÉNNIS Linn.

and *var. ε cruciata*, having small, linear petals, shorter than the stamens. The flowers open fully, after sundown, and remain so until the sun is well up in the morning, then wither and fall. Much has been written concerning the property inherent in the petals of many species of this genus, of emitting a "phosphorescence" at night, the flowers being distinguishable at a goodly distance beyond non-refractory objects by their whitish luminosity. In regard to this phosphorescence a word or two is in place. That the petals do emit light on a dark night is not fanciful; still it is not due to a property of giving out spontaneous light (phosphorescence), but to a process of storing up sunlight during the day, and retaining it at night—a property identical with that exhibited by *hepar sulphuris calcarea*, and the sulphides of barium and strontium.*

The young roots of the evening primrose are said to be edible and pleasant, either pickled or boiled, having "a nutty taste, quite similar to that of rampion (*Campanula rapunculus*), and are used in Germany and some parts of France, either stewed or raw, in salads, like celery." (Porcher.) Lindley states, that the young mucilaginous twigs are used in the same way.

About the only previous use of this plant in medicine was a strong decoction of the dried herb as an external application in infantile eruptions, and as a general vulnerary. Dr. Winterburn† states it to be a curative in spasmodic asthma, pertussis, gastric irritation, irritable bladder, and chronic exhaustive diarrhœas.

PART USED AND PREPARATION.—The whole fresh plant, as it is coming into bloom, is chopped and pounded to a pulp and weighed. Then two parts by weight of alcohol are taken, the pulp mixed thoroughly with one-sixth part of it, and the rest of the alcohol added. After having stirred the whole, it is poured into a well-stoppered bottle, and allowed to stand eight days in a dark, cool place.

The tincture, obtained from this mass by filtration, should have a clear reddish-orange color by transmitted light, an odor similar to that of wet hay, a taste at first mucilaginous, then astringent and bitter, and an acid reaction.

CHEMICAL CONSTITUENTS.—*Œnotherin*. This body, claimed as a principle by Chicoisneau, is evidently an extract, which probably contains all of the principles of the plant except the acrid body, which is dissipated by heat. It has not yet been analyzed, but would doubtless show a resin, a bitter principle, and a special acid. Mucilage is present in large percentage.

Potassium nitrate, $K NO_3$.—Crystals of this salt are readily extracted from an alcoholic tincture of the root.‡

PHYSIOLOGICAL ACTION.—The brain symptoms following a dose of 60 drops of the fluid extract of Œnothera in a woman of 40, as chronicled by Dr. Nute,§ are very interesting, and should stimulate a desire for a fuller proving.

---

* Calcined oyster shells emit stored sunlight, on account of the sulphide of calcium in their composition. This fact is largely utilized in the manufacture of luminous clock-faces, match-safes, door-plates, and the like. These objects, when placed in the sunlight during the day, are visible at night.

† "The Evening Primrose," a paper read before the *Ills. State Hom. Soc'y. Am. Homœopath*, 1883, p. 317.

‡ Claussen, *Am. Jour. Phar.*, 1884, p. 365.　　　§ *U. S. Med. and Surg. Journ.*, vol. ix, p. 395.

236 [60–3]

This individual experienced extreme vertigo, inability to sit or stand erect, semi-unconsciousness, loss of muscular power, numbness and peripheral prickling, rigors, occasional muscular cramps in the abdomen and extremities, and great exhaustion. These symptoms were followed by a free movement of the bowels, and a copious discharge of urine. Dr. Winterburn* judges that the drug has a special action upon the pneumogastric nerve, and, reflexly, an irritative action upon its pulmonary and laryngeal branches.

DESCRIPTION OF PLATE 60.

1. Top of flowering plant; Chemung, N. Y., Sept. 4th, 1879.
2. Pistil.
3. Fruit.

* *U. S. Med. and Surg. Journ.*, vol. ix, p. 395.

GENUS.—**OPUNTIA**,* TOURN.

SEX. SYST.—ICOSANDRIA MONOGYNIA.

61

OPUNTIA.

PRICKLY PEAR.

SYN.—OPUNTIA VULGARIS, MILL.; O. ITALICA, TEN.; O. HUMIFUSUS, AND O. MARITIMA AND HUMIFUSA, RAF.; O. INTERMEDIA, SALM.; CACTUS OPUNTIA, LINN.

COM. NAMES.—PRICKLY PEAR, INDIAN FIG.

A TINCTURE OF THE FRESH FLOWERS AND GREEN OVARIES OF OPUNTIA VULGARIS, LINN.

Description.—This curious, low, pale, prostrate, spreading plant is characterized as follows: *Branches* (?) more or less assurgent; *joints* flat, broadly ovate, the younger ones leafy, the older prickly; *leaves* minute ovate-subulate, appressed, deciduous, arranged spirally about the joints; *axils* more or less bristly with numerous short, barbed prickles; *spines* rarely present, when found they are whitish in the north and yellowish southward, and vary from two-thirds to one and one-quarter inches long. *Inflorescence* consisting of a few sessile, solitary flowers along the apical ridge of the joints; *flowers* large, sulphur-yellow, not ephemeral; *perianth* not united into a prolonged tube, but regular and spreading. *Sepals* ovate-lanceolate, tapering to a point. *Petals* ample, the inner roundish. *Stamens* numerous, shorter than the larger petal; *filaments* glabrous; *anthers* linear, versatile. *Ovary* 1-celled, obovate; *style* cylindrical, narrowed at the base; *stigmas* about 6, in two sets, clavate. *Fruit* an obovoid, nearly smooth, crimson, pulpy and edible berry, having a deep depression at the apex showing the scars of the perianth. *Seeds* numerous, flattish-reniform, with a rounded ridge extending over the arch opposite the hilum; *embryo* curved around the thin albumen; *cotyledons* large, becoming foliaceous.

Cactaceæ.—This large and peculiar family of thick and fleshy plants is represented in North America by 5 genera, containing in all 142 species and 39 recognized varieties. Its characteristics are as follows: *Stems* globular or columnar and angled, composed of numerous compressed joints. *Leaves* usually absent or represented by spines, thorns or bristles. *Flowers* solitary, sessile. *Sepals* and *petals* similar and evolute, numerous and imbricated in several rows, all adherent to the ovary. *Stamens* numerous; *filaments* long and slender, inserted into a ring formed by the union of the sepals and petals. *Styles* united into one; *stigmas* numerous. *Fruit* a berry; *seeds* numerous, campylotropous, finally becoming separate from the placentæ and loose in the pulp; *placentæ* several, parietal; *albumen* scanty.

---

* A Theophrastian name for some species growing in the country of the Opuntiani, whose chief city was Opus, near Phocis.

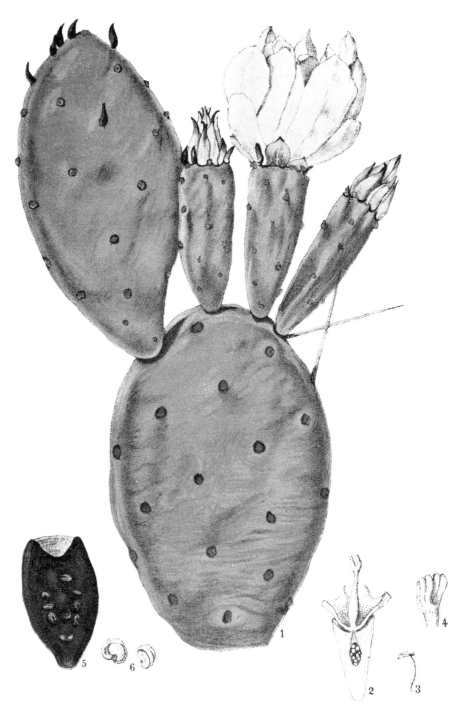

Ɛ.m. ad nat del.et pinxt.

OPÚNTIA VULGÀRIS, Mill.

The proven plants of this order are : the Jamaican *Cactus grandiflorus*, Linn. ; the beautiful Night-blooming Cereus, whose ephemeral flowers are remarkable for their exceeding size and fragrance ; *Cereus Bonplandii*, Parm. ; and *C. serpentinus*, Haw. No other species are used in medicine, though many furnish both food and drink to those compelled to pass over the barren wastes which this order mostly habits, the pulpy fruits and succulent joints, deprived of their coat of mail, being acid and aqueous to a high degree. Mr. J. R. Dodge* speaks as follows of the species used by the American Aborigines :

"*Echinocactus Wislizeni*.—A section of the stem is often employed as a cook-ing vessel. The seeds are small and black, but, when parched and pulverized, make good gruel and even bread. The pulp of the fruit is rather sour, and not much eaten. Travellers in passing through the cactus wastes often resort to this plant to quench their thirst, its interior containing a soft, white, watery substance, of slightly acid taste, which is rather pleasant when chewed. It is a common sight to see on each side of the road these plants with a large perforation made by the thirsty traveller. An Indian, when travelling, and wishing to make a meal, selects a large plant, three feet or more long and two in diameter, cuts it down and hol-lows it out so as to form a trough ; into this he throws the soft portions of the pulpy substance which surrounds the central woody axis, and adds meat, roots, seeds, meal, fruits, or any edible thing on hand ; water is added, and the whole mixed together ; stones are then highly heated and dropped into the mixture, and, as they cool, are taken out, licked clean, reheated, and returned to the cooking ves-sel, until the mixture is thoroughly boiled. This is a favorite dish with the Yabapais and Apaches of Arizona. The Papajo Indians pare off the rind and thorns of large plants of this species of cactus, letting it remain several days to bleed, when the pulp is pared down to the woody axis, cut up into suitable pieces, and boiled in syrup of the *Cereus giganteus* or *Cereus Thurberi*. If a kind of sugar which is made by the Mexicans is attainable, it is employed instead of the syrup, thus form-ing a good preserve. These pieces, when taken out of the liquid and dried, are as good as candied citron, which they much resemble in taste and substance.

"*Prickly pear* (*Opuntia Engelmani, O. vulgaris, O. Camanchica, O. Rafines-quii, O. occidentalis*).—The fruit of these species of cactus is much eaten by all the Indians of New Mexico, Arizona, California and Utah, under the common Spanish name of *tunas*, great quantities being dried for use in the winter. These plants grow in arid desert localities which produce nothing better ; they are large and of a bright red to purple color ; of a rather pleasant, sweet, somewhat acid taste, and have thin skins and rather large seeds, which are discarded. The skin is studded with bunches of very fine downy spines, which the Indians brush off with a bunch of grass. The Apaches use wooden tongs to gather the fruit, to prevent being scratched by these spines or the thorns of the plant. The Pawnees and Papajoes dry the unripe fruit of the *Opuntia* for future use, to be cooked with meat and other substances. The fresh unripe fruit is often boiled in water from ten to twelve hours, until soft, when it becomes like apple-sauce ; then, being allowed to ferment a little, it becomes stimulating and nutritious. Some Indians roast the leaves of the *Opuntia* in hot ashes, and, when cooked, the outer skin,

---

* *U. S. Agric. Repts.*, 1870, 417–418.

with the thorns, is easily removed, leaving a slimy, sweet, succulent substance, which is eaten. Hunger and destitution frequently compel Indians and white men to live for many days on this food. A yellowish white gum often oozes out of the leaves of the *Opuntia*, which is also eaten."

History and Habitat.—This species is indigenous to the sandy fields of the Atlantic and Pacific seaboards, as well as the arid lands of the southwestern portion of North America; it is also found in Europe. It habits rocky places and dry sands, where it flowers in June and July at the north.

The fruit is edible and at the same time a pleasant diuretic, though it renders the urine a bloody tinge; the taste is acid and cool, much resembling the Pomegranate. Rafinesque states* that the split joints make a good emollient application for acute rheumatism, and, when baked, for chronic ulcers, gout, and recent wounds; the juice and gummy exudation, he says, is used in gravel. Dr. Porcher says† he is informed that a decoction of the joints is mucilaginous, and much used in Alabama as a demulcent drink in pulmonic and pleuritic affections. Merat‡ claims that the cut joints are discutient.

PART USED AND PREPARATION.—The fresh flowers and green ovaries are chopped and pounded to a pulp and weighed. Then two parts by weight of alcohol are taken, the pulp thoroughly mixed with one-sixth part of it and the rest of the alcohol added. The whole is then poured into a well-stoppered vial, and allowed to stand eight days in a dark, cool place. The tincture, separated from this mass by filtration, should have a slightly opaque straw-color by transmitted light; a slight odor of the flowers; a bitterish and astringent taste; and an acid reaction.

CHEMICAL CONSTITUENTS.—An analysis of the fruit was made by Mr. W. W. Light,§ and resulted in the determination of: Tartaric acid, $C_4H_6O_6$; citric acid mucilage, and coloring-matter. In the seeds a fixed oil, a fat acid, albumen, starch and glucose were found, but no glucoside nor alkaloid.

PHYSIOLOGICAL ACTION.—According to the experiments made by Drs. Burdick,|| Kunze and Fitch,¶ with doses varying from a small portion to a drachm of the tincture, the effects are as follows: Mental disturbances; acute pain in the globe of the eye; epistaxis; nausea in both stomach and bowels as if diarrhœa would set in; urging to stool; urine red, increased; coldness; and various pains, principally about the joints.

DESCRIPTION OF PLATE 61.

1. Two joints in flower and leaf, Salem, Mass., July 3d, 1885.
2. Section of flower, stamens and floral envelope removed.
3. Stamen.
4. Stigma.
5. Fruit.
6. Seeds.

(3, 4 and 6 enlarged.)

---

* *Med. Flora*, 2, 243.　　† *Resourc. South. Fields and Forests*, 66.　　‡ *Dict. Univ. de Mat. Med.*, vi, 11.
§ *Am. Jour. Phar.*, 1884, 3.　　|| *N. A. Jour. of Hom.*, 1874 48.　　¶ *Trans. Ec. Med. Soc.*, 1875.

GENUS.—**ERYNGIUM,*** TOURN.

SEX. SYST.—PENTANDRIA DIGYNIA.

62
ERYNGIUM.

BUTTON SNAKEROOT.

SYN.—ERYNGIUM YUCCÆFOLIUM, MICHX.; E. AQUATICUM, LINN. (IN PART).

COM. NAMES.—BUTTON SNAKEROOT, RATTLESNAKE MASTER, ERYNGO, CORN SNAKEROOT; (FR.) PANICANT D'EAU; (GER.) WASSERMANNS-TREU.

A TINCTURE OF THE ROOT OF ERYNGIUM YUCCÆFOLIUM, MICHX.†

Description.—This peculiar, sedge-like perennial grows to a height of from 1 to 6 feet. *Stem* smooth, erect, and grooved. *Leaves* linear, six inches to two feet long, and one-half to one inch wide, taper-pointed, coriaceous, rigid, parallel-veined, gramineous, and remotely bristly-fringed upon the margins. *Inflorescence* in a terminal compound umbel, each peduncle bearing a compact head; *heads* broadly ovate; *bracts* entire, paleaceous, not spinous; *flowers* inconspicuous, white, all fertile, closely sessile; *leaves* of the *involucels* mostly entire, and shorter than the heads. *Calyx* 5-toothed; *teeth* persistent. *Petals* connivent, oblong, emarginate. *Styles* filiform. *Fruit* top-shaped, covered with little scales or tubercles, having no ribs and scarcely any vittæ, the inner face of each mericarp flat or nearly so.

Umbelliferæ.—This large and very natural order, of herbs, represented in North America by 50 genera and 187 species, is characterized as follows: *Stems* usually hollow and striate. *Leaves* alternate, mostly compound; *petioles* sheathing or expanding at the base. *Inflorescence* in terminal, compound umbels, often subtended by a whorl of bracts (*involucre*), usually also subtending the umbellets (*involucel*); *flowers* small, in many genera dichogamous. *Calyx* adherent to the whole face of the ovary: *limb* minute, entire or 5-toothed. *Petals* 5, usually inflexed at the point, imbricate or valvate in æstivation. *Stamens* 5, alternate with the petals, and inserted with them upon the disk. *Ovary* 2-carpelled, surmounted by the fleshy disk that bears the petals and stamens; *ovules* 2, anatropous; *styles* 2, distinct, or united at their thickened bases; *stigmas* simple. *Fruit* a cremocarp, consisting of 2 coherent achenia (*mericarps*) which separate along the middle interval (*commissure*), and are usually suspended from the summit of a slender

---

* Ἐρυγεῖν, *erygein*, to belch, from carminative properties.

† A much better name than *E. aquaticum*, Linn., as the plant never is truly aquatic with us.

prolongation of the axis (*carpophore*) ; *mericarps* marked lengthwise by 5 primary ribs, and often with 5 secondary intermediate, in the interstices or intervals between these ribs are commonly lodged few or many oil-tubes (*vittæ*), which are longitudinal canals in the substance of the fruit, containing aromatic oil. *Seeds* suspended from the summit of the mericarp ; *embryo* minute ; *albumen* hard. The flowers in this order are so minute, and so nearly alike in all genera, that the differentiation is usually, in great part, based upon the cremocarps.

Besides the seven species treated of in this work, we have provings of the following plants : The Persian Ammoniacum (*Dorema Ammoniacum*, Don.), a fetid, stimulating, discutient gum-resin ; the European Celery (*Apium graveolens*, Linn.), which, though an acrid poison when growing in wet places, is a delightful salad when cultivated ; the Thibetan Asafœtida (*Narthex Asafœtida*, Falc.), a fetid, stimulant, and antispasmodic gum-resin ; the Central European Athamantha (*Peucedanum Oreoselinum*, Mœnch), an aromatic and powerful stimulant ; the North European and Asiatic Water Hemlock (*Cicuta virosa*, Linn.), a dangerous, acrid, narcotic poison ; the European Sea Holly (*Eryngium maritimum*, Linn.), a sweet, aromatic, tonic and diuretic ; the Italian Giant Fennel (*Ferula glauca*, Linn.), a stimulating antihysteric ; the Mediterranean Fennel Seed (*Fœniculum officinale*, Allioni.), an aromatic stimulant and carminative ; the European and North Asiatic Cow-Parsnip, Branca Ursina (*Heracleum Sphondylium*, Linn.), an acrid vesicant ; the subtropical Indian Pennywort (*Hydrocotyle Asiatica*, Linn.), noted as a remedy for leprosy, ichthyosis, and rheumatism ; the European Masterwort (*Imperatoria ostruthium*, Linn.), a febrifuge, antiperiodic, and masticatory in toothache ; the European Hemlock Dropwort (*Œnanthe crocata*, Linn.), a narcotico-acrid poison of great virulence ; the Sardinian Parsley (*Petroselinum sativum*, Hoff.), a noted diuretic pot-herb ; the European Water Dropwort (*Phellandrium aquaticum*, Linn.), which partakes of the poisonous nature of Œnanthe, but is less dangerous ; the Levantine Bibernell or Burnet Saxifrage (*Pimpinella Saxifraga*, Linn.), an astringent, masticatory, also used to remove freckles ; the Central Asiatic Sumbul (*Ferula Sumbul*, Hook., f.), a Russian "specific" for cholera, that failed and was afterward used as an antihysteric, and remedy for hypersecretive mucous membranes ; the Northern Europe and Asiatic Caraway (*Carum Carui*, Linn.), a well-known aromatic stimulant and condiment ; and lastly, the European Water Parsnip (*Sium latifolium*, Linn.), an acrid, narcotic poison.

Many other species are used in general medicine.* The European Turbith (*Laserpitium latifolium*, Jacq.), yields an acrid, bitter, caustic, and violently purgative gum-resin. The European genus *Anthriscus*, yields two species, *A. sylvestris*, Hoff., and *A. vulgaris*, Pers., that are acrid, narcotic poisons ; while *A. Cerefolium*, Hoff., is an agreeable pot-herb, called Chervil. The South Russian *Cachrys odontalgica*, Pall., is, as its name denotes, a remedy for aching carious teeth. The Indian and Levantine Fructus Ptychotis (*Carum Ajowan*, Bentl.), is carminative, and the oil antiseptic. The European and Levantine genus *Pim-*

---

* Concerning this order it is noteworthy, that those which grow near water are generally acrid, narcotic poisons, while those seeking dry soils are little else than carminative.

62.

℃.m. ad nat del. et pinxt.   ERÝNGIUM YUCCÆFÒLIUM , Michx.

pinella yields the well known Anise (*P. Anisum*), an aromatic stimulant and carminative, as well as *P. dissecta*, Retz., and *P. magna*, Linn., which have properties similar to those of P. Saxifraga, mentioned above. The genus *Ferula*, which includes *Narthex*, yields the following substances, beside Sumbul and Asafœtida mentioned above: African Gum Ammoniacum from *F. tingitana*, Linn.; Persian Galbanum is produced by *F. Galbaniflua*, and *F. rubricaulis*, Boiss.; it saction is considered to be intermediate between asafœtida and ammoniacum. Asafœtida is also produced by *F. Scorodosma*, Bentl., and *F. alliacea*, Bois. (*F. Asafœtida*, Linn., cannot be decided upon. It was founded upon Kæmpfer's descriptions and fragmentary specimens, neither of which are conclusive.—Bentley). The European genus, *Peucedanum*, contains, beside Athamantha, the following medicinal species: Sulphur-wort (*P. officinale*, Linn.), reputed diuretic and antispasmodic; Marsh Parsley (*P. palustre*, Mœn.), a famous Courland remedy for epilepsy; and Dill (*P. graveolens*, Hiern.), a stimulant and carminative. The European and Asiatic Coriander (*Coriandrum sativum*, Linn.), is an aromatic stimulant and carminative; the Levantine Cumin (*Cuminum Cyminum*, Linn.), a stimulant, carminative, and discutient. The European genus, *Daucus*, yields the common Carrot (*D. Carrota*, Linn.), whose seeds are diuretic, and root a well known esculent; while the Sicilian *D. gummifer*, Lam., and Corsican *D. Gingidum*, Linn., are supposed to yield the Bdellium of the old Pharmacopœias.* Opoponax is a fetid deobstruent, and antispasmodic gum-resin, produced by the juice of *Pastinaca Opoponax*, Linn. The Alpine Lovage (*Ligusticum levisticum*, Linn.), is carminative, stimulant, diuretic, and emmenagogue. The root of the European *Astrantia major*, Linn., is acrid and purgative. The European Eringo (*Eryngium campestre*, Linn.), is considered by Boerhaave, the first of aperient, diuretic roots. It has been also recommended in gonorrhœa, hepatic and intestinal obstructions, and suppression of the menses, and considered aphrodisiac; its scope is considered larger than that of the Sea Holly mentioned above. The Italian Bracala (*Angelica nemorosa*, Ten.), furnishes the Neapolitans with a remedy for the itch. Samphire, a saline aromatic, is the product of *Crithum maritimum*, Linn. Alexanders are the aromatic fruits of the European *Smyrnium Olusatrum*, Linn., formerly used instead of celery.

Asa Dulcis—in contradistinction to Asa Fetida—which enjoyed the highest reputation among the ancients, as an antispasmodic, emetic, deobstruent, and diuretic,† is yielded by *Thapsia garganica*, Linn., or the nearly allied *T. sylphium ;* the resin of the root is said to be fully as active and thorough a vesicant as croton oil; it deserves a careful proving. Numerous other species have held a place in medicine, and deserve mention, but the above list covers their action.

Beside the edible species already mentioned, carrots, parsnips, celery, and chervil, many other plants of this order are eaten. *Prangos fabularia*, Lindl., is suggested by Royle to be the Συλφιον of the Greeks, mentioned by Alexander's

---

* India Bdellium is referred to *Balsamodendron mukul*, and African Bdellium to *B. Africanum*, Arn. (Burseraceæ).

† This was the Laser cyrenaicum of Cyrene, a drug in high reputation among the ancients for its medical uses; it had miraculous powers assigned to it, such as neutralizing the effects of poison, curing envenomed wounds, restoring sight to the blind, and youth to the aged. So great was its reputation that the princes of Cyrene caused it to be struck on the reverse of their coins; and the Cyrenian doctors were reckoned among the most eminent in the world. Its value was estimated by its weight in gold.—Lindley.

historians as a highly nutritious food for cattle, and even man, of heating and fattening qualities. The American Aborigines use several species, prominent among which Mr. Dodge* mentions the following:

"*Dill* (*Peucedanum graveolens*, Wats.), called by the Snakes and Shoshone Indians *Yampah*.—This spindle-shaped root grows in low, timbered bottoms, and is esteemed as the best of its kind when used for food. It is analogous to the parsnip, and is an article of commerce among the Indians. The seeds are used to flavor soup."

"*Podosciadium Californicum*, Gray.—The tubers of this species form one of the dainty dishes of the Oregon Indians. They are black, but when boiled like potatoes they burst open lengthwise, showing a snowy-white farinaceous substance, which has a sweet, cream-like taste, with a slight parsley flavor. It is an excellent root, the cultivation of which might prove useful among the whites."

"*Kouse root* (*Peucedanum ambiguum*, Nutt.).—The root of this plant is dug in April or May when in bloom. It grows on hills and mountains which are so poor that grass will not grow upon them. When fresh it is like the parsnip in taste, and as it dies becomes brittle and very white, with an agreeable taste of mild celery. It is easily reduced to flour. When its brown epidermis is removed, innumerable small dots are revealed. Both the roots and the flour will keep several months. It is sometimes called bread or biscuit root by travelers, and Kouse root by the Indians of Oregon and Idaho. The Canadians know it by the name of *Racine blanc*. After the bread has been made a short time, its taste is not unlike that of stale biscuits. When the roots have been pounded fine, the flour is pressed into flat cakes, one foot wide, three feet long, and from a quarter to half an inch thick, of an oblong rectangular form, with a hole in the middle by which they are fastened on the saddles when traveling. The cakes have a ribbed appearance, caused by being laid on sticks stretched over the tent fires, for the purpose of smoke-drying or baking the bread. When broken up the bread has a coarse, granulated appearance, especially when not ground very fine, and is very insipid."

History and Habitat.—Eryngium Yuccæfolium is indigenous to North America, where it ranges from New Jersey to Wisconsin and southward. It habits damp or dry prairies and pine barrens, and blossoms in July and August.

This species was valued highly by the Aborigines as an alexiteric, and, combined with Iris versicolor, as a febrifuge and diuretic; since their time it has come into use by first the laity, then the physician, as a stimulant, diaphoretic, sialogogue, expectorant, diuretic, and alterative. A decoction of the root has been found useful in dropsy, nephritic and calculous disorders; chronic laryngitis and bronchitis; irritation of the urethra, vaginal, uterine, and cystic mucous membranes; gonorrhœa, gleet, and leucorrhœa; mucoid diarrhœa; local inflammations of the mucous membranes; exhaustion from sexual depletion with loss of erectile power, seminal emissions, and orchitis. By some physicians it has been preferred to Seneka snakeroot for its sphere, and by others it has been considered fully equal to Contrayerva. The powdered root is said to make a fine escharotic

* *U. S. Agric. Rep.*, 1870, pp. 405-7.

application to fungoid growths and indolent ulcerations, preventing gangrene, and stimulating them to resolution.

The plant is not officinal in the U. S. Ph.; in the Eclectic Dispensatory the preparation recommended is *Decoctum Eryngii*.

PART USED AND PREPARATION. — The fresh root, gathered after the fruits are fully ripe, is chopped and pounded to a pulp and weighed. Then two parts by weight of alcohol are taken, the pulp mixed thoroughly with one-sixth part of it, and the rest of the alcohol added. After having stirred the whole well, pour it into a well-stoppered bottle, and allow it to stand for eight days in a dark, cool place. The tincture, separated by decanting, straining, and filtering, has a clear reddish-orange color by transmitted light; an odor much like that of an old chest that has been shut up with oil-cloth for some time; a bitterish, acrid, and terebinthic taste; and an acid reaction. It leaves a sensation deep in the throat, much like that following Senega.

CHEMICAL CONSTITUENTS.—This root yields its properties to both water and alcohol, and probably contains an acrid, volatile oil, a bitter principle, and sugar. No analysis has been made of the root; the tincture, however, shows the presence of a small amount of resin.

PHYSIOLOGICAL ACTION.—According to the experiments of Drs. C. H. McClelland, C. H. Coggswells, and W. G. Jones, Eryngium causes, in doses of from 5 to 150 drops of the tincture: Depression of spirits; vertigo and headache; irritation of the palpebral mucous membrane, followed by purulent discharges; inflammation of the eustachian tube, followed by a discharge of fetid pus; a similar condition of the nasal and pharyngeal mucous membranes; nausea and burning in the stomach; colic; constipation, with tenesmus; frequent desire to urinate, with a decrease in quantity daily passed; stinging, burning sensation in the urethra, severe pain in left testicle, depression of sexual desire, followed by excitation, lewd dreams, pollutions, and discharges of prostatic fluid; a sensation of dyspnœa, and constriction of the throat;* and slight increase in the heart's action.

DESCRIPTION OF PLATE 62.

1 and 2. Whole plant, from St. Augustine, Fla., Aug. 2d, 1886.
3. Flower.
4. Calyx and styles.
5 and 6. Petals.
7 and 8. Stamens.
9. Fruit.
(3–9 enlarged.)

* This symptom followed my tasting the tincture for the above description, and became, in half an hour, so strong as to be decidedly uncomfortable.—C. F. M.

63

PASTINACA.

PARSNIP.

SYN.—PASTINACA SATIVA, LINN.
COM. NAMES.—GARDEN PARSNIP OR PARSNEP; (FR.) PANAIS POTAGER;
(GER.) PASTINAKE.

A TINCTURE OF THE FRESH ROOT OF PASTINACA SATIVA, LINN.

Description.—This usually cultivated biennial herb grows to a height of from 3 to 6 feet. *Root* conical, long and slender, fleshy and succulent. *Stem* smooth, deeply and plentifully grooved. *Leaves* pinnately compounded of 3 to 8 pairs of shining leaflets; *leaflets* ovate or oblong, obtuse cut-toothed or coarsely serrate, the terminal 3-lobed, all somewhat pubescent beneath; *petioles* sheathed. *Umbels* large and flat; *involucre* and involucels small or absent; *flowers* all perfect, none radiant. *Calyx-teeth* obsolete. *Petals* yellow, roundish, entire, involute; *point* broad and retuse. *Fruit* oval, flat, with a thin, single-winged margin; *carpels* minutely 5-ribbed, 3 of which are dorsal and equidistant, 2 lateral and at or near the margin; *vittæ* as long as the carpel, 1 in each sulcus, 2 in the commissure; *albumen* flat.

History and Habitat.—The Parsnip is a well-known culinary root, introduced into this country from Europe. It has now run wild in fields and waysides throughout the central and eastern parts of the United States, where it flowers from July to October.

The root is succulent, nutritious, sweet and in its cultivated state very pleasant to many, but when wild or in its second year's growth, it is rank and acrid poisonous, causing emesis and inflammation of the alimentary tract, followed by flatulent colic and diuresis. The seeds have been used in agues, with what curative action I cannot state.

In the north of Ireland a kind of beer is made by brewing the roots with hops; a good wine is also made in some places from them; and by distillation a sort of rum is produced similar to that of the sorghum product.

PART USED AND PREPARATION.—The roots of the second year's growth, or those of wild individuals, are prepared and macerated as in the previous plant. The resulting tincture is almost colorless, being but slightly tinged with yellow; is very gummy, has a peculiar honey-like odor, a sweet taste, and an acid reaction.

---

* *Pastus,* nourishment.

CHEMICAL CONSTITUENTS.—No analysis has yet been made to determine an active principle. Sugar abounds in the root, also starch and a gummy extractive.

PHYSIOLOGICAL ACTION.—Several cases of poisoning are recorded from the use of the wild or old roots. The symptoms following their ingestion are: Illusions of sight, dilated pupils, vertigo, difficult breathing, weak, slow pulse, and quiet delirium dependent upon the visions. In Dr. Pupcke's cases, where seven children ate of the cooked wild roots,* " all labored under 'delirium tremens,' they were in constant motion, talked incessantly, without knowing what they said, and fancied they saw objects which had no existence; they fought with each other, and occasionally had attacks of convulsive laughter; they rejected everything that was offered them, and were obliged to be restrained by force."

All the symptoms of the drug point to severe gastric irritation, with reflex action upon the brain and spinal cord.

DESCRIPTION OF PLATE 63.

1. Summit of a wild individual in young fruit, Binghamton, N. Y., June 26th, 1885.
2. Part of stem.
3. Face of flower.
4. Petal.
5. Stamen.
6. Ripe pistil.
7. Root.
8. Seed.
9. Section of a carpel.
(3–6 and 8–9 enlarged.)

---

* *Pharm. Jour.*, 1848, 184.

63.

1 2 3 4 5 6 7 8 9

ℭ︎𝔪. ad nat del.et pinxt.

PASTINÀCA SATÌVA, Linn.

64

ANGELICA ATROPURPUREA.

GREAT ANGELICA.

SYN.—ARCHANGELICA ATROPURPUREA, HOFF.; ANGELICA ATROPUR-
PUREA, LINN.; A. TRIQUINATA, MX.; IMPERATORIA LUCIDA, NUTT.
COM. NAMES.—COMMON ANGELICA,† HIGH ANGELICA, MASTERWORT.‡
(GER.) PURPURFARBIGE ANGELICA.

A TINCTURE OF THE WHOLE PLANT ARCHANGELICA ATROPURPUREA, HOFF.

Description.—This strong-scented, perennial herb grows to a height of from
4 to 6 feet. *Root* somewhat conical. *Stem* very stout, smooth, dark-purple, and
hollow. *Leaves* 2 to 3 ternately-compound; *leaflets* 5 to 7 pinnate, ovate, sharply
cut-serrate, acute, and pale beneath, the three terminal ones often confluent and
somewhat decurrent at the base. *Inflorescence* a globular compound umbel. *Involucre* little or none; *involucels* of very short, subulate leaflets. *Calyx* with very
short teeth. *Petals* ovate, entire, with the sharp tips inflexed. *Fruit* smooth;
carpels somewhat compressed, furnished with 3 rather prominent dorsal ribs, and
the two lateral ones prolonged into marginal wings; *vittæ* not on the pericarp,
but surrounding the seed and adherent to its surface; *seed* convex upon the back
and flattish upon the face, very loose in the pericarp. Read description of the
order under 62.

History and Habitat.—The Great Angelica is indigenous to North America,
from Pennsylvania and Wisconsin northward, where it habits low grounds along
streams, and flowers in June.

When fresh the roots are poisonous, and are said to have been used for
suicidal purposes by the Canadian Indians; when dried, however, they lose this
quality, and are then considered carminative, diuretic, emmenagogue and stimulant. The dried root was often used, especially in combination with other and
better-known diuretics, in anasarca and various diseases of the urinary organs;
and alone in flatulent colic and suppressed menstruation. Dr. Schell claims§ that

---

* This name alluded to its supposed high *angelic* properties.

† The common Garden Angelica is *A. archangelica.*

‡ The true Masterwort is the European *Imperatoria ostruthium*, Linn.; the Cow Parsnip, *Heracleum lanatum*, Linn.,
is often wrongly called by this name.

§ *Fam. Guide to Health,* 1856, corroborated in *Am. Jour. Hom. Mat. Med.,* i. 272.

64.

ℰℳ.ad nat.del.et pinxt. ARCHANGÉLICA ATROPURPÙREA , Hoffm.

doses of 15 to 20 grains of the dried root will cause a disgust for all spirituous liquors. The stems were often made into a candied preserve in some sections of the country—a practice now nearly extinct. Its uses, all in all, have been greatly similar to those of the Garden Angelica (*Angelica officinalis*, Hoff.; *A. archangelica*, Linn.).

PART USED AND PREPARATION.—The whole plant, when in seed, is chopped and pounded to a pulp, and treated as in the preceding species. The tincture, after filtration, has a clear greenish-orange color, a somewhat terebinthic odor, a sweetish taste, and neutral reaction.

CHEMICAL CONSTITUENTS.—This plant has not been specifically examined for the determination of its principles. Its oils, however, may be, in all probability, compared with those of *Angelica archangelica*.

PHYSIOLOGICAL ACTION.—Uninvestigated.

DESCRIPTION OF PLATE 64.

1. Whole plant 9 times reduced, Binghamton, N. Y., July 6th, 1885.
2. Portion of upper stalk, showing petiole.
3. Flower (petals removed).
4. Pistil.
5. Horizontal section of fruit.

(3–5 enlarged.)

GENUS.—**ÆTHUSA**,* LINN.

SEX. SYST.—PENTANDRIA DIGYNIA.

65

ÆTHUSA.

FOOL'S PARSLEY.

SYN.—ÆTHUSA CYNAPIUM, LINN.; CICUTARIA TENUIFOLIA, RAII.; C. FATUA, LOB.; CORIANDRUM CYNAPIUM, CRANTZ.

COM. NAMES.—FOOL'S PARSLEY, DOG'S PARSLEY, DOG POISON, GARDEN HEMLOCK, LESSER HEMLOCK, SMALL HEMLOCK; (FR.) LA PETITE CIQUË; (GER.) KLEINER SCHEILING, HUNDSPETERSILIE.

A TINCTURE OF THE WHOLE PLANT ÆTHUSA CYNAPIUM, LINN.

Description.—This fetid annual herb attains a growth of from 8 inches to 2 feet. *Stem* erect, unspotted, striate, and fistulous. *Leaves* dark green, 2-3-ternately compound, many cleft; *divisions* pinnate, wedge-lanceolate, obtuse. *Umbels* terminal and opposite the petioles; *rays* very unequal; *involucre* none; *involucels* one-sided, 3-leaved, the leaves erect while the buds are immature, but become long, narrow, and pendent when in full flower and fruit. *Flowers* white; *calyx teeth* obsolete; *petals* obovate, appearing emarginate, or even obcordate, by the inflexion of the tip. *Fruit* ovate-globose, not much if at all flattened either way; *carpophore* 2-parted; *mericarps*, each with 5 thick, sharply-keeled ridges; *vittæ*, single in the deep intervals, and 2 in the commissure at its base.

History and Habitat.—The Fool's Parsley is indigenous to Europe and Siberia, from whence it has been introduced into this country where it now grows, still sparingly, along roadsides and waste places about cultivated grounds, in New England, and from there to Pennsylvania, flowering in July and August.

On account of the many cases of poisoning by the inadvertent use of this herb for parsley, from which it is easily distinguishable,† very little use has been made of it by physicians. By the early writers it is so often confounded with Conium, that it is very difficult to trace its history. The first author to characterize it was Hermolaus Barbarus, who called it *Cicuta terrestris minore;* it is also mentioned by Matthiolus, Jonston, Jungius, Müller, and others, all speaking of its peculiar effects when eaten. Its action has been generally considered like that of *Conium*, but milder, and its principal, if not its only use, was in some forms of obstinate cutaneous disorders. It is not mentioned in the U. S. Ph., nor is it found in the Eclectic Dispensatory.

---

* Αἰθύσσω, *aithusso,* to set on fire; in reference to the acrid taste of the plant.

† Æthusa has much darker-green foliage than Parsley, a nauseous smell, white flowers, and the leaf-sections are much more acute.

PART USED AND PREPARATION.—The whole fresh plant, when in flower and fruit, is treated as directed under Eryngium (62). The resulting tincture has a clear, orange-brown color by transmitted light; a fetid, disagreeable odor; an acrid taste; and an acid reaction.

CHEMICAL CONSTITUENTS.—*Cynapin.* This alkaloid was discovered by Ficinus, who describes it as crystallizing in prisms that are soluble both in alcohol and water, but not in ether, and as having an alkaline reaction, and forming a crystallizable salt with sulphuric acid.* Walz describes an alkaloid, resulting as a volatile oily liquid, in which he is upheld by the experiments of Bernhart,† who succeeded in isolating a like substance, which he describes as having a strong alkaline reaction, an exceedingly penetrating, offensive odor, and as being soluble in alcohol. The body seems, as yet, to have received no further investigation.

PHYSIOLOGICAL ACTION.—The following excerpt, from one of the prominent botanical journals,‡ being of late date, serves to introduce this rubric:

" '*Fool's Parsley' not Poisonous.* — For several centuries the plant *Æthusa Cynapium*, L., has been the object of suspicion, and classed among poisons by botanists and toxicological writers. But now Dr. John Harley, of England, comes forward and presents a vindication of what he calls 'an innocent and harmless plant.' In the St. Thomas' Hospital Reports, he relates a number of facts to prove the correctness of his conclusions. The juices of the plant, from the root as well as from the leaves, were obtained by expression just before flowering, and also after the plants had reached maturity and set fruit. Being thus provided with a supply of material, representing the active properties of the plant, he exhausted it upon four patients,—one a little girl, four years old, who took the extract in quantities ranging from 2 drachms to 2 ounces; himself, who took it in quantities ranging from 2 to 4 fluid ounces; and two other adults, who were the subjects of spasmodic wry-neck. These two took one or other of the juices, in doses ranging from 1 to 8 fluid ounces. Effects were anxiously looked for, but absolutely none followed in any of the cases. Dr. Harley therefore feels compelled to assert that *Æthusa Cynapium* of Sussex, Essex, Kent, Surrey, and Hertfordshire, is not only absolutely free from the noxious properties attributed to it, but that it is pleasant to sight, smell, and taste, and, in the absence of the more fragrant and succulent plants, might well be used as a pot-herb or salad. He is satisfied, further, that his conclusions are independent both of locality and season, and that the only influence which these conditions have on Fool's Parsley, as on hemlock (*Conium maculatum*), is to increase or diminish its succulency. Dr. Harley, some years ago, made some observations on the last-mentioned plant, and came to the same conclusion in regard to its innocuous nature that he has concerning that of the *Æthusa*. In connection with this, it may be stated that *Conium maculatum*, in northern latitudes—Russia for example—is eaten with impunity, although precaution is taken to first boil it in several waters. This subject of the harmlessness, under certain conditions, of plants reputed to be poisonous, recalls to mind the

---

* Wittstein.   † *Arch. de Phar.*, 1880, 117 (*Am. Jour. Phar.*, 1880, 204).   ‡ *Bull. Torr. Club*, 1881, 9.

statement of Linnæus, in his *Flora Lapponica*, that the Norlanders prepare from the leaves of *Aconitum Napellus* a broth, which they éat without any injurious effects resulting therefrom."

The following cases of poisoning by the drug, serve, however, to show its action upon the system:

"A boy, six years of age, having eaten some of this herb, by mistake for Parsley, at 4 o'clock in the afternoon, commenced immediately to cry out in great pain, and complained of great cramps in the stomach. Whilst taking him home the whole body became excessively swollen, and of a livid hue; the respiration became difficult and short, and he died toward midnight. Another child was poisoned in the same manner, but he was fortunate enough to vomit up the herb. This, however, did not prevent many symptoms manifesting themselves; he talked wildly, and in his delirium he thought he saw numbers of dogs and cats."—(*Orfila*, vol. ii, p. 324.)

"Gmelin has related the case of a child who died in eight hours, in consequence of having eaten the Æthusa. The symptoms were spasmodic pains in the stomach; swelling of the belly; lividity of the skin; and difficult breathing."—(*Chris.*, p. 365.)

"A woman gave two of her children soup, in which some of this was boiled. They were both seized with severe pain in the abdomen, and next morning there was perfect unconsciousness; the lower jaw was spasmodically fixed; abdomen tumid; vomiting of a bloody mucus, and constant diarrhœa; cold extremities; convulsions; and death in twenty-four hours. Post-mortem appearance: redness of the lining-membrane of the œsophagus, and slight vascular congestion of stomach and duodenum."—(*Medic. Jahrbuch.*)

"Another child, who had eaten the bulbs by mistake for young turnips, was suddenly seized with pain in the abdomen, followed by nausea, without vomiting; could not swallow; vacuity; inability to answer questions; lower jaw fixed; insensibility and death an hour after the commencement of the symptoms."—(*Med. Times*, August 23, 1845.)

"A healthy, strong man, about thirty-five years of age, a publican, ate a handful of Fool's Parsley, with nearly the same quantity of young lettuce, about 1 o'clock P. M.; in about ten minutes he was affected with a pain in the stomach and bowels, attended with a rumbling. He walked out in the fields, but was seized with such languor, weariness, and weakness, that he supported himself with difficulty. He was much troubled with giddiness in the head; his vision was confused, and sometimes objects appeared double. At 7 o'clock he got an emetic, which brought up, he supposes, all the Fool's Parsley, but none of the lettuce; this relieved him of the unpleasant symptoms in the stomach, but the other sensations continued, and he passed a restless night. Next day he had much pain in his head and eyes, which last were inflamed and bloodshot. He had different circumscribed swellings in his face, which were painful and inflamed, but they were transient, and flew from place to place. On the Saturday his eyes were highly inflamed, painful, and entirely closed by the surrounding inflammation. He was bled, which gave him much relief in his face and eyes. From this time until the Monday, he continued to get better, but had, even then, pain, heat, and inflammation of the eyes, with œdematous swelling of the cheeks; his remaining symptoms went off gradually."—(*Lowe.*)

Riviere relates that a person died after taking this plant. "His tongue was black; a brownish serosity was found in the stomach; the liver was hard, of a yellow color; the spleen livid; but the body was not at all emphysematous."

The symptoms of poisoning by this drug show, according to Schulze, that its chief action is upon the medulla spinalis.

On Animals.—Seven ounces of the juice of the leaves were given to a strong dog, and the œsophagus tied. Twenty minutes thereafter the dog became sick; in half an hour it did not seem to affect him much, when suddenly he stretched out his limbs and lay upon his stomach; in a few minutes he tried to arouse himself, but his efforts were in vain. The muscles of the limbs, particularly of the posterior, refused to obey the will, but the organs of sense exercised their functions; the pupils were scarcely dilated; the pulsations of the heart were slow and strong. This state lasted a quarter of an hour, and then the extremities were agitated by convulsive movements; the animal threw himself from one side to the other, his senses began to be enfeebled, and the œsophagus and fauces were spasmodically contracted. This state of stupor increased, and the animal died an hour after taking the poison. On opening the body the heart was found to be contracted, and the left ventricle contained fluid and black blood; the lungs were a little less crepitant than natural. The stomach was found full of the poison, but there was no alteration of the digestive canal.*

DESCRIPTION OF PLATE 65.

1. End of flowering plant.
2. Bract of the involucel.
3. Flower.
4. Stigmas.
5. Fruit.
6. Dorsal view of a mericarp.
7. Commissural view of same.
8. Section of same.
   (2, 4, and 6 enlarged.)

* *Orfila*, vol. ii, 323.

65.

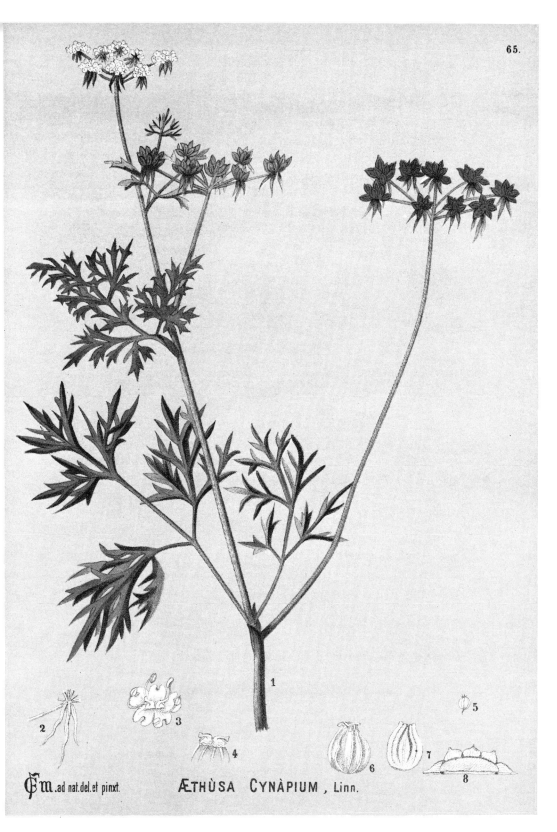

1

2

3

4

5

6

7

8

℈m.ad nat.del.et pinxt.   ÆTHÙSA CYNÀPIUM, Linn.

N. ORD.—UMBELLIFERÆ.

GENUS.—**THASPIUM**,* NUTT.

SEX. SYST.—PENTANDRIA DIGYNIA.

66

ZIZIA.†

MEADOW PARSNIPS.

SYN.—THASPIUM AUREUM, NUTT.; ZIZIA AUREA, KOCH.; SMYRNIUM
AUREUM, LINN.; SMYRNIUM LUTEUM, MUHL.; SMYRNIUM ACU-
MINATUM, SMITH; SISSON TRIFOLATUM, MICHX.; SISSON AU-
REUS, SPRENG.

COM. NAMES.—MEADOW PARSNIP, GOLDEN MEADOW PARSNEP, GOL-
DEN ALEXANDERS, ROUNDHEART; (GER.) GOLDEN PASTINAKE.

A TINCTURE OF THE WHOLE PLANT THASPIUM AUREUM, NUTT.

Description.—This erect, perennial herb attains a height of from 1 to 3 feet.
Root tap-shaped, 2 to 4 inches long by ½ to ¾ of an inch in diameter, yellow
internally. *Leaves* 1- to 2-ternately parted or divided; *lower leaves* on long
petioles, sometimes simple or more or less cordate; *upper leaves* sessile or nearly
so; *leaflets* 1 to 2 inches long, oblong-lanceolate, cut serrate, the *bases* elongated
cuneate. *Inflorescence* axial or terminal compound umbels, on long, naked peduncles; *involucre* inconspicuous or absent; *pedicels* 10 to 20 elongating in fruit; *involucels* minute, few-leaved; *flowers* deep, orange-yellow. *Calyx teeth* obscure.
Petals oblong, terminated by an inflexed tip. *Fruit* oval-oblong, somewhat flattened or laterally contracted; *ridges* 10-winged; *transverse section* orbicular; *vittæ*
solitary in each sulcus, and 2 in the commissure. Read description of the natural
order, under Eryngium, 62.

History and Habitat.—The Meadow Parsnip is quite a common indigenous
plant on the moist banks of streams, and in open, wet woods, where it flowers in
June and July. I find no mention of this plant in medical literature. The genus
is spoken of by Rafinesque‡ as vulnerary, antisyphilitic, and sudorific.

PART USED AND PREPARATION.—The whole fresh plant (the prover
used only the root) is chopped and pounded to a pulp and weighed. Then two
parts by weight of alcohol are taken, the pulp mixed thoroughly with one-sixth
part of it, and the rest of the alcohol added. After having stirred the whole well,
pour it into a well-stoppered bottle, and allow it to stand eight days in a dark,
cool place.

---

* A play upon the genus *Thapsia*, named from the Isle of Thapsus.
† I have retained the name under which the plant was proven. See second synonym.
‡ *Med. Bot.*, vol. ii, p. 267.

₵ℳ.ad nat.del.et pinxt.   THÁSPIUM AÚREUM Var APTERUM, Gray.

The tincture, separated from this mass by straining and filtering, should have a deep brownish-orange color by transmitted light, no distinguishing odor, a slightly bitter taste, and strong acid reaction.   It leaves a numb, furry sensation upon the tongue, something like the impression left by tincture of aconite.

PHYSIOLOGICAL ACTION.—The Meadow Parsnip appears to uphold the general action of the Umbelliferæ, and act specifically in a similar manner to Æthusa.   The symptoms of those proving the drug under the direction of Dr. E. E. Marcy are those of a nerve irritant.   The only report of a toxic quantity being taken is that by Judge Gray of a young lady who ate a large root.   In this case violent vomiting followed immediately, ejecting the root in time to ward off any farther action.*

DESCRIPTION OF PLATE 66.†

1. 1a to 1b, upper part of plant, Ithaca, N. Y., June 3d, 1880.
2. Flower (enlarged).

---

* Marcy, in *Ency. Pure Mat. Med.*, vol. x, p. 634.

† This Plate has been titled *Thaspium aureum*, var. *apertum ;* but the seed, the only characteristic of var. *apertum*, having been omitted, it reverts to its proper title—*i. e.*, *Thaspium aureum*, Nutt.

Shortly after taking note of the physical properties of the tincture here recorded,—during which I made many futile attempts to detect a characteristic odor and taste, and took probably about 10 minims,—the tongue felt fuzzy and numb. This sensation was followed by a feeling as if the tongue had been scalded with hot tea ; my eyes began to water and smart ; I ceased writing, and threw myself upon my lounge (12 M.) ; my face then began to feel suffused with blood and soon became hot, especially the cheeks and forehead ; drowsiness followed, and I fell into a distressingly dreamy sleep, lasting an hour.   When I awoke (1.30 P. M.) all symptoms had passed away except the scalded sensation of the tongue, which lasted fully an hour longer.

N. ORD.—UMBELLIFERÆ.

GENUS.—**CICUTA**,* LINN.

SEX. SYST.—PENTANDRIA DIGYNIA.

67

CICUTA MACULATA.

WATER HEMLOCK.

SYN.—CICUTA MACULATA, LINN.; CICUTARIA MACULATA, LAM.; SIUM DOUGLASII, (?) D. C.

COM. NAMES.—AMERICAN WATER HEMLOCK, SNAKEWEED, BEAVER POISON, MUSQUASH ROOT, SPOTTED COWBANE, DEATH OF MAN, CHILDREN'S BANE; (FR.) CIQUE D'AMERIQUE; (GER.) AMERIKA-NISCHER WASSERSCHIERLING.

A TINCTURE OF THE FRESH ROOTS OF CICUTA MACULATA, LINN.

Description.—This poisonous marsh perennial attains a growth of from 3 to 6 feet. *Root* a fascicle of several oblong, thick and fleshy tubers. *Stem* stout and smooth, fistulate, streaked with purple (*not maculate*), or when growing in open places deep purple, and in shady situations wholly green. *Leaves* bi-ternately compound, the lower on long petioles; *leaflets* oblong-lanceolate, pointed, and sometimes lobed; *margins* mucronately coarse-serrate, the veins ending in the notches. *Inflorescence* in long peduncled, axillary umbels; *involucre* few leaved or wanting; *involucels* 5 to 6 leaved; leaflets linear; *flowers* white. *Calyx* minutely 5-toothed; *teeth* acute. *Petals* obcordate, with an inflexed, pointed tip. *Fruit* aromatic, almost globular, geminate, and a little contracted at the sides. *Carpels* with 5 strong, flattish ribs, the lateral ones marginal; *vittæ* large, single in the intervals, double in the commissure; *seeds* terete. Read description of the order under Eryngium, 62.

History and Habitat.—The Water Hemlock is indigenous to the United States from Florida and Mississippi northward, where it grows in wet places, and flowers in June and July.

Cicuta had, until the publication of Dr. Bigelow's work,† been considered more as a poison than a drug, a few practitioners only using very small doses as a substitute for conium, and some of the laity, little knowing its toxic properties, as a gargle in sore throat. Rafinesque claims that its roots were eaten by such Indians as were tired of life and desired a speedy demise. Later the powdered leaves were employed to a limited extent to alleviate the pain of scirrhus cancers. Cicuta plays no part in any system of medicine except the homœopathic.

---

* The ancient Latin name, in reference to the hollow stems of this genus, the name Cicuta designating the hollow joints of reeds from which pipes were made.

† *Am. Med. Bot.*, Boston, 1817.

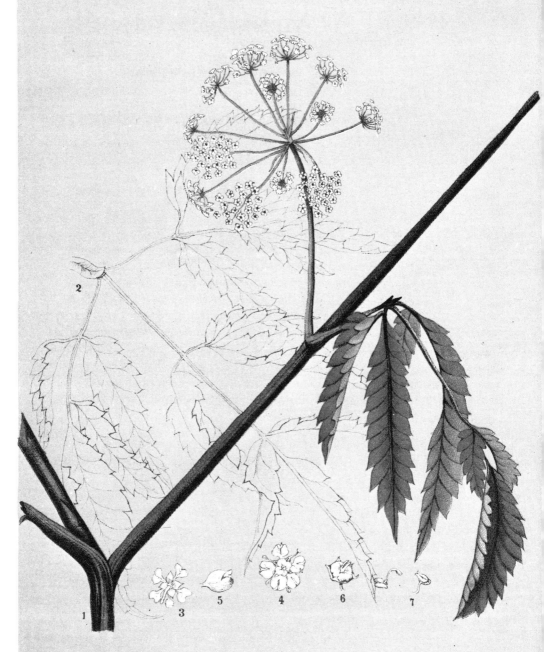

Ͼ.ᴍ..ad nat del.et pinxt.

CICÙTA MACULÀTA, Linn.

The specific name *maculata* is badly chosen, as the stems, as far as I have observed, are never spotted, nor do I find any record of such a marking having been noticed; Dr. Bigelow modestly offers the name *fasciculata*, which is true of the roots, and should be adopted, being much less like that of conium. Great similarity is said to exist between this species and the European *C. virosa*. Not having had an opportunity to examine the latter, I am at present unable to differentiate between them. According to descriptions, *C. virosa* has not a fasciculate root, and its umbels are larger in every way and much denser.

PART USED AND PREPARATION.—The fresh roots, chopped and pounded to a pulp, are treated as in the preceding drug. The resulting tincture has a clear yellowish-amber color by transmitted light, the peculiar odor of the fresh root, a sweetish taste, and an acid reaction.

CHEMICAL CONSTITUENTS.—Dr. Bigelow's examination of the root is the only attempt so far made toward an analysis; he procured a volatile oil and a yellow, inflammable resin. Mr. J. E. Young succeeded in obtaining a volatile alkaloid from the fruits, which he regarded as identical with *conia*. A glance, however, at the chemistry of *C. virosa* will not be out of place here:

Cicutina.—This volatile alkaloid found in all parts of the plant by Wittstein, Polex, and others, remains as yet very imperfectly investigated; it is simply mentioned by Wittstein as having been obtained in an aqueous solution.

Oil of Cumin.—This compound of several hydrocarbons, first obtained from the fruit of *Cuminum cyminum*, Linn., is proven by Trapp to be identical with the oil of this species. Two of the hydrocarbons are identified as follows: *Cicuten*, $C_{10}H_{16}$ (Van Ankum), boils at 166° (330.8° F.), is dextrogyrate, sp. gr. at 18° (64.4° F.), 0.87038, and is soluble in alcohol, ether, and chloroform; *Cymol*, $C_{10}H_{14}$, a colorless oil of great refractory power and the odor of lemons, having a sp. gr. at 15° (59° F.) of 0.86, and a boiling point at 172° (341.6° F.).

Cicutoxin.—This amorphous, resinous body, in all probability identical with that found by Bigelow in the root-juice of *C. maculata*, was isolated and named by Trojanowski.

PHYSIOLOGICAL ACTION.—Many cases of poisoning from the root of this species have been reported, all showing, by the symptoms, that cicuta produces great hyperæmia of the brain and spinal cord.

The following case, reported by letter to Dr. Bigelow by Dr. R. Hazeltine (1818),* gives all the symptoms noted by observers in other cases: A boy had eaten of certain tuberous roots, gathered in a recently-ploughed field, supposing them to be artichokes, but which were identified as the roots of Cicuta maculata. His first symptom was a pain in the bowels urging him to an ineffectual attempt at stool, after which he vomited about a teacupful of what appeared to be the

* Bigelow, *Am. Med. Bot.*, vol. iii., 181.

recently-masticated root, and immediately fell back into convulsions which lasted off and on continuously until his death. The doctor found him in a profuse sweat and "convulsive agitations, consisting of tremors, violent contractions and distortions, with alternate and imperfect relaxations of the whole muscular system, astonishing mobility of the eyeballs and eyelids, with widely-dilated pupils, stridor dentium, trismus, frothing at the mouth and nose, mixed with blood, and occasionally violent and genuine epilepsy." The convulsive agitations were so powerful and incessant, that the doctor "could not examine the pulse with sufficient constancy to ascertain its character." At the post-mortem no inflammation was observed, the stomach was fully distended with flatus, and contained "about three gills of a muciform and greenish fluid, such as had flowed from the mouth ; this mass assumed a dark green color on standing."

DESCRIPTION OF PLATE 67.

1. Part of flowering branch, Binghamton, N. Y., July 2d, 1885.
2. Leaf.
3. Flower, showing calyx.
4. Face of flower.
5. Petal.
6. Pistil and calyx.
7. Stamens.
     (3–7 enlarged.)

68

CONIUM.

POISON HEMLOCK.

SYN.—CONIUM MACULATUM, LINN.; C. MAJOR, BAUH.; CORIANDRUM CICUTA, CRANTZ.; C. MACULATUM. ROTH.; CICUTA MACULATA, LAM. (not Linn.); C. VULGARIS MAJOR, PARK.; CICUTARIA VULGARIS, CLUS.

COM. NAMES.—WILD OR POISON HEMLOCK, STINK-WEED,† SPOTTED POISON PARSLEY, HERB-BENNET; (FR.) GRAND CIQUE, CIQUE ORDINAIRE; (GER.) SCHIERLING.

A TINCTURE OF THE FRESH PLANT, EXCLUDING THE ROOT, OF CONIUM MACULATUM, L.

Description.—This large, unsavory, biennial herb, grows to a height varying from 2 to 6 feet. *Root* fusiform, sometimes forked. *Stem* erect, hollow, smooth, and striate, stout below, corymbosely branching above, the whole dotted and splashed with crimson beneath the white, pulverent, easily detached coating that pervades the whole plant except the leaves and flowers. *Leaves* generally large, decompound, somewhat deltoid in outline; *common petioles* with broad striate sheathing bases; *segments* lanceolate pinnatifid; *lobes* bright green, acute and regularly serrate. *Inflorescence* terminal, flat-topped, compound umbels; *involucre* about 3-leaved; *leaves* lanceolate, acuminate, deflexed; *involucels* about 5-leaved, shorter than the umbellets, and situated to the outside of them; *leaves* lanceolate; *rays* numerous, straight; *flowers* small, white. *Petals* obtuse or somewhat obcordate, the apices incurved. *Calyx teeth* obsolete, the limb forming a thickened crowning ring in fruit. *Stamens* but slightly longer than the petals; *anthers* white. *Fruit* orate, turgid, laterally flattened, the crown retaining the divergent styles, each of which, together with its dilated base, greatly resembles the depicted head-gear of the mediæval court jester. *Carpels* with 5 prominent, nearly equal, papillose ribs, the lateral ones marginal; *vittæ* none; *seed* with its inner face marked by a deep and narrow longitudinal sulcus.

History and Habitat.—Conium is indigenous to Europe and Asia. It, however, has become thoroughly naturalized in this country, where it grows in waste places, usually by river-sides. It blossoms during July and August.

---

* Κώνειον, *koneion ;* from κῶνος, *konos*, a top, judged by Hooker to be so named on account of the whirling vertigo caused by the poison.

† A name more commonly applied to *Datura Stramonium.*

The history of this fetid, poisonous plant, dates back to about the fifth century before Christ. From the careful observations of many pharmacographists and historians, there seems little doubt that the Grecian State potion used at Athens as a mode of execution of those condemned to death by the tribunal of Areopagus, was principally, if not wholly, composed of the fresh juice of the leaves and green seeds of this plant. It is the κόνειον which destroyed Thermanes, one of the thirty, Phocion, and Socrates, whose disciple he had been. Plato, in describing the potion, does not give it a specific name, nor mention its source, but terms the potion φαρμακον, which means any strong drug, and not necessarily a poisonous one. In the writings of Eratosthenes also, it appears that the words κινειν κωνειον mean to drink poison, and κωνειον πεπωκοτα, having drunk poison. Ælian states that Cean old men, who, when they had become useless to the State, and tired of the infirmities of life, invited each other to a banquet, after which they drank κωνειον and died together. Although none of these accounts give the derivation of the potion, and notwithstanding the fact that Dioscorides' description of the plant is too general to distinguish the umbelliferous species he refers to, yet there are important reasons why we should feel perfectly satisfied that the Grecian κωνειον was the Conium of our materia medica : first, Sibthorp says * that Conium grows plentifully between Athens and Magara, and that no other plant of near so violent qualities grows in Greece; secondly, *Cicuta virosa*—supposed, by those who doubt Conium being the origin of the potion, to be the κωνειον—does not grow in Greece. The cicuta of later writers, is a Latin name, applied by the Romans to any and all poisonous umbelliferæ, and even to other widely separate toxic plants ; this term was unknown to the Greeks ; thirdly, Dr. J. H. Bennett's case of poisoning by Conium gave symptoms almost identical with those given in the description of the death of Socrates ; fourthly, later provings of Conium on man and animals, all point to it as being answerable to the symptoms mentioned. Cicuta causes convulsions even to opisthotonos, and sudden stiffness and immobility of the limbs ; while Conium causes creeping muscular paralysis, with mayhap slight trembling, but no spasm ; lastly, the words of the man who prepared the potion : " We only *bruise* as much as is barely sufficient for the purpose," would seem to indicate a simple; a man who spoke so clearly and definitely would hardly have used the word " bruise " had opium been added to the preparation, as some of the upholders of Cicuta claim, in trying to explain why spasms did not occur in this case.

The first use of Conium in medicine is that of Dioscorides, who used it as a collyrium mixed with wine, and as a cataplasm in herpes and erysipelas. Pliny states † that the leaves keep down all tumors ; and Anaxilaus claims that by anointing the mammæ they ceased to grow. Avicenna ‡ praised it as an agent for the cure of tumors of the breasts. It remained, however, for Baron Störck (1760) to introduce Conium into more general use; he found it effectual in curing scirrhus, ulcers, cancer, and many other chronic forms of disease. Bayle § collected from various sources 46 cases of cancerous disease cured, and 26 ameliorated by the use of this drug. Conium has been recommended in jaundice, tic-douloureux,

* *Prod. Flor. Gr.,* i, 187.   † *Nat. Hist.,* b. xxvi, c. 16.   ‡ *Lib.* ii, 662.   § *Bib. Therap.,* iii, 618.

syphilitic affections, enlargement of glands, especially those of a scrofulous nature, as a sedative in mania, chorea, epilepsy, laryngismus stridulus, pertussis, and various forms of nervous diseases.

Like all other drugs used by the dominant school of medicine then and now, many physicians failed to get any effect whatsoever from this drug in the diseases specified by Störck and others; so frequent were the failures that most careful and protracted experiments in gathering, curing, preserving, and preparing the drug were resorted to, analyses were made, essays written, and finally serious doubts expressed as to Baron Störck's cases;* without once a thought that it might be adaptability to his cases, and not pharmaceutical preparation that caused the drug to cure. It is well known to us as homœopathists that Baron Störck had a "peculiar notion" as to the adaptability of drugs to diseased conditions, a notion very like the law that guides us to-day.† I can personally testify to the cure of one well-marked case of mammary scirrhus, by Conium. The case is as follows: Mrs. B—— complained to me of having experienced, for some months past, sharp stitching pains in the left mamma, extending thence in all directions, but especially through to the shoulder-blade, and upward and outward into the axilla; these stitches would awaken her at night, causing her sleep to be interfered with seriously. On examining the breast I found the nipple retracted and surrounded by a hard nodular lump, just movable, and about the area of a silver dollar. Her mother died of "a cancer of the breast" several years before. I prescribed Conium in a potency, one dose per diem. Within six weeks the subjective symptoms entirely passed away, four months after, the "tumor" was much softer and the nipple less cupped. The remedy was then stopped, and upon examining her to-day (nearly four years after the first dose), I find no vestige of the growth whatever, the mamma appearing entirely normal.

Concerning the root of this virulent plant, Lepage ‡ corroborates the assertion of Orfila, that the amount of alkaloid therein is very small; this accounts for the following experiences: Ray relates § that Mr. Petiver ate half an ounce, and Mr. Healy four ounces without experiencing any remarkable effect. Curtis says: ‖ "Mr. Alicorn assures me that he has tried this (eating the roots) in every season of the year, and in most parts of our island, without feeling any material difference; and Mr. T. Lane informs me that he also, cautiously, made some experiments of the like kind, without any inconvenience; after many successive trials, he had some of the larger roots boiled, and found them as agreeable eating at dinner with meat as carrots, which they somewhat resembled;" Mr. Steven, a Russian botanist, states that the Russian peasants eat it with impunity, and concludes that the colder the climate the less poisonous is the root. Pliny says: ¶ "as for the stems and

---

* Woodville says (*Med. Bot.*, i, 108): " . . . . Nay, it never succeeded so well as when under his own direction or confined to the neighborhood in which he resided, and to the practice of those physicians with whom he lived in habits of intimacy and friendship. [A base imputation, unworthy of the author.—C. F. M.] The general inefficiency of Hemlock experienced in this country, induced physicians at first to suppose that this plant, in the environs of Vienna and Berlin, differed widely from ours, and this being so stated to Dr. Störck he sent a quantity of the extract, prepared by himself, to London, but this proved equally unsuccessful, and to differ in no respect from the English extract."

† Note also Baron Störck's use of Stramonium, as cited under that drug. ‡ *Jour. Phar. et Chim.*, 1885, 10.
§ *Phil. Trans.*, xix, 634. ‖ *Flor. Londinensis.* ¶ *Nat. Hist.*, b. 26, c. xii.

stalks, many there be who do eat it, both green and also boiled or stewed between two platters." Notwithstanding all this, many children have been poisoned from eating the roots.

Conium is official in the U. S. Ph., as *Abstractum Conii ; Extractum Conii Alcoholicum ; Extractum Conii Fluidum*, and *Tinctura Conii*. In the Eclectic Materia Medica the preparations are : *Extractum Conii Alcoholicum ; Unguentum Conii* and *Emplastrum Belladonnæ Compositum.**

PART USED AND PREPARATION.—The entire fresh plant, with the exception of the root, should be gathered while the fruits are yet green, and prepared as in the preceding drug. The resulting tincture should have a clear madder color by transmitted light, and give an odor somewhat similar to that of the bruised leaves, a taste at first sweetish, then similar to the odor, and an acid reaction.

CHEMICAL CONSTITUENTS.—*Conia,*† $C_8H_{15}N$. This volatile alkaloid was discovered by Giseke in the leaves and fruit of this plant; Geiger, however, was first to purify it. Conia is a limpid, colorless, oily liquid, having the specific gravity of .89, and boiling at 163.°5 (328.°3 F.). It possesses a nauseous and sharp taste, and a disagreeable odor. It is soluble in cold water, in which solution it becomes turbid on the application of heat.

Methylconine, $C_8H_{14}NCH_3$. This alkaloid is also sometimes present in conium. It bears great resemblance to conia.

Conydrine,‡ $C_8H_{17}ON$. A crystalline alkaloid melting at 120.°6 (249° F.), and boiling at 225° (437° F.).

Paraconine, $C_8H_{15}N$. This fourth alkaloid, isomeric with conia, differs from it only in being a tertiary base devoid of rotary power. Paraconine is liquid, and boils at 160°–170° (320°–338° F.). (*Ut supra*, Schorlemmer.)

Oil of Conium, $C_8H_{16}N_2O$. A pale, yellow oil extracted from the seeds. This oil is also formed when nitrogen trioxide is passed into conia and the resulting liquid decomposed by water.

Conic Acid.—This body, yet uninvestigated, exists in all parts of the plant and holds in solution the alkaloids present.

PHYSIOLOGICAL ACTION.—No more fitting introduction to the action of this virulent spinal irritant could be written than the description, in Plato's "Phædo," of the death of Socrates: "And Crito, hearing this, gave the sign to the boy who stood near; and the boy departing, after some time returned, bringing with him the man who was to administer the poison, who brought it ready bruised in a cup. And Socrates, beholding the man, said : 'Good friend, come hither ; you are experienced in these affairs—what is to be done ?' 'Nothing,' replied the man, 'only when you have drank the poison you are to walk about until a heaviness takes

---

* Rosin, Belladonna, Conium, and Iodine.   † Conine, Conicina, Conein, Coniin, Conicin.

‡ Conydrina, Conhydria, Conhydrin.

place in your legs; then lie down—this is all you have to do.' At the same time he presented the cup. Socrates received it from him with great calmness, without fear or change of countenance, and regarding the man with his usual stern aspect he asked: 'What say you of this potion? Is it lawful to sprinkle any portion of it on the earth, as a libation, or not?' 'We only bruise,' said the man, 'as much as is barely sufficient for the purpose.' 'I understand you,' said Socrates; 'but it is certainly lawful and proper to pray the gods that my departure from hence may be prosperous and happy, which I indeed beseech them to grant.' So saying, he carried the cup to his mouth, and drank it with great promptness and facility.

"Thus far most of us had been able to refrain from weeping. But when we saw that he was drinking, and actually had drank the poison, we could no longer restrain our tears. And from me they broke forth with such violence that I covered my face and deplored my wretchedness. I did not weep for his fate so much as for the loss of a friend and benefactor, which I was about to sustain. But Crito, unable to restrain his tears, now broke forth in loud lamentations, which infected all who were present, except Socrates. But he observing us, exclaimed, 'What is it you do, my excellent friends? I have sent away the women that they might not betray such weakness. I have heard that it is our duty to die cheerfully, and with expressions of joy and praise. Be silent, therefore, and let your fortitude be seen.' At this address we blushed, and suppressed our tears. But Socrates, after walking about, now told us that his legs were beginning to grow heavy, and immediately lay down, for so he had been ordered. At the same time the man who had given him the poison examined his feet and legs, touching them at intervals. At length he pressed violently upon his foot, and asked if he felt it. To which Socrates replied that he did not. The man then pressed his legs and so on, showing us that he was becoming cold and stiff. And Socrates, feeling it himself, assured us that when the effects had ascended to his heart, he should be gone. And now the middle of his body growing cold, he threw aside his clothes, and spoke for the last time: 'Crito, we owe the sacrifice of a cock to Æsculapius. Discharge this, and neglect it not.' 'It shall be done,' said Crito; 'have you anything else to say?' He made no reply, but a moment after moved, and his eyes became fixed. And Crito, seeing this, closed his eyelids and mouth."

Another case very similar to this was met with by Dr. J. H. Bennett.* A man ate a large quantity of Hemlock plant by mistake for parsley; soon afterwards there was a loss of power in the lower extremities, but he apparently suffered no pain. In walking he staggered as if he was drunk; at length his limbs refused to support him, and he fell. On being raised, his legs dragged after him, or when his arms were lifted they fell like inert masses, and remained immovable; there was perfect paralysis of the upper and lower extremities within two hours after he had taken the poison. There was a loss of power of deglutition, and a partial paralysis of sensation, but no convulsions, only slight occasional motions of the left leg; the pupils were fixed. Three hours after eating the hemlock the respiratory movements had ceased. Death took place in three and one-quarter hours. It

* *Med. and Surg. Jour. Edin.*, 1845, 169.

was evidently caused by gradual asphyxia from paralysis of the muscles of respiration, but the intellect was perfectly clear until shortly before death.

The sequence of symptoms would seem to show in all of the many cases of poisoning by this plant that the drug acts primarily upon the spinal cord, causing a paralysis first of the anterior then posterior branches, and that from below upward until the medulla is reached.

On Animals.—Linnæus states that sheep will eat of the leaves, but horses and goats refuse them. Ray says that the thrush will feed upon the seeds, even when grain is plenty. Orfila* found that the powder and extract were generally harmless when given to animals, but that the juice or leaves of the fresh plant produced the most violent symptoms and death. Moiroud† gave a decoction of four ounces of the dried plant to a horse which had eaten three and a half pounds of the plant without effect. It caused dejection, stupor, dilation of the pupils, trembling, spasmodic trembling of muscles, grinding of teeth and copious sweats. It would seem, from experiments upon animals, that Conium is more poisonous to carnivora than to graminivora.

Post-mortem.—In Dr. Bennett's case, there was slight serous effusion beneath the arachnoid membrane. The substance of the brain was soft on section ; there were numerous bloody points, but the organ was otherwise healthy. The lungs were engorged with dark-red fluid blood ; the heart was soft and flabby. The mucous coat of the stomach, that contained a green, pultaceous mass of the herb, was much congested, especially at the cardiac extremity ; here there were numerous extravasations of dark blood below the epithelium, over a space about the size of the hand. The intestines presented patches of congestion on .the mucous coat. The blood throughout the body was fluid and of a dark color.

DESCRIPTION OF PLATE 68.

1. Top of a flowering branch divested of three of its umbels, Binghamton, N. Y., June 29th, 1884.
    2. Stalk at the root.
    3. Flower.
    4 and 5. Stamens.
    6. Young fruit.
    7. Section of ovary.
    8. Pollen, x 250.
        (3–6 enlarged.)

---

* *Tox. Gén.*, ii, 309. † *Pharm. Vét.*, 359.

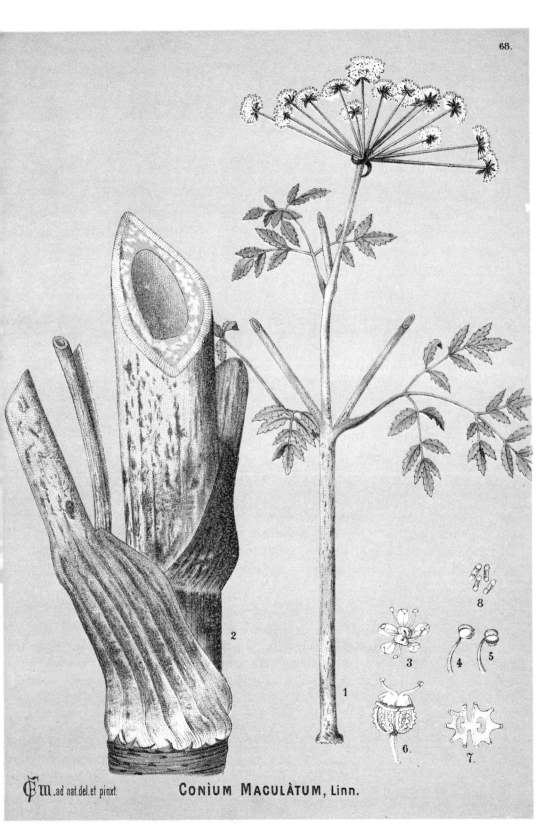

CONIUM MACULATUM, Linn.

.ad nat.del.et pinxt.

N. ORD.—ARALIACEÆ.

GENUS.—**ARALIA,*** TOURN.

SEX. SYST.—PENTANDRIA PENTAGYNIA.

69

ARALIA RACEMOSA.

SPIKENARD.

SYN.—ARALIA RACEMOSA, LINN.

COM. NAMES.—SPIKENARD, AMERICAN SPIKENARD, PETTYMORREL, LIFE-OF-MAN, PIGEON-WEED; (FR.) NARD D'AMERIQUE; (GER.) AMERIKANISCHER ARALIE.

A TINCTURE OF THE FRESH ROOT OF ARALIA RACEMOSA, LINN.

Description.—This aromatic perennial attains a growth of from 2 to 5 feet.†
Root large, thick, spicy-aromatic; *bark* thick, whitish internally. *Stem* ligneously herbaceous, smooth, bifurcating, much branched, and devoid of prickles. *Leaves* very large, odd-pinnately compound; *leaflets* ovate-cordate, doubly-serrate, acuminate, slightly downy; *stipules* wanting, or represented by a serrate stipular membrane at the bifurcation of the branches and sometimes at the bases of the petioles. *Inflorescence* numerous axillary, compound, racemose panicles, or thyrsi. *Flowers* monœciously polygamous or perfect. *Calyx* coherent with the ovary; *teeth* 5, short, projecting upward between the petals. *Petals* 5, epigynous, obovate acute, reflexed-spreading, caducous. *Stamens* 5, epigynous, situated opposite the calyx teeth; *filaments* slender; *anthers* 2-celled, opening longitudinally. *Ovary* globular, 5-celled, somewhat 10-ridged; *ovules* anatropous, suspended, 1 in each cell; *styles* 5, closely clustered, sometimes united at the base, or in the sterile flowers entirely united; *stigmas* capitellate, or simply a stigmatic surface to the apex of each style. *Fruit* globular, aromatic, baccate drupes, retaining the persistent and now divaricate styles; *embryo* minute.

Araliaceæ.—Many characters of this natural order are identical with the preceding (Umbelliferæ), its distinguishing points are: Herbs, shrubs, or trees. *Leaves* sometimes simple but mostly compound or decompound. *Inflorescence* panicled or racemose umbels; *flowers* in our species more or less polygamous. *Calyx: limb* very short or wanting. *Petals* 5, not inflexed. *Stamens* 5. *Fruit* a berry or drupe with usually more than two cells; *carpels* not separating; *albumen* generally sarcous.

This family affords, beside the two species represented here, the following plants used in medicine and the arts: The common Ivy (*Hedera Helix*), at one time held in great repute as a preventive of drunkenness and antidote to the

---

* Derivation unknown.

† J. F. James mentions a plant 7 to 8 feet high, with leaves 3 feet long, and fruit 15 to 18 inches, in *Bot. Gaz.*, 1882, p. 122.

effects of "heady" wines; its blackish, gummy resin is used as a constituent of some varnishes (Griffith); the Amboyian *Hedera umbellifera* (*Aralia umbellifera*, Lam.) yields a powerfully aromatic camphoraceous resin; and the Ceylon *H. terebinthacea* one resembling turpentine. The American aromatic tonics False Sarsaparilla (*Aralia nudicaulis*) and the Angelica tree (*A. spinosa*) have just been dismissed from the Pharmacopœia of the United States. Among the edible plants of this family are the Chinese *Diamorphantus edulis*, *Gunnera scabra*, and *G. macrocephala*. The useful species of *Panax* are noted under the next drug.

History and Habitat.—Spikenard is indigenous to Canada, and the United States southward to the mountains of South Carolina and westward to the Rockies. It grows along the rocky but rich banks of well shaded streams, and flowers in July.

Concerning the previous use of this species, which was not so extensive as that of *A. spinosa*, *nudicaulis*, and *hispida*, Rafinesque says:* " *A. racemosa* is used by the Indians as carminative, pectoral and antiseptic, in coughs, pains in the breast (chest), and mortification; the root with horse-radish is made in poultice for the feet in general dropsy. The juice of the berries and oil of the seeds is said to cure earache and deafness, poured in the ears." Culpepper says:† "It is good to provoke urine, and cureth the pains of the stone in the reins and kidneys." In domestic practice it has been made into a composite syrup with the root of *Inula helenium*, and used as a remedy in chronic coughs, asthma, and rheumatism; a tincture of the root and fruit has also been used as a stomachic.

No preparation of this plant is now officinal in the U. S. Ph. or Eclectic Materia Medica.

PART USED AND PREPARATION.—The fresh root, the part used is large and thick, the bark is about $\frac{3}{16}$ inch in thickness, white internally and shows on section, many yellow resin cells, it readily peels off the ligneous layer surrounding the main bulk of the root. The central portion is somewhat dense, dotted with scattered bundles of woody fibre and surrounded by a ligneous sheath $\frac{1}{16}$ inch thick.

The tincture is prepared by chopping and pounding the root to a pulp, macerating it for eight days in two parts by weight of alcohol and filtering. It results as a clear, slightly brownish-orange liquid by transmitted light, having the peculiar, somewhat terebinthic odor of the root, a bitter astringent taste, and an acid reaction.

CHEMICAL CONSTITUENTS.—No analysis of this plant has been published as far as I can determine. The analysis of *A. spinosa*, by Holden,‡ Elkins,§ and Lilly,‖ will give us some idea of the probable nature of the phytochemistry of this species.

* *Med. Flor.*, vol. 2, p. 175.   † *Complete Herbal*, London, 1819.
‡ *Am. Jour. Phar.*, 1880, p. 390.   § *Idem*, p. 402.
‖ *Period. cit.*, 1882, p. 433.

Araliin.—This *saponin*-like glucoside was discovered by Holden and purified by Lilly. It results as a slightly acrid, inodorous, whitish powder; soluble in water, insoluble in cold, strong alcohol, ether, and chloroform. Its watery solution yields a dense, persistent froth on agitation. It precipitates whiter from its solution in boiling alcohol when cold. Boiled with very dilute hydrochloric acid, it breaks down into glucose and *Araliretin* (Holden), a white, insoluble, tasteless and odorless, amorphous product.

Alkaloid.—Elkin announced an alkaloid principle separable as a yellowish, amorphous, semi-transparent, bitter mass, soluble in water and ether, and answering to Mayer's test. Lilly failed to procure this precipitable body, but isolated a " bitter principle " having all its characteristics except that it was crystalline.

Oil of Aralia (Elkins, Lilly).—An aromatic, somewhatc amphoraceous, acid body, having the characteristic odor of the root.

An acrid resin, soluble in alcohol and ether, insoluble in water ;*† tannin ;* glucose ;†‡ pictin ;†‡ gum ;† fat ;* and starch,†‡ were also determined.

PHYSIOLOGICAL ACTION.—The only account of the action of this drug that we have, is a proving by Dr. Sam'l A. Jones, of Ann Arbor, § in whom a dose of 10 drops of the tincture caused a severe asthmatic fit, characterized by dry, wheezing respiration ; obstructed inspiration ; a sense of impending suffocation and inability to lie down during the attack ; profuse night sweat during sleep ; nausea ; prostration ; and difficult expulsion of small, soft stool, accompanied by the abdominal sense of oncoming diarrhœa. I have had the pleasure of seeing drop doses of the tincture promptly relieve a similar case, in my own practice, in a half hour, and exert a beneficial effect in warding off recurring attacks.

DESCRIPTION OF PLATE 69.

1. Portion of a fruiting stem, Binghamton, N. Y., Oct. 12, 1882.
2. A leaf, half natural size.
3. A flower.
4. Bird's-eye view of flower after removal of the anthers.
5. Styles.
6. Stamen.
7. Pollen x 300.
8. Section of the root.
    (3–6 enlarged.)

---

* Holden, *loc. cit.*   † Elkins, *loc. cit.*   ‡ Lilly, *loc. cit.*   § Hale's *New Remedies*, p. 53.

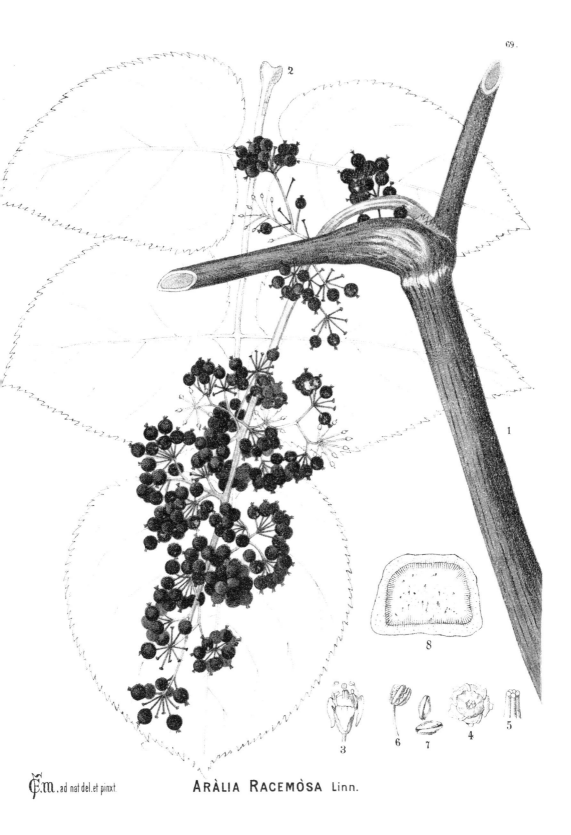

69.

2

1

8

3   6   7   4   5

ℰ.m. ad nat del. et pinxt.   ARÀLIA RACEMÒSA Linn.

70

GINSENG.

JIN-CHEN.

SYN.—ARALIA QUINQUEFOLIA, GRAY; A. CANADENSIS, TOURN.; PA-
NAX QUINQUEFOLIUM, LINN.; P. AMERICANUM, RAF.; AURELIANA
CANADENSIS, LAFIT; GINSENG QUINQUEFOLIUM, WOOD; GIN-SENG
CHINENSIBUS, JARTOUX.

COM. NAMES.—GINSENG, TARTAR-ROOT, FIVE-FINGER, RED BERRY,
MAN'S HEALTH; (FR.) GINSENG D'AMERIQUE; (GER.) KRAFTWUR-
ZEL.

A TINCTURE OF THE DRY ROOT OF ARALIA QUINQUEFOLIA, GRAY.

Description.—This herbaceous perennial grows to a height of about 1 foot. *Root* large, sometimes forked, but generally consisting of a fleshy, somewhat fusiform body, from the larger end of which is given off an irregular, cylindrical, knotty portion, narrower at its abrupt juncture with the main root, and showing the scars of previous stem-growths. Both parts are transversely wrinkled, closely above and sparsely below. *Stem* simple, erect; *leaves* 3, palmately 5-divided; *leaflets* obovate, thin, serrate, and pointed, in two sets, 3 large and 2 small, all long petioled. *Inflorescence* a single terminal, naked, peduncled umbel; *flowers* few, diœciously-polygamous. *Calyx-limb* very short, obscurely 5-toothed; *teeth* triangular acute. *Petals* 5, spreading, ovate-oblong. *Styles* 2 to 3, erect or spreading. *Stamens* 5. *Fruit* a cluster of bright-red, 2-celled, more or less reniform, fleshy berries, each retaining its calyx-limb and styles; *endocarp* thin.

This portion of the genus Aralia is the genus *Panax** of Linnæus. It has many characters, which have given rise to opportunities for forming distinct genera from its species, though its close resemblance to the Aralias serves to hold it there.

History and Habitat.—The American Ginseng grows in the rich, cool woods of central and northern North America, where it flowers in July.

There is great similarity in the American and Chinese individuals of this species, but the place of growth or mode of drying seems to more or less affect the properties of the roots, especially if the accounts of the usefulness of the Oriental product can be credited. Father Jartoux, who spent much time, and had special privileges accorded him in the study of this plant, remarks, that so high is it held in esteem by the natives of China that the physicians have written volumes upon its virtues, and deem it a necessity in all their best prescriptions, ascribing

---

* Παν, *pan*, all; ακος, *akos*, a remedy; as the Chinese and Tartar species were considered panaceas.

to it medicinal properties of inestimable value, and a remedial agency in fatigue and the infirmities of old age. So great is the plant esteemed in China that the Emperor monopolizes the right of gathering its roots. The preparation of the best roots for the Chinese market is a process which renders them yellow, semi-transparent, and of a horny appearance; this condition is gained by first plunging them in hot water, brushing until thoroughly scoured, and steaming over boiling millet seed. The root thus prepared is chewed by the sick to recover health, and by the healthy to increase their vitality; it is said that it removes both mental and bodily fatigue, cures pulmonary complaints, dissolves humors, and prolongs life to a ripe old age,—for all of which the root has often brought in the markets ten times its weight in silver. Father Jartoux * finally became so satisfied that the use of the root verified all that was said of its virtues, that he, in his own case, adds testimony as to its relief of fatigue and increase of vitality. Those roots that are bifurcated are held by the natives to be the most powerful; it was to this kind—which they considered to resemble the human form—that they gave the name *Jin-chen, like a man.* Strange as it may seem, the American Indian name of the plant, *garant-oquen,* means the same.

The plant is becoming rare in this country, and in fact wherever it is found, on account of the value it brings in the markets. In 1718 the Jesuits of Canada began shipping the roots to China; in 1748 they sold at a dollar a pound here and nearly five in China; afterward the price fluctuated greatly on account of a dislike in China of our product; and finally its gathering has nearly ceased, though fine sun-dried roots will now bring nearly a dollar per pound at New York.

Panax was dismissed from the U. S. Ph. at the last revision, and is simply mentioned in the Eclectic Materia Medica.

PART USED AND PREPARATION.—The genuine Chinese or the American root, dried and coarsely powdered, is covered with five times its weight of alcohol, and allowed to stand eight days, in a well-stoppered bottle, in a dark, cool place, being shaken twice a day. The tincture, poured off and filtered, has a clear, light-lemon color by transmitted light, an odor like the root, a taste at first bitter then dulcamarous, and an acid reaction.

CHEMICAL CONSTITUENTS.—Panaquilon, $C_{12}H_{25}O_9$.—This peculiar body, having a taste much like *glycyrrhizin* but more amarous, may be extracted from the root. It results as an amorphous, yellowish powder, soluble in water and alcohol, but not in ether, and precipitable by tannin. It breaks down under the action of sulphuric acid, which, in extracting three molecules of water, causes it to give off carbonic dioxide and yield a new body as follows:

$$\text{Panaquilon.} \qquad \text{Panacon.}$$
$$C_{12}H_{25}O_9 = CO_2 + (H_2O)_3 + C_{11}H_{10}O_4.$$

PHYSIOLOGICAL ACTION.—Ginseng causes vertigo, dryness of the mucous membranes of the mouth and throat, increased appetite, accumulation of flatus

* *Phil. Trans.,* 28, 239.

with tension of the abdomen, diarrhœa, decreased secretion of urine, sexual excitement, oppression of the chest and a dry cough, increased heart's action and irregular pulse, weakness and weariness of the limbs, increased general strength, followed by weakness and prostration, somnolence, and much chilliness.

DESCRIPTION OF PLATE 70.

1 and 2. Whole plant, Pittsburgh, Pa., June 28th, 1885.
　　　　3. Section of flower.
　　　　4. Part of calyx, a petal and stamen.
　　　　5 and 6. Fruit.
　　　　7. Section of rhizome.
　　　　　　(3, 4, and 6 enlarged.)

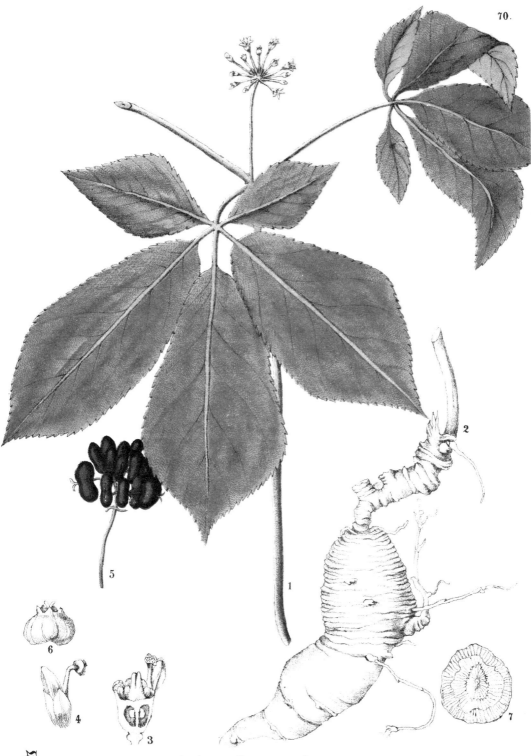

℃m.ad nat.del.et pinxt. ARÀLIA QUINQUEFÒLIA, Gray.

71

CORNUS FLORIDA.

FLOWERING DOGWOOD.

SYN.—CORNUS FLORIDA, LINN.; BENTHAMIDIA FLORIDA, SPACH.

COM. NAMES.—FLOWERING DOGWOOD, DOG TREE, BOX TREE, NEW ENGLAND BOXWOOD, CORNEL, BITTER REDBERRY; (FR.) CORNUILLIER À GRANDES FLEURS; (GER.) GROSSBLÜTHIGE CORNEL.

A TINCTURE OF THE FRESH BARK OF CORNUS FLORIDA, LINN.

Description.—This small but beautiful forest tree, grows to a height of from 10 to 30 feet; its form is usually somewhat bent, scraggy, and loosely branched; but if transplanted when young to open places, it grows into a beautiful full, umbrella-like tree, with an immense spread of branches. *Bark* greyish, cracked into small, more or less rectangular pieces; that of the branches is smooth, red, and shows strongly the scars of previous leaves. *Inflorescence* terminal, peduncled, involucrate, greenish heads; *involucre* white and showy; *lobes* 4, petaloid, obcordate or furnished with deep notches, having a discolored and thickened margin. *Flowers* perfect, appearing with the leaves; *calyx* tubular; *lobes* 4, minute, triangular and somewhat obtuse; *petals* 4, oblong, obtuse, spreading, but at length recurved in such a manner as to cause each flower, when magnified, to bear great resemblance to a plain Ionic capital. *Stamens* 4, erect; *filaments* slender and filiform; *anthers* oval, versatile, 2-celled. *Style* erect, slender, clavate, shorter than the stamens; *stigma* terminal, obtuse. *Fruit* a few oval, red drupes, containing each a 2-celled and 2-seeded nutlet.

Cornaceæ.—This small order is composed of shrubs or trees (rarely herbs) having the following characters: *Leaves* mostly opposite, rarely alternate; *stipules* none. *Inflorescence* cymose, or (in two species of Cornus) capitate and subtended by a showy, white involucre; *flowers* perfect or polygamous. *Calyx* tubular and coherent with the ovary; *limb* minute, 4-toothed. *Petals* valvate in the bud, equal in number to the calyx teeth or sometimes wanting. *Stamens* as many as the petals and alternate with them; in the perfect flowers they are borne on the margin of an epigynous disk; *filaments* usually ascending, sometimes erect. *Ovary* 1 to 2-celled; *ovules* one in each cell, anatropous, hanging from the apex of its cell; *styles* united into one. *Fruit* a 1 to 2-seeded drupe; *seeds* oval; *testa* coriaceous; *albumen* sarcous; *embryo* axial, nearly the length of the albumen; *cotyledons* foliaceous.

---

* *Cornu,* a horn, alluding to the density of the wood.

Cm.ad nat.del.et pinxt. CÓRNUS FLÓRIDA, Linn.

This family is represented by only two genera, *Cornus* and *Nyssa*, the latter having diœcious and partly apetalous flowers.

Beside the three species treated of in this work, the following are useful: The European and Asiatic Cornellian Cherry (*Cornus mas*, Linn.), the fruits of which were formerly fermented as a beverage, and are now used in Turkey in the concoction of a kind of sherbet; and the North European *Lus-a-chrasis* (*C. succica*, Linn.), the berries of which are claimed by the Highlanders to have the power of enormously increasing the appetite. The berries of the Red Osier Dogwood (*C. stolonifera*, Michx.; *C. sanguinea*, Linn.), are claimed by Murion* to yield about one-third their weight of a pure, limpid oil, resembling olive, and fit for table use or for burning.

History and Habitat.—The flowering dogwood is common in the deep woods of North America from the 43° north latitude southward, eastward, and westward; it is especially common in the South, where it extends from Florida westward to the Mississippi. Its principal central localities are the States of New Jersey, Pennsylvania, Maryland, and Virginia, where it flowers in May, generally from the 15th to the 22d, and fruits in September. A peculiar feature in the blossoming of this species is the great regularity in time of appearance of its short-lived blossoms; so characteristic is this that the Indians always planted their corn when the blossoms appeared.

Notwithstanding the small diameter of the trunk of the dogwood, its wood is nevertheless quite valuable, on account of its great density and susceptibility of polish. It has been used for every purpose generally filled by the European Boxwood, such as engravers' blocks, cog-wheels, forks, spoons, rules, etc., etc. The twigs have long been used as a dentifrice; of this use Barton says: † "The young branches stripped of their bark, and rubbed with their ends against the teeth, render them extremely white. The Creole negroes, who inhabit Norfolk, in Virginia, in great numbers, are in constant practice of using dogwood twigs in cleansing their teeth; the striking whiteness of these, which I have frequently observed, is a proof of the efficacy of this practice. The application of the juice of these twigs to the gums, is also useful in preserving them hard and sound." The bark of the root afforded the aborigines a scarlet pigment.

The previous medicinal use of dogwood bark dates from the discovery of this country, as it was then used by the Indians, who called the tree *Mon-ha-can-ni-min-schi*, or *Hat-ta-wa-no-min-schi* by the Delawares. The bark has proven tonic, astringent, and slightly stimulating; being a stomachic tonic and anti-periodic, said to possess an action very like that of Peruvian bark, and differing from the latter only in quantity of action. Eberle states‡ that 35 grains equal 30 grains of cinchona bark, and Barton says,§ "It may be asserted with entire safety, that as yet there has not been discovered within the limits of the United States any vegetable so effectually to answer the purpose of Peruvian bark in the management of intermittent fever as *Cornus florida.*" The dose of the dried and powdered

---

* *Jour. de Pharm.*, 10.   † *Med. Bot.*, i., 55.   ‡ *Therapeutics*, i., 304.   § *Collections.*

bark is placed at from 20 to 30 grains, and caution is necessary against its being too fresh, as it then disagrees seriously with the stomach and bowels. The bark is also considered a tonic, stimulant, and antiseptic poultice for indolent ulcers, phlegmonous erysipelas, and anthrax.

The officinal preparation of the U. S. Ph. is *Extractum Cornus Fluidum;* in the Eclectic Materia Medica the preparations are: *Decoctum Cornus Floridæ, Extractum Cornus Floridæ, Extractum Cornus Floridæ Fluidum,* and *Pilulæ Quiniæ Compositæ.**

PART USED AND PREPARATION.—The fresh bark, especially that of the root, is to be chopped and pounded to a pulp and weighed. Then two parts by weight of alcohol are taken, the pulp thoroughly mixed with one-sixth part of it, and the rest of the alcohol added. After having stirred the whole well, pour it into a well-stoppered bottle and allow it to remain eight days in a dark, cool place.

The tincture separated from this mass by filtration, presents a magnificent, clear, crimson color by transmitted light. It has a vinous odor, a sharply astringent cinnamon like taste, and a strongly acid reaction.

CHEMICAL CONSTITUENTS.—*Cornic Acid.* This acid was discovered by Carpenter (1830), who judged it alkaloidal and gave it the name *Cornin.* Geiger[†] (1836) investigated the principle and determined it to be a crystalline acid; his observations were corroborated by Frey[‡] (1879). It crystallizes in nearly white, silky forms, very bitter and soluble in alcohol and water. The crystals deliquesce when exposed to the air, and when subjected to heat upon platinum foil they melt readily, become black, and finally burst into a flame and burn without residue.

Oil of Cornus.—The ripe berries, when boiled and pressed, are said to yield a limpid oil; this body is uninvestigated.

Tannic,[1345] and gallic acid,[125] a neutral resin crystallizing in shining needles,[1234] gum,[134] extractive,[1235] fatty matter,[2] oil,[2] wax,[2] red coloring matter,[2345] cornic acid,[2345] and a bitter principle,[3] have been determined.

PHYSIOLOGICAL ACTION.—The fresh bark in doses of from 20 to 40 grains causes increased action of the heart, heat of the skin, and severe pain in the bowels. The American Indian, true to the principle that seems to have guided him in the use of all medicines, used the bark for fever and colic. The symptoms so far developed in proving are: sensations of fullness of the head with headache; nausea and vomiting; violent pain in the bowels with purging; and increased bodily temperature, followed by hot sweat.[6] Dr. Chas. A. Lee sums up the action of the drug as follows:[7] "The physiological effects of Cornus bark are: increased frequency of pulse, exalted temperature, diaphoresis, sensation of fullness or pains in the

---

* Sulphate of Quinia, extract of Cornus florida, Tartaric acid, and alcoholic extract of Cimicifuga.
† M. Geiger, *Ann. der Pharm.,* XIV., 206.
‡ *Am. Jour. Phar.,* 1879, 390.
1 Walker, *Inaug. Diss.* ² Cockburn, *Am. Jour. Phar.,* 1835, 114. ³ Tilden, *Jour. Mat. Med.,* i., N. S., 294.
⁴ Geiger, l. c. ⁵ Frey, l. c. ⁶ Hale, *New Rem.,* 242. ⁷ *The Jour. of Mat. Med.,* l. c.

head, and, if the dose be too large, gastric derangement. Of these the most strongly marked are the increased temperature of the skin, and the general perspiration. Some experimenters have observed a constant tendency to sleep, which has continued for several hours. This does not indicate any specific narcotic properties, but is the result of the cerebral fullness. Whether the remote effects are owing to sympathy, propagated from the gastic centre, or are the direct effects of the introduction of the active principles into the blood, is not certainly known; although the latter is most probable, since the cold infusion or the alcoholic extract produces the same effects. But whatever doubt there may be in regard to its true mode of operation, it is very evident that the bark has properties calculated to invigorate the vital forces, and the organic nervous energy, without unduly stimulating the circulating system."

DESCRIPTION OF PLATE 71.

1. End of a flowering branch, Newfield, N. Y., May 15th, 1880.
2. Flower.
3. Section of calyx and ovary.
4. Fruiting branch.

(2 and 3 enlarged.)

72

CORNUS CIRCINATA.

ROUND LEAVED DOGWOOD.

SYN.—CORNUS CIRCINATA, L'HER.; C. RUGOSA, LAM.; C. TOMENTULOSA, MICHX.

COM. NAMES.—ROUND LEAVED CORNEL OR DOGWOOD, ALDER DOGWOOD, PENNSYLVANIA DOGWOOD, GREEN OSIER, SWAMP SASSAFRAS; (FR.) CORNOUILE À FEUILLES RONDIE; (GER.) RUNDBLÄTTERIGE CORNEL.

A TINCTURE OF THE FRESH BARK OF CORNUS CIRCINATA, L'HER.

Description.—This shrubby species grows from 6 to 10 feet high. *Stem* erect; *bark* greyish, verrucose; *branches* green, opposite, straight, and slender—the younger ones bright green splashed with red, those of the previous year somewhat crimson and more or less warty. *Leaves* all opposite, round-oval, acuminate, woolly beneath, larger than those of any other species; *ribs* and *veins* prominent below and correspondingly indented above. *Inflorescence* terminal, in open, more or less flat, spreading cymes; *flowers* white. *Calyx teeth* very short. *Petals* ovate-lanceolate, at length spreading. *Stamens* longer than the petals. *Style* about two-thirds the length of the stamens; *stigma* capitate. *Fruit* an incomplete cyme of spherical, light blue drupes, each hollowed at the insertion of the pedicel and where it retains the remains of the persistent style.

History and Habitat.—The Round Leaved Dogwood grows in copses where the soil is rich, being indigenous from Canada to the Carolinas, and west to the Mississippi; flowering in the north in June.

The medicinal use of this species is far less extensive than the last, preceding. The Drs. Ives claim * that the bark is tonic, and astringent to a far greater degree than any other species of the genus, and that it resembles Cinchona lance-folia (Pale Bark) in its action. It has proven, in their hands, an excellent remedy for chronic dyspepsia [*sic*] and diarrhœa. An ounce of the bark will yield in the neighborhood of 150 grains of a very strongly-bitter extract; far greater in quantity, and more bitter than that of *C. florida.*

Cornus circinata was dismissed from the U. S. Ph. at the last revision.

PART USED AND PREPARATION.—The fresh bark is gathered and treated as in the preceding species.

---

* Dr. A. W. Ives, *N. Y. Rep.*, 1822; Dr. E. Ives, *Trans. Am. Med. Assoc'n*, iii, 312.

The tincture resulting is clear, and of a slightly brownish-orange color. Its odor is very like that of Rhubarb; its taste sharply astringent and bitter, and its reaction acid.

CHEMICAL CONSTITUENTS.—*Cornin.* This acid differs from that of *C. florida* only in the fact that it remains associated with tannin in spite of most careful re-crystallization, and other means of purification.*

The other constituents mentioned in the preceding species are all, without doubt, duplicated in this. Gibson isolated sugar, coloring-matter, *cornin* and tannin.

PHYSIOLOGICAL ACTION.—Here again great similarity exists between the species. *C. circinata* causes drowsiness and depression of spirits; congestion of the head; nausea and faintness; flatulency; copious bilious stools and urine, with yellowness of the sclera, face and hands; coldness of the extremties; itching, red rash, upon the whole surface, especially the trunk, with flashes of heat and chill, followed by perspiration.

DESCRIPTION OF PLATE 72.

1. End of a flowering branch, Binghamton, N. Y., June 16th, 1885.
   2. Flower.
   3 and 4. Stamens.
   5. Stigma.
   6. Portion of the stem, showing mode of branching.
   7. Part of a fruiting cyme.
   8. Seed.
(2–5, and 8 enlarged.)

* Robert Gibson, Jr., *Am. Jour. Phar.*, 1880, 433.

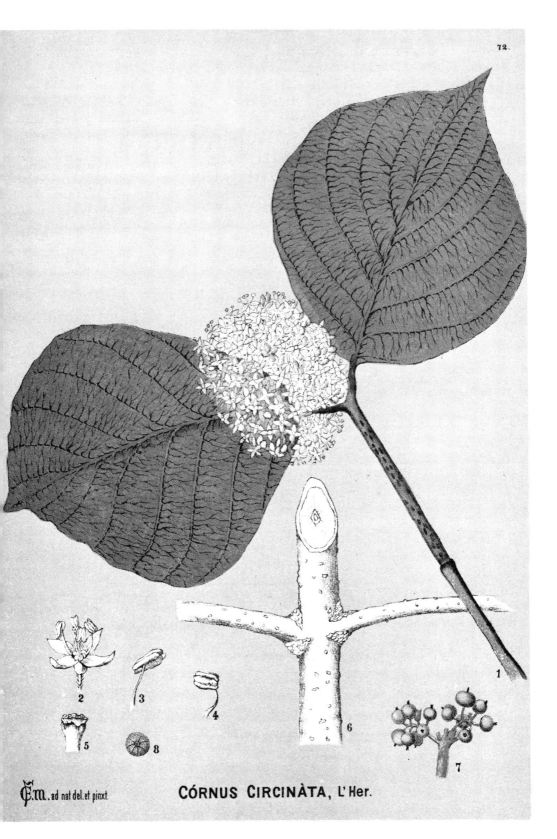

72.

2

3

4

5

8

6

1

7

CÉ.M. ad nat del. et pinxt.

CÓRNUS CIRCINÀTA, L'Her.

73

CORNUS SERICEA.

SILKY DOGWOOD.

SYN.—CORNUS SERICEA, LINN.; C. AMOMUM, DU ROI; C. CYANOCAR-
PUS, MOEN.; C. LANUGINOSA, MICHX.; C. OBLIQUA, RAF.

COM. NAMES.*—SWAMP OR FEMALE DOGWOOD, SILKY OR BLUEBERRY
CORNEL, KINNIKINNIK; (FR.) CORNOUILLE SOYEUX; (GER.) SUMPF-
CORNEL.

A TINCTURE OF THE FRESH BARK OF CORNUS SERICEA, LINN.

Description.—This water-loving shrub grows to a height of from 6 to 12 feet. *Branches* spreading, dark-purplish (not brilliant red); *branchlets* silky-downy. *Leaves* narrowly ovate or elliptical, pointed, smooth above, silky-downy below and often rusty-hairy upon the ribs. *Inflorescence* a flat, close, woolly-pubescent, long-peduncled cyme; *flowers* creamy-white. *Calyx teeth* lanceolate, conspicuous. *Petals* lanceolate-oblong, obtuse. *Stigma* thick, capitate. *Fruit* pale blue, globose. Read description of Cornaceæ, p. 71.

History and Habitat.—The Swamp Dogwood is indigenous to North America, from Florida to Mississippi and thence northward, where it grows in wet places, generally in company with Cephalanthus and Viburnum dentatum. It flowers northward in June, and ripens its azure fruit in September.

The use of this species in general medicine has mostly been as a substitute for *C. florida*, than which it is less bitter, while being more astringent. The Cree Indians of Hudson's Bay call the plant *Milawapamule*, and use the bark in decoction as an emetic in coughs and fevers. They also smoke the scrapings of the wood, and make a black dye from the bark by boiling it with iron rust.† A favorite tobacco mixture of the North American Indians, called *Kinnikinnik*, is composed of scrapings of the wood of this species, mixed with tobacco in the proportion of about one to four. A good scarlet dye is made by boiling the rootlets with water.

PART USED AND PREPARATION.—The fresh bark, including that of the root, is treated like that of the first-mentioned species; the resulting tincture has

---

* The names Red Willow, Red Osier, Red Rod, and Rose Willow, are often given to this species, but they should only designate *C. stolonifera*, Michx.

† E. M. Holmes in *Am. Jour. Phar.*, 1884, 617.

1

2

3

4

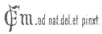.ad nat.del.et pinxt.

CÓRNUS SERÍCEA, Linn.

a beautiful madder color by transmitted light, an odor greatly like that of sugar-cane when the juices are slightly soured, an extremely astringent and bitterish taste, and an acid reaction.

CHEMICAL CONSTITUENTS.—At present we can only call attention again to this rubric under *C. florida.* The bitterness, however, of this species is less than its congener, while its astringency is greater.

PHYSIOLOGICAL ACTION.—This species seems to act stronger upon the heart than *C. florida,* and to cause more cerebral congestion.

DESCRIPTION OF PLATE 73.

1. End of a flowering branch, Binghamton, N. Y., June 20th, 1885.
2. Flower.
3. Stigma.
4. Fruit.
(2 and 3 enlarged.)

74
TRIOSTEUM.

FEVER-WORT.

SYN.—TRIOSTEUM PERFOLIATUM, LINN.; TRIOSTEUM MAJUS, MICHX.
COM. NAMES.—FEVER-WORT, OR ROOT; HORSE-GENTIAN, OR GINSENG;
WHITE GINSENG; TINKER WEED, OR DR. TINKER'S WEED; BAS-
TARD, FALSE, OR, WILD IPECAC;† WILD COFFEE; SWEET-BITTER;
CINQUE; (FR.) TRIOSTE; (GER.) DREISTEIN.

A TINCTURE OF THE FRESH ROOT OF TRIOSTEUM PERFOLIATUM, LINN.

Description.—This coarse, leafy, perennial herb, grows to a height of from 1 to 4 feet. *Root* thick and sarcous, sub-divided into several horizontal sections; *stem* simple, hollow, glandularly pubescent; *leaves* opposite, ample, ovate-spatulate, sinuate, acuminate, abruptly narrowed and connate or almost perfoliate at the base, prominently reticulate veined and downy pubescent upon the under surface, and hairy above. *Inflorescence*, axillary whorls at the middle of the stem; *flowers* 1 to 6, dull or reddish purple, sessile. *Bracts* linear; *calyx* persistent; *lobes* linear-lanceolate, foliaceous. *Corolla* elongated cylindro-tubular, curved, gibbous at the base, scarcely longer than the calyx lobes, viscidly pubescent; *limb* more or less equally 5-lobed. *Stamens* 5, inserted upon the tube of the corolla; *filaments* hairy; *anthers* sagittate. *Ovary* generally 5-celled, each cell 1-ovuled; *ovules* suspended; *style* filiform, hairy; *stigma* 3 to 5-lobed. *Fruit* drupaceous, dry, orange-colored; *nutlets* 3-angled and 3-ribbed, 1-seeded; *endocarp* osseous, *testa* membranaceous.

Caprifoliaceæ.—A large family of shrubs and a few perennial herbs. *Leaves* opposite and destitute of stipules when normal. *Flowers* generally 5-merous, regular, or sometimes in the corolla irregular, hermaphrodite; *calyx* adnate to the ovary; *corolla* with its lobes imbricate in aestivation. *Stamens* as many as the lobes of the corolla, alternate with them, and inserted upon its tube. (Exc. *Adoxa* and *Linnaea*.) *Ovary* 2 to 5- or, by abortion, 1-celled; *ovules* anatropous, when only one then suspended and inverted; *raphe* dorsal. *Embryo* small in the axis of the fleshy albumen.

The following remedies belonging to this family are of special interest to us

---

* Τρεῖς, *treis*, three; ὀστέον, *osteon*, a bone; the fruit having three nutlets, shortened from *Triosteospermum*, Dill.
† Applied also to many species of Euphorbia, and to *Gillennia trifoliata*, Moench. (Rosaceæ.)

74.

1

2

3

4

5

6

7

8

9

℃m.ad nat.del.et.pinxt. TRIÓSTEUM PERFOLIÀTUM, Linn.

beside the two under consideration: the European Moschatel (*Adoxa Moschatel-lina*, Linn.), also found in Arctic America and sparsely in the Rocky Mountains; the European Elder (*Sambucus nigra*, Linn.), a native also of Asia and Northern Africa; and the European Fly Woodbine (*Lonicera Xylosteum*, Linn.). Two American species were proven too late for representation in this work, they are the Snowberry (*Symphoricarpus racemosus*, Michx.), a valuable remedy in vomiting pregnancy, as many suffering ladies have testified in my practice; and the High Cranberry (*Viburnum opulus*, Linn.), now proving valuable in many forms of uterine affections and puerperal diseases.

Outside of our Materia Medica the order contains: The Dwarf Elder (*Sambucus ebulus*, Linn.), probably the most active of that genus; and the Bush Honey-suckle (*Diervilla trifida*, Mœnch.).

History and Habitat.—The feverwort is indigenous to North America from Canada southward and westward to Alabama, growing on open woodlands in limestone soils; not really plentiful in any locality. It blossoms in June, and ripens its characteristically arranged fruit in September.

It was in all probability the Southern species *T. augustifolium*, Linn., that was principally used as an emetic in earlier days, and this is doubtless the plant sent to Pluckenet as *Dr. Tinker's Weed*, and gravely commented on by Poiret as follows:* "Ses racines et celles de l'espece précédente passent pour émétiques; le docteur Tinker est le premier qui les a mises en usage, et qui a fait donner à cette plante par plusieurs habitans de l'Amerique septentrional le d' *herbe sauvage du docteur Tinker.*" Triosteum is stated by Rafinesque to have been one of the aboriginal medicamentæ, called *Sincky*. A decoction is said to have been used by the Cherokee Indians in the cure of fevers (Porcher). The bark of the root has long been esteemed as an emetic and smoothly-acting cathartic, the former in doses of from 40 to 60 grains, the latter in half that amount; its cathartic action was claimed to be fully as sure as jalap. Dr. J. Kneeland calls attention to this plant as an application to painful swellings, regarding which he says:† "My attention was first called to it by a gentleman of observation and intelligence, who derived his knowledge of its value indirectly from the Onondaga Indians. So strongly did he back his claims with facts on cases of whitlow or felon, successfully treated, that I applied the bruised root, moistened, to the first well-marked case of onychia or felon which came to me for treatment. The young man upon whose hand it was, had not slept much for two nights. The whole hand was much swollen; the middle finger, tense and throbbing, was the centre from which the pain and swelling extended. It had been poulticed and thoroughly soaked in weak lye for three days, and still grew worse. We applied the *Triosteum, and nothing else.* After six hours' application he slept; the throbbing and tensive pain gradually diminished after the first application; in two days' time the swelling disappeared from the forearm and hand; in four days the finger affected, the whole palm, and the centre of the dorsum of the hand peeled, and complete resolution took place, no

---

* Bigelow, *Am. Med. Bot.*, I, p. 90. † *Loc. cit.*, *The Jour. of Mat. Med.*, Vol. I., N. S., 1859, 240.

pus having formed. In another case, wherein it was tried, only two applications were required to relieve the pain and throbbing, and complete resolution followed." Dr. Mulenberg says* that the dried and toasted berries of this plant were considered by some of the Germans of Lancaster County, Pa., an excellent substitute for coffee when prepared in the same way; having great respect for German taste I tried an infusion, but came to the conclusion that it was not the Lancaster County Germans' taste that I held in regard.

Triosteum is one of the drugs dismissed from the U. S. Ph., at the last revision.

PART USED AND PREPARATION.—The fresh root, gathered in Autumn, is chopped and pounded to a pulp and weighed. Then two parts by weight of alcohol are taken, the pulp mixed well with one-sixth part of it, and the rest of the alcohol added. After first stirring, the whole is poured into a well-stoppered bottle, and allowed to stand eight days in a dark, cool place.

The tincture thus formed after filtration has a beautiful, clear, reddish-orange color by transmitted light, a bitterish odor and taste, and an acid reaction.

CHEMICAL CONSTITUENTS.—The only analysis thus far made of the root is that by Dr. John Randall, communicated to the Linnæan Society of New England. His conclusions were that no pure resin exists in the plant, nor did he determine a volatile oil or free acid. The leaves under his manipulation yielded the most extract, and the root more than the stems. The sensible qualities of the root, however, he found to be essentially different from those of the herb. Water yields a greater quantity of extract than alcohol.

PHYSIOLOGICAL ACTION.—In Dr. Williamson's proving of the drug the prominent effects were: Nausea; vomiting; copious watery stools apparently proceeding from the small intestines, accompanied by stiffness of the lower extremities and cramps in the calves; aching in the bones; coldness and stiffness of the feet, and general perspiration.†

DESCRIPTION OF PLATE 74.

1. Top of plant, Binghamton, N. Y., June 15th, 1884.
2. A portion of the middle of the flowering plant.
3. A flower.
4. Opened corolla.
5. Pistil.
6. Stamen.
7. Pollen, x 200.
8. Fruit.
9. Seeds.

(3–6, 8 and 9, enlarged.)

* Barton, *Med. Bot.*, 1, p. 63.   † Allen, *Ency. Pure Mat. Med.*, 10, p. 25.

N. ORD.—CAPRIFOLIACEÆ.

Tribe.—SAMBUCEÆ.

GENUS.—**SAMBUCUS**,* TOURN.

SEX. SYST.—PENTANDRIA TRIGYNIA.

75

SAMBUCUS CANADENSIS.

ELDER.

SYN.—SAMBUCUS CANADENSIS, LINN.; S. NIGRA, MARSH (NOT LINN.); S. HUMILIS, RAF.; S. GLAUCA, GRAY (NOT NUTT.).
COM. NAMES.—ELDER BUSH, ELDER BERRY; (FR.) SUREAU DU CANADA; (GR.) CANADISCHE HOLLUNDER.

A TINCTURE OF THE BUDS, FLOWERS, SHOOTS, AND LEAVES OF SAMBUCUS CANADENSIS, LINN.

Description.—This common, glabrous, suffrutescent perennial, usually attains a growth of from 6 to 10 feet. *Stems* somewhat ligneous, hollow, pithy, generally dying down to the ground, or persistent for a few years; *bark* verrucose; *pith* dense and bright white after the first year. *Leaves* compound, imparipinnate; *stipules* rare; *leaflets* 5 to 11, mostly 7, petiolulate, from ovate-oval to oblong-lanceolate, serrate, acuminate, the lower sometimes with a lateral lobe; *stipels* not uncommonly present, narrowly linear, and tipped with a callous gland. *Inflorescence* terminal, broad, flat, or depressed, 5-rayed, compound cymes; *flowers* small, creamy-white, and sickishly odorous. *Calyx* minute, 5-lobed; *lobes* somewhat deltoid, acute. *Corolla* rotate, or somewhat urceolate; *limb* broadly spreading; *lobes* 5, obtuse. *Stamens* 5, alternate with the lobes of the corolla, and attached to the base of its tube. *Stigmas* 3; *styles* capitate. *Fruit* a baccate, sweet and juicy, dark-purple drupe, never red, but later becoming black; *bloom* slight. *Nutlets* 3, small, 1-seeded, punctate-rugulose; *seed* suspended; *testa* membranaceous.

History and Habitat.—This species is indigenous to North America, where it extends from New Brunswick westward to Saskatchewan, southward to Florida and Texas, and to the mountains of Colorado, Utah, and Arizona. It grows in rich alluvial soils, blossoming in July and fruiting in September.

Our species is not sufficiently distinct from the European *S. nigra*, Linn., from which it differs only in being less woody, and having more loose cymes, larger flowers and more compound leaves. The bracteate inflorescence, considered specific, does not seem to be a constant feature. The American species was introduced into England in 1761.

---

* Σαμβύκη, *sambuke,* an ancient musical instrument, said to have been made of the wood.

75.

.ad nat.del.et pinxt.

SAMBÙCUS CANADÉNSIS, Linn.

The pith of the Elder has many offices to fill in the arts and manufactures; the berries make a really pleasant wine; and, among the poorer class of people (it must be more from necessity than choice), they are made into pies, like the huckleberry.

In domestic medicine this plant forms almost a pharmacy in itself, and has been used substantially as follows: A decoction of the flowers and leaves, or an ointment containing them, was used as an application to large wounds to prevent deleterious consequences from flies; the leaf-buds proved themselves a violent and unsafe cathartic; the flowers, in a warm infusion are stimulant, excitant, and sudorific; in cold, diuretic, alterative, and laxative (Elderblow Tea); they were also employed, in ointment, as a discutient; the inner bark is a severe hydrogogue cathartic, emetic, deobstruent, and alterative, valuable in intestinal obstruction and anasarca; the berries proved aperient, diuretic, diaphoretic, and cathartic, valuable in rheumatic gout, scrofula, and syphilis—the juice making a cooling, laxative drink.

In pharmacy the leaves have been used to impart a clear green tint to oils, etc. (*Oleum Viride, Unguentum Sambuci foliorum*), and the flowers for perfumes.

Sambucus Canadensis (*flores*) are officinal in the U. S. Ph.; in the Eclectic Materia Medica the preparations are: *Aqua Sambuci, Syrupus Sarsaparillæ Compositus,* Unguentum Sambuci,* and *Vinum Sambuci.*†

PART USED AND PREPARATION.—Equal parts of the fresh flower-buds, flowers, young twigs, and leaves are taken, and treated as in the preceding drug (p. 74-3). The resulting tincture has a clear orange-brown color by transmitted light; it retains the sweetish odor and taste of the flowers; and has an acid reaction.

CHEMICAL CONSTITUENTS.—*Viburnic Acid.* This body, identical with valerianic acid,‡ was proven to exist in the bark of this species by C. G. Traub,§ who succeeded in obtaining its characteristic odor, and valerianate of zinc after the addition of the sulphate of that metal.

Oil of Sambucus.—This volatile body, found in the flowers of *S. nigra,* was proven by Traub to also exist in the bark of this species. It is described as a thin, light-yellow body, having the odor of the flowers, a bitter, burning, afterward cooling taste; becoming of a butter-like consistence, and solidifying at 0° (32° F.) to a crystalline mass.

Tannin, sugar, fat, resin, and a coloring-matter were also determined.

PHYSIOLOGICAL ACTION.—Dr. Ubelacker's experiments with from 20 to 50 drops of the tincture gave the following symptoms of physical disturbance: Drawing in the head, with anxious dread; flushed and blotched face; dryness

---

* See p. 92-2, foot-note to *Syrupus Araliæ Compositus*, as the syrup is now called.

† This so-called *Hydragogue Tincture* contains Elder-bark, Parsley-root, and Sherry.

‡ See p. 155-3.

§ *Am. Jour. Phar.*, 1881, 392.

and sensation of swelling of the mucous membranes of the mouth, pharynx, larynx, and trachea; frequent and profuse flow of clear urine; heaviness and constriction of the chest; palpitation of the heart; pulse rose to 100, and remained until perspiration ensued; sharp, darting rheumatic pains in the hands and feet; exhaustion and profuse perspiration, which relieved all the symptoms.

DESCRIPTION OF PLATE 75.

1. End of flowering branch, Binghamton, N. Y., July 20th, 1885.
2. Flower, showing calyx.
3. Face of flower.
4. Stamen.
5. Pistil.
6. A portion of fruiting cyme.
7. Seed.
(2–5 and 7 enlarged.)

N. ORD.—RUBIACEÆ.
GENUS.—**CEPHALANTHUS**,* LINN.
SEX. SYST.—TETRANDRIA MONOGYNIA.

76
CEPHALANTHUS.

BUTTON BUSH.

SYN.—CEPHALANTHUS OCCIDENTALIS, LINN.
COM. NAMES.—BUTTON BUSH, BUTTON-WOOD,† CRANE WILLOW, POND-DOGWOOD, SNOWBALL,‡ GLOBE FLOWER;§ (FR.) BOIS DE PLOMB, CEPHALANTHE D'AMERIQUE; (GER.) KNOPFBUSCH, AMERIKAN-ISCHE WEISSBALL.

A TINCTURE OF THE FRESH BARK OF CEPHALANTHUS OCCIDENTALIS, LINN.

Description.—This smooth or pubescent‖ shrub attains a growth of from 5 to 15 feet. *Stem* diffusely branching; *bark* smooth and reddish on the branchlets, rough and yellowish on the stems; *branches* opposite. *Leaves* large, opposite, and ternate, both arrangements often appearing upon the same branch, petiolate, ovate, or ovate-lanceolate, pointed, dark-green, and smooth; *stipules* intermediate, ovate, sometimes toothed. *Inflorescence* dense, axillary and terminal, globular heads; *peduncles* longer than the diameter of the heads; *flowers* creamy-white, sessile upon a globose, hirsute receptacle. *Calyx* tube inversely pyramidal; *limb* 4-toothed. *Corolla* slender, tubular, or funnel-form; *margin* 4-toothed; *teeth* erect, imbricate in æstivation. *Stamens* 4, hardly exserted. *Style* filiform, greatly exserted; *stigma* capitate, globose. *Fruit* small, dry, pyriform, 2 to 4 celled, cleaving from the base to form 2 to 4 1-seeded divisions; *seeds* pendulous, crowned with a cork-like arillus; *embryo* straight in the axis; *albumen* somewhat cartilaginous; *cotyledons* leaf-like.

Rubiaceæ.—This large and important order has but few representatives in North America, but yields many valuable drugs in the hotter climates. It is characterized as follows: Herbs or shrubs. *Leaves* opposite, entire, or sometimes whorled and astipulate; *stipules* intermediate and connective. *Calyx* coherent with the ovary. *Corolla* regular, tubular. *Stamens* as many as the lobes of the corolla, and inserted upon its tube. *Ovary* 2 to 4 celled. *Seeds* anatropous or amphitropous.

The important medicinal plants of this family are: The cinchonas or Peruvian barks, *i.e.*, pale bark (*Cinchona officinalis*, Linn.), Calisaya bark (*Cinchona Calisaya, Wedd.*), red bark (*Cinchona succiruba, Pav.*), Columbian bark (*Cinchona*

---

* Κεφαλή, *kephale*, a head; ἄνθος, *anthos*, a flower.
† The true button-wood is the sycamore, a large tree growing along rivers (*Platanus occidentalis, Linn.*).
‡ The true snowball is *Symphoricarpus racemosus, Mich.* (Caprifoliaceæ).
§ The true globe flower is *Trollius laxus, Salisb.* (Ranunculaceæ).
‖ *Var. pubescens, Raf.*

cordifolia, Mut.), lancifolia bark (*Cinchona lancifolia, Mut.*), crown bark (*Cinchona condaminea, D. C. var. crispa* and *var. Chahuarguera*), gray bark (*Cinchona micrantha, Ru. et Pav.*), and many minor species; Gambier, or pallid catechu (*Uncaria Gambier, Rox.*), coffee (*Coffea Arabica, Linn.*), ipecacuanha (*Cephælis Ipecacuanha, A. Rich.*), Cainca (*Chiococca racemosa, Linn.*), madder (*Rubia tinctoria, Linn.*), bitter bark (*Pinckneya pubens, Mich.*), cleavers (*Gallium aparine, Linn.*) and others of minor import.

History and Habitat.—The button bush is indigenous to the United States and Canadas, growing as far south as Florida and Louisiana, and west to Missouri. It habits the borders of wet places, and flowers from July to August. The flowers of cephalanthus, especially those of the more southern individuals, are pleasantly odorous, the perfume being likened to that of jessamine. Rafinesque mentions several varieties of this species, the only one apparently deserving special designation being *var. macrophylla, Raf.*, distinguishable by having larger leaves, and an hirsute corolla; he stations this plant in Louisiana.

The medical history of Cephalanthus is not important; it has been used with accredited success in intermittent and remittent fevers, obstinate coughs (Elliott), palsy, various venereal disorders (Merat), and in general as a tonic, laxative, and diuretic.

PART USED AND PREPARATION.—The fresh bark of the stem, branches, and root* is chopped and pounded to a pulp and weighed. Then two parts by weight of alcohol are taken, the pulp thoroughly mixed with one-sixth part of it, and the rest of the alcohol added. After having stirred the whole well, pour it into a well-stoppered bottle, and let it stand eight days in a dark, cool place.

The tincture, separated from the above mass by filtration, has a light, clear, orange-brown color, by transmitted light, a bitter, astringent taste, and an acid reaction.

CHEMICAL CONSTITUENTS.—An analysis of the bark by E. M. Hattan† yielded:

An uncrystallizable bitter principle, soluble in both water and alcohol.
A fluorescent body, forming apicular crystals, soluble in water and alcohol.
Two resins (uninvestigated), and tannin.

PHYSIOLOGICAL ACTION.—We have a proving of this drug by Dr. E. D. Wright,‡ but it is not complete enough to give us an idea of the action. It would seem, from the close resemblance and botanical relation of this plant to the cinchonas, that a more thorough proving might develop in it a very useful addition to our remedies.

DESCRIPTION OF PLATE 76.

1. End of flowering branch, Binghamton, N. Y., June 18th, 1883.
2. Flower (enlarged).

---

* The bark of the root apparently contains the greatest proportion of the bitter principle of the plant.
† *Am. Jour. Phar.*, 1874, p. 357.   ‡ *Am. Hom. Obs.*, 1875, p. 177.

76.

1

2

℥m.ad nat.del.et pinxt. GEPHALÁNTHUS OCCIDENTÀLIS, Linn.

GENUS.—**MITCHELLA**,* LINN.

SEX. SYST.—TETRANDRIA MONOGYNIA.

77

MITCHELLA.

PARTRIDGE-BERRY.

SYN.—MITCHELLA REPENS, LINN.; MITCHELLA UNDULATA, S. & Z.;
SYRINGA BACCIFERA, ETC., PLUK.

COM. NAMES.—PARTRIDGE-BERRY, SQUAW-BERRY, SQUAW-VINE, TWO-
EYED CHEQUER-BERRY, REEPING CHECKER-BERRY, WINTER-
CLOVER, DEER-BERRY.

A TINCTURE OF THE WHOLE FRESH PLANT, MITCHELLA REPENS, LINN.

Description.—This pretty little plant, creeping about in the moss at the foot of our forest trees and decayed stumps, attains a growth of from 6 to 14 inches. *Root* cylindrical, branched, horizontal, and noduled at the insertion of the tufted, oppo-site rootlets. *Stem* glabrous, branching widely, and rooting at each axilla. *Leaves* orbicular-cordate or oval and subcordate, sometimes having a whitish line over the midrib; dark, evergreen, slender, petioled; *stipules* minute, somewhat triangular awl-shaped. *Inflorescence* terminal; *flowers* in pairs with united ovaries, some-times solitary and double (fig. 3); the flowers on one plant may have included stamens and an exserted style, while another show an included style and exserted stamens. This fact has led Mr. Thos. Meehan† to consider the species diœcious. The first form, he alleges, to be that of the female; the last, the male plant. As far as my observation extends, I have as yet been unable to discover a plant that bore no fruit, and all parts examined appear to be fully developed internally as well as externally. *Peduncle* short, or, in the double form, almost wanting. *Calyx* 4-toothed. *Corolla* slender, funnel-form; *limb* 4-lobed; *lobes* spreading or reflexed, densely clothed with white hairs upon the upper face and in the throat and tube of the corolla. *Stamens* 4; *filaments* inserted upon the corolla; *anthers* oblong. *Style* single filiform; *stigmas* 4, linear. *Fruit* a fleshy, edible, globose, baccate, double drupe, retaining the persistent teeth of both calices, and remaining fresh on the plant all winter; *nutlets* 8 (4 to each ovary), small, seedlike, and bony. Read description of the order, under Cephalanthus, 76.

History and Habitat.—The Partridge-berry is indigenous to North America, from the Canadas to the extreme southern limits of the United States, and has been found in Mexico and Japan. It grows in moist woods, especially those abounding in evergreens. It flowers in July.

---

* In commemoration of Dr. John Mitchell, an early and excellent American botanist.
† *Am. Jour. Phar.*, 1868, p. 554.

MITCHÉLLA RÈPENS , Linn.

 ad nat.del.et pinxt

Mitchella is one of the many plants used by the American Aborigines as a parturient, frequent doses of a decoction being taken during the few weeks just preceding confinement. It has also been found to be a valuable diuretic and astringent, and to have an especial affinity to various forms of uterine difficulties.

The plant is not mentioned in the U. S. Ph. In the Eclectic Materia Medica its preparations are : *Extractum Mitchellæ* and *Syrupus Mitchellæ Compositus.**

PART USED AND PREPARATION.—The whole fresh plant is chopped and pounded to a pulp and weighed. Then two parts by weight of alcohol are taken, the pulp well mixed with one-sixth part of it, and the rest of the alcohol added. After a thorough mixture, the whole is poured into a well-stoppered bottle, and allowed to stand eight days in a dark, cool place.

The tincture, separated by filtering the mass, should have a deep orange-red color by transmitted light, an odor between that of Scotch snuff and oil of wintergreen, an astringent taste, and an acid reaction.

CHEMICAL CONSTITUENTS.—No analysis has been made, as far as I can determine, of this plant. The tincture, made as above, contains a large percentage of tannin, and a resin precipitable by water.

PHYSIOLOGICAL ACTION.—The symptoms, as recorded by Drs. F. C. Duncan and P. H. Hale,† show that Mitchella causes a general congestion, with dryness and burning of the mucous membranes of the alimentary tract. The clinical results would seem to show a tonic action upon involuntary muscular fibres. The drug merits more extended proving.

DESCRIPTION OF PLATE 77.

1. Whole plant (somewhat reduced); Pamrapo, N. J., June 8th, 1879.
    2. A pair of flowers (somewhat enlarged).
    3. A double flower (somewhat enlarged).

---

* Mitchella, Helonias, Viburnum op., and Caulophyllum.
† Allen, *Ency. Pure Mat. Med.*, vol. vi, p. 373.

78

EUPATORIUM PURPUREUM.

PURPLE BONESET.

SYN.—EUPATORIUM PURPUREUM, TRIFOLIATUM, AND MACULATUM, LINN.; E. VERTICILLATUM, MUHL.; E. TERNIFOLIUM, ELL.

COM. NAMES.—PURPLE BONESET, THOROUGH-WORT, OR HEMP-WEED; JOE-PYE,† OR JOPI-WEED; TRUMPET-WEED; QUEEN OF THE MEADOW;‡ GRAVEL-ROOT; (GER.) PURPURFARBENER WASSER-HANF.

A TINCTURE OF THE FRESH ROOT OF EUPATORIUM PURPUREUM, L.

Description.—This common herb varies greatly in form and foliage, the type being very tall and graceful. *Stem* rigidly erect, 6 to 12 feet high,§ stout, simple, and either hollow or furnished with an incomplete pith; it is punctate in lines and purple above the nodes, or often covered with elongated spots (*E. maculata*, Linn.). *Leaves* verticillate, mostly in fives, nearly destitute of resinous punctæ, oblong-lanceolate, acutish or acuminate, coarsely serrate, roughish and reticulate-veiny; *petioles* distinct or merely represented by the contracted bases of the leaves. *Inflorescence* a terminal, dense, compound corymb; *heads* very numerous, 5 to 10-flowered. *Involucre* flesh-colored, cylindrical; *bracts* thin, membranaceous, somewhat scarious when dry, and faintly 3-striate, obtuse; they are closely imbricated in three rows, the exterior successively shorter. *Receptacle* flat, not hirsute. *Style* bulbous at the base, much exserted. *Achenia* smooth, glandular.

Eupatorium.—This vast genus contains in North America alone 39 species and 16 distinct varieties; other species are found in South America, Asia, Africa, and Europe. It is composed mostly of perennial herbs, but contains a few annuals, and shrubs in warmer regions. *Leaves* mostly opposite and simple, resinous and bitter, rarely alternate, whorled, or divided. *Heads* small, homogamous, discoid, and corymbosely-cymose or paniculate, rarely solitary; *involucre* cylindrical or somewhat campanulate; *scales* numerous, purple, blue, or white, never really yellow, though sometimes ochroleucous. *Flowers* hermaphrodite and homochromous; *corolla* tubular and regular, 5-toothed; *anthers* included, not caudate; *receptacle* naked and flat. *Style* cylindraceous, branched, the branches exserted, more or less thickened upward and very minutely pubescent. *Pappus* a single

---

* Mithridates Eupator, king of Pontus, who was first to use the plant as a remedy.
† An Indian by this name cured typhus in New England, with this plant, by powerful sweating.
‡ The Queen of the Meadow is more properly *Spiræa salicifolia*, Linn. (Rosaceæ).
§ The individual represented in the plate was nearly 10 feet high, growing in an open, rich field.

series of slender but somewhat stiff and rough capillary bristles. *Achenia* 5-angled, not striate.

The species of this genus used in medicine are, beside the two under consideration, the American *E. aromaticum*, Linn., *sessilifolium*, Linn., *tencrifolium*, Willd., and *ageratoides*, Linn., all considered tonic, diaphoretic, and antiperiodic, the latter being the supposed cause of the "trembles" in cattle ; *E. rotundifolium*, Linn., a palliative in consumption ; the Texan *mata* (*E. incarnatum*, Walt.) is said to be diuretic, and is used for flavoring tobacco ; while *E. fœniculceum*, Willd., *leucolepsis*, T. & G., and *hyssopifolium*, Linn., are considered to be antidotes to the poisonous bites of reptiles and stings of insects. The European *E. cannabinum*, Linn., is diuretic, emetic, and purgative ; the South American *E. glutinosum* is one of the sources of the substance known as *Matico*;* the Jamaican *E. nervosum* is regarded as an almost certain cure for cholera, typhus, typhoid, and small-pox ; while the Brazilian *aya-pana* (*E. ayapana*, Vent.) is an aromatic tonic and febrifuge, and is considered a sure remedy—if timely used—for antidoting the effects of the bites of poisonous reptiles and insects ; this last is said to be the most powerful species of the genus, and as such, it should be carefully proven.

Compositæ.—This immense and purely natural order, consists of herbs, and rarely shrubs and trees; it comprises one-tenth of all known phænogamous plants, and one-eighth of those of North America, where it has 237 genera and 1610 species, of which 1551 are indigenous. Its members are easily distinguished as such, even by general observation ; but many of the genera and species require close and careful study for their identification.

Since this work was begun, and too late for revision, Prof. Asa Gray's almost phenomenal volume,† including this order, appeared. In his careful and laborious revision of the order many changes were instituted in the arrangement and names of the tribes and genera, making the following table necessary to an understanding of the order as it stands at present :

NEW ARRANGEMENT.	THIS WORK.	OLD ARRANGEMENT.	NEW ARRANGEMENT.	THIS WORK.	OLD ARRANGEMENT.
TRIBE.	GENUS.	TRIBE.	TRIBE.	GENUS.	TRIBE.
Eupatoriaceæ.	78, 79. Eupatorium.	(Same.)	Anthemideæ.	87, 88. Artemisia.	Senecionideæ.
Asteroideæ.	80. Erigeron.	"	Senecionideæ.	90. Erechthites.	(Same.)
Inuloideæ.	89. Graphalium.	Senecionideæ.	"	91. Senecio.	"
"	81. Inula.	Asteroideæ.	Cynaroideæ.	92. Arctium.	Cynareæ (Lappa).
Helianthoideæ.	82. Ambrosia.	Senecionideæ.	Cichoriacæ.	93. Cichorium.	(Same.)
"	83. Helianthus.	"	"	94. Prenanthes.	" (Nabalus).
Anthemideæ.	84. Anthemis.	"	"	95. Taraxacum.	"
"	85. Achillea.	"	"	96. Lactucca.	"
"	86. Tancetum.	"			

* The officinal matico, however, is derived from *Piper angustifolium*, R. & P. (Piperaceæ).
† *Synop. Flora of N. A.*

Description.*—"*Flowers* in an involucrate head on a simple receptacle, 5-merous, or sometimes 4-merous; with *lobes* of the epigynous *corolla* valvate in the bud; *stamens* as many as corolla lobes and alternate with them, inserted on the tube; *anthers* connate into a tube (syngenesious); *style* in all fertile flowers 2-cleft or lobed at the summit and bearing introrse-marginal *stigmas;* *ovary* 1-celled, a single anatropous *ovule* erect from the base, becoming an exalbuminous *seed* with a straight *embryo*, the inferior *radicle* shorter and narrower than the *cotyledons;* the *fruit* an akene. Tube of the *calyx* wholly adnate to the ovary; its *limb* none, or absolute, or developed into a cup or teeth, scales, awns, or capillary bristles. *Corolla* with nerves running to the sinuses, then forking and bordering the lobes, rarely as many intermediate nerves. *Anthers* commonly with sterile tip or append-age; the cells introrse, discharging the pollen within the tube; this forced out by the lengthening of the *style*, which in hermaphrodite and male flowers is commonly hairy-tipped or appendaged. *Pollen-grains* globose, echinulate, sometimes smooth, in CICHORIACEÆ 12-sided. *Leaves* various; no true stipules. *Development* of the flowers in the head centripetal; of the heads when clustered or associated, more or less centrifugal, *i. e.*, heads disposed to be cymose. *Juice* watery, in some resinous, in the last tribe milky.

"Heads *homogamous* when all its flowers are alike in sex; *heterogamous* when unlike (generally marginal flowers female or neutral, and central hermaphrodite or by abortion male); *androgynous* when of male and female flowers; *monœcious* or *diœcious* when the flowers of separate sexes are in different heads, either on same or different plants; *radiate* when there are enlarged ligulate flowers in the margin; wholly *ligulate* when all the flowers have ligulate corollas, *discoid* when there are no enlarged marginal corollas. When these exist they are sometimes called the *ray;* the other flowers collectively occupy the *disk*. The head (compound flower of early botanists), in Latin *capitulum*, is also named *anthodium*. Its involucre (periclinium of authors) is formed of separate or sometimes connate reduced leaves, *i. e.*, *bracts* (*squamæ* or scales); the innermost of these bracts subtend the outer-most or lowest flowers. The axis within or above these is the *receptacle* (*clinan-thium*), which varies from plane to conical or oblong, or even cylindrical or subu-late. When the receptacle bears flowers only it is naked, although the surface may be *alveolate, foveolate* or merely *areolate*, according as the insertion of the ovaries or akenes is surrounded or circumscribed by honeycomb-like or lesser elevations, or, when these project into bristles, slender teeth or shreds, it is *fimbril-late;* it is *paleaceous* when the disk flowers are subtended by bracts; these usually chaff-like, therefore called *paleæ, chaff*, or simply bracts of the receptacle. In place of calyx-limb there is more commonly a circle of epigynous bristles, hairs or awns; the *pappus*, a name extended to the calyx-limb of whatever form or texture; its parts are bristles, awns, palae, teeth, etc., according to shape and texture. Corollas either all *tubular* (usually enlarging above the insertion of the stamens into the *throat*, and 4 to 5-lobed at summit, mostly regular), or the marginal ones strap-shaped, *i. e., ligulate*, the elongated limb (*ligule*) being explanate, and 3 to 5-toothed

* I use Prof. Gray's full description of the order from the volume above referred to, Vol. I., pt. 2, 48.

at the apex.   Such are always female or neutral, or, when all the flowers of the head have ligulate corollas, then hermaphrodite.   Anthers with basal auricles either rounded or acute, or sometimes produced into tails (*caudate*).   Branches of the style in female flowers and in some hermaphrodite ones margined with stigma, *i. e.*, stigmatic lines, quite to the tip ; in most hermaphrodite flowers these lines shorter, occupying the lower portion, or ending at the appendage or hairy tip."   The largest subdivision or series of this order is the TUBULIFLORÆ, wherein the hermaphrodite flowers have tubular and regular flowers.   The LABIATIFLORÆ have corollas of all, or only of the hermaphrodite flowers, bilabiate.   The LIGULIFLORÆ have all flowers hermaphrodite and all corollas ligulate.

Beside the 19 medicinal species treated of in this work, and those spoken of under the description of the genus Eupatorium, we have provings of the following : Wyethia (*Wyethia, Helenoides,* Nutt.) ; the New Zeyland *Puka-puka* (*Brachyglottis repens,* Forsk.) ; the Arctic American Grindelia (*Grindelia squarrosa,* Dunal.); the European Mountain Arnica (*Arnica montana,* Linn.); the Spanish Pellitory (*Pyrethrum Parnethium,* Linn.); the European Coltsfoot (*Tussilago Farfara,* Linn.); and the Italian Sweet-scented Coltsfoot (*T. fragrans,* Linn.); the European Daisy (*Bellis perennis,* Linn.); the South European Marigold (*Calendula officinalis,* Linn.); the Blessed Thistle (*Carduus Benedictus,* Linn. ; *Centaurea Tagana,* Willd.); Chamomilla, the German Chamomile (*Matricaria Chamomilla,* Linn.); and Cina, the European Wormseed (*Artemisia Cina,* Berg.; *A. santonica,* Linn., Artemisia Contra.).*

Outside of our materia medica many valuable, and secondary, drugs are used ; prominent among them we find : the American Daisy-fleabane (*Erigeron heterophyllum,* Muhl.), a reputed remedy for gravel, hydrothorax, and gout; and *E. Philadelphicum,* Linn., a powerful emmenagogue.   The German Pellitory (*Anacyclus officinarum,* H.D.B.), a powerful irritant, sialagogue and stimulant.   The East Indian *Veronia anthelmintica,* Willd., is considered a most powerful vermifuge ; the Indian *Elephantopus scaber,* Linn., is used on the coast of Malabar in dysuria ; the Mexican *Xoxonitztal* or *Yoloxiltic* (*Piqueria trinervia,* Cav.) is said to be a valuable antiperiodic.   Many species of *Liatris* are considered powerful diuretics, especially *L. squarrosa,* Willd., and *L. odoratissima,* Willd.   The Brazilian *Coracoa de Jesu* (*Mikania officinalis,* Mart.) is claimed to be an excellent stomachic-tonic ; and the South American *M. Guaco,* H. & B., and the Brazilian *Erva da Cobra* (*M. opifera,* Mart.), are considered efficacious antidotes to the bites of the cobra de capello, and those of malignant insects.   The common European Fleabane (*Pulicaria dysenterica,* Gærtn.) is said to have once cured the Russian army of dysentery.   Two species of *Bidens,* viz.: the European *B. tripartita,* Linn., and the Carolinian *B. Chrytsanthemoides,* Michx., together with the South American *Spilanthes oleracea,* Jacq. (*Bidens fervida,* Lam.), produce acrid and copious salivation.   The Mayweed, *Maruta cotula,* D.C.), so common almost generally throughout the North Temperate Zone, is fetid and blistering, and causes copious vomiting and

---

* Bentley and Trimen, in their work on " Medicinal Plants," consider that the true source of *Santonine* is from the Russian and Asiatic *Artemisia pauciflora,* Weber (*A. Cina,* Willk., not Berg.).

diaphoresis; it should be proven. The Egyptian and Palestine *Babouny* or *Zeysoum* (*Santolina fragrantissima*, Forsk.) is substituted in Cairo for chamomile, and used in eye affections. The Chinese and Japanese *Artemisia Indica*, Willd., is said to be a powerful deobstruent and antispasmodic. The East Indian *Emila sonchifera*, D.C., is used in India as a febrifuge. Thus throughout the order almost every genus has its useful species, especially in their native localities.

Among the edible vegetables afforded by the order, we find the Jerusalem Artichoke (*Helianthus tuberosum*, Linn.); * the European salsify (*Tragopogon porrifolius*, Linn.); Endive and Chiccory, mentioned under Cichorium Intybus, 93; and Lettuce (*Lactuca sativa*, Linn.).

History and Habitat.—Eupatorium purpureum is indigenous to North America. Its northern range extends from New Brunswick to Saskatchewan; thence it grows southward to Florida and westward to New Mexico, Utah, and British Columbia. It grows in rich, low grounds, where it blossoms throughout the summer months.

The previous use of the purple flowered boneset was very similar to that of its congener, E. perfoliatum. It, however, has proven especially valuable as a diuretic and stimulant, as well as an astringent tonic. It proves useful in dropsy, strangury, gravel, hematuria, gout and rheumatism; seeming to exert a special influence upon chronic renal and cystic trouble, especially when there is an excess of uric acid present (King).

The preparations of the Eclectic Materia Medica are: *Decoctum Eupatorii Purpurei; Infusum Eupatorii Purpurei*, and *Infusum Epigeæ Composita.*†

PART USED AND PREPARATION.—The fresh root should be chopped and pounded to a pulp and weighed. Then two parts by weight of alcohol are taken, the pulp thoroughly mixed with one-sixth part of it, and the rest of the alcohol added. After having stirred the whole well, pour it into a well-stoppered bottle, and allow it to stand eight days in a dark, cool place.

The tincture separated from this mass by filtration has a clear, orange color by transmitted light. It is slightly bitter and astringent, has a somewhat tere-binthic odor, and an acid reaction.

CHEMICAL CONSTITUENTS.—No specific analysis to determine a special principle has been made of this plant. The chemistry of E. perfoliatum is probably applicable more or less to this species.

Eupurpurin.—This so called oleoresin was precipitated from a tincture of the root by Merrell. The body is thrown down when the alcoholic tincture is poured into twice its volume of water and the alcohol is filtered off. It results as a thick,

---

* The true artichokes, however, are, the succulent receptacle of the South European *Cynaria Scolymus*, Linn., and *Cardoons, i. e.*, the leafstalks of *C. carunculus.*

† Epigæa, Eupatorium purpureum, Aralia hispida, and Althea officinalis.

dark greenish-brown mass, having a nauseous taste, and exhibiting, as far as known, the full action of the root. It contains all those principles of the root not soluble in water.

PHYSIOLOGICAL ACTION.—Eupatorium purpureum—in doses of from 10 to 60 drops of the tincture—causes increased secretion of the glands of the mouth; nausea; crampy pains in the stomach and bowels; aching or cutting pains in the bladder with a sensation of fullness and soreness, and a constant desire to void urine, with scanty discharge; increased heart's action; and a general feeling all through the system of languor, soreness, faintness, and weakness, with yawning and intense desire to sleep.*

DESCRIPTION OF PLATE 78.

1. Whole plant, 15 times reduced, Chemung, N. Y., September 10th, 1879.
2. One of the smaller branches of the corymb.

---

* Mrs. Dresser's experience with the drug. Hale, *New Rem.*, l. c.

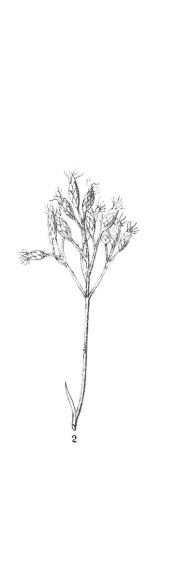

2

1

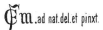.ad nat.del.et pinxt.   EUPATÒRIUM PURPÙREUM, Linn.

79

EUPATORIUM PERFOLIATUM.

BONESET.

SYN.—EUPATORIUM PERFOLIATUM, LINN.; E. CONNATUM, MICHX.; E. SALVIÆFOLIUM, SIMS; E. VIRGINIANUM, PLUK.

COM. NAMES.—BONESET, THOROUHWORT, AGUE-WEED, VEGETABLE ANTIMONY, INDIAN SAGE, FEVERWORT,* CROSSWORT, SWEATING WEED, THOROUGH-WAX;† (FR.) EUPATORIE PERFOLIÉE, HERBE PARFAITE, HERBE À FIÈVRE; (GER.) DURCHWACHSENER WASSER-HANF.

A TINCTURE OF THE WHOLE FRESH PLANT, EUPATORIUM PERFOLIATUM, L.

Description.—This familiar plant grows to a height of from 2 to 4 feet. *Stem* stout, cylindrical, or somewhat terete, fastigiately branched above, and villous-pubescent throughout; *leaves* connate perfoliate, divaricate, narrowly lanceolate and acuminate; they are prominently one-ribbed, rugose, copiously studded with resinous dots, finely and closely crenulate-serrate, dark and shining green above and soft-pubescent or almost cottony beneath. *Inflorescence* a dense, somewhat convex, compound, capitate, corymbose cyme; *heads* small, very numerous; *bracts* narrowly-lanceolate, hairy, and furnished with slightly scarious, acutish tips; *flowers* mostly 10; *corolla* tubular-campanulate; *teeth* broadly triangular. *Akenes* small glandular, oblong-linear, smooth, and bluntly 5-angled; *pappus* shorter than the corolla. The description of *Eupatorium* as given under the preceding drug should be read in connection with this.

History and Habitat.—Boneset is a common plant, indigenous to North America, where it ranges from New Brunswick to Dakota in the North, to Florida and Louisiana in the South. It grows in marshy places on the borders of lakes, ponds, and streams, where it blossoms from July to September.

There is probably no plant in American domestic practice that has more extensive or frequent use than this. The attic, or woodshed, of almost every country farm-house, has its bunches of the dried herb hanging tops downward from the rafters during the whole year, ready for immediate use should some member

---

* The true Feverwort with us is *Triosteum perfoliatum* (Caprifoliaceæ).
† The true Thoroughwax is *Bupleurum rotundifolium*, Linn. (Umbelliferæ).

79.

℃.m. ad nat del. et pinxt.

EUPATÒRIUM PERFOLIÀTUM, Linn.

of the family, or that of a neighbor, be taken with a cold. How many children have winced when the maternal edict: "drink this boneset; it'll do you good," has been issued; and how many old men have craned their necks to allow the nauseous draught to the quicker pass the palate! The use of a hot infusion of the tops and leaves to produce diaphoresis, was handed down to the early settlers of this country by the Aborigines, who called it by a name that is equivalent to ague-weed. It was first introduced, as a plant, into England in 1699; but was not used in medical practice, even in this country, until about the year 1800, but it now has a place in every work on Medical Botany which treats of North American plants.

Eupatorium perfoliatum is diaphoretic only when given in generous doses of the hot infusion; a cold decoction is claimed to be tonic and stimulant in moderately small, laxative in medium, and emetic in large doses. It is also said to be anti-dyspeptic and anti-rheumatic. It is prominently adapted to cure a disease peculiar to the South, known as break-bone fever (Dengue), and it is without doubt from this property that the name boneset was derived. This herb has also been found to be curative in intermittent fever, bilious fever, bilious colic, typhus, and typhoid conditions, influenza, catarrhal fever, rheumatism, lake fever, yellow fever, and remittent types of fevers in general. Many of the earlier works allude to this species as being diuretic, and therefore of great use in dropsy; this is evidently an error of substitution, the previously described drug being the species used.

Dr. Barton, who had made this species one in general use in his practice, observes as follows: "The late Samuel C. Hopkins, M.D., who resided in the village of Woodbury, N. J., and had an extensive practice in a range of fifteen or twenty miles of a populous tract of country, in which, from the low and marshy nature of the soil—exposure of many of the inhabitants holding fisheries, to the water and other pernicious causes—intermittent and typhus fevers were very prevalent, and the latter particularly malignant. The Doctor was among those partial to the sweating plan of treating this fever, and his unusual success in a multitude of cases for five or six years in succession, is strongly in favor of that mode of practice. The boneset was the medicine used in producing this effect. He prescribed it freely in warm and cold decoction, but preferred the warm. He assured me that in many instances his sole reliance was upon this plant, which was occasionally so varied in its manner of exhibition as to produce emesis, and frequently was intentionally pushed to such extent as to excite free purging. Its diaphoretic effect, however, he deemed it indispensable to ensure, and therefore preferred in general giving it warm." *

My friend, Dr. Henry S. Sloan, of this city, relates his personal experience with this drug as follows: When a young man, living in the central part of this State, he was attacked with intermittent fever, which lasted off and on for three years. Being of a bilious temperament, he grew at length sallow, emaciated, and hardly able to get about. As he sat one day, resting by the side of the road, an old lady of his acquaintance told him to go home and have some thoroughwort

---

* Barton, *Med. Bot.*, ii, 136.

"fixed," and it would certainly cure him. (He had been given, during the years he suffered, quinine, cinchonine, bark and all its known derivatives, as well as chologogues, and every other substance then known to the regular practitioner, without effect; the attacks coming on latterly twice a day.) On reaching home, with the aid of the fences and buildings along the way, he received a tablespoonful of a decoction of boneset evaporated until it was about the consistency of syrup, and immediately went to bed. He had hardly lain down when insensibility and stupor came on, passing into deep sleep. On awaking in the morning, he felt decidedly better, and from that moment improved rapidly without farther medication, gaining flesh and strength daily. No attack returned for twenty years, when a short one was brought on by lying down in a marsh while hunting.

From my own experience, as well as what I have learned from others, I feel confident that as an "antiperiodic" this drug will be indicated much more frequently in the United States than quinine, and exhibit its peculiar action in a curative manner, not palliative as is most common in the latter substance when exhibited *ex patria*. I have observed that boneset acts more surely in intermittent fever, when the disease was contracted near its habitat, *i. e.*, by streams, ponds, and lakes in the United States east of the 85° west longitude, and north of the 32° north latitude. It may be stated that this is true of most plants used in medicine, and probably accounts for many failures of foreign drugs in domestic diseases: witness Conium, Cinchona, etc., etc.*

The officinal preparation in the U. S. Ph., is *Extractum Eupatorii Fluidum*. In the Eclectic Materia Medica the following preparations are recommended: *Extractum Eupatorii, Infusum Eupatorii*, and *Pilulæ Aloes Compositæ*.

PART USED AND PREPARATION.—The whole fresh plant, gathered just as it is coming into flower, is prepared as in the preceding drug. The resulting tincture is opaque; in thin layers it exhibits a deep, slightly orange-brown color by transmitted light. It has a nauseous, penetrating, bitter, and astringent taste, and imparts a sensation to the tongue very similar to that of ginger; it retains the peculiar odor of the plant, and has an acid reaction.

CHEMICAL CONSTITUENTS.—*Eupatorine.*—This glucoside was extracted from a percolate of the dried tops and leaves of this plant by G. Latin;[5] it was also appreciated in most of the analyses referred to below, but was not isolated, being spoken of as a bitter principle only. Eupatorine is described as a slightly acid, amorphous body, soluble in alcohol and boiling water, yielding a red precipitate when boiled with sulphuric acid, and a white precipitate with the cold acid. Its farther physical and chemical properties are as yet undetermined.

Bitter extractive;[1267] Tannin;[123456] Volatile oil;[1456] Free acid;[2] Gallic acid;[2] Resin;[267] Gum;[23567] Sugar;[157] and a bitter principle,[234567] have also been

* This refers only to drugs exhibited for their physiological or toxic action.

[1] Bigelow, *Am. Med. Bot.*, i, 35.   [2] Anderson, *Inaug. Thesis.*   [3] Peterson, *Am. Jour. Phar.*, 1851, 206.
[4] Bickley, *ibid.*, 1854, 459.   [5] Latin, *ibid.*, 1880, 392.   [6] Parsons, 1859, *Rep. to U. S. Com. of Agric.*
[7] Tilden's Analysis, *Jour. of Mat. Med.*, ii, N. S. 243.

determined. The last-named substance is spoken of by some observers as being resinous, others as resinoid, and again as crystallizable. I judge it to have been in all the Eupatorine of Latin, either mixed with some part of the other constituents, or more or less pure.

PHYSIOLOGICAL ACTION.—The symptoms shown by those who have partaken of large doses of an infusion of the tops and leaves, show that this drug causes at first an irritation of the vaso-motor system, followed by a relaxed condition of the capillaries, and an increase of the heart's action, again followed by severe congestion and higher temperature. The symptoms are: Faintness, with loss of consciousness, ending in lethargic sleep; pain, soreness, and throbbing in head; soreness of eyeballs, with sharp pains and photophobia; buzzing in the ears; catarrhal influenza; face red or sallow, and sickly in appearance; tongue white cottony coated; thirst especially preceding the stage of chill; vomiting, especially as the chill passes off; violent colic pains in the upper abdomen; urine dark-colored and scanty, with frequent micturition; oppression of the chest with difficult breathing; stiffness, soreness and deep aching in the limbs, the long bones especially, feel as if pounded or broken; sleepiness, with yawning and stretching, from which the patient awakes with a severe headache; skin bathed in copious sweat. The soreness and deep pains of Eupatorium are most general, and the skin feels numb and as if it would cleave from the bones.

The adaptability of this drug to various forms of disease of paludal origin can readily be understood.

DESCRIPTION OF PLATE 79.

1. Summit of stem, from Greenville, N. J., July 26th, 1879.
2. Flower-head.
3. Floweret.
4. Anther.
5. Fruit.
(2–4 enlarged.)

80

ERIGERON.

CANADA FLEABANE.

SYN.—ERIGERON CANADENSE, LINN.; E. PANICULATUS, LAM.; E. PUSIL-
LUS, NUTT.; E. STRICTUM, D. C.; SENECIO CILIATUS, WALT.
COM. NAMES.—CANADA FLEABANE, HORSE-WEED, BUTTER-WEED,
COLT'S TAIL, PRIDE-WEED, SCABIOUS; (FR.) ERIGERON DE CANADA;
(GER.) CANADISCHES BERUFKRAUT.

A TINCTURE OF THE WHOLE PLANT, ERIGERON CANADENSE, LINN.

Description. — This common annual herb grows to a height of from 1
to 4 feet, according to the soil. *Stem* strict, striate, varying from sparsely
hispid to almost glabrous; *branches* mostly superior, short, slender, ascending.
Leaves all sessile, alternate, and more or less ciliate-hispid; the lower often somewhat spatulate, 3-nerved, and sparingly incised; upper leaves linear-lanceolate
acute at each end. *Inflorescence* in a more or less dense terminal panicle; *heads*
very small, cylindrical, many flowered, and radiate; the *face* flat or hemispherical;
peduncles and *pedicels* short; *involucre* almost glabrous; *scales* linear-lanceolate,
nearly equal, little imbricated, all reflexed in fruit; *receptacle* flat or convex, naked,
and pitted. *Ray florets* white, fertile, crowded in a single row, a little exserted
and surpassing the branches of the style; *tube*, elongated-cylindrical; *ligule* very
short, ascending, 2-toothed. *Disk florets* bisexual; *corolla tubular*, mostly 4-
toothed; *filaments* very short, filiform; *anthers* cylindrical, half exserted, not
tailed, the connective prolonged at the apex; *style* short, branched; *stigmas* spreading. *Achenia* oblong, flattened, usually pubescent, 2-nerved; *pappus* simple, a
single row of capillary bristles.

History and Habitat.—Erigeron is indigenous to the eastern and central belt
of North America, where it is common in dry soils, from Canada to Texas; from
thence southward, through South America, as far as Argentine Republic.
In part to recompense Europe for the miserable dock weeds she has sent us, we
have returned her this species, which has now spread through Asia to the sea.
It is also introduced in South Africa, Australia, and many of the Pacific islands.
It flowers, with us, in July and August, maturing its profusion of parachute-like
seeds in autumn.

---

* Ἦρ, *Er*, spring; γέρων, *geron*, an old man; on account of the hoary appearance of some vernal species.

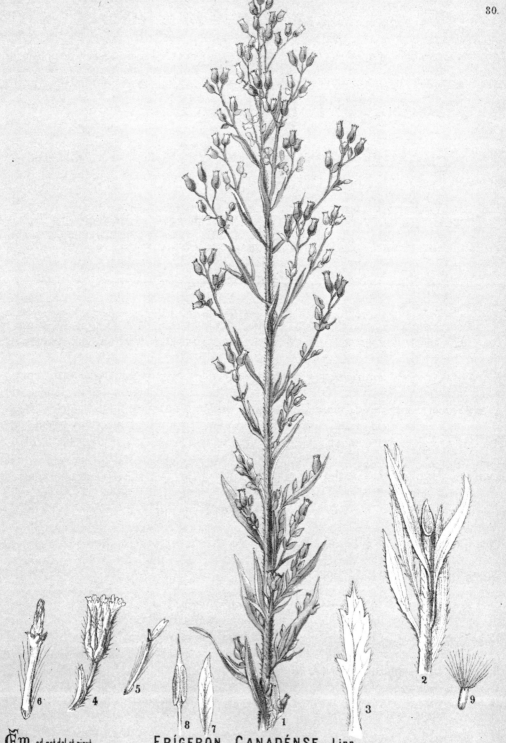

C.m. ad nat del. et pinxt.

ERÍGERON CANADÉNSE, Linn.

The applicability of a decoction of this herb to many forms of diarrhœa was well known to the Aborigines, and is now used in that disease by the Cree Indians of Hudson Bay. It was introduced in the practice at the New York Almshouse, in 1872, by Dr. Gilbert Smith, for a type of diarrhœa that often prevailed there, and met with very great success.

The decoction has proven tonic, stimulant, astringent and diuretic, and been found useful in dropsies and many forms of urinary disorders, both renal and cystic,—such as gravel, diabetes, dysury, strangury, and urethritis; *E. heterophyllum*, and *Philadelphicum* have, however, greater power than *Canadense* in this direction. The oil of the plant is acrid, and, though not astringent, is, nevertheless, an extraordinary styptic; it was introduced by Eclectic practice, and is an efficient agent in the treatment of hemorrhoids, passive hemorrhage, diarrhœa, dysentery, hemoptysis,* hematemesis, hematuria, and menorrhagia; as well as an excellent palliative in the treatment of sore throat, with swelling of the glands, boils, tumors, rheumatism and gonorrhœa. The dose of the oil is from four to six drops in water, repeated not oftener than every hour, if much is to be required.

The officinal preparation of the U. S. Ph., is *Oleum Erigerontis;* in the Eclectic Dispensatory, *Oleum Erigerontis* and *Infusum Erigerontis.*

PART USED AND PREPARATION.—The whole fresh plant, gathered during its flowering season, is treated as in the two preceding species. The resulting tincture has a clear, brownish-orange color by transmitted light; a somewhat aromatic odor; a slightly bitter and astringent taste; and an acid reaction.

CHEMICAL CONSTITUENTS.—No analysis of the plant has yet been made that individualizes the bitter principle first separated by De Puy,† who also determined, in this species, gallic and tannic acids, and an essential oil, and proved that all the qualities of the herb were extracted by cold water or alcohol.

Oil of Erigeron Canadense.—This body may be extracted by distilling the fresh herb with water. It results as a colorless or pale yellow liquid, gradually becoming darker and thicker by age or exposure, and having an aromatic, persistent odor, an acrid taste, and a neutral reaction. It boils at 178° (352.4° F.); has a sp. gr. of from .845 to .850, and is readily soluble in water or alcohol. This oil

---

* In the autumn of 1883, I was called hastily to attend Miss X. I found her sitting upon the floor, her arm resting upon a chair and her head bending over a common-size foot bath-tub, and every few moments a large quantity of bright red blood would gurglingly issue from her mouth. She had been spitting such quantities for over three-quarters of an hour, and the tub was over half-filled with foamy blood, and, I judge, a large quantity of saliva. I immediately mixed about a drachm of tincture of Erigeron in half a goblet of water, and gave her two teaspoonfuls of the mixture every five minutes, while getting the history of the case. She had been subject to these hemorrhages, which did not occur at the menstrual epoch, for some months past, though they were much less in quantity than the present one. Her family history was consumptive and hemorrhagic, and her physical strength always below medium. The hemorrhage now being arrested (after the second dose) leaving her terribly exsanguinated, I had her removed to her bed, and put her on light liquid food in large quantities. This treatment was followed by Erigeron in a potency for a month, one dose nightly, upon which her strength improved; and, up to the last time I saw her, three years after, no subsequent hemorrhage occurred. Her menstrual flux, which had been much too copious and early, was also corrected; and her general health, as she expresses, a thousand times better than at any time since her monthlies commenced.

† *Inq. into Bot. Hist., Chem. Prop., and Med. Qual. Erig. Can.,* 1815.

contains less oxygen than that obtainable from *E. heterophyllum*, and consists mainly of a terpene ($C_{10}H_{16}$), which, after distillation over sodium, boils at 176° (348.8° F.), and has a sp. gr. of .8464 at 18° (64.4° F.).[*]

PHYSIOLOGICAL ACTION.—The symptoms arising during the experiments of Dr. W. H. Burt,[†] were mainly as follows: Cephallagia; smarting of the eyes; roughness of the pharynx; soreness of the throat; abdominal distress, and colic; increased urine; aching of back and extremities; and prostration.

DESCRIPTION OF PLATE 80.

1. Inflorescence, Binghamton, N. Y., Aug. 18th, 1886.
2. A portion of the mid-stem.
3. Lower leaf.
4. Flower-head.
5. Ray-floret.
6. Disk-floret.
7. Scale of the involucre.
8. Stamen.
9. Fruit.
(4–9 enlarged.)

[*] *Am. Jour. Phar.*, 1883, 372 (*Berichte*, 1882, 2854).
[†] *Am. Hom. Obs.*, 1866, p. 357.

Tribe.—ASTEROIDEÆ.

GENUS.—**I N U L A,*** LINN.

SEX. SYST.—SYNGENESIA, POLYGAMIA SUPERFLUA.

81

I N U L A.

ELECAMPANE.†

SYN.—INULA HELENIUM, L. CORVISARTIA HELENIUM, MERAT.
COM. NAMES.—ELECAMPANE, SCABWORT, (GER.) ALANT, (FR.) AUNEE.

TINCTURE OF THE FRESH ROOT OF INULA HELENIUM, *L.*

Description.—This strikingly beautiful perennial attains a height of from 3 to
6 feet. *Root* thick, mucilaginous, more or less tap-shaped, about 6 inches long,
and 1 to 2 inches thick in the largest part, having a curled furrow commencing
about an inch from the stem end, and running nearly to the tip; somewhat branching, the branches generally longer than the main root, but not so thick. The
bark is rough, laminated or flakey, showing upon section a thickness of from one-
sixteenth to one-eighth of an inch. The inner portion is radiate with numerous
bundles of fibres, and dotted generally with yellowish resin-cells. *Stem* erect,
stout, rounded, downy above, branching? near the top. *Leaves* alternate, large,
sometimes reaching a length of 18 inches and a breadth of from 4 to 6 inches;
those near the root are ovate, petioled, the others sessile partly clasping; all green
above, and whitish downy beneath. *Peduncles* of the flower-heads are given off
from the axils of the upper leaves, they are long, thick, sometimes furnished with
a pair of small leaves midway in their length; such are the so-called branches, and
bear usually more than one flower-head on separate pedicles. *Involucre* dense,
woolly, the outer scales broadly ovate, sometimes leaf-like, the inner becoming at
length linear. *Flower-heads* large, solitary or corymbose, all at or near the summit of the plant; the somewhat convex, naked, flat receptacles measuring about 1
inch in diameter. The heads are many-flowered, the *ray-florets* numerous and
arranged generally in a single series, pistillate, but often infertile; the *rays* ligulate, unequally three-notched at the tip, and generally clasping the pistil forming
a tube. *Disk-florets* many, tubular, perfect, the tube 5 toothed or lobed. *Stamens*
five, inserted on the corolla, their *Anthers* syngenesious, with two serrate tails at
the base. *Ovary* oblong; *Style* 2-cleft at the apex. *Achenia* terete or 4-sided,
the sides smooth; *pappus* simple, composed of bristly hairs. A general description of the Compositæ will be found under Eupatorium purpureum.

---

* INULA, a Latin classical name for this plant, probably a contraction of the word HELENIUM, ἑλέςνον, which was applied to the same species. Mediæval, ENULA.

† Ante-Linnæan name ENULA CAMPANA, from which Elecampane.

81.

GM. ad nat. del. et pinxt.

INULA HELENIUM. Linn.

History and Habitat.—Inula was one of the most famous of ancient medicines, and continued in vogue in the old school until very recent times. It owed the reputation it gained to its stimulant qualities. As far back as the Hippocratic writings, it is stated to be a stimulant to the brain, the stomach, the kidneys, and the uterus.

This plant is a native of Southern England, now thoroughly naturalized in Europe and our country. It grows here spontaneously in the Northern States, in damp places along road-sides, the borders of gardens and about the ruins of old buildings. It flowers in July and August, and is a strikingly beautiful plant, reminding one forcibly of its near relative, the sunflower.

Inula is simply mentioned in the U. S. Ph. The Eclectic officinal preparations are: *Decoctum Helenii*, and *Extractum Helenii Alcoholicum*. Inula is also one of the components of *Syrupus Araliæ Compositus*.

PART USED AND PREPARATION.—The fresh roots gathered in autumn (those of the second year's growth in preference, as the older ones are too woody) are chopped and pounded to a pulp and weighed. Then two parts by weight of alcohol are taken, and having mixed the pulp thoroughly with one-sixth part of it, the rest of the alcohol is added; after having stirred the whole well, and poured it into a well-stoppered bottle, it is allowed to stand eight days in a dark, cool place. The tincture is then separated by decanting, straining and filtering.

Thus prepared it is, by transmitted light, of a clear amber color, has a decided bitter and astringent taste, and an acid reaction to litmus.

CHEMICAL CONSTITUENTS.—Inulin,* $C_6 H_{10} O_5$. This amylose principle is found in the plants of many genera of the order Compositæ; but as it occurs in greater percentage in this genus, I describe it here. It will be noticed that this substance has the same composition as starch, still, though it takes the place of that body in the roots of this order of plants, it acts in many ways entirely different; for instance, it dissolves readily in hot water, but forms a clear solution, not an opaline pasty mass, its reaction with a solution of iodine gives a brown, not a blue color. It does not form in the plant as granular shell-like bodies as does starch, but is in solution in the plant juice. Inulin may be thrown down from its watery solution by alcohol, forming thus globular masses of white needle-like crystals, called in the dried plant "Sphæro-crystals." Upon boiling this substance with a dilute acid, it is rapidly converted into levulose, but not at lower temperature. It is considered by Kiliani to be an anhydride of levulose.

Elecampane Camphor, formerly called Helinin, was given the composition $C_{16} H_{28} O_{10}$. Kallen succeeded in resolving it into two crystallizable bodies which he describes as follows:

Helinin, $C_6 H_8 O$, a principle devoid of odor or taste, crystallizing in needles and fusing at 230°F., and

Alant-Camphor, (Inulol, Inulöid, Elecampane-camphor), $C_{10} H_{16} O$, not supposed to be a pure substance; it has an odor and taste resembling peppermint, and fuses at 147.2° F. (*Et supra*, Wittstein.)

---

* Alantin, Menyanthin, Elecampin, Dahlin, Datiscin.

324 [81–3]

Synanthrose, $C_{12}H_{22}O_{11}$.—This saccharose body occurs according to Schorlemmer in the tubers of Inula and other Compositæ. It is a non-crystalline powder, light, deliquescent, and having no sweet taste.

Inulic Acid.—Exists in larger quantities than inulol; it is probably the anhydride of some acid peculiar to this plant.

Resin.—A brown, bitter, nauseous acrid body, aromatic when warm, soluble in alcohol and ether; wax, gum, salts of K, Ca, and Mg, and a trace of volatile oil have also been determined.

PHYSIOLOGICAL ACTION.—Inula has been held to be a stimulant to the secretory organs, but the effects produced—according to Fischer[*]—in those who partook of the juice of the root, show the opposite effect! His scheme of prominent symptoms is as follows: Confusion of the head, with nausea and vertigo on stooping; burning of the eyeballs; dryness of the mouth and throat; increased peristaltic action of the intestines, with griping or tensive pain; dragging in the rectum and female genitalia; much urging to urinate, with scanty results; severe pain in the lumbar region, with sleeplessness and coldness. The more minute action of the drug seems to fully carry out the above, which shows Inula to be anything but diaphoretic, diuretic, or expectorant in a physiological sense.

DESCRIPTION OF PLATE 81.

1. Whole plant five times reduced, from Waverly, N. Y., August 11th, 1880.
2. Flower-head.
3. Disk flower (enlarged).
4. Stamen (enlarged).
5. Ray-floret (enlarged).
6. Section of the root.
7. Seed.

[*] Vide Allen, " Encyc. Mat. Med.," Vol. V, p. 113.

82

AMBROSIA ARTEMISIÆFOLIA.

RAG-WEED.

SYN.—AMBROSIA ARTIMISIÆFOLIA, LINN.; A. ELATIOR, LINN.; A. ABSYNTHIFOLIA AND PANICULATA, MICHX.; A. HETEROPHYLLA, MUHL.; IVA MONOPHYLLA, WALT.

COM. NAMES.—RAG-WEED, ROMAN WORMWOOD, CARROT-WEED, WILD OR BASTARD WORMWOOD, HOG-WEED, CONOT-WEED, BITTER-WEED; (FR.) AMBROSIE; (GER.) TRAUBENKRAUT.

A TINCTURE OF THE WHOLE HERB AMBROSIA ARTEMISIÆFOLIA, LINN.

Description.—This annual, pubescent or hirsute weedy-herb, attains a growth of from 1 to 3 feet. *Stem* erect, at first simple, then paniculately branched. *Leaves* opposite and alternate, thinnish, bipinnatifid, or pinnatifidly parted, those of the inflorescence often entire, all smooth above and pale or hoary beneath; *divisions* irregularly pinnatifid or entire. *Flowers* unisexual on the same plant. *Sterile heads* numerous, gamophyllous, arranged in centripetal, racemose spikes, all more or less recurved-pedicelled and not subtended by bracts; *involucre* truncate, saucer-shape or campanulate, not costate but indistinctly radiate veined; *border* irregularly 4 to 6 toothed; *corolla* obconical, the border 5-toothed; *stamens* 5; *filaments* short; *anthers* deltoid, slightly united, their short appendages inflexed; *abortive style* columnar, the apex dilated and penicillate, strongly exserted. *Fertile heads* 1 to 3, apetalous, glomerate in the axils of the upper leaves and below the male spikes; *involucre* open, nutlet-like; *corolla* reduced to a ring around the base of the style; *style* bilamellar, exserted. *Akenes* turgid-ovoid, triangularly compressed, short-beaked, and crowned with from 4 to 6 short teeth or spines; *pappus* wanting.

History and Habitat.—This too-common, truly American weed, is indigenous from Nova Scotia to Saskatchewan, Washington Territory, and southward to Brazil. It habits waste fields, roadsides, and dry places, and blossoms from the latter part of July to October.

The former uses of this plant were but slight, its principal use being as an antiseptic emollient fomentation; its bitterness caused its use in Maryland as a substitute for quinine, but not successfully. J A. Zabriskie, of Closter, N. J.,

---

* Ἀμβροσια, *ambrosia*, the food of the gods; the gods know why!

claims it to be a successful application to the poisonous effects of Rhus if rubbed upon the inflamed parts until they are discolored by its juice.* Being very astringent, it has also been used to check discharges from mucous surfaces, such as mercurial ptyalism, leucorrhœa, gonorrhœa, and especially in septic forms of diarrhœa, dysentery, and enteritis. It lays some claim also to being stimulant and tonic, and is recognized in the Mexican Pharmacopœia as an emmenagogue, febrifuge, and anthelmintic. Of late years much attention has been called to the species of this genus, especially this and *A. trifida*, as being, through their pollen, the cause of hay fever, many people affected with this troublesome disorder laying the charge direct; certain it is that when the pollenation of the plant is begun the disorder generally commences in those subject to it, and only ceases when the plants are out of flower, unless the patient is able to sojourn to mountain heights out of the limit of their growth. We have had the pleasure of curing two patients of this disease, both of whom had asthmatic symptoms at the height of the trouble, with drop doses of the tincture *tres in dies*.

PART USED AND PREPARATION.—The whole fresh plant, when in the height of its sexual season, should be carefully gathered to retain all the pollen possible, and macerated for fourteen days in twice its weight of absolute alcohol, being kept in a dark, cool place, well corked, and shaken twice a day. The tincture thus prepared should, after pressing, straining, and filtering, have a clear orange-red color by transmitted light; an odor like chocolate; a similar taste, followed by bitterness; and an acid reaction.

CHEMICAL CONSTITUENTS.—This plant has not yet been investigated as to its specific chemical nature; Tannin, and an essential oil, itself uninvestigated, being all we possess of knowledge in this direction.

PHYSIOLOGICAL ACTION.—Ambrosia appears to have a decided irritant action upon mucous membranes, not only by its pollen directly applied, but also upon its ingestion in infusion and tincture. The plant certainly deserves thorough and extended experimentation.

DESCRIPTION OF PLATE 82.

1. Whole young plant, Binghamton, N. Y., Aug. 15th, 1886.
2. A leaf.
3. Male involucre.
4. Face of same, showing sterile flowers.
5. Sterile flower.
6. Sterile style.
7. Stamen.
8. Anther.
9. Female flower.
10. Fruit.
11. Horizontal section of akene.
(3–11 enlarged.)

* *New Rem.*, 1879, 239.

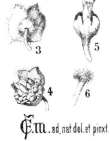

ℭ.ℳ. ad. nat del. et pinxt.

AMBRÒSIA ARTEMISIAEFÒLIA, Linn.

83

HELIANTHUS.

SUNFLOWER.

SYN.—HELIANTHUS ANNUUS, LINN.

COM. NAMES.—SUNFLOWER; (GER.) SONNENBLUME; (FR.) LE TOURNE-
SOL.

TINCTURE OF THE RIPE ACHENIA OF HELIANTHUS ANNUUS, LINN.

Description.—This commonly cultivated plant, springing from an annual
root, attains a height of from 3 to 18 or more feet, and bears numerous large flower-
heads on long peduncles. *Stem* erect, rounded and rough, bearing opposite
leaves below and alternate ones above. *Leaves* petioled, broadly ovate or heart-
shaped, from 5 to 10 inches long, and 4 to 8 inches broad, rough and conspicuously
3-ribbed. *Peduncles* long, gradually thickening into a funnel-form base at the
involucre. *Involucre* composed of ovate aristate, hirsute scales, imbricated in
several rows. *Flower-heads* many, nodding, bearing innumerable ray and many
disk florets; they range from 6 to 12 inches in diameter with a flat or convex disk.
Ray-florets numerous, ligulate and neutral. *Disk-florets*, all perfect and fertile,
with short 5-lobed tubes, decemneurate. *Pollen* grains ovate, beset with numerous rows of spines. *Ovary* 1-celled; *style* invested with stiff hairs; *stigma* 2-
branched, with subulate appendages. *Achenia* ovate-oblong or cuneiform, somewhat quadrangularly compressed, without margins, each achenium bearing 2 ear-
like chaffy scales, sometimes accompanied by an accessory pair, all of which fall
away when the seed is ripe. A description of the natural order will be found
under Eupatorium purpureum.

History and Habitat.—The sunflower is one of the natives of tropical
America, that has become popular in cultivation in many countries, both on account of its beautiful flowers, whose bright chrome rays, in their many modes of
curling and reflexing in a circle about the handsome seal-brown disk, render it
attractive as a garden ornament, as well as the many uses to which the seeds
are put. From points where it is cultivated it often spreads about in many places
by spontaneous growth, blossoming from July until August. The white central
pith of the stalk contains nitre; this fact has led to its use as a diuretic, and recommended it also as a form of moxa. The leaves, when carefully cared for and

---

* ἥλιος, *the sun*, ἄνθος, *a flower.*

33.

꿇ꠓ. ad nat. del. et. pinxt.

HELIANTHUS ANNUUS. Linn.

successfully dried, have been used as a substitute for tobacco in cigars, the flavor of which is said to greatly resemble that of mild Spanish tobacco. The seeds have been extensively used for fattening poultry; fowls eat of these greedily on account of their oily nature. How much a fact it may be that a growth of this plant about a dwelling protects the inhabitants against malarial influences is not yet proven, though strongly asserted by many. An infusion of the stems is claimed to be anti-malarial, and with some forms will probably prove such. A further proving of the tincture is greatly needed, as it would doubtless show an adaptability in this direction. Helianthus has no place in the U. S. Ph. In the Eclectic Materia Medica the infusion of the seeds is used as a mild expectorant, and the expressed oil as a diuretic.

PART USED AND PREPARATION.—The ripe seeds. The seeds when ripe are of a dark purplish color, more or less 4-sided and 4-angled by compression; they are about half an inch in length by one-eighth in breadth. The husk is whitish internally and the kernel sweet, oily and edible. The tincture is made by coarsely powdering the ripe seeds, covering the mass with five parts by weight of dilute alcohol, and allowing it to remain at least eight days in a well-corked bottle, in a dark, cool place, being shaken twice a day. The tincture is then decanted, strained and filtered.

Thus prepared it is by transmitted light a very pale straw-color, has no characteristic taste, and has an acid reaction to litmus-paper.

CHEMICAL CONSTITUENTS.—The analysis of this plant by Wittstein, in 1879, was made exclusive of the seeds, and has therefore no interest to us. The fruit contains by his analysis from twelve to twenty-four per cent. of fixed oil, having a light straw-color, mild taste, and watery consistence, its specific gravity being .926°. It becomes turbid at ordinary temperatures and solidifies at —16°.

Helianthic Acid.—$C_7H_9O_4$, in the form of a slightly colored powder, has been extracted from the kernels; it is soluble both in water and alcohol.

PHYSIOLOGICAL ACTION.—Very little or nothing is known of the physiological action of this plant, which would necessarily be slight. It causes dryness of the mucous membranes of the mouth, throat, and fauces, excites vomiting, heat and redness of the skin, and some slight inflammation of the cuticle. A thorough proving of the *whole plant* is greatly to be desired, as without doubt another remedy would be found in it to add to our excellent list for intermittents.

DESCRIPTION OF PLATE 83.

1. Whole plant, seven times reduced, from a cultivated specimen. Binghamton, N. Y., Sept 8, 1882.
2. Flower head.
3. Floweret (enlarged).
4. Young seed.
5. Mature seed.
6. Scale of involucre.
7. Ray.
8. Pollen grain x 200.

84

ANTHEMIS NOBILIS.

ROMAN CHAMOMILE.

SYN.—ANTHEMIS NOBILIS, LINN.; A. AUREA, D. C.; CHAMOMILLA NO-
BILIS, GODR.; CHAMÆMELUM NOBILE, ALL.; ORMENIS NOBILIS,
GAY.

COM. NAMES.—TRUE CHAMOMILE, GARDEN CHAMOMILE,† CORN FEVER-
FEW ‡; (FR.) CHAMOMILE ROMAINE; (GER.) RÖMISCHE KAMILLEN.

A TINCTURE OF THE WHOLE PLANT ANTHEMIS NOBILIS, LINN.

Description.—This low, aromatic perennial, seldom rises to any great height above the ground. *Stems* smooth or slightly pubescent, the sterile creeping, the fertile somewhat ascending; *branches* numerous, hairy. *Leaves* alternate, sessile, pinnately bi- or tri-ternately compound, and dissected into filiform segments. *Heads* heterogamous, many-flowered, and rather large, terminal and solitary upon the branches; *peduncles* long, pubescent; *involucre* hemispherical, consisting of 2 or 3 rows of comparatively small, imbricated bracts, the outer successively shorter; *receptacle* oblong, with blunt, chaffy bracts subtending most of the florets. *Disk-florets* numerous, yellow, bi-sexual; *corolla* tubular, slightly gibbous below, enlarged above to bell-shaped, and having a few oil glands upon its surface; *limb* 5-lobed; *stamens* 5; *anthers* tailless at the base; *style* slender, bifurcated. *Ray-florets* 15 to 20, white, fertile; *ligules* 3-toothed at the apex; *style-branches* stigmatic at their truncate, penicillate extremities. *Akenes* terete, glabrous, marked by 3 indistinct ridges upon their inner faces, the truncate summit naked; *pappus* none, the persistent base of the corolla, however, appearing like a coronal body of that nature.

History and Habitat.—This European immigrant has, as yet, spread but little in this country, it being only occasionally found spontaneous near gardens, where it blossoms in July and August.

On account of many species being nearly related to this one, and the ancient descriptions of so meagre a type, the history of this plant, which has, without doubt, been used as long as any other, is not traceable with any chance of correct-ness. In later times, however, it has been regarded important, by both physicians and the laity, and judged more active than Chamomilla, which it greatly resembles

---

* Ἀνθεμίς, *anthemis*, a Greek name for some allied plant.
† Our Chamomilla is *Matricaria Chamomilla*, Linn.
‡ Garden Feverfew is *Matricaria Parthenium*.

in its action. As a stomachic tonic and carminative, it has been found useful in atonic dyspepsia, gastro-intestinal irritation, intermittent and typhoid fevers, and colic, and is claimed to be an effectual preventive of incubus. A warm infusion acts as a prompt emetic, emptying the stomach without enervating the system. Fomentations of the steamed leaves make a kindly application in local pains, neuralgic, podagric, uterine, or abdominal. Hot infusions are sudorific and emmenagogue, but are very apt to cause profuse diarrhœa. The oil of the plant is considered anti-spasmodic, useful in hysteric complaints ; stimulant, and anti-flatulent ; and is often combined with purgative pills, to prevent griping.

The flower-heads are official in the U. S. Ph.; in the Eclectic Dispensatory the preparations are : *Extractum Anthemidis, Extractum Anthemidis Fluidum, Infusum Anthemidis*, and *Oleum Anthemidis ;* it is also a component of *Vinum Symphytii Compositum.**

PART USED AND PREPARATION.—The fresh-flowering plant is treated as directed for the root of Inula.† The tincture resulting has a light, brownish-orange color by transmitted light ; the pleasant, aromatic odor of the bruised plant ; a taste at first sourish and pine-apple-like, then bitter ; and acid reaction.

CHEMICAL CONSTITUENTS.—From various analyses, this herb has been found to contain a volatile and fixed oil, a resin, tannin, and a bitter principle judged by Flückiger to be a glucoside.

Oil of Anthemis.—This volatile body has a bluish or greenish tint, becoming brownish or yellowish by age. It has a specific gravity of about 0.91, is composed principally of the angelates and valerates of butyl and amyl, and yields the following bodies :

Angelicaldehyde, C_7H_8O, and a hydrocarbon, $C_{10}H_{16}$, having a lemonaceous odor, and boiling at 175° (347° F.).

Angelic Acid, $C_5H_8O_2$.—According to the analysis of Fittig, this body, first discovered in *Angelica Archangelica*, exists in the oil of Anthemis, of which it constitutes nearly 30 per cent. It crystalizes in large, colorless prisms, having a peculiar aromatic odor, and an acid and burning taste. The crystals melt at 45° (113° F.), boil at 191° (375.8° F.), and are soluble in both water and alcohol. By heating this body, with hydriodic acid and phosphorus, to 200° (392° F.), it is converted into valerianic acid.

Tiglic Acid, $C_5H_8O_2$.—This isomer of the above, and of *Methylcrotonic Acid*, was discovered in Croton Oil. It exists, according to E. Schmidt, in company with the above ; and it is more than possible that it is identical with it, its boiling point and that of its ethyl-ether being the same. (Flück. and Han., Schorlemmer and Wittstein.)

---

* Comfrey Root, Solomon's Seal, Helonias Root, Chamomile Flowers, Colombo Root, Gentian Root, Cardamom Seeds, Sassafras Bark, and Sherry Wine.

† Page 81-2.

84.

C.m. ad nat del.et pinxt.

ÁNTHEMIS NÓBILIS , Linn.

PHYSIOLOGICAL ACTION.—According to the experiments made with the tincture by Dr. Berridge, Anthemis causes the following symptoms of disturbance: Pain and fullness in the head, lachrymation, rawness of the throat, a feeling of warmth in the stomach and desire for food, followed by qualmishness and nausea; some abdominal pain, freeness of the bowels, increased urine; higher heart's action, lassitude, and a general feeling of chilliness.

DESCRIPTION OF PLATE 84.

1. End of a fertile branch, from an escaped garden plant.
2. Ray-floret.
3. Disk-floret.
4. Stamen.
5. Scales of receptacle.
6. Stigmas.
7. Achenium.
8 and 9. Longitudinal section of akene.
(3–9 enlarged.)

85

MILLEFOLIUM.

YARROW.

SYN.—ACHILLEA, MILLEFOLIUM, LINN. ACHILLEA SETACEA, W. & KIT.

COM. NAMES.—COMMON YARROW, MILFOIL, NOSEBLEED ; (FR.) MIL-LEFEUILLE; (GER.) SCHAFGARBE, SCHAFRIPPE.

A TINCTURE OF THE FRESH PLANT ACHILLEA MILLEFOLIUM, LINN.

Description.—This very common roadside herb rises to a height of from 6 to 20 inches, from a slender, creeping, perennial root, which, beside a multitude of filiform rootlets, gives off several long, reddish stolons. The *stem* is simple or nearly so, erect, slightly grooved and roughly hairy. *Leaves* alternate ; those from near the root wide-petioled, 2 to 6 inches long ; those of the stem proper, shorter, sessile or nearly so, and all in their general outline more or less lanceolate oblong, twice pinnately parted, the divisions linear, crowded and 3 to 5 cleft. *Peduncles* 3 or more ; pedicels many, forming small, crowded, flat-topped corymbs at the summit of the plant. *Heads* many-flowered, radiate. *Involucre*, of 2 to 3 imbricated rows of ovoid-oblong scales, with a prominent midrib and brownish, scarious edges. *Rays* 4 or 5, pistillate, with a short, obovate, reflexed limb, more or less 3-lobed. *Disk-florets* 8 to 12, bisexual. *Calyx* limb obsolete. *Corolla* tubular, the summit slightly inflated, 5-lobed, the lobes revolute, acute. *Stamens* 5, inserted upon the tube, and rising slightly above the face of the corolla. *Anthers* adnate, without tails at the base. *Style* long, upright, slender, rising above the anthers. *Stigma* 2-cleft, the divisions recurved and fringed at their tips. *Receptacle* small, usually flat and chaffy. *Achenia* oblong, flattened by compression, shining and slightly margined. *Pappus* none. For a description of the natural order see Eupatorium purpureum, 78.

History and Habitat.—Yarrow is an abundant weed in old, dry pastures, along roadsides and in fields in the northern parts of America, extending in this country, as well as in Western Asia and Europe, high in the colder latitudes. It came to us from Europe, being now fully naturalized. The white or sometimes pink flower-heads blossom all summer. Among the Pah-Ute Indians, according to Dr. Edward Palmer, this plant is much used in decoction for weak and disordered stomachs. Linnæus says, that for a time the Swedes used Yarrow in lieu of hops in the manufacture of beer, and claimed the beer thus brewed to be a greater intoxicant. Millefolium has been dismissed from the U. S. Ph. In the Eclectic practice it is used in an infusion, tincture, or the essential oil.

* The virtues of this genus are said to have been discovered by Achilles.

PART USED AND PREPARATION.—The whole fresh plant should be gathered when flowering begins, excluding all old and woody stems, and chopped and pounded to a pulp; then in a new piece of linen press out thoroughly all the juice and mix it by brisk succussion with an equal part by weight of alcohol. Allow the mixture to stand eight days in a dark, cool place, then filter. The tincture thus prepared should be by transmitted light of a clear reddish-orange color; its odor peculiar, resembling that of malt yeast, pungent and agreeable, like the fresh plant; to the taste acrid and slightly bitter, and shows an acid reaction to test papers.

CHEMICAL CONSTITUENTS.—*Achillein* $C_{20} H_{38} N_2 O_{15}$. The body formerly designated by this name was a mixed alcoholic extract of no definite character, containing all of the unvolatilized principles of the plant; from this mass the true alkaloid was isolated by Von Planta and its composition, as above, determined. Achillein has no definite crystalline form; it is soluble in water, alcohol and ether, and has a bitter taste.

Oil of Achillea.—This oil is readily obtained by aqueous distillation of the plant; that from the flowers and green parts of the herb has a beautiful dark blue color and a specific gravity 0.92; that from the achenia is greenish-white, while from the root it is either colorless or slightly yellow. The oil from the green parts, if cold, is of a butter-like consistence, strongly odorous, and with a taste similar to that of the herb itself.

Achilleic Acid.—A strongly acid, odorless, liquid body, with a density of 1.0148 when fully concentrated, crystallizing in colorless quadrilateral prisms, soluble in water. (*Et supra*, Wittstein.)

The plant contains besides the above principles tannin and a resinoid body uninvestigated. It is considered by Griffith that the plant as naturalized in the Northern United States is more active in its properties than its European progenitors.

PHYSIOLOGICAL ACTION.—Yarrow seems to have a decided action upon the bloodvessels, especially in the pelvis. It has been proven to be of great utility in controlling hæmorrhages, especially of the pelvic viscera, where hæmorrhage is caused by it. Its common European name, Nosebleed, was given from the fact that the early writers claimed hæmorrhage of the nose followed placing its leaves in the nostrils; this may have been either due to its direct irritation, or the use of Achillea ptarmica, its leaves being very sharply serrate and appressed-toothed. Millefolium causes burning and raw sensations of the membranes with which it comes in contact, considerable pain in the gastric and abdominal regions, with diarrhœa and enuresis.

DESCRIPTION OF PLATE 85.

1. Leaf from near the root.
2. Flower-head (enlarged).
3. Ray-floret (enlarged).
4. Top of plant from South Waverly, N. Y., June 8th, 1880.
5. Disk-floret and bract (enlarged).
6. Stamens (enlarged).

CFm.ad nat.del.et pinxt.

ACHILLÈA MILLEFÒLIUM, Linn.

86
TANACETUM.

TANSY.

SYN.—TANACETUM VULGARE, LINN.
COM. NAMES.—TANSY OR TANSEY; (FR.) TANAISIE; (GER.) RAINFARN.

A TINCTURE OF THE LEAVES AND FLOWERS OF TANACETUM VULGARE, LINN.

Description.—This robust, acrid-aromatic perennial, grows to a height of from 2 to 3 feet. *Stem* erect, glabrous or somewhat pubescent, leafy to the summit. *Leaves* alternate, 2 to 3 pinnately dissected, glandularly dotted; *divisions* very numerous, confluent, decurrent, incisely-serrate, with many small lobes interposed along the common petiole; *teeth* cuspidate, acuminate. *Inflorescence* capitate, in dense, terminal, corymbiform cymes; *heads* numerous, depressed-hemispherical, heterogamous; *involucre* composed of several imbricated rows of dry, minute scales; *flowers* all fertile, the corollas sprinkled with resinous dots. *Marginal florets* terete, pistillate; *rays* inconspicuous, oblique, 3-toothed. *Disk florets* densely crowded, perfect; *corolla* tubular; *border* 5-toothed; *anthers* tailless, with broad, obtuse tips. *Style* deciduous, the branches truncate with obscure, conical tips. *Pappus* a coroniform, dentately 5-lobed border. *Akenes* 5-ribbed, with a large epigynous disk.

History and Habitat.—This common European plant has escaped from gardens in many places in this country, especially, however, in the more eastern States, where it flowers from July to October.

. Tansy has been used in medicine, especially as a carminative tonic, since the middle ages, its use at the present time being almost entirely laic and among country folk. Bergius† recommended a cold infusion of the tops as a tonic in convalescence from exhausting diseases, dyspepsia, jaundice and periodic fevers. A warm infusion has been found to be antihysteric, antiflatulent, carminative and stimulant, and largely used in amenorrhœa, dysmenorrhœa and abdominal cramps. Dr. Clark spoke highly of its relief of gout.‡ Hoffman recommended the seeds in 10 to 40 grain doses as an anthelmintic not inferior to cina, for which action the leaves are often applied to the abdomen as a fomentation. Dr. Clapp speaks of

---

* Altered from ἀθανασία, *athanasia*, not dying; the name of a genus of Compositæ having the nature of an " everlasting " plant.

† *Mat. Med.,* 664.   ‡ *Essays Phys. et Lit., 3, 348.*

the infusion as being almost narcotic, soothing nervous restlessness and often producing quiet sleep.* The hot infusion has also been considered diuretic and diaphoretic, and found useful in dropsy. A fomentation of the leaves is often used with salutary effect in swellings, tumors, local inflammations and dysmenorrhœa. The oil, in doses of from 10 drops to a drachm or more, is one of the most frequently-used abortives by ignorant people—a practice at all times serious and often dangerous; even if desisted in, after one or more attempts, the development of the fœtus is very liable to be interefered with; hemorrhage also often occurs—not so dangerous generally as that following the use of nutmegs, but very often serious.

The leaves and tops are officinal in the U. S. Ph.,—in the Eclectic Materia Medica the preparation relied upon is *Infusum Tanaceti;* it is also a component of *Tinctura Laricis Composita.*†

PART USED AND PREPARATION.—Equal parts of the fresh leaves and blossoms are to be treated as directed under Inula (page 81–2). The resulting tincture, after filtration, should have a clear greenish-orange color by transmitted light; it should retain the peculiar odor and taste of the plant to a high degree; and show an acid reaction.

CHEMICAL CONSTITUENTS.— *Oil of Tansy.* This peculiar yellow, or greenish-yellow volatile oil, possesses fully the odor and taste of the plant; it is lighter than water, its sp. gr. being 0.952; it is soluble in alcohol, and will deposit a camphor on standing.

Tanacetin, $C_{11}H_{16}O_4$.‡—This bitter, amorphous principle is found principally in the flowers; it is soluble both in alcohol and water—most readily, however, in the latter.

Tanacetumtannic Acid, $C_{23}H_{29}O_{31}$. — This specific tannin has also been isolated by Leppig; § of its characteristics I am unacquainted.

Leppig § also found in this species: a resin and gallic, citric, malic, oxalic and meta-arabinic acids.

PHYSIOLOGICAL ACTION.—Many serious, and not a few fatal, cases of poisoning, by oil of tansy, are reported, among which the following will show the sphere of toxic action held by this drug: A young woman had been in the habit of using tansy tea, made from the herb, at nearly every menstrual period, for difficult menstruation. . . On this occasion about two and a half drachms of the oil was poured into half an ordinary tin cupful of water; this, with the exception of a small portion of the water containing about one-half drachm of the oil, was taken at one dose. Convulsions were almost at once produced, and when Dr. Bailey was sent for the patient was unconscious, foaming at the mouth, and in

---

* *Catalogue,* 800.
† See foot-note, p. 33–3.
‡ O. Leppig, *Chem. Zeitung,* 1862, 328 (*Am. Jour. Phar.,* 1885, 288).
§ *Ibid,*

violent tonic spasms, with dilated pupils, frequent and feeble pulse.   Constant kneading on the stomach had produced partial emesis, and then ipecac, mustard, and large draughts of hot water, emptied the stomach.   Two drachms of magnesia were then given, and a full dose of acetate of morphine; consciousness then returned, no unfavorable symptoms followed, and, after thirty-six hours, without additional medication she was entirely restored.*

A married woman aged 28, accustomed to taking 5-drop doses without inconvenience, took from 15 to 20 drops.   Shortly after, she complained of dizziness, agonizing pain in the head and burning in the stomach; a sense of cold numbness crept over her limbs, increasing until it amounted almost to paralysis; convulsions followed, during which she vomited twice, freely, and finally uttered a shriek and fell senseless to the floor.   She continued in this comatose condition for over an hour, when, on again vomiting, she recovered consciousness.†

A woman took half an ounce of the oil; the most violent, rigid kind of clonic spasms occurred once in about twelve minutes, coming on generally and instantly, and continuing about one minute.   They were attended with slight, if any motion of the arms; it might be called a trembling.   The arms were peculiarly affected, and invariably in the same way; they were thrown out forward of, and at right angles with, the body; the hands at the wrists bent at right angles, with the fore-arm supinated, the points of the fingers nearly in contact, the fingers straight and slightly bent at the metatarsophalangeal joints.   The muscles of respiration were strongly affected during each paroxysm; air was forced from the chest slowly but steadily, and made a slight hissing noise as it escaped from between the patient's lips.   During the intermission of spasm, the muscles were perfectly flexible, and the transition seemed very sudden.   The jaws were the only exception to this rule; they were, for the first hour and a quarter, rigidly closed, and were with difficulty opened, but after that were subjected to the same action as the rest of the body—when the spasms were on they were rigid; when off, they were relaxed.   After the patient grew weaker, the spasms were more frequent, but had about the same severity and length. Death ensued in two hours.‡

A young woman took two tablespoonfuls of the oil to procure abortion, after which, those who saw her related, that she suffered from symptoms much resembling apoplexy.   Two weeks afterward, the vaginal walls of the labia were found inflamed to such extent that one of them resulted in an enormous abscess; the sclerotic coat of the eye was also so congested that it had a dark purple, glassy appearance, and was so badly swollen that the cornea seemed to be depressed.§

A girl aged 21 years, took 11 drachms of the oil to produce an abortion. Total unconsciousness soon followed; at intervals of 5 or 10 minutes the body was convulsed by strong spasms, in which the head was thrown back, the respiration suspended, the arms raised and kept rigidly extended, and the fingers contracted.   After this state of rigidity had continued for about half a minute, it was

---

* Dr. W. W. Bailey, in the *St. Louis Courier of Medicine*, April, 1885.
† A. D. Binkerd, M.D., *Med. and Surg. Rep.*, 1870, 588.
‡ C. T. Hildreth, M.D., *Med. Mag.*, 1834 (*Am. J. of Med. Sci.*, 1835, 256).
§ E. M. Hale, M.D., *West. Hom. Obs.*, 1869, 345.

usually succeeded by tremulous motion often sufficient to shake the room, together with very faint and very imperfect attempts at inspiration. The whole interval, from the commencement of the convulsion to the first full inspiration, varied from a minute to a minute and a half. Respiration was hurried, labored, stertorous, and obstructed by an abundance of frothy mucus, which filled the air passages and was blown from between the lips in expiration ; the breath had a strong odor of Tansy. Occasionally the tongue was wounded by the teeth, and the saliva slightly tinged with blood. Immediately after a convulsion the countenance was very pallid and livid, from the suspension of respiration, and the pulse, which, during the spasm, was quite forcible, full and rapid, was now exceedingly reduced in strength and frequency. The pulse and color then gradually returned, until the next spasm came on. It was very common, a few seconds after the termination of a convulsion, for the head to be drawn slowly backward, and the eyelids at the same time stretched wide open, at which times the eyes were very brilliant; pupils of equal size, widely dilated, and immovable; and the sclerotics injected. A little inward strabismus was noticeable, of the right eye, as was, also, occasionally slow, lateral, rolling motion of the eye-balls. The mouth and nose were at times drawn a little to the right side. In the intervals of the convulsions, the limbs were mostly relaxed, but the jaws remained clenched. The skin was warm, but not remarkable as to moisture. The victim died in three hours and a half.*

On Animals.—Dr. Ely Van DeWarker records cases of the action of the oil upon dogs. In one case two drachms were given, causing salivation, vomiting, dilation of the pupils, muscular twitchings, followed by clonic spasms, and a cataleptic condition from which the animal recovered. Recovery also followed a half ounce after the same class of symptoms, but, however, on repeating the dose, the already poisoned animal was plunged into a long and fatal convulsion. Postmortem examination disclosed the cerebral veins and spinal cord itself highly congested, and serous effusions had taken place in the pia mater. The lungs were found to be engorged, the left heart empty, and the right distended with dark, liquid blood. Congestion of the kidneys had also taken place, and the bladder was found contracted.†

The safe maximum dose of the oil is indeterminable, a few drops only sometimes proving serious.

The symptoms occurring in a number of cases of poisoning and experiments, were substantially as follows : Mental confusion, loss of consciousness ; vertigo, with cephalalgia ; at first contraction, then wide dilation, of the pupils, staring, immovable eye-balls ; ringing in the ears ; face congested ; roughness of the mouth and throat, difficult deglutition ; eructations, nausea, free vomiting, and burning of the stomach ; sharp colic pains in the abdomen ; diarrhœa ; constant desire to urinate—urine at first suppressed, then profuse ; respiration hurried and laborious ; pulse at first high, then very low and irregular ; numbness of

---

* J. C. Dalton, Jr., M.D., *Am. Jour. Med. Sci.*, 1852, p. 136.
† *The Detection of Criminal Abortion.*

the extremities; tonic and clonic spasms, and nervous tremblings; drowsiness and cold sweat. Death appears to ensue from paralysis of the heart and lungs.

DESCRIPTION OF PLATE 86.

1. Summit of an escaped plant, Binghamton, N. Y., July 21st, 1886.
    2. A flower-head.
    3. A flower-head, longitudinal section.
    4. A floret.
    5. Anther.
        (4 and 5 enlarged.)

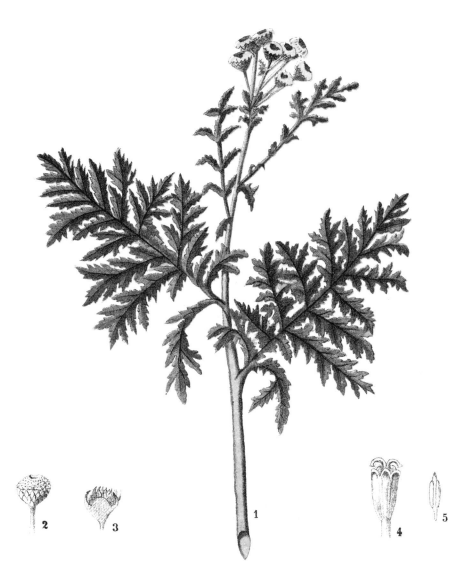

1

2   3

4   5

℮.m. ad nat del. et pinxt.

TANACÈTUM VULGÀRE.

87
ARTEMISIA VULGARIS.

MUGWORT.

SYN.—ARTEMISIA VULGARIS, LINN.; A. HETEROPHYLLUS, NUTT.; A. INDICA CANADENSIS. BESS.
COM. NAMES.—MUGWORT; (FR.) COURONNE DE ST. JEAN; (GER.) BIFUSS.

A TINCTURE OF THE ROOT OF ARTEMISIA VULGARIS, LINN.

Description.—This perennial herb grows to a height of from 2 to 3 feet. *Stem* erect, furrowed, paniculately branched. *Leaves* mostly glabrous and green above, white-woolly beneath and on the branches, the lower laciniate, the median pinnatifid, the upper lanceolate to linear; *divisions* often cut-lobed or linear-lanceolate. *Inflorescence* glomerate, in open, leafy panicles; *heads* numerous, small, ovoid, heterogamous; *flowers* all fertile; *involucre* mostly oblong, campanulate; *bracts* scarious, sparingly arachnoid, but mostly glabrate. *Corolla* smooth. *Receptacle* naked. Otherwise agreeing in minutiæ of florets and sexual organs with the following species, p. 88.

History and Habitat.—The Common Mugwort is an immigrant from Europe in most of its situations here, but is considered apparently indigenous at Hudson's Bay by Prof. Gray. It is naturalized in Canada and the Atlantic States, where it frequents old fields and gardens, roadsides, and waste places, and flowers from September till October.

Hippocrates very frequently mentions Artemisia as of use in promoting uterine evacuations. Dioscorides and Galen used it as a fomentation for amenorrhœa and hysteria—a practice then in vogue among the women of China. German physicians have urged the drug in epilepsy, but it has nevertheless fallen entirely into disrepute, being now very seldom, if ever, used in any disease.

That torturous, barbaric practice, the use of the Moxa, is closely related to this plant, as it was one of the substances, in connection with *A. Chinensis*, used in the manufacture of that pastile.

The Mexican Pharmacopœia is now, we believe, the only one recognizing this drug.

. ad nat del. et pinxt.

ARTEMÍSIA VULGÀRIS, Linn.

PART USED AND PREPARATION.—The fresh root is chopped and pounded to a pulp and weighed. Then two parts by weight of alcohol are taken, the pulp thoroughly mixed with one-sixth part of it, and the rest of the alcohol added. After thorough succussion, the whole is poured into a well-stoppered bottle, and allowed to stand eight days in a dark, cool place. The tincture thus prepared should, after straining and filtering, have a deep yellowish-brown color by trans-mitted light; a characteristic, uncomparable odor—that of the bruised leaves; an aromatic, slightly bitter taste; and an acid reaction.

CHEMICAL CONSTITUENTS.—No analysis has, as far as we are able to ascertain, been made of this plant since Baierus found that by fermentation, dis-tillation, and mixture with water, a fragrant sapid liquor was obtained, with a thin fragrant oil upon the surface.

PHYSIOLOGICAL ACTION.—Mugwort is said to cause increase of epileptic spasms; irritation of the nervous system; profuse sweat, having a fetid, cadaver-ous odor, resembling garlic; violent contractions of the uterus; labor-like pains; prolapsus and rupture of the uterus; miscarriage; metrorrhagia; and increase of lochial discharges.*

DESCRIPTION OF PLATE 87.

1. A portion of a panicle, from Salem, Mass., August 10th, 1885.

---

* Noak and Trinks.

N. ORD—COMPOSITÆ.

Tribe.—SENECIONIDEÆ.

GENUS.—**ARTEMISIA**,* LINN.

SEX. SYST.—POLYGAMIA SUPERFLUA.

88

ABSINTHIUM.†

WORMWOOD.

SYN.—ARTEMISIA ABSINTHIUM, LINN.; ABSINTHIUM VULGARE, PARK.;
A. OFFICINALE, LAM.

COM. NAMES.—WORMWOOD; (FR.) ABSINTHE; (GER.) WERMUTH.

A TINCTURE OF THE LEAVES AND FLOWERS OF ARTEMISIA ABSINTHIUM, LINN.

Description.—This bitter, aromatic, frutescent perennial, attains a growth of
2 to 4 feet. *Stem* stiff, almost ligneous at the base and paniculately branched;
branches of two kinds, some fertile, others barren. *Leaves* alternate, 2 to 3 pinnately parted, finely pubescent with close silky hairs, the uppermost lanceolate,
entire; *leaflets* oblong or lanceolate, obtuse and entire, sparingly toothed or
incised. *Inflorescence* in long, leafy panicles; *heads* numerous, small, heterogamous, on slender nodding pedicles; *involucre* canescent; *bracts* of two kinds, 1 to
2 loose, narrow, herbaceous ones, and several that are roundish and scarious;
florets many, all discoid, the central hermaphrodite, the marginal pistillate. *Corollas* tubular glabrous; *limb* nearly entire in the marginal florets, 5-toothed, and
spreading in the central. *Style* 2-cleft, in the marginal florets bilamellar, with the
inner surfaces stigmatic, in the central bifurcated with only the tips stigmatose,
fringed or fimbriate. *Anthers* tipped with an acuminate appendage, not inflexed.
Receptacle flattish, beset with long woolly hairs; *akenes* obovoid or oblong; *pappus*
none.

History and Habitat.—This European synonym of bitterness has escaped
from gardens in many places in North America, especially, however, in Nova
Scotia, New England, and at Moose Factory, Hudson's Bay. It blossoms with us
from the latter part of July to October.

Wormwood has been used in medicine from ancient times. Dioscorides and
Pliny considered it to be a stomachic tonic, and anthelmintic. Boerhaave, Linnæus,
Haller, and all of the earlier writers speak of its good effects in many disorders,
such as, intermittents, hypochondriasis, gout, scurvy, calculus, and hepatic and
splenic obstructions. Bergius, in recounting its virtues, says it is "antiputredi-
nosa, antacida, anthelmintica, resolens, tonica, et stomachia." The famous "Port-

---

* Artemisia, the Greek Diana, goddess of chastity, as the plant was thought to bring on early puberty. Pliny says
the name is in honor of Artemisia, queen of Mausolus, king of Caria.

† ʼΑψίνθιον, *apsinthion*, the classical name of many species of the genus.

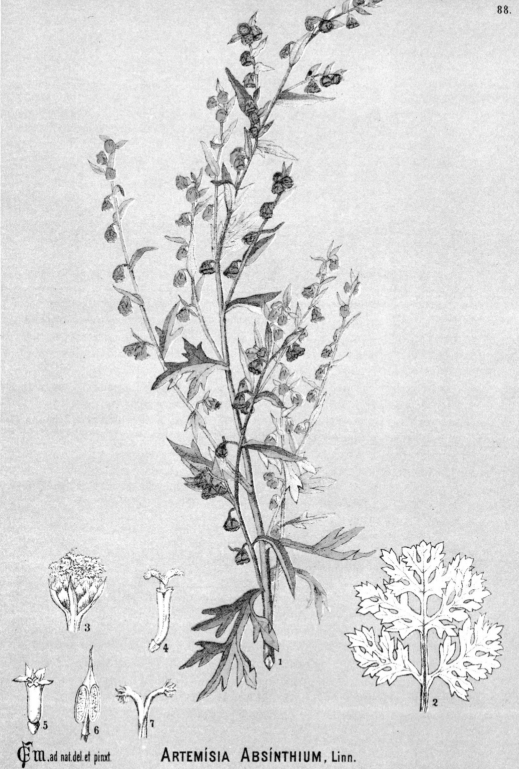

88.

ℭℳ.ad nat.del.et pinxt. ARTEMÍSIA ABSÍNTHIUM, Linn.

land powder," once noted for its efficacy in gout, had this drug as its principal ingredient. A decoction has ever been found a most excellent application for wounds, bruises, and sprains, relieving the pain nicely in most cases; every reader will recall "wormwood and vinegar" in this connection. Latterly it has been found diuretic, discutient, and antispasmodic in epilepsy.

The bitterness of the herb is communicated to the milk of cows who may browse upon it, and also to mothers' milk if the drug be taken.

Brewers are said to add the fruits to their hops to make the beer more heady; and rectifiers also to their spirits. Absinthe forms one of the favorite drinks for those who love stimulating beverages; it is compounded of various aromatics as follows: Green anise (Pimpinella anisi), Star anise (Illicum anisatum), Large absinth (Artemisia absinthium), Small absinth (Artemisia pontica), Coriander (Coriandum sativum), and Hyssop (Hyssopus officinalis); these are distilled together until the distillate comes over reddish, then the following herbs and products are steeped in the distillate to color and flavor it: Peppermint (Mentha piperita), Balm (Melissa officinalis), Citron peel (Citrus medicus), and Liquorice root (Glycyrrhiza glabra).

The leaves and tops of the plant are recognized in the U. S. Ph., and the officinal preparation is *Vinum Aromaticum.** It is officinal in the Eclectic Materia Medica as *Absinthine* and *Infusum Absynthii.*

PART USED AND PREPARATION.—The fresh young leaves and the blossoms are treated as in the preceding species. The resulting tincture is opaque; in thin layers it has a beautiful crimson color; its odor is terebinthic and pleasant; its taste extremely and penetratingly bitter; and its reaction acid.

CHEMICAL CONSTITUENTS.—*Volatile Oil of Wormwood.* This oil, isomeric with camphor, consists principally of *absinthol*, $C_{10}H_{16}O$. It is dark green, acrid, and bitter, retains the odor of the plant, boils at 205° (401° F.), has a sp. gr. of 0.973, and is soluble to almost any extent in alcohol.

Absinthin, $C_{20}H_{28}O_4$.—This bitter principle when first extracted forms in yellow globules, which soon crystallize and become a bitter, neutral, inodorous, friable powder, fusing at 120° (248° F.) to 125° (257° F.). It is soluble in alcohol, slightly also in water, and forms no sugar on decomposing with a mineral acid.

Succinic Acid,† $C_4H_6O_4$.—This acid, together with citric and malic acids, exists in the leaves and fruit of the plant, from which it may be isolated in inodorous, moderately acid, klinorhombic prisms, that fuse at 180° (356° F.), boil at 235° (455° F.), and are soluble in alcohol and twenty-five parts water.

Potassium Chloride, KCl.—This salt has been determined in the plant,‡ from which it may be isolated in yellowish cubes and octahedrons.

---

* One part each of Lavender, Origanum, Peppermint, Rosemary, Sage, and Wormwood.
† Absinthic Acid of Braconnot.
‡ Kunsmuller, *Ann. de Chim.*, vi, 35, from the ash; Claassen, *Am. Jour. Sci.*, 1882, 323, from the extract.

Braconnot also determined a green and a bitter resin, albumen, starch, a tasteless nitrogenized body, a bitter nitrogenized body, and nitre.*

PHYSIOLOGICAL ACTION.—A druggist's clerk took about half an ounce of the oil; he was found on the floor perfectly insensible, convulsed, and foaming at the mouth; shortly afterward the convulsions ceased, the patient remained insensible with the jaws locked, pupils dilated, pulse weak, and stomach retching. After causing free emesis and applying stimulants the man recovered, but could not remember how or when he had taken the drug. According to Dr. Legrand, the effects prominent in absinthe drinkers are: Derangement of the digestive organs, intense thirst, restlessness, vertigo, tingling in the ears, and illusions of sight and hearing. These are followed by tremblings in the arms, hands, and legs, numbness of the extremities, loss of muscular power, delirium, loss of intellect, general paralysis, and death. Dr. Magnan, who had a great number of absinthe drinkers under his care, and who performed many experiments with the liquor upon animals, states that peculiar epileptic attacks result, which he has called "absinthe epilepsy." †

Post-Mortem.—Great congestion of the cerbro-spinal vessels, of the meninges of the brain, extreme hyperæmia of the medulla oblongata, injection of the vessels of the cord, with suffusion of the cord itself. The stomach, endocardium, and pericardium show small ecchymoses.‡

DESCRIPTION OF PLATE 88.

1. End of a flowering branch, escaped at Binghamton, N. Y., Aug. 10th, 1885.
2. A lower leaf.
3. Flower head.
4. Marginal floret.
5. Central floret.
6. Anther.
7. Style of central floret.
   (3–7 enlarged.)

* Thomson, *Organic Chem.*, 1838, 864.
† *Et supra, Taylor On Poisons*, 1885, 652.
‡ *Jour. of Physiological Med.*, 9, 525; in Allen, *Ency. Mat. Med., loc. cit.*

Tribe.—SENECIONIDEÆ.

GENUS.—**GNAPHALIUM,*** LINN.

SEX. SYST.—SYNGENESIA SUPERFLUA.

89

GNAPHALIUM.

EVERLASTING.

SYN.—GNAPHALIUM POLYCEPHALUM, MICHX.; G. OBTUSIFOLIUM, LINN.; G. CONOIDEUM, LAM.

COM. NAMES.—FRAGRANT EVERLASTING, LIFE EVERLASTING, OLD FIELD BALSAM, WHITE BALSAM, INDIAN POSEY, CAT FOOT, SILVER LEAF, NONE-SO-PRETTY; (FR.) IMMORTELLE, LE COTONNIÈRE; (GER.) IMMERSCHÖN RUHKRAUT.

A TINCTURE OF THE WHOLE PLANT GNAPHALIUM POLYCEPHALUM, MICHX.

Description.—This persistent, annual herb, usually grows to a height of from 1 to 3 feet. *Stem* erect, terete, and floccose-woolly; *branches* numerous at the summit, either glabrous or minutely viscid-pubescent when the wool is off. *Leaves* alternate, closely serrate or slightly amplexicaul, but never decurrent, somewhat aromatic, thinnish, all lanceolate or linear, narrowed at the base, and mucronately acute or acuminate at the tip, soon bare and green, or viscid-puberulent above; *margins* entire, often finely undulate. *Inflorescence* in terminal-paniculate, or cymose, glomerules; *heads* numerous, ovate-conoidal before expansion, then obovate, all discoid and heterogamous; *involucre* woolly only at the base; *bracts* oblong, obtuse, thin, dull white, becoming somewhat rusty-colored, pluriserially-imbricate, without tips or appendages; *receptacle* flat, chaffless, and bractless. *Flowers* fertile throughout, arranged in several rows; *corona* filiform-tubular, shorter than the style; *anthers* with slender tails. *Hermaphrodite flowers,* very few; *styles* two-cleft, the branches mostly truncate. *Akenes* terete, lightly 3- to 4-nerved, smooth and glabrous; *pappus* a single row of scabrous, capillary bristles, each free at the base and falling separately.

History and Habitat—This species is indigenous to North America, where it ranges from Florida and Texas northward to Canada and Wisconsin. It grows upon old fields and in quite open, dry woods, and blossoms from July to October.

The Everlastings formed a part of aboriginal medication, and from there they descended to the white settlers, who, in conjunction with the more or less botanic physicians, used them about as follows: The herb, as a masticatory, has always been a popular remedy, on account of its astringent properties, in ulceration of the

---

* Γνάφαλον, *gnaphalon,* a lock of wool; from the floccose appearance of any torn or broken end.

mouth and fauces, and for quinsy. A hot decoction proves pectoral and some-what anodyne, as well as sudorific in early stages of fevers. A cold infusion has been much used in diarrhœa, dysentery, and hemorrhage of the bowels, and is somewhat vermifugal; it is also recommended in leucorrhœa. The fresh juice is considered anti-venereal. Hot fomentations of the herb have been used like Arnica, for sprains and bruises, and form a good vulnerary for painful tumors and un-healthy ulcers. The dried flowers are recommended as a quieting filling for the pillows of consumptives.

Of *Antennaria plantaginifolia*, Hook. (Gnaphalium plantaginifolium, Linn.), Rafinesque says: "For a small fee, the Indians, who call this plant *Sinjachu*, will allow themselves to be bitten by a rattlesnake, and immediately cure themselves with this herb."

Gnaphalium is not official in the U. S. Ph.; in the Eclectic Dispensatory, the preparation recommended is: *Infusum Gnaphalii.*

PART USED AND PREPARATION.—The whole fresh plant, gathered when the flowers are still young, should be treated as directed for the root of Inula.* The resulting tincture should have a brownish-orange color by transmitted light; a pleasant, slightly balsamic odor; a taste at first aromatic, then bitter; and an acid reaction.

CHEMICAL CONSTITUENTS.—No analysis to determine the character of the bitter principle has been made. The herb contains a little resin, a volatile oil, a bitter principle, and tannin; and yields all its sensible qualities to both water and alcohol.

PHYSIOLOGICAL ACTION.—The symptoms following the ingestion of from 15 drops to a half ounce of the tincture, at the hands of Dr. Woodbury,† were essentially as follows: Slight abdominal griping, vomiting and purging; profuse diarrhœa, dark-colored offensive passages. Experiments with small doses of the triturated dry flowers and leaves, at the hands of Dr. Banks,‡ corroborated the above symptoms, though the result was less severe, and gave the following symp-toms beside: Giddiness, especially on rising; dull, heavy expression of counte-nance; diminished appetite; rumbling of flatus, increased urine; sexual excite-ment; intense sciatic pain; weakness, and languor.

DESCRIPTION OF PLATE 89.

1. Summit of plant, Binghamton, N. Y., Aug. 10th, 1886.
2. A leaf (from a plant gathered by Chapman in Florida).
3. Outer } scale of involucre.
4. Inner }
5. Floret.
6. Stigmas.
7. Seed.

(3–7 enlarged.)

89.

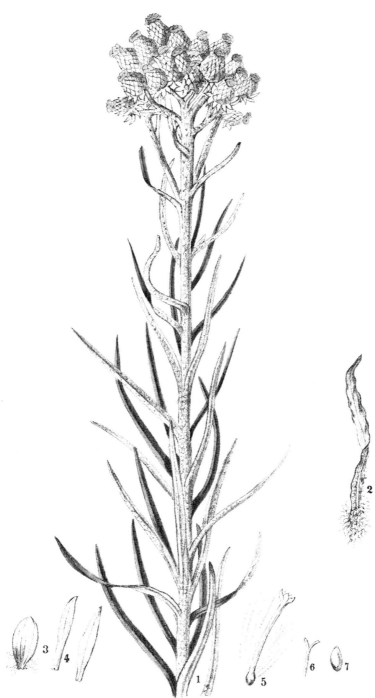

2

3 4 1 5 6 7

CM.ad nat.del.et pinxt. GNAPHÀLIUM POLYCÉPHALUM, Michx.

90

ERECHTHITES.

FIREWEED.

SYN.—ERECHTHITES HIERACIFOLIA, PREALTA, AND ELONGATA, RAF.;
SENECIO HIERACIFOLIUS, LINN.; CINERARIA CANADENSIS, WALT.
COM. NAMES.—FIREWEED; (FR.) HERBE DE FEU; (GER.) FEUERKRAUT.

A TINCTURE OF THE WHOLE PLANT ERECHTHITES HIERACIFOLIA, RAF.

Description.—This rank, glabrous, or slightly hairy annual, usually grows from 1 to 7 feet high. *Stem* stout, erect, virgate, sulcate, and leafy to the top. *Leaves* alternate, sessile, tender, and thin, all narrowly or broadly lanceolate and acute; *margins* sharply denticulate or somewhat pinnately incised; *bases* of the upper leaves somewhat auriculate and partly clasping. *Inflorescence* in a loose, terminal, corymbose panicle; *heads* about one-half inch long, cylindraceous, heterogamous, and discoid; *involucre* a single row of erect, linear, acute scales; *bracteoles* few, setaceous; *flowers* numerous, white, or ochroleucous, the outer female, the inner hermaphrodite. *Corollas* all slender and tubular. *Female florets:* corolla-tube filiform, the limb slightly dilated, and 2- 4-toothed. *Hermaphrodite flowers:* corolla-tube filiform, the limb short, cyathiform, 4- 5-lobed. *Anthers* tailless. *Style-branches* narrow, tipped with a conical pubescence. *Receptacle* flat and naked. *Pappus* white and copious; *bristles* soft, fine, and elongated. *Akenes* oblong, somewhat striate, tapering at the end.

History and Habitat.—This coarse, homely, indigenous weed ranges from Newfoundland and Canada southward to South America; it grows in moist, open woods, upon enriched soil, and blossoms in July and September. Its vulgarism, Fireweed, is given it on account of its seeking newly-burned fallows, there growing in its greatest luxuriance.

The whole plant is succulent, bitter, and somewhat acrid, and has been used by the laity principally as an emetic, alterative, cathartic, acrid tonic, and astringent, in various forms of eczema, muco-sanguineous diarrhœa, and hemorrhages. The oil, as well as the herb itself, has been found highly serviceable in piles and dysentery.

In the Eclectic Dispensatory, the preparations recommended for use are: *Oleum Erechthiti* and *Infusum Erechthiti.*

---

* Derived from the ancient name of some troublesome groundsel.

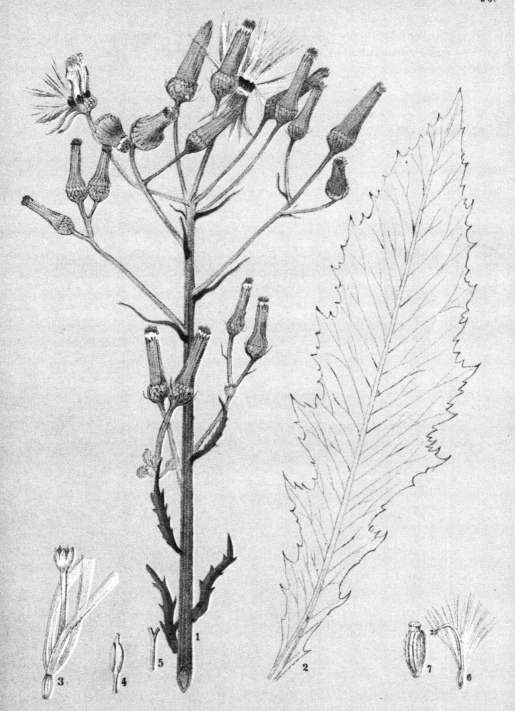

℅.ɯ. ad nat del. et pinxt.

ERECHTHÌTES HIERACIFÒLIA, Rat.

PART USED AND PREPARATION.—The whole fresh, flowering plant is treated as recommended for the next drug.*

The resulting tincture has a clear, beautiful, reddish-orange color by transmitted light; a sourish odor, resembling that of claret wine; a taste at first sourish, then astringent and bitter; and an acid reaction.

CHEMICAL CONSTITUENTS.—In all probability, the principal virtues of the plant reside in its peculiar volatile oil, though no analysis to determine other bodies has been made.

Oil of Erechthites.—This fluid, transparent, yellowish oil, is obtained by distilling the plant with water. It has a strong, fetid, peculiar, slightly aromatic odor, and a bitterish, burning taste. Its sp. gr. is 0.927. It is soluble in both alcohol and ether. According to Beilstein, and Wiegand,† it consists, almost exclusively, of terpenes, boiling between 175° and 310° F. (79.5°–154.4°).

PHYSIOLOGICAL ACTION.—The symptoms of disturbance caused by doses of from 12 to 200 drops of the tincture, at the hands of T. J. Merryman,‡ were in substance as follows: Uneasiness approaching nausea; griping in the bowels, followed by three copious, yellow, mushy, fecal stools, followed again by constipation; increased flow of urine, containing a large amount of mucus; stimulation of the genital organs, followed by erections; and pains in the extremities.

DESCRIPTION OF PLATE 90.

1. Summit of plant, Binghamton, N. Y., Aug. 27th, 1886.
2. A middle leaf.
3. A floret.
4. Stamen.
5. Stigmas.
6. Fruit.
7. Akene.
(3–7 enlarged.)

* Senecio, page 91–2.
† *Berichte*, 1882, 2854; *Am. Jour. Phar.*, 1883, 372.
‡ E. M. Hale, *Trans. Hom. Med. Soc., N. Y.,* 1868, 78.

N. ORD. COMPOSITÆ.

Tribe.—SENECIONIDEÆ.

GENUS.—**SENECIO**,* LINN.

SEX. SYST.—SYNGENESIA SUPERFLUA.

91

SENECIO.

GOLDEN RAGWORT.

SYN.—SENECIO AUREUS, LINN.; SENECIO GRACILIS, PURSH.; SENECIO
FASTIGIATUS, ELL.

COM. NAMES.—GOLDEN RAGWORT, GROUNDSEL, SQUAW-WEED, LIFE-
ROOT, FALSE VALERIAN, GOLDEN SENECIO, FEMALE REGULA-
TOR, FIREWEED,† UNKUM; (FR.) SENEÇON; (GER.) GOLDENES
KREUZKRAUT.

A TINCTURE OF THE ENTIRE, FRESH, FLOWERING PLANT, SENECIO AUREUS, LINN.

Description.—This early spring perennial, usually attains a growth of about
1 or 2 feet. *Root* small, thin, horizontal; *rootlets* numerous, slender. *Stem* usually
free of woolliness at the flowering season, floccose woolly when young. *Leaves*
alternate; *radical leaves* on long, slender petioles, *blade* mostly rounded and undivided, *base* somewhat truncate or almost cordate, *margin* crenate, under surface
pinkish-purple; *cauline leaves*, lowermost similar to the root-leaves with the addition of 2 or 3 lobelets opposite along the petiole, *blade* subcordate, crenate, pinkish beneath; *middle leaves* lyrately divided and passing gradually to laciniate-
pinnatifid, *bases* semi-auriculate, clasping; *superior leaves* linear-lanceolate, linear, sessile, and lastly bracteolate. *Inflorescence* numerous superior-axillary and
finally corymbose, long-peduncled, ray-bearing heads; *heads* radiate, many-flowered; *receptacle* flat and naked. *Ray florets* 8–12, conspicuous, ovoid, pistillate.
Disk florets numerous, perfect, tubular; *corolla* 5-lobed; *lobes* revolute, obtuse.
Involucre of a few lanceolate scales arranged in a single row; *pappus* of many,
soft, capillary bristles. *Anthers* tailless. *Style* bifurcated; *stigmas* recurved. *Akenes*
quite glabrous or only microscopically hairy on the angles, neither rostrate nor
winged. Read description of the order, under Eupatorium purpureum, 78.

History and Habitat.—The Golden Ragwort is common everywhere, the
primary form mostly in swampy spots and on the wet borders of streams. It
flowers from May until June.

Like many another of our partially-proven plants, the medical history is very
superficial. Senecio has been found useful in Aboriginal medicine as an anti-

* The old Latin name for the plant, from *senex*, an old man, on account of the hoary pappus. This large and
widely-distributed genus contains in North America 57 species and 15 varieties, all but 3 of which are indigenous; of the
varieties, 6 belong to *S. aureus*.

† The true fireweed is *Erechthites hieracifolia, Raf.* (90).

hemorrhagic, abortivant and vulnerary. Later it has been recommended as a substitute for ergot, as an excellent drug to control pulmonary hemorrhage, generally as a diuretic, pectoral, diaphoretic, tonic, and a substance to be thought of in various forms of uterine trouble.

The plant has no place in the U. S. Ph. The officinal preparations in the Eclectic Materia Medica are: *Decoctum Senecii, Extractum Senecii Fluidum,* and *Senecii Oleo-resinæ.*

PART USED AND PREPARATION.—The entire, fresh, flowering plant, is chopped and pounded to a pulp and weighed. Then two parts by weight of alcohol are taken, the pulp mixed thoroughly with one-sixth part of it, and the rest of the alcohol added. After having stirred the whole, pour it into a well-stoppered bottle, and let it stand eight days in a dark, cool place.

The tincture, separated from this mass by filtration, has a brownish-orange color by transmitted light, the peculiar odor of the bruised herb, a sweetish then slightly bitter taste, and a strong acid reaction.

CHEMICAL CONSTITUENTS.—*Senecin,* an arbitrary oleo-resin, of unknown constitution. No analysis of the plant has been made, as far as I can determine.

Upon adding the tincture to water a decided deposit of resin takes place, and tincture of iron shows the presence of tannin, even in a mixture of four drops of the drug-tincture in a drachm of alcohol.

PHYSIOLOGICAL ACTION.—We have several provings of this drug, but its action is not determinable from them.

DESCRIPTION OF PLATE 91.

1. Whole plant, Ithaca, N. Y., May 24th, 1880.
2. Disk floret (enlarged).
3. Ray floret (enlarged).

1

3

2

Ⓒ.m. ad nat del. et pinxt.

SENÈCIO AÙREUS Linn.

Tribe.—*CYNARODEÆ.*

GENUS.—**ARCTIUM**,* LINN.

SEX. SYST.—SYNGENESIA POLYGAMIA ÆQUALIS.

92

LAPPA.†

BURDOCK.

SYN.—ARCTIUM LAPPA, LINN.; A. MAJUS, SCHK.; LAPPA OFFICINALIS, ALLIONI; L. MAJOR, GÆRTN.; L. OFFICINALIS, VAR. MAJOR, GRAY; BARDANA MAJOR, GER.

COM. NAMES.—COMMON BURDOCK, CLOTBUR;‡ BAT WEED; (FR.) GLOU-TERON, BARDANE; (GER.) KLETTE.

A TINCTURE OF THE FRESH ROOT OF ARCTIUM LAPPA, LINN.

Description.—This coarse, rank, biennial emigrant, grows to a height of about 3 or 5 feet. *Root* deep, sub-cylindrical, almost black externally and white within. *Stem* stout; *branches* numerous, widely spreading. *Leaves* alternate, ample, orbicular-cordate, unarmed; green and smooth above, whitish cottony beneath, all marked with prominent, crimson veins; *petioles* stout, those of the lower leaves deeply channelled upon the upper side. *Inflorescence* somewhat cymose or clustered; *heads* many flowered, homogamous, tubulifloral, herma-phrodite; *involucre* globular, strongly imbricate; *bracts* all spreading, coriaceous, and nearly smooth, divided into three portions from below upward, viz.: *base* dilated appressed, with a ridge marking its outer median line, the edges some-what serrated; *arista* long, slender and smooth, the apex coverted into a strongly incurved *hook* of a horny consistence, sharp and transparent. *Corolla* pink, equally or somewhat unequally five-cleft; *lobes* long, narrow, and acute. *Stamens* exserted, united by their anthers (except the tips) into a purple tube enclosing the style; *filaments* smooth, distinct; *anthers* tailed at the base and furnished with an elon-gated, connate, cartilaginous apex. *Style* long, filiform, thickened at the apex where it bifurcates into partly distinct, slender, smooth branches without appen-dages, and stigmatic to the apex on the inner side. *Receptacle* flat or convex, densely setose. *Akenes* somewhat bony, inversely pyramidal, transversely wrin-kled, and attached by the very end of the pointed base; *pappus* composed of numerous, short, rigid, barbellate bristles, which are finally separately deciduous.

---

* Ἄρκτος, *arktos* (Celtic *arth*), a bear, from a fancied resemblance in the rough, shaggy, fruiting heads.

† Λαβεῖν, *labein*, to lay hold of, Celtic *llap*, a hand, signifying the tenacious hold the burr takes upon fabrics and the coats of animals. Ray says (*Hist.*, 232; *Syn.*, 196), Lappa dici potest vel απο τυ λαβειν prehendere vel λαπτειν lambere.

‡ The clotburs are properly species of *Xanthium*.

History and Habitat.—This common weed is indigenous to Europe and Asia, growing there as here—about roadsides and dwellings. Since its introduction into this country it has spread rapidly westward, its seeds being numerous and readily carried about by both man and animals. It flowers from June to October. The herb is so rank that man, the jackass, and caterpillar are the only animals that will eat of it. The young stems, stripped of their rind, may be eaten raw or boiled, as a salad with oil, or a potage with vinegar. (Withering.)

The previous uses of this plant have been a decoction of the root in pulmonary catarrh, rheumatism, gout; and a depurant in scrofula, scurvy, venereal eruptions, lepra, and kindred affections, in which it is even now considered better in many cases than sarsaparilla. It is also diuretic. The powdered seeds have been used as a diuretic, and application for the cure of styes. Woodville says* that he "never had an opportunity of observing the effects of the root, except as a diuretic, and in this way we have known it succeed in two dropsical cases, where other powerful medicines had been ineffectually used; and as it neither excites nausea or increases irritation, it may occasionally deserve a trial where more active remedies are improper."

The root is official in the U. S. Ph.; in the Eclectic Materia Medica the following preparations are given: *Infusum Arctii; Extractum Arctii;* and *Syrupus Araliæ Compositus.*†

PART USED AND PREPARATION.—The fresh root gathered in Autumn, before the frost has touched the plant deeply, should be chopped and pounded to a pulp and weighed. Then two parts by weight of alcohol are taken, the pulp well mixed with one-sixth part of it, and the rest of the alcohol added. After the whole has been thoroughly stirred, pour it into a well-stoppered bottle and allow it to stand eight days in a dark, cool place.

The tincture, separated from this mass by filtration, should be clear and transparent. It should have a slighly brownish-orange color by transmitted light, and an acid reaction. This tincture gives no odor or taste by which it may be identified.

CHEMICAL CONSTITUENTS.—*Lappine.*—This peculiar bitter principle was discovered by Messrs. Trimble and Macfarland,‡ and judged by them an alkaloid, as it answered to several of the alkaloid tests. It is described as an amorphous, intensely bitter body, with a faintly alkaline reaction. Its solubility and peculiar physical properties are as yet uninvestigated; it cannot, however, be soluble in cold alcohol to any great extent, as our tincture does not show its presence, at least to the taste.

Oil of Lappa.§—This fixed oil exists in the seeds in the proportion of 15.4 per cent. It is yellow, bland, not soluble in cold alcohol, and has a sp. gr. of .930.

* *Med. Bot.,* i, 34.

† Containing *Aralia Spinosa* and *nudicaulis* (root), Sassafras (root bark), Rumex crispus (root), Burdock (root), Sambucus (flowers), Guaiacum (wood), and Iris (root).

‡ *Am. Jour. Phar.,* 1885, p. 127.　　§ Ibid.

Inulin,* tannin, a gummy extractive, nitrate of potash,† a resin soluble in water, and another in alcohol, have been determined.

PHYSIOLOGICAL ACTION. — The only symptom of importance so far recorded from the action of this drug, is an increased secretion of milky urine, with frequent desire and copious discharges.

DESCRIPTION OF PLATE 92.

1. A flowering branch, Binghamton, N. Y., August 1st, 1884.
2. Floweret.
3 and 4. Bract.
5. Seed.
6. Bristle of Pappus.
7. A thoroughly dried horn.
(2–7 enlarged.)

---

* See under Inula Helenium, 81.

† Loudon says that the mature green herb, when burnt, will yield fully one-third its quantity of a pure, white, alkaline salt equal to the best potash.

ℭ𝔪.ad nat.del.et pinxt.

LÁPPA OFFICINÀLIS,VAR. MÀJOR,Gray.

93

CICHORIUM.

CHICCORY.

SYN.—CICHORIUM INTYBUS, LINN.; CICHORIUM SYLVESTRE SIVE OFFIC. BAUH.

COM. NAMES.—WILD OR BLUE SUCCORY OR CHICCORY, WILD EN-DIVE; (FR.) CHICOREÉ SAUVAGE; (GER.) CICHORIE, WEGEWART.

A TINCTURE OF THE FRESH ROOT OF CICHORIUM INTYBUS, L.

Description.—This partially naturalized, branching, perennial herb, grows to a height of from 2 to 4 feet. *Root* deep, more or less fusiform, woody, branching, and surcharged with milky juice. *Stem* bristly, hairy; *branches* rigid and stout; *leaves* alternate, those from the root runcinate, the lower stem leaves oblong-lan-ceolate, dentate, and partly clasping, those on the branches varying from auricu-late-lanceolate to mere bracts. *Inflorescence* axillary and terminal heads; *heads* 2 or 3 sessile, several-flowered, homogamous, or single and raised upon a hollow peduncle. *Involucre* double, the outer row composed of 5 short, spreading scales; the inner of 8 or 10. *Flowerets* all ligulate and perfect; *ligules* 5-toothed, bright blue, becoming pinkish, then whitish, as the day advances. *Stamens: filaments* white, slender, and unconnected; *anthers* deep blue. *Stigmas* 2, circinate, dark blue. *Akenes* turbinate, striate, angular, and glabrous; *pappus* composed of numerous short, chaffy scales, forming a sort of crown.

History and Habitat.—This European emigrant grows chiefly near the eastern coast, from whence it is spreading somewhat inland. It flowers through-out the months of July, August, and September. Its blossoms present a beau-tiful sight in early morning or on cloudy days, but fade and wither during bright sunshine. The principal previous use of this plant has been that of the root as an adulteration of, or substitute for, coffee. This use, it appears, originated with the Egyptians and Arabians, who also used the bleached leaves as a salad, the boiled or baked roots as pottage, and made a flour for bread from them when dried. Endive (*Cichorium Endivia*), so much used in many countries as salad, was at one time thought to be merely a cultivated state of this species. The specific names Endivia and Intybus both appear to spring from the same Arabic word designating the herb, *hendibeh*. As regards the use of chiccory, Dickens says in his " Household Words : " " The great demand for chiccory has led to its very extensive cultivation in this country; considerable sums of money have been

---

* The Latinized Arabian name *Chickouryeh.*

93.

℮m.ad nat.del.et pinxt.

CICHÒRIUM ÍNTYBUS, Linn.

expended on the kilns and machinery required to prepare it for the markets, and a large amount of capital is profitably employed upon this branch of English agriculture. . . . The bleached leaves are sometimes used as a substitute for endive, and are commonly sold as an early salad in the Netherlands. If the roots, after being taken up, be packed in sand in a dark cellar, with their crowns exposed, they will push out shoots, and provide through the winter a very delicate blanched salad, known in France as *Barbe de Capucin*. When chiccory is to be used for coffee the roots are partly dried, cut into thin slices, roasted and ground. The ground chiccory thus made is used by many poor upon the continent as a substitute for coffee by itself. It has not, of course, the true coffee flavor, but it makes a rich and wholesome vegetable infusion of a dark color, with a bitterish, sweet taste, which would probably be preferred by a rude palate to the comparatively thin and weak, and at the same time not very palatable infusion of pure coffee of the second and third quality. By the combination of a little chiccory with coffee the flavor of the coffee is not destroyed, but there is added to the infusion a richness of flavor and a depth of color—a body—which renders it to many people much more welcome as a beverage than pure coffee purchased at the same price." In times of scarcity chiccory certainly would make a better substitute than many other substances used, as, for instance, during the war of the Rebellion, when—especially in the South—beans, peas, rye, sweet potatoes, corn, cotton seed, pea-nuts, etc., were utilized.

The medical history of chiccory is of little value to us. A free use of the root and leaves produces, according to Lewis, a mild catharsis, rendering aid in jaundice and obstruction of the bowels. It has also been used as a diuretic and detergent in gravel, and a refrigerant in hectic fevers and agues.*

PART USED AND PREPARATION.—The fresh root, gathered while the plant is budding to blossom, is to be treated as in preceding drug. The resulting tincture has a clear orange color by transmitted light, an acid bitter taste, and acid reaction.

CHEMICAL CONSTITUENTS.—The activity of the plant, without doubt, lies wholly in its milk-juice, which has not yet been investigated.

PHYSIOLOGICAL ACTION.—We have no record of toxical effects of Cichorium; its disturbance of the system is very slight, and that appears to be wholly confined to a slight increase of glandular secretions.

DESCRIPTION OF PLATE 93.

1. Part of a flowering branch, Binghamton, N. Y.,† Sept. 10th, 1884.
2. A portion of the main stem.
3. Floweret.
4. Akene.
5. Stigma.
6. Section of the root.
7. Pollen grain, x 150.

(3–6 enlarged.)

---

* Rafinesque, *Med. Bot.*, II, p. 206.   † Where it has escaped to the streets in many localities.

Tribe.—CICHORIACEÆ.

GENUS.—**PRENANTHES,*** VAILL.

SEX. SYST.—SYNGENESIA ÆQUALIS.

94

NABALUS.

RATTLESNAKE ROOT.

SYN.—PRENANTHES SERPENTARIA, PURSH.; P. ALBA, VAR. SERPEN-
TARIA, TORR.; P. GLAUCA, RAF.; NABALUS ALBUS, VAR. SERPENTA-
RIUS, GRAY; NABALUS SERPENTARIUS, HOOK.; N. TRILOBATUS,
CASS, AND D. C.; N. FRAZERI, D. C.; N. GLAUCUS, RAF.; HARPALYCE
SERPENTARIA, DON.; ESOPON GLAUCUM, RAF.

COM. NAMES.—RATTLESNAKE ROOT, WHITE LETTUCE, LION'S FOOT,
GALL-OF-THE-EARTH, DEWITT SNAKEROOT, DROP FLOWER, CAN-
CER WEED; (FR.) LAITUE BLANC, PIED D'LEON; (GER.) WEISSER
LATTICH.

A TINCTURE OF THE WHOLE PLANT PRENANTHES SERPENTARIA, PURSH.

Description.—This variable perennial herb, grows to a height of from 1 to 3 feet. *Root* very bitter, fusiform, thickened or more or less tuberous; *stem* stout, upright, glabrous or a little hirsute, sometimes purple-spotted or splashed. *Leaves* alternate, diversely variable, dilated, often decurrent upon the petiole, rather thin and pale beneath; deeply sinuate-pinnatified, or 3-parted, and the terminal lobe 3-cleft; the margin a little rough-ciliate; the cauline nearly all long, slender, petioled; the upper more or less lanceolate; the lower and radical truncate, cordate, or hastate at the base. *Inflorescence* corymbosely thyrsoid-paniculate; *heads* drooping, mostly glomerate at the summit of ascending or spreading floral-branchlets or peduncles, 8 to 12 flowered; *involucre* cylindrical, green, rarely purplish-tinged; *scales* 5 to 14, in a single row, with a few small bractlets at their base; *receptacle* naked. *Flowers* all perfect, pendulous, purplish, greenish-white or ochroleucous; *corolla* ligulate; *style* long and slender; *stigmas* much exserted. *Akenes* linear-oblong or terete, truncated, and finely serrate; *pappus* sordid, straw-color, or whitish,† composed of rough capillary bristles.

History and Habitat.—This botanically difficult species, assumes, in its mode of growth and shape of leaf, all the forms from *P. alba* to *P. altissima*, including two varieties (*nana* and *barbata*); hardly two plants in any one district being found with constant characters except, mayhap, those of the glomerules and pappus. Thus, now, *P. serpentaria* includes in itself what were once considered

---

* Πρηνής, *prenes*, drooping; ἄνθη, *anthe*, flower.

† As a shade of color cannot be absolutely kept through several thousand copies in lithography, some of the plates may not represent the pappus correctly.

to be 17 distinct species and varieties ; and affords an interminable field of work for a botanist of Rafinesquian tendencies. The Rattlesnake Root is indigenous to North America, where it ranges from New Brunswick and Canada, to Florida, being especially abundant northward. It habits the sterile soil of open grounds and hilly wood-borders, and blossoms in August and September.

As Gall-of-the-Earth, it has been known in domestic practice from an early date, and is said to be an excellent antidote to the bite of the rattlesnake and other poisonous serpents,—one who searches through the domestic literature of medicinal plants, wonders why the bite of snakes ever has a chance to prove fatal.—As an alexiteric, the milky juice of the plant is recommended to be taken internally, while the leaves, steeped in water, are to be frequently applied to the wound ; or a decoction of the root is taken. A decoction of the root has been found useful in dysentery, anemic diarrhœa, and as a stomachic tonic.

Prenanthes is officinal in none of the pharmacopœias.

PART USED AND PREPARATION.—The whole plant, gathered during the flowering season, is treated as directed under Lappa.* The resulting tincture has a beautiful deep-orange color by transmitted light; an odor similar to that of the root; a bitter, astringent taste ; and an acid reaction.

CHEMICAL CONSTITUENTS.—No analysis of this species has been made to determine a specific principle. An analysis of the root of *P. alba*—too nearly allied to this species—by Neri. B. Williams,† showed the presence of resins, tannin, extractive, gum, and waxy matters.

DESCRIPTION OF PLATE 94.

1. Inflorescence, Binghamton, N. Y., Aug. 25th, 1886.
2. A lower leaf.
3. A portion of leaf-margin.
4. Flower.
5. Involucral scales.
6 and 7. Floret.
(3–7 enlarged.)

---

* Page 92-2.   † Thesis, *Am. Jour. Phar.*, 1886, 117.

ℭ𝔪.ad nat.del.et pinxt.　PRENÀNTHES SERPENTÁRIA , Pursh.

95

TARAXACUM.

DANDELION.

SYN.—TARAXACUM DENS-LEONIS, DESF.; TARAXACUM OFFICINALIS, WEBER; TARAXACUM VULGARE, SCHR.; LEONTODON† TARAXACUM, LINN.; LEONTODON DENS-LEONIS, LAM.; LEONTODON VULGARE, LAM.; LEONTODON OFFICINALIS, WITH.; DENS-LEONIS, RAII.; HEDYPNOIS TARAXACUM, SCOP.

COM. NAMES.—DANDELION,‡ PUFF-BALL;§ (ENG.) PISSABED; (FR.) DENT DE LION, PISSENLIT COMMUNE; (GER.) LÖWENZAHN, PFAFFEN-ROHRLEIN.

A TINCTURE OF THE FRESH ROOT OF TARAXACUM DENS-LEONIS, DESF.

Description.—This vernal, tufted, perennial herb, springs from a vertical tap-shaped *root*, furnished with numerous short, thickened rootlets. *Leaves* radical, varying from spatulate to lanceolate, pinnatifid, runcinate, or irregularly dentate. *Inflorescence* several many-flowered heads, each raised upon a scape that elongates during and after anthesis; *scape* slender, naked, cylindrical, fistulous, 6 to 18 inches long in fruit. *Involucre* double, the outer portion composed of numerous short scales; the inner of a single row of linear, erect scales. *Receptacle* naked. *Akenes* terete, oblong, ribbed; *ribs* roughened by numerous, ascending tubercles; *apex* abruptly conical or pyramidal, prolonged into a slender, filiform beak; *pappus* borne upon the summit of the beak, and composed of copious, soft, white, capillary bristles. Read description of the order, under Eupatorium purpureum, 78.

History and Habitat.—The Dandelion is a native of Greece, or, at least, of Europe and Asia Minor, and has become by introduction a common herb in fields, pastures, lawns and open grounds everywhere in this country, where it blossoms in early spring and fruits in the summer. The growth of this plant furnishes an instance of a beautifully provisional Nature. During the expansion of the flower, the outer scales of the involucre reflex, after anthesis the inner row contracts until it covers the forming pappus; then while the fruit is maturing the beaks gradually extend by growth and raise the pappus, until finally the inner involucre

---

* Ταράσσω, *tarasso*, to disorder, in allusion to its action upon the system.

† Λεον, *leon*, lion; οδους, *odous*, a tooth; from a supposed likeness of the leaf incisions to a lion's tooth.

‡ Americanized from (Fr.) Dent de lion.

§ On account of the separability of the akenes from the receptacle. The true puff-ball is *Lycoperdon Bovista*.

in turn reflexes, disclosing the fruit as a beautiful, white, globular, feathery head, exposing upon its coronate receptacle the ripe seeds ready to be dissipated and wafted to new fields by the first summer zephyr that passes by.

Tufts of this plant are eagerly gathered by the poor, in early spring, and cooked, furnishing thus an excellent and palatable pot-herb; they are also in many localities bleached like, and used in lieu of, endive,* as a salad. The leaves are eaten raw or cooked by the Digger and Apache Indians, who value them so highly that they scour the country for many days' journeys in search of sufficient to appease their appetites. So great is their love for the plant, that the quantity consumed by a single individual exceeds belief.† In many parts of Europe, especially in Germany, the dried roots "are roasted and substituted for coffee by the poorer inhabitants, who find that an infusion prepared in this way can hardly be distinguished from that of the coffee berry."‡

Taraxacum has been used in medicine from ancient times; it is one of those drugs, overrated, derogated, extirpated, and reinstated time and again by writers upon pharmacology, from Theophrastus' αφάκη and κιχοριον to the present day. It has been considered as a mild detergent, aperient, and diuretic; Bergius recommends it in hepatic obstruction, hypochondriasis, and icterus; and many authors give it repute in dropsy, pulmonic tuberculosis, various skin disorders, gastric derangements, biliary calculi, incipient visceral scirrhus, etc., etc. Children often play with the scapes at making chains, bracelets and "curls." The curls are formed as follows: A split is started in four directions at the smaller end of a scape, into which the tongue is deftly and gradually inserted, causing a slow separation into sections that curl backward, revolutely, being kept up to their form by the tongue, when the scape is curled to the end it is drawn several times through the operator's mouth and partially uncurled into graceful ringlets. In its manufacture a child usually gets full benefit of the milky, bitter juice, and, if susceptible, verifies the common name of the plant as applied in England: ... *quasi lectiminga et urinaria herba dicitur—plus lotii derivat in vesicam quám pueruli retinendo sunt, præsertim inter dormiendum, eòque tunc imprudentes et inviti stragula permingunt.*§

Taraxacum is official in the U. S. Ph., its preparations being: *Extractum Taraxaci* and *Extractum Taraxaci Fluidum.* The same preparations are officinal in Eclectic pharmacopœias, also *Decoctum Taraxaci,* and *Pilulæ Taraxaci Compositæ.*||

PART USED AND PREPARATION.—The fresh root, gathered in March, July or November, is chopped and pounded to a pulp and pressed out in a piece of new linen. The expressed juice is then, by brisk agitation, mingled with an equal part by weight of alcohol. This mixture is allowed to stand eight days in a dark, cool place.

The tincture, separated from the above mass by filtration, should have a light orange color by transmitted light, a bitter, somewhat acrid taste, and an acid reaction.

---

* *Cichorium endiva.*
† Dodge, *U. S. Agric. Rep.*, 1870, p. 423.
‡ Murray, *App. Med.*, p. 107.
§ *Raii Hist. Pl.*, p. 244.
|| Sanguinaria, Podophyllin, Taraxacum, and Mentha viridis.

CHEMICAL CONSTITUENTS.—*Taraxacin.* This body, when extracted from the roots or milky juice, forms in a bitter amorphous mass, soluble in alcohol, ether, and water. It was discovered by Polex in 1839, and named by Kromayer, who corroborated the discovery in 1861.

Taraxacerin, $C_8 H_{16} O$.—(Kromayer, 1861). This crystalline principle is said to resemble *lactucerin.** It is soluble in alcohol, but not in water.

Levulin, $C_6 H_{10} O_5$.—(Dragendorf). This amylose principle has the same composition as *inulin*,† but differs in that it is soluble in water and devoid of rotary power.

Inosite, $C_6 H_{12} O_6 (H_2 O)_2$.—(Marmé, 1864). This hydride of glucose was determined in the leaves and scapes, but not in the root. It forms transparent rhombic crystals, losing their water of crystallization when exposed to the air. It is soluble in water, the solution having a sweet taste.

Leontodonium ‡ is simply, or in great part, the inspissated juice of the plant, and in a measure the principles *en masse.* *Mannite*, $C_6 H_8 (O H)_6$, has been proven by Messrs. T. and H. Smith (1849) to be present only after a sort of fermentation had taken place in the juice.§ This is probably the change that takes place to a greater or less extent, when the roots are undergoing the winter changes.

Taraxacum also contains, according to many assayists,‖ caoutchouc, resin, gum, mucilage, free acid, sugar, wax, and the usual plant constituents.

PHYSIOLOGICAL ACTION.—Although this plant has received the attention of scientists of all nations from remote times, still I know of no attempt having been made to determine its toxic action.

The symptoms caused by repeated doses are, in general: mental excitement, vertigo and headache, blotchy white coated tongue, nausea and colic; frequent urination; general sticking or stitching pains; sleepiness, chilliness and sweating. These symptoms point to a peculiar action upon the liver, causing inaction of that organ. Its action upon the skin in causing an exanthem seems to be dependent greatly upon the amount of gastric irritation.

DESCRIPTION OF PLATE 95.

1. Whole plant, Bergen, N. J., May 14th, 1879.
2. Root.
3. Ray floret (enlarged).
4. Disk floret (enlarged).
5. Fruit.
6. Seed (enlarged).
7. Section of root (enlarged).

---

* See Lactuca, 96.
† See Inula, 81.
‡ Kromayer, 1861.
§ *Et supra*, Flück. & Han., *Pharmacographia*, in part.
‖ Sprengel, Frickhinger, Squire, Polex, John, Overbrook, T. and H. Smith, Dragendorf, Kromayer, Marmé, and Widemann.

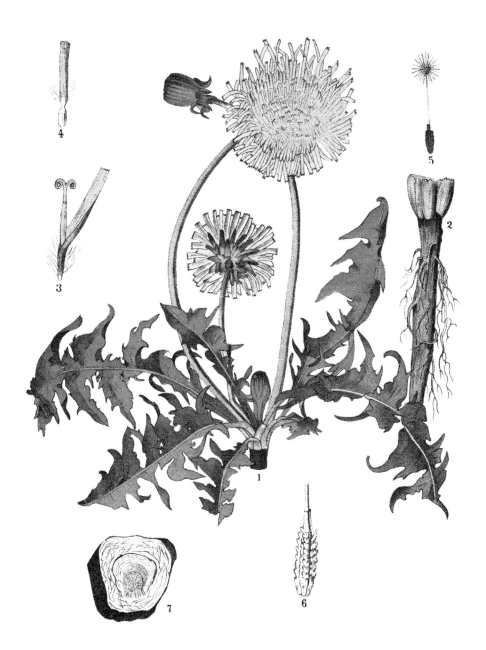

1 2 3 4 5 6 7

CM.ad nat.del.et pinxt.　TARÁXACUM DENS-LEÒNIS, Desf.

96

LACTUCA.

LETTUCE.

SYN.—LACTUCA CANADENSIS, LINN.; L. ELONGATA, MUHL. (TYPE); L. ELONGATA, VAR. LONGIFOLIA. T. & G.; L. CAROLINIANA, WALT.; L. LONGIFOLIA, MICHX.; GALATHENIUM ELONGATUM, NUTT.; SONCHUS PALLIDUS, WILLD.

COM. NAMES.—WILD LETTUCE, FIRE-WEED,† TRUMPET-WEED,‡; (FR.) LAITUE DU CANADA; (GER.) CANADISCHE LATTICH.

A TINCTURE OF THE WHOLE PLANT, OF VARIOUS SPECIES, INCLUDING THIS.

Description.—This glabrous, glaucescent biennial, grows to a height of from 4 to 9 feet. *Stem* erect, very leafy to the top, and copiously supplied with milky juice. *Leaves* alternate, mostly sinuate, pinnatifid below, lanceolate and entire above, all partly clasping by a sagittate base, and pale beneath; *midrib* naked, or rarely with a few sparse bristles; *margins* entire or sparingly dentate, especially near the base; *terminal lobe* elongated. *Inflorescence* in a terminal, narrow, elongated, leafless panicle; *heads* 12- to 20-flowered; *flowers* pale yellow, all perfect: *involucre* a half-inch or less high, cylindraceous, irregularly calyculate, and slightly imbricated in two rows. *Corolla* ligulate in all the flowers of the head; *tube* hairy; *ligules* obscurely, if at all, notched at the apex. *Receptacle* naked. *Akenes* blackish, broadly oval, flat, wingless, rather longer than the beak, obscurely scabrous-rugulose, and lightly 1-nerved in the middle of each face; *beak* filiform, abrupt at the base, and expanded at the apex; *pappus* of soft, silvery-white hairs, on the dilated apex of the beak.

History and Habitat.—Wild Lettuce is indigenous to North America, where it extends from Nova Scotia and Canada to Saskatchewan, and southward to Upper Georgia. It habits rich moist grounds along the borders of fields, thickets, and roads, where it blossoms in July and August.

This species has been used in early practice as an anodyne, diaphoretic, laxative, and diuretic, in many diseases, principally, however, in hypochondria, satyriasis, nymphomania, phthisis pulmonalis, ascites, anasarca, and nervous complaints in general.

---

* Latin, *lac*, milk; on account of the milky juice.

† Many plants have been given this name in different localities, on account of their growing particular burned fallows, *Enechthites hieracifolius, Senecio aureus, Hieracium Canadense*, and this.

‡ This name also designates *Eupatorium purpureum.*

Lactucarium, or Lettuce Opium, being of the same nature, no matter from what species it is obtained, consists of the inspissated milky juice of various species of Lactuca. The yield varies greatly with the species; greatest in *L. virosa,* and diminishing as follows: *L. scariola, L. altissima, L. Canadensis, L. sativa.* Dr. Coxe, of Philadelphia, was the first to call the attention of the profession to this substance as a substitute for commercial opium;* his reasoning and experiments were based upon the product of *L. sativa.* Although Lettuce has been considered narcotic from ancient times, still it is but slightly soporific, and hardly deserves a tithe of the reputation writers have made for it.

Lactucarium from *L. virosa* is still officinal in the U. S. Phar., but will, without doubt, be dropped at the next revision.

PART USED AND PREPARATION.—The whole fresh plant, just as the blossoms open, is chopped and pounded to a pulp and weighed. Then two parts by weight of alcohol are taken, the pulp thoroughly mixed with one-sixth part of it, and the rest of the alcohol added. After stirring the whole well, it is poured into a well-stoppered bottle, and allowed to stand eight days in a dark, cool place. The tincture formed thus, after straining and filtering, has a deep orange-red color by transmitted light; the odor of canned tomatoes; a slightly bitter and astringent taste; and an acid reaction.

CHEMICAL CONSTITUENTS.—*Lactucarium,* or *Thridace,* as noted above, represents in itself all the active principles of the plant, being a mixture of different organic and about ten per cent. inorganic bodies. It is not fully soluble in any vehicle, and merely softens on the application of heat. Subjected to analysis, it yields:

Lactucerin,† $C_{19}H_{30}O$.‡—This compound body composes nearly half the whole weight of Lactucarium. It forms in slender, colorless, microscopic, odorless and tasteless acicular crystals, insoluble in water, soluble in boiling alcohol and cold ether, and melting at 232° (449.6° F.).

Lactucin, $C_{11}H_{12}O_3(H_2O)$.—This body, which proves not to be a glucoside, gives to Lactucarium its intensely bitter taste. It forms, when purified, white, bitter, pearly scales, insoluble in ether, soluble in alcohol and in hot water.

Lactucic Acid.—This very acid body, isolated by Pfaf and Ludwig, results as an amorphous light yellow or brownish mass, only crystallizing after long standing.

Lactucopicrin, $C_{44}H_{64}O_{21}$.—This bitter amorphous substance seems to be formed by the oxidation of *Lactucin.* It is soluble in alcohol and water.

Beside the above, Lactucarium also contains a yellowish-red tasteless resin; a greenish-red acrid resin; caoutchouc; gum; oxalic, citric, malic, and succinic acids; sugar; mannite; asparagin; and a volatile oil.

* *Trans. Am. Philosoph. Socy.,* 1799, 387.
† Lactucon.
‡ Flückiger, $C_{14}H_{24}O$; Franchimont, $C_{16}H_{26}O$.

PHYSIOLOGICAL ACTION.—Lactucarium, in large doses, causes: Delirium; confusion of the brain, vertigo, and headache; dimness of vision; salivation; difficult deglutition; nausea and vomiting, and retraction of the epigastric region, with a sensation of tightness; distension of the abdomen, with flatulence; urging to stool followed by diarrhœa; increased secretion of urine; spasmodic cough, oppressed respiration, and tightness of the chest; reduction of the pulse ten to twelve or more beats; unsteady gait; great sleepiness; and chills and heat, followed by profuse perspiration.

DESCRIPTION OF PLATE 96.

1. Whole plant, eighteen times reduced, Binghamton, N. Y., July 26th, 1885.
2. A portion of the panicle.
3. An upper leaf.
4. Outline of a lower leaf.
5. Flower-head.
6. A floret.
7. Anther.
8. Fruit.
     (6 and 7 enlarged.)

Ċ.m. ad nat del. et pinxt.

LACTÙCA CANADÉNSIS, Linn.

97

LOBELIA CARDINALIS.

CARDINAL FLOWER.

SYN.—LOBELIA CARDINALIS, LINN.; L. COCCINEA, STOKES; TRACHE-
LIUM AMERICANUM, PARK.

COM. NAMES.—CARDINAL FLOWER, SCARLET OR RED LOBELIA, HIGH-
BELIA; (FR.) LOBELIE CARDINALE; (GER.) ROTHE KARDINALS
BLUME.

A TINCTURE OF THE WHOLE PLANT LOBELIA CARDINALIS, LINN.

Description.—This showy perennial grows to a height of from 2 to 4 feet.
Stem minutely pubescent or glabrous, commonly simple. *Leaves* oblong-ovate, to
oblong-lanceolate, tapering at both ends, sessile, and irregularly serrate or serrulate. *Inflorescence* a dense, terminal, more or less one-sided virgate raceme;
flowers large and showy, intense red, or rose-color, sometimes pure white; *pedicels*
erect or ascending; *bracts* of the upper portion linear-lanceolate, of the lower,
leafy. *Calyx* smooth; *tube* short, hemispherical, much shorter than the lobes;
lobes linear-subulate. *Corolla*† gamopetalous, tubular; *tube* about 1 inch long,
straight; *limb* bilabiate; *upper lip* 2-parted to the base, the cleft extending down
to the calyx, the lobes erect, linear-lanceolate; *lower lip* 3-cleft, spreading plane or
slightly recurved, the segments oblong-lanceolate. *Stamens* free from the tube of
the corolla, monadelphous almost to the base, exserted through the cleft in the
corolla tube, which they again enter between the two upper lobes; *filaments* red;
anthers syngenesious, curved, blue, the two larger ones naked at the tip, the other
three ciliate. *Capsule* hemispherical, thin-walled, 2-celled, and loculicidally 2-valved
at the summit. *Seeds* numerous, oblong, rugulose-tuberculate, similar to those of
L. inflata.

Lobeliaceæ.—This large family, closely related to *Campanulaceæ,* is represented
in North America, by 7 genera and 31 species, characterized in general as follows:
Herbs (when not Tropical) with acrid, milky juice. *Leaves* alternate, simple;
stipules none. *Inflorescence* racemose; *flowers* 5-merous, perfect. *Calyx* adnate
to the ovary; *limb* divided down to the ovary, or entire; *lobes* persistent when
present. *Corolla* regular and perigynous, inserted with the stamens just where
the calyx leaves the ovary; *limb* disposed to become bilabiate; *lobes* 5, valvate in

---

* Dedicated to Mathias de L'Obel, a Flemish herbalist, Botanist to James I.
† In describing this organ, I adopt the position it stands in while flowering. See *Lobeliaceæ.*

the bud, or in some cases induplicate, commonly deeper cleft or completely split down between two of the lobes (this cleft is generally upon the lower face of the corolla when the bud is young, but becomes superior, by a twisting of the pedicel, during its maturation). *Stamens* 5, epigynous, as many as the lobes of the corolla and alternate with them, usually both monadelphous and syngenesious; *filaments* generally free from the corolla, but not invariably so; *anthers* 2-celled, introrsely dehiscent, firmly united around the top of the style. *Ovary* wholly inferior, or sometimes half free, 2-celled, with the placentæ projecting from the axis (sometimes 1-celled with 2 parietal placentæ); *ovules* anatropous; *style* filiform, entire; *stigma* commonly 2-lobed, and girt with a ring of more or less rigid hairs, at first included, then exserted.* *Fruit* capsular and loculicidal, or baccate and indehiscent; seeds indefinitely numerous; *embryo* small or narrow, straight and axial; *albumen* copious, fleshy.

Many species of this order are acrid, narcotic poisons, only a few being, so far, used in medicine, among which the West Indian *Rebenta Cavallos* (*Hippobroma longifolia*, Don.) is noted for its poisonous properties. If taken internally it speedily brings on hypercatharsis, while the juice, if touching the mucous membrane, quickly causes acute inflammation; and *Tupa Fenillaei*, Don., is said to bring on nausea in one simply smelling of its flowers. The three species described in this work are, however, all that are much used.

History and Habitat.—The Cardinal Flower is indigenous to North America, from New Brunswick to Saskatchewan, southward east of the Mississippi to Florida, and southwest to the borders of Texas. It rears its magnificent spike of gorgeous flowers along the muddy banks of streams, during the early autumn months. It was introduced into Great Britain from Virginia, on account of its beauty, in 1629.

Shœpf mentions the use of the root of this species, by the Cherokee Indians, for syphilis; and Dr. Barton speaks of their successful use of it as an anthelmintic By some early physicians it was considered fully equal to Spigelia Marilandica, in this direction. This species is, however, seldom used now, *L. inflata* taking its place entirely. It is considered, however, to possess marked anthelmintic, nervine, and antispasmodic properties.

PART USED AND PREPARATION.—The whole fresh plant, gathered when coming into blossom, is treated as in the next species. The resulting tincture has a clear yellowish-brown color by transmitted light; a sweetish, herbaceous odor and taste; and an acid reaction.

CHEMICAL CONSTITUENTS.—No special examination of this plant having been made, we can do no better at present than to refer to the chemistry of *L. inflata*, page 99–3.

---

* See pp. 98–98-2.

DESCRIPTION OF PLATE 97.

1. Top of a flowering plant, Binghamton, N. Y., Aug. 10th, 1886.
   2. A middle leaf.
   3. Flower.
   4. Stamens.
   5. Section of the stamen-tube.
   6. Stigma.
   7. Open stigma.
   8. Fruit.
   9. Section of the ovary.
      (4–9 enlarged.)

Œm.ad nat.del.et pinxt.

LOBÈLIA CARDINÀLIS , Linn.

GENUS.—**LOBELIA,** LINN.

SEX. SYST.—PENTANDRIA MONOGYNIA.

98
LOBELIA SYPHILITICA.*

GREAT BLUE LOBELIA.

SYN.—LOBELIA SYPHILITICA, **LINN.**; LOBELIA CŒRULEA? LOBELIA GLANDULOSA, LINDL.; LOBELIA REFLEXA, STOKES.

COM. NAMES.—GREAT LOBELIA, BLUE LOBELIA, BLUE CARDINAL FLOWER; (FR.) LOBELIE SYPHILITIQUE; (GR.) GEMEINE LOBELIE.

A TINCTURE OF THE WHOLE FRESH PLANT, LOBELIA SYPHILITICA, LINN.

Description.—This erect, perennial herb attains a growth of from 1 to 3 feet, its conspicuous racemes being generally from one-third to one-quarter the length of the whole plant. *Stem* simple, leafy to the base of the raceme, and somewhat hairy, especially upon its angles. *Leaves* sessile, ovate-lanceolate, irregularly denticulate-serrate, acute at the base, from 2 to 6 inches long, and about 1 inch wide; thin, and more or less appressed hairy. *Inflorescence* supra-axillary, composed of a long, at first leafy, then morphologically bracted, dense spike or raceme; *pedicels* shorter than the bracts; *flowers* light blue, nearly 1 inch long, extending beyond the leafy bracts. *Calyx* five-cleft, hirsute, shorter than the tube of the corolla, with reflexed, conspicuous, two-cleft auricles at the sinuses; *tube* hemispherical, short; *lobes* one-half the length of the corolla. *Corolla* with a straight, sub-cylindrical tube, more or less two-lipped, having a deep fissure at the superior margin; *upper lip* of two erect, slightly diverging lobes; *lower lip* spreading and three-lobed by incision. *Fruit* a globose pod, free above, but enclosed by the loose, persistent calyx; two-celled, opening at the apex; *seeds* many. For a description of the Natural Order, see Lobelia cardinalis, 97.

History and Habitat.—The great blue lobelia habits the borders of marshy places and wet spots in pasture lands and meadows, pretty generally throughout the United States, to which it is indigenous; flowering from July to September. In some localities it is called *high belia*, in unconscious pun upon its lowlier but more frequently-used companion, L. inflata, or *low belia*, as they term it. The lobelias furnish one of the best examples of the system of cross-fertilization in plants. The stamens, especially their anthers, grow into a tube, enclosing the stigma, and apparently making self-fertilization positive. A closer study, however, reveals the following conclusive points: The stigma is two-lobed, the recep-

---

* Dr. Hale, in his "New Remedies," treats of this drug as Lobelia cœrulea. Dr. Allen remarks that—as there are a number of blue lobelias, and beside this the true *cœrulea* grows at the Cape of Good Hope, and may yet be proven—*syphilitica* should always designate this drug.

98.

2

3

4

5

1

Ĕ.m. ad nat del. et pinxt.

LOBÈLIA SYPHÍLITICA, Linn.

tion surfaces—in the earlier stages of growth and while enclosed in the anther tube—are tightly pressed together and fringed with close, bristly hairs, all together resembling the mouth of a full-bearded man, with lips compressed. The tube of anthers opens by a pore at the tip and discharges the ripened pollen directly through this pore when it is irritated by the back of any insect that may creep into the throat of the corolla after nectar. As the pollen is discharged, the stigma, by elongation of the style, presses forward, keeping up the discharge by acting as a swab, until the cell is completely empty; then, as it projects beyond the pore, the compressed lips open and roll back, standing ready to collect the pollen from the back of some insect that has been on a visit to a neighboring plant.

The former uses of this plant were the same as those of L. inflata, than which it is less active. The natives of North America are said to have held this plant a secret in the cure of syphilis, until it was purchased from them by Sir William Johnson, who took a quantity to Europe, and introduced it as a drug of great repute in that disease. European physicians, however, failed to cure with it, and finally cast it aside, though Linnæus, thinking it justified its Indian reputation, gave the species its distinctive name, *syphilitica*. The cause of failure may be the fact that the aborigines did not trust to the plant alone, but always used it in combination with may-apple roots (*Podophyllum peltatum*), the bark of the wild cherry (*Prunus Virginica*), and dusted the ulcers with the powdered bark of New Jersey tea (*Cenothus Americanus*). Another chance of failure lay in the volatility of its active principle, as the dried herb was used. It is not officinal in the U. S. Ph., nor in the Eclectic Materia Medica.

PART USED AND PREPARATION.—The whole fresh plant is chopped and pounded to a pulp and weighed. Then two parts by weight of alcohol are taken, the pulp thoroughly mixed with one-sixth part of it and the rest of the alcohol added. The whole, after thorough mixture, is poured into a well-stoppered bottle and allowed to stand eight days in a dark, cool place. The tincture is then separated by straining and filtering. Thus prepared, it has a beautiful, clear, light-brown color by transmitted light, a slightly bitter taste and tingling sensation upon the tongue, and a strong acid reaction.

CHEMICAL CONSTITUENTS.—The chemical properties of this plant will probably be found to differ from those of L. inflata only in quantity. An analysis by M. Boissel resulted in the separation of fatty and butyraceous matters, mucilage, sugar, earthy salts, and a volatile bitter principle.

PHYSIOLOGICAL ACTION.—No data upon this is obtainable. We will do well, perhaps, to again consult L. inflata, which, in virulence of action, is the type of the genus in the Northern States.

DESCRIPTION OF PLATE 98.

1. Whole plant, once reduced; from Chemung, N. Y., September 9, 1879.
    2. Apex of receme.
    3. Flower (somewhat enlarged).
    4. Fruit.
    5 Pollen, with end view x 380.

Tribe.—LOBELIEÆ.

GENUS.—**LOBELIA**, LINN.

SEX. SYST.—PENTANDRIA MONOGYNIA.

99

LOBELIA INFLATA.

INDIAN TOBACCO.

SYN.—LOBELIA INFLATA, LINN.; RAPUNTIUM INFLATUM, MILL.

COM. NAMES.—WILD OR INDIAN TOBACCO, EYE-BRIGHT,* BLADDER
POD,† EMETIC ROOT OR WEED, PUKE WEED, ASTHMA WEED; (FR.)
LOBÉLIE ENFLÉE; (GER.) LOBELIE.

A TINCTURE OF THE WHOLE FRESH HERB LOBELIA INFLATA, L.

Description.—This well-known milky, acrid, biennial or annual herb, varies
greatly in its growth, generally, however, its height is from 8 inches to 2 feet.‡
Root slender, yellowish-white; *stem* erect, somewhat angled, lined or winged,
leafy, paniculately branched, especially above, and divergently hirsute, principally
below; *leaves* sessile, veiny, acute, and irregularly or obtusely toothed; they vary
from ovate or oblong below to foliaceous or even subulate bracts above, longer
than the pedicels. *Inflorescence* loose, terminal, spike-like racemes; *flowers* small,
inconspicuous, irregular. *Calyx* persistent 10-veined, not auriculate nor appendaged in the sinuses; *lobes* linear-subulate, nearly as long as the corolla, and springing from a decided ring involving the throat of the tube. *Corolla* marcescent,
about two lines long, pale blue externally, somewhat violet within; *lobes* 5, the two
upper lanceolate, erect, the three lower ovate, acute, and projecting. *Stamens* 5,
epigynous, projecting with the style (which they enclose) through the complete
slit in the upper median line of the corolla tube. *Capsule* 2-celled, oval, glabrous,
much inflated, longitudinally 10-nerved and roughened between the nerves by
transverse rugæ, they greatly exceed their pedicels in length; *seeds* numerous,
oblong, rough, of a brilliant brown color and reticulated with honey-yellow intermixed lines; *placentæ* central. A description of the genus is incorporated in that
of Lobelia Cardinalis, 97.

History and Habitat.—Indian Tobacco is common in dry open fields from
Hudson's Bay westward to Saskatchewan and southward to Georgia and the
Mississippi, where it flowers from July to October. Linnæus first noticed this

---

* The true eye-bright is *Euphrasia officinalis, L. (Scrophulariaceæ).*

† The true bladder-pod is *Vesicaria Shortii, T. & G. (Cruciferæ).*

‡ I met many individuals this season (1885), scarcely 3 inches high, simple stemmed, and in full flower and fruit.
I judge this depauperate form to be the *var. simplex* of Rafinesque.

species in the Transactions of the Upsal Academy in 1741.[1] It was introduced into England in 1859, and noticed medically by Schoepf in 1787, his observations being mostly founded upon the use of the plant by the American aborigines as an emetic, and application for "sore eyes." It afterward became in frequent use by Botanic physicians, and in 1813 was more or less prominently brought before the medical profession by the Rev. D. Cutler, as a valuable remedy in asthma. Its use was not carried into England until 1829.

The name Indian Tobacco might have arisen either from the peculiar tobacco-like sensation imparted to the tongue and stomach on chewing the leaves, or from the fact that the American Indians often smoked the dried leaves to produce the effect of the drug.

Lobelia has been recommended and used in the Botanic practice particularly, either alone or compounded with other drugs, for almost every disease known, and has proven curative in some cases, palliative in more, useless in many, and a deadly poison in more cases than one. Its action, as will be seen farther on, is, as in all narcotics, principally upon the brain, thus making it anything but a desirable emetic, as which it is most frequently used. From the power it exhibits to relax the whole system, it has been found very valuable in spasms, tetanus, croup, strangulated hernia, whooping cough, and even hydrophobia. Samuel Thomson claims to have discovered the virtues of the plant, though without doubt his first ideas of its emetic property were gathered from the Indians. He went so far as to claim it curative in all disorders, giving it with such a reckless hand that he fatally poisoned one of his patients, a certain Ezra Lovett, for which he was arrested on the charge of murder, escaping punishment because said Lovett was foolish enough to take the prescription of a man who claimed to carry such potent (?) drugs as "*well-my-gristle*" and "*ram-cats.*"

Lobelia Inflata is official in the U. S. Ph., as: *Acetum Lobeliæ; Extractum Lobeliæ Fluidum;* and *Tinctura Lobeliæ;* and in the Eclectic Materia Medica as above, and as: *Cataplasma Lobeliæ et Ulmus;*[2] *Enema Lobeliæ Composita;*[3] *Extractum Lobeliæ Fluidum Compositum;*[4] *Linimentum Stillingiæ Compositum;*[5] *Lotio Lobeliæ Composita;*[6] *Oleum Lobeliæ; Pilulæ Aloes Compositæ;*[7] *Pulvis Lobeliæ Compositus;*[8] *Tinctura Hydrastis Compositæ;*[9] *Tinctura Lobeliæ Composita;*[10] *Tinctura Lobeliæ et Capsici;*[11] *Tinctura Sanguinariæ Acetata Composita;*[12] *Tinctura Sanguinariæ Composita,* and *Tinctura Viburni Composita.*[13]

PART USED AND PREPARATION.—The whole plant gathered in September, or when the last flowers are developing and the lower capsules are ripe,

---

[1] *Trans. Upsal,* 1741, t. I, p. 43. [2] Lobelia, Elm, and Lye.
[3] Tinctura Lobeliæ et Capsici ʒss, water ℥ss. [4] Lobelia, Skunk-cabbage, and Sanguinaria.
[5] Oils of Stillingia, Cajeput, and Lobelia. [6] Bayberry bark, Lobelia leaves and seeds, and Yellow Dockroot.
[7] Boneset, Mandrake, Ginseng, Aloes, Soap, Gamboge, and Capsicum and Lobelia seeds.
[8] Lobelia, Blood-root, Skunk-cabbage, Ipecac, and Capsicum.
[9] Hydrastis and Lobelia.
[10] Lobelia, Wild Ginger (*Asarum Canadense* ?), Blood-root, Skunk-cabbage, and Pleurisy-root.
[11] Lobelia, Capsicum, and Skunk-cabbage root.
[12] Blood-root, Lobelia, Skunk-cabbage root, and Vinegar.
High Cranberry bark, Lobelia seed, Blood-root, Skunk-cabbage seed, Capsicum, and Stramonium seed.

should be treated as in the preceding species. The resulting tincture should be of a clear reddish-orange color by transmitted light, and have a very acrid penetrating tobacco-like taste, a peculiar characteristic odor, and an acid reaction.

CHEMICAL CONSTITUENTS.—*Lobelina.*[1] This alkaloidal body was discovered by Calhoun,[2] though Procter was first to isolate it.[3] Bastic,[4] working without a previous knowledge of its discovery, also isolated the principle. Lobelina exists after separation, especially when carefully sealed, as an oily, yellowish fluid having a decided alkaline reaction, this is especially noticeable in its watery solution. Its taste is acro-pungent, very like that of nicotia. It exhibits, even in very small doses, the poisonous action of the herb. It is somewhat volatile, decomposing and losing its acridity at a temperature above 100° (212° F.) either alone or in the presence of dilute acids or caustic alkalies. It is soluble in water, alcohol, and ether. Lobelina neutralizes acids, and except with acetic, forms crystallizable salts, more soluble in water than the alkaloid itself.

Lobelacrin.—This glucoside (?) was discovered by Pereira [5] and corroborated by Enders.[6] Lewes (1878), who made a thorough analysis of this drug, suggests that this body may be *Lobeliate of Lobelina*, a salt of lobelina formed by the free acid in the plant itself. Lobelacrin, according to Enders, exists as acrid, brownish, verrucose tufts, decomposing rapidly in water at 100° (212° F.), and resolving under the action of acids or alkalies into sugar and

Lobelic Acid.—This acid is crystallizable, non-volatile, soluble in water, alcohol, and ether, and yields an insoluble plumbic and soluble baric salt.

Lobelianin.—This body, so named by its discoverer, Pereira, is now considered to be the volatile oil, *Lobeliin,* a compound body isolated by Reinsch, and now considered indefinite.

Oil of Lobelia.—This oil may be extracted from the seeds, which, when bruised between heated rollers, generally yield about 30 per cent. According to Procter its specific gravity is 0.940, and its drying quality and consistence quite similar to that of linseed oil. Dr. John King states [7] that the oil possesses all the medicinal qualities of the seed.

Beside the foregoing, caoutchouc,[8][9][10] extractive,[8][10] resin,[9][10][11] and fat,[9] have been determined.

PHYSIOLOGICAL ACTION.—Thanks to much reckless prescribing by many so-called Botanic physicians, and to murderous intent; as well as to experimentation and careful provings, the action of this drug is pretty thoroughly known. Lobelia

[1] *Lobelin, Lobeline.*

[2] *Journ. Phil. Coll. Pharm.*, 300.

[3] *Am. Jour. Phar.*, 1838, p. 98; and farther *ibid.*, 1871, p. 1; and 1851, p. 456.

[4] 1850. *Ibid.*, 1851, p. 270.

[5] *Mat. Med.*, Vol. 2, part 2, p. 12.

[6] 1871, in an analysis made for the authors of the *Pharmacographia*, l. c., p. 400.

[7] *Am. Disp.*, 1880, p. 492.

[8] Bigelow, *Am. Med. Bot.*, 1817, Vol. 1, p. 179.

[9] Reinsch.

[10] Pereira, *l. c.*

[11] Procter, *l. c.*

in large doses is a decided narcotic poison, producing effects on animals generally, bearing great similitude to somewhat smaller doses of tobacco; and *lobelina* in like manner to *nicotia*. Its principal sphere of action seems to be upon the pneumogastric nerve, and it is to the organs supplied by this nerve that its toxic symptoms are mainly due, and its "physiological" cures of pertussis, spasmodic asthma, croup and gastralgia gained. Its second action in importance is that of causing general muscular relaxation, and under this it records its cures of strangulated hernia (by enemata), tetanic spasms, convulsions, hysteria, and, mayhap, hydrophobia. Its third action is upon mucous surfaces and secretory glands, increasing their secretions.

The prominent symptoms of its action are: great dejection, exhaustion, and mental depression, even to insensibility and loss of consciousness; nausea and vertigo; contraction of the pupil; profuse clammy salivation; dryness and prickling in the throat; pressure in the œsophagus with a sensation of vermicular motion, most strongly, however, in the larynx and epigastrium; sensation as of a lump in the throat; incessant and violent nausea, with pain, heat, and oppression of the respiratory tract; vomiting, followed by great prostration; violent and painful cardiac constriction; griping and drawing abdominal pains; increased urine, easily decomposing and depositing much uric acid; violent racking paroxysmal cough with ropy expectoration; small, irregular, slow pulse; general weakness and oppression, more marked in the thorax; violent spasmodic pains, with paralytic feeling, especially in the left arm; weariness of the limbs, with cramps in the gastrocnemii; and sensation of chill and fever. Death is usually preceded by insensibility and convulsions.

Post-mortem.—The stomach is found congested and filled with fluid, and the brain engorged with blood.

DESCRIPTION OF PLATE 99.

1. Whole plant, Chemung, N. Y., September 9th, 1879.
2. Flower.
3. Fruit.
4. Seed natural size and magnified 100 diam.
(2–3 enlarged.)

Œ.m. ad nat del.et pinxt.

LOBÈLIA INFLATA, Linn.

Tribe.—ERICINEÆ.

GENUS.—**ARCTOSTAPHYLOS,*** ADANS.

SEX. SYST.—DECANDRIA MONOGYNIA.

100
UVA-URSI.

BEARBERRY.

SYN.—ARCTOSTAPHYLOS UVA-URSI, SPRENG.; A. OFFICINALIS, WILLD.; ARBUTUS UVA-URSI, LINN.; DAPHNIDOSTAPHYLIS FENDLERIANA, KLOT.

COM. NAMES.—BEARBERRY, MOUNTAIN BOX, RED BERRY, UPLAND CRANBERRY, BEAR'S GRAPE, RED-BERRIED TRAILING ARBUTUS, WHORTLEBERRY,† HETH, UNIVERSE; (FR.) BUSSEROLLE, RAISIN D'OURS; (GER.) BÄRENTRAUBE.

A TINCTURE OF THE LEAVES OF ARCTOSTÁPHYLOS UVA-URSI.

Description.—This peculiar boreal shrub is seldom erect except that it throws its young shoots upward for from 3 to 8 inches. *Stems* numerous, depressed or trailing; *branches* various, the sterile from 2 to 3 feet long and compactly leafy, the fertile shorter; *bark* mahogany color, scaling off in irregular patches; *roots* thick, ligneous, and creeping. *Leaves* alternate, coriaceous, thick, shining, and evergreen, turning mahogany color when aged, those of the erect branchlets more or less vertical, all oblong spatulate, entire, retuse, and tapering to a short-petioled base. *Inflorescence* in few-flowered, terminal clusters or racemes; *bracts* and *bracteoles* persistent, finally becoming rigid; *flowers* pale, rose-colored, drooping. *Calyx* reddish, persistent, free from the ovary; *lobes* 5, roundish. *Corolla* urceolate, pellucid at the base, deciduous; *tube* inflated, hairy inside, hypogynous; *lobes* 5, short acute, recurved. *Stamens* 10, included; *anthers* large, upright, introrse, the cells opening by terminal pores and appendaged upon the dorsal surface by 2 reflexed awns. *Ovary* 4 to 10 celled; *ovules* solitary in each cell. *Fruit* a glabrous, depressed-globose berry or drupe, about the size of a pea; *pulp* mealy and insipid; *nutlets* 5, when the fruit is baccate, or united firmly into a 5-several celled stone when drupaceous; whether distinct or coherent, the nutlets are bony and 1-nerved upon the dorsal surface.

Ericaceæ.—This chiefly boreal family is represented in North America by 34 genera, 135 species, and 32 recognized varieties, thus producing half the ericaceous genera of the globe, but only one-eighth of the total number of species. The order is characterized as follows: The growth comprises trees, shrubs, and

---

* Ἄρκτος, *arktos,* a bear; σταφυλή, *staphyle,* a grape or berry.
† Generally applied to species of *Vaccinium,* especially *V. Vitis Idæa,* Linn.

ℭ.m. . ad nat del.et pinxt.   ARCTOSTÁPHYLOS UVA-ÚRSI, Spreng.

some perennial herbs, all having alternate, simple, and undivided leaves, and no stipules. *Flowers* symmetrical, 4- to 5-merous, perfect; *calyx* imbricated or valvate in the bud. *Corolla* gamopetalous, or not rarely 4- to 5-petalous, regular or irregular, hypogynous except in *Vacciniæ*, imbricated or convolute in the bud. *Stamens* free from the corolla or nearly so, as many or twice as many as its lobes; *filaments* distinct; *anthers* introrse or becoming introrsely inverted, 2-celled, usually opening by pores or chinks, and generally awned or somehow appendaged; *pollen* usually composed of 4 united grains. *Ovary* 4- to 10-celled; *placentæ* axial, except in *Monotropeæ*; *ovules* solitary or numerous, anatropous; *style* single; *stigma* entire or merely lobed, except in *Clethra*, where it is 3-cleft. *Fruit* capsular, baccate, or drupaceous; *embryo* small or minute; *albumen* fleshy; *cotyledons* small or undeveloped.

Our only proven species of this order, except the six represented in this work, are: The European, Asiatic, and British-American Labrador Tea (*Ledum Palustre*, Linn.); and the Russian intoxicant and anti-rheumatic Yellow Rosebay (*Rhododendron chrysanthemum*, Linn.).

Other medicinal species are: The American Rosebay (*Rhododendron maximum*, Willd.), an astringent, and by some accounted narcotic and poisonous; the Swiss *R. ferrugineum*, Linn., an antiarthritic; and the Persian *R. ponticum*, Linn., supposed to be one of the plants whose nectar renders the honey of Trebisond poisonous—an influence also said to be contributed to by *Azalea pontica*, Linn., of this order. The North American Alpine Azalea (*Loiseleuria procumbens*, Desv.) is, like all of the order, astringent; and Marsh Tea (*Ledum latifolium*, Ait.), used in dysentery, diarrhœa, tertian ague, and in some places to render beer heady, though it is said to bring on delirium. The fruit of the Strawberry Tree of the Levant (*Arbutus Unedo*, Linn.), when made into wine, is said to be narcotic—a property also ascribed to the wine of Whortleberries (*Vaccinium uliginosum*, Linn.), which is very intoxicating. The leaves of the European and North American *Andromeda polifolia*, Linn., are an acrid and dangerous narcotic, and are said to kill sheep if browsed upon.

Many species of the order furnish our tables with fine refreshing berries, viz.: The Blue Berry (*Gaylussacia frondosa*, T. & G.); the Huckleberry (*G. resinosa*, T. & G.); the Blue Huckleberries (*Vaccinium Pennsylvanicum*, Lam., *vacillans*, Solander, and *corymbosum*, Linn.); and the Cranberries (*Vaccinium macrocarpon*, Ait., and *V. Oxycoccus*, Linn.); the latter are also refrigerant, and a fine palliative dressing for acute erysipelas.

Among the Western Aborigines the Manzañita, the fruit of *Arctostaphylos tomentosa*, Dougl., is extensively eaten in a fresh or dried state. When dried it is husky but sweet, and is often ground and made into sun-baked bread, or, mixed with corn-meal and cactus syrup, fermented and drank; the cranberry and blue huckleberry are also prized; while the smoke-dried fruits of *Vaccinium myrtillus*, and *V. stamineum*, Linn., are largely stored for winter food.

History and Habitat.—The Bearberry is indigenous to North America, where it extends from New Jersey, Pennsylvania, Wisconsin, and Northern California, northward to the Arctic Circle. In Europe it extends northward from North-western Ireland, Yorkshire, and Central Russia; in Asia also northward from Lower Siberia and Kamtschatka, its northerly range includes Iceland and Greenland. Its choice of growth is barren, but healthy ground, among rocks, where it flowers in May.

The principal substitutive leaves for the Uva-Ursi of commerce are those of *Vaccinium Vitis Idæa*, Linn., of which Mr. J. H. Sears says:[*] "This is the plant that the Shakers gather instead of the Uva-Ursi; they go 40 or 50 miles for it when Uva-Ursi is abundant in their own ground. Uva-Ursi is common at Groton, Mass.; still the Shakers of that vicinity go to Danvers, where there is a small patch of *Vitis Idæa*, which they gather instead." Comparing the leaves of specimens sent by Mr. Sears, I find the following distinction:

UVA-URSI.	VITIS IDÆA.
Bearberry.	Cowberry.
Blade, oblanceolate to oblong, never spatulately narrowed, as in Vitis Idæa; reticulately broad-veined beneath, not dotted.	*Blade*, narrowly oblanceolate, seldom, if ever, tending toward oblong; very distinctly black-dotted and narrow-veined beneath.
	The character of the leaves being toward the apex crenate and distinctly revolute,[†] is not at all constant, nor is it distinctive.

Uva Ursi is an ancient astringent, though used but little until the 13th century by the "physicians of Myddfai." Clusius described the plant, in 1601, as the Ἄρκτου σταφυλή of Galen, useful as an hemostatic; it was not much used, however, until about the middle of the eighteenth century, when it began to prove, in the hands of De Haen and Gerhard, an excellent remedy in nephritic disorders. It was admitted to the London Pharmacopœia in 1763. From this time it came into more or less general use as an astringent tonic and diuretic in various diseases, particularly, however, in dysuria, chronic vesical catarrh, cystitis with or without ulceration, calculous disorders, and kindred affections, as well as in irritations of the genital tracts, such as gleet, gonorrhœa, leucorrhœa, blenorrhœa, etc. In all these disorders, however, it proved itself simply palliative in most cases, and many times fell into disuse. Dr. Bourin, of Oxford, recommended it highly in phthisis, but it only abated the hectic fever from reduction of the heart's action. In late years it has been called attention to as a uterine excitant, very useful in prolonged parturition from atony; it is claimed that it is fully as sure as Secale, while the contractions resulting are more prolonged, while less painful, and dangerous to the child. The general dose in nephritic complaints has been: of the powdered leaves, Ðij to ʒj, and of the decoction, *coch. mag.* ij to iv, *quater in die;* and in parturition, grs. xv, in infusion, a cupful every hour, one, or at most two doses, being fully sufficient.

The American Aborigines smoke the dried leaves with tobacco, making a mixture called *Sagack-homi* in Canada, and *Kinikinik* among the Western tribes; this is the *Larb* of the Western hunters.

---

[*] In a letter from Peabody Academy of Science to the author.
[†] Bentley and Trimen, *Med. Pl.*, 163.

The leaves of Uva-Ursi are officinal in the U. S. Ph., as well as *Extractum Uva-Ursi Fluidum ;* in Eclectic practice the preparation is *Decoctum Uva-Ursi.*

PART USED AND PREPARATION.—The fresh leaves, particularly those of the sterile branches, gathered in September or October, are to be chopped and pounded to a pulp and weighed. Then take two-thirds' part by weight of dilute alcohol, add to it the pulp with constant agitation, and strain the whole through a piece of new linen. The grainy menstruum thus obtained should be allowed to stand eight days, in a well-stoppered bottle, in a dark, cool place, before filtering.

The tincture obtained by filtration should be opaque, and have, in thin layers, a deep blackish-brown color by transmitted light ; its odor should be heavily herbaceous and slightly terebinthic ; its taste extremely astringent and slightly bitter ; and its reaction acid.

CHEMICAL CONSTITUENTS.—According to many observers, especially Prof. Murray and Dr. J. S. Mitchell, water is the best menstruum with which to extract the principles of this plant. The large amount of tannin contained in the leaves causes them to be extensively gathered in Iceland, Sweden, and Russia for tanning fine grades of leather.

[*Arbutose.*[*]—Treat the mixture of several successive decoctions of the coarsely-powdered leaves of Uva-Ursi with subacetate of lead, thereby precipitating the tannin and extractive matters. Decolorize the liquid with sulphydric acid, and evaporate quickly. This process decomposes a certain quantity of arbutin and a sticky crystalline mass is produced (Arbutose), containing 55 per cent. *arbutin*, 35 per cent. glucose, and 10 per cent. water. After drying this body in air as far as possible, and treating it with charcoal, followed by successive quantities of alcohol and distilled water, crystallized arbutin may be obtained.]

Arbutin,[†] $C_{25}H_{34}O_{14}$.[‡]—This glucoside, in an impure state, was first determined by Hughes,[§] and called by him *Ursin ;* Kawalier, however, in 1853, isolated the body in a pure state, and gave it the name it now bears. Arbutin crystallizes in handsome, white, shining, radiate forms, odorless, bitter, and neutral ; they lose water at 100° (212° F.), fuse at 160° (338° F.), are soluble in water, slightly soluble in alcohol, and insoluble in ether. By heating the crystals with peroxide of manganese they are resolved as follows :

$$\underset{\text{Arbutin.}}{C_{25}H_{34}O_{14}} = \underset{\text{Kinone.}}{4C_6H_4O_2} + \underset{\text{Formic Acid.}}{CH_2O_2} + \underset{\text{Water.}}{4H_2O}.$$

Kinone,[||] $C_6H_4O_2$.—This very volatile body readily sublimes in brilliant golden-yellow acicular crystals, possessing a suffocating smell. They are slightly soluble in cold, freely soluble in hot, water, in alcohol, and in ether.

---

[*] Lewin, *Pharm. Jour.*, 3, xiv, 490.

[†] Kawalier, $C_{32}H_{44}O_{19}$. Strecker, $C_{12}H_{16}O_7$.

[‡] Hlasiwetz and Habermann.

[§] J. C. C. Hughes, in *Am. Jour. Phar.*, 1847, 90.

[||] *Quinone.*

Arbutin, during its passage through the body, undergoes the following change,* which is also brought about outside the body by the action of emulsin, or by boiling with dilute sulphuric acid:

Arbutin.   Water.   Glucose.   Hydrokinone.   Methyl-hydrokinone.

$$C_{25}H_{34}O_{14} + 2H_2O = C_6H_{12}O_6 + C_6H_4(OH)_2 + C_6H_4(OH.OCH_3).$$

Hydrokinone,† $C_6H_6O_2$.—This dioxybenzene forms in colorless rhombic prisms, melting at 169°–172° (336.2°–341.6° F.), and subliming, partly decomposed, at higher temperatures.

In the mother-liquor, after the crystallization of Arbutin, the following substances are found:

Ericolin, $C_{34}H_{56}O_{21}$.—This amorphous, very bitter glucoside results as a yellowish-brown mass, softening at 100° (212° F.), and resolving, under the action of dilute sulphuric acid, as follows:

Ericolin.   Water.   Glucose.   Ericinol.

$$C_{34}H_{56}O_{21} + 4H_2O = 4C_6H_{12}O_6 + C_{10}H_{16}O.$$

Ericinol, $C_{10}H_{16}O$, is a yellowish, or nearly colorless resinifying oil, having a peculiar odor.‡ It also exists free in the volatile oils of many Ericaceæ; that from *Ledum* having a blue-green color, a disagreeable odor, a burning and bitter taste, and boils at 240°–250° (464°–482° F.). On boiling it with hydrated lime it yields a hydrocarbon of the composition $C_{20}H_{16}$.§

Urson, $C_{20}H_{32}O_2$.‖—This colorless, tasteless, crystalline body melts at 198°–200° (388.4°-392° F.), sublimes at higher temperatures without visible change, is insoluble in water, and slightly soluble in alcohol and ether.§

Gallic, or *Trioxybenzoic, Acid,* $C_7H_3O_2(OH)_3$.—This acid occurs in a free state in this and many other plants, and, in combination with tannic acid, in numberless others; it dissolves in 100 parts of cold water, from which it crystallizes in fine, silky needles, slightly acid and astringent. Gallic acid gives a deep blue color with ferric salts, melts at 200° (392° F.), and resolves at 210° (410° F.), as follows:

Gallic Acid.   Carbonic Dioxide.   Pyrogallic Acid.

$$C_7H_3O_2(OH)_3 = CO_2 + C_6H_6O_3.$$

Tannin.—This glucoside is generally considered to have the composition $C_{14}H_{10}O_9$, which proves it an anhydride of gallic acid, and its true name Digallic Acid.¶ The difficulty of obtaining tannin pure renders its composition, however, somewhat doubtful; when as pure as possible it results as a porous, greenish-yellow, friable mass, freely soluble in water, less so in alcohol, and insoluble in ether. The tannic acids, so called, are a group of bodies widely diffused through the vegetable kingdom, the species containing them usually lending a portion of

---

* M. von Mering, *Arch. f. d. gesam. Physiol.* 1877, 276.   § Wittstein.   ‖ Trommsdorf.
† Arctuvin, Quinhydrone, Hydroquinone, Hydrochinone.   Gallic Acid.   Water.   Tannin.
‡ Gmelin, *Chem.*, xvi, 28.   ¶ $(C_7H_6O_5)_2 - H_2O = C_{14}H_{10}O_9$.

their name to specify the body as found in them—(*Caffee*-tannic Acid, *Quino*-tannic Acid, *Catechu*-tannic Acid, *Kino*-tannic Acid, etc.). With gelatine, these tannins form an insoluble compound; and with ferric chloride they yield bluish-black or green precipitates. They combine readily with animal skin, giving it the property of resisting putrefaction, which forms part of the process called tanning.

Resin, gum, pyrocatechin,* extractive matters, and the usual plant constituents, are also found.†

PHYSIOLOGICAL ACTION.—Should we prescribe on the palliative principle, and at the same time believe in disinfection by killing germs, I could hardly point to a drug more adapted to diseases of the kidneys, bladder, and urethra than *arbutin*, which is changed in the renal tract to hydrokinone, a sort of phenol, which is in itself a germicide, the arbutin being more or less innocuous and at the same time a diuretic; it has, however, caused an eruption of the skin.‡

Uva-Ursi itself causes vomiting and purging, involuntary passage, bloody and green urine, and reduces the heart's action; further than this little is known of its direct effects.

DESCRIPTION OF PLATE 100.

 1. End of a flowering branch.
 2. Fruiting branch, Salem, Mass., Nov. 22, 1886.
 3. Leaf, under surface.
 4. Flower.
 5. Longitudinal section of flower.
 6. Pistil.
 7. Stamen, front and side view.
 8. Drupe.
 9. Pyrenæ consolidated into a stone.
10. Transverse section of a pyrena.
12. Longitudinal section of a seed.
13. Horizontal section of a seed.
14. Section of ovary.
15. Separate pyrena.
(4–15 enlarged.)

---

* See page 40–2.

† Further bibliography in this department: *Gray's Elements;* Gmelin, *Chem.,* xv, 419, xvi, 28; *Phar. Jour.,* 3, v, 401; *Am. Jour. Phar.,* xxvii, 334; 1873, 197; 1886, 385; 1885, 139; *Chem. Gaz.,* 1853, 61; Wittstein, *Org. Constit. Plants;* Schorlemmer, *Chem. Carb. Comp.*

‡ Lewin, *ibid.*

Tribe.—ANDROMEDEÆ.

GENUS.—**EPIGÆA**,* LINN.

SEX. SYST.—DECANDRIA MONOGYNIA.

101

EPIGÆA.

TRAILING ARBUTUS.

SYN.—EPIGÆA REPENS, LINN.

COM. NAMES.—TRAILING ARBUTUS, MAY FLOWER, GRAVEL PLANT, GRAVEL WEED, GROUND LAUREL, MOUNTAIN PINK, WINTER PINK.

A TINCTURE OF THE FRESH PLANT EPIGÆA REPENS, LINN.

Description.—This fragrant spring flower, blossoming amid the verdure of its previous year's growth is prostrate or trailing* from a mass of perennial red-brown, fibrous *roots* thickly beset with a tangle of rootlets; the *stem* is rounded and conspicuously hairy, the bark and hairs having a rusty color. *Leaves* alternate, evergreen, reticulate, ovate-cordate and entire, from 1 to 2 inches long, and relatively one-half as wide, the edges and under surface rusty hairy. *Inflorescence* apical or axillary; the *flowers* spring from dry, scaly bracts, and have a delicate pink, a deep rose-color, or are in some cases white, and emit a fragrant, spicy aroma. *Sepals* 5, dry, nearly separate, ovate-lanceolate, acute. *Corolla* monopetalous, salver-form, with 5 ovate, spreading lobes, the tube hairy inside. *Stamens* 10, shorter than the corolla; *filaments* hairy at the base; *anthers* linear, opening longitudinally; *pollen* of compound grains as in the preceding, but smaller. *Ovary* globular, depressed, 5-celled, many-seeded; *style* slender, forming a zone about the minutely 5-lobed stigma. *Capsule* 5-lobed, 5-celled, 5-angled, many-seeded, inclosed in the persistent calyx; *placentæ* large, 2-celled; *seeds* ovate.

History and Habitat.—Upon rich, damp, mossy banks throughout the central part of North America east of the Mississippi, under the shade and protection of low pines and hemlocks, in the early sunny days of spring, sometimes even peeping from under a snow-bank, appear the sweet-scented flowers of this much-sought-after little plant; so closely do the prostrate spreading stems cling to and mingle with the mosses, to which they in their rusty hairiness bear great similitude, that one of its common names in some localities is *Moss Beauty*. Epigæa flowers until May, and ripens its fruit in July.

It is stated that in lithic acid gravel, and some forms of nephritis, cystitis and vesical catarrh, its use has often been of greater benefit than uva-ursi or buchu.

---

* ἐπί, *upon*, γῆ, *the earth.*

Epigæa has no place in the U. S. Ph.   In the Eclectic Materia Medica its officinal preparations are *Extracium Epigeæ Fluidum*, and *Infusum Epigeæ ;* it is also the principal component of *Infusum Epigeæ Compositum*, together with Eupatorium purpureum, Aralia hispida, and Radix althæa officinalis, this being one of their much used diuretics.

PART USED AND PREPARATION.—The fresh leaves, or the whole plant gathered when budding to blossom, being chopped and pounded to a pulp and weighed, two parts by weight of alcohol are taken, the pulp mixed with one-sixth part of it, and the rest of the alcohol added.   After thorough succussion the whole is poured into a well-stoppered bottle and allowed to stand for eight days in a dark, cool place.   The tincture is then decanted, strained and filtered.

Thus prepared it is opaque, showing in thin layers a deep brown color ; it has a pleasant woody taste, is slightly astringent, and of a decided acid reaction.

CHEMICAL CONSTITUENTS.—The three glucosides, *urson, ericolin,* and *arbutin* (*vide* Uva-ursi, 100).   *Formic acid* and a body having properties similar to *gallic acid* have been determined in this plant.

Tannic Acid.—The amount of this body existing in epigæa is given by Bowman as 3.5 per cent.

Ericinol.—$C_{10} H_{16} O$, a pale-yellow, aromatic oil, is also present.

PHYSIOLOGICAL ACTION.—Epigæa, so far as is determined at present, shows no important symptoms of physiological disturbance of the system.   The provings are scanty ; the only one so far published was made upon myself, and may be found in the " Hom. Physician," Oct., 1881, vol. 1, No. 10, pp. 486–9.

DESCRIPTION OF PLATE 101.

1. Flowering branch, from Waverly, N. Y., April 3, 1880.
    2. Flower showing calyx (enlarged).
    3. Section of flower (enlarged).
    4. Stamen (enlarged).
    5. Pollen grains x 380.

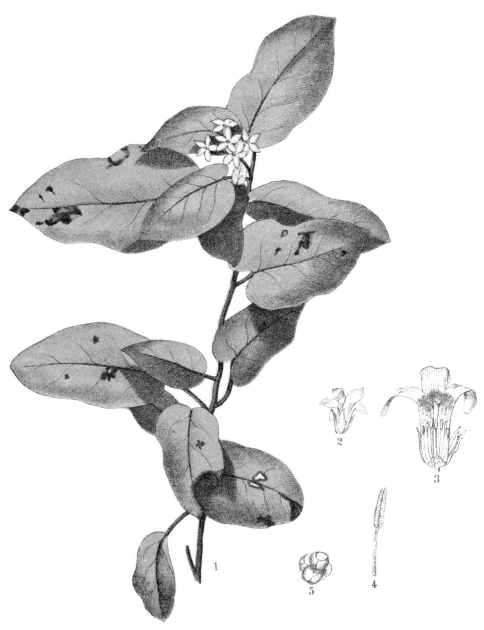

Œm. ad nat. del. et pinxt.

EPIGÆA RÈPENS, Linn.

Tribe.—ANDROMEDEÆ.

GENUS.—**GAULTHERIA**,* LINN.

SEX. SYST.—DECANDRIA MONOGYNIA.

102

GAULTHERIA.

WINTERGREEN.

SYN.—GAULTHERIA PROCUMBENS, LINN.; GAULTHERIA HUMILIS, SALISB.; GAULTIERA REPENS, RAF.

COM. NAMES.—CREEPING WINTERGREEN, CHECKER BERRY, PARTRIDGE BERRY, BOX BERRY, SPICE BERRY, TEA BERRY, MOUNTAIN TEA,† JERSEY TEA, GROUND HOLLY, AROMATIC WINTERGREEN, GROUSE BERRY, DEW BERRY, RED BERRY. HILL BERRY, (FR.) THE du CANADA; (GER.) BERGTHEE.

A TINCTURE OF THE FRESH LEAVES OF GAULTHERIA PROCUMBENS, LINN.

Description.—This well-known perennial, spicy-aromatic evergreen grows, in its upright height, from 3 to 5 inches, the true *stem* creeping, generally below the surface, and resembling a root. The flowering branches upright, stem-like, naked below and leafy at the top. *Leaves* alternate, upon very short petioles, obovate or oval, with a wedge-shaped base and very finely serrate edges; thick, smooth and shining. *Inflorescence* axillary; *flowers* usually single, sometimes more, upon nodding, two-bracted pedicels from the base of the upper petioles. *Calyx* five-lobed. *Corolla* inflated-cylindrical or pear-shaped, hairy within, with five small revolute teeth. *Stamens* ten, included within the tube of the corolla; *filaments* flat, hairy, curving toward the style; *anthers* large, introrse, two-celled with two awns at the apex of each cell, opening by a terminal pore. *Ovary* smooth, five-lobed, five-celled, depressed, situated upon an hypogenous disk; *placenta* axillary; *style* simple, cylindrical, thick, longer than the stamens; *stigma* blunt, apparently entire, but in reality faintly marked into five lobes. *Fruit* a depressed, five-lobed, -celled and -valved, many-seeded pod, invested, when ripe, by the now thickened and fleshy calyx, thus forming a globose, bright red, edible berry, having a depression at its apex, surrounded by crenations formed of the thickened calyx teeth. *Seeds* situated upon the axis, minute, very irregularly shaped, the average being rounded-triangular, with concave or convex surfaces; *testa* light-yellow, with fine hexagonal reticulations. A description of the Ericaceæ will be found under Uva-Ursi, 100.

---

* Dedicated to Dr. Gaultier of Quebec. The orthography of whose name, after passing through botanical works as " Gaulthier " and "Gautier," was finally settled by the records of Quebec, searched by Prof. Brunet, as " Gaultier." (Gray)

† The leaves of this plant formed one of the substitutes for *Thea Chinensis* during the Revolutionary War.

History and Habitat.—The wintergreen is indigenous to the eastern portion of the United States, growing from Maine to South Carolina, and westward to Central Kentucky, especially among the mountains in the shade of pines, flowering in July. The strange fruit hangs, and retains its bright color, until the next spring, then rots upon the pedicels or drops to the ground, thus allowing the escape of the seeds. The common names given to *Gaultheria procumbens, Chimaphila umbellata*, and *Mitchella repens* are very confusing, being interchanged in different sections of the country. The berries when fresh, and the young leaves, are very pleasant to the palate, being esteemed highly by many, and forming an article for sale by hucksters in some localities. They form, especially among the mountains of Pennsylvania, together with those of *Mitchella*, the principal food of partridges, grouse and deer, in the late autumn months.

Distillation of the oil of wintergreen, for use as a flavoring extract—to which its principal commercial value is due—is confined to men of limited means, in those districts where its growth is most abundant. The apparatus used is simple and movable, being shifted as the supply of leaves gives out. It consists usually of a copper whiskey-still. This is placed near some rivulet with a sufficient fall to keep the cooler filled. It is entirely invested by brick, with the exception of the cap, filled with leaves covered with water, and heated by an open fire beneath. The volatile oil, together with the steam, passes through the condensing worm into the receiver, which is kept filled with water. The oil is collected by a separating funnel, placed in the bottom of the receiver, and the water used over and again to economize the product. The average yield is ten pounds from a ton of the leaves; greater in dry seasons.

Most of the so-called oil of wintergreen is made from young birch trees (*Betula lentæ*), in a similar manner to the process described above. Mr. G. W. Kennedy decides* that there is but little variance between the oil of wintergreen and that of birch. This, as far as he determined after many tests, consists only in a slight difference in the boiling point.

Gaultheria is only mentioned in the U. S. Ph., no officinal preparation being given. In the Eclectic Materia Medica it meets with the same lack of popularity.

PART USED AND PREPARATION.—The fresh leaves, gathered in summer, are chopped and pounded to a pulp and weighed. Then two parts by weight of alcohol are taken, the pulp thoroughly mixed with one-sixth part of it and the rest of the alcohol added. The whole is then poured into a well-stoppered bottle and allowed to remain for eight days in a dark, cool place. The tincture is then separated by straining and filtering. Thus prepared, it is of a deep brownish red color by transmitting light through thin layers, or black and opaque when in quantity. It retains the pleasant odor of the plant. The taste peculiar to the plant is covered at first by its great astringency, but gradually becomes apparent as the natural condition of the tongue returns. Its acidity is marked.

CHEMICAL CONSTITUENTS.—The general constituents of this plant are the same as those described under Uva-Ursi, 100, *viz.*, arbutin, urson, ericolin and tannin.

* *Am. Jour. Phar.*, 1882, p. 49.

Oil of Gaultheria. This body is a mixture of the volatile oil of the plant, salicylate of methyl, gaultherilene and gaultheric acid, forming the heaviest of the known essential oils, its sp. gr. being 1.173. Unless purified by macerating in animal charcoal, it has a reddish color, and boils at 200° (392° F.).

Gaultherilene, $C_{10}H_{16}$. This hydrocarbon is one of the constituents of the mixed oil.

Gaultheric acid. Methyl-salicylic acid, $C_6H_4 \begin{cases} O.CH_3 \\ CO_2H. \end{cases}$ This methyl-ether of salicylic acid, is obtained from the oil of wintergreen through the agency of an alkali. It crystallizes in plates, melting at 98.5° (209.3° F.). It is isomeric with the next, from which it differs by being a strong acid.

Salicylate of methyl, $C_6H_4 \begin{cases} OH \\ CO.COH_2. \end{cases}$ This body constitutes the principal part of the compound oil distilling over after the passage of the volatile body when the temperature is raised to 222° (431.6° F.). It exists as an oily liquid, possessing a very pleasant penetrating odor and a sweet, aromatic, refreshing taste. (Schorlemmer, Wittstein.) All of the above constituents are soluble in alcohol.

PHYSIOLOGICAL ACTION.—The following digest of the action of Gaultheria is from Dr. T. J. Gallaher (*Med. Ex.*, 8, 347) and Drs. W. E. Townsend and Hooker (*Rec. Boston Soc. Med. Imp.*), the first from an overdose of the oil, the last from large amounts of the essence: Stupidity, swelling of the tongue and very active inflammation of the stomach, attended with a highly morbid desire for food, with a painful tenderness in the epigastric region and violent retching and vomiting whenever anything entered the stomach; slow, laborious breathing, with loud respiration, but no stertor; hot skin, high pulse and restlessness.

DESCRIPTION OF PLATE 102.

1. A branch in flower, Binghamton, N. Y., July 21st, 1883.
2. A fruiting branch in October.
3. Flower (enlarged).
4. Flower (section enlarged).

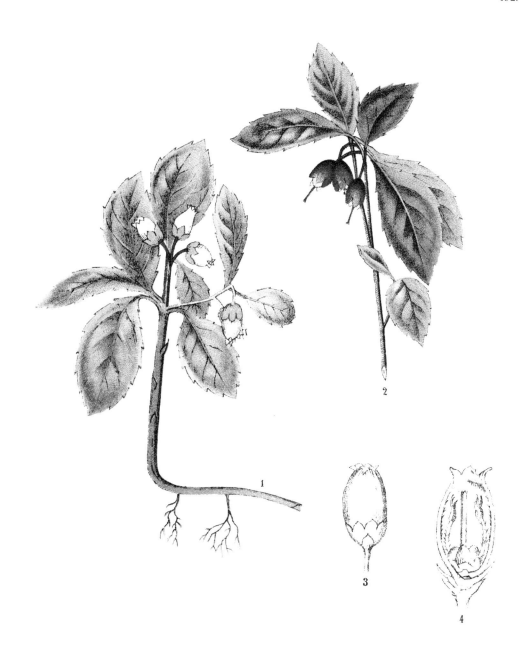

1

2

3

4

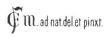.ad nat.del.et pinxt.

GAULTHERIA PROCUMBENS, Linn.

Tribe.—RHODOREÆ.

GENUS.—**KALMIA**,* LINN.

SEX. SYST.—DECANDRIA MONOGYNIA.

103

KALMIA.

MOUNTAIN LAUREL.

SYN.—KALMIA LATIFOLIA, LINN.; CISTUS CHAMÆRHODODENDROS, ETC., PLUK.; LEDUM FLORIBUS BULLATIS, ETC., TREW.

COM. NAMES.—MOUNTAIN LAUREL, AMERICAN LAUREL, CALICO-BUSH, SPOONWOOD, BIG IVY, ROSE LAUREL, ROUND-LEAVED LAUREL, SHEEP-LAUREL,† LAMB-KILL,† WICKE; (FR.) GRANDE KALMIE; (GER.) GROSS KALMIE.

A TINCTURE OF THE FRESH LEAVES OF KALMIA LATIFOLIA, LINN.

Description.—This beautiful evergreen shrub attains a height of from 4 to 10 or more feet. *Stem* smooth; *branches* more or less terete, irregular, and tortuous. *Leaves* more or less scattered but tending to alternation, they are thick, coriaceous, glabrous, dark and shining green both sides; in form they are elliptical or ovate-lanceolate, acute at both ends and entire. *Inflorescence* simple or clustered, naked, umbel-like corymbs, terminal upon the branchlets; *pedicels* long, arising from leaf-like bracts; *flowers* clammy-pubescent. *Calyx* rotate, persistent, somewhat smaller than the fruit; *limb* 5-parted; *teeth* deltoid. *Corolla* somewhat hypocrateriform, infundibular, or campanulate; furnished with 10 mammæ, into the internal depressions of which the anthers are held until irritated; *tube* short; *limb* 5-lobed; *lobes* semi-ovate, acute. *Stamens* 10; *filaments* smooth, filiform; *anthers* 2-celled, each opening by a large apical pore or chink. *Ovary* globose; *style* terminal, filiform; *stigma* capitate. *Fruit* a globose, 5-celled, pubescent, coriaceous capsule; *seeds* many, oblong; *testa* thin and somewhat loose.

History and Habitat.—The laurel bush is indigenous to North America, growing from Canada and Maine southward and westward to Ohio, and on the mountains as far as Florida. Its large clusters of beautiful flowers, embosomed in the rich, dark green foliage so characteristic of the plant, is one of the most attractive points of beauty of our mountain woods in May and June. In southern Pennsylvania, on the Alleghanies, this shrub often attains the dimensions of a small tree, sometimes reaching as high as 30 feet. The wood when dry is hard and dense, somewhat like that of the box (*Buxus*), and is used for the manufacture of household implements, such as ladles, spoons, forks, etc.; for the handles of small tools, and for cog-wheels and the like.

---

* Peter Kalm, a Swedish botanist and a pupil of Linnæus.   † More properly names applied to *K. angustifolia.*

The previous uses of this plant in medicine were of a very limited character. A decoction was used in domestic practice for various forms of tinea capitis, psora and herpes; also in secondary syphilis. It has been recommended in inflammatory fevers as a cardiac depressor; its astringency was utilized also by the application of the drug in diarrhœas and hemorrhages of the bowels.

Kalmia is not officinal in the U. S. Ph.; in the Eclectic Materia Medica its preparations are: *Decoctum Kalmiæ; Tinctura Kalmiæ;* and *Syrupus Phytolaccæ Compositus.* *

PART USED AND PREPARATION.—The fresh leaves, gathered while the plant is in blossom, are treated as in the preceding species. The tincture thus prepared is opaque; in thin layers it has a deep brownish-orange color; it retains the peculiar odor of the bruised leaves, has an extremely astringent and somewhat bitter taste, leaves a slightly scalded sensation upon the tongue, and has a strong acid reaction.

CHEMICAL CONSTITUENTS.—A special active principle has not as yet been determined in this plant. The analyses of Bigelow,† Bullock,‡ and Kennedy,§ resulted in the determination of *Arbutin,*‖ tannic acid,†‡ resin,†‡ fat,‡ gum,†‡ wax,‡ an acid body uninvestigated,‡ extractive,‡ yellow coloring matter,‡ a mannite,‡ and the usual plant constituents.

PHYSIOLOGICAL ACTION.—Laurel leaves have always been deemed poisonous, especially by the Indians and the laity. Their action upon sheep, especially lambs, has given two of its vernacular names, *Sheep-laurel* and *lamb-kill.* Catesby says:¶ "deer feed upon its green leaves with impunity; yet when cattle and sheep, by severe winters deprived of better food, feed on the leaves of this plant, a great many of them die annually." And Kalm gives the following:** "The leaves are poison to some animals, and food for others; experience has taught the people, that when sheep eat of these leaves, they either die immediately, or fall very sick, and recover with great difficulty. The young and more tender sheep are killed by a small portion, but the older ones can bear a stronger dose. Yet this food will also prove mortal to them if they eat too much of it. The same noxious effect it shows in regard to calves, . . . they fall very sick, swell, foam at the mouth and can hardly stand. The sheep are most exposed to be tempted with these leaves in winter, . . . being greedy of all greens; especially if snow still lies upon the ground. Horses, oxen, and cows, which have eaten them, have likewise been very ill after the meal." He farther adds that these leaves form a winter food for stags, and if killed during the time of feeding and the entrails given to dogs to eat, they "become quite stupid, and, as it were, intoxicated, and often fall so sick that they seem to be at the point of death; but the people who have eaten the venison have not felt the least inconvenience." Dr. Bigelow states, as do other observers, that it is a common belief that the flesh

* Phytolacca, Ampelopsis, Cimicifuga, and Kalmia.
† *Am. Med. Bot.*, vol. 1, p. 136.
‡ *Am. Jour. Phar.*, 1848, p. 264.
§ *Am. Jour. Phar.*, 1875.
‖ Kennedy (see Uva Ursi, 100).
¶ *Op. cit.*, p. 137.
** *Travels in North America*, vol. 1, p. 335.

of the Partridge, after feeding upon the leaves and fruits, becomes of itself poisonous; this Wilson the ornithologist denies on trial, though other observers declare it a fact. Dr. Bigelow judges that the illness caused in animals is due to the indigestibility of the plant; other authors think that those persons made ill by eating the flesh of the partridge under the circumstances mentioned, are made so from a decomposed state of the meat. Beck* appears to deem the flesh poisonous from eating the berries as above.

From the experience of nearly all persons who have experimented upon themselves with a tincture or decoction of the leaves, it is obvious that the effects produced on cattle after grazing on the leaves, and on persons eating of "poisoned" partridges, are due to the plant itself, not to indigestion or putrefaction. Dr. Bigelow's later observations,† agree *in toto* with our provings. He gives the following as its action: "The flesh of the bird impairs the functions of the brain and acts directly as a sedative poison, secondarily affecting the digestive and circulatory organs." The symptoms arising in those proving the drug are: Vertigo and headache; almost complete loss of sight; pale, somewhat livid countenance; salivation and difficult deglutition; thirst, nausea and vomiting, with oppression and pressure in the region of the stomach; difficult respiration with great palpitation and fluttering of the heart, followed by an irregular, feeble, and slow pulse; weakness, weariness and pains in the limbs; coldness of the surface and great prostration.

DESCRIPTION OF PLATE 103.

1. End of flowering branch, Waverly, N. Y., June 15th, 1880.
2. Flower.
3. Pistil.
4. Stamen.
5. Pollen x 200.
(3 and 4 enlarged).

Kalmia Angustifolia, Linn., seems from the experience of others to be the most poisonous species, its habitat is the same as that of K. latifolia. It may be the confusion of species that causes so much doubt upon the questions of toxicology. It is stated‡ that a few drops of a saturated tincture of the plant caused the death of a rattlesnake when poured upon it. We cannot be certain that our preparations and those of the provers were made from K. latifolia alone; therefore I append a differentiation for future reference in experimentation, judging that a thorough revision and re-proving of the two species separately, would be vastly important to us.

KALMIA.

K. LATIFOLIA.	K. ANGUSTIFOLIA.
(Calico-bush, Mountain Laurel.)	(Sheep-laurel, Lamb-kill.)
Height 4 to 30 feet.	*Height* 2 to 4 feet.
Leaves alternate or scattered, ovate-lanceolate or elliptical, acute, bright, rich green both sides.	*Leaves* opposite or in whorls of three, narrowly oblong, obtuse, light green above, pale to whitish beneath.
Inflorescence terminal, clammy, pubescent; *flowers* pink to nearly white.	*Inflorescence* lateral, slightly glandular; *flowers* red, and nearly two-thirds smaller.
Fruit a depressed glandular capsule.	*Fruit* a depressed smooth capsule, upon a recurved pedicel.

* *Medical Jurisprudence*, p. 864.   † Nearly 40 years after the publication of his *Am. Med. Bot.*, quoted above.
‡ By Dr. Barton.

103.

𝕮.𝕸. ad nat del. et pinxt.

KÁLMIA LATIFÒLIA, Linn.

104

CHIMAPHILA.

PIPSISSEWA.

SYN.—CHIMAPHILA UMBELLATA, NUTT., CHIMAPHILA CORYMBOSA, PURSH., PYROLA UMBELLATA, LINN., PYROLA FRUCTICANS, PARKINSON.
COM. NAMES.—PIPSISSEWA, WINTERGREEN, PRINCE'S PINE, BITTER WINTERGREEN, GROUND HOLLY; (FR.) PYROLE OMBELLÉE; (GER.) DOLDENBLÜTHIGES HARNKRAÜT, ODER WINTERGRÜN.

A TINCTURE OF THE FRESH PLANT *CHIMAPHILA*, EITHER *UMBELLATA* OR *MACULATA*, OR BOTH, AS THE PROVINGS HAVE BEEN MADE WITHOUT DISCRIMINATION.

Description.—This small, slightly woody, nearly herbaceous evergreen perennial, springs from a long, cylindrical, creeping, yellowish *root*, about one-eighth to one-quarter of an inch in diameter, giving off numerous fine rootlets, and sending up many branches, which terminate in leafy and flowering stems alternately. *Stem* simple, or sometimes branched at the base, 3 to 6 inches high before the flowering season. *Leaves* mostly in several imperfect whorls, or sometimes scattered about the upper portion of the stem; they are dark green above, paler below, thick, shining, wedge-lanceolate, acute at the base, sharply saw-toothed, amaculate, short-petioled, and from one and a half to two inches long, by one-quarter to one-half an inch broad. *Peduncle* from 3 to 6 inches long, erect, smooth, terminating in from 4 to 7 *pedicels* covered with a very fine down, nodding in flower, erect in fruit, and forming a loose umbel or corymb. *Calyx* much smaller than the corolla; *sepals* five, blunt, persistent, slightly hairy. *Corolla* of five *petals* rounded, concave and spreading. *Stamens* ten, free, inserted under the pistil; *filaments* at first convex, obovate, fleshy, then concave, filiform and hairy; *anthers* large, extrorse in the bud but becoming inverted in flower, more or less conspicuously 2-horned, 4-celled, and opening by two pores; *pollen* grains white, compounded of four more or less globose granules. *Ovaries* 5, connected about a fleshy receptacle in such a manner as to form a depressed globose mass, surrounded at its base by a glandular zone; *ovules* many, small, anatropous; *style* very short, rounded and wedge-shaped, the apex entering into the summit of the substance between the ovaries; *stigma* broad, convex, discoid, faintly marked by

* χεῖμα, *winter,* φιλέω, *to love.*

1

2

3

4

5

ℭℳ.ad nat.del.et pinxt.

CHIMÁPHILA UMBELLÀTA, Nutt.

5 crenations. *Pod* depressed-globose, 5-lobed, 5-celled and 5-valved, loculicidal from the apex downward ; *seeds* innumerable, minute.

Chimaphila Maculata, Pursh.—This species differs from the foregoing as follows: Peduncles from 1 to 5 flowered. Leaves ovate-lanceolate, obtuse at the base, the edges widely toothed, their upper surface white-maculate. A description of the natural order will be found under Arctostaphylos Uva-ursi.

History and Habitat.—This hardy little plant seeks the deep shaded portion of woodlands, where it flourishes best in the loamy formations of rotted leaves. It abounds throughout the central portion of North America, the forests of Siberia and the Northern countries of Europe. It blossoms here in June and July, fruiting in September. It is used among the aborigines of this country as a tonic and diuretic, as well as for rheumatic and scrofulous disorders, and latterly as an application to scrofulous and other open sores. Chimaphila is still retained in the U. S. Ph. as *Extractum Chimaphilæ Fluidum*. In the Eclectic Materia Medica its officinal preparation is *Decoctum Chimaphilæ ;* it is also a component of *Syrupus Stillingiæ Compositus*.

PART USED AND PREPARATION.—The fresh plants while in flower are chopped and pounded to a pulp and weighed. Then two parts by weight of alcohol are taken, the pulp mixed thoroughly with one-sixth part of it, and the rest of the alcohol added. After stirring the whole well it is poured into a well-stoppered bottle and allowed to stand eight days in a dark, cool place. The tincture is then decanted, strained and filtered.

Thus formed it is opaque ; thin layers have a deep, rich, reddish-brown color ; it is decidedly bitter, slightly astringent, and has an acid reaction to litmus.

CHEMICAL CONSTITUENTS.—The chemistry of this plant corresponds with that of Arctostaphylos Uva-ursi (vide Uva-ursi, plate 100), differing probably little except in also containing the following principle, determined by Fairbank :

Chimaphilin.—On the aqueous distillation of the stems in a retort, a deposit of golden-yellow, odorless, tasteless crystals takes place upon the neck, the chemical nature of which has not yet been determined ; their physical features are : a slight solubility in water, and a free solution in alcohol. The percentage of tannin in this plant is somewhat less than in Uva-ursi.

PHYSIOLOGICAL ACTION.—Here again Uva-ursi should be consulted. Chimaphila does not cause nausea and vomiting to the extent of Uva-ursi, while its diuretic action is greater. Its physiological action as such is undetermined.

DESCRIPTION OF PLATE 104.

1. Whole plant in fruit.
2. Flowering stem, Binghamton, N. Y., June 26, 1883.
3. Stamen (enlarged).
4. Fruit (enlarged).
5. Seed (enlarged).

105

MONOTROPA.

INDIAN PIPE.

SYN.—MONOTROPA UNIFLORA, LINN.; MONOTROPA MORISONIANA, MICHX.; MONOTROPA MORISONI, PERS.

COM. NAMES.—INDIAN PIPE, TOBACCO PIPE, PIPE PLANT, CORPSE PLANT, ICE PLANT, BIRD'S NEST,† NEST PLANT, FIT-ROOT, CONVULSION-ROOT, OVA-OVA; (GER.) EINBLÜTHIGE MONOTROPA.

A TINCTURE OF THE WHOLE FRESH PLANT MONOTROPA UNIFLORA, L.

Description.—This strange waxy or bluish-white, fleshy, inodorous, semi-parasitic herb, grows from 2 to 8 inches high. *Rootlets* very numerous, forming a ball of densely-matted fibres. *Stems* several from each clump of rootlets, simple, subcylindrical and smooth. *Leaves*, none; their place supplied below by numerous small triangular scales, which gradually enlarge and become ovate-spatulate foliaceous bracts toward the summit of the stem, where they pass into the *inflorescence*, composed of a single, terminal, declined flower, which becomes horizontal, then inclined as it performs its life-work, and rigidly erect in fruit. *Flower* slightly pubescent, entirely devoid of color except where the yellow anthers and flesh-colored pistil are disclosed. *Sepals* replaced by 2 to 5 bracteolate, irregular, lanceolate, caducous bodies; *petals* 5, erect, gouge-shaped, saccate at the base, marcescent. *Stamens* 10, shorter than the petals, each alternating at the base with a short, recurved, nipple-like process of the base of the ovary; *filaments* awl-shaped, pubescent; *anthers* horizontal, reniform, becoming one-celled and opening by transverse chinks; *pollen* simple, showing 1 to 2 translucent depressed spots.‡ *Style* columnar, short and thick; *stigma* naked, discoid, obtusely 5-angled, with a funnel-form depression in the centre. *Fruit* an erect, ovoid, 8- to 10-grooved, 4- to 5-celled loculicidal pod; *placentæ* large and sarcous; *seeds* very numerous, minute, subulate; *testa* loose, cellular, translucent. A description of the Ericaceæ will be found under Uva Ursi 100.

History and Habitat.—The Indian pipe grows in deep, rich, shady woods—especially those in which the beech abounds—from Florida to Mississippi, and thence northward, flowering in July in the North and from August to September in the South. This curious herb well deserves its name of *corpse plant*, so like is it to

---

* Μόνος, *monos ;* τρόπος, *tropos ;* one turn, from the facing of the flower.

† More applicable to *Daucus carota*, on account of the resemblance of the fruiting umbels to that structure.

‡ The pollen of Monotropa uniflora bears a striking resemblance in this regard to that of *Pendicularis Canadensis*.

the general bluish waxy appearance of the dead; then, too, it is cool and clammy to the touch, and rapidly decomposes and turns black even when carefully handled. The whole plant when wounded—especially, however, the floral envelope—emits a clear glutinous fluid. Attempts to preserve it in alcohol turn it a bluish-black, and tinge the preservative a deep reddish-violet hue, while the drying process turns it jet-black, leaving very little semblance to its natural appearance. The medical history of the plant begins with its use by the American Aborigines as an application in "sore eyes;" they valued a mixture of the juice with water highly as a soothing and often curative measure. Of this property Dr. Kunze* says in corroboration: "This is a drug very highly recommended† for overcoming nervous irritability, epilepsy, chorea, etc., when used in large doses—inwardly, of course—and for ophthalmic as well as other inflammations of delicate mucous surfaces outwardly applied, either in its fresh state or the preserved juice. I have myself used it very much in ordinary cases of inflamed eyes, both chronic and acute, and have never seen, or even before heard any evil effects following the most indiscriminate use.‡ Have applied it to the eyes of infants when only three days old, in *Ophthalmia purulenta infantum*, as well as in old age in every variety of so-called constitutions, and even where not successfully employed no ill effects have ever been observed thereafter." He farther on describes an incidental cure which is of interest botanically and medically: "Fourteen years ago—it was in the early part of July—I went woodcock-shooting with two friends, near Hackensack, N. J., and while taking some luncheon in a beech grove along the course of Saddle River, I found a large patch of ground literally covered with *Monotropa uniflora* in full bloom; it covered a space some five feet wide by nine feet long, a beautiful sight of snow-white stems and nodding flowers. Being in need of some just then, I proceeded to fill my game-bag, and to the question, what it was used for, answered: 'Good for sore eyes;' little thinking that the party addressed was suffering from a chronic inflammation of the eye-lids, the edges of which had a very fiery-red appearance. No sooner said than he proceeded to take in his game-bag a supply also, and he made very good use of it, as I ascertained afterwards. His inflamed lids were entirely cured in four weeks' time, and he has had no further trouble since, by applying the fresh juice of the stems he obtained while it lasted." Dr. King mentions the drug§ as "tonic, nervine, sedative and antispasmodic." The former uses of the herb in spasms of children, epileptiform and chorea-like, gave it the popular names so characterizing it. Dr. Stewart claimed that the dried herb was an excellent substitute for opium, "easing pain, comforting the stomach, and causing sleep." In spasmodic affections the usual dose is a teaspoonful of the dried root in powder; to this is often added the appropriate dose of valerian.

No mention is made of this drug in the U. S. Ph., and no officinal preparation appears in the Eclectic Materia Medica.

---

* *Bot. Gaz.*, 1878, Vol. iii, No. 6, pp 53, 54.
† In King's *Am. Disp.*, and Howard's *Botanic Medicine*.
‡ This clause he uses in discussing Mr. A. H. Young's case of poisoning, which I shall quote under the proper rubric.
§ *American Dispensatory*, 1880, p. 530.

Œ̃m.ad nat.del.et pinxt.

MONÓTROPA UNIFLÒRA, Linn.

PART USED AND PREPARATION.—The whole fresh flowering plant is treated as in the preceding drug. The resultant tincture has a brilliant orage-red color by transmitted light, a bitterish odor, a decidedly sweet taste, and a slightly acid reaction.

CHEMICAL CONSTITUENTS.—No analysis of this plant has, as far as I am able to determine, been made. The European species, also found here, *Monotropa hypopitys*, a tawny, many-flowered form, yields a volatile oil and *Salicylate of Methyl*.*

PHYSIOLOGICAL ACTION.—The only account of poisoning by this plant is that of Mr. A. H. Young.† This case was discussed by Dr. R. E. Kunze, as before mentioned, who was of the opinion that in the gathering the young lady handled *Rhus toxicodendron ;* Mr. Young then again consulted the patient‡ and found that she was not susceptible to Rhus poison, and farther, that she had not personally gathered the plant, but met with her ill-fortune while examining it at home. As Mr. Young had the identical plant in his herbarium, he searched for rootlets of Rhus tox. clinging to the plant, but found none, and states it as his conviction that the case, though standing alone, is veritable. He says: "During the month of September a young lady brought me a plant which she said had poisoned her, and she desired its name. With some surprise, and perhaps I should have had none after considering its fostering food and close resemblance to the Fungi, I found the plant to be *Monotropa uniflora*. The circumstances of the case are as follows: The young lady while examining the plant, accidentally crushed the stem, and some of the juice was driven upon her lips. The mucous portions which were somewhat chapped became very much irritated, and began to inflame and swell considerably, while in two or three places upon the epidermal skin of the lip small ulcerous sores were formed. The effect remained some four or five days and then gradually healed. The whole effect was very much like a mild case of poisoning with *Rhus toxicodendron*." As we have no proving of this drug, we cannot as yet corroborate this case ; there is, however, no plant in our country that promises so good results from provings.

DESCRIPTION OF PLATE 105.

1. Whole plant, Binghamton, N. Y., July 21st, 1884.
2. Flower with petals removed.
3. Petal.
4 and 5. Anthers.
6. Pollen, x 300.
7. Pistil.
8. Bird's-eye view of stigma.
9. Longitudinal section of pistil.

(2-9 enlarged.)

---

* See Gaultheria, p. 102-3.   † *Bot. Gaz.*, 1878, Vol. iii, No. 1, p. 37.   ‡ *Ibid.*, No. 9, p. 79.

106
PRINOS.

BLACK ALDER.

SYN.—ILEX VERTICILLATA, GRAY; PRINOS VERTICILLATUS, LINN.; P. GRONOVII, MICHX.; P. CONFERTUS, MŒN.

COM. NAMES.—BLACK ALDER, FEVER BUSH, WINTERBERRY, VIRGINIAN WINTERBERRY; (FR.) APALACHINE À FEUILLES DE PRUNIER; (GER.) VIRGINISCHE WINTERBEERE.

A TINCTURE OF THE BARK AND FRUIT OF ILEX VERTICILLATA, GRAY.

Description. — This upright or ascending, much-branched shrub, usually attains a growth of from 4 to 8 feet. *Leaves* thin and deciduous, not spiny, in form obovate, oval, or cuneate-lanceolate, acute at the apex and base, uncinately serrate, and downy upon the veins underneath; *petioles* about one-quarter the length of the blade. *Inflorescence* diœcious; *flowers* all short peduncled, white, appearing with the leaves. *Sterile flowers* in small axillary umbels; *calyx-lobes* ciliate; *petals* mostly 4 to 6; *stamens* 6 to 7; *ovary* abortive. *Fertile flowers* aggregated or solitary; *petals* mostly 5 to 8; *ovary* conical, about 6-celled; *stigma* 4- to 6-lobed. *Fruit* a globose, bright vermilion berry, about the size of a large pea, crowded upon the branches so as to appear whorled; *nutlets* about 6, smooth and even, or dorsally furrowed or ridged. *Embryo* minute, nearly globose.

Aquifoliaceæ.—This small order, to which Prinos is but lightly wedded, and represented in North America by but 2 genera and 14 species, is characterized as follows: Shrubs or trees with their *leaves* simple, mostly alternate, and generally coriaceous and evergreen. *Flowers* small, axillary, 4- to 8-merous, white or greenish, often polygamous by abortion. *Calyx* minute, free from the ovary, 4- to 9-toothed. *Stamens* as many as the divisions of the corolla and alternate with them, the filaments attached to their very base; *anthers* adnate, opening lengthwise. *Corolla* hypogynous, rotate, or almost or quite 4- to 8-parted, imbricated in the bud. *Ovary* 4- to 8-celled; *ovules* anatropous; *stigmas* 4 to 8 or united into 1, nearly sessile. *Fruit* a baccate 4- to 8-seeded drupe; *seeds* solitary in each cell, suspended; *embryo* minute; *albumen* fleshy.

Our only other proven species in this order is the South American Maté, or Paraguay Tea (*Ilex Paraguayensis*, St. Hil.), the leaves of which are used like Chinese tea, and are considered slightly nervine, diaphoretic, and diuretic. In

---

* The ancient name of the holly oak.

general medicine the following species are more or less useful: The English Holly (*Ilex aquifolium*, Linn.), and the American co-species, *I. opaca*, Ait., have been considered nearly equal to Peruvian Bark in intermittent fevers and jaundice. The *Cassena* of the American aborigines, *I. Cassene*, Linn., and *I. Dahoon*, Walt., are emetic, and enter into the ceremonies of the natives as holy plants, which the males only were allowed to use as purifiers of the body. The Carthaginian *Myginda Uragoga*, Swartz., is said to be a most powerful diuretic. The juice and leaves of the Indian *Monetia Barleroides*, Linn., are considered by Hindoo doctors to be anti-catarrhal and anti-asthmatic; and the unripe fruit of the Brazilian *Ilex macoucoua*, Linn., are so rich in tannin as to be used as a substitute for galls.

History and Habitat.—The Black Alder is common in thickets at the margins of pools and marshy places, from western Florida northward; during its flowering season, in April and May, it is hardly distinguishable, to those who are not well acquainted with it, from the surrounding bush; but when the autumnal frosts have deprived all vegetation of its leaves, then the fruiting plant stands out like a flaming spot in the dreary waste, striking, even to the most careless observer, in its beauty.

This is another of the growing list of plants handed down to us by the aborigines, who used the bark both internally and externally as a tonic, astringent, and antiseptic, and is probably as well known to domestic practice as any indigenous shrub. In intermittent fever it has often proved as generally applicable as Peruvian Bark, and in such low typhoid forms associated with diarrhœa, and in later stages, where ulceration and hemorrhage are present, it is a very valuable agent. In general debilitated conditions of the system after long fevers, and where the body is depleted by exhausting discharges, it is also very useful, as well as in gangrenous affections and jaundice. Certain forms of chronic herpetic eruptions and ulcers are also benefited by its use as an external application. The berries are purgative and vermifuge, forming one of the pleasantest adjuvants in children's remedies, for the expulsion of lumbrici. Shoepf first noted the plant as having the above field of utility, and also mentioned its usefulness in anasarca.

The bark is official in the U. S. Ph.; in the Eclectic Dispensatory the preparation recommended is *Decoctum Prinos*.

PART USED AND PREPARATION.—The fresh bark and fruit, gathered before the first autumnal frost, are chopped and pounded to a pulp and weighed. Then two parts by weight of alcohol are taken, the pulp thoroughly mixed with one-sixth part of it, and the rest of the alcohol added. The whole is then poured into a well-stoppered bottle, and allowed to stand eight days in a dark, cool place, being shaken thoroughly twice each day. After decanting, straining, and filtering, the resulting tincture has a greenish-brown color by transmitted light; an herbaceous odor; a bitter taste, and an acid reaction.

CHEMICAL CONSTITUENTS.—Beside a bitter principle, the nature of which has not yet been determined, this species contains about 4.8 per cent. tannin; a

Ẽꝿ. ad nat del.et pinxt.   ÌLEX VERTICILLÀTA, Gray.

resin soluble in alcohol, another insoluble in alcohol; coloring-matter; albumen; gum, and sugar.*

PHYSIOLOGICAL ACTION.—The berries caused nausea, vomiting, and purging, in two children who ate of them, but whom I had no further chance to watch. In a case reported† of the effects attending the ingestion of about twenty-five berries, the following symptoms supervened: Sensation of nausea in the stomach not amounting to real sickness nor interfering with the appetite; vomiting of bile without retching; profuse evacuation of the bowels, consisting of their natural contents, diluted with an immense quantity of greenish liquid, attended with no pain or uneasiness; another similar but less profuse evacuation followed in about half an hour, after which the patient felt remarkably well, but as though he had lost ten or twelve pounds in weight. Following this, his appetite and digestion seemed much better than usual.

DESCRIPTION OF PLATE 106.

1. End of a flowering branch, Binghamton, N. Y., May 5th, 1886.
    2. Under side of leaf-margin.
    3. Flower.
    4. Calyx.
    5. Stamen.
    6. Pistil.
    7. Fruiting branch.
    8. Nutlet.
    (2–6 and 8 enlarged.)

---

* Tilden analysis, *Jour. Mat. Med.*, vol. 1, N. S., 329.   † *Bost. Med. and Surg. Jour.*, 1833, 383.

107

PLANTAGO.

PLANTAIN.

SYN.—PLANTAGO MAJOR, LINN.; PLANTA GOVULGARIS, GER.; Ἀρνόγλωσσον, DIOSCOR.

COM. NAMES.—PLANTAIN, BROAD-LEAVED PLANTAIN, RIB-GRASS, RIB-WORT, WAY-BREAD (WAY-BRED); (FR.) PLANTAIN ORDINAIRE; (GER.) GROSSER WEGETRITT.

A TINCTURE OF THE WHOLE FRESH PLANT, PLANTAGO MAJOR, L.

Description.—This cosmopolitan immigrant varies greatly in its growth, some individuals only attaining a height of 2 inches, others 18. *Root* perennial, fasciculate. *Leaves* all radical, broad, ovate, ovate-cordate or oblong, sometimes slightly toothed, 5 to 7-ribbed; *petioles* deeply channelled, smooth or slightly hairy. *Inflorescence* 1 to several long and slender, bracted, densely floral, sub-cylindrical spikes, each raised upon a naked scape; *flowers* all alike and perfect. *Sepals* 4, imbricated, persistent, membranaceous, and margined. *Corolla* whitish, thin, marcescent; *lobes* reflexed after flowering. *Stamens* 4, rarely 2, much exserted; *filaments* long filiform, lengthening suddenly when the anther is ripe; *anthers* 2-celled, early deciduous. *Pistil* dichogamous, *i.e.*, protruding from the flower tube before the anthers are ripe;† *ovary* 2-celled; *stigma* more or less unilateral, fringed. *Fruit* a 2 to 16-seeded pyxis, opening by a complete transverse fissure, the top falling off like a cap, and the thin partition escaping with the seeds; *seeds* somewhat fusiform; *albumen* sarcous; *embryo* straight, enclosed.

PLANTAGINACEÆ.—This small anomalous family of low acaulescent herbs is principally represented by the genus Plantago. Its members are characterized by having: *Leaves* all radical and ribbed. *Flowers* spiked upon a simple scape; *calyx* 4-cleft, persistent; *corolla* tubular or hypocrateriform, scarious and veinless. *Stamens* 4, inserted upon the tube of the corolla alternate with its lobes; *filaments* persistent, long and weak. *Ovary* 2-celled; *ovules* amphitropous; *style* single, long, and stigmatose. *Fruit* a membranaceous pyxis; *dehiscence* circumscissile; *seeds* 1 to several in each cell; *embryo* large, mostly straight; *albumen* sarcous.

The mucilaginous principle of the seeds of Plantago renders them somewhat valuable in medicine. The Indian plantain *Plantago Isphagula* (*P. decumbens*, Forsk) furnishes seeds from which a mucilaginous drink is prepared and used as an emollient; this species is mentioned in the native Materia Medica. The seeds of

---

* The ancient Latin name.   † A help in cross-fertilization.

the European and Barbarian *P. Psyllium*, the Hungarian *P. arenaria*, and the South European *P. Cynops*, are spoken of by Lindley as a good substitute for linseed and marsh-mallows. The leaves and roots of the common rib-grass *P. lanceolata* are considered expectorant and vulnerary; the Scottish Highlanders attach great value to this plant as a healing application to fresh wounds.

History and Habitat.—The common plantain grows in rich, moist soils, in Europe, India, and America, where it is considered truly indigenous north of Lake Superior. It flowers throughout the summer months, fruiting as it flowers. It is said that the American Indians gave this plant the name of "White Man's Foot," in allusion to its method of introduction, and its trait of accompanying the civilizer and literally growing in his footsteps. This character also gave rise to the vulgarism "way-bred."

The previous medical uses of plantain are chiefly those of a general vulnerary and demulcent; thus it became in great demand in the coughs attending various pulmonary and bronchial diseases as well as an application to recent wounds and chronic sores. The seeds were used in the former instance, the leaves in the latter. A decoction of the roots was recommended by Bergius in tertian intermittents, one ounce to four being taken when the chill came on. An infusion of the seeds in milk has been much used by the laity to check various hemorrhages from mucous surfaces, diarrhœa, dysentery, and leucorrhœa. The fibrous strings in the petioles have been extolled* as an almost certain cure for aching carious teeth, if placed in the ear on the affected side. It is said that these fibres turn black if the pain is relieved, but remain green if not. Boerhaave says that in his own experience he has found that plantain leaves placed upon the feet will ease the pain and fatigue engendered by long walks. Plantain has also been highly praised as an antidote to the effects of bites of venomous reptiles and insects; it is stated by Duncan† to be one of the principal ingredients in the remedy of the negro Cæsar, for the discovery of which he received a large reward from the Assembly of South Carolina. To complete this review of the uses of this herb no better expression could be used than that of Mérat :‡ "En fin, on a porté la racine des plantains en amulet pour guérir on prévenir une multitude des maladies."

PART USED AND PREPARATION.—The fresh plant, gathered when coming into flower, is chopped and pounded to a pulp and weighed. Then two parts by weight of alcohol are taken, the pulp mixed thoroughly with one-tenth part of it, and the rest of the alcohol added. After having stirred the whole, pour it into a well-stoppered bottle, and let it stand eight days in a dark, cool place.

The tincture separated from this mass by filtration is opaque, in thin layers it has a deep reddish-brown color by transmitted light. It retains the peculiar odor of the plant, has a sourish astringent taste and an acid reaction.

CHEMICAL CONSTITUENTS.—*Mucilage.*—This substance exists plentifully in the seeds of all species, from which it may be extracted by water, and pre-

---

* Dr. Reutlinger to Dr. E. M. Hale, *New Rem.*, p. 500.   † *New Edinburgh Dispensatory.*
‡ *Dict. de M. Med.*, Supplement, 1846, p. 567.

℃.m. ad nat del. et pinxt.

PLÀNTAGO MÀJOR, Linn.

cipitated from its watery solution (impure) by alcohol. Dry pure mucilage is a yellowish, tough, opaque body, swelling upon the addition of water, and finally dissolving into a ropy mass. The vegetable mucilages vary in their behavior toward reagents according to the plant from which they are extracted; they all, however, break down under the action of dilute sulphuric acid, first into gum, then sugar.

The whole plant has not been analyzed.

PHYSIOLOGICAL ACTION.—The principal symptoms caused by this drug are, according to Dr. F. Humphreys: headache; excessive digging, boring pain in carious teeth; severe dryness of the fauces and pharynx; colic; urging to urinate, with copious discharges; looseness of the bowels; weakness and oppression of the chest; restless sleep; and a strong fever, with a high pulse which finally becomes weak and intermittent.

DESCRIPTION OF PLATE 107.

1. Whole plant once reduced, Bergen, N. J., July 18th, 1879.
2. Flower.
3. Pistil.
4. Stamen.
5. Pollen, x 250.

(2–4 enlarged.)

N. ORD.—PRIMULACEÆ.
Tribe.—PRIMULEÆ.
GENUS.—ANAGALLIS,* TOURN.
SEX. SYST.—PENTANDRIA MONOGYNIA.

108
ANAGALLIS.

PIMPERNEL.

SYN.—ANAGALLIS ARVENSIS, LINN.
COM. NAMES.—COMMON SCARLET OR RED PIMPERNEL, POOR MAN'S
  WEATHER-GLASS, RED CHICKWEED; (GER.) HÜHNERDARN; (FR.)
  MOURON.

A TINCTURE OF THE WHOLE PLANT ANAGALLIS ARVENSIS, LINN.

Description.—This low, spreading or prostrate annual herb, grows from 6 to 20 inches in length. *Stem* square, glabrous, branching; *leaves* opposite, entire, ovate, and sessile, dotted upon the under surface. *Inflorescence* axillary; *flowers* ranging on different plants from scarlet to white through the shades of blue and purple; *peduncles* filiform, longer than the leaves, 1-flowered, bractless. *Calyx* 5-parted; *lobes* lanceolate-subulate; *margins* rough. *Corolla* rotate, 5-parted, longer than the calyx; *tube* little or none; *lobes* broad, obovate, obtuse, fringed with stipitate glands. *Stamens* 5, inserted upon the base of the corolla; *filaments* purple, bearded; *anthers* broadly oblong. *Ovary* free from the calyx; *ovules* amphitropous. *Fruit* a globular, membranaceous, circumcissile capsule or pyxis; *seeds* many, somewhat triangular; *testa* rough with minute veruccæ.

Primulaceæ.—This small family of herbs is represented in North America by 12 genera, comprising 38 species and 15 varieties; it is characterized as follows: *Leaves* simple, alternate, opposite, or whorled. *Flowers* regular, symmetrical, and perfect; *perianth* hypogynous. *Calyx* persistent. *Corolla* rotate, hypocrateriform, or campanulate. *Stamens* of the same number as the lobes of the corolla and opposite them; *filaments* inserted upon the tube of the corolla; *anthers* introrse. *Ovary* 1-celled, free from the calyx; *style* columnar, undivided; *stigma* undivided; *ovules* sessile on a free central placenta. *Seeds* numerous; *albumen* copious, fleshy; *embryo* straight, small.

The only other plant of this order in our Materia Medica is the European Sow-Bread (*Cyclamen Europæum*, Linn.). In general and household practice the flowers of the European Cowslip (*Primula officinalis*, Jacq.) have been used as a sedative, and placed in wine to render it soporific.

---

* Ἀνάγελάω, *anagelao*, to laugh; from its supposed quality of causing hilariousness.

History and Habitat.—The Pimpernel is naturalized in this country from Europe, and has established itself along both the Atlantic and Pacific coasts in dry, sandy soil, where it blossoms from June to August.

Anagallis formerly held a place in the pharmacopœias of Great Britain as a detergent, vulnerary, and cephalic; and was much prized by the ancients in gout, gravel, convulsions, and the plague. Gelin and many others considered it highly anti-hydrophobic, and reported many cures of this dire malady by its use, even after dangerous symptoms supervened. The plant also enjoyed much reputation at one time as an anti-epileptic, sudorific, and diuretic in dropsy; it has, however, entirely passed out of the minds of general practitioners. Pliny and Dioscorides thought highly of the Pimpernel in the removal of intestinal and hepatic obstructions; and it was, most probably, from the happier condition of the mind following such action, that the latter called the plant ἀνάγελάω.

PART USED AND PREPARATION.—The whole fresh, flowering plant (the scarlet-flowered form) is chopped and pounded to a pulp, enclosed in a piece of new linen, and subjected to pressure. The expressed juice is then briskly agitated with an equal weight of alcohol, and allowed to stand eight days in a dark, cool place. The tincture, prepared by filtering the above mass, has a slight olivaceous color by transmitted light; a sweetish somewhat nauseous herbaceous odor; a nutty and slightly astringent taste; and an acid reaction.

CHEMICAL CONSTITUENTS.—*Cyclamin*, $C_{20}H_{24}O_{13}$. This glucoside forms in small white crystals, or in an amorphous, lustreless, friable mass; it is very acrid, has a rancid taste, and a neutral reaction. Cyclamin is not volatile, is soluble in water and alcohol, but not in ether. Its aqueous solution is quite saponaceous. This glucoside breaks down under the action of mineral acids as follows:

$$\underset{\text{Cyclamin.}}{C_{20}H_{24}O_{13}} = \underset{\text{Glucose.}}{C_6H_{12}O_6} + \underset{\text{Cyclamiretin.}}{C_{14}H_{10}O_6} + \underset{\text{Water.}}{H_2O.}$$

PHYSIOLOGICAL ACTION.—The whole plant is acrid and poisonous, as the following experiment of Orfila shows:

"At eight o'clock in the morning, three drachms of the extract of pimpernel, dissolved in an ounce and a half of water, were introduced into the stomach of a robust dog. At half-past twelve he had a motion. At six in the evening he was dejected. At eleven sensibility appeared diminished. The next morning at six he was lying upon the side, and appeared to be dead; he might be displaced like an inert mass of matter. He expired half an hour later. The mucous membrane of the stomach was slightly inflamed; the interior of the rectum was of a bright color; the ventricles of the heart were distended with black coagulated blood; the lungs presented several livid spots, and their texture was preternaturally dense. Two drachms of the same extract, applied to the cellular texture of a dog's thigh, produced death in twelve hours; and the heart and lungs presented the same appearances as in the other." The following symptoms, recorded by Schreter, show the character of its action upon man: Lively mood with extra mental vigor;

.ad nat.del.et pinxt.

ANAGÁLLIS ARVÉNSIS, Linn.

stitching headache with sticking pains in the eyeballs; dryness of the throat; tickling, prickling along the urethra, causing desire for coition; prickling in the chest; general drawing rheumatic pains; sleeplessness; trembling and shivering; and trembling of the heart.

DESCRIPTION OF PLATE 108.

1. Whole plant, Salem, Mass., July 25th, 1875.
2. Fruit.
3. Same, showing dehiscence.
4. Seed.
(2–4 enlarged.)

GENUS.—**CATALPA**,* LINN.

SEX. SYST.—DIANDRIA MONOGYNIA.

109

CATALPA.

INDIAN BEAN.

SYN.—CATALPA BIGNONIOIDES, WALT.; BIGNONIA CATALPA, LINN;
CATALPA SYRINGÆFOLIA, SIMS; CATALPA CORDIFOLIA, DUHAM·

COM. NAMES.—CATALPA, INDIAN BEAN, BEANTREE.

A TINCTURE OF EQUAL PARTS OF THE FRESH INNER BARK AND LEAVES OF
CATALPA BIGNONIOIDES, WALT.

Description.—This magnificent umbrageous tree, beautiful in blossom, pictur-esque in fruit, attains a height of from 20 to 40 feet, its short trunk and spreading branches making it one of our finest shade trees, noted for the persistence of its fruit, the pods often hanging until new ones are formed. The *stem* is deliquescent, and has a fine gray corrugated bark, more or less glossy and warty; the *wood* commercially has but little value, though it is light, fine-textured, and capable of taking a fine polish. The *branches* are large and very irregular in their mode of growth. *Leaves* large, opposite or in whorls of three, long-petioled, simple, entire, heart-shaped and pointed; they are smooth above and downy beneath, especially upon the midrib. *Inflorescence* open, compound, showy panicles, of large, striking flowers, upon the ends of the branches. *Calyx* deeply 2-lipped or 2-parted, the segments being ovate, scaphoid, and blunt-pointed. *Corolla* monopetalous, cam-panulate, inflated, deciduous; the repand five-lobed, divergent border, irregu-lar and 2-lipped. *Stamens* sometimes didynamous with a rudimentary fifth, but more frequently with only one fertile pair; *filaments* incurved, as long as the tube of the corolla and inserted upon it; *anthers* with two diverging cells; *pollen*-grains compounded of many globular bodies all united in the form of a globe. *Pistil* compound; *ovary* 2-celled, free, upon a fleshy discoid base; *style* single; *stigma* capitate, or consisting of two lips or plates. *Fruit* a woody, subcylindrical, slender pod, from 4 to 12 inches long, pendulous and persistent, 2-celled, the septum contrary to the valves; *seeds* numerous, densely packed and superimposed, flattened by compression, membraneous, with fringe-tipped alæ; *embryo* flat, *al-bumen* none.

History and Habitat.—Catalpa, like all the other genera of this order of plants, is tropical; its most northern range is Kentucky, where it grows in many places spontaneously, flowering in July, and fruiting in October. It is cultivated in many places in the Middle and Eastern States, attaining a full growth and ap-

---

* The Indian name.

parently as healthy and perfect as in its own climate. Its uses as a drug have been but slight, its provings as yet show nothing of great importance, a mild cathartic action being the only result of large doses of a decoction of the inner bark. It has been used as an anthelmintic. Catalpa has no place in the U. S. Ph., nor Eclectic Materia Medica.

PART USED AND PREPARATION.—The fresh inner bark and leaves are chopped and pounded to a pulp and weighed. Then two parts by weight of alcohol are taken, the pulp thoroughly mixed with one-sixth part of it, and the rest of the alcohol added. After stirring the whole well, and pouring it into a well-stoppered bottle, it is allowed to stand eight days in a dark, cool place. The tincture is then separated by decanting, straining and filtering. Thus prepared, it has a clear orange-brown color by transmitted light, a bitter astringent taste and an acid reaction.

CHEMICAL CONSTITUENTS.—The bark of this plant contains an amorphous bitter principle, the chemistry of which has not been determined; it has a nauseous taste, and is soluble in alcohol. Beside this, sugar and tannin are present in small amount. The plant seems to impart all its properties to hot water and to alcohol.

PHYSIOLOGICAL ACTION.—Unknown. It has been said that it is dangerous to long inhale the odor of the tree, which however is false, at least in this locality the emanations cause no symptoms whatever.

DESCRIPTION OF PLATE 109.

1. Panicle from a specimen in DeWitt Park, Ithaca, N. Y., June 12, 1880.
2. Medium-sized leaf.
3. Pistil (enlarged).
4. Stamens (enlarged).
5. Medium-sized fruit.
6. Seed.
7. Pollen x 380.

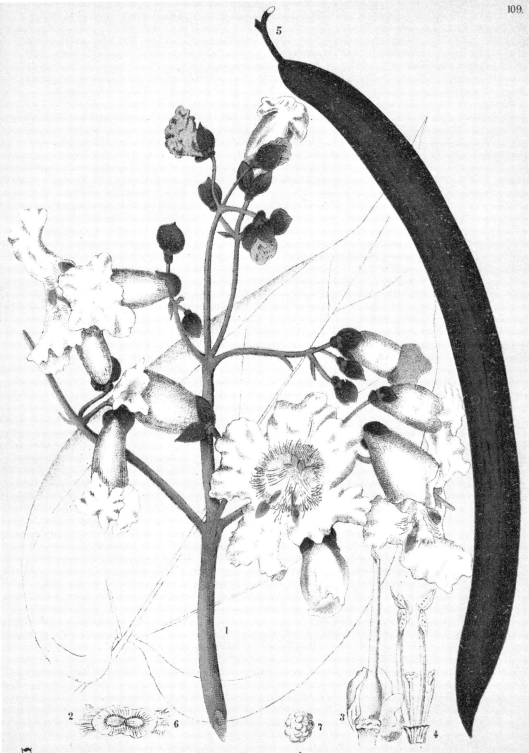

5

1

2   6   7   3   4

C.M. ad nat.del.et pinxt.   CATÁLPA BIGNONIOÍDES, Walt.

Tribe.—*VERBASCEÆ.*

GENUS.—**VERBASCUM,**[*] LINN.

SEX. SYST.—PENTANDRIA MONOGYNIA.

110

VERBASCUM.

MULLEIN.

SYN.—VERBASCUM THAPSUS, LINN.; TAPSUS BARBATUS, GER.

COM. NAMES.—COMMON MULLEIN; HIGH TAPER; COW'S LUNG WORT; FLANNEL PLANT; (FR.) MOLÈNE, BOUILLON-BLANC; (GER.) KÖNIGS-KERZE, WOLLKRAUT.

A TINCTURE OF THE WHOLE FRESH HERB, VERBASCUM THAPSUS, LINN.

Description.—This densely woolly, pale green biennial weed, grows to a height of from 3 to 6 feet or more. *Stem* stout, simple, and very straight; *leaves* alternate, crowded, oblong, acute, entire or nearly so, and so far decurrent at the base that the stem appears winged. *Inflorescence* a simple, dense, terminal, cylindrical spike, from 1 to 2 feet in length. *Flowers* ephemeral, closing during sunshine. *Calyx* 5-parted; *lobes* lanceolate, acute. *Corolla* open or concave, somewhat rotate, the tube scarcely apparent; *lobes* 5, broad, acute, nearly equal. *Stamens* 5; *filaments* curved, the lower two longest and naked, the lateral pair longer than the upper one, and the latter three bearded; *anthers* 5, 1-celled by confluence. *Style* cylindrical, curved; *stigma* capitate, or merely a stigmatose dilation of the apex of the style. *Pod* globular, septicidally 2-valved; *valves* 2-cleft; *seeds* numerous, wrinkled.

Scrophulariaceæ.—This large family of herbs, or rarely small shrubs and trees, is noted for its many narcotic-poisonous species. In its general character it bears some resemblance to the Labiateæ, but is separated from that order by many intervening families. It is characterized as follows: *Leaves* either opposite or alternate, sometimes whorled; *stipules* none. *Inflorescence* various; *primary* centripetal; *secondary* centrifugal when present; *flowers* perfect, more or less irregular and bilabiate; *calyx* and *corolla* 5-merous, the former persistent, the latter personate; sometimes, however, they are 4-merous, but all four stamens are not always present, and in one genus (*Synthyris*) the corolla is entirely wanting. *Stamens* didynamous or diandrous, rarely 5 and perfect (*Verbascum*), when any are abortive it is usually the superior one; *filaments* inserted upon the tube of the corolla. *Ovary* 2-celled; *placentæ* axial; *ovules* several to numerous, rarely one,

---

[*] Altered from *Barbascum*, the old Latin name, signifying the bearded pubescence.

ℰ.𝔪.ad nat del.et pinxt.

VERBÁSCUM THÁPSUS , Linn.

anatropous or amphitropous; *style* single and undivided; *stigma* usually entire, sometimes 2-lobed or 2-lipped. *Fruit* generally capsular, 2-celled. *Seeds* small, rarely winged; *embryo* usually small and straight; *albumen* copious, sarcous.

Beside the six genera represented in this work, we have provings of two important members of this Order, viz.: the European Fox-glove (*Digitalis purpurea*, Linn.), remarkable for its accumulative power in the system, and its action upon the heart; and the European Hedge Hyssop (*Gratiola officinalis*, Linn.), whose active principle so nearly resembles that of Veratrum.

The following species are more or less noted in medical literature as secondary plants: the tropical Indian anti-rheumatic *Herpestes Monniera*, H.B.K.; the Peruvian tonic and febrifuge *Tumpu* (*Calceolaria trifida*, Vahl.), and emetic and purgative *C. pinnata*, Linn.; the Guayanian Bitter Blain (*Vandellia diffusa*, Linn.), highly valued by the natives as an emetic and purgative in malignant fever and dysentery; and the Malabar specific for gonorrhœa, *Torenia Asiatica*, Linn. Several other species of *Digitalis* are said to possess the full action of *D. purpurea*, among which the following are prominent: The Swiss *Digitalis ambigua*, Murr.; the Levantine *D. orientalis*, Lam.; the German *D. purpurascens*, Roth.; and the Italian *D. ferruginea*, Linn. The European Water-Betony (*Scrophularia aquatica*, Linn.) is noted in France as the *herbe du siége*, from its having been the sole support at one time of the garrison of Rochelle during the celebrated siege by Cardinal Richelieu in 1628.

History and Habitat.—The common Mullein is a native of the Isle of Thapsos, now found in most parts of Europe. In North America it has become thoroughly naturalized, principally though, in the Eastern United States, where it frequents waste grounds and dry fields. It flowers throughout the summer months, its fruit being fully ripe in October.

Verbascum has been known as a medical plant from ancient times. The Φλόμος of Hippocrates and other ancient writers is supposed to be this species, though Sibthorp states that it is the male Λευχη φλόμος; Sprengel judges that the emale is the mullein and the male the *V. undulatum*.*

The principal use of this herb in medicine has been as an anodyne-pectoral, and remedy for catarrhal coughs and diarrhœas. Dr. Home† concludes upon trial that it " is useful in diminishing or stopping diarrhœa of an old standing, and often in easing the pains of the intestines." Rafinesque‡ sums up its uses as follows: "Leaves soft, like velvet; equal to flannel in rheumatism for frictions; formerly thought to cure agues; emollient in poultice; good discutient to reduce swelled and contracted sinews. Tea sub-astringent, bitterish, used for diarrhœa; strong decoction in wash for piles, scalds, and wounds of cattle. Blossoms better than leaves, anodyne, antispasmodic, repellant, pectoral, make a perfumed tea useful for coughs, hemoptysis, hemorrhage and proctalgy." The flowers placed in a bottle and set in the sunshine are said to yield a fatty matter valuable as a cure for hemorrhoids. The plant is just now being introduced as a valuable

---

* Hamilton, *Flora Hom.*, II., 218. † Woodville, *Med. Bot.*, II., 203. ‡ *Med. Flora*, II., 273.

remedy in pulmonary phthisis, articles appearing from time to time in various medical and scientific periodicals upon this point. Dr. F. J. B. Quinlan regards the plant as having a distinct weight-increasing power in early cases of pulmonary consumption. The hot decoction, he claims, causes a comfortable sensation, which, patients who have taken it, experience a decided physiological need of. " It eases phthisical cough, some patients scarcely requiring cough medicines at all " who use this remedy. "Its power of checking phthisical looseness is very marked, and it also gives great relief to the dyspnœa. It is, however, useless in advanced cases, and has no effect in checking night sweats."* The leaves are considered to be diuretic, demulcent, anti-spasmodic, and anodyne; and the seeds are said to pass readily and rapidly through the intestinal canal, thus proving useful for the removal of obstructions.

Verbascum plays no part in the U. S. Ph.; in the Eclectic Materia Medica its preparation is *Cataplasma Verbasci.*

PART USED AND PREPARATION.—The fresh plant, gathered in July, when coming into blossom, should be chopped and pounded to a pulp and weighed. Then two parts by weight of alcohol are taken, the pulp thoroughly mixed with one-sixth part of it, and the rest of the alcohol added. After having stirred the whole well, pour it into a closely-stoppered bottle, and allow it to stand eight days in a dark, cool place. The tincture separated by filtration should be opaque, in thin layers it has a deep reddish-brown color by transmitted light. It should have a sweetish, herbaceous odor, a smoothish astringent taste, and decided acid reaction.

CHEMICAL CONSTITUENTS.—An analysis of the flowers by Morin yielded a yellow volatile oil, a fatty acid, free malic and phosphoric acids and their -ate salts of lime, a yellow resinous coloring matter, and the general plant constituents, including an uncrystallizable sugar. The leaves contain mucilage.

PHYSIOLOGICAL ACTION.—Many of the symptoms caused by from 30 to 40 ounces of a tincture of the fresh leaves daily, are characteristic of the action of this drug. In Hahnemann's experiments the following prominent effects are noted; Vertigo on pressing the left cheek with the hand; dull pressure at the left infra-maxillary condyle, with painful tearing and drawing in the ear; sensation as if the temporal eminences were crushed with pincers;† numbness in the left ear, with a sensation as if the ear would be drawn inward; severe drawing, pressure, and numbness of the left malar bone, temple and zygoma; root of tongue coated brown; urging to urinate, with decreased secretion; constrictive and pressive pains in the bones and muscles, and weakness of the lower limbs. The action of

---

* *Am. Jour. Phar.*, 1883, 268; from *Brit. Med. Jour.*

† I judge from my own experiments with plants, that the pains similar to crushing of bones with excruciating tearing sensation, is due to the Malic acid contained in them. I have never noted the symptom as arising from experiments with drugs not containing this body. The minor symptoms of disinclination to work, sleepiness after dinner, general shiftlessness, etc., of Verbascum arose also in my experimentation with the *Sheep sorrel* (*Oxalis stricta*, Linn.), which contains Malic among other vegetable acids.

Verbascum seems to be a somewhat peculiar irritation of the temporo-facial branch of the seventh pair of cranial nerves and a somewhat narcotic action upon the brain.

Hahnemann observes that the narcotic effects of the drug wore off in about two hours in his experiments. The seeds of Verbascum Lychnitis and Thapsus have often been employed to stupefy fish.

DESCRIPTION OF PLATE 110.

1. Upper portion of a young plant, Pamrapo, N. J., June 29th, 1879.
2. Flower.
3. Pistil.
4. Anther of beardless stamen.
5. Bearded stamen.
6. Pollen, x 2 50.
7. A portion of the root.

(3-5 enlarged.)

111

LINARIA.

TOAD FLAX.

SYN.—LINARIA VULGARIS, MILL.; ANTIRRHINUM LINARIA, LINN.

COM. NAMES.—TOAD FLAX, FALSE FLAX, YELLOW FLAX, RANSTED, JACOB'S LADDER, CONTINENTAL WEED, BUTTER AND EGGS; (GER.) FRAUENFLACHS, LEINKRAÜT, LOWENMAUL; (FR.) LINAIRE COMMUNE.

A TINCTURE OF THE FRESH PLANT LINARIA VULGARIS, MILL.

Description.—This too-common roadside weed grows to a height of from 1 to 3 feet, from a perennial root. *Root* woody, creeping, white and fibrous. *Stem* erect and simple. *Leaves* pale green, glaucous, arranged alternately, or more or less scattered or whorled upon the stem; sesile, linear-lanceolate, with an acute tip, and vary from 1 to 3 inches in length. *Inflorescence*, a terminal, densely-flowered, spiked raceme; flowers 1 inch long, bright yellow, with a chrome-colored palate. *Calyx* five-parted, shorter than the spur of the corolla. *Corolla* tubular, masked with a projecting, bifid palate, that nearly closes the ringent throat. *Upper lip* two-cleft. *Lower lip* trifid, the middle lobe smallest. *Spur* awl-shaped, situated upon the lower side of the base. *Stamens* four, didynamous. *Anthers* two-celled. *Pollen* grains oval, with a deep sulcus and induplicate edges. *Fruit* a thin, two-celled ovoid capsule, opening by two slits below the apex. *Seeds* numerous, flattened, with a nearly complete winged margin. For description of the natural order Scrophulariaceæ, see Verbascum Thapsus, 110.

History and Habitat.—This pernicious, widely-spreading weed, doubtless has its origin in Europe. It is now but too thoroughly naturalized here; its injurious-ness, flowever, being somewhat mitigated by its choice of ground, growing as it does only in waste places, dry sandy fields, and along the embankment of rail-roads and roadways. It blossoms through the summer months, fruiting as it flowers. Linnæus states (*Flor. Suec.*) that a decoction of this plant in milk was used as a fly poison. Its previous medical uses were internally for jaundice and anasarca, and externally for hemorrhoids, but it has dropped out of use entirely, except with us.

PART USED AND PREPARATION.—The whole fresh plant, gathered when in full flower, is chopped and pounded to a pulp and weighed. Then two parts by weight of alcohol are taken, the pulp mixed thoroughly with one-sixth part of it and the rest of the alcohol added. The whole is then poured into a well-stop-

---

* The leaves of some species resembling those of flax (*Linum*).

pered bottle and allowed to stand for eight days in a dark, cool place. The tincture is then separated by straining and filtering. Thus prepared, it has a very deep brownish-red color by transmitted light, a taste at first cooling and sour, then like weak tea, and a very acid reaction.

CHEMICAL CONSTITUENTS.—I am unable to find any chemical data regarding this plant, with the exception of the flowers; they have been analyzed, but show nothing of the active principle, which probably lies in its acid.

PHYSIOLOGICAL ACTION.—The true action, physiologically, of this plant is not known. The provings have been carefully made, and show symptoms of some importance, but are not sufficient to determine its sphere.

DESCRIPTION OF PLATE 111.

1. Upper part of a plant from W. Brighton, S. I., July 5th, 1879.
      2–4. Flowers.
      3. Section of flower.
      5. Root.
      6. Pollen x 380.
      7. Seed (enlarged).

Œ.m. . ad nat del. et pinxt.

LINÀRIA VULGÀRIS, Mill.

GENUS.—**SCROPHULARIA,*** TOURN.

112
SCROPHULARIA.

FIG-WORT.

SYN.—SCROPHULARIA NODOSA, LINN.; SCROPHULARIA MARILAND-
ICA, LINN.; SCROPHULARIA NODOSA, VAR. AMERICANA, MICHX.;
SCROPHULARIA LANCEOLATA, PURSH.

COM. NAMES.—FIG-WORT, SCROFULA-PLANT, HEAL-ALL, HOLMES-
WEED, SQUARE-STALK, CARPENTER'S SQUARE; (FR.) SCROPHU-
LAIRE; (GER.) KROPFWURZ, SCROPHELNPFLANZE.

A TINCTURE OF THE WHOLE FRESH PLANT SCROPHULARIA NODOSA, LINN.,
OR VAR. MARILANDICA, GRAY, OR BOTH.

Description.—This rank perennial herb grows to a height of from 2 to 4 feet. *Stem* clearly quadrilateral, with slight obtuse ridges at the angles, glabrous through-out. *Leaves* opposite, ranging from oval below to lanceolate above, doubly serrate, and cordate or nearly so at the base. *Inflorescence* a primarily nodding terminal panicle, of loose, 3 to 6-flowered cymes; *flowers* small, lurid, brownish- or greenish-purple. *Calyx* deeply 5-cleft into ovate, equal lobes. *Corolla* globose, contracted at the throat, and furnished with a two-lipped border; *petals* 5, the *upper lip* of two erect, equal lobes, the *lower lip* composed of a lateral equal pair, shorter however than those of the upper, and a lower reflexed, spreading lobe, closely appressed to the tube. *Stamens* 4, curled inward with the anthers closely sur-rounding the ovary; they become erect when ripening, and finally decline. The rudiment of a fifth stamen forms a protuberance at the summit and in the throat of the corolla-tube. *Filaments* pubescent, broader above than below; *anthers* with two confluent cells, opening transversely at the apex. *Fruit* a 2-celled, ovoid, septicidal, many-seeded pod; *seeds* black, rough, and dotted with minute pits. Read description of the N. Order under Verbascum, 110.

History and Habitat.—The Fig-wort grows along the borders of woods and dry roadsides, from Utah eastward throughout the United States and Canada, flowering from June to September. The European *Scrophularia nodosa* and our *var. Marilandica* seem to differ but slightly in their parts and properties from the species under consideration. This herb is said to serve as a soothing poultice to inflamed tumors, suppurating mammæ, ulcers, burns, hemorrhoids, etc.; it is also used alone and as a component of salves, for itch, various eruptions, and "scabs"

---

* On account of its repute in scrofula.

2

3   4   5   6

1

𝕮m.ad nat.del.et pinxt.   SCROPHULÀRIA NODÒSA, Linn.

in swine, as well as a tonic and deobstruent in hepatic and glandular disorders. All parts of the plant have a heavy, rank odor when bruised, resembling that of the elder (*Sambucus*).

Scrophularia is not mentioned in the U. S. Ph.; in the Eclectic Materia Medica it is official as *Decoctum Scrophulariæ*, and as a component of *Syrupus Rumecis Compositus*, and *Tinctura Corydalis Composita*.

PART USED AND PREPARATION.—The whole fresh plant, gathered just before flowering, should be chopped and pounded to a pulp and weighed. Then two parts by weight of alcohol should be taken, the pulp thoroughly mixed with one-sixth part of it, and the rest of the alcohol added. After having stirred the whole, pour it into a well-stoppered bottle and let it stand eight days in a dark, cool place. The tincture, separated by straining and filtering, should have a beautiful deep crimson color by transmitted sunlight, a rank, acrid odor and taste, and strong acid reaction.

CHEMICAL CONSTITUENTS.—SCROPHULARIN; this principle, the chemistry of which has not yet been determined, was extracted from a decoction of the fresh plant by Walz.* It crystallizes in bitter scales, soluble in both alcohol and water.

Scrophularosmin; this stearoptene was also discovered by Walz in an aqueous distillate of the plant.

Walz's analysis also yielded *acetic acid*, $C_2H_4O_2$; *propionic acid*, $C_3H_6O_2$; *pectin*, $C_{32}H_{48}O_{32}$; and a red *coloring matter*.

PHYSIOLOGICAL ACTION.—According to Dr. Blakely,† this drug, in repeated doses of from 20 drops to a teaspoonful of the tincture, causes: Fullness of the head, and vertigo; free bleeding of the gums; salivation; increased appetite; colic; general weariness; sleepiness; and sallow skin.

In this experimenter the drug seemed to expend its force upon the liver.

DESCRIPTION OF PLATE 112.

1. Panicle.
2. Second pair of leaves from panicle.
3. Flower, under side.
4. Corolla opened to show sexual organs.
5. Ripe stamen (enlarged).
6. Pollen, x 250.

Binghamton, N. Y., June 8th, 1884.

---

* Mayer in Am. Jour. Phar., 1863, p. 295.

† N. A. Jour. Hom., 1866, p. 187.

113

CHELONE GLABRA.

TURTLE-HEAD.

SYN.—CHELONE GLABRA, LINN.; CHELONE OBLIQUA, LINN.

COM. NAMES.—TURTLE-HEAD, SNAKE-HEAD, SHELL-FLOWER, BAL-
MONY, SALT-RHEUM WEED; (FR.) CHELONE; (GER.) GLATTE,
CHELONE.

A TINCTURE OF THE FRESH PLANT CHELONE GLABRA, LINN.

Description.—This beautiful swamp herb grows to a height of from 2 to 6 feet, from a creeping perennial root. The *stem* is smooth, upright, somewhat obtusely four angled, and branching laterally, particularly near the top. It is a question though, whether it is really a branching herb, or whether the so-called branches are merely elongated peduncles of the lateral axillary flower spikes. The *leaves* are opposite, either sessile or very short petiolate, broadly lanceolate, serrate and pointed, ranging from 2 to 4 inches in length and of various breadths. The *inflorescence* consists of a dense, bracted spike, terminal upon the stem and its branches?; the flowers are sessile, closely imbricated with concave, rounded-ovate, sharp-pointed bracts and bractlets. *Calyx* of five deeply parted or distinct imbricated sepals. *Corolla* tubular, with either equal or unequal lateral inflations, the mouth either a little open or widely gaping; *upper lip* broad-arching, keeled in the middle, and either entire or notched at the apex; *lower lip* 3-lobed at the apex, the middle lobe narrow or sometimes smallest. *Stamens* consisting of four didynamous, included, fertile or complete ones and one sterile or rudimentary; *filaments* flat, woolly, the rudimentary fifth much smaller than the other four; *anthers* heart-shaped, acuminate, completely connected in pairs by the adhesive cottony wool; *pollen* more or less cylindrically "hat-shaped," the sulcus being between the crown and the rim. *Pistil* as a whole, projecting beyond the stamens; *ovary* 2-celled, ovoid; *style* long, slender and cylindrical; *stigma* small and blunt. *Fruit* a 2-grooved, 2-celled ovoid capsule, opening by dehiscence through the partition, each half carrying a section with it bearing the placentæ. *Seeds* numerous, winged and margined. A description of the natural order may be found under Verbuscum thapsus, 110.

---

* χελώνη, tortoise, from the resemblance of the corolla to the head of that reptile.

History and Habitat.—This strikingly erect plant, native of Canada and the United States, grows—though not in great abundance in any one locality—about the margins of swampy places and along the wet edges of open woods, flowering from August to September. The flowers are large and without odor, they vary from white to cream, rose or purplish; varieties have been at different times named both on account of the color of the flowers and the mode of growth, but they are too indistinctly separate to afford a place and name. *C. alba; C. rosea; C. purpurea; C. lanceolata;* and *C. obliqua.*

Balmony has for years been a favorite tonic, laxative and purgative, among the aborigines of North America and Thomsonian physicians; without sufficient reason however as a tonic, in the doses usually employed.

Chelone has no place in the U. S. Ph. In the Eclectic Materia Medica it is officinal as *Decoctum Chelonis.*

PART USED, AND PREPARATION.—The fresh herb as a whole, is chopped and pounded to a pulp and weighed. Then two parts by weight of alcohol are taken, the pulp mixed with one-sixth part of it, and the rest of the alcohol added. After thorough stirring, and pouring the whole into a well-stoppered bottle, it is allowed to stand eight days in a dark, cool place. The tincture is then separated by straining and filtering. Thus prepared, it has a clear orange-brown color by transmitted light, a bitter taste and highly acid reaction.

CHEMICAL CONSTITUENTS.—No analysis has been made of this plant; all parts of it are very bitter, and as it yields this property to alcohol and water, we may consider at least, that the active body is soluble in these liquids.

DESCRIPTION OF PLATE 113.

1. Whole plant five times reduced, from Binghamton, N. Y., August 15th, 1882.
   2. Apex of stem in flower.
   3. Pistil (enlarged).
   4. Fertile stamen (enlarged).
   5. Rudimentary stamen (enlarged).
   6. Pollen x 380.

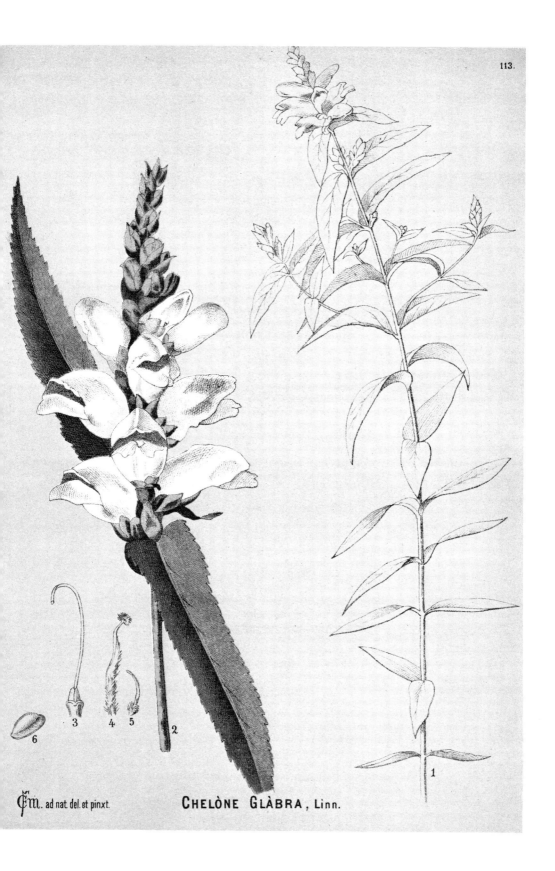

1 2 3 4 5 6

Cm. ad nat. del. et pinxt.   CHELÒNE GLÀBRA, Linn.

114

LEPTANDRA.

CULVER'S PHYSIC.

SYN.—VERONICA VIRGINICA, LINN.; V. PURPUREA, STEUD.; V. SIBI-
RICA, LINN.; V. JAPONICA, STEUD.; LEPTANDRA VIRGINICA, NUTT.;
PÆDEROTA VIRGINICA, TORR.; CALLISTACHYA VIRGINICA, AND
EUSTACHYA ALBA, RAF.
COM. NAMES.—CULVER'S ROOT OR PHYSIC, BLACK ROOT, TALL SPEED-
WELL, HIGH VERONICA. WHORLY WORT, QUINTEL, HINI; (FR.)
VERONIQUE DE VIRGINIE; (GER.) VIRGINISCHER EHRENPREIS.

A TINCTURE OF THE FRESH ROOT OF VERONICA VIRGINICA, LINN.

Description.—This graceful perennial herb grows to a height of from 1 to 7 feet. *Root* horizontal, blackish, sometimes branched, scarred upon its upper surface by the previous growths, and giving off from the nether numerous long and fibrous rootlets. *Stem* simple, strict, and glabrous. *Leaves* whorled in numerous clusters of from 3 to 9; short petioled, lanceolate, acute, tapering at both ends, finely serrate, and often downy beneath especially upon the veins. *Inflorescence* in from 1 to 9 terminal, panicled, spike-like, densely-flowered racemes; *flowers* small, nearly sessile; *bracts* very small, subulate. *Calyx* 4-parted, persistent; *sepals* lanceolate, acute. *Corolla* salver-form, pubescent within, the tube much longer than the 4-parted limb, and greatly exceeding the calyx; *lobes* erect, acute, the upper broadest, the lower narrowest. *Stamens* 2, far exserted; *filaments* hairy, inserted low down upon each side of the upper lobe of the corolla and about twice its length; *anthers* rather large, 2-celled; *cells* confluent at the apex. *Ovary* superior, 2-celled; *style* columnar, entire, exserted, persistent; *stigma* solitary, capitate. *Fruit* an oblong-ovate, 2-celled pod, not notched at the apex nor much flattened; *dehiscence* by 4 apical teeth, at length becoming somewhat loculicidal; *seeds* numerous, black, oval, and terete; *testa* minutely reticulated.

History and Habitat.—This most graceful and attractive of all American Veronicas, habits moist wooded banks from Canada and the valley of Winnipeg, to Georgia, Alabama, and Missouri. It blossoms contemporaneously with Cimicifuga early in July, and, when viewed at a distance, the two plants appear to be the same, while either has a beauty and grace which would render it poetically suitable for a fairy's wand. The species also grows in Japan and Eastern India, and varies

---

* Dedicated to St. Veronica; or, perhaps, a play upon Betonica.

somewhat in color of anther and perianth in different localities. Culver's Physic was introduced into English gardens in 1714, and has been somewhat planted in this country.

This is one of the many American Aboriginal remedies handed down by them to the botanics, and extensively, therefore, used in domestic practice from our earliest settlements. In a fresh state the root gained a great reputation as a drastic purge and abortivant, but its action was too uncertain and severe; in this state it was also frequently employed in intermittents, and was thought to be a prophylactic against future attacks. The use of the fresh drug has, however, almost ceased in general practice, giving place to the dried root, and an extrac-tive called *Leptandrin.* Doses of from 20 to 60 grains of the powdered root have been used as a stomachic tonic, laxative, and antiperiodic; in dyspepsia, torpidity of the liver, debilitated conditions of the alimentary tract, typhoid and intermittent fever, and some forms of dysentery and diarrhœa. Speaking of the drug in the light of sixty years ago, Rafinesque says:* "The root alone is medical; it is bitter and nauseous, and is commonly used in warm decoction as purgative and emetic, acting somewhat like the *Eupatorium* and *Verbena hastata;* some boil it in milk for a milder cathartic, or as a sudorific in pleurisy. A strong decoction of the fresh root is a violent and disagreeable, but effectual and popular remedy in the Western States, for the summer bilious fevers."

The officinal preparations of the U. S. Phar. are: *Extractum Leptandræ* and *Extractum Leptandræ Fluidum.* In the Eclectic Materia Medica the same preparations are recommended, and the following also advised: *Extractum Leptandræ Hydroalcoholicum* and *Tinctura Leptandræ.*

PART USED AND PREPARATION.—The fresh root of the second year, gathered after fruition, should be chopped and pounded to a pulp and weighed. Then two parts by weight of alcohol are to be taken, the pulp thoroughly mixed with one-sixth part of it, and the rest of the alcohol added. After stirring the whole well, transfer it to a well-stoppered bottle, and allow it to macerate eight days in a dark, cool place, shaking twice a day.

The tincture, prepared from this mass by pressing and filtering, has a deep reddish-orange color by transmitted light; a somewhat earthy odor; no characteristic taste; and an acid reaction.

CHEMICAL CONSTITUENTS.—*Leptandrine.*† This bitter principle, separated by Wayne,‡ retains the characteristic odor of the root. It is crystallizable when free from coloring-matter, and is soluble in water, alcohol, and ether.

Tannin, gum, resin, volatile oil, and mannite,§ a volatile alkaloid, citric acid, and a saponin-like body having a glucosidal nature,‖ have also been determined.

---

* *Med. Flora*, 2, 22.
† This name is proposed, that the substance may not be confounded with "*Leptandrin*," the extract of the tincture now on the market.
‡ *Proc. Am. Phar. Assoc.*, 1856, 34.
§ Wayne, *Am. Jour. Phar.*, 1859, 557.
‖ Mayer, *Am. Jour. Phar.*, 1863, 298.

PHYSIOLOGICAL ACTION.—Full doses of the recent root of Leptandra cause dimness of vision, vertigo, vomiting, and purging of bloody or black, tarry, papescent feces. Dr. Burt's experiments with from 1 to 40 grains "Leptandrin" and 20 to 160 drops of the fluid extract gave the following symptoms: Headache, smarting of the eyes and lachrymation; yellow-coated tongue; nausea, burning and distress in the stomach; severe abdominal pains with great desire for stool; profuse black, fetid discharges from the bowels; general lassitude; hot, dry skin; and sleepiness,

Leptandra proves itself to be a severe irritant to the gastric and intestinal mucous surfaces, and a stimulant to the absorbent system.

DESCRIPTION OF PLATE 114.

1. Whole plant, 6 times reduced, Binghamton, N. Y., July 27th, 1885.
2. Summit of single-racemed plant.
3. Third whorl of leaves from top of No. 1.
4. Limb of corolla.
5. Flower.
6. Calyx and pistil.
7. Stamen.
8. Anther.
9. Bract and calyx.
10. Fruit.
11. Horizontal section of ovary.
12. Seed.

(4–12 enlarged.)

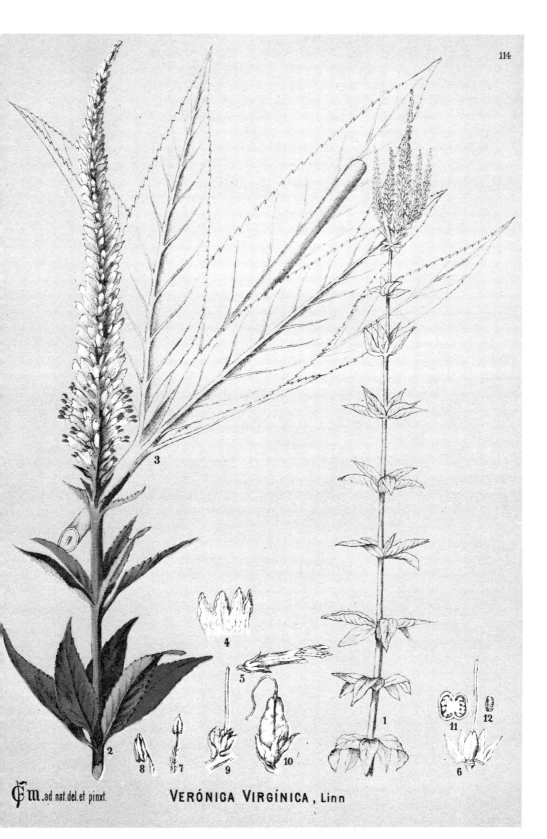

Cm.ad nat.del.et pinxt.

VERÓNICA VIRGÍNICA, Linn

Tribe.—EUPHRASIEÆ.

GENUS.—**EUPHRASIA**,* TOURN.

SEX. SYST.—DIDYNAMIA ANGIOSPERMIA.

115

EUPHRASIA.

EYEBRIGHT.

SYN.—EUPHRASIA OFFICINALIS, LINN.; E. CANDIDA, SCHŒN.; EUPHRA-
GIA ALBA, BRUN.

COM. NAMES.—EYEBRIGHT, EUPHRASY; (FR.) EUPHRAISE; (GER.) AUGEN-
TROST.

A TINCTURE OF THE HERB EUPHRASIA OFFICINALIS, LINN.

Description.—This low annual only grows to a height of a few inches. *Stem* erect, hairy; *branches* opposite. *Leaves* opposite, varying from roundish-ovate to oblong; *margin* incisely dentate, that of the upper or floral leaves with strongly setaceous teeth; in the lower leaves tending more to crenate. *Inflorescence* spicate; *bracteoles* none; *flowers* small, whitish. *Calyx* tubular-campanulate, 4-cleft; *lobes* acute, pointed. *Corolla* purple-striped, dilated at the throat, bilabiate, the lips subequal; *upper lip* erect, barely concave, 2-lobed, the sides revolute; *lobes* emarginate; *lower lip* external in the bud, spreading, 3-lobed; *lobes* emarginate, the middle one largest and yellow. *Stamens* 4, didynamous, rising under the upper lip of the corolla; *anthers* 2-celled; *cells* equal, distinct, each mucronate at its base. *Style* filiform; *stigma* entire. *Fruit* an oblong, flattened, loculicidal capsule; *seeds* numerous, pendulous, oblong, and longitudinally sulcate.

History and Habitat.—Euphrasia is indigenous to Europe and North America. With us its growth is depauperate and its stations few. It ranges, here, from the north-eastern coast of Maine over the alpine summits of the White Mountains and Adirondacks; thence northward and westward along the upper shore of Lake Superior to the Aleutian Islands. In many of these locations a dwarf form, with very small flowers, is found. It flowers in July and August.

Though this herb has always been known under a name of Greek originl still no mention of the plant is made by Dioscorides, Pliny, Galen, or even by the Arabian physicians. F. Bauhin says that it was known as a remedy for the eyes about the year 1380.† Arnoldus Villanovanus, who died in 1313, was the author of *" Vini Euphrasiati tantopere celebrati."* How long before him Euphrasia was in repute for eye diseases, is impossible to say; but in Gordon's *" Liticium Medi-cinæ,"* published in 1305, among the medicines for the eyes Euphragia is one, and is recommended both outwardly in a compound, distilled water, and inwardly as a

---

* Εὐφρασία, *euphrasia*, cheerfulness; as to its effect upon the spirits through its benefit to the sight.
† *Phytop.*, 442

syrup.* Euphragia is not mentioned in the *Schola Salernitana*, compiled about 1100. The earliest notice of Euphrasia, as a medicine, is in the works of Tragus.† It was employed as a remedy in diseases of the eyes, by Fuschius, Dodonæus, Haller, and others, and has been a vulgar remedy in these diseases from time immemorial, throughout the whole of Europe. Fuschius recommended it in suffusions and cataracts. The Highlanders, of Scotland, make an infusion of it in milk, and anoint the patient's eyes with a feather dipped in it. Hoffman employed it in jaundice; Villanova and Velebt, in weakness of the eyes. In 1836, Kramehfeld‡ employed it, with success, in rheumatic and catarrhal inflammation of the eyes and their lids; in cough, hoarseness, earache, and headache, which have succeeded catarrhal affections; and glandulous, catarrhal, and scrofulous blepharophthalmia.§

Woodville says:|| " Euphrasia derives its name from its reputed efficacy in various disorders of the eyes, for which it was used both externally and internally, and has long been so much celebrated as to be considered almost in the character of a specific, the '*verum oculorum solamen.*' But as there cannot possibly be a general remedy for all diseases of the eyes, the absurd and indiscriminate recommendation of Euphrasia as such, must receive but little credit from those who practice medicine on rational principles. It must be acknowledged, however, that some authors have stated peculiar complaints of the eyes, in which the use of this plant was thought more remarkably evident; and, judging by these, we should say that eyes, weakened by long-continued exertion, and those that are dim and watery, as in a senile state, are the cases in which Euphrasia promises most advantage; nor are old people to despair, for according to Hildanus and Lanzonus, several, at the age of seventy and eighty years, were recovered from almost entire blindness." He further remarks that the Icelanders are in the constant habit of using the juice of the plant in all affections of the eyes; and adds that, "though the great reputation which Eyebright formerly supported for several ages, must have induced some practitioners to have used it; yet we do not find a single instance of its efficacy recorded in modern times. How far this remark ought to invalidate the positive testimonies in its favor, we leave others to determine."

Dr. John King remarks¶ that four fluid ounces of the infusion morning and night, upon an empty stomach, has cured epilepsy.

PART USED AND PREPARATION. — The whole fresh flowering plant, above the root, gathered from barren, sunny spots, should be treated as directed for Verbascum, Scrophularia, and Chelone (*ante,* pp. 110–2, 112–2, 113–2). The resulting tincture has a deep brownish-red color by transmitted light; a pleasant, vinous odor; a bitter, astringent taste; and an acid reaction.

CHEMICAL CONSTITUENTS.—*Euphrasia-Tannic Acid*, $C_{32}H_{40}O_{17}$. — This peculiar tannin gives a dark-green precipitate with ferric salts, and is only obtainable by combination with lead. It is precipitable by glue, and tartrate of antimony (Wittstein).

---

* Allston, *Mat. Med.,* 7, 139.   ‡ *Ozann's Journal.* || *Med. Bot.,* 2, 369.
† Sprengel, *op. cit.*   § Hamilton, *Flor. Hom.,* 1, 275.   ¶ *Am. Disp., loc. cit.*

The volatile oil, and acrid and bitter principle, have not as yet been chemically analyzed.

PHYSIOLOGICAL ACTION.—The symptoms caused by doses varying from 10 to 60 drops of the tincture, observed by several German experimenters,* were substantially as follows: Confusion of the mind and cephalalgia; violent pressure in the eyes with lachrymation and itching, redness and swelling of the margins of the lids, violent burning of the lids, dimness of vision, sensation as though the eye were covered with mucus; weakness, and photophobia; sneezing and fluent coryza; odontalgia; nausea; constipation; hoarseness, violent cough, with profuse expectoration, and difficult breathing; yawning and sleeplessness; profuse secretion of urine; and sweat.

DESCRIPTION OF PLATE 115.

1. Whole plant, once enlarged, Kearsarge, N. H., July 24th, 1883.
2. Calyx.
3. Flower.
4. Stamen.
5. Seed.
(2–5 enlarged.)

---

* See *Allen's Encyc.*, 4, 254.

2

3

4

5

€.m. ad nat del.et pinxt.

EUPHRÀSIA OFFICINÀLIS, Linn.

Tribe.—SATUREIÆ.

GENUS.—**MENTHA**,* LINN.

SEX. SYST.—DIDYNAMIA GYMNOSPERMIA.

116
MENTHA PIPERITA.

PEPPERMINT.

SYN.—MENTHA PIPERITA, SMITH, VAR. OFFICINALIS, KOCH; M. VIRIDI-AQUATICA, SHULTZ; M. OFFICINALIS AND HIRCINA, HULL; M. PALUS-TRIS, RAII.

COM. NAMES.—PEPPERMINT; (FR.) MENTHE POIVREE; (GER.) PFEFFER-MÜNZE.

A TINCTURE OF THE WHOLE PLANT MENTHA PIPERITA.

Description. — This glabrous or somewhat hairy, pungent, perennial herb, grows to a height of from 1 to 2 feet. *Rootstock* creeping, spreading, and multi-plying; *stem* suberect. *Leaves* ovate-oblong to oblong-lanceolate, sharply serrate, acute, and rounded at the base; *petioles* distinct. *Inflorescence* in numerously glomeruled, terminal and superaxillary, leafless, and at last interrupted, ovate spikes; *flowers* small, distinctly pedicellate; *bracts* hispid, mostly longer than the verticillasters, the upper linear. *Calyx* campanulate, naked in the throat; *limb* 5-toothed; *teeth* hispid. *Corolla* 4-lobed, hardly irregular, except that the upper lobe, though never galeate nor concave, is broader than the others and emarginate; *tube* short, inclined. *Stamens* 4, included, similar and nearly equal, erect, straight, and distant; *anthers* 2-celled; *cells* parallel, without a thickened connective. *Style* long, exserted.

Labiatæ. — This large family of square-stalked aromatic herbs, and low shrubs, represented in North America by 50 genera, comprising 231 species and 45 recognized varieties, is characterized as follows: *Stems* square; *leaves* opposite, or sometimes verticillate, simple, and usually dotted with immersed glands filled with volatile oil; *stipules* none. *Inflorescence* thyrsoidal; the general evolution of the clusters in the axils of leaves or primary bracts centripetal; that of the cymes or glomerules centrifugal; the leaves being opposite and the clusters nearly or quite sessile, a whorl-like appearance is made (verticillaster); *flowers* perfect; *hypogynous disk* usually present, or represented by 1 or 4 gland-like lobes. *Calyx* tubular, gamosepalous. *Corolla* irregular and more or less bilabiate; *lobes* imbri-cated in the bud, the posterior or upper exterior, the middle lower innermost. *Stamens* didynamous or diandrous, borne upon the tube of the corolla, distinct or

---

* Μίνθη, *Minthe,* daughter of Cocytus, whom, through jealousy, Proserpine changed into one of these plants.

rarely monadelphous ; the fifth, or anterior, and in diandrous species the adjacent pair also, rudimentary or sterile ; rarely the four fertile stamens are equal. *Pistil* dimerous, each carpel deeply 2-parted or lobed ; *ovary* 4-parted or lobed ; *lobes* uniovulate ; *ovul s* mostly amphitropous or anatropous and erect ; *style* filiform, mostly 2-cleft and 2-stigmatose at the apex. *Fruit* 4 akene-like nutlets, surrounding the base of the stigma, in the bottom of the persistent calyx ; *nutlets* smooth or barely roughish. *Embryo* straight except in *Scutellarineæ* ; *cotyledons* plane or plano-convex ; *radicle* inferior ; *albumen* slight or none.

The proven plants of this order, besides the six treated of in this work, are : the Mediterranean Germander (*Teucrium Marum*, Linn.), a noted feline aphrodisiac ; the European, West Asiatic, and North African Pennyroyal (*Mentha pulegium*, Linn.), which is deemed emmenagogue, and antispasmodic ; the South American Alfavaca (*Ocimum canum*, D. C.), which is used, in Brazil, as a sudorific, especially in diseases of the kidneys, bladder, and urethra ; the East Indian *Ocimum Basilicum*, Linn., used by the natives as a palliative for the pains of parturition ; Sweet Marjoram (*Origanum Marjorana*, Linn.), a cultivated form of *O. vulgare ;* the Cape *Plectranthus fruticosus*, L. Herit. ; the Mediterranean Rosemary (*Rosmarinus officinalis*, Linn.), an antihysteric and emmenagogue ; and the European and Siberian Betony (*Stachys Betonica*, Benth.), a sternutatory, emetic and purgative.

A large number of species of this order have figured, more or less, in general and domestic practice, as stimulant, antispasmodic, carminatives, and jucunda for unpleasant drugs. A few of them only will be mentioned here, that the order may be well understood. The European, Asiatic, and African Lavender (*Lavendula vera*, D. C.), a carminative, antihysteric, and antiflatulent. The European Spearmint (*Mentha viridis*, Linn.), which is also considered stomachic ; the European, Asiatic, and African Marjoram (*Origanum vulgare*, Linn.), a mild tonic, diaphoretic, and emmenagogue ; and the Mediterranean Thyme (*Thymus vulgaris*, Linn.), lauded as a local stimulant and rubefacient, in carious teeth, rheumatism, sprains, etc. The leaves of the Mediterranean Sage (*Salvia officinalis*, Linn.), are well known as a light, bitter tonic, anti-emetic, diaphoretic, and astringent. The American Horsemint (*Monarda punctata*, Linn.), is considered diaphoretic, emmenagogue, diuretic, and rubefacient. The European and West Asiatic Catmint, or Catnip (*Nepeta Cataria*, Linn.), so well known in all country households, has been used, from time without date, as a stimulant, antispasmodic, and emmenagogue, in chlorosis, amenorrhœa, and various low type female disorders. Like Marum Verum it is a feline aphrodisiac. The European Horehound (*Marubium vulgare*, Linn.), is diaphoretic, diuretic, pectoral, and emmenagogue, and much used in confections, for asthma, phthisis, tussis, night-sweats, as well as in uterine and visceral affections. The South European Hyssop (*Hyssopus officinalis*, Linn.) ; Balm (*Melissa officinalis*, Linn.) ; Summer and Winter Savories (*Satureia hortensis*, and *montana*, Linn.) ; and Dittany of Crete (*Origanum Dictamnus*, Linn.), are all considered antiflatulent, antihysteric, antispasmodic, emmenagogue, etc., and are used in chlorosis, amenorrhœa, hypochondriasis, and kindred affections. The

European and Asiatic Motherwort (*Leonurus Cardiaca*, Linn.), which has but lately been brought before us, as Homœopaths, has been esteemed much, as the above species, beside being valued in Russia, as a remedy in rabies. The East Indian *Anisomeles Malabarica*, R. Br., is an excellent diaphoretic. The American Dittany (*Cunila mariana*, Linn.), was used, by the Aborigines, as an antiperiodic and alexiteric. The genus *Ocimum* furnishes plants of various properties; the Sierra Leone *viride*, Willd., and Indian *sanctum*, Linn., are febrifugal; the Japanese *crispus*, Thunb., antirheumatic, and the Indian *suave*, Willd., useful in infantile catarrh.

A number of the above species, and a multitude of others, are better known to the housewife and perfumer than to us as physicians.

History and Habitat.—Peppermint is nowhere considered truly indigenous, though probably its native haunt is the basin of the Mediterranean. It grows as an escaped plant in all European countries, as it does with us, in ditches and along brooks; there is nothing to prove that it is not a cultivated variety of *M. viridis*, into which it is said to revert if not properly reset. It was first said to be found in England about the year 1700, by Dr. Eales. The cultivation of the plant was begun in Great Britain about 1750, and on the Continent in 1770; it was afterward quite extensively planted in Surrey, Cambridgeshire, Lincolnshire, and Hertfordshire, in England; Sens, in France; Cölleda, in Germany; and New York, Ohio, and Michigan, in the United States. The yield of oil, for which alone the plant is cultivated, is from .5 to 1.5 per cent. of the production (from 8 to 16 lbs. per acre); and the annual product of the world is estimated at about 90,000 lbs.*

Peppermint began its usefulness, in medicine, at about the same period of its cultivation, and was then considered specific in renal and vesical calculus, dyspepsia, and diarrhœa; being considered a stomachic, tonic, stimulant, antispasmodic, and carminative. It was found useful in bowel troubles, especially those associated with flatulency, colic, retching, vomiting, spasmodic actions, and hysteria. Its rubefacient action is intimately associated with what may be considered anodyne properties, when the trouble is neuralgic or rheumatoid, and the affected nerves or muscles are somewhat superficial. Facial and sciatic affections are greatly relieved by fomentations of the leaves, or rubbing the oil, or menthol, directly over the course of the nerve itself; the action is temporary, but decidedly happy.

The principal use of the essence or oil is as a flavoring for confections, and a jucund ingredient of prescriptions containing nauseous, and especially griping drugs.

The leaves and tops are officinal in the U. S. Ph., as well as *Spiritus Menthæ Piperitæ*, and *Vinum Aromaticum*.† In Eclectic practice, the preparations are: *Aqua Menthæ Piperitæ, Extractum Rhei Fluidum,‡ Infusum Mentha Piperitæ, Mistura Camphoræ Composita,§ Mistura Cajeputi Composita,‖ Oleum Menthæ Piperitæ, Pulvis Rhei Compositus,¶ Tinctura Olei Menthæ Piperitæ.*

---

* Todd, *Proc. Am. Pharm. Assoc.* 1876, 828.
† Lavender, Origanum, Peppermint, Rosemary, Sage, and Wormwood.
‡ Rhubarb and Peppermint.
§ Camphor, Opium, Peppermint, and Spearmint.
‖ Cajeput, Cloves, Peppermint, and Anise.
¶ Rhubarb, Bicarbonate Potash, and Peppermint.

PART USED AND PREPARATION.—The whole fresh, flowering plant is chopped and pounded to a pulp and weighed. Then two parts by weight of alcohol are taken, the pulp mixed thoroughly with one-sixth part of it, and the rest of the alcohol added. After stirring the whole well, and pouring it into a well-stoppered bottle, it is allowed to stand eight days in a dark, cool place.

The tincture, separated from this mass by pressure and filtration, should have a clear orange-brown color by transmitted light; retain the odor of the plant; have an oily feel; a bitterish, slightly astringent, mint-like taste; and an acid reaction.

CHEMICAL CONSTITUENTS.—*Oil of Peppermint.* This essential oil of the leaves is either colorless, pale yellow, or greenish, turning brown with age. It is liquid, has a sp. gr. of 0.84–0.92, boils at 188°–193° (370.4°–379.4° F.), has a strong, agreeable odor, and a powerful aromatic taste, at first biting, then cold, especially upon strong inhalation of air over the tongue; this effect is followed by a peculiar numbness characteristic of this product. The oil is soluble in water and in alcohol. It consists of a solid and liquid portion, and contains from 0.5 to 5 per cent. of a hydrocarbon ($C_{10}H_{18}$ + or — O), which is said to prevent the crystallization of menthol.

The oil of commerce is often adulterated with that of pennyroyal, with intent, or that of *Mentha arvensis, Erigeron Canadense,* or *Erechthites hieracifolia,* by carelessness. The tests for the oil are given by the *Oil and Drug News* as follows: On the addition to the oil of an equal part of a mixture of two parts chloral-hydrate, dissolved in one part of C. P. sulphuric acid and a drop or two of alcohol, a cherry-red coloration follows if the oil is pure; but, if pennyroyal is present, a dark olive-green color ensues; and D. Reagan says* that the pure oil is but slowly absorbed by blotting paper, but when the three plants above mentioned are mixed with it the absorption is rapid.

If the presence of the hydrocarbon above mentioned is very slight, the oil cooled to — 4 (+ 24. 8° F.) will deposit.

Pipmenthol,† $C_{10}H_{20}O$, a stearopten of the exquisite odor of Peppermint, composed of fine hexagonal crystals, melting at 36° (96.8° F.), and boiling at 210° (410° F.).‡

[*Menthol.*—Under this name is understood the Chinese Oil of Peppermint, which is distilled from *Mentha Javanica,* Bl., which is so pure that it almost wholly yields this product. Chinese menthol is very like that of other countries, but differs essentially in melting at 42° (107.6° F.), and boiling at 212° (413.6° F.). The import of this substance in 1884 was 4000 lbs., since when it has greatly increased.]

Menthene, $C_{10}H_{18}$.—On distilling menthol with phosphorous pentoxide, this body results as a levogyrate liquid, boiling at 163° (325.4° F.).

An almost odorless resin, and tannin, have also been determined.

---

* *Am. Jour. Phar.,* 1885, 600.   † Peppermint Camphor.   ‡ Henry Trimble, *Am. Jour. Phar.,* 1883, 486.

PHYSIOLOGICAL ACTION.—The symptoms of disturbance caused in Dr. Demeures' experiments are substantially as follows: Headache, with confusion; shooting pains in the region of fifth-nerve terminals; throat dry and sensitive; dry cough on inspiration; and external muscular soreness of the neck. Dr. Demeures judges that this drug is to dry cough what arnica is to bruised and strained muscles.

DESCRIPTION OF PLATE 116.

1. End of an early flowering plant, Binghamton, N. Y., July 26th, 1885.
2. Flower.
3. Section of calyx.
4. Section of corolla.
   (2–4 enlarged.)

CFM.ad nat.del.et pinxt.

MÉNTHA PIPERÌTA, Linn.

117

LYCOPUS.

BUGLE-WEED.

SYN.—LYCOPUS VIRGINICUS, LINN.; L. UNIFLORUS, MICHX.; L. PUMI-LUS, VAHL.; L. MACROPHYLLUS, BENTH.; L. VIRGINICUS, VAR. PAU-CIFLORUS, BENTH.; L. VIRGINICUS, VAR. MACROPHYLLUS, GRAY.

COM. NAMES.—BUGLE-WEED, WATER HOREHOUND, GIPSY-WEED, GIPSY-WORT, PAUL'S BETONY, WATER BUGLE; (FR.) LYCOPE DE VIRGINIE; (GER.) VIRGINISHER WOLFSFUSS.

A TINCTURE OF THE WHOLE HERB LYCOPUS VIRGINICUS, L.

Description.—This common perennial weed usually attains a growth of from 6 to 24 inches. *Stem* erect, obtusely angled, stoloniferous, and glabrous or very slightly pubescent; *stolons* long, filiform, often tuberous at the apex, produced from the base of the summer stems. *Leaves* ovate or oblong-lanceolate, coarsely serrate especially in the middle, acute at both ends, and tapering at the base into a short petiole. *Inflorescence* in sessile, axillary, capitate-verticillastrate glomerules; *bracts* very short, resembling the calyx-teeth; *flowers* whitish or tending toward purple. *Calyx* campanulate, only slightly shorter than the corolla, and naked in the throat; *teeth* 4 to 5, ovate or lance-ovate, obtuse or slightly acutish, 3-nerved. *Corolla* bell-shaped, small, short, and hardly irregular; *lobes* 4, nearly equal, the upper entire and broader than the others, but neither galeate or concave. *Stamens* inserted, straight, erect, equidistant, only two furnished with anthers; *anthers* with two parallel cells. *Style* bulbous at the base, bifurcating at the apex, the inner surfaces of the lobes stigmatic. *Fruit* composed of 4 3-sided nutlets, truncate at the top and acute at the base, the lateral margins thickened, the superior 4-crenated; *areola* basal, small.

History and Habitat.—The Virginian Bugle-weed is indigenous to North America, where it ranges from Labrador to Florida, Missouri, and northwestward to British Columbia and Oregon. It grows in low, damp, and shady grounds, and blossoms from July to September. This is one of the species that caused Rafinesque to vagarize, he disported with it to such an extent that it was forced to yield him 5 new species and 16 varieties "some of which might even be deemed species."

---

* Λύκος, *Lykos*, wolf: πούς, *pous*, foot; from suppositional resemblance.

The medical history of this species seems to hang upon the laurels of *L. vulgaris* of Europe. It was first mentioned by Schoepf,* but Drs. Pendleton and Rogers† first presented it in tangible form as an agent in incipient phthisis with hemoptysis. Rafinesque‡ thought exceeding well of its general properties, and as a means of producing diaphoresis without debility; he judged it a tonic sedative, and found it very useful in hemoptysis, and internal inflammation; he further claims that it acts somewhat like Digatalis, lowering the pulse, without producing any bad effects, nor accumulating in the system. Dr. Williams speaks of the plant§ as being " one of the most valuable styptics (hemostatics?) we possess in our vegetable Materia Medica. Most writers accept the idea that the plant is narcotic; we, however, infer, both from our own experience and that of others, that it is only sedative in that it removes, by checking hemorrhage, that nervous excitability and mental fear always accompanying such conditions. It is certainly an excellent hemostatic, very useful in generous doses, striving for its primary effect in epistaxis, hemoptysis, hematemesis, and menorrhagia. But two days have passed, at this writing, since we checked one of the most serious cases of epistaxis in our practice by the exhibition of teaspoonful doses of the tincture, one drachm to the ounce of water, ten minutes between doses; three doses alone were sufficient, after two hours of hemorrhage and the patient (a healthy man) greatly reduced. Dr. King says,§ Lycopus is decidedly beneficial in the treatment of diabetes, having cured when other means were useless, and has been of service in chronic diarrhœa and dysentery.

This valuable remedy was dismissed from the U. S. Phar. at the last revision; in the Eclectic Materia Medica the officinal preparation is *Infusum Lycopus*.

PART USED AND PREPARATION.—The whole fresh flowering herb is treated as in the preceding drug. The resulting tincture has a clear brown color by transmitted light; an herbaceous odor; an astringent and slightly bitter taste; and an acid reaction.

CHEMICAL CONSTITUENTS.—The analysis of the Tildens‖ determined the presence of a peculiar bitter principle, insoluble in ether, another soluble in ether, the two forming more than ten per cent. of the whole solid extract; tannin, and the usual plant constituents. The plant, according to the observations of myself and others, contains also a volatile oil. The properties of the plant are given up to water, and all seem to remain on drying except the last.

PHYSIOLOGICAL ACTION.—The symptoms caused in the human body by doses varying from ten drops to three drachms of the tincture, and of a wineglassful of the infusion¶ all point to the drug as increasing the tonicity of the capillaries and diminishing the vis-a-tergo in the larger vessels and the action of the heart itself. The symptoms, other than those of circulation, were: Nausea; flatulence,

---

* *N. Y. Med. and Phys. Jour.*, I, 179.
† *Med. Flor.*, II, 20.
‡ *Am. Med. Assoc.*, 1849, 902.

§ *Am. Disp.*, 1870, 494.
‖ *Jour. of Mat. Med.*, vol. I, N. S. 1859, 326.
¶ Allen, *Encyc. Mat. Med.* VI, 69.

griping, and diarrhœa ; decrease of sp. gr. of urine to as low as 1004, with diminished quantity, causes deposits of mucus, but no albumen ; fleeting rheumatic
pains, and pleurodynia ; sensations of cardiac constriction ; slight fever ; and
sleeplessness.

DESCRIPTION OF PLATE 117.

1 and 2. Whole plant, Binghamton, N. Y., July 31, 1885.

     3. Flower.

     4. Face of corolla.

     5. Stamen.

     6. Pistil.

     7. Fruit.

     8.   outer view.

     9. Akene,   inner view.

    10.   lateral view.

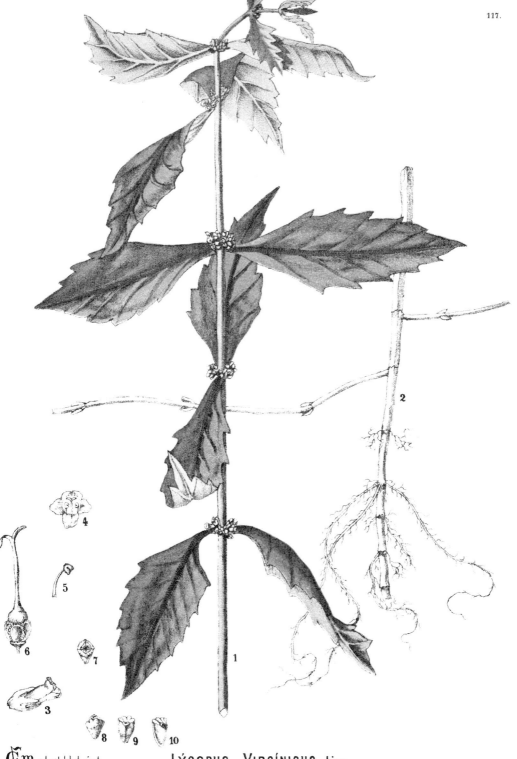

ℭ𝔪.ad nat.del.et pinxt. LÝCOPUS VIRGÍNICUS, Linn.

Tribe.—SATUREIEÆ.

GENUS.—**HEDEOMA**,* PERS.

SEX. SYST.—DIANDRIA MONOGYNIA.

118

HEDEOMA.

AMERICAN PENNYROYAL.

SYN.—HEDEOMA PULEGIOIDES, PERS.; MELISSA PULEGIOIDES, LINN.;
CUNILA PULEGIOIDES, LINN.; ZIZIPHORA PULEGIOIDES, R. & S.

COM. NAMES.—MOCK PENNYROYAL, TICK-WEED, SQUAW MINT, STINK-
ING BALM; (FR.) POULIOT D'AMERIQUE; (GER.) AMERIKANISCHER
POLEY.

A TINCTURE OF THE WHOLE PLANT HEDEOMA PULEGIOIDES, PERS.

Description.—This common, annual herb, grows to a height of from 6 to 12
inches. *Stem* erect, minutely pubescent, branching; *hairs* retuse. *Leaves* oblong-
ovate, obscurely serrate, the floral similar, all narrowed at the base into a slender
petiole. *Inflorescence* in loose, few-flowered, axillary whorls, often having the
appearance of terminal racemes; *flowers* very small, pedicillate. *Calyx* ovoid or
tubular, gibbous at the base, 13-nerved, bearded in the throat, and more or less
two-lipped; *upper-lip* 3-toothed, broad and spreading; *teeth* triangular; *lower-lip*
2-cleft, divisions setaceous-subulate, and hispid-ciliate. *Corolla* bluish, pubescent,
scarcely exceeding the calyx; *tube* naked within; *limb* 2-lipped, the throat evenly
open; *upper-lip* erect, flat, and notched at the apex; *lower-lip* spreading, 3-cleft.
Stamens 4, the inferior (fertile) pair the longer; *fertile filaments* ascending parallel
and under the upper-lip; *sterile* tipped with a little head, destitute of cells or pollen.
Anthers of fertile stamens, 2-celled. *Fruiting calyx* ovate-campanulate, strongly
gibbous, the throat closed with a ring of villous hairs. *Nutlets* 4, ovoid, brown,
slightly compressed.

History and Habitat.—This species is indigenous to North America, where it
ranges from Canada to Iowa, and southward. It grows upon the most arid spots
of open woods and fields, and blossoms from July to September.

The American Pennyroyal differs largely from the European *Mentha pulegium* in its botanical characters, but its action, as a medicine, is very like it. Our
species is extensively used, in domestic practice, as an aromatic stimulant and carminative in colic of children; a diaphoretic in the beginning of colds (Pennyroyal
Tea); and in large doses of a hot infusion, together with the pediluvium, in amenorrhœa. In the latter trouble, if of recent occurrence, it will often bring on the
menses nicely; and, combined with a gill of brewer's yeast, it frequently acts well

---

* Ἡδύοσμον, *hedyosmon*, from ἡδύς, *hedys*, sweet; ὀσμή, *osme*, smell.

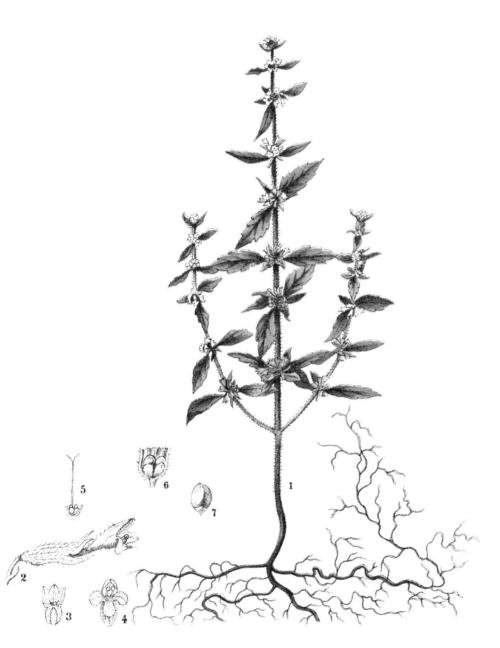

℃m.ad nat.del.et pinxt.

HEDEÒMA PULEGIOIDES , Pers.

as an abortivant, should the intender be not too late with her prescription. The oil is anti-emetic, anti-spasmodic, and rubefacient in rheumatism; with raw linseed oil, it makes an excellent dressing for recent burns. The oil has been recommended as an ointment to keep off gnats, ticks, fleas, and mosquitoes; many who have camped in the northern woods, have anointed their hands, neck, and face with this body, to guard against the pests of that region, but with only partial success.

The herb and *Oleum Hedeomæ* are officinal in the U. S. Ph.; in the Eclectic Dispensatory, the oil and *Decoctum Hedeomæ* are recommended.

PART USED AND PREPARATION.—The whole fresh plant, at the flowering period, is treated as described for the root of Collinsonia.* The resulting tincture has a deep orange color by transmitted light; retains the odor and taste of the plant to a high degree; and has an acid reaction.

CHEMICAL CONSTITUENTS.—*Oil of Hedeoma.*—This body is easily obtainable by distilling the fresh herb with water. It results as an almost colorless, light-yellow liquid, becoming darker with age. It retains the odor and taste of the herb, is neutral, has a sp. gr. of 0.941,† and is readily soluble in alcohol.

PHYSIOLOGICAL ACTION.—A case of poisoning by the oil is reported by Dr. Toothacker,‡ of a woman who took, at intervals, doses of a teaspoonful of the oil; she presented the following symptoms: Severe headache; difficult deglutition; great nausea, severe retchings, but inability to vomit; intolerable bearing down, labor-like pains, with tenderness of the abdomen; constipation; dyspnœa; semi-paralysis of the limbs; nervous weakness, and prostration.

DESCRIPTION OF PLATE 118.

1. Whole plant, Binghamton, N. Y., July 21st, 1885.
2. Flower.
3. Calyx.
4. Mouth of corolla.
5. Pistil.
6. Fruiting calyx.
7. Nutlet.
(2–7 enlarged.)

---

* Page 119–2.   † The sp. gr. of the oil of *Mentha pulegium* is 0.925.   ‡ *Phil. Jour. of Hom.*, 2, 655.

N. ORD.—LABIATÆ.
Tribe.—SATUREIEÆ.
GENUS.—**COLLINSONIA**,* LINN.
SEX. SYST.—DIANDRIA MONOGYNIA.

119

COLLINSONIA.

STONE-ROOT.

SYN.—COLLINSONIA CANADENSIS, LINN.; C. DECUSSATA, MŒN.; C. OVALIS, PURSH.

COM. NAMES.—STONE-ROOT, HORSE-WEED, HORSE-BALM, OX-BALM, KNOT-ROOT, KNOB-ROOT, GRAVEL-ROOT, RICH-WEED,† RICH-LEAF, HEAL-ALL,‡ HARDHACK;§ (FR.) BAUME DE CHEVAL; (GER.) CANA-DISCHE COLLINSONIE.

A TINCTURE OF THE ROOT OF COLLINSONIA CANADENSIS, LINN.

Description.—This glabrous perennial herb grows to a height of from 2 to 4 feet. *Root* nodular, depressed, and very hard and stone like; *stem* erect, somewhat 4-angled. *Leaves* opposite, petioled, ample, thin, varying from broadly ovate to oblong, tapering at the base, pointed at the apex, very veiny, and coarsely, sharply, and irregularly serrate. *Inflorescence* a naked, terminal, racemose, glandular-puberulent panicle; *flowers* lemon-yellow and lemon-scented. *Calyx* ovate, short, 10-nerved, lengthened in fruit, bearded midway in the throat, and containing a little honey-gland that partly surrounds, and is larger than, the two upper nutlets; *lips* 2, the upper flattened and 3-toothed, the lower 2-parted. *Corolla* elongated, somewhat infundibuliform, and having a bearded ring at the insertion of the filaments; *lips* 2, the lower larger, pendent, irregularly fimbriate, and bearded down the inner median line. *Stamens* 2 (the posterior pair wanting), much exserted, not declined, and spirally coiled in the bud; *filaments* long and straight, somewhat divergent; *anthers* introrse, 2-celled, the cells divaricate and contiguous. *Style* long, filiform, protruding toward one or the other stamen, and bifurcated at the apex into unequal lobes. *Seeds* triticose, carunculate.

History and Habitat.—The Stone-Root is indigenous to North America, where it ranges from Canada to Wisconsin, and southward to Florida, being particularly abundant in the North, and along the Allegheny Mountains. It habits rich woods, and flowers from July to September. The original specimen of this plant was sent to Peter Collinson, a promoter of science in England, by John Bartram, in 1735; he afterward forwarded it to Linnæus, who named the species in his honor.

---

* In honor of Peter Collinson, F.L.S. (See "History and Habitat.")
† The true Rich-weed is *Pilea pumila*, Gray (Urticaceæ).
‡ Properly, *Brunella vulgaris*, Linn.
§ This vulgarism denotes *Spirea tomentosa*, Linn. (Roseaceæ).

Collinsonia was first introduced as a medicine by Schoepf, who praised its virtues in lochial colic, snake-bites, rheumatism, and dumb ague. Rafinesque states that the Aborigines used the plant as a vulnerary, and that Dr. Mease claimed to cure dropsy with an infusion of the root in cider;* he further states that, "in the mountains of Virginia, Kentucky, Tennessee, and Carolina, this genus is considered as a panacea, and used outwardly and inwardly in many disorders; it is applied in poultice and wash for bruises, sores, blows, falls, wounds, sprains, contusions, and taken like tea for headaches, colics, cramps, dropsy, indigestion, etc." Drs. A. French and Beers speak highly of it in pains of the bladder, ascites, and dropsy of the ovaries; also as a powerful tonic in putrid and malignant fevers, and in leucorrhœa. Dr. Hooker judges the principle so volatile that all infusions should be made in a tight vessel. Dr. Scudder speaks highly of the plant in chronic diseases of the respiratory tract, and says that it relieves pulmonary irritation, and acts as a stimulant expectorant. "In irritation of the pneumogastric nerve," he says, "heart disease, and that peculiarly distressing asthma simulating, and sometimes attending, phthisis, it has a superior influence in quieting irritation, giving increased strength to the patient. In hemorrhoids, where there is rectal irritation, with the feces in part scybalous and part semifluid, no constipation being present, it cures in doses of from one to two drops of the tincture in water, three or four times a day."

The officinal preparations in the Eclectic Materia Medica are: *Infusum Collinsonæ* and *Tinctura Collinsonæ*.

PART USED AND PREPARATION.—The fresh root is chopped and pounded to a pulp and weighed. Then two parts by weight of alcohol are taken, the pulp mixed thoroughly with one-sixth part of it, and the rest of the alcohol added. After stirring the whole well, it is poured into a well-stoppered bottle, and allowed to stand eight days in a dark, cool place. The tincture so prepared is, after straining and filtering, of a brilliant reddish-orange color by transmitted light; has no characteristic odor; a ligneous taste; and an acid reaction.

CHEMICAL CONSTITUENTS.—An analysis of the root and leaves of this species, by C. N. Lochman,† resulted in the separation of a resin soluble in ether and partly in alcohol, wax, tannin, mucilage, and starch. A volatile oil is also present. The *collinsonin* of the pharmacies is the solid matter of the root, combined with chloride of sodium—not a specific principle, as might be supposed.

PHYSIOLOGICAL ACTION.—Dr. Dowle's experiment,‡ in which he took a teaspoonful and a half of the powder, gave the following symptoms: Numbness of the face and arms, with a sensation of enlargement of the parts; nausea; faintness and giddiness; an exhilaration something like that of whiskey; increased urine; and scybalous stool. Dr. E. M. Hale's provings add to the above the following effects: Headache with throbbing; yellow-coated tongue; vomiting; colic with desire for stool; and copious yellow bilious stools with tenesmus.

---

* Dr. Mease's account of the drug is set forth in his *Enclyclopædia*, vol. II, 177.
† *Am. Jour. Phar.*, 1885, 228.   ‡ *U. S. Med. Investigator.*

Œm.ad nat.del.et pinxt.

COLLINSÒNIA CANADÉNSIS, Linn.

Collinsonia appears to act as an irritant to the pneumogastric and vaso-motor nerves, and to mucous membranes in general, increasing the secretions of the latter, and causing inflammatory action to follow the congestion excited by its action.

DESCRIPTION OF PLATE 119.

1. Top of a flowering plant, Binghamton, N. Y., July 2d, 1885.
    3. Under surface of a flower.
    4. Upper surface.
    5. Anther.
    6. Stigmas.
    7. Calyx in section.
    8. Seed.
        (3–8 enlarged.)

Tribe.—STACHYDEÆ.

GENUS.—**SCUTELLARIA**,* LINN.

SEX. SYST.—DIDYNAMIA GYMNOSPERMIA.

120
SCUTELLARIA.

SKULL CAP.

SYN.—SCUTELLARIA LATERIFOLIA, LINN.
COM. NAMES.—VIRGINIAN SKULL CAP, MAD-DOG SKULL CAP, HOOD-
WORT, MAD-WEED, MAD-DOG WEED, BLUE PIMPERNEL; (FR.) SCU-
TELLAIRE; (GR.) HELMKRAUT.

A TINCTURE OF THE WHOLE PLANT SCUTELLARIA LATERIFOLIA, LINN.

Description.—This common perennial herb grows to a height of from 1 to 2 feet. *Root* fibrous; *stem* 4-sided, smooth, except upon the softly pubescent angles, upright, and much branched or simple. *Leaves* opposite, ovate-lanceolate or ovate-oblong, pointed, closely serrate, and rounded or somewhat cordate at the base; *petioles* about one-fourth the length of the blade. *Inflorescence* in opposite, axillary, unilateral, leafy racemes; *leaves*, first pair similar to those of the stem, the rest gradually reduced to bracts; *flowers* small, blue, single, in the axils of the floral leaves. *Calyx* in anthesis campanulate, 2-lipped; *lips* entire. *Corolla* bilabiate, erect; *tube* elongated, curved upward, dilated at the throat, and naked within; *lips* short, equal in length, the upper arched and having two lateral divisions connected with its basal sides, the lower spreading, convex, notched at the apex. *Stamens* 4, parallel, ascending under the upper lip, the superior pair shorter; *anthers* approximated in pairs, ciliate, those of the lower pair 1-celled by abortion, the upper 2-celled and cordate. *Style* 2-forked, the upper arm wanting or very small. *Fruiting calyx* closed, the upper lip with a helmet-like, and at length concave and enlarged, appendage on the back, the whole splitting at maturity, the upper lip usually falling away. *Nutlets* 4, wingless, depressed, tubercular, and situated upon a slightly elevated and bent gyno-base, inclining the fruit to the upper sepal; *seed* transverse; *embryo* curved; *radicle* short, incumbent upon one of the cotyledons.

History and Habitat.—Scutellaria is indigenous to North America, where it ranges from Canada to Florida and westward to British Columbia, Oregon, and New Mexico; it habits the borders of wet places, and flowers during July and August.

---

* *Scutella*, a saucer or shallow dish, alluding to the fruiting calyx.

About the first introduction of this plant into medicine was the experiments of Dr. Vandesveer, in 1772, who claimed to have found it curative and prophylactic in canine rabies, his reported cases being fourteen hundred; this seems a large number to fall to the lot of one physician; his son after him claimed the cure of forty cases more in three years. On account of the apparently slight properties inherent in this species by physical examination its worthiness was greatly doubted and the plant much railed against, even by many who never tried it. Following Vandesveer, many empirics and regulars used the remedy with success, while many others wrote essays against its being relied upon as an antihydrophobic. Dr. White, of Fishkill, assured Rafinesque that the plant preserved him from rabies after being bitten by a dog from whose bite others died. Rafinesque states his full belief in the prophylactic prowess of the plant, and adds that many laymen and physicians claim that the plant never fails to ward off or cure the disease. The dose given was a gill of the infusion four times a day, and the plant applied to the wound. Dr. S. W. Williams, whose cry of "charlatan" and "quack" was always raised upon the slightest pretext, lends his support to the probable virtue of the plant. Mr. Youatt, a distinguished veterinary surgeon, spoke highly of its virtues in this direction, but omitted it entirely from his treatise on canine rabies. The natural order Labiatæ yields species of many of its genera that are valued by the aborigines of countries in which they grow as antihydrophobics. Some value should at least be considered under these circumstances, as native medication is always the result of long and more or less successful experiment.

The plant has proved itself a useful antispasmodic, nervine, and tonic in chorea, convulsions, tetanus, tremors, delirium tremens, wakefulness in chronic disorders, and many other diseases when a tonic combining nervine powers might be deemed necessary; it is also considered diaphoretic and diuretic.

Scutellaria is officinal in the U. S. Ph. as *Extractum Scutellariæ Fluidum;* in the Eclectic Materia Medica it is recommended in the same preparation as well as *Extractum Scutellariæ Alcoholicum, Infusum Scutellariæ, Extractum Scutellariæ Composita,** and *Pilulæ Valerianæ Compositæ.†*

PART USED AND PREPARATION.—The whole fresh blossoming plant, gathered in August, when fruiting is well advanced, is treated as in the preceding species.‡ The resulting tincture is opaque. In thin layers it has a deep brown color by transmitted light: its taste is extremely bitter and very astringent; and its reaction acid.

CHEMICAL CONSTITUENTS.—According to the analysis of Cadet, this species contains: α, a greenish-yellow fixed oil, soluble in ether; β, an essential oil; γ, a bitter principle, soluble in water, alcohol, and ether; δ, a peculiar volatile matter; ε, a peculiar astringent principle; ζ, albumen; η, a sweet mucoid body; and the usual plant constituents.

---

* Scutellaria, Cypripedium, Humulus, and Lactuca.
† Scutellaria, Valeriana, Chamomilla, Eupatorium, Quinine, and Capsicum.
‡ Page 119–2.

120.

𝕮.𝖒. ad nat del et pinxt.   SCUTELLÀRIA LATERIFLÒRA , Linn.

[*Scutellarine.**—This unclassifiable substance is a precipitate, by alum, of the evaporated tincture made with 76 per cent. alcohol, after dilution with several times its bulk of water. It results as a neutral non-resin, in the form of a greenish†-brown, gritty, resinous powde r, insoluble in water, and partly soluble in alcohol and ether. It is said to retain the activity of the plant as far as known.]

PHYSIOLOGICAL ACTION.—Gordon's experiments with from 10 to 60 drops of the tincture resulted substantially as follows: Mental confusion and stupor ; headache and vertigo ; photophobia with dilated pupils ; scanty urine, with difficult micturition ; variable pulse with final reduction of the heart's action from 70–72 to 52 with intermission ; general languor and tremulousness ; followed by wakefulness and restlessness.

DESCRIPTION OF PLATE 120.

1. Upper portion of plant, Binghamton, N. Y., July 31st, 1886.
2. Flower.
3. Lower } stamen.
4. Upper }
5. Calyx.
6. Fruiting calyx.
7. Fruiting calyx, showing fruit.
8 and 9. Nutlets.
(2–9 enlarged.)

* Scutelline, so called, is valueless.   † Chlorophyll.

N. ORD.—LABIATÆ.
Tribe.—STACHYDEÆ.
GENUS.—**LAMIUM**,* TOURN.
SEX. SYST.—DIDYNAMIA GYMNOSPERMA.

121

LAMIUM.

DEAD NETTLE.

SYN.—LAMIUM ALBUM, LINN.
COM. NAMES.—DEAD NETTLE, WHITE ARCHANGEL; (FR.) L'ORTIE BLANCHE; (GER.) WEISSE TAUBNESSEL, WEISSBIENENSANG.

A TINCTURE OF THE LEAVES AND FLOWERS OF LAMIUM ALBUM, LINN.

Description—This more or less erect, hairy, and very leafy perennial herb, grows to a height of 1 foot or more. *Stem* decumbent at the base. *Leaves* ovate, acuminate, coarsely and doubly serrate, with a cordate or truncate base; *petioles* manifest upon the upper, and long, upon the lower part of the plant. *Inflorescence* in several axillary whorls; *flowers* large. *Calyx* tubular-campanulate, about 5-nerved; *teeth* 5, nearly equal, very slender, and awl-pointed, but not spinescent. *Corolla* white, about 1 inch long; *tube* curved upward from an obliquely-contracted base, having a ring of hairs inside; *throat* rather narrow; *upper lip* oblong, fornicate, narrowed at the base; *lateral lips* small, broadened down to the throat, and each bearing upon its upper margin a spur-like appendage that appears like a projection from the throat; *lower lip* spreading, 3-lobed, the middle lobe notched at the apex, and contracted into an almost stipitate claw at the base. *Stamens* 4, ascending under the galeate upper lip of the corolla, and not deflexed after anthesis, the anterior (inferior) pair longer, both pairs parallel and fertile; *anthers* hirsute, approximate in pairs; *cells* 2, divergent, opening lengthwise. *Style* filiform, forked at the apex into 2 divergent, stigmatose, pointed lobes. *Nutlets* somewhat triquetrous, sharply 3-angled, truncate, and hollowed out at the apex.

History and Habitat.—The Dead Nettle comes to us from Great Britain, France, and Germany, where it grows in waste places and along hedges; with us it is becoming naturalized in Eastern New England, where it takes up its usual habitat, and blossoms in July and August.

The very unpleasant odor and bitter taste of this species causes it to be exempt from use by grazing cattle; yet Linnæus says that in Sweden it is gathered by the peasants and cooked as a pot-herb, the process of boiling dissipating, in the most part, the principles of the plant.

---

* Λαῖμος, *laimos*, the throat, alluding to the ringent corolla; or *lamia*, a witch, hag, or demon, to which the flower is likened in appearance.

Although this plant has been used from ancient times, and is mentioned by Dioscorides and Pliny, yet it has received but little thought or experiment. The principal uses as a drug are all mentioned in a few words by Gerarde, who says :* "Archangel, stamped with vinegar, and applied in manner of a pultis, taketh away Wens and hard swellings ; the King's Evill, inflammation of the kernels under the ears and jawes, and also hot fierie inflammation of the kernels of the necke, arm-holes, and flanks. It is good to bathe those parts with the decoction of it . . . . . The later Phisitions thinke that the white flowers do staie the whites, and for the same purpose divers do make of them a conserve."

PART USED AND PREPARATION.—Two parts of the fresh leaves, and one part of the fresh blossoms are to be chopped and pounded to a pulp, enclosed in a piece of new linen, and subjected to pressure. The expressed juice should then be thoroughly mixed with an equal part by weight of alcohol. After allowing the mass to macerate eight days in a well-stoppered bottle, in a dark, cool place, the tincture may be separated by filtration. This tincture should be opaque. In thin layers, it has a reddish-brown color by transmitted light ; its odor is sourish and herbaceous, reminding one of old buckweat honey-comb ; its taste very like its odor, and followed by a bitterishness ; and its reaction strongly acid.

CHEMICAL CONSTITUENTS.—Lamium contains a bitter principle and a volatile oil, but neither have as yet been isolated.

PHYSIOLOGICAL ACTION.—Little is known of the action of this plant, the provings of Hahnemann and others giving few characteristic symptoms. Its action seems to be spent upon the mucous membranes in general, and upon the female generative organs in particular, where it causes a sort of inflammatory excitement.

DESCRIPTION OF PLATE 121.

1. Top of plant, from Salem, Mass., Aug. 6th, 1885.
2. A leaf, under surface.
3. Flower.
4. A portion of the corolla, showing the appendage.
5 and 6. Anthers.
7. Stigma.
8 and 9. Carpels.

(3–9 enlarged.)

* *Herball*, p. 568.

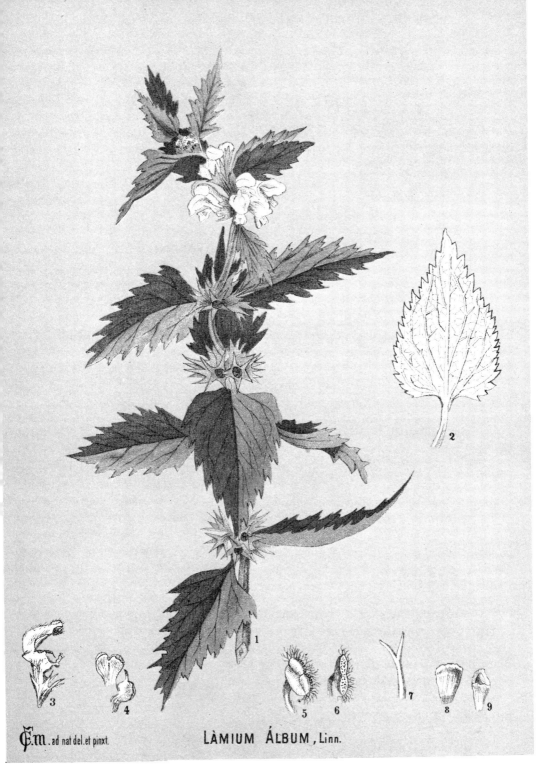

121.

3   4   5   6   7   8   9   1

Ɛ.m. ad nat del.et pinxt.

LÀMIUM ÁLBUM, Linn.

Tribe.—*HYDROPHYLLEÆ.*

GENUS.—**HYDROPHYLLUM,*** TOURN.

SEX. SYST.—PENTANDRIA MONOGYNIA.

122

HYDROPHYLLUM.

WATERLEAF.

SYN.—HYDROPHYLLUM VIRGINICUM, LINN.
COM. NAMES.—VIRGINIAN WATERLEAF, BURR FLOWER.

A TINCTURE OF THE WHOLE FRESH PLANT HYDROPHYLLUM VIRGINICUM, LINN.

Description.—This smoothish perennial herb grows to a height of from 1 to 2 feet. *Rootstock* creeping, scaly-toothed by the withered sheathes of previous stems. *Stems* generally simple, sometimes 2-forked; *leaves* ample, pinnately divided, and conspicuously petioled; *leaflets* 5 to 7, ovate-lanceolate or oblong in general outline, sharply and irregularly cut-toothed, the lower pair mostly 2-parted, the upper three confluent, all acuminate or acute. *Inflorescence* in terminal and upper axillary cymose clusters; *flowers* pinkish-white; *peduncles* forked, longer than the petioles of the leaves from whose axils they spring. *Calyx* deeply 5-parted, naked at the sinuses; *teeth* narrowly linear, bristly ciliate. *Corolla* campanulate, 5-cleft, the lobes convolute in the bud; *tube* furnished with five adnate appendages fixed to the midrib of each petaloid lobe, the incurved free margins approximated by interlocked hairs, thus forming a sort of nectariferous tube. *Stamens* exserted; *filaments* long, filiform, bearded about the middle by a few long hairs; *anthers* linear, versatile. *Ovary* bristly hairy, 1-celled; *ovules* amphitropous, enveloped by the dilated fleshy placentæ. *Style* exserted, bifurcated at the summit; *stigmas* 2, capitate, minute. *Fruit* a spherical, loculicidal capsule about the size of a pea. *Seeds* 4, or generally fewer by abortion; *testa* pitted or reticulated; *albumen* cartilaginous.

Hydrophyllaceæ.—This large and innocent family of commonly hairy herbs is represented in North America by 14 genera, comprising 115 species, and 17 recognized varieties. *Leaves* mostly alternate; *stipules* absent. *Inflorescence* in more or less unilateral, mostly bractless cymes or scorpioid racemes; *flowers* regular, 5-merous and 5-androus, blue or white. *Calyx* sometimes with nearly separate sepals, the sinuses often appendaged. *Stamens* borne on the base of the corolla and alternate with its lobes. *Ovary* entire, 1-celled, or sometimes 2-celled

---

* ὕδωρ, *hudor*, water; φυλλον, *phyllon*, leaf; the application doubtful.

122.

𝕲.𝔪. ad nat del.et pinxt. HYDROPHÝLLUM VIRGÍNICUM , Linn.

by union of the placentæ in the axis; *placentæ* 2, parietal; *ovules* amphitropous or anatropous, pendulous or nearly horizontal. *Styles* 2, or single and 2-cleft. *Fruit* a 2-valved, 2 to many-seeded capsule; *seeds* pitted or reticulated; *embryo* small; *albumen* copious.

History and Habitat.—The Waterleaf is indigenous to North America, where it ranges from Canada southward to the mountains of North Carolina and northward to Alaska, seeking moist, shady grounds, and flowering from June to August. The young leaves serve in some localities as a salad, called Shawanese Lettuce, and are eaten as a potage in other places, under the name of John's Cabbage. We have no previous medical history of this plant, or any other species of the order.

PART USED AND PREPARATION.—The fresh flowering plant is chopped and pounded to a pulp and weighed. Then two parts by weight of alcohol are taken, the pulp mixed thoroughly with one-sixth part of it, and the rest of the alcohol added. After stirring the whole well, it is poured into a well-stoppered bottle, and allowed to macerate for eight days in a dark, cool place. The tincture thus formed after filtration has a deep crimson-brown color by transmitted light, a peculiar bitterish odor, an astringent taste, and an acid reaction.

PHYSIOLOGICAL ACTION.—The only account of the action of this plant is that furnished by Dr. P. B. Hoyt,* who records the following symptoms caused in himself: Dull headache; burning, smarting, and itching of the eyelids with profuse lachrymation; agglutination of the lids in the morning; injection of the sclera, and photophobia.

DESCRIPTION OF PLATE 122.

1. End of flowering plant, Binghamton, N. Y., June 1st, 1885.
2. Flower.
3. Petal and appendage.
4. Stamen.
5. Nectary.
6. Pistil.
7. Style and stigmas.
8. Leaf.
   (3-7 enlarged.)

---

* *Am. Hom. Obs.*, xi, 101.

123
CONVOLVULUS.

BINDWEED.

SYN.—CONVOLVULUS ARVENSIS, LINN.
COM. NAMES.—BINDWEED; (FR.) LE LISERON; (GER.) DIE WINDE.

A TINCTURE OF THE WHOLE PLANT CONVOLVULUS ARVENSIS, L.

Description.—This low perennial attains a growth of from 2 to 5 feet. *Root* deeply and extensively creeping; *stem* nearly glabrous, procumbent or twining over surroundings; *leaves* ovate-oblong, sagittate tending to hastate, entire, the basal auriculate lobes acute. *Inflorescence* axillary; *peduncles* mostly 1-flowered *flowers* matinal, white tinged with rose; *bracts* remote from the flower, subulate. *Calyx* naked at the base; *sepals* equal, rounded. *Corolla* about three-quarters of an inch long, open infundibuliform, more or less plicate at the sinuses and obscurely 5-notched. *Stamens* included; *filaments* dilated at the base. *Ovary* entire; *style* single, persistent; *stigmas* 2, filiform, mostly spreading or revolute. *Fruit* a 2-celled globose capsule. *Seeds* 2 in each cell; *cotyledons* broad, foliaceous.

Convolvulaceæ.—This large and well-distinguished family of mostly tropical or subtropical plants, is represented in North America by 8 genera, containing in all 73 species and 17 recognized varieties. The order is composed of herbs or shrubs with stems that generally twine or trail. *Leaves* alternate, petioled (absent in *Cuscuta*); *stipules* none. *Inflorescence* truly axillary, the peduncles 1-flowered or cymosely 3- many-flowered; *flowers* regular and perfect, 5-merous or rarely 4-merous. *Calyx* persistent; *sepals* mostly distinct, imbricated. *Corolla* with an entire or lobed limb. *Gynœcium* generally 2-carpelled. *Stamens* as many as the lobes of the corolla and inserted low upon its tube. *Hypogynous disk* evident, annular. *Ovary* 2- to 6-celled; *style* single, sometimes divided; *stigma* terminal or introrse. *Fruit* capsular or fleshy; *seeds* comparatively large; *embryo* filling the testa; *albumen* mucilaginous, surrounding, or surrounded by, the embryo.

In this order our proven plants are: The Oriental Scammony (*Convolvulus Scammonia*, Linn.), whose root yields an irritant but nearly tasteless purgative, often given to children as an anthelmintic on account of the smallness of the requisite dose for purging; Jalap, the dried tubercules of the Mexican *Exogonium Purga*, Benth., is a certain, powerful, and speedy drastic purgative used as above;

---

* From *convolvulo*, to twine.

it has a griping effect, however, making it less pleasant than Scammony; and Convolvulus Duartinus, the common Morning Glory (*Ipomœa Bona-nox*, Linn.), a native of the tropics, so extensively planted north as an ornamental "vine."

Many other genera furnish plants more or less used in general medicine, viz.: The North African *Ipomœa Nil*, Roth., whose seeds, in 50-grain doses, prove purgative, and in action greatly resemble Jalap; the East Indian *Ipomœa Turpethum*, R. Br., the Jamaican *I. tuberosa*, Linn., and the St. Domingo *I. cathartica*, Poir., are all used in their countries as purgatives, though the latter is generally too strong in its action to be safely given. The leaves of the Madras *Argyreia bracteata*, Wall., are used by the natives in decoction as fomentations for scrofulous enlargements. The root of the tropical *Batatas paniculata*, Chois., is cathartic; while those of the East Indian *B. edulis* are wholesome, and, as cultivated in the warmer climates, form an article of commerce known as Sweet Potatoes. Our common Bracted Bindweed (*Calystegia sepium*, R. Br.) has a purgative root, as has also the European *C. Soldanella*, Röm. & S. Oil of Rhodium, a bitter essential oil, used to attract rats and mice to traps, also to adulterate oil of roses, is distilled from the sternutatory wood of *Convolvulus* (Breweria, Rhodoriza) *scoparius*, Linn.

History and Habitat.—This too common European plant has become naturalized in the North-eastern United States, where it flowers in June. It is said to be a sure indication that the soil is dry in all localities that it chooses as its habitat.

This plant has been used much like Jalap and Scammony, in 40-grain doses of the jointed and vermiculate roots, as a diuretic and gentle laxative.

PART USED AND PREPARATION.—The whole fresh flowering plant, in a slightly wilted condition, is chopped and pounded to a pulp and weighed. Then two parts by weight of alcohol are taken, the pulp mixed thoroughly with one-sixth part of it, and the rest of the alcohol added. After having stirred the whole well, it is poured into a well-stoppered bottle, and allowed to stand eight days in a dark, cool place.

The tincture, separated from this mass by pressing and filtering, has a deep reddish-brown color by transmitted light; a somewhat nauseous odor; a slightly astringent, tea-like taste; and an acid reaction.

CHEMICAL CONSTITUENTS.—*Convolvulin*. This so-called resinoid, obtained from the roots of this species, is as yet of doubtful chemical nature. It remains to be determined whether it contains the principles found in Jalap, Scammony, etc.

PHYSIOLOGICAL ACTION.—The few symptoms so far determined in this drug, point to it as an irritant to the mucous membranes of the alimentary tract, and a stimulant to the neighboring secretory glands. Convolvulus causes eructations, flatulent colic, and liquid stools very similar to those following Jalap.

DESCRIPTION OF PLATE 123.

1. End of flowering plant, Salem, Mass., July 20th, 1885.
2. Anther.
3. Pistil.
4. Section of ovary.
(2–4 enlarged.)

Œm.ad nat.del.et pinxt.

CONVÓLVULUS ARVÉNSIS, Linn.

GENUS.—**SOLANUM**,* TOURN.

SEX. SYST.—PENTANDRIA MONOGYNIA.

124

DULCAMARA.†

BITTERSWEET.

SYN.—SOLANUM DULCAMARA, LINN.   DULCAMARA FLEXUOSA,
MOENCH.   RAMUS NOVELLUS, L.

COM. NAMES.—BITTERSWEET, WOODY NIGHTSHADE, VIOLET BLOOM;
(FR.) DOUCE-AMERE; (GER.) BITTERSÜSS.

A TINCTURE OF THE FRESH GREEN BRANCHES ABOVE THE WOODY STEM, OF
SOLANUM DULCAMARA, LINN.

Description.—This beautiful and falsely dreaded shrubby herb, seldom reaches a length of more than 5 feet, unless well supported in a hedge or by a wall; it then may extend to various lengths, in some cases reaching 18 feet or more. *Root* woody, irregularly creeping and branching, pale yellow. *Stem* herbaceous or shrubby, flexuous, pubescent, scarcely climbing. *Branches* many, weak, flexuous and somewhat angular, with a dull green bark, destitute of thorns or spines. *Leaves* alternate, petiolate, from 2 to 3 inches long, the upper surface smooth, the under usually pubescent; the lower few leaves are either ovate or ovate-cordate, the upper vary from hastate to auriculate, all entire. *Flowers* drooping, on lateral, branching, extra-axillary peduncles, forming a loose spreading corymb with bractless pedicels. *Calyx* small, 5-parted. *Corolla* plaited, and valvate or induplicate in the bud; when expanded it is wheel-shaped, 5-cleft, with the acute-lanceolate lobes reflexed, each with two green ovate spots at its base. *Stamens* exserted, mostly equal, their filaments inserted upon the tube of the corolla. *Filaments* short, more or less triangular. *Anthers* large, erect, blunt, bright yellow, converging into a cone about the style, and opening by two pores or chinks at the apex. *Pollen* grains minute, ovoid and induplicate. *Ovary* rounded, 2-celled, containing many ovules upon the axis. *Ovules* curved (campylotropous), sometimes merging into the amphitropic form. *Style* simple, filiform, protruding beyond the tube formed by the anthers. *Stigma* single. *Fruit* a 2-celled, bright scarlet, oval, translucent, thin-skinned, bitter and juicy berry. *Seeds* numerous, whitish, somewhat plano-convex, their surfaces minutely pitted.

History and Habitat.—This very common plant prefers moist banks, old fences and hedges, the slightly higher ground on the margins of swampy spots, and disused ground about old dwellings; blossoming in June and July. Its place

---

* Derivation unknown.

† Dulcis, *sweet;* amarus, *bitter.*

among American plants is doubtful; by some authors it is considered indigenous, by others as advanced from Europe; judging from its locations here, I am inclined to favor the latter idea. It is found in the greater part of Europe, in North Africa, and Asia Minor, and the northern parts of India and China. The genus Solanum is very interesting, containing as it does some of our most useful table vegetables, noxious weeds, and excellent remedies. Notably among the edible vegetables are the potato, *Solanum tuberosum*, the tomato, *Solanum lyco-persicon*, and the egg plant, *Solanum melongena*, all extensively cultivated and having their origin doubtless in the tropical regions of South America. From the common names, Bittersweet and Nightshade, confusion has often arisen among the laity in mistaking it for Belladonna (Deadly Nightshade), and *Celastrus*, the staff-vine, often called Bittersweet; but Belladonna does not grow sponta-neously in this country, and Celastrus is too widely different to be confused with Dulcamara except in name.

Dulcamara is still retained in the U. S. Ph., as *Extractum Dulcamaræ Fluidum*. In the Eclectic Materia Medica its preparations are *Decoctum Solani* and *Extractum Dulcamara*.

PART USED AND PREPARATION.—The fresh, green branches that are still pliant, and their leaves, should be gathered just as the plant is budding to blossom, and chopped and pounded into a pulp, inclosed in a piece of new linen and pressed. The juice thus expressed should, by brisk succussion, be mingled with an equal part by weight of alcohol. This mixture should then be allowed to stand at least eight days in a well-stoppered bottle, in a dark, cool place, and filtered before using.

Thus prepared it is by transmitted light of a pale chestnut color, having at first a decidedly bitter, then sweet taste, and an acid reaction.

CHEMICAL CONSTITUENTS.—Solania, $C_{43}H_{71}NO_{16}$, fully described under Solanum nigrum, 125, is undoubtedly also a separate principle in this species. Wittstein claims it to be easily obtainable from the young shoots of the plant.

Dulcamarin.*—$C_{22}H_{34}O_{10}$. This glucoside, extracted from Wittstein's so-called alkaloid Dulcamarin, $C_{65}H_{100}N_2O_{29}$, is in the form of a permanent, slightly yellow powder, odorless, with at first an exceeding bitter, then a lasting sweet taste. It melts with heat, decomposing at 205° (401° F.), and is soluble in water, alcohol and ether, insoluble in chloroform and benzol. Dulcamarin readily sepa-rates in boiling with a mineral acid into dulcamaretin ($C_{16}H_{26}O$), and glucose.

Pfaff's analysis of 100 parts of the dried stems resulted as follows:

Dulcamarin,	21.817	Resin containing Benzoic Acid,	2.74
Vegeto-animal matter,	3.125	Gum, Starch, and Salts of Lime,	2 00
Gummy extractive,	12.029	Extractive and Lime Salts,	4.00
Gluten and green wax,	1.4	Woody Fibre,	62.00
	(Excess,	9.111)	

---

* Picroglycion, Dulcarin.

PHYSIOLOGICAL ACTION.—The first action of this drug is somewhat narcotic, but of short duration in this sphere. Upon the circulation the action is quite marked, it causing venous congestion, attended with great pain, heat, nausea and vomiting, and sudden prostration. The head droops and oscillates forth and back, the patient is giddy, the heart palpitates, the mouth and fauces become hot and dry, and the face and ears cyanotic. Post mortem: the medulla is found as to its substance healthy, though there is great injection of the blood-vessels above and below it. One clearly defined case of poisoning by the berries of this plant is reported in the *Lancet* of June 28th, 1856, p. 715, in which the identity of the plant seems to have been certain, and that the berries of Solanum nigrum, which are much more poisonous, took no part, resulted in the death of a boy aged 4. The following symptoms were noted: after eleven hours, during which no symptoms of importance were observed, he was attacked with vomiting, purging and convulsions, which continued throughout the day, the child being insensible during the intervals. He died convulsed in about 24 hours. The vomited matters were of a dark greenish color, and of a bilious character.

Notwithstanding numerous cases reported of poisoning by this plant it cannot justly be considered as generally poisonous, as most animals and persons who have eaten of it or its fruit, show no serious symptoms.

It is to be deplored that the berries were not incorporated in the tinctures proven, as they seem to be the most toxic part of the plant.

DESCRIPTION OF PLATE 124.

1. Flowering branch. Ithaca, N. Y., May 31, 1880. Fruit added later in the season.
   2. Flower (enlarged).
   3. Pistil (enlarged).
   4. Stamens (enlarged).
   5. Section of Ovary.
   6. Pollen grains x 380.

124.

𝕱𝔪. ad nat.del.et pinxt.

SOLANUM DULCAMARA, Linn.

125

SOLANUM NIGRUM.

BLACK NIGHTSHADE.

SYN.—SOLANUM NIGRUM, LINN.; S. PTEROCAULON, DUNAL.; S. CRE-
NATO-DENTATUM, PTYCANTHUM, AND INOPS, D. C.

COM. NAMES.—COMMON OR GARDEN NIGHTSHADE, BLACK NIGHT-
SHADE, DEADLY NIGHTSHADE;* (FR.) MORELLE NOIR; (GER.)
SCHWARZER NACHSCHATTEN.

A TINCTURE OF THE WHOLE HERB SOLANUM NIGRUM, LINN.

Description.—This low, weedy, annual herb grows to a height of from 1 to 2
feet. *Stem* angular, glabrous, pubescent when young, diffusely spreading or
branching, and more or less rough on the angles; *branches* mostly twisted.
Leaves ovate, cuneate, somewhat obtusely, acutely, or acuminately tipped, and
usually much perforated by insects; *margin* varying from coarsely, crenately, or
irregularly toothed, to entire. *Inflorescence* in small, pedunculate, lateral, and
extra-axillary, umbel-like, drooping cymes; *flowers* quite small, white or whitish.
Calyx much shorter than the corolla, merely spreading in fruit; *teeth* ovate, acutish. *Corolla* wheel-shaped, 5-parted, valvate in the bud; *petals* oblong-lanceolate,
reflexed, closely studded with minute papillæ upon the upper surface. *Stamens*
exserted; *filaments* very short, more or less hairy inside; *anthers* large, connivent
around the style, blunt, opening by two terminal pores. *Ovary* globular, 2-celled;
style columnar, mostly included, hairy at its base; *stigma* capitate. *Fruit* a small
cluster of blue-black, globular berries, each about the size of a large pea. *Seeds*
numerous, flattened; *embryo* slender, curved; *cotyledons* semiterete, not larger than
the radicle.

Solanaceæ.—This large, well-known order, whose representatives grow mostly
in tropical and subtropical regions, furnishes North American botany with 14 genera,
101 species, and 24 recognized varieties. The order is characterized as follows:
Herbs, shrubs, or even trees, commonly rank-scented, and having a watery juice.
Leaves alternate, never truly opposite, though, being often unequally geminate
they have the appearance of being opposite; *stipules* none. *Inflorescence* properly
terminal and cymose, but variously modified, sometimes scorpioid-racemiform;
pedicels not bracted, or, if bracted, then not in the axils. *Flowers* perfect and
mostly regular, 5- 4-merous. *Corolla* with its lobes induplicate-valvate, plicate,

---

* Belladonna alone answers to this name: it does not grow wild in this country.

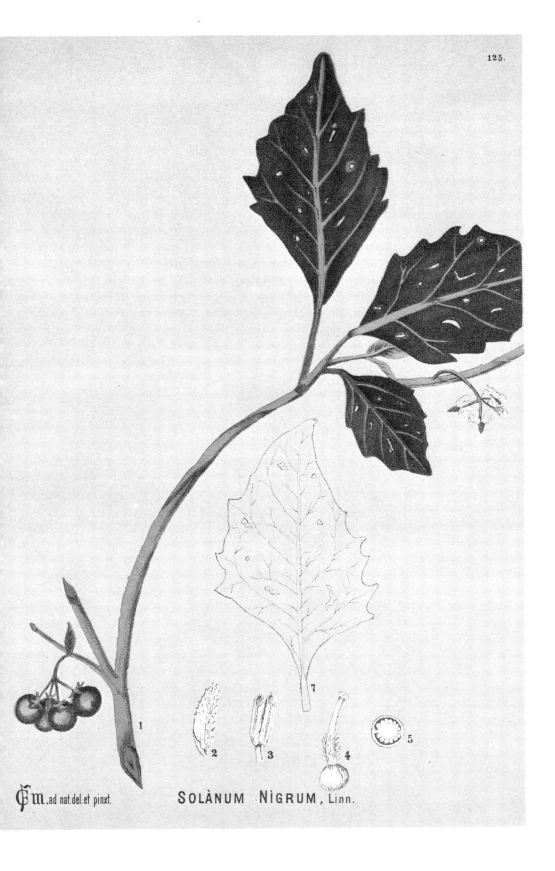

Cm.ad nat.del.et pinxt.

1 2 3 4 5 7

SOLÀNUM NÌGRUM, Linn.

or very rarely imbricate in the bud. *Ovary* wholly free, normally 2-celled ; *placentæ* axillary ; *ovules* indefinitely many, anatropous or amphitropous ; *style* undivided ; *stigma* entire or sometimes bilamellar. *Fruit* either capsular or baccate ; *embryo* terete and incurved or coiled, or sometimes almost straight ; *albumen* fleshy ; *cotyledons* rarely much broader than the radicle.*

This order furnishes our Materia Medica with twenty drugs, which are, beside the five here described : The European Belladonna, or Deadly Nightshade (*Atropa Belladonna*, Linn.) ; the Tropical Cayenne Pepper (*Capsicum Annuum*, Linn.) ; the Pacific coast Tree Stramonium (*Datura arborea*, Linn.) ; the Chinese Datura (*D. ferox*, Linn.), probably the most poisonous species in the family ; the Indian Datura (*D. metel*, Linn.) ; the Tropical American Tomato, or Love-apple (*Lycopersicum esculentum*, Mill.) ; the true Mandrake of Southern Europe (*Atropa mandragora*, Linn.) ; the South Brazilian *Arrebenta Cavallos* (*Solanum Rebenta*, Vell.) ; the Southern and West Indian Apple of Sodom, or Nipple Nightshade (*S. mammosum*, Linn.) ; the Brazilian *Juquerioba*, or *Gyquirioba* (*S. oleraceum*, Vell.) ; the European Jerusalem Cherry (*S. pseudo-capsicum*, Linn.) ; the common Potato (*S. tuberosum*, Linn.) and its diseased state (*S. tuberosum ægrotans*), due to the growth of a fungus known as *Peronospora infestans ;* the Peruvian *Floripondio* (*Datura sanguinea*, R. et Pav.) ; the Australian Corkwood Tree (*Duboisia myoporoides*, R. Br.), and Pituri (*D. Hopwoodi*, Von M.).

Numerous drugs, still unproven but used in general practice, belong to this order, notably, the Indian Guinea Pepper (*Capsicum fastigiatum*, Blume), which, with the Indian Goat Pepper (*C. frutescens*, Linn.), is a much more powerful stimulant than Cayenne, and often produces violent pain and purgation. The genus *Solanum* further furnishes to medicine the Indian expectorant, *S. Jacquiri*, Willd. ; the West Indian astringent, *S. Bahamense*, Linn. ; the Brazilian active cathartic and vulnerary, *Juripeba* (*S. paniculatum*, Linn.) ; the South American sudorific, *S. cernuum*, Vell. ; and many other species used in their native countries as purgatives, diuretics, deobstruents, and vulneraries. The fruit of the West Indian Calabash Tree (*Crescentia Cujete*, Linn.) yields a pulp that is considered at once vulnerary and pectoral. In the south of Europe the White Henbane (*Helleborus albus*, Linn.) is considered much more active than *H. niger ;* and Arabia yields, according to Foreskäl, a species, *H. Datura*, used by the natives to produce intoxication, and supposed to be the *nepenthes* of Homer. The genus *Cestrum* contains many active species, those especially notable being, the South African *C. venenatum*, Thursb., used by the Hottentots as a poison for their spears, and to poison their bait for wild beasts ; *C. macrophyllum*, Vent., and *C. nocturnum*, Lam., are also toxic, and have been used with some effect in chorea ; while *C. Hediunda*, Lam., and *C. auriculatum*, L. Her., are febrifugal. Many species of *Physalis* are valuable, especially the South European *P. flexuosus*, Linn., which is said to be narcotic, diuretic, and alexiteric ; and the Winter Cherry, *P. Alkekengi*, Linn., which has been considered an excellent diuretic from the days of Dioscorides ; Ray considered it also anti-podagric. The bitter leaves of the Peru-

---

* Description of Prof. Asa Gray, in *Synop. Flora of N. A.*, vol. ii, pt. i, p. 224.

vian *Saracha umbellata*, Jacq., are used as an anodyne emollient. In New Grenada the Matrimony Vine (*Lycium umbrosum*) is adjudged an excellent remedy in erysipelas; and, lastly, the South American *Himeranthus uncinatus* is esteemed by the natives as an aphrodisiac, stimulating the ingester to venery.

History and Habitat.—Black Nightshade is a cosmopolite; in this country it grows in damp and shady waste grounds, generally throughout the eastern section, where it flowers from July to frosty weather.

This species has been used in general practice, especially as a resolvent, from A. D. 54 (Dioscorides) to within a few years. The principal use of the plant has been in dropsy; gastritis; glandular enlargement; nervous affections; general inflammations of mucous membranes; herpetic, scorbutic, and syphilitic eruptions; and as a narcotic. The Arabs use the bruised leaves, with adeps, as an application to burns, bullæ, and felons. In Dalmatia the root is used to cure hydrophobia, and is fried in butter and eaten to produce sleep; while in Bohemia the blossoming plant is hung over the cradle of infants to act as an hypnotic. Orfila claims the extract equal in power and energy to lactucarium. In Spain patients are often said to be cured of phthisis by burying them up to the neck in garden loam, then, after removal, rubbing the body thoroughly with an ointment of the leaves of this species.

PART USED AND PREPARATION.—The whole plant, gathered when, in early autumn, it is in both flower and fruit, is treated as in the preceding species.

The resulting tincture has a brownish-orange color by transmitted light, no distinguishing odor, a slightly astringent and woody taste, and an acid reaction.

CHEMICAL CONSTITUENTS.—*Solania,** $C_{43}H_{71}NO_{16}$. This peculiar body, having, according to all observers up to date, both alkaloidal and glucosidal reactions, needs much careful investigation before either its chemical or physical nature can be fully understood. It is readily obtainable from all species of the genus Solanum, but is especially prevalent in this. According to Wittstein, it crystallizes in white, flat, quadrangular prisms of mother-of-pearl lustre, or results as an amorphous powder of like appearance; it is inodorous, and has a bitter, disagreeable, long-lasting, rancid, and acrid taste. It is soluble to only a slight extent in water, its solution becoming frothy on agitation; readily dissolves in alcohol; and is insoluble in ether. It shows a decided glucosidal nature by breaking down under the action of heat and hydrochloric acid, as follows:

$$\underset{\text{Solanin.}}{C_{43}H_{71}NO_{16}} + \underset{\text{Water.}}{(H_2O)_3} = \underset{\text{Glucose.}}{(C_6H_{12}O_6)_3} + \underset{\text{Solanidine.†}}{C_{25}H_{41}NO.}$$

PHYSIOLOGICAL ACTION.—Numerous cases of poisoning have been reported, among which the following will serve to show the action of the plant:

Three children who had eaten the berries complained of headache, vertigo, nausea, colic, and tenesmus. There was copious vomiting of a greenish-colored

---

* Discovered in the plant in 1821 by M. Desfosses, *Jour. de Pharmacie*, vi, 374, and vii, 414.

† This body is a very strong base, and crystallizes in long needles (Schorlemmer).

matter, thirst, dilated pupils, stertorous respiration, convulsions, and a tetanic stiff-ness of the limbs. Death followed in all cases but one only during the acute symptoms.*

A boy, after eating the berries, suffered horrible symptoms, dilation of the pupil, burning in the stomach, delirium, agony, trembling of the limbs, cold sweat, and death.†

Gataker‡ commenced his experiments with the drug by giving a grain, which acted gently as an evacuant by sweat, urine, and stool; on increasing the dose until it was quite large, it produced vomiting, profuse perspiration, or too copious urination or diarrhœa, and sometimes dimness of vision and vertigo.

A family, having eaten of the leaves, were attacked with swelling of the face, accompanied by burning heat, and followed by gangrene.§

A boy, aged eight years, ate some of the black berries of this plant, which induced a state of stupor and coma, attended with fever. He complained of great pain in the pit of the stomach, and was harassed with nausea and retchings.||

A little girl ate some of the berries. She was found entirely insensible, lying in a deep, *apoplectic stupor*, all the muscles relaxed, the face flushed and the pulse full and irregular. She continued in this state about six hours, then gradually recovered.¶

Four of the ripe berries caused deep sleep in a child (age not given).**

Two boys, aged two and three years, having eaten of the berries, had con-vulsions and spasms; they stretched their hands during the spasms, as if they would grasp something, carrying their hands to their mouths, chewing and swal-lowing, etc.††

Thus Solanum Nigrum acts as an irritant to the brain and spinal cord, and secondarily upon the circulation through the vaso-motor system; the irritation seems greatest upon the sensory nerves and less upon the motor. Its action upon the brain is quite parallel with that of Belladonna, but evidently greater than Stra-monium or Hyoscyamus. Its action upon the eye is more like that of Stramonium than Belladonna, and directly opposite to that of Gelsemium.

DESCRIPTION OF PLATE 125.

1. Part of a fruiting and flowering branch, Binghamton, N. Y., Sept. 1st, 1885.
2. A petal.
3. An effete stamen.
4. Pistil.
5. Horizontal section of the ovary.
(2–5 enlarged.)

---

* Orfila. *Taylor on Poisons*, p. 648.
† K. Ch. Grelin. *Florce bedensic*, p. 520.
‡ *Versuch. u. Bemerk. des Edin.*, pp. 95 and 98.
§ Rucker, *De effect, Solani in Commerc, Morci.*, p. 372.

|| *Alibert, Nouveaux Éléments de Thérapeutique.*
¶ *Eberle, Therapeutics.*
** *Ibid.*
†† *Journal de Clinic Medical.*

GENUS.—**HYOSCYAMUS**,* TOURN.

SEX. SYST.—PENTANDRIA MONOGYNIA.

126
HYOSCYAMUS.

HENBANE.

SYN.—HYOSCYAMUS NIGER, LINN.; H. FLAVUS, FUCHS.; H. PALLIDUS, KIT.; H. VULGARIS, RAII.; H. LETHALIS, SALISB.; H. AGROSTIS. COM. NAMES.—BLACK HENBANE, HOGBEAN, STINKING NIGHTSHADE, POISON TOBACCO; (FR.) JUSQUIAME NOIR; (GER.) BILSENKRAUT.

A TINCTURE OF THE WHOLE HERB HYOSCYAMUS NIGER, LINN.

Description.—This annual, or biennial, heavy-scented, viscid-pubescent, or villous herb, usually attains a growth of from 1 to 2 feet. *Root* fusiform; *stem* rigid. *Leaves* oblong, acute, the lower large, spreading upon the ground, sinuate-toothed and angled, the upper more or less amplexicaul and partly decurrent, the uppermost tending to be entire and bract-like, subtending the flowers. *Inflorescence* in secund, scorpioid, leafy spikes; *flowers* numerous, sessile. *Calyx* large, tubular-campanulate or urceolate; *border* 5-cleft, spreading; *teeth* equal, broadly triangular, acute. *Corolla* oblique, funnel-form, dull yellowish, strongly reticulated with anastomosing purple veins; *limb* spreading, inclined to be unequally 5-lobed and plaited; *lobes* shallow, rounded, and more or less acute. *Stamens* 5, declined, all perfect, and slightly exserted; *filaments* inserted upon the corolla-tube near its base and continuing attached for about half their length, where they are also hairy; *anthers* purple, turned upon their backs, and opening by a longitudinal chink. *Style* filiform; *stigma* dilated-capitate. *Capsule* membranaceous, 2-celled, enclosed by the persistent calyx, which is now many-costate and reticulate-veiny; *dehiscence* by an apical circumscissile line, the top falling away like a lid. *Seeds* very numerous, roundish-oval, slightly hollowed upon each side; *testa* conspicuously reticulated; *embryo* much curved, axile; *albumen* copious.

History and Habitat.—Henbane is indigenous to Europe and Western Asia, from whence it was introduced into this country by the English settlers, in the seventeenth century. It grows, with us, near dwellings and settlements, from Nova Scotia and Canada, southward to the environs of New York City and Brooklyn, where it blossoms from June to August. The seeds are notably tenacious of life; hence the plant is often found in localities after having disappeared years before.†

---

* Ὑς, ὑός, *Hus, hyos,* a hog; κναμος, *kyamos,* a bean; because it does or does not poison swine—an open question.

† Dr. Bigelow says: "About ten years since (1807), a drain, which intersects the Common in Boston, was opened for the purpose of repairs. In the following season a distinct row of very luxuriant plants of Henbane covered the whole of this drain, although none of them had been observed to grow in the vicinity the preceding year. The seeds which produced these plants had probably been buried for more than fifteen years."—*Am. Med. Bot.,* 1, 161.

Hyoscyamus—principally *H. albus*, Linn.—was medicinal among the ancients, and the Ὑοσκύαμος μελας of Dioscorides, who rejected *H. niger* as being too highly poisonous for use. The white species is also, according to Sprengel, described by Hippocrates. Pliny speaks of Henbane, as follows :* " Moreover, unto Hercules is ascribed Henbane, which the Latins call Appollinaris ; the Arabians, Altercum or Altercangenon ; but the Greeks, Hyoscyamus. Many kinds there be of it, the one beareth black seed, flowers standing much upon purple, and this herbe is full of prickes ; and in very truth such is the Henbane that groweth in Galatia. The common Henbane is whiter, and brauncheth more than the other, taller also than the poppie. * * * All the sort of these alreadie named trouble the braine, and put men besides their right wits ; besides that, they breed dizziness of the head. As touching the fourth, it carieth leaves soft, full of down, fuller and fatter than the rest : the seed also is white, and it groweth by the seaside. Physicians are not afraid to use this in their compositions, no more than that which has red seed. Howbeit, otherwiles, this white kind especially, if it bee not thoroughly ripe, prooveth to be reddish, and then it is rejected by the physicians. For, otherwise, none of them all would be gathered, but when they bee fully drie. Henbane is of the nature of wine, and therefore offensive to the understanding, and troubleth the head. Howbeit, good use there is, both of the seed it selfe as it is in substance, and also of the oile or juice drawne out of it apart. And yet the stalk, leaves, and roots are employed in some purposes. For mine owne part, I hold it to be a dangerous medicine, and not to be used but with great heed and discretion. For this is certainly knowne, that, if one take in drinke more than four leaves thereof, it will put him beside himself. An oile (I say) is made of the seed thereof, which, if it be but dropped into the eares, is ynough to trouble the braine. But, strange it is of this oile, that, if it be taken in drinke, it serveth as a counter poison. See how industrious men have been to prove experiments, and made no end of trying all things, insomuch as they have found meanes, and forced very poysons to be remedies." The Arabian physicians also rejected *H. niger* as a medicinal drug ; but in later years it gradually took the place of the white.

In Europe, the history of Henbane is remote. It is spoken of by Benedictus Crispus (A. D. 681) ; Macer. Floridus (10th Cent.) ; in Anglo-Saxon works (11th Cent.) ; " Physicians of Myddvai (13th Cent.) ; and *Arbolayre*, a French herbal (15th Cent.) ; from which time it fell into disuse, until brought again to the notice of physicians, in 1762, by Baron Störck.†

Hyoscyamus is now quite generally used by physicians of all schools, prescribing in the so-called physiological manner, as a sedative in various affections, such as epilepsy, hysteria, mania, febris nervosa, angina pectoris, etc. ; as an anodyne in rheumatism, arthritis, podagra, neuralgia, gastralgia, colica pictorum, cephalalgia, etc. ; as an anti-spasmodic in asthma, croup, pertussis, phthisical coughs, and irritable conditions of such organs as are mostly supplied with involuntary muscular fibres, as the diaphragm, heart, lungs, uterus, bladder, and urethra ; and as an hypnotic in all cases where opium would be used, did it not disagree. It is

---

* *Holland's Trans.*, 1601, 215. (Hamiltòn.)   † Flückiger and Hanbury, *Pharmacographia*, 463.

also claimed, in this connection, that Hyoscyamus rather tends to keep the bowels open, than to constipate like opium. Hyoscyamus leaves are often used as fomentations or cataplasms for painful swellings, such as irritable ulcers, indurated glands, and tumors, as well as in severe chordee, orchitis, etc. The doses given, are: 10 grains of the powdered leaves; 5 to 10 grains of the extract; one-half to 1 drachm of the tincture; or very small doses of Hyoscyamine.

The laity have often used the smoke of the smouldering leaves in odontalgia, by directing it into the caries by means of a paper funnel; but as convulsions, delirium, and other frightening symptoms have followed in some cases, this practice is now seldom resorted to.

The following preparations and *Hyoscyami Folia*, are officinal in the U. S. Ph.: *Abstractum Hyoscyami ; Extracta Hyoscyami Alcoholicum* and *Fluidum*, and *Tinctura Hyoscyami. Hyoscyaminæ Sulphas* is also recommended. In the Eclectic Dispensatory, a tincture and the two extracts are mentioned.

PART USED AND PREPARATION.—The fresh herb, gathered just before flowering, or after the seed pods are well formed and the summit of the plant is still flowering, is treated in the manner laid down for Dulcamara.* The resulting tincture has a clear brownish-orange color by transmitted light; the strong, heavy odor of the plant; an unpleasant, slightly bitter taste; and an acid reaction.

CHEMICAL CONSTITUENTS.—*Hyoscyamine,*† $C_{15}H_{23}NO_3$.‡ This noted, mydriatic, highly poisonous alkaloid, was first detected by Brandes; Geiger and Hesse procured it in an impure state from the herb in 1833, but it was not isolated in a pure state until 1871, when Höhn extracted it from the seeds, which are richer in this principle than the herb. It is described as an oily liquid, concreting later into verrucose-tufted crystals, which Duquesnel has succeeded in crystallizing into stellately grouped, acicular prisms. The crystals fuse at 90° (194° F.), and are soluble in ether, chloroform, alcohol, and water. Hyoscyamine is decomposed by caustic alkalies; and in aqueous solution, when boiled with Baryta, it splits into the two following bodies:

Hyoscine, $C_6H_{13}N$.— This volatile, oily liquid, of an alkaline reaction, having a narcotic odor, is now claimed, by Ladenburg, to be identical with *Tropine* (Belladonna); and that *Hyoscine* proper is a second alkaloid of Hyoscyamus, yielding different salts than either *Hyoscyamine* or *Tropine ;* and

Hyoscinic Acid, $C_9H_{10}O_3$.—This crystalline body, melting at 105° (221° F.), is isomeric with *Tropic Acid* (Belladonna) and may yet be found to be identical with it.

Oil of Hyoscyamus.—This thin, inodorous, greenish-yellow liquor, is obtainable from the seeds by pressure. It has a sp. gr. of 0.913, and is soluble in 60 parts of alcohol.

* Page 124–2.　　† Hyoscyamia, Duboisin.　　‡ Höhn and Reichardt; other authorities, $C_{17}H_{23}NO_3$.

Potassium Nitrate, KNO₃.—Crystals of this salt were isolated from this plant by Attfield.*

PHYSIOLOGICAL ACTION. — All parts of this plant are poisonous; the seeds, however, are the most active, the root next, and, lastly, the leaves and flowers. The effluvium arising from the cut and bruised leaves has been known to cause of itself, vertigo, stupor, and syncope.

On Animals.—Orfila states that the drug acts upon dogs much the same as upon man, producing dilation of the pupils, weakness of the posterior extremities, staggering, and insensibility. Moirond states that, given in large quantities to horses, it causes slight dilation of the pupils, spasmodic movements of the limbs, and increased heart's action. On cats it acts much the same as upon dogs. Upon gallinaceous birds it is supposed to have a baneful action; while cows, sheep, goats, rabbits, and many other animals are said to be but slightly affected.

On Man.—The action of Hyoscyamus upon man, is that of a powerful narcotic poison, a severe, cardiac, and cerebral stimulant, and tends to produce general paralysis of the nervous system. Of the delirium produced, Dr. Harley remarks —as Dioscorides had before him—that it greatly resembles that produced by alcoholic intoxication.

The symptoms in general, resulting from taking the drug, are: Lively, wild, or busy delirium, tending more to the grotesque than to the harmful type; the patient laughs, talks, gesticulates, dances, etc., and carphologia is often noticed; vertigo and confusion; eyes red, wild, and sparkling, with dilation of the pupils; insensibility of the retina, and illusions of sight; redness of the face; dryness of the mucous membranes of the mouth and fauces; paralysis of the tongue; difficult deglutition; nausea and vomiting; tympanitic distention of the abdomen; diarrhœa, and involuntary passages; paralysis of the bladder, and retention of urine; dry cough; rapid, irregular heart's action; trembling of the upper limbs, weakness of the legs; convulsions; insomnia; chill, fever, and sweat.

The following cases of poisoning by this drug, will serve to show its method of action: Nine persons, having eaten the roots of Hyoscyamus, were seized with alarming symptoms: "Some were speechless, and showed no other signs of life than by convulsions, contortions of their limbs, and the *risus sardonicus;* all having their eyes starting out of their heads, and their mouths drawn backwards on both sides; others had all the symptoms alike; however, five of them did open their mouths, now and then, but it was to utter howlings. The madness of all of these patients was so complete, and their agitations so violent, that, in order to give one of them an antidote, I was obliged to employ six strong men to hold him while I was getting his teeth asunder, to pour down the remedy. Upon their recovery, all objects appeared to them as scarlet, for two or three days."—(Dr. Patouillat, *Phil. Trans.*, 40, 446.)

---

* *Pharm. Jour.*, 1862, 447. For authorities upon the Chemistry of Hyoscyamus, and further study, see Bibliographical Index, in the Appendix.

Seven persons ate broth, in which the leaves of Hyoscyamus had been boiled; symptoms of intoxication soon followed: "I saw them about three hours after having eat it; and then three of the men were become quite insensible, did not know their comrades, talked incoherently, and were in as high a delirium as people in the rage of a fever; all of them had low, irregular pulses, slavered, and frequently changed color; their eyes looked fiery, and they catched at whatever lay next them, calling out that it was going to fall."—(Dr. Stedman, *Phil. Trans.*, 1750.)

Wepfer relates that several monks made a repast on the roots of wild endive (Cichorium Intibus), among which were mixed, by mistake, two roots of Henbane. In a few hours some experienced vertigo, others a burning of the tongue, lips, and throat; severe pains were also felt in the iliac regions, and in all the joints. The intellectual faculties and the organs of vision were perverted, and they gave themselves up to actions which were mad and ridiculous. In other cases, a haggard countenance, dilation of the pupils, difficulty of breathing, small and intermittent pulse, loss of speech, trismus, and temporary loss of intellect have been the principal symptoms; while the extremities have been observed to be cold and nearly paralyzed.—(Orfila 2, 135.)

A woman, æt. 34, swallowed, in mistake for a black draught, an ounce and a half of the *tincture* of Hyoscyamus, made apparently from the biennial plant, and resembling the pharmacopœial tincture. (The annual plant is said to make a weaker tincture.) In *ten minutes* she had a hot, burning, pricking sensation in the hands, feet, and legs; became giddy and delirious, and complained of great dryness in the throat. Shortly after, in attempting to get out of bed, she found her legs were powerless. A purplish rash appeared over the body, particularly about the neck and face, which were much swollen. The draught was taken at 5 A.M. At 9 A.M. Dr. White found her almost insensible and unable to speak. The tongue was swollen, brown, and dry, and put out with difficulty; the face swollen and scarlet; the pupils were so dilated that the iris was a mere thread-like ring; the skin hot and dry. The poison had been taken on an empty stomach. There was no sickness. In three hours she passed a motion smelling strongly of this drug, but the odor was not perceived in the urine. She could not see distinctly. All motion in the extremities was lost, and their sensibility was diminished. At 4 P.M. she was delirious, and there was a sickness; 11 P.M., shivering and coldness of the skin. At 9 A.M. the next day she could see and articulate better. The iris was half a line in breadth. Brandy, opium, ammonia, and other remedies were used, and she gradually improved. It was six days before she acquired a partial use of her legs, and could not then stand without being supported on both sides. She had quite lost her memory, and talked in a rambling manner. She was unable to remember for a minute a single sentence or word she had uttered or read.—(Dr. White, *Lancet*, July 5, 1873, p. 8.)

Two men ate the young shoots of the plant. The first effect was that the earth seemed to pass suddenly from under them; the tongue became paralyzed, and their limbs were cold, torpid, paralyzed, and insensible; the arms were in a state of spasmodic action; the pupils were dilated, the look was fixed and vacant;

breathing difficult; the pulse small and intermittent. Beside these symptoms, there was the spasmodic grin (*risus sardonicus*), with delirium ; and the jaws were spasmodically closed. Under treatment the men recovered in the course of two days.—(Orfila, 4ème ed., vol. 2, p. 264.)

A woman collected in a field a quantity of the roots by mistake for parsnips. They were boiled in soup, of which nine persons in the family partook without remarking any particular taste. Very shortly afterward the whole of these persons felt uneasy, and complained of a bitter, acrid taste in the mouth, with nausea. The pupils of the eyes were dilated, and there was indistinctness of vision. These symptoms were followed by great restlessness, convulsions, and continued delirium. The patients successively lost the power of vision, hearing, and voice, and were affected with stupor and insurmountable somnolency.—(*Ed. Med. and S. J.*, Oct., 1844, p. 562.)

Post-Mortem.—Orfila quotes a case of fatal poisoning by the roots, and Wibmer one by the leaves. The appearances were those of general congestion of dark-colored liquid blood in the venous system, such condition being found in the lungs and brain. There are commonly found no traces of irritation or inflammation in the stomach or bowels.

"The differential diagnosis of the three mydriatics in the treatment of head affections is fairly stated by Dr. Phillips. In cases of cerebral hyperæmia, the severer forms are removed by Belladonna, while Hyoscyamus proves its value when there is little or no congestion, but much excitement. So in the case of delirium ; the forms of this disorder, for which Hyoscyamus is adapted, are the milder and less inflammatory ones, whereas the severer cases are better dealt with by Belladonna and Stramonium. Hyoscyamus is specially useful again in those cases of delirium with hallucinations which are accompanied with little or no cerebral congestion, but where there is great excitability of the nervous system, and where there is reason to fear that the operation of opium would prove injurious."—(Hughes, *Pharmacodynamics*, p. 414.)

DESCRIPTION OF PLATE 126.

   1. A flowering and fruiting branch, from near Boston, July 27th, 1884.
      2. Opened corolla.
      3. Stamen.
      4. Opened calyx, showing pistil.
      5. Horizontal section of the ovary.
      6. Fruiting calyx.
      7. Fruit.
      8. Longitudinal section of fruit.
      9. Dehiscent fruit.
   10. Seed.
   11. Longitudinal section of seed } × 50 diameters.
          (2–9 enlarged.)

E.m. ad nat del. et pinxt.

HYOSCÝAMUS NÌGER, Linn.

127

STRAMONIUM.†

THORN-APPLE.

SYN.—DATURA STRAMONIUM, LINN.; STRAMONIUM SPINOSUM, GER.; S. FŒTIDUM, SCOP.; S. VULGATUM, GAERT.

COM. NAMES.—THORN-APPLE, DEVIL'S APPLE, MAD APPLE, APPLE OF PERU, JAMESTOWN OR JIMSON WEED, STINK-WEED; (FR.) POMME ÉPINEUSE OU L'ENDORMIE; (GER.) STECKAPFEL.

A TINCTURE OF THE FRESH RIPE SEED OF DATURA STRAMONIUM, L.

Description.—This rank, glabrous, annual, bushy berb, grows to a height of from 2 to 4 feet. *Root* tapering, somewhat branched. *Stem* very smooth, subcylindrical, green and succulent, at first bifurcating, then dichotomously branching. *Leaves* alternate, and at times opposite, upon the same plant, in reality more or less scattered; all more or less cordate at the base, but in many instances unequal, in this case one side of the base is prolonged decurrently along the upper side of the petiole. In outline the leaves are ovate, very irregularly sinuate, and laciniately toothed or angled; they are smooth, deep green above, pale beneath, and all the older ones are plentifully perforated by the ravages of worms. *Inflorescence* solitary in the forks of the branches; *flowers* erect, 2 to 4 inches long, raised upon a short rigid peduncle. *Calyx* tubular, prismatic, half-persistent, circumscissile, *i. e.*, separating transversely above the base, the upper portion falling away, the lower remaining persistent and forming in fruit a peltate border to the under side of the capsule; *limb* 5-toothed. *Corolla* infundibuliform, delicate, creamy white, convolute-plicate in æstivation; *limb* plaited, larger and spreading, 5-toothed; *sinuses* long subulate-pointed. *Stamens* 5, included; *filaments* long and filiform, inserted upon the tube of the corolla; *anthers* adnate, oblong and pointed. *Style* slender, longer than the stamens, but not exserted; *stigma* clavate, 2-lipped. *Fruit* an erect, globose-ovoid and more or less quadrilateral, divergently echinate, 2-celled pod; *pericarp* coriaceous; *valves* 4; *placentæ* 2, thick, projected from the axis into the middle of each cell, where each division becomes somewhat expanded into two placentiferous lines at the middle, thus rendering the pod in reality 4-celled, except at its apex. *Seeds* very numerous, rather large, laterally flattened horizontally, and somewhat reniform; *testa* crustaceous, scrobiculate-rugose; *embryo* much curved.

---

* The Arabic name *Tatorah* (Indian *Daturo*), given to *D. fastuosa*, Linn.

† Στρυχνομανικον, *strychnomanikon*, referring to its causing madness.

C.m..ad nat del. et pinxt.

DATÙRA STRAMÒNIUM, Linn.

History and Habitat.—Stramonium is judged by De Candolle to be indigenous to the Old World, probably to the borders of the Caspian Sea and the adjacent regions. It is one of the many Solanaceous plants whose origin is exceedingly doubtful. This species is now only found near the habitations of man, and then generally in garbage heaps where the soil is loose but rich, being in reality a true weed of civilization, scattered throughout almost all of the temperate and warmer regions of the globe. It was at one time seriously maintained that America was its birthplace, but in no locality here does it at all approach a situation that has the semblance of a natural site; so thoroughly does it cling to waste heaps that the American Aborigines named it *The White Man's Plant* in allusion to its only place of growth, *i. e.*, near the homes of the civilized. With us in the North, it blossoms from July to October, and ripens its capsules from September to November.

The first notice of Stramonium is, in all probability, that of Fuchsius (1542), who states that it was introduced into Germany from Italy.* Gerarde (who received some of the seeds from Lord Zouch, who sent them from Constantinople, about the end of the 16th century), cultivated the plant in England.

Baron Störck was first to introduce the plant into medicine, to any extent. He used it internally in mania and epilepsy. "If," he says, "Stramonium produces symptoms of madness in a healthy person, would it not be desirable to make experiments in order to discover whether this plant, by its effects on the brain in changing the ideas and the state of the sensorium (*i. e.*, of the part, whatever it may be, which is the centre of action of the nerves upon the body)—should we not, I say, try whether this plant would not restore to a healthy state those who are suffering from alienation of mind? and if by the change which Stramonium would cause in those who suffer from convulsions, by putting them into a contrary state to that in which they were, would it not cause their cure?" Bergius states † that he frequently saw maniacs restored to saneness of mind, which they never afterward lost, by the continued use of the extract of Stramonium; and that by the same means he effectually cured the delirium so often attendant upon child-birth.

In general practice Stramonium has been used as a narcotic, soothing drug, in chorea (Wedenberg); epilepsy (Odhelius); neuralgia; and tic-douloureux; and as an ointment, for the same purpose, in recent burns and scalds, nymphomania and rheumatism. One of its principal uses, however, has been that of the dried leaves, smoked as cigarettes, during the spasm of asthma, a practice highly recommended by Dr. Bigelow.

The officinal parts of this plant in the U. S. Ph., are: *Stramonii Folia* and *Stramonii Semen;* of the latter the preparations are: *Extractum Stramonii; Extractum Stramonii Fluidum,* and *Tinctura Stramonii.* In the Eclectic Materia Medica the following preparations are recommended: *Cataplasma Stramonii; Extractum Stramonii Alcoholicum; Tinctura Stramonii; Unguentum Stramonii.* The drug also plays a part in their *Tinctura Viburnii Composita* and *Unguentum Stramonii Compositum.*‡

---

* Sprengel, *Hist. Rei. Herb.*, ii, 326.   † *Bull. des Plantes Vén. et Susp. de Fr.*, i, 38; and *Mat. Med.*, l. c.
‡ Dulcamara, Stramonium, Cicuta, Belladonna, Rumex, and Oleum Terebinthinæ.

PART USED AND PREPARATION.—The ripe seeds are powdered and covered in a well-stoppered bottle, with five parts by weight of alcohol, and allowed to stand for eight days in a dark, cool place; vigorously shaking the vial twice a day.

The tincture separated from this mass by filtration is clear, and has a beautiful brownish-orange color by transmitted light. The slight odor it exhales is not characteristic; it has no peculiar taste, but leaves a numb feeling upon the tongue very similar to that caused by carbolic acid. Its reaction is acid.

Should the bottle be left longer before filtration, the tincture will become stronger each day until it is opaque. Then in thin layers it exhibits a beautiful orange-red color by transmitted light, and when looked down upon presents a brilliant iridescent, grass-green film, which does not change during agitation, although it appears like a stratum separable from the rest of the preparation. This last preparation is, of course, unofficinal, but is mentioned simply to show that our tincture does not represent the full strength of the seed.

CHEMICAL CONSTITUENTS.—*Datura-Atropine* or *Daturine.*—This body was discovered in Stramonium by Geiger and Hesse in 1833. A. von Planta in 1850 proved it identical with *Atropine,*[*] not only in solubility and fusibility, but also in its chemical composition ($C_{17}H_{23}NO_3$), and many physical properties. It differs, however, sufficiently to suggest to Herr Schmidt that we should distinguish the two products by prefixing the name of the plant from which each is derived. Ledenburg [†] says, doubtless Daturine, Hyoscyamine, Atropine, and Duboisine are identical.

The following points of difference are, however, distinguishable between the two alkaloids: The crystals are said to differ somewhat in form;[‡] datura-atropine is levogyrate, while atropa-atropine is non-rotary;[§] platinic chloride precipitates atropa-atropine salts, but not salts of datura-atropine, and picric acid precipitates datura-atropine, but not atropa-atropine;[||] atropa-atropine is said to be twice as poisonous as datura-atropine;[¶] and it is claimed that datura-atropine is thrice as powerful a dilatant of the pupil as its isomer, and that the dilation lasts longer.[**]

Atropa-atropine or *atropine,* $C_{17}H_{23}O_3$ as purified after its extraction from the flowering Belladonna, forms prisms, having a nauseous, bitter and burning taste, and causing a dryness of the mouth and fauces, with constriction of the throat. Even in very small doses it produces congestive headache and dilatation of the pupil. It is readily soluble in alcohol, less so in water; its solubility is increased in each by the addition of heat. It fuses at 90° (194° F.); and at 140° (284° F.) it breaks down, the greater portion being destroyed; by farther heating on platinum-foil it bursts into a flame, and the slight residue soon vanishes.

Stramonin.—This chemically uninvestigated body was separated from the tincture of the seeds, by Trommsdorf.[††] It is described as a white, tasteless powder; sparingly soluble in alcohol, insoluble in water and fusing at 150° (302° F.).

---

[*] *Am. Jour. Phar.*, XXIII., 38. [†] *Berichte. der Chem. ges.*, 1880, 380. [‡] Erhard, 1866.

[§] Poehl, *Petersb. Med. Wochensch.*, 1877, No. 20. [||] Poehl, l. c. [¶] Schroff.

[**] Jobert, *Ann. de Therap.*, 1863, 28. [††] Wittstein, l. c.

Brandes, in his analysis of the seeds, extracted a fixed oil, fat oil, fatty matter, wax, resin insoluble in ether, red extractive matter, uncrystallizable sugar, gum, gummy extractive, malic acid, and various uncharacteristic bodies.

PHYSIOLOGICAL ACTION.—Datura Stramonium acts very powerfully upon the cerebro-spinal system, causing a line of symptoms showing it to be a narcoto-irritant of high degree. The symptoms collated from many cases of poisoning by this drug are : Vertigo, with staggering gait, and finally unconsciousness ; stupor and deep sleep, with stertorous breathing ; mania, with loquaciousness or melancholia ; hallucinations of terrifying aspect, the patient bites, strikes and screams, and throws the arms about, or picks and grasps at unattainable objects ; congestive headaches, with dull beating and throbbing in the vertex. The pupils are dilated, and the patient suffers from photophobia, diplopia and hemeralopia ; the eyes are wide open, staring, and set, or are contorted, rolling, and squinting. The face becomes red, bloated, and hot, the mouth spasmodically closed, and the tongue dry and swollen ; the patient suffers greatly from thirst, but the sight of water throws him into a spasm and causes great constriction of the throat, foaming at the mouth, and other symptoms similar to those of hydrophobia. There is often nausea, but seldom vomiting. The sexual functions are often excited, more especially in women, in whom it causes nymphomania. Spasms of the muscles of the chest are of frequent occurrence ; inspiration is slow and expiration quick. Paralysis of the lower limbs and loss of speech, with twitchings and jerkings of muscles often mark a case. Its action will be seen to be similar to that of Belladonna, yet differing in many respects.

A few of the many cases of poisoning by this plant will serve to show its mode of action :

Beverly states* that some of the soldiers sent to Jamestown to quell the rebellion of Bacon, gathered the young sprouts of Stramonium and ate them as a potage, " the effect of which was a very pleasant comedy, for they turned natural fools upon it for several days. One would blow up a feather in the air, another would dart straws at it with fury ; another, stark naked, was sitting up in a corner like a monkey, grinning and making maws at them ; a fourth would fondly kiss and paw his companions, and smile in their faces with a countenance more antic than any in a Dutch droll. A thousand simple tricks they played, and after eleven days returned to themselves again, not remembering anything that had passed." J. R. Dodge states† that " *Datura meteloides* grows abundantly on the Colorado River, in Arizona, and that the Mohave Indians gather the leaves and roots, bruise and mix them with water, and after being allowed to stand several hours, the liquid is drawn off. It is a highly narcotic drink, producing a stupefying effect, which is not very easy to remove. The Mohaves will often drink this nauseous liquid, as they are very fond of any kind of intoxication." The California Indians use a decoction of this species to stimulate young females in dancing. The Pah-Utes call the plant *Main-oph-weep;* they ferment in the sun a watery infusion of the

---

* *Hist. of Virginia*, 121.   † *U. S. Agric. Rep.*, 1870, 423.

bruised seeds, and drink the liquor for the purpose of intoxication.* Dr. Schlesier met a case† in which the subject, a boy, æt. 4, mistook the fruit of Stramonium for poppy heads, and ate a quantity of them. "Soon afterwards his face was flushed, his eyes were glistening and in constant motion, the pupils much dilated, and the countenance was that of an intoxicated person. He sat up in bed quite unconscious, but continually babbling and occasionally starting up suddenly, his hands apparently directed at imaginary objects in the air. His pulse was very slow; there was no fever, but intense thirst and violent perspiration from incessant motion." Dr. Turner‡ describes the effects upon two children who had eaten the seeds: "In an hour and a half they were fully under the influence of the poison. They were lying on their backs, eyes bright, pupils widely dilated and insensible to light, conjunctiva injected, faces deeply suffused, and of a dark-crimson color; difficulty of breathing, inability to articulate, and in a state of complete insensibility, broken occasionally by a paroxysm, during which they would utter some indistinct sounds and throw their hands about, as if trying to ward off some threatening evil. They then fell into a comatose state, but were easily roused into a state of violent excitement; they grasped at imaginary objects; there was picking of the bedclothes, with paroxysms of excessive laughter."

The Thugs, a society of stealthy fanatic murderers of India, often employ *D. fastuosa* and *alba* to render their intended victims unconscious.

On Animals.—Orfila found that half an ounce killed a dog within twenty-four hours; and a quarter of an ounce applied to an open wound in another, killed him in six hours. The symptoms in each case showed that the effects were produced upon the nervous system in general.

Post-mortem.—The blood was found to be semi-fluid throughout the body, the few coagula that are met with in the auricles and large veins are very thoroughly formed and easily broken down. A slight injection of the mucous membrane of the larynx, pharynx, and upper portion of the œsophagus was observed. The rima glottidis was thickened and very turgid. The alimentary tract, however, was found absolutely normal.§

From the symptoms caused by this drug, its homœopathic adaptability to hydrophobia will be at once evident. There is no drug so far proven that deserves as thorough and careful a trial in this dread disease as Stramonium. The following, from a letter written by the Catholic Bishop of Singapore to the *Straits Times*, has just come to my notice. This bishop says he thinks it his duty to publish the remedies used in the missions in Tonquin for the cure of hydrophobia. These, he says, consist first, in giving as much star-aniseed as may be contained on a cent piece; and secondly, in making the patient take some water in which a handful of the leaves of stramony, or thorn-apple, or pear-apple, is infused. These will cause an access of the convulsions or delirium, during which the patient must be tied; but on its abatement he will be cured. If the remedy act too violently, either by

---

* Dr. Edward Palmer in *Am. Nat.*, 1878, 650. † Canstatt's *Jahrbuch*, 1844, 297.

‡ *Am. Jour. of Med. Sci.*, 1864, 552. § Mr. Duffin's case (his youngest daughter), *Lancet*, 1845, 195.

too much being administered, or on account of there being no virus of real hydrophobia, the consequences may be ameliorated by making the patient drink an
infusion of licorice root, a most precious antidote against poisoning by stramony.
In 1869, the bishop relates, a very honorable member of the clergy of Paris was
bitten by a pet dog, which died thirty hours afterwards with the most characterized convulsions of rabies. The following day he felt the first symptoms of the
dreadful disease, and these augmented in intensity every day. The priest, however, applied at once all sorts of known remedies, ancient and modern, and even
employed a very small dose of stramony. Each time he used the latter the pro-
gress of the disease ceased for some hours, even days, and then continued its
ravages with greater intensity than before. When the fatal issue was at hand,
just at the crisis of the disease, when the paroxysms had attained the greatest
violence, the patient, with almost superhuman energy, began chewing a pinch of
dried stramony leaves, swallowing the juice. The effect was not long in making
itself felt. In half an hour the disease had attained its height, the patient being
delirious during the convulsions ; but on the following day he was perfectly cured.
"The same remedy," concludes the bishop, "is used in India, and is always successful."

DESCRIPTION OF PLATE 127.

1. End of a flowering branch and portion of the main stem, Jersey City, N. J., July 10th, 1884.
   2. Stamen.
   3. Ovary.
   4. Stigma.
   5. Pollen x 200.
   (2–4 enlarged.)

N. ORD.—SOLANACEÆ.

Tribe.—NICOTIANEÆ.

GENUS.—**NICOTIANA,*** LINN.

SEX. SYST.—PENTANDRIA MONOGYNIA.

128

TABACUM.

TOBACCO.†

SYN.—NICOTIANA TABACUM, LINN., NICOTIANA MACROPHYLLA, SPRENGEL, LEHM., HYOSCYAMUS PERUVIANUS, GERARD.
COM. NAMES.—TOBACCO; (FR.) TABAC; (GER.) TABAK.

A TINCTURE OF THE LEAVES OF NICOTIANA TABACUM, L. A TINCTURE OF THE ALKALOID NICOTINUM.

Description.—This largely cultivated, rank, acrid, annual herb, the base of the most wide-spread of all narcotic habits, grows to a height of from 4 to 6 feet at its flowering season. *Root* long, fibrous and tap-shaped. *Stem* erect, simple, cylindrical, solid and viscid-pubescent. *Leaves* alternate, bright-green upon the upper surface, paler beneath, those of the base more or less petioled, large and broad, ovate and from one and one-half to two feet long, by from 10 to 18 inches broad; those of the upper part of the plant more or less amplectant, oval-oblong or oval-lanceolate, all entire acute and glandularly pubescent. *Inflorescence* a terminal spreading panicle of rose colored or white flowers; *bracts* lanceolate, acute. *Calyx* inflated-tubular or campanulate, 5-cleft, viscid-hairy; *teeth* narrow-lanceolate, acute. *Corolla*; *tube* funnel-form, clammy-pubescent, from one and one-half to two inches long; *limb* salver-form, plaited, 5-cleft, the lobes acute and broadly triangular. *Stamens* 5, equal or nearly so; *filaments* inserted upon the base of the corolla and nearly as long as the tube; *anthers* small, opening longitudinally. *Ovary* ovate, 2-celled; *style* slender, about equal in length to the filaments; *stigma* capitate, 2-lobed. *Fruit* a 2-celled ovate capsule, situated in the cup of the persistent calyx; *dehiscence* septicidal from the apex; *valves* 2, becoming at length separated; *pericarp* papyraceous, thin. *Seeds* innumerable, minute, subcylindrical; *testa* sinuously, raised-reticulate.

History and Habitat.—There seems to be little doubt that tobacco is a native of some portion of South or Central America, where it appears to have been used by the natives as a narcotic from prehistoric times. The first intimation history gives of its use, is the account of the Spaniards with Columbus, who, upon landing at St. Domingo, in 1492, discovered the natives smoking cylinders of the dried leaves, which they called *cohiba*. In 1498 its use was again noted by them upon

* Jean Nicot, *vide* History and Habitat, p. 128-2.   † Origin somewhat doubtful, *vide idem*.

the British West Indian Island of Tobago. It was either from this island, or from the native word meaning pipe, *tobaco*, that the specific name was derived. Tobacco was quite extensively used by the Spaniards in Yucatan as early as 1520, and from there its use was introduced into Spain by Hernandez de Toledo in 1559; about this time also, it was first grown in Europe, at Lisbon, and from there in 1560, Jean Nicot, ambassador to France, sent seeds, mentioning them as the germs of a medicinal plant of great value. From this circumstance Linnæus honored him with its generic name, *Nicotiana*. In 1585 its use by the Canadian Indians was discovered, and in 1586 it was brought to England by Sir Francis Drake and Sir Walter Raleigh and his companions. About the year 1600 the plant was introduced into Java, Turkey, India and China, though some historians feel confident that the Chinese had used the leaves long before this period, attempting thus to more fully substantiate the theory often promulgated that the Chinese had visited the western shores of America long before the discovery of the eastern coasts by the Spaniards. The rapidity with which this plant has traveled from one extremity of the temperate and torrid zones to the other, notwithstanding the act of English Parliament, the Popish bull, the Russian knout and death, the commands of the priests and sultans of Turkey and Persia, and the edict of the hwang-ti of China, is almost incredible, the very opposition that attended its first introduction into all countries seemed only to urge its onward rush, until it has gained to-day a prominence greater than any other known plant.

Besides the true Virginian tobacco (*Nicotiana Tabacum, L.*) for which the genus was composed, the following species and varieties have been determined: *N. rustica, L.*, a species with greenish-yellow flowers, cultivated in Mexico, India, Syria, and Turkey (*Latakia*), and found escaped in the northern United States; *N. Tabacum, var. undulata, Sendtner*, found in Brazil; *N. quadrivalvis, var. multivalvis, Gray*, a relic of aboriginal cultivation in Oregon; *N. Palmeri*, an Arizonian species (Palmer); *N. Clevelandi*, a Californian species (Cleveland); *N. Plumbaginifolia, Viv.*, a Mexican species (Berlandier); *N. fructicosa, L.*, a beautiful species with sharply pointed capsules; *N. persica, Lindl.*, cultivated as the fragrant Shiraz or Persian tobacco; *N. repanda, Willd.*, furnishing the fine Havana and Cuban leaves; *N. quadrivalvis, Pursh.*, used by the Indians along the Missouri river, and called by them *nonchaw*; *N. nana, Lindl.*, the plant of the Rocky Mountain tribes; *N. chinensis*, as cultivated in China and Japan; *N. trigonophylla, Dunal, N. Bigelovii, Watson*, and *N. attenuata, Torrey*, the leaves of all of which being used by the Indians of Utah, Arizona, New Mexico and Southern California, and said to be stronger than the cultivated plants (Palmer); *N. lancifolia, Willd.*, and *N. Ybarrensis, HBK.*, to which Prof. Asa Gray refers the *Yaqui Tobacco*, cultivated in Arizona (Palmer); and N. *petiolata*, a variety of cultivation in the United States.

The tobacco plant flowers in temperate regions from June to August, varying with the locality and season.

Tobacco can be raised in its proper soil at almost any point between the equator and the 50th degree N. or S. latitude, the better grades however not above the 35th degree, and the best between the 15th and 35th degrees, north.

The production of this narcotic for its specific use as before intimated is enormous, and increasing rapidly from year to year, the United States alone raising 472,061,175 lbs. in 1880, or nearly double the product for 1870. The estimated annual production of the globe is placed at about 3,000,000 tons! which, taking the world's population at present (1882) to be 1,433,887,600, would furnish each individual, without regard to age, sex, or condition, with over 4½ lbs.

As an habitual narcotic its modes of use are various. I place them here in the order of their harmfulness: Chewing without expectorating, inhalation of the smoke, chewing and expectorating, insufflation of snuff, and smoking without inhalation. The leaves are prepared for use,—after passing through processes which tend slightly to militate against the poisonous properties,—in the form of twists soaked in molasses or liquorice, for chewing, called *plugs;* shredded leaves more or less pure, for chewing or smoking, called *fine-cut;* finely-broken leaves, sometimes bleached, for smoking, termed *granulated tobacco;* rolled into cylindrical forms, either pure or saturated with nitre, as *cigars* and *cheroots;* rolled into small cylinders and wrapped in paper, as *cigarettes;* pulverized and kept dry or damp for insufflation or chewing, as *snuff;* and many other minor forms.

Its exhibition internally as a drug, must be conducted with the greatest care and watchfulness according to the susceptibility of the patient and the potence of the preparation. It was formerly quite esteemed as an anthelmintic, emetic, antispasmodic, cathartic, and sialagogue. Externally its forms of application were many in hemorrhoids, various skin diseases of man and beast, spasma glottidis, rheumatism, ulcers, tumors, and kindred affections.

Its official form in the U. S. Ph. is now simply *Folia Tabaci;* its former officinal preparations were dismissed at the 6th revision, 1882. In the Eclectic Materia Medica the preparations are *Infusum Tabaci, Oleum Tabaci* and *Unguentum Tabaci.*

PART USED AND PREPARATION.—The generic effects of Nicotiana being almost, if not quite identical in each species, and as the physiological effects have been gathered from all sources, varieties, and uses, the leaves of any fully-developed plant may be used. Place the dried and finely-cut leaves in a bottle, cover them with five parts by weight of alcohol, and allow them to stand at least eight days, well stoppered, in a dark, cool place. The tincture may then be pressed out and filtered. If prepared from Havana leaves, which contain the smallest percentage of nicotia, it presents a clear orange-brown color by transmitted light, the characteristic penetrating odor and taste of the plant, and only a slight acid reaction.

Nicotinum.—A Solution of one part by weight of the volatile alkaloid *nicotia* in 99 parts of absolute alcohol.

CHEMICAL CONSTITUENTS.—Nicotia,* $C_{10}H_{14}O_2$. This volatile alkaloid exists in the leaves and seeds of all species of the genus nicotiana, from which it may be extracted by aqueous or alcoholic distillation. The process best calculated to extract the full amount is Laiblin's modification of that of Schlœsing,†

---

* Nicotina, nicotin, nicotylia, nicotine, tabacine.   † *Annal. d. chem.,* vol. 196, p. 130.

substantially as follows: The cut leaves and stems are placed in some convenient apparatus, covered to a good depth with water, and allowed to digest 24 hours or more, then heated by means of superheated steam for half an hour, filtered and pressed. The mass is again dealt with in the same way, and the resultant liquids united and evaporated to one-third. Ten per cent. of the original weight of the tobacco of slaked caustic lime is now added, and the whole subjected to distillation by steam, until the disgusting odor of nicotia is no longer perceptible from the still. The distillate is now neutralized by a known weight of oxalic acid and evaporated to a thin syrup, the requisite amount of potassa to neutralize the known quantity of acid is now added, which causes a separation of the crude nicotia; this is collected and the menstruum treated with ether to extract the remaining alkaloid. Both resultants are now mixed, purified by distillation with hydrogen, solution in ether, shaking with powdered oxalic acid, solution again in ether, decomposing with potassa and redistillation in hydrogen. The distillate (Nicotia) is a colorless pure liquid, having a peculiar repulsive acrid odor not resembling tobacco, a burning taste, strong alkaline reaction, turning brown when exposed to light and air, and a specific gravity of 1.048 at 0° C. (32° F.). It boils at 250° C. (482° F.), is soluble to any quantity in water, alcohol or ether, and completely saturates acids.

The question as to the presence of nicotia in tobacco smoke, a point quite necessary to determine, seems still unsettled, many chemists of note having failed to detect its presence, while others find it in considerable quantity without apparent trouble. Vohl and Eulenberg (1871) conclude that nicotia is completely decomposed in the process of smoking, while Kissling (1882) in a comprehensive essay* criticises their process, and judges that their analysis was incorrect. He also criticises the analyses of Heubel, Le Bon and Pease, who found nicotia, and reports its presence in his own analysis. The smoke contains, according to Vohl and Eulenberg, who have made careful analyses,† *pyridine*, $C_5 H_5 N$; *piccoline*, $C_6 H_7 N$; *lutidine*, $C_7 H_9 N$; *collidine*, $C_8 H_{11} N$; *parvoline*, $C_9 H_{13} N$; *coridine*, $C_{10} H_{15} N$; *rubidine*, $C_{11} H_{17} N$; and *viridine*, $C_{12} H_{19} N$; all of which are bases occurring in coal-tar, and in Dippel's oil (*Oleum Animale Dippelii*), a product of the dry distillation of bones and other animal matter. Besides these another hydrocarbon, $C_{38} H_{18}$; carbonic anhydride; hydrocyanic acid; sulphuretted hydrogen; acetic anhydride; formic, propionic, butyric, valeric and carbolic acids; creosote; several hydrocarbons of the acetylene group; ammonia; methane and carbonic oxide were found present.

Oleum Tabaci.—This empyreumatic, tarry liquid doubtless contains many of the hydrocarbons mentioned above, and mixed with nicotia is in great part that subsidence found in the smoker's pipes.

Nicotianin.—Tobacco Camphor.—$C_{20} H_{32} N_2 O_3$. Hermbstadt (1823) observed floating separate upon the surface of an aqueous distillate of tobacco leaves, white laminæ, to which he gave the above name. Nicotianin consists of white, scale-like crystals, having a bitter aromatic taste, soluble in water, alcohol and ether, and emitting a tobacco-like odor.

---

* Quoted in *Jour. Chem. Soc.*, August, 1882.
† *Vierteljahrsschr. f. gerichtl. und offentl. Medicin*, N. ed., Vol. 14, p. 249.

Nicotinic Acid.—$C_5H_4N,CO.OH$, was first discovered by Huber, who subsequently recognized it as *carbopyridenic acid*. Weidel afterward separated this principle from nicotia by the use of nitric acid, and deemed his product identical with that of Huber; he gave it the formula $C_{10}H_8N_2O_3$.* Laiblin, however, (1879)† after successive tests favors the formula of Huber. This acid forms colorless, sublimable crystals, possessing a strongly acid taste.

Oil of Nicotiana Tabacum.—The fixed oil of the seeds, according to Wittstein, is golden-yellow, mild and inodorous, having a density of 0.917. A corresponding or identical oil, $C_{11}H_{22}O_2$, is found (Zeise) in *Oleum Tabaci*.

Tabacose.—The presence of this tobacco sugar has been determined by Prof. Attfield‡ in amounts varying in different samples, from about 5–10 per cent. The precise nature of this saccharose body is not yet known.

Besides the above the plant contains gum, mucilage, tannin, and from 15 to 30 per cent. of inorganic matters, salts of potassium, calcium and magnesium, as sulphates, phosphates, malates, nitrates and probably citrates, these latter differing in quantity according to the nature of the soil in which the individual grows, and showing it to be a very exhaustive crop.

PHYSIOLOGICAL ACTION.—The important question of whether the use of tobacco in moderation is harmful or not, has been decided in the negative by many of the highest authorities. It would seem that he who can use it at all, and who notes no symptoms from its moderate exhibition, is not particularly injured. In this as with all other drugs, it must be remembered, that what is moderation in one individual is often excess in another, and that, therefore, the dose, whether taken as a remedy or otherwise, must in all cases be suited to the particular individual under consideration. Concerning the many essays that are written upon this subject, the fact that all of them show to a careful reader whether the writer is a user or not, renders them very unsatisfactory and more or less faulty through partisanship.

Chronic effects.—It is almost an impossibility to gain a systematic knowledge of the chronic effects of tobacco poisoning, though the sources of information upon this subject would seem at first to be excellent. The effects produced upon smokers are almost useless in the study of the *drug* itself, and it is only in that class of chewers who swallow the juice, that positive data could be looked for; still here, as well, we are at a loss to determine facts, for in manufacturing the narcotic processes are used which alter the product greatly; nevertheless some few symptoms seem to be more or less common to all who have been for protracted periods subjected to the drug. Mental anxiety and irritability, with at times confusion of ideas; dilation of the pupils; ringing in the ears; increased secretion of saliva; uncertainty of speech; dryness of the throat; at times weakness of the stomach and nausea; increased secretion of urine; dry cough especially at night; præcordial oppression with palpitation of the heart and at times an irregular pulse; trembling of the extremities when held long in one position; general

* Laiblin, *Jour. Chem. Soc.*, October, 1879, quoted from *Liebig's Annalen*.　　† Ibid.
‡ *Pharm. Jour. Trans.*, Jan. 12, quoted in *Am. Jour. Phar.*, 1884, p. 147.

anæmic condition of the blood; spasmodic contractions or jactation of single muscles; sensations of exhaustion and especially lassitude; sleepiness; profuse perspiration, and sensitiveness to cold.

It would seem to be a fact, that in habitual users of this or any other toxic drug, the drug acts more or less as its own antidote, for immediately upon discontinuance of its use the preponderance of its symptoms arise.

The effects of tobacco or its alkaloid nicotia in toxic quantities, when taken into the stomach, injected into the rectum, or applied to a denuded surface are:

Ante-mortem.—Faintness, vertigo and trembling, with extreme nausea, torpor, stertorous breathing, weak irregular pulse, relaxation of the muscles, and vomiting; followed by severe spasms or paralysis, advancing coldness of the extremities, collapse with cold sweat, and death.

Post-mortem.—Excessive cadaveric rigidity, a general contraction and congestion of all hollow organs; the heart, stomach, intestines, kidneys and bladder; a congestion of the cerebellum, liver, portal and mesenteric veins, and mucous membranes either as a whole or only in patches. The blood is found everywhere very dark and liquid.

On Animals.—Johnston states* that the Hottentots are said to kill snakes by placing a drop of the empyreumatic oil of tobacco upon their tongues. Death follows instantly as by an electric shock, or a dose of hydrocyanic acid. The action of nicotia upon small species seems to be in general almost as instantaneous as above; especially upon the *carnivora*, where its action seems more intense.

Tobacco, then, from the foregoing facts, acts as a severe irritant to the ganglionic centers, producing thence an action at first paralytic, then spasmodic, affecting the sympathetic, motor and vaso-motor systems.

DESCRIPTION OF PLATE 128.

1. Whole plant, eight times reduced, from a cultivated specimen. Chemung, N. Y., Sept. 11, 1879.
   2. Flower.
   3. Fruit.
   4. Seed (somewhat enlarged).
   5. Section of fruit.

---

*Chem. of Com. Life, Vol. II., p. 28.

3

2

4

5

1

𝕰.m. ad nat del.et pinxt.   NICOTIÀNA TABACUM, Linn.

Tribe.—MENYANTHEÆ.

GENUS.—**MENYANTHES,*** TOURN.

SEX. SYST.—PENTANDRIA MONOGYNIA.

129
MENYANTHES.

BUCK BEAN.

SYN.—MENYANTHES TRIFOLIATA, LINN.; MENYANTHES VERNA, RAF.;
TRIFOLIUM PALUDOSUM, GER.; TRIFOLIUM FIBRINUM, G. PH.
COM. NAMES.—BUCK BEAN, BOG BEAN, MARSH TREFOIL, MARSH CLO-
VER, WATER SHAMROCK, BITTER ROOT; (FR.) MENYANTHE TREFLE,
TREFLE D'EAU; (GER.) BACHSBOHNE, BITTERKLEE, FIEBERKLEE.

A TINCTURE OF THE WHOLE FRESH PLANT MENYANTHES TRIFOLIATA, LINN.

Description.—This beautiful bog perennial is characterized as follows: *Root-stalk* horizontal, creeping, long, thick, sub-cylindrical, and conspicuously marked by the remains of the sheaths of previous petioles; *roots* long, at first stout and simple, then attenuated and greatly branched. *Leaves* alternate, trifoliate, midribs very prominent and conspicuously pale; *petioles* long and thick at the base, where they are surrounded by large membranaceous sheathing bracts; *leaflets* oval or oblong, situated at the summit of the petiole; *margins* entire, or sometimes slightly crenate or obscurely serrate. *Inflorescence* a simple, terminal, pyramidal raceme; *scape* naked, arising from the axils of the previous year's leaves; *bracts* ovate, membraneous, obtuse, shorter than the pedicels; *flowers* 10 to 15, white or pinkish. *Calyx* persistent, much shorter than the corolla; *limb* 5-parted, the segments oblong-obtuse. *Corolla* deciduous, infundibuliform; *limb* 5-parted, spreading, its whole upper surface densely bearded; *æstivation* induplicate. *Stamens* scarcely one-half the length of the corolla; *anthers* oblong, sagittate. *Style* slender, persistent, somewhat exserted; *stigma* capitate, 2-lobed. *Fruit* a 1-celled, ovoid capsule; *pericarp* thin, pale brown; *dehiscence* irregular, but more or less loculicidal; *placentæ* in the middle of the valves. *Seeds* numerous, minute; *testa* hard, rough, and shiny.

Gentianaceæ.—A large order of smooth herbs, having a colorless, bitter juice, and scattered throughout all portions of the globe. *Leaves* generally opposite, sessile, and entire (Exc. Menyantheæ); *stipules* wanting. *Inflorescence* solitary, cymose or racemose; *flowers* regular and showy. *Calyx* persistent; *corolla* marcescent, funnel- or salver-form. *Stamens* as many as the lobes of the corolla, and inserted upon its tube. *Styles* united or absent; *stigmas* 2-lobed. *Ovary* 1-celled

---

* Μηνίανθος, μήνη, *mene*, month; ἄνθος, *anthos*, flower; from its reputed power in promoting menstruation.

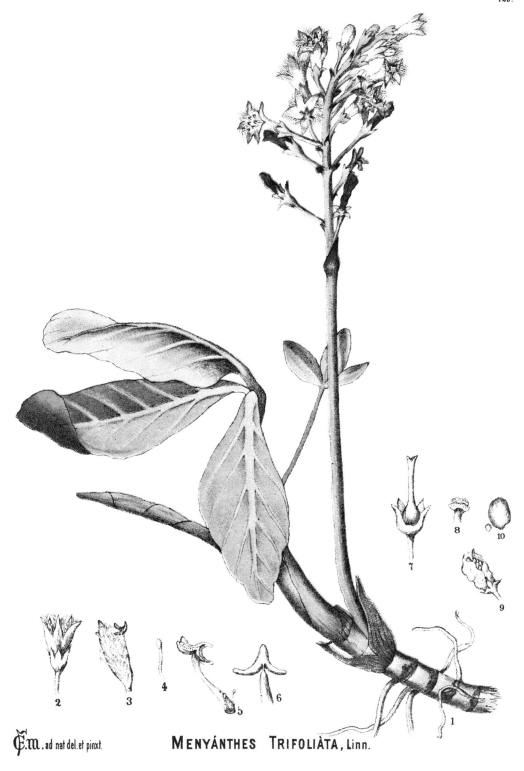

2   3   4   5   6   7   8   9   10   1

C.M. ad nat del. et pinxt.

MENYÁNTHES TRIFOLIÀTA, Linn.

or imperfectly 2-celled; *placentæ* 2, parietal, or sometimes the whole inner surface of the ovary placentiferous. *Fruit* a 2-valved capsule; *dehiscence* septicidal. *Seeds* small, anatropous; *embryo* minute, straight, and axial; *albumen* sarcous.

Besides Menyanthes, this order furnishes our Materia Medica three other proven species, viz.: The Chilian Centaury or Canchalagua (*Erythræa Chilensis*, Pers.); the Austrian Cross-wort (*Gentiana cruciata*, L.); and the European Yellow Gentian (*Gentiana lutea*, L.).

Many other species are used in medicine, principal among which are the following species of Gentiana, which often figure as substitutes for *G. lutea:* The North American *G. Catesbaei*, Walt.; and the European *G. amarella*, L.; *campestris*, L.; *purpurea*, L.; *pannonica*, Murr.; and *punctata*, L. The Indian *Gentiana Kurroo*, Royle, is used in its country in a similar manner to *G. lutea* in Europe. The North American Columbo (*Frazera Carolinensis*, Walt.) has, when fresh, properties quite similar to *G. lutea;* as have also the European Centaury (*Erythræa Centaurium*, Pers.), and *Chlora perfoliata*, L. The Indian Chiretta (*Ophelia Chirayta*, Don) is bitter, tonic, and febrifuge, and is used by English physicians in India as a substitute for Cinchona. The East Indian *Cicendia hyssopifolia*, Wright & A., is tonic and stomachic. The American Centaury (*Sabbatia angularis*, Pursh.) is a bitter tonic and febrifuge, often employed in remittent and intermittent fevers. The South American *Lisianthus purpurascens*, Aubl., *pendulus*, Mart., *grandiflorus*, Aubl., and *amplissimus*, Mart., are claimed to be extremely bitter tonics, esteemed as febrifuges and anthelmintics, as are also the European *Villarsia nymphæoides*, Vent., and the Cape of Good Hope *V. ovata*, D. C. The Guianian *Coutoubea spicata*, and *C. ramosa*, Aubl., are bitter tonics, much used as emmenagogues, anthelmintics, and for the removal of intestinal obstructions. *Limnanthemum Indica* is accounted a holy plant by the Chinese, in consideration of its many virtues; *L. nymphoides* is febrifugal; while the leaves of *L. peltata* are eaten in Japan as a potage.

A peculiar property pervades the whole of this natural order—the species when fresh are all emetic and cathartic, and, when dry, tonic and stomachic in varying degrees.

History and Habitat.—The Buck Bean is a native of the temperate regions of the Northern Hemisphere, from Alaska throughout the northern portions of North America, south of Greenland, Iceland, Scotland, Norway, Sweden, Russia, and eastward to the confines of Siberia. In the United States it extends southward as far as Wisconsin in the west and Pennsylvania in the east. It habits freshwater bogs, marshes, and ditches which retain water throughout the summer season, and blossoms in May and June.

The previous uses of the dried plant in medicine were all dependent more or less upon its so-called tonic action; while in a fresh state it was used as an energetic cathartic. As early as 1613 a Swedish writer, Johannes Franckenius, states that a decoction of the herb removes all visceral obstructions, acts as an emmenagogue and diuretic, kills intestinal worms, and is an efficacious remedy in scrofula. Besides its use in amenorrhœa, Menyanthes was considered valuable in the treatment of atonic dyspepsia, and derangements of the digestive tract, as well as a useful remedy in remittent and intermittent fevers.

Cullen speaks of the root as efficacious in obstinate cutaneous affections of a seemingly cancerous nature; Boerhaave claims to have relieved gout in his own case by drinking the juice of the plant in whey. Dr. Alston remarks "that this plant has remarkable effect in the gout in keeping off the paroxysms, though not to the patient's advantage." The general use of Menyanthes has been mostly as a substitute for gentian and columbo.

In Sweden the leaves are often used in brewing; two ounces of which are said to equal a pound of hops, for which they are substituted. Linnæus notes that in Lapland, in times of scarcity, the dried and powdered roots have been used, mixed with meal, in bread-making; he, however, characterizes the result as "amarus et detestabilis," which one can readily imagine, as neither dryness nor heat removes the bitterness of the roots.

PART USED AND PREPARATION.—The whole fresh plant, gathered when budding to blossom, is to be chopped and pounded to a pulp, enclosed in a piece of new linen and subjected to pressure. The expressed juice is then, by brisk agitation, mingled with an equal part by weight of alcohol. This mixture should then be poured into a well-stoppered bottle, and allowed to stand eight days in a dark, cool place. The tincture, separated from the mass by filtration, should be opaque, and in thin layers present a deep olive-green color by transmitted light. It should have a strong herbaceous odor, a lasting, extremely bitter taste, and a strong acid reaction.

CHEMICAL CONSTITUENTS.—Menyanthin, $C_{33}H_{54}O_{16}$.[*] This uncrystallizable glucoside is derivable from the whole plant; when pure it exists as a white, bitter powder that is freely soluble in water and alcohol, but insoluble in ether. Menyanthin softens at 60°–65° (140°–149° F.), becomes liquid at 115° (239° F.), and carbonizes at higher temperatures.

Menyanthol, C_8H_8O.—This body, together with a brown resin and glucose, is formed by the destruction of Menyanthin with dilute sulphuric or muriatic acid. It results as an oily liquid, possessing a burning taste and a penetrating odor, similar to that of oil of bitter almonds.

Menyanthic Acid.—When Menyanthol is exposed to the air for some time it is oxidized to a white crystalline mass of unknown chemical composition, which is at present provisionally known by this name.

The analysis of Trommsdorf[†] resulted in the separation of albumen, resin, malic acid, "a peculiar matter precipitated by tannin," gum, inulin, and a bitter principle, which Brandes[‡] succeeded in gaining as an amorphous mass of mostly yellowish-white grains (impure Menyanthin). Tilden's analysis[§] corresponds with that of Trommsdorf, but does not specify the amylose body found as inulin.

---

[*] Kromayer and Froehde, *Phar. Jour.*, ser. 2, vol. iii., 579.

[†] *Ann. de Chim.*, lxxii., 191.

[‡] *Phar. Jour.*, ser. 1, vol. ii., 660.

[§] *Jour. Mat. Med.*, N. S., vol. ii., 90.

PHYSIOLOGICAL ACTION.—Large doses of the root of this plant cause profuse vomiting and purging, together with exhausting diaphoresis. Smaller doses cause confusion and vertigo, pressive headache, dimness of vision, contraction of the pupil, twitching of the facial muscles, a sensation of coldness in the stomach and œsophagus, followed by nausea, distension and fulness of the abdomen, with griping, constipation, frequent desire to urinate with scanty discharge, oppression of the chest with increased respiration and accelerated pulse, cramps in the legs, sleeplessness, coldness of the extremities, followed by fever without thirst, and extreme weakness of the whole body.

DESCRIPTION OF PLATE 129.

1. Whole plant, Appalachin, N. Y., June 2d, 1885.
   2. Flower.
   3. Petal and stamen.
   4. A hair of the corolla.
   5. Stamen, with open anther.
   6. Anther, showing under surface.
   7. Pistil.
   8. Stigma.
   9. Fruit.
   10. Seed, natural size and enlarged.
   (2–8 enlarged.)

GENUS.—**GELSEMIUM**,* JUSS.

130

GELSEMIUM.†

YELLOW JESSAMINE.

SYN.—GELSEMIUM SEMPERVIRENS, AIT.; GELSEMIUM LUCIDUM, POIR.: GELSEMIUM NITIDUM, MICHX.; GELSEMIUM SEU JASMINUM LUT. ODOR. ETC., CATESBY; BIGNONIA SEMPERVIRENS, LINN.; ANONYMOS SEMPERVIRENS, WALT; LISIANTHUS SEMPERVIRENS, MILL.
COM. NAMES.—YELLOW JESSAMINE OR JASMINE, FALSE JASMINE, WILD JESSAMINE, WOODBINE;‡ (FR.) JASMIN JAUNE; (GER.) GELBER JASMIN.

A TINCTURE OF THE FRESH ROOT OF GELSEMIUM SEMPERVIRENS, AIT.

Description.—This beautiful, evergreen, woody, twining plant, often attains great heights, its growth depending somewhat upon its chosen support. *Root* long, ligneous, varying from nearly two inches in diameter to a few lines; *root-bark* of a cinnamon-brown color, and about two lines in thickness; *wood* light-yellow. *Stems* branching, at first with a more or less smooth, light slate-colored bark, then smooth and purplish. *Leaves* opposite, persistent, on short petioles; shining, lanceolate or ovate-lanceolate, bright green above and pale beneath; *stipules* inconspicuous. *Inflorescence* small axillary clusters; *flowers* sweet scented, on scaly bracted pedicels. *Calyx* small; *lobes* 5, imbricated, nearly distinct, ovate and acute. *Corolla* large, from 1 to 1½ inches long, open funnel-form; *lobes* 5, nearly equal, rounded and imbricated. *Stamens* 5, inserted on the base of the corolla-tube; *filaments* equal; *anthers* long, sagittate, adnate, and extrorse. *Ovary* elliptical, smooth, compressed, 2-celled; *ovules* several in each cell, ascending; *style* long and slender; *stigmas* 2, each bifurcated, the lobes linear and equal. *Fruit* an ovoid oblong, beaked, pendent capsule; *pericarp* papyraceous, splitting septicidally into two scaphoid valves. *Seeds* many, imbricated, light-brown, surrounded by a thin, flat, membranous border, which is prolonged at one extremity into a slightly wrinkled wing.

Loganiaceæ.—This order is composed of herbs, shrubs, or trees, and forms a connective between the orders *Gentianaceæ, Apocynaceæ, Scrophulariaceæ,* and *Rubiaceæ.* Its distinguishing characteristics are: *Leaves* opposite and entire; *stipules* present or represented by a stipular line. *Flowers* regular and perfect, 4-5-merous and androus. *Ovary* free from the calyx.
The Loganiaceæ of our Materia Medica are: Ignatia (*Strychnos Ignatii,*

---

* Gelsemino, the Italian for Jessamine.   † Not Gelsemi*n*um.
‡ The only woodbine in this country is *Lonicera grata, Ait.* (Caprifoliaceæ).

Berg.) ; Nux (*Strychnos Nux-Vomica, Linn.*) ; Indian pink (*Spigelia Marilandica, Linn.*), and Spigelia (*Spigelia anthelmia, Linn.*).

History and Habitat.—The yellow jessamine of the southern United States grows from Virginia southward, extending into Mexico. It flowers in March and April, and some years a second time, at least I am given to understand that such is the case in the State of Georgia. Although its support somewhat regulates the extent of the growth of this climbing vine, still it extends beyond the limits of the support in such a manner as to form beautiful trails and fringes ; this occurs even above trees that are over 50 feet high. The beautiful yellow flowers, the odor of which is said to be narcotic, yield a delightful perfume, which may be extracted by a process similar to that used for procuring oil of rose (Porcher).

The medical history of this plant is quite modern, having been brought into notice, according to Dr. King, by a Mississippi planter, for whom in his illness the root was gathered in mistake for that of another plant ; after partaking of an infusion serious symptoms arose, so alarming in their character that his friends expected his death ; upon his revival, however, it was apparent that the attack of bilious fever from which he had been suffering had disappeared. This accidental cure came to the knowledge of a pretender, who prepared a proprietary nostrum from the plant, called the "Electric Febrifuge." Dr. Porcher, of South Carolina, noting the use of gelsemium in the works of Elliott and Frost, brought it again into notice through the mediumship of a report on the medical botany of his state, made to the Am. Med. Ass'n, in 1849. The first provings were made by Dr. Henry (1852), whose work was followed by many provers, the principal among them being Dr. E. M. Hale, whose "Monograph on Gelsemium" has been a most efficient help to the true knowledge of this valuble American addition to our medicamentæ.

Gelsemium is official in the U. S. Ph. as *Extractum Gelsemii* and *Tinctura Gelsemii*, and in the Eclectic Materia Medica as *Tinctura Gelsemini*.

PART USED AND PREPARATION.—Under this rubric it should be borne in mind that "root-gatherers" often mingle with Gelsemium root that of a similar twiner growing in like manner and localities ; this plant is known as *White Jessamine* or *White Poison Vine*. The following comparison will suffice to distinguish them :

Yellow Jessamine.	*White Jessamine.*
Flowers yellow.	*Flowers* dirty-white.
Stem-bark smooth and uniformly gray.	*Stem-bark* maculate and striate with white.
Tendrils wanting.	*Tendrils* present on the lower stem.
Leaves ovate-lanceolate, acute at both extremities.	*Leaves* ovate, taper-pointed, heart-shaped at the base.
Petioles (leaf-stalks) short.	*Petioles* (leaf-stalks) long.
Root fibrous, in section showing a yellowish wood.	*Root* not so fibrous, in section showing white wood.
Taste pleasantly bitter.	*Taste* bitter and nauseous.

PREPARATION.—Small sections of the fresh root, cut from where the whole diameter is not greater than that of a goose-quill,* are to be chopped and weighed.

---

* The woody portion of the root contains none of the alkaloid; this fact was determined by Eberle (1869), and corroborated by Gerrard (1883).

Then two parts by weight of alcohol are taken, the chopped root mixed thoroughly with one-sixth part of it, and the rest of the alcohol added. After having stirred the whole well, allow it to stand in a well-stoppered bottle for at least eight days in a dark, cool place.

The tincture, separated from this mass by filtration, should have a clear, slightly brownish, orange color by transmitted light, an odor like that of an enraged honey bee, a pleasantly bitter taste, and a slightly acid reaction.

CHEMICAL CONSTITUENTS.—Gelsemine,* $C_{12} H_{14} NO_2$. This alkaloid, extracted from an alcoholic percolate of the powdered root, was determined by Kollock (1855).† Sonnenschein (1876) gave it the formula $C_{11} H_{19} NO_2$, but Gerrard (1883)‡ judges that the alkaloid used by him must have been impure, as his careful determinations result in the formula given above. Gelsemine, according to Gerrard and others, is a colorless, bitter, odorless, amorphous, brittle, transparent body, without definite crystals, fusing into such mass at a little below 200° C. (392° F.). It is soluble in alcohol, slightly also in boiling water, forms crystalline soluble salts with acids, and gives no color reactions with sulphuric or nitric acids.

Gelsemic Acid.§—$C_{30} H_{34} O_{19}$. Sonnenschein (1876) claimed that this body was identical with the glucoside *æsculin*,|| but Wormley (1882),¶ after careful chemical and physiological analyses, determines that it is similar to, but not identical with, that body. According to the latter observer gelsemic acid is readily crystallizable into needles, but slightly soluble in water, and soluble in alcohol, ether, and chloroform. Kollock** determined, beside gelsemine, a dry and a fatty resin, volatile oil, and a yellow coloring matter.

PHYSIOLOGICAL ACTION.—Many cases of poisoning by the inadvertent use of this drug are reported, from which, together with the experiments of Wormley,†† we glean the following rationale of its action :

The following symptoms are entailed by doses of from one drachm to an ounce of the fluid extract: Nausea, with ineffectual attempts to vomit ; dimness of vision or diplopia, especially on turning the head to one side ; congestion of the face ; spasms of the larynx and pharynx ; restlessness ; great prostration ; feeble, irregular, and intermittent pulse ; irregular and slow respiration with gasping ; loss of muscular power, with incoördination ; extremities at first hot and dry, then cold and moist ; dilated pupils insensible to light ; eyes fixed and protruding ; inability to raise the eyelids. Death follows without previous loss of consciousness or convulsions.

Post-Mortem.—Venous congestion ; collapsed lungs that are otherwise natural ; the adipose tissue is found suffused with bile ; blood dark, grumous, and enfibrinated ; the brain and spinal cord are found pale and anæmic. By this it will be seen that there are no characteristic post-mortem appearances.

---

* *Gelsemina, gelsemia, gelseminia.*   † *Am. Jour. Phar.*, 1855, p. 203.
‡ A. W. Gerrard, *Am. Jour. Phar.*, 1883, p. 256.   ₰ *Gelseminic acid.* || See Æsculus Hippocastanum, 43.
¶ T. G. Wormley, *Am. Jour. Phar.*, 1882, p. 357.   ** Ibid.   †† *Am. Jour. Phar.*, Jan., 1870.

Gelsemium then lowers the rate of the action of the heart and lungs, thus reducing the bodily temperature; dilates the pupil by paralyzing the motor oculi (differing here from Belladonna, which also dilates the pupil, but does so by irritating terminal filaments from the carotid and cavernous plexuses of the sympathetic system). Its action on the motor oculi causes also a loss of accommodation, and paralysis of the epicylia; this paralysis is gradually followed by a general paralytic action until the animal becomes impassive, but remains conscious until death. Gelsemium seems to act exactly opposite to Conium, the former destroying all reflex action from the centre to the periphery, the latter from the periphery to the centre. The natural antidote to this drug seems to be black coffee rather than opium; alcoholic stimulants and heat should also be plied.

DESCRIPTION OF PLATE 130.

1. End of flowering stem, Augusta, Ga.,* May 23d, 1883.
    2. A portion of the stem.
    3. Calyx and bracts (enlarged).
    4. Stamens (enlarged).
    5. Pistil (enlarged).
    6. Section of the ovary (enlarged).
    7. Fruit.

* From one of a number of living specimens, kindly sent me together with the fruit, by Miss Mary C. Cuthbert

Œm. ad nat del. et pinxt.   GELSÉMIUM SEMPÉRVIRENS, Aiton.

GENUS.—**SPIGELIA**,* LINN.

SEX. SYST.—PENTANDRIA MONOGYNIA.

131
SPIGELIA MARILANDICA.

PINK ROOT.

SYN.—SPIGELIA MARILANDICA, LINN.; S. OPPOSITIFOLIA, STOKES; S. AMERICANA, MONRO; LONICERA MARILANDICA, LINN.
COM. NAMES.—MARYLAND PINK ROOT, INDIAN PINK, WORM GRASS, PERENNIAL WORM GRASS, SNAKE ROOT, CAROLINA PINK ROOT, STAR BLOOM; (FR.) SPIGÉLIA DE MARYLAND; (GER.) NORDAMERIKANISCHER SPIGELIE.

A TINCTURE OF THE FRESH ROOT OF SPIGELIA MARILANDICA, LINN.

Description.—This Southern perennial herb usually grows to a height of from 1 to 2 feet. *Root* fibrous, twisted; *stems* several from the same root, simple, 4-angled and glabrous. *Leaves* opposite, membranaceous, ovate to ovate-lanceolate, acuminate, closely sessile by a rounded base, entire, one or two pairs of veins basal, the rest more or less pinnate; *stipules* small, interpetiolar. *Inflorescence* in a terminal, sometimes branched, unilateral, scorpioid spike; *flowers* showy, erect; *pedicels* single or geminate; *bracts* minute and subulate, or wanting; *peduncle* short and naked. *Calyx* 5-parted; *lobes* very slender and narrow. *Corolla* scarlet without, yellow within, elongated-tubular, 15-nerved; *tube* somewhat clavate; *lobes* 5, ovate-lanceolate, about one-quarter the length of the tube. *Stamens* 5, inserted above the middle of the corolla-tube; *filaments* short, slightly exserted; *anthers* erect, linear-oblong, 2-celled at the base. *Ovary* superior, smooth, compressed; *ovules* numerous; *placenta* peltate, stipitate; *style* long, the lower portion flattened, the upper cylindrical, the two parts articulated, and the lower persistent, farther exserted than the stamens; *stigma* simply the somewhat inflated hairy end of the style. *Capsule* didymous, compressed contrary to the partitions, circumcissile above the cupule-like base, the two carpels somewhat loculicidally 2-valved. *Seeds* few, peltate, closely packed, and angled by mutual pressure; *embryo* short and straight; *albumen* fleshy.

History and Habitat.—This beautiful plant is indigenous to North America, where it extends from Southern New Jersey to Wisconsin, and southward to Florida and the borders of Texas; it is, however, rare north of central Virginia. It grows in rich soil on the borders of woods, and blossoms from May to July, according to its station.

---

* In honor of Adrian Spiegel, the probable originator of *Herbaria*.

Among the Aborigines, even before the discovery of America, this plant was valued as an anthelmintic; the colonists of the South received their information concerning its properties from the Cherokees, who called it *unsteetla*, and from the Osages, who used it also as a sudorific and sedative, under the name of *mikaa*. It was first introduced to the notice of physicians by Dr. Garden, who wrote several letters concerning its properties in 1763-6 to Dr. Hope. Drs. Lining and Chalmers, about this period, also contributed largely to its introduction. These physicians, and many others, have lauded the effects of the root upon lumbricoids, but all agreed that its efficacy was only certain when sufficient fresh root was taken to cause purgation; therefore, if such an effect did not take place, calomel or rhubarb were given to gain such action. This caused many others, who failed with the drug, to demean it, and search for its vaunted effects in the accessory drugs given; Spigelia, however, rose above all protests as an efficient vermifuge. Bergelius found it useful also in convulsions; and Ives and Barton considered it a valuable drug in encephalic forms of fever in children.

The *root* and *Extractum Spigeliæ Fluidum* are officinal in the U. S. Ph.; and in the Eclectic Dispensatory, *Extractum Spigeliæ et Sennæ Fluidum*, and *Infusum Spigeliæ*.

PART USED AND PREPARATION.—The fresh root, gathered just before the flowers expand, is treated as directed under Gelsemium (page 130–2). The resulting tincture has a clear and beautiful reddish-orange color by transmitted light; no characteristic odor; an astringent and slightly bitter taste, and an acid reaction.

CHEMICAL CONSTITUENTS. — Many analyses have been made of this species — none, however, that show the characteristics of the active principle. The following constituents of importance have been determined: An uncrystallizable, bitter substance, having alkaloidal characters, called by some *Spigeline*, an acrid resin, fixed and volatile oils, extractive matter, and a peculiar tannin.* The properties of the root seem to be much greater than those of the herb, and also appear to be well extracted by either water or alcohol.

PHYSIOLOGICAL ACTION.—Dr. Barton says† Pink Root induces, occasionally, violent narcotic effects, such as dimness of sight, giddiness, dilated pupils, spasmodic motions of the muscles of the eye, and even convulsions. Dr. Chalmers attributes the loss of two children by convulsions to this drug. Dr. Thompson found large doses to produce, in himself, acceleration of the pulse, flushed face, drowsiness, and stiffness of the eyelids.

Bureau‡ found that the drug acted as an acrid narcotic poison upon rabbits and other animals.

Dr. Hedge Thompson,§ above referred to, found the following symptoms to be produced upon man, after the ingestion of varying doses, all considered large:

* See *Proc. Am. Phar. Assoc.*, 1857, 132; *Jour. de Phar.*, ix, 197; *Am. Jour. Phar.*, 1857, 511; *Phar. Jour.*, i, v, 354; *Am. Chem. Jour.*, i, 104; and *Am. Jour. Phar.*, 1884, 570.
† *Veg. Mat. Med.*, ii, 80.
‡ *De la famillie des Loganiacees*, 130.
§ *Exp. diss. on the Spigelia Marilandica*, 1802.

Acceleration of the heart's action, followed soon by a notable reduction and irregularity; nausea; inflammation of the palpebræ, followed by a sensation of stiffness therein; languor, and drowsiness.

Dr. Spalsbury* records the effects of three doses of an infusion as follows: A peculiar, wild, staring expression of the eyes, giving the countenance a very singular, in fact, ludicrous, appearance; strabismus of the right eye; great dilation of the pupils; face, especially about the eyes, including the lids, much swollen; tongue pointed and tremulous; pulse 110 and irregular; on attempting to rise a general tremor came on, which passed off in a few seconds, leaving the patient apparently quite exhausted; and the skin hot and dry. Lining states that the only muscles of the eye affected, according to his experience, were the adductors and abductors.

These symptoms point to the drug as an irritant to the inhibitory nerves, especially the thoracic plexus, and give no farther narcotic symptoms than the natural counter-effect of such irritation.

Description of Plate 131.

1. Top of plant in flower, from near Charleston, S. C., June 7th, 1886.
   2. Calyx.
   3. Opened corolla.
   4. Stamen.
   5. Section of lower portion of corolla-tube.
   6. Style and stigma.
   7. Section of ovary.
   8. Fruit.
   9. Seed.
   (2–9 enlarged.)

---

* *Bost. Med. and Surg. Jour.*, lii, 72.

131.

SPIGÈLIA MARILÁNDICA, Linn.

ₑₘ. ad nat del. et pinxt.

GENUS.—**APOCYNUM**,* TOURN.

SEX. SYST.—PENTANDRIA DIGYNIA.

132

APOCYNUM ANDROSÆMIFOLIUM.

DOG'S BANE.

SYN.—APOCYNUM ANDROSÆMIFOLIUM, LINN.

COM. NAMES.—DOG'S BANE, BITTER ROOT, INDIAN HEMP, MILK WEED, FLY-TRAP, HONEY BLOOM, WANDERING MILK WEED, CATCH-FLY, SPREADING DOG'S BANE, AMERICAN IPECAC, BLACK INDIAN HEMP.

TINCTURE OF THE FRESH ROOT OF APOCYNUM ANDROSÆMIFOLIUM, LINN.

Description.—This upright perennial shrub-like herb, grows from 2 to 4 feet in height, branching profusely, and emitting when wounded in any part a milky juice. The *root* is long, more or less cylindrical, with a diameter of from one-eighth to three-quarters of an inch, sparsely branched, and covered with a quantity of fine fibres. It is light-brown externally, wrinkled throughout its length, and transversely fissured; the bark is thin, amorphous, the wood somewhat porous, white and tasteless; the milky juice permeates its whole substance. *Stem* smooth, at first simple, then divergently branched, and forked. *Leaves* opposite, smooth and green above, paler and more or less whitish pubescent beneath; they are ovate, acute, mucronate, from 2 to 3 inches long, and about 1 inch broad. *Petioles* about one-quarter of an inch in length. *Inflorescence* upright or nodding paniculate cymes at the ends of the branches, and in the axils of the terminal leaves. *Pedicels* from 2 to 3 lines long, with minute subulate bracts at their bases. *Calyx* entirely free from the ovaries, five-parted, with ovate-lanceolate, acute lobes, much shorter than the corolla, not glandular. *Corolla* convolute, and sinistrally twisted in the bud, monopetalous, bell-shaped, white tinged with red, five cleft; *limb* spreading; *lobes* ovate, obtuse, reflexed, each bearing at its base a triangular nectariferous scale, free only at the tip. *Stamens* five, inserted at the base of the corolla, alternate with the glands; *filaments* distinct, very short, ligulate, pubescent inside; *anthers* sagittate, with an acute hyaline tip, sometimes slightly coherent, and adhering by their faces to a zone or ring at about the middle of the stigma, 2-celled, the cells opening longitudinally. *Pollen* granular. *Ovaries* 2, oblong, generally distinct, rarely united; *stigma* sessile or nearly

* An ancient name of the dog's bane composed of ἀπὸ, *from,* κύων, *a dog;* as it was thought to be poisonous to this animal.

so, ovoid, obtuse and obscurely 2-lobed. *Follicles* 2, from 2 to 4 inches long, cylindrical, slender, and pendant; generally remaining united by their apices until fully ripe. *Seeds* numerous, crowned with a long silky coma at their summit. The apocynaceæ are chiefly tropical, acrid, poisonous plants, represented in the gardens by the Oleander and the Periwinkle, and wild in the northern United States by *Amsonia, Forsteronia* and *Apocynum.*

History and Habitat.—This rather common plant is found from Canada to Georgia, and Missouri. It grows along fences, and over old fields, flowering in June and July, the pods forming well before the blossoms have all fallen.

The names catch-fly and fly-trap are derived from the fact that the flowers of both this and A. cannabinum have a power, without special utility, of imprisoning insects. Dr. Darwin supposed this quality to be due to an irritability of the internal organs, but upon careful observation it is plainly seen that the capture is entirely accidental, the flower and plant remaining neutral. In consequence of the convergence of the anthers and their adherence to the zone of the stigma, a narrow fissure is formed, very contracted at the apex, the insect in search of honey from the nectaries at the base of the corolla, inserts its proboscis between the short filaments of the stamens, thus when about to leave its feast the proboscis is sometimes caught in this fissure; once fast, the greater the insect struggles the more firmly is it wedged, until its self-deliverance becomes impossible. Thus mosquitos, gnats and small flies may frequently be found dead in the flower-tubes.

The only previous use of this herb is said to be that of the Indians, who employed it in syphilis. Rafinesque says: "From its stem may be obtained a thread similar to hemp, which can be woven into cloth; from its pods, cotton; from its blossoms, sugar." The quantity of the last two articles is small, it is true, but might serve in an emergency.

This drug has been dismissed from the U. S. Ph., on account of lack of knowledge of its action. With the Eclectics it is used as *Decoctum Apocyni; Extractum Apocyni Alcoholicum;* and *Apocynin* their so-called alka-resinoid.

For obvious reasons, when desired as a tonic, diaphoretic or laxative agent, a decoction prepared as follows is the most effectual: Take a suitably sized earthen or porcelain-lined vessel and place in it one oz. of the sliced plant, roots, stems and leaves, to which add one pint of pure cold water; place the vessel in a pot of water and let it come to a boil, and remain so for at least an hour, replenishing as fast as it evaporates, with hot water, then strain the decoction from the inner vessel before it cools. It should be covered with a tight lid while heating, and after bottling should be always kept tightly corked; even then it is worthless after standing a few days. Dose, a tablespoonful three times a day.

PART USED AND PREPARATION.—The fresh root is chopped and pounded to a pulp and weighed. Then two parts by weight of alcohol are taken, and after thoroughly mixing the pulp with one-sixth part of it, the rest of the alcohol is added. After having stirred the whole, pour it into a well-stoppered bottle and let it stand eight days in a dark, cool place. The tincture is then separated by decanting, straining and filtering.

Thus prepared, it has a light reddish-brown color by transmitted light, a very bitter taste, and a slight acid reaction to litmus.

CHEMICAL CONSTITUENTS.—Very little is known of the constitution of this plant, it not having been very thoroughly analyzed. According to Bigelow it contains:

Red coloring matter, soluble in water, slightly soluble in alcohol.

A bitter principle, soluble in water and alcohol.

Volatile oil, caoutchouc and fixed oil.

PHYSIOLOGICAL ACTION.—Here also investigation has been neglected. Apocynum A. is an emetic without causing nausea, a cathartic, and quite a powerful diuretic and sudorific; it is also expectorant and considered antisyphilitic.

DESCRIPTION OF PLATE 132.

1. Part of plant, from McLean, N. Y., June 15th, 1880, showing the mode of branching.
    2. End of branch in flower.
    3. Follicles.
    4. Seed.
    5. Flower (enlarged).

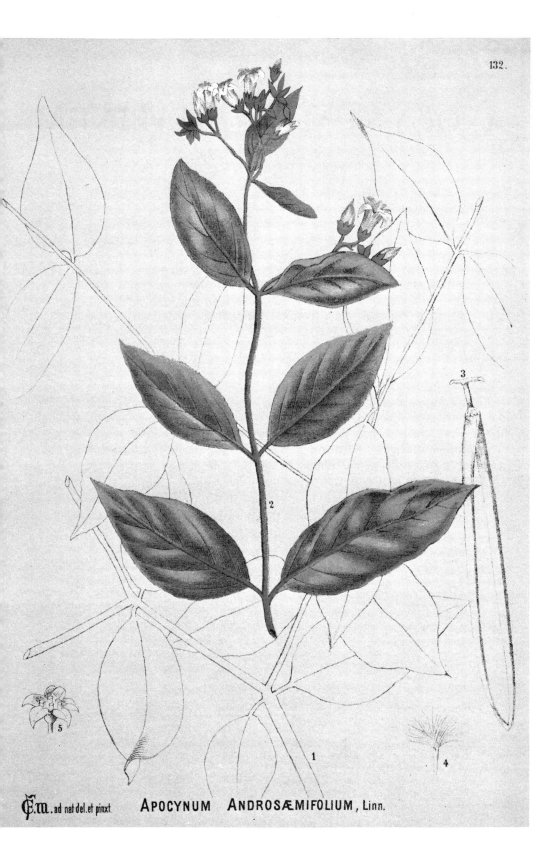

Œ.m..ad nat del.et pinxt.   APOCYNUM ANDROSÆMIFOLIUM, Linn.

133

APOCYNUM CANNABINUM.

CANADIAN HEMP.

SYN.—APOCYNUM CANNABINUM, LINN.; APOCYNUM HYPERICIFOL-
IUM, AIT.; APOCYNUM SYBERICUM, JACQ.; APOCYNUM PUBES-
CENS, R. BR.

COM. NAMES.—AMERICAN INDIAN HEMP,* DOG'S BANE,† OLD-AMY
ROOT, GENERAL MARION'S WEED, SNAKES' MILK, CANADIAN
HEMP, AMERICAN HEMP;‡ (CANADIAN) HOUATTE; (FR.) CHANVRE
DU CANADA; (GER.) CANADISCHE HANF.

A TINCTURE OF THE FRESH ROOT OF APOCYNUM CANNABINUM, LINN.

Description.—This species attains a height of from 2 to 4 feet. *Stem* erect, glabrous, or downy pubescent; *branches* upright or ascending, leafy to the top. *Leaves* varying from nearly oval to oblong and sometimes even lanceolate; *base* rounded, obscurely cordate, or acute; *petioles* usually present, short, but sometimes wanting. *Inflorescence* terminal, erect, many and densely flowered, cymes, shorter than the leaves; *flowers* smaller than those of the preceding species. *Calyx: lobes* lanceolate. *Corolla* greenish-white; *tube* not longer than the calyx lobes; *lobes* nearly erect, not reflexed. *Follicles* from 3 to 5 inches long.

In this description only the more distinctive and differential points are given; the generic description is embodied in that of the preceding species. As these two plants are so often classed as one by collectors in general, and as their action is quite different, I append a differentiation:

A. androsæmifolium.	*A cannabinum.*
1. *Stem* divergently branching or bifurcating.	1. *Stem* assurgently branching, not bifurcating.
2. *Root: bark* dark brown; *wood* white, tenacious, fibrous; *pith* of about the diameter of the thickness of the bark, sometimes greater.§	2. *Root: bark* grayish-brown; *wood* yellowish, soft, porous; *pith* minute or not evident.§
3. *Leaves* ovate, distinctly petioled; those at the bases of the branches like those upon them—*i. e.*, an opposite, petioled pair.‖ (Plate 132, Fig. 1.)	3. *Leaves* ranging from ovate to nearly lanceolate, sometimes sessile or nearly so; those at the bases of the branches single, sessile, and larger.‖ (Plate 133, Fig. 2.)
Inflorescence loose, spreading cymes; *flowers* greenish-white, with rose-colored maculations or striæ, or full pale rose-color;¶ *corolla: tube* longer than the calyx lobes; *lobes* reflexed or spreading.	*Inflorescence* close, erect cymes; *flowers* greenish-white, smaller; *corolla: tube* not longer than the calyx lobes; *lobes* erect.

* This plant is often termed Indian hemp, a name only applicable to *Cannabis Indica*, as it designates that plant alone. American Indian hemp might possibly apply, if we consider the first two words a compound word, and write it American-Indian hemp.

† Dog's-bane as properly belongs to *A. androsæmifolium*, as Canadian hemp does to this species.

‡ American hemp and American Indian hemp (so written) refer to Cannabis Indica as cultivated in America.

§ Manheimer, in *Am. Jour. Phar.*, 1881, p. 354.

‖ A purely distinctive point, no mention of which appears in any of the works I have examined.

¶ The author regrets that a misinterpretation occurred, causing the lithographer to alter his originally rose-colored flowers to green in Fig. 2, Plate 132.

Apocynaceæ.—This family of chiefly tropical plants of poisonous nature, has the following characteristics: Trees, woody shrubs, or herbs, exuding when wounded, a milky, acrid juice. *Leaves* entire, feather-veined, arranged alternately, oppositely, or in whorls; *stipules* wanting. *Inflorescence* terminal or axillary cymes, or panicles; *flowers* 5-merous and 5-androus, perfect and regular. *Calyx* free from the ovary, persistent. *Corolla* gamopetalous; lobes convolute or twisted in the bud. *Stamens* equal in number to the corolla lobes and alternate with them; *anthers* distinct or nearly so, encircling the stigma and sometimes adhering to it, 2-celled, introrsely and longitudinally splitting; *filaments* distinct, inserted upon the tube of the corolla; *pollen* of loose grains, sometimes glutinous. *Ovaries* 2, united or distinct, biplacentiferous; *ovules* numerous or few, anatropous or amphitropous; *style* single, common to both ovaries; *stigma* single, capitate, the receptive surface consisting of a ring encircling the under surface of the stigma. *Carpels* 2, distinct or united; *seeds* numerous, comose or acomose; *albumen* sparse; *embryo* straight and comparatively large.

This family contains in North America 9 genera, 21 species, and 2 varieties. Beside the two under consideration, the following species have a place in the Homœopathic Materia Medica: Dita bark (*Alstonia scholaris*); Oleander (*Nerium oleander*); Tanghinia (*Tanghinia Madagascariensis*, Pet. Th.; *T. venenifera*, Poir; *Cerbera tanghina*, Hook.); the Antillesian Ahovai-baum (*Thevetia nereifolia*, Juss.; *Cerbera thevetia*, Linn.); Toxicophlœa (*Toxicophlœa Thunbergi*); Upas (*Strychnos tieute*); Periwinkle (*Vinca minor*, Linn.); and Echites (*Echites suberecta*, Jacq.).

History and Habitat.—The habitat of both indigenous species is generally given as the same—*i. e.*, sandy soils and the borders of old fields and open woods. I have noticed that *A. androsæmifolium* answers well to this habitat, but that *A. cannabinum* is found much more abundant in marshy places and on the banks of rivers, particularly where they are subjected to submergence during high water. Their geographical range is: from the Canadas southward to Georgia and Florida, and westward to California, A. cannabinum extending the farther south of the two. The two species blossom together in June and July, fruiting as they flower.

This species yields the better and tougher "hemp" of the two, and is more utilized. Porcher quotes* the *Rural Cyc.* as follows:

"This plant has been proved by Prof. Thouin, of Paris, to possess a stronger fibre than that of hemp; and is used by the American Indians for making cordage, fishing-nets, and coarse cloth." He further states: "The decoction affords a permanent dye, brown or black, according to the mordant used."

In general and domestic practice this species has been used and lauded as an excellent diuretic,† also as an hydragogue cathartic, emetic, and diaphoretic, in proper relative dosage.

The root is official in the U. S. Ph. In the Eclectic Materia Medica the preparation is: *Tinctura Apocyni.*

---

* *Resources of the Southern Fields and Forests*, p. 484.
† See page 132-2, concerning decoction.

PART USED AND PREPARATION.—The preparation is made from the root in the same manner as that of the preceding species. The resulting tincture has a deep reddish-orange color by transmitted light, a rank odor, an extremely bitter and penetrating taste, and an acid reaction.

CHEMICAL CONSTITUENTS.—*Apocynin.* This partly crystalline, bitter principle has been isolated by both Dr. Knapp and Dr. Griscom; its chemical nature has not yet been determined. It is not a glucoside, but for the present is supposed to hold a place in close relation to that class of bodies. It is insoluble, or only slightly soluble, in water.

Apocynëin.—This amorphous glucoside greatly resembles *saponin* in its physical properties.* It is fully soluble in water. Its chemical nature is only slightly known.

Beside the two bitter principles, Dr. Griscom (1832) found in the root, tannic and gallic acids, gum, resin and wax.

PHYSIOLOGICAL ACTION.—Apocynum cannabinum has long been noted for its hydragogue properties, the results obtaining in this direction through its peculiar action upon the mucous membranes of the intestinal canal. What its action may be upon serous membranes is still to be determined. Its action in causing diuresis and diaphoresis (the latter only present when it causes emesis), is another point in the dark, concerning which more light is greatly to be desired. When nausea and vomiting occur, the action of the heart is greatly diminished, and a sense of mental depression and oppression of the chest almost naturally result. Apocynum apparently acts simply as an evacuant, and affects the organic trouble causing the dropsical condition for which it is usually given, little, or not at all.

DESCRIPTION OF PLATE 133.

1. End of fruiting and flowering branch, Binghamton, N. Y., July 22d, 1882.
2. Part of stem, showing mode of branching.
3. Flower (enlarged).
4. Flower after removal of the perianth (enlarged).
5. Flower after removal of the stamens (enlarged).
6. Side view of stamen (enlarged).
7. Seed.
8. Section of the root.

* *Am. Jour. Phar.* 1883, p. 368.

133.

Œm. ad nat.del.et pinxt.   APÓCYNUM CANNÁBINUM Linn.

134

ASCLEPIAS CORNUTI.

COMMON MILKWEED.

SYN.—ASCLEPIAS SYRIACA,† LINN. A. CORNUTI, DEC.
COM. NAMES.—COMMON MILKWEED, SILKWEED, WILD COTTON,
VIRGINIAN SWALLOW-WORT; (FR.), ASCLEPIADE A LA SOIE,
HERBE A LA OUATE; (GER.), SCHWALBENWURZEL, SEIDEN-
PFLANZE.

A TINCTURE OF THE FRESH ROOT OF ASCLEPIAS CORNUTI, DEC.

Description.—This stout, upright, perennial herb, grows from 4–5 feet high, is leafy to the top, and bears superior lateral as well as terminal umbels of dusky red flowers.

The *root* extends horizontally to a length of from 1–2 feet, is externally of a grayish-brown color, somewhat branched, and from one-quarter to one inch thick, giving off a few scattered rootlets, or is marked by their scars; it is often knotty from branches that have failed to develop. It has no specific odor, but is decidedly bitter to the taste. It breaks with a short fracture when dry, disclosing a soft, porous, yellow-tinged wood, with broad medullary rays and a thin white bark. The *stem* is simple, or nearly so, cylindrical, stout and smooth, emitting when wounded a copious, white, mucilaginous juice which soon congeals. The *leaves* are about 4–8 inches in length, oppositely arranged upon the stem, oval-oblong, entire, slightly pointed and short petioled; they are of a dark rich green color above, pale and minutely downy beneath. *Inflorescence*, many-flowered umbels, upon long, drooping, downy peduncles, from the base of the petioles of the upper leaves. The *calyx* and *corolla* are deeply 5-parted, reflexed, and spreading, the former persistent, the latter deciduous. The *crown* consists of 5 hooded, fleshy bodies (termed nectaries by Linnæus), situated upon the stamen tube, each containing an incurved horn. Specifically these hoods are ovate, obtuse, having a tooth or lobe upon each side of the horn, which is short and claw-like. *Stamens* 5, inserted upon the base of the corolla; *filaments* united into a tube inclosing the pistil; *anthers* adherent to the stigma (forming a distinguishing feature of this large order of plants, of which Asclepias is the type); they are composed of two vertical cells, tipped with a membrane-like appendage, each containing a flattened, pear-shaped, waxy, pollen-mass. *Ovaries* 2, tapering into two

---

* The Greek name of Æsculapius, to whom it is dedicated.
† Syria; but as this is a purely American species, we should use the name by Decaisne.

very short *styles*, surmounted at their apices by a large, depressed, 5-angled, fleshy mass, which takes the place of a *stigma* common to the two, having five cloven glands upon its angles. *Pollen*-masses of adjacent anther-cells, extricated by the agency of insects, form pairs, which hang by a fine prolongation of their summits from the glands of the stigmatose body, ejecting copious pollen-tubes into its junction with the styles. *Follicles* 2, one of them often abortive, ovate, soft, woolly, and covered with weak spines. *Seeds* anatropous, margined, flat, furnished with long silky hairs at the hilum; all imbricated downward over the large placenta, which separates from the raphe when mature. *Embryo* large, the thin albumen containing broad leaf-like cotyledons.

History and Habitat.—This very common herb grows in rich or sandy ground, along roadsides and in waste places everywhere in Canada and the United States, flowering during the summer months. Few genera are more beautiful or complex in their structure than this, still the plants of this order are so peculiar that even the youngest student of botany will recognize them at a glance. That they are so plentiful cannot appear strange after an examination of the seeds, whose silky coma when expanded forms them into veritable parachutes; balanced by the pendant seeds, they mount gracefully to immense heights, whence they are wafted far and wide by the lightest zephyr until, dampened by dew or rain, they fall to the ground. The young sprouts, just as they appear above the ground in spring, are highly esteemed among housewives as a pot-herb, being cooked similarly to asparagus, for which they are an excellent substitute. The juice when applied to the skin forms a tough, adhesive pellicle; this has led to its use by the laity as a covering for ulcers and recent wounds to promote cicatrization. In a memoir on the cultivation of this plant, by J. A. Moller, in Tilloch's Magazine, vol. viii, p. 149, may be found the following: "Its chief uses were for beds, cloth, "hats, and paper. It was found that from eight to nine pounds of the coma of the "seeds occupied a space of from five to six cubic feet, and were sufficient for a bed, "coverlet, and pillows. The shortness of the fibre prevented it from being spun "and woven alone, it however was mixed with flax, wool, etc., in certain stuffs to "advantage. Hats made with it were very light and soft. The stalks afforded "paper in every respect resembling that obtained from rags. The plant is easily "propagated by seeds or slips. A plantation containing thirty thousand plants "yielded from six to eight hundred pounds of coma."

This plant, together with many other excellent drugs, has been dismissed *sine curâ* from the U. S. Ph. The Eclectic Dispensatory recommends its use in a fluid extract, dose from 10 drops to a fluidrachm; in amenorrhœa, dropsy, retention of urine, asthma, dyspepsia, cough, dyspnœa, etc.

The use of the Asclepiadeæ in general in pleurisy is not well proven, though their action upon the nerves might lead to empirical use in pleurodynia.

PART USED AND PREPARATION.—The fresh root, already described, is gathered when in full vigor, chopped and pounded to a pulp and weighed. Then two parts by weight of alcohol are taken, and after thoroughly mixing this pulp with one-sixth part of it, the rest of the alcohol is added. After having stirred the whole, pour it into a well-stoppered bottle and let it stand eight days in a dark cool place. The tincture is then separated by decanting, straining, and filtering.

Thus prepared it has a light orange-yellow color by transmitted light, a bitter and slightly astringent taste, quite similar to half ripe butternuts, and a slightly acid reaction.

CHEMICAL CONSTITUENTS.—Asclepione,* $C_{20} H_{34} O_3$. This resinoid principle was determined by List in the juice of the plant; also by W. L. Hinchman (Am. Jour. Phar. 1881, p. 433) in the roots; as white, verrucose, odorless, tasteless, iridescent crystals; decomposing at 194° (219.2° F.) and volatilizing at higher temperatures. They are soluble in chloroform, ether and alcohol; insoluble in water. The roots, according to the latter authority, contain *asclepione, caoutchouc, fixed oil, tannin, glucose*, a *bitter principle* not isolated, *gum, starch*, and *volatile oil*. The milky juice of the whole plant contains the same bodies found in the root. The acid of the plant seems to be in close relation with the undetermined bitter principle.

PHYSIOLOGICAL ACTION.—A. cornuti is diuretic (increasing the solid constituents as well as the watery portion of the urine) and diaphoretic, not by stimulating but by lowering the action of the heart. It is thought to act directly upon the vaso-motor system, often in this sphere lessening local congestions. Its minute action can best be studied in the published provings. Anodyne properties have been attributed to this drug, but this is totally unsupported at present.

DESCRIPTION OF PLATE 134.

1. Upper part of plant, from Binghams, N. Y., June 21st, 1880.
   2. A cluster of follicles.
   3. A flower (enlarged).
   4. Seed (somewhat enlarged).

---

* There seems to be a similarity between this body and Lactucerin, *vide*, 96.

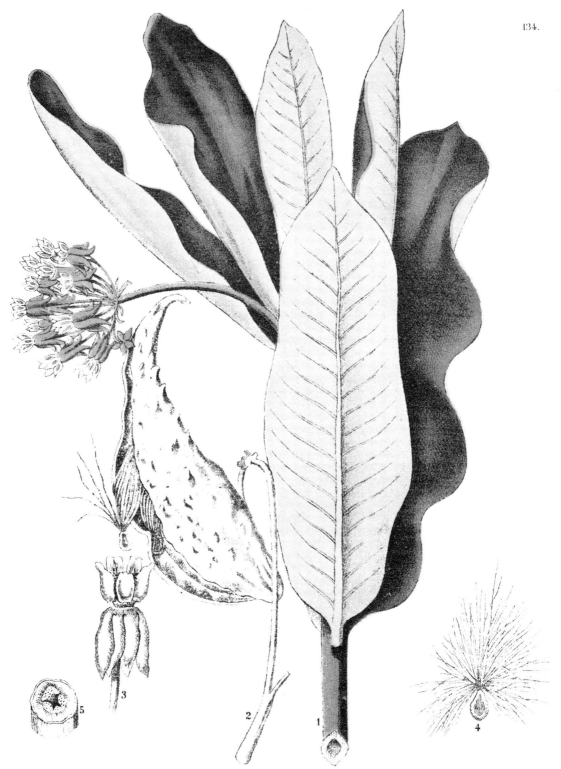

134.

𝔉𝔪. ad nat.del.et pinxt.

ASCLEPIAS CORNUTI, Decaisne.

135

ASCLEPIAS TUBEROSA.*

PLEURISY-ROOT.

SYN.—ASCLEPIAS TUBEROSA, LINN.; ASCLEPIAS CAULE ERECT. DIVAR. VILLOS., ETC., HORT. CLIFF.; APOCYNUM NOVÆ ANG. HIRSUT. ETC., HERM. LUGDB.

COM. NAMES.—PLEURISY-ROOT, BUTTERFLY WEED, ORANGE SWAL-LOW-WORT, ORANGE MILK-WEED, ORANGE APOCYNUM, WIND ROOT, WIND WEED, COLIC ROOT, WHITE ROOT; (FR.) ASCLEPIADE TUBEREUSE; (GER.) KNOLLIGE SCHWALBENWURZ.

A TINCTURE OF THE FRESH ROOT OF ASCLEPIAS TUBEROSA, LINN.

Description.—This attractive plant grows to a height of from 1 to 2 feet. *Root* large, sarcous, fusiform and branching. *Stems* numerous, erect or oblique, roughish·hairy, branching superiorly, and leafy to the top ; they form an exception to Asclepiadeæ in general by being almost or entirely devoid of milky juice. *Leaves* numerous, scattered, some falling opposite ; they may vary from linear to linear- or oblong-lanceolate, be sessile or very short petioled, hirsute, mostly acute or subacute, and undulately wrinkled along the margin. *Inflorescence* terminal cymose or corymbose clusters of short peduncled umbels ; *flowers* showy, greenish- or orange-chrome. *Calyx* much smaller than the corolla ; *sepals* reflexed, subulate, hidden under the lobes of the corolla. *Petals* or divisions of the corolla oblong, at first extended then reflexed. *Crown* elevated conspicuously above the base of the corolla ; *hoods* or *cuculli* erect, narrowly oblong, sessile, somewhat broadened at the base, and about twice the length of the column ; *horns* subulate, slender, nearly erect. *Column* short. *Anthers* shorter than the cuculli ; *wings* truncate, broadest at the base. *Pods* lanceolate, acuminate, hoary.

Asclepiadaceæ.—This large family differs mainly from the preceding, and all Exogens, in the arrangement of the essential organs and fecundating element. It consists of shrubs and herbs having acrid, bitter, milky (exc. *Asclepias tuberosa*) juice, containing *caoutchouc*. It answers in general to the characters of leaf, flower, and fruit exhibited in the Apocynaceæ (*vide ante, p. 133–2*).

Leaves destitute of stipules ; their place generally supplied by hairs. *Inflorescence* terminal, axillary or somewhat racemose clusters of cymose or umbelli-

---

* In executing this plate with the stem and leaves natural size, it became necessary to remove two flower clusters, which greatly diminishes its value to the botanist, though the representation is still characteristic of *A. tuberosa*.

form flowers; *bracts* minute. *Corona** consisting of 5 parts or lobes (hoods), usually present and situated between the corolla and the stamens, adnate to the one or the other. *Disk* (hypogynous) wanting; *stamens* mostly monadelphous, their tube forming the *column; anthers* introrse, 2- or incompletely 4-celled, in Asclepias flattened, opening lengthwise (c. Fig. 6), and surmounted by a small membranous appendage (d. Fig. 6). *Styles* 2, generally distinct as far as the stigmatic body; *stigma* or *stigmatose disk* fleshy, consisting of a central portion or body common to both styles, from which are produced 5 corpuscles or glands, alternate with the anthers (e. Fig. 6). *Pollinia* (Fig. 4) waxy masses of coherent, granular, compressed hexagonal, pollen cells. Each of the masses is furnished with a fine prolongation, these meet in pairs, the point of juncture being tipped with a minute, black, coriaceous appendage, sharply cleft at its inferior edge, the sides prolonging like the barbs of an arrowhead; this appendage is situated between the apices of two contiguous anthers, and is connected with the stigmatic glands. Thus when the pollen is withdrawn two anthers yield a cell's contents each to the mass. *Fruit* a pair of follicles except when aborted; *seeds* few or many, compressed, imbricate, generally margined, and furnished with a soft coma; *embryo* straight; *cotyledons* foliaceous; *albumen* thin. A general description of Asclepias is incorporated in that of A. cornutum, 134.

A word in regard to cross-fertilization in Asclepias. While drawing figure 2, plate 135, holding the flower by its peduncle, a large blue-bottle fly alighted upon the crown, as he did so one of his legs slipped down between two hoods,—which neatly curve to such a shape that the foot of an insect is guided directly into the crevice between two adjacent anther cells—and upon attempting to withdraw it he was unable to do so. Noting this, I teased him into many strong tugs and pulls, but the more he struggled the tighter his foot became wedged, until finally after about ten minutes' hard work he flew off with a little yellow spot attached to the extremity. I caught him, plucked off the leg, and examined it under a lens; the claws were firmly wedged into the little cleft, before mentioned as existing in the coriaceous appendage of the pollen-masses. I afterward examined numerous heads of *Asclepias cornuti*, nearly always finding many captive insects, especially *Muscæ*, some dead and others struggling; and watched many more fly off with the fecundating element trailing after them. Others, too, arrived with pollen-masses, and by the same interesting procedure as described, left their burdens in the crown, thus executing without design the will of Nature.

The plants of this order that are of particular interest to us, beside the two under consideration, are: Cundurango (*Gonolobus Cundurango*), the Spanish *Mataperro* (the plant that—being announced and lauded as a cure for cancer—caused such a furor in medical and general circles in 1871; now considered worthless in cancer or any other disorder by those who were foremost in its advancement and use); and the curled-flowered Calatropis (*Calatropis gigantea*), a native of the East Indies. The other prominent medicines in this order are: The Indian emetic *Secamone emetica*, and purgative *S. Thunbergii*. The acrid juice of Syrian Peri-

---

* Crown, nectary, lepanthium.

ploca (*Periploca Graeca*) has been used as a stimulating application for ulcers, and in Greece as a wolf poison.   Lindley states* that the East Indian *Tylophora asthmatica* is either emetic or purgative in the proper dosage, and constitutes a valuable Indian remedy.   Many species of *Gonolobus* act as drastic purges, and some are used by the Aborigines as arrow poisons.   The Ceylon Indian or Country Sarsaparilla, *Hemidesmus Indicus*, is spoken of by Lindley† as being quite as efficient in its usage as the American root, and adds: "A great deal of it is consumed in London and considered a fine sort."   The genus *Cynanchum* affords several purgatives, one of which, the Syrian *Cynanchum erectum* (*Marsdenia erecta*), is stated to be very poisonous, and used by the natives as a means of murder or suicide; *Arghel* (*Cynanchum Argel*) is often used to adulterate Alexandrian Senna, and to this Lindley ascribes the griping and other unpleasant effects of the commercial Senna; while the leaves of the East Indian *Cynanchum extensum* (*Daemia extensa*) are employed as an anthelmintic, and the juice in asthma.   Thus throughout the order almost all species are used in the practice of their native countries; while to the arts some yield excellent fiber for the manufacture of rope, and others (especially *Cynanchum ovalifolium*), caoutchouc in good quantity and of fine quality.

History and Habitat.—Asclepias tuberosa is common from Canada southward; growing at first near the coast on sandy fields, but spreading inland as the soil grows drier and less rich.   It flowers northward during the earlier months of summer, and fruits in September.   The procumbent form, more common southward, formerly classed with this species, is now recognized as *var. decumbens*, Pursh.   The Western Indians boil the tubers for food; prepare a crude sugar from the flowers, and eat the young seed-pods after boiling them with buffalo meat.   Some of the Canadian tribes use the young shoots as a pot-herb after the manner of asparagus.‡

The pleurisy-root has received more attention as a medicine than any other species of this genus, having been regarded, almost since the discovery of this country, as subtonic, diaphoretic, alterative, expectorant, diuretic, laxative, escharotic, carminative, anti-spasmodic, anti-pleuritic, stomachic, astringent, anti-rheumatic, anti-syphilitic, and what not?   It has been recommended in low typhoid states, pneumonia, catarrh, bronchitis, pleurisy, dyspepsia, indigestion, dysentery, helminthiasis, and obstinate eczemas, in doses of from 20 to 40 grains of the powdered root.

Schoepf first brought it before the medical profession, followed by Drs. Barton, Chapman, Eberle, and Parker, each of whom found it often reliable, especially in cases where an expectorant or diaphoretic seemed requisite.   In colic and rheumatic pains its exhibition met with much success.   Dr. Chapman states§ that it is distinguished by great certainty and permanency of operation, and is well suited to excite perspiration, etc.   Prof. Barton esteemed it as one of the most important of our indigenous remedies.   Dr. Benj. Parker says:‖ "The powdered root frequently acts as a mild purgative, but it is particularly valuable for its virtues as an

* *Flor. med.*, p. 542.   † *Idem*, p. 544.   ‡ J. R. Dodge in *U. S. Agric. Rep.*, 1870, p. 405.
§ *Elementary Therapeutics*, Vol. 1, p. 351.   ‖ *Thatcher Disp.* in *Barton's Veg. Mat. Med.*, Vol. 1, p. 247.

expectorant, diaphoretic, and febrifuge." "From the successful employment of the pleurisy-root for twenty-five years, he has imbibed such confidence that he extols it as possessing the peculiar and almost specific quality of acting on the organs of respiration, powerfully promoting suppressed expectoration, and thereby relieving the breathing of pleuritic patients in the most advanced stage of the disease; and in pneumonic fevers, recent colds, catarrhs, and diseases of the breast in general, this remedy has in his hands proved equally efficacious." Dr. Griffith concludes[*] that "from all that can be gathered on the subject, it may be deemed one of the most useful of our native articles, and deserves a full and unbiassed trial." Other and more recent writers as usual have looked with doubt upon all its given qualities, except mayhap its utility as an expectorant and diaphoretic. The provings, however, point to it as a valuable remedy in certain forms of dry coryza, indigestion, colic, diarrhœa, dry coughs, pleurisy, general rheumatic pains, and certain skin affections. In one case only in my own practice have I seen the indications for its use, that a case of chronic indigestion, accompanied by dry cough and intercostal rheumatic pains; it acted promptly and efficaciously, bringing relief within a few hours, and immunity of the disorder within a month.

The root is officinal in the U. S. Ph. Its preparations in the Eclectic Materia Medica are: *Extractum Asclepidis Alcoholicum,* and *Fluidum; Infusum Asclepidis; Pulvis Asclepiæ Compositus;*[†] *Pulvis Ipecacuanhæ Compositus;*[‡] *Tinctura Lobeliæ Composita;*[§] and *Asclepidin* or *Oleo-Resina Asclepidis.*

PART USED AND PREPARATION.—The tincture is prepared from the fresh root in the same manner as that of the preceding species. It has a brownish-orange color by transmitted light, darker therefore than that of *A. cornuti;* a slightly bitter taste; preserves the characteristic odor of the root, and has a decided acid reaction.

CHEMICAL CONSTITUENTS.—An analysis of the root by Alton Clabaugh[‖] resulted in the separation of a fixed oil saponifiable by caustic alkalies; a peculiar odorous, crystalline, sublimable stearopten melting at 160° F., and soluble in alcohol, ether, and chloroform; a bitter principle insoluble in alcohol; another yellowish-brown bitter principle soluble in alcohol; a yellowish-white body possessing the taste of the drug, soluble in alcohol; together with starch, gummy and coloring matters, and a resin, thus corroborating the former analysis of Elam Rhodes.

PHYSIOLOGICAL ACTION.—The following symptoms occurring after taking doses of from 20 to 50 drops of the tincture, are recorded by Thos. Nichol.[¶] Deficient appetite, with pain and weight in the pit of the stomach; soreness and colic, followed by flatulence; soft fœtid stools, preceded by rumbling in the bowels; dry, hard, hacking cough, with painful respiration; sharp, shooting pains, espe-

* *Med. Bot.,* p. 455.   † Pleurisy-root, Spearmint, Sumach Berries, Bayberry Bark, Skunk Cabbage, and Ginger.
‡ Pleurisy-root, Ipecacuanha, Blood Root, and Nitrate of Potassa.   § See foot-note to Lobelia inflata, 99.
‖ *Am. Jour. Phar.,* 1882, p. 5.   ¶ Hale, *New Remedies,* 2d Ed.

cially between the ribs and about the heart, aggravated by deep inspiration and by motion of the arms; darting, shooting pains in the extremities, followed by a sense of languor and debility.

From this it is evident that *A. tuberosa* has a decided action upon the body, especially the mucous membranes of the alimentary tract. Just what this action is, is as yet undeterminable.

DESCRIPTION OF PLATE 135.

1. End of flowering plant with two clusters removed, Jamaica, L. I., July 17th, 1884.
2. Flower, somewhat enlarged.
3. Hood and horn (enlarged).
4. Pollen-masses, showing connective (x 25).
5. Stigmatic body (enlarged).
6. A portion of the column, showing:
   a. The connective of the pollen-masses.
   b. Cleft between the anther cells.
   c. Anther.
   d. Membranous appendage.
   e. Stigmatic lobe.

℄.m̃. ad nat.del.et pinxt.

ASCLÈPIAS TUBERÒSA, Linn.

136
CHIONANTHUS.

FRINGE TREE.

SYN.—CHIONANTHUS VIRGINICA, LINN.
COM. NAMES.—FRINGE TREE, SNOW FLOWER, POISON ASH, OLD MAN'S
BEARD, SNOWDROP TREE; (FR.) CHIONANTHE; (GER.) SCHNEE-
BAUM, ODER SCHNEEBLUME.

A TINCTURE OF THE FRESH BARK OF CHIONANTHUS VIRGINICA, LINN.

Description.—This beautiful southern shrub grows to a height of from 6 to 10 feet, and may be characterized as follows: *Leaves* smooth or downy-pubescent, oblong- or ovate-lanceolate, and narrowed into a petiole; *margin* entire. *Inflorescence* loose, axillary, leafy-bracted panicles, appearing with the leaves, than which they are longer; *flowers* delicate, more or less arranged in threes, each on a drooping pedicel. *Calyx* small, 4-cleft, persistent; *lobes* linear-lanceolate. *Corolla* wheel-shaped, 4-cleft; *lobes* long, linear, and almost separate. *Stamens* 2, included, inserted just at the base of the corolla; *anthers* larger than the young pistil, 2-celled; *filaments* no longer than the anthers. *Style* short; *stigma* 4-notched. *Fruit* an ovoid, blackish, fleshy drupe, covered by a delicate bloom; *seeds* 1 to 3.

Oleaceæ.—A small family of trees or shrubs, represented in North America by 6 genera, 29 species, and 7 varieties. *Leaves* opposite, simple or pinnate, extipulate, deciduous. *Flowers* perfect, polygamous or diœcious. *Calyx* 4-toothed, sometimes obsolete. *Corolla* 4-lobed or petaled, sometimes wanting; *æstivation* valvate. *Stamens* 2 or abnormally more. *Ovary* 2-celled, with 2 suspended ovules in each cell; *style* single or none. *Fruit* a 1–2 seeded samara, berry, or drupe. *Embryo* straight; *albumen* hard, sometimes wanting.

The only proven plant in this order, beside those here considered, is the White Jessamine (*Jasminum officinale*, Linn.), the authority for the use of which I am unable to determine. Prominent in this order stands the Levantine and South European Olive (*Olea Europæa*, Linn.), which yields, beside its valuable fruit and oil, a bark that is highly spoken of by De Candolle as a substitute for

---

* χιών, *chion*, snow; ἄνθος, *anthos*, flower.

Cinchona, and a gummy substance much esteemed as a vulnerary. The South European Flowering Ash (*Fraxinus Ornus*, Linn.) exudes from its branches a dulcamarous substance called *Manna*, a gentle laxative, useful in cases of genito-urinary affections attended by constipation ; it has, however, the usual drawback of causing flatulent colic.* Calabrian manna, considered by Fothergill to be of even better quality than the last, is a product of *F. excelsior*, Linn.; *F. rotundifolia* is also manniferous. The fruit of the Persian Lilac (*Syringia vulgaris*, Linn.†) is, according to Curveiller, a remarkably good tonic and febrifuge when extracted.

The leaves of the South European *Phyllyrea latifolia* have been found to relieve headache, when soaked in vinegar and applied with a compress ; the leaves of the British Privet (*Ligustrum vulgare*) are often used in the same manner; both are astringents.

History and Habitat.—The Fringe Tree is indigenous to the United States, where it ranges from the southern portions of Pennsylvania southward to Florida and Texas. It habits rich woods along the borders of streams, flowering in June.

The previous use of the bark of this shrub as an astringent vulnerary, and the bark of the root as a tonic after long and exhaustive diseases, is one that has a great merit. The bark in infusion is a remedy that was too often neglected for foreign drugs in the treatment of typhoid forms of fever and intermittents, especially those of bilious character. This bark has often also proved itself a trustworthy diuretic, and Prof. Griffith deems it possessed of acro-narcotic properties. Rafinesque claims that the root makes a cataplasm that will cause the healing of wounds without suppuration. Dr. F. S. Smith, of Lock Haven, Pa., who has used the fluid extract of the bark in his practice, judges it one of the best remedies at his command in certain forms of bilious sick headaches ; and Dr. E. M. Hale is of the opinion that in all the diseases mentioned above Chionanthus will often prove to be the similimum.

PART USED AND PREPARATION.—The fresh bark, including that of the root, is chopped and pounded to a pulp and weighed. Then two parts by weight of alcohol are taken, the pulp thoroughly mixed with one-sixth part of it, and the rest of the alcohol added. The whole is then poured into a well-stoppered bottle, and allowed to stand eight days in a dark, cool place.

The tincture, separated from this mass by pressure and filtration, has a beautiful, slightly orange-red color by transmitted light, a bitterish barky odor, a bitter taste, and an acid reaction.

PHYSIOLOGICAL ACTION.—According to Drs. Lawsche and Scudder, the symptoms following the ingestion of this drug are substantially as follows : Severe frontal headache, bruised, sore sensation in the eyeballs ; nausea, bitter eructa-

---

* Armenian manna is derived from *Quercus Persica*, J. & S., and *Quercus vallonea*, Kat (Cupuliferæ); Australian manna, from *Eucalyptus viminalis*, Lab. (Myrtaceæ) ; Tamarisk manna, *Tamarix gallica*, Linn. (Tamiricaceæ) ; Persian manna, from *Alhagi camelorum*, Fisch. (Leguminosæ) ; and Briançon manna, from *Pinus Larix*, Linn. (Coniferæ).

† Our common purple Lilac is *var. violacca*, and the white, *var. alba*, both natives of Persia.

tions and retching, followed by pressure to stool; tongue coated greenish-yellow; uneasy sensations throughout the alimentary tract; vomiting of ropy, bitter, dark-green, bilious matter; blackish evacuations of the bowels; slow pulse; cold perspiration, and great general weakness.*

DESCRIPTION OF PLATE 136.

1. End of a flowering branch, Landisville, N. J., June 7th, 1885.
2. A flower.
3. A flower with broken petals, showing essential organs.
4. Stamen.
5. Pistil and calyx.

(2–5 enlarged.)

---

* Dr. Scudder in *Eclectic Med. Jour.*, May, 1876; Dr. Lawche in *N. A. Jour. of Hom.*, 1883, p. 612.

136.

℃.m. ad nat del. et pinxt.　CHIONÁNTHUS VIRGÍNICA, Linn.

137

FRAXINUS.

WHITE ASH.

SYN.—FRAXINUS AMERICANA, LINN.; F. ACUMINATA AND JUGLANDI-
FOLIA, LAM.; F. EPIPTERA, MICHX.; F. DISCOLOR, MUHL.; F. CANA-
DENSIS, GAERTN.; F. ALBA, MARSH.
COM. NAMES.—AMERICAN WHITE ASH; (FR.) LE FRÉNE BLANC; (GER.)
WEISSE ESCHE.

A TINCTURE OF THE FRESH BARK OF FRAXINUS AMERICANA, LINN.

Description.—This beautiful timber tree usually attains a growth of from 40 to 60 feet or more; *trunk* generally naked for about half the whole growth; *bark* gray, furrowed, and transversely fissured with great regularity; *branchlets* gray and glabrous; *buds* rust-colored. *Leaves* opposite, odd-pinnately compound, and over a foot in length; *leaflets* 7 to 9, short-stalked, varying from ovate to oblong-lanceolate; all acuminate, entire or sparsely denticulate, pale or whitish, and often pubescent beneath, especially upon the mid-rib; *petioles* glabrous. *Inflorescence* densely paniculate, especially in the male—all developed from special buds, from the upper axils of the previous year's growth; *Flowers* diœcious, apetalous; *Male flowers : Calyx* minute, campanulate, with 4 sharp teeth, or sometimes obsolete or wanting; *stamens* 2 to 4; *filaments* shorter than the large anthers; *anthers* linear-oblong, mucronate. *Female flowers : Calyx* small, persistent; *stamens* even, abortive ones rarely present; *style* erect; *stigma* 2-lobed, *lobes* revolute; *ovary* 2-celled, *ovules* a pair from the summit of each cell, one usually abortive. *Fruit* a dry samara about an inch and a half long; *body* oblong, cylindraceous, terete, barely acute at the base, merely 1-nerved, not margined, about one-half as long as the lanceolate or oblanceolate, slightly emarginate, apical wing. *Seed* oblong, filling the cell; *cotyledons* elliptical; *radicle* slender.

History and Habitat.—The White Ash abounds in rich or moist woods from Canada southward to Florida, and westward to Louisiana, where it flowers on the appearance of the leaves. It was introduced into English gardens in 1723, but does not flourish there as here in its native climate.

The wood is very tough, fine-grained and elastic, and, were it not for its weight, would make fine cabinet material. It weighs 35 lbs., 10 oz. per cubic foot, and has a sp. gr. of .570. Ash furnishes material for the most strained parts of wagons, as well as for all the heavier agricultural implements.

---

* Φράξις, *phraxis,* separation; as the wood splits with facility.

An infusion of White Ash bark has been much used in cases where an astringent tonic was deemed necessary; it also proves cathartic, and has been found useful in constipation, especially of dropsical subjects. It has received much praise in mastitis, and enlargement of the spleen, as well as in some forms of eczema, and in gouty affections. There is a belief extant in the South that the seeds prevent accumulation of fat.

Dr. Porcher quotes some unmentioned author as follows: The leaves of this plant "are said to be so highly offensive to the rattlesnake, that that formidable reptile is never found on land where it grows; and it is the practice of hunters and others, having occasion to traverse the woods in the summer months, to stuff their boots or shoes with White Ash leaves, as a preventive of the bite of the rattlesnake." My father relates that, among the settlers of Orange Co., N. Y., it was always asserted that the Aborigines used to defend themselves from this snake by carrying White Ash leaves about their persons. How much dependence might be placed in this prophylactic, it is hard to tell.

PART USED AND PREPARATION.—The fresh bark of the young twigs, as well as that of the root, is treated in the same manner as that of the previous species.*

The tincture has a clear, beautiful, reddish-orange color by transmitted light; an odor resembling that of arnica tincture; an astringent, then very bitter, taste; and an acid reaction.

CHEMICAL CONSTITUENTS.—There is, as yet, considerable doubt concerning the principles constituting this bark, yet the experiments of H. M. Edwards,† J. M. Bradford,‡ Jos. C. Roberts,§ and especially Edward Kremers,|| point to, at least, a great similarity between this species and *Fraxinus excelsior* and *nigra*, which, in part, yield the following:

Fraxin, $C_{32}H_{36}O_{20}$.—This glucoside is found also in the bark of *Æsculus*. Fraxin forms in tufts of white, lustrous, acicular forms, slightly bitter and acrid, losing water at 110° (230° F.), fusing at 320° (608° F.) and decomposing. It is sparingly soluble in cold water and alcohol, the aqueous solution giving a beautiful blue fluorescence. Dilute acids resolve the body as follows:

$$\underset{\text{Fraxin.}}{C_{32}H_{36}O_{20}} + (H_2O)_2 = \underset{\text{Sugar.}}{(C_6H_{12}O_6)_2} + \underset{\text{Fraxetin.¶}}{(C_{10}H_8O_5)_2}.$$

Mannite,** $C_6H_8(OH)_6$.—This saccharose body, found in many plants, as noted on page 136-2, was identified in this species by Kremers and others. It may be extracted from manna by boiling that substance in alcohol, from which it crystallizes in tufts of long, rhombic needles, possessing a pleasant, sweetish taste. The crystals from our species were found by Kremers to fuse at 162°–163° (323.6°–325.4° F.), and decompose at higher temperature, taking fire and leaving

* Page 136-2.
† Am. Jour. Phar., 1882, pp. 99, 283.
‡ Ibid., p. 282.
§ Ibid., 1885.
|| Contrib. Pharm. Univ. Wis., No. 2, 1866, p. 19.
¶ A crystalline body, as yet uninvestigated, having a slightly acerb taste.
** The Fraxinin of Keller.

a black residue, which finally volatilized. Mannite from *F. ornus* crystallizes as above, loses no weight at 120° (248° F.), fuses at 165°–166° (329°–330.8° F.), boils at 200° (392° F.), a portion volatilizing ; another losing two atoms of the compound radical OH, and becoming a syrupy mass of *mannitan* ($C_6H_8O(OH)_4$), which, if left to itself, reverts to mannite by its hygroscopic power ; the rest remaining unchanged ; if, however, the temperature is raised to 250° (482° F.), the mass swells up and is destroyed. This body, as isolated from our species, is soluble in cold water and boiling alcohol, and insoluble in ether, which is also true of the old-world product.

Oil of Fraxinus.—A small quantity of this volatile body has been isolated or noted by all experimenters upon the bark. It is described by Roberts as somewhat aromatic, bland, and having a yellow color.*

Fraxitannic Acid, $C_{13}H_{16}O_7$.—This body, extracted by Gintl and Reinitzer,† from the leaves of *F. excelsior*, has not been proven in the bark of our species, but the analyses made, except that of Edwards, seem to point to its existence. It is described as an amorphous, yellow-brown, brittle body, soluble in alcohol and water, and precipitable, like other tannins on saturation with common salt, but not by tartar emetic.

[An alkaloid is suspected by Edwards, Roberts, and Kremers, but remains to be proven a separate principle from Fraxin.]

An acrid and a neutral resin, starch, gum, etc., have also been determined by the above experimenters.

PHYSIOLOGICAL ACTION. — The experiments of Dr. Wright‡ gave the following effects from four ounces and a half of the tincture taken in three days : Vertigo and headache, followed by fever ; fever sores upon the lips ; constipation ; scanty urine ; pedal cramps ; and wakefulness.

DESCRIPTION OF PLATE 137.

1. A female flowering spray, Binghamton, N. Y., May 1st, 1886.
2. Female flower.
3. Section of ovary.
4. Fruit.
(2 and 3 enlarged.)

* That from the leaves of *F. excelsior* has the odor of syringia flowers, boils at 175° (237° F.), and has the composition $C_{10}H_{20}O_2$.—*Montash. Chem.*, iii, 745-762, from *Am. Jour. Phar.*, 1883, 371.
† *Ibid.*
‡ *U. S. Med. Investig.*, 1875, 326.

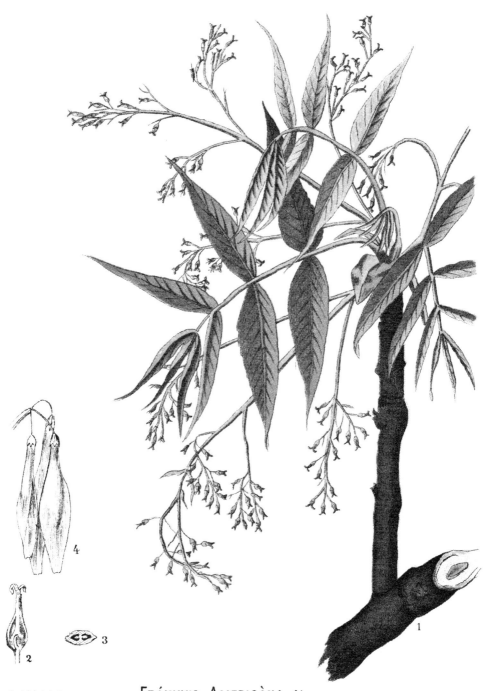

Œ.m . ad nat del.et pinxt.   FRÁXINUS AMERICÀNA , Linn.

138
SERPENTARIA.

VIRGINIAN SNAKE-ROOT.

SYN.—ARISTOLOCHIA SERPENTARIA, LINN.; A. SERPENTARIA, VAR. BARTONII, DUCH.; A. OFFICINALIS, NEES.; A. SAGITTATA, MUHL.; A. HASTATA, NUTT.; ENDODÆCA SERPENTARIA & BARTONII, KLOT.

COM. NAMES.—SNAKE-ROOT,† OR WEED; SERPENTARY ROOT, BIRTHWORT, SNAGREL; (FR.) SERPENTAIRE OU COULEUVRÉE DE VIRGINIE; (GER.) SCHLANGENWURZEL.

A TINCTURE OF THE DRIED ROOT OF ARISTOLOCHIA SERPENTARIA, L.

Description.—This small, aromatic perennial herb, grows to a height of from 8 to 15 inches. *Root* somewhat horizontal, more or less knotty, giving off—principally from its under surface—a multitude of long, fibrous, branching rootlets, its dorsum showing the scars of previous stems. *Stems* few or single, erect, flexuous, pubescent, branching at the naked or nodular and bracteolate base. *Leaves* petioled, thin, ovate, ovate-lanceolate, or nearly halbred-shaped, entire, acuminate; *base* cordate, or auriculate. *Stipules* none. *Inflorescence* single, terminal, upon bracted, flexuous peduncles, arising from the base of the stem; *flowers* apetalous, irregular. *Calyx* tubular, sigmoid, pubescent, and adherent to the ovary; *tube* somewhat dumb-bell shaped, *i. e.*, dilated at the apex, gibbous at the base above the ovary, and narrowly constricted in the throat; *limb* flat, more or less obtusely 3-lobed, the opening looking obliquely upward. *Stamens* 6; *anthers* 12 (contiguous in pairs, appearing but 6), sessile, adnate to the back of the stigma. *Style* very short and thick; *stigma* short and sarcous, divided into 3 to 6 flattened lobes, with a thickened apical margin. *Fruit* a naked, somewhat cylindrical, slightly 6-angled, 6-valved, septicidal capsule; *pericarp* smooth, dark brown, and papyraceous; *seeds* several in each cell, somewhat flattened-pear-shaped, carunculate about the fundus, and channelled upon the upper surface, where the *raphe*—a white, thick, fleshy body—runs along its centre.

Aristolochiaceæ.—A small family of twining shrubs, or low herbs, principally natives of South America, but having a few scattering species in the warmer parts

---

* Αρις'ος, *aris'os*, excellent; λοχός, *lochos*, a parturient female; from the medical qualities of *A. Clematitis*, which is said to hasten the delivery of the placenta, and accelerate lochial discharges.

† The American Snake-roots are, beside this species, Black Snake-root (*Sanicula Canadensis*, and *Marilandica*, Linn.), *Umbelliferæ*; White Snake-root (*Eupatorium ageratoides*, Linn.), *Compositæ*; Seneca Snake-root (*Polygala Senega*, Linn.), *Polygalaceæ*; and Button Snake-root (various species of *Liatris* (Compositæ), and *Eringium Yuccæfolium*, Michx., Umbelliferæ. These do not include the Rattlesnake roots.

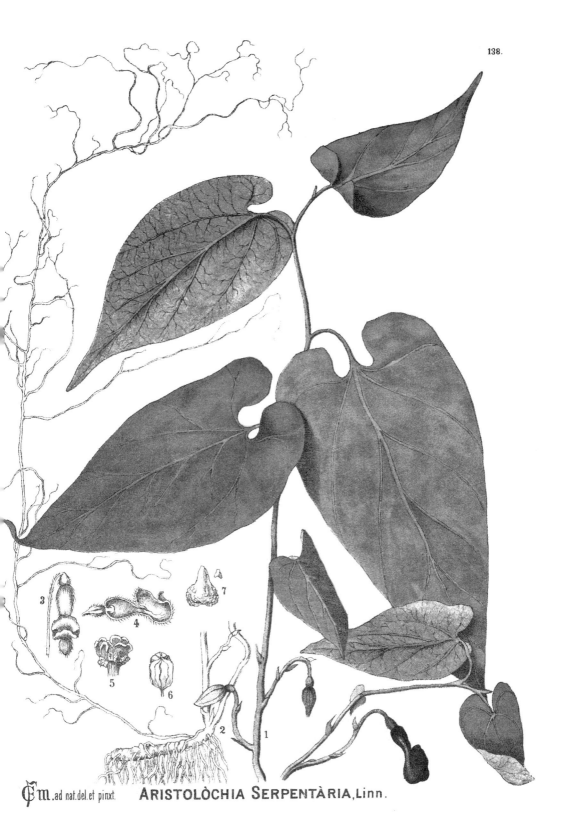

3

4

7

5

6

2

1

ℭ𝔐.ad nat.del.et pinxt. ARISTOLÒCHIA SERPENTÀRIA, Linn.

of both hemispheres. *Leaves* alternate, petioled, generally cordate, entire, and deciduous; *stipules* opposite the leaves, or wanting. *Aestivation* valvate; *flowers* brown or lurid, perfect, and usually solitary. *Calyx* tubular, conspicuously petaloid, coherent with the ovary; *limb* coriaceous, regular or irregular. *Stamens* 6 or 12, somewhat united with the style, or more or less distinct, inserted upon an epigynous disk; *filaments* short, or wanting; *anthers* adnate, extrorse, 2-celled; *dehiscence* longitudinal. *Ovary* 6-celled; *style* short and thick, or wanting; *stigmas* radiating, more or less lamellate. *Fruit* a 3- to 6-celled, dry capsule, or succulent berry. *Seeds* numerous, rounded or angular, anatropous; *raphe* prominent and fleshy; *embryo* minute, basal; *albumen* sarcous.

The only plant of this order, outside the genus *Aristolochia*, in our Materia Medica, is the European emetic, cathartic, diuretic, and sternutatory *Asarabacca* (*Asarum Europæum*, Linn.). The American Wild, or Indian Ginger (*A. Canadense*, Linn.), though not exhibiting the action of the European species to any great extent, except, mayhap, the errhine power, will, without doubt, soon be added to our medicaments.

History and Habitat.—Serpentaria is indigenous to North America, ranging from the State of Connecticut to Indiana, and thence southward. It grows in rich, shady woods, and blossoms in July. The flowers of this plant, like those of Asarum, are usually hidden beneath the dry leaves and loose top-mould of its chosen localities.

Strange as it may seem, almost all the species of this large genus are esteemed, by the natives of the countries in which they grow, as remedies against the poisonous effects of snake bites (Alexiterics); this use being fully known to each nation without previous communication with each other. Only one species has been proven beside Serpentaria, viz.: The Brazilian Snake-root *Aristolochia* (*Milhomens*) (*A. cymbifera*, Mart.), which was formerly considered alexiteric, antiparalytic, antiperiodic, and aphrodisiac. Among the more or less prominent species are: The Texan or Red River Snake-root, *A. reticulata*, Nutt., the chemistry of which has been proven by Wigand* to be nearly identical with that of Serpentaria; the North European *A. clematitis*, Linn., once noted for its emmenagogue and febrifugal properties; the South European *A. pistolochia*, having properties similar to those of Serpentaria, and *A. longa*, Linn., *A. bœtica*, Linn., and *A. rotunda*, Linn., used in Germany as emmenagogues, antiarthritics, and stimulants. The South American *A. trilobata*, Linn., is said to be superior in quantity and quality of action to Serpentaria, it being an energetic sudorific in doses of 6 to 20 grains. The Brazilian *A. anguicida*, Linn., is thought, by Humboldt and Lindley, to be the source of the celebrated alexiteric *guaco* of the Colombians; it is stated that a few drops of the juice of this plant, placed in the mouth of a snake, will stupefy it, and a larger dose cause its death. The East Indian *Gardigavapoo* (*A. bracteata*, Retz.), is anthelmintic and antipsoric; and *A. Indica*, Linn., emmenagogue, antiarthritic and stomachic. Other alexiterics are *A. bilobata* (Brazil),

---

* *Am. Jour. Phar.*, xvi, 10.

A. sempervirens, Linn. (Colombia), *A. fragrantissima*, Ruiz. (Peru), *A. grandiflora*, Swartz (Jamaica), *A. macroura*, Gomez (Brazil), *A. tomentosa*, Sims (U. S.), *A. hirsuta*, Muhl., and *A. Sipho*, L'Her. (N. A.).

The medical history of Serpentaria begins with Cornutus' first notice of the plant in 1635,* augmented by Parkinson in 1640. These authors, together with Dale (1693) and Geoffroy (1741), speak in high terms of its alexiteric properties. The root was admitted into the London Pharmacopœia in 1650.

Serpentaria has been classed among the diuretics and warm stimulating tonics and diaphoretics, and used with some success in the treatment of low forms of fevers, especially those of a septicæmic type, this use resulting from its alexipharmic properties. It was also used in intermittents and remittents before Quinine had been isolated from bark. Of this use Sydenham says :† "To cure tertians *in poor people who are not able to bear the charge of a long process* (Ital. ours), take of Virginia Snake-weed, finely powdered, one scruple, of white wine, three ounces, mingle them; let the sick take it two hours before the fit, and being well covered with clothing, let him sweat three or four hours, and let it be repeated twice as the fit approaches."‡ Serpentaria was also often given in mixture with Peruvian Bark, thus rendering the latter more active, and at the same time preventing the ill effect of bark upon the stomach; of this Dr. Chapman says,§ that "in some patients such is the irritability of the stomach, that bark, in substance, cannot be retained even in the smallest dose. In such cases we resort to it in decoction or compounded with Serpentaria, which, I think, renders the mixture quite as pleasant to the taste, as would cloves or cinnamon, as comfortable to the stomach, and perhaps more efficacious. *Combinations* too of this sort *will cure intermittents when the bark, alone, fails*" (Ital. ours). Serpentaria was also used in bilious, typhoid, and typhus fevers, small-pox, erysipelas, pneumonia, amenorrhœa, and in fact wherever a stimulating diaphoretic was deemed advisable. It was also considered a stimulating and antiseptic poultice for open, indolent wounds, ulcers, etc.; of this use Dr. Porcher wisely remarks :|| "This antiseptic power of certain vegetables should be compared with their medicinal effects when prescribed internally."

The officinal preparations of this drug in the U. S. Ph., are: *Extractum Serpentariæ Fluidum ; Tinctura Serpentariæ* and *Tinctura Cinchonæ Composita.¶* The Eclectic preparations are: *Infusum Serpentariæ ; Extractum Serpentariæ Fluidum ;* and *Tinctura Serpentaria Composita.***

PART USED AND PREPARATION.—The dried root, coarsely powdered, is covered by five parts by weight of alcohol, and kept eight days in a well stoppered bottle, in a dark, cool place, being shaken thoroughly twice a day.

---

* *Canadensium Plantarum Historia,* l.c.

† 1679.

‡ Did Sydenham already know, by experience, that the general exhibition of Peruvian Bark in fevers was only applicable to the wealthy who could stand the cost of a long attendance ?

§ *Element. Ther.,* ii, 411.

|| *Resources South. Field and Forests,* l.c.

¶ Cinchona rubra, Citrus medicus, and Aristolochia serpentaria.

** Aristolochia serp., Ipecacuanha, Crocus sat., Camphora, and Opium or Cypripedium.

The tincture, separated from this mass by decantation, pressure, and filtration, should have a beautiful, deep reddish-orange color by transmitted light.   Its odor should be decidedly terebinthic, resembling exactly that of the root before extraction; its taste warm, camphoraceous, terebinthic, and at last very penetratingly bitter; and its reaction acid.

CHEMICAL CONSTITUENTS.—*Aristolochin.* This amorphous yellowish body has a bitter and slightly acrid taste, and is soluble both in water and alcohol.[3]

Oil of Serpentaria.—This yellowish-brown oil is obtained by aqueous distillation of the roots.   It is lighter than water, and has an odor and taste resembling a mixture of valerian and camphor.[3]

Aristolochia-camphor.—This body, greatly resembling pure camphor, is deposited upon the cool sides of the receiver of the products of an aqueous distillation of the root.[4]

Gum,[1 2 3] coloring matter,[1] bitter-principle,[1 3 4] oil,[1 5] resin,[1 2 3 4] extractive,[1 2] and the volatile oil,[2 3 4] have been determined in this species.

PHYSIOLOGICAL ACTION.—Jörg determined as a result of his experiments* that Serpentaria caused an excitation of the alimentary tract with subsequent determination of blood to all the abdominal viscera, more frequently followed by flatulence than mucous secretion.   The symptoms usually following doses of from 2 to 5 scruples of the root were: Copious salivation; eructations; great nausea, and vomiting; a sense of weight in the stomach; distention of the abdomen, with colic and borborygm, frequent expulsion of flatulence, tenesmus and solid stools, with itching at the anus; a sensation of heat, and weight in the head followed by cephalagia; violent and frequent desire to urinate with greatly increased discharges of pale, watery urine.

DESCRIPTION OF PLATE 138.

1–2. Whole plant from Pittsburgh, Pa., June 18th, 1885.
2. Root, and one full length rootlet.
3. Face view of flower.
4. Longitudinal section of calyx.
5. Style, stigma and stamens.
6. Fruit.
7. Seed.
(5 and 7 enlarged.)

[1] Tilden's analysis, *Jour. of Mat. Med.*, ii, N. S., 203.
[2] Buckholz.
[3] Chevallier, *Jour. de Phar.*, 1820, 565.
[4] Bigelow, *Am. Med. Bot.*, iii, 85.
[5] Lewis, *ibid.*
* *Materialien zu einer Künftigen Heilmittellehre*, 1825.

139

PHYTOLACCA.

POKE WEED.

SYN.—PHYTOLACCA DECANDRA, LINN.; P. VULGARIS, DILL.; P. AMERI-
CANA, BOERHA.; BLITUM AMERICANUM, MUT.

COM. NAMES.—POKE WEED OR ROOT,† SKOKE, GARGET, CROWBERRY,‡
PIGEON-BERRY, JALAP, CANCER-ROOT,§ AMERICAN NIGHTSHADE,
POCAN OR COKAN (*Virginian tribes*), COCUM (*Northern tribes*), CHONGRAS,
(*Louisiana*); (FR.) MORELLE A GRAPPES, HERBE DE LA LAQUE; (GER.)
AMERIKANISCHE SCHARLACHBEERE OR KERMESBEERE.

A TINCTURE OF THE FRESH ROOT OF PHYTOLACCA DECANDRA, LINN.

Description.—This smooth, purplish stemmed perennial, grows to a height of
from 4 to 10 feet. *Root* large, fleshy, fusiform, verrucose, and variously branched,
the apex or head showing the scars of the previous stems ; the body is easily cut
or broken, its section being white, marked by annular rings and distinct radii,
and the bark very thin, almost papyraceous. *Stem* stout, cylindrical, hollow and
branching; *pith* sectioned by numerous discoid septa, thin in the centre, but so
thickened at the edges as to cause the interspaces to be fusiform. *Leaves* alternate or scattered, ample, ovate-lanceolate, acute at each end; *petioles* thick. *Inflorescence* terminal, many flowered racemes, which become lateral and opposite
the leaves as the growth proceeds; *peduncles* ascending; *pedicels* divaricate, usually
three-bracted, sometimes branched. *Calyx* white ; *sepals* 5, petaloid, ovate-obtuse,
concave and incurved. *Corolla* none. *Stamens* 10, somewhat shorter than the
lobes of the calyx ; *filaments* subulate ; *anthers* elliptical, 2-lobed. *Ovary* green,
composed of 10 carpels closely united into a ring; *styles* 10, short, separate, recurved
at the apex ; *stigma* simply a stigmatose surface on inner aspect of the recurved
portion of the style. *Fruit* a deep purple, depressed-globose, juicy, 10-celled
berry, marked with 10 slight furrows ; *seeds* 10, one in each cell, vertical ; *embryo*
curved in a circle around the albumen ; *cotyledons* linear ; *albumen* farinaceous.

Phytolaccaceæ.—The special characters of this small family are embodied in
the above description of its principal and typical genus. The order differs little
from the next (Chenopodiaceæ), mostly in having alternate entire leaves, a several
celled ovary, compounded of as many carpels united into a circle, and forming a
berry in fruit.

---

* Φυτον, *phyton*, plant; *lac*, lake; from the coloring properties of the berries.
† A perversion of the Indian name.   ‡ The true crowberry is *Empetrum nigrum*, Linn. (Empetraceæ).
§ This name properly designates the American species of *Epiphegus* and *Conopholis* (*Orobanche*), both of which
are members of the *Orobanchaceæ*, and are now being proven.

Five other species of Phytolacca are more or less used and have properties similar to ours, viz.: the Mexican and West Indian *P. octandra*, the berries of which are used in lieu of soap; the African *P. Abyssinica;* the recurved leaved *P. dodecandra;* the East Indian *P. icosandra;* and the South American tree-like *P. dioica.*

History and Habitat.—The poke is indigenous to North America, where it is common in light, rich soils, and flowers throughout the summer months. It has become a common weed in all the countries bordering upon the Mediterranean sea, both north and south, undoubtedly introduced from America.

The medical uses of poke-root were handed down to domestic and botanic practice by the aborigines, who valued the plant not only as an emetic, but also as an efficient remedy in gonorrhœal and syphilitic rheumatism.

Phytolacca, among the earlier American writers upon medicinal plants, was considered fully equal to Ipecacuanha as an emetic; its use, however, often caused narcotic effects, very injurious to the system. Its emetic action usually followed doses of 10 grains of the powdered root; both emesis and catharsis were effected by from 20 to 30 grains. The serious difficulties, however, in its employment were a slowness to begin its operation, and also to suspend its catharsis when once begun; it became often necessary to check its action upon the bowels with some preparation of opium. It was considered, however, to be the proper cathartic to use in partial paralysis of the bowels.

The root with lard was found to be an excellent ointment for the cure of many forms of skin diseases, notably: psoriasis, eczema capitis, and tinea circinata; also as a stimulant vulnerary in syphilitic ulcers, and a softening application in mastitis, as well as scrofulous swellings of glands in general. It was also considered an excellent poultice to cause rapid suppuration in felons.

A tincture of the berries was found to be often curative, or at least in some cases palliative, of syphilitic and gonorrhœal rheumatism, as well as non-specific chronic forms of that disease.

As an inevitable result of its uses as above, it was experimented with as a cure for cancer and malignant tumors, but its success in the cure of these terrible maladies never became notable.

I noted in my readings several years ago that the berries had been used for pies by frugal housewives, and often since have half determined to try poke-berry pastry; discretion has, however, always overruled valor, and the much-thought-of pie is still unmade and uneaten. The young shoots, however, make an excellent substitute for asparagus, and I much prefer them, if gathered early and discriminately.

The officinal forms of Phytolacca in the U. S. Ph. are: *Phytolaccæ Bacca* and *Phytolaccæ Radix.* In the Eclectic Materia Medica we find *Cataplasma Phytolaccæ; Decoctum Phytolaccæ; Extractum Phytolaccæ; Pilulæ Phytolaccæ Compositæ;* * *Syrupus Phytolaccæ Compositus;*† *Tinctura Phytolaccæ; Tinctura Cimicifugæ Composita; Unguentum Phytolaccæ;* and *Vinum Phytolaccæ Compositum.*‡

---

* Phytolacca, Stillingia, and Stramonium.   † Phytolacca, Ampelopsis, Cimicifuga, and Kalmia.
‡ Phytolacca and White turpentine.

PART USED AND PREPARATION.—The fresh root gathered in Autumn, is chopped and pounded to a pulp and weighed. Then two parts by weight of alcohol are taken, the pulp thoroughly mixed with one-sixth part of it, and the rest of the alcohol added. After stirring the whole well, it is placed in a well-stoppered bottle and allowed to stand eight days in a dark, cool place.

The tincture separated from the above by filtration, should have a clear, light yellowish-orange color by transmitted light, a bitterish odor and taste, and a very slight acid reaction.

CHEMICAL CONSTITUENTS.—*Phytolaccine.* Although an acrid principle was deemed present by all previous analysts of the root of this plant, it seems to have remained in some doubt prior to the analysis of Edmond Preston.* His analysis yielded small crystals, almost white when purified, giving precipitates with the four alkaloidal reagents—phosphomolybdic acid, tannin, iodohydrargyrate of potassium, and auric chloride, and were entirely dissipated when fused and subjected to further heat upon platinum foil. They proved entirely soluble in alcohol, moderately so in water, and fully in nitric, sulphuric, and hydrochloric acids, giving, however, no characteristic color test. He also found the hydrochlorate salt, as nearly colorless, strongly acid, acicular crystals, moderately soluble in alcohol, and fully so in water.

Phytolaccic Acid.—There seems to be little doubt that A. C. Erhard's analysis determines such an acid to exist in the root.† Its crystals were in his analysis, however, combined with potassium. A. Terreil ‡ found the same acid salt of potassium in an alcoholic extract of the berries. Isolated, it was amorphous, yellowish-brown, transparent, non-deliquescent and very soluble in water and alcohol. An analysis of the berries, however, by Cramer, elicited no acid answering to the above, but instead, one proving itself to be malic.§ Concerning this acid M. Braconnot says:‖ The alkali of this plant is neutralized by an acid having considerable affinity to the malic, but with a few shades of difference. With lime and lead malic acid forms flocculent precipitates, very easily soluble in distilled vinegar; but those with the *phytolaccic acid* are insoluble. He farther judges this peculiar acid to be probably a body between malic and oxalic acids, or an oxygenized malic.

Beside the above, potash exists in such large per cent. that some thought has been devoted to the advisability of its manufacture from the roots. Starch, tannin, gum, sugar, resin, and fixed oil have also been determined.¶

The coloring matter of the berries has been largely experimented upon, with a view to its utility as a dye. No mordant, however, is found that will fix its color. With alum, it is somewhat fast but not permanent; with urine, it dyes blue; and alone, it is very fugitive, although very brilliant at first. M. Braconnot, in his experiments with the juice of the berry, turned yellow by the addition of lime-water, found it to be one of the most delicate tests for acids: four times as

* *Am. Jour. Phar.*, 1884, 567. † *New Remedies*, 1879, 258.
‡ *Compt. rend.*, xci., pp. 856-8; *Am. Jour. Phar.*, 1881, 325.
§ Walter Cramer, *Am. Jour. Phar*, 1881, 598. ‖ *Annals de Chimie*, vol. LXXII.
¶ Donnelly, *Am. Jour. Phar.*, 1843, 165; Pape, *Ibid.*, 1881, p. 579; Preston, l. c.; Erhard, l. c.

sensitive as an infusion of litmus, but its use limited, as freshness of the juice is absolutely necessary.

PHYSIOLOGICAL ACTION.—The principal primary action of Phytolacca is upon the stomach as an emetic; this action is remarkably slow, it being from an hour to two hours after its ingestion before emesis occurs. The next effects noticed are upon the nervous system. The toxic symptoms from an overdose are: more or less nausea, violent vomiting and purging, great thirst and discomfort in the epigastric region, feeble pulse, dimness of vision, vertigo, drowsiness, great prostration and coldness of the periphery, followed by convulsion, and in one case, death.

The grated fresh root applied to the skin causes a sensation of heat and smarting, followed by redness and finally vesication.

On animals, Dr. Schultz found that the juice of the root in repeated trials resulted only in emesis, catharsis, and drowsiness.

Compiling the symptoms occurring in various cases of poisoning, voluntary and involuntary, the most prominent and duplicating effects are as follows: mental indifference and stupor, dullness, giddiness, and vertigo; severe pressive headache with soreness; dilation of the pupil, with dimness of vision and photophobia; paleness of the face; tongue white-coated, with a very red tip; it feels rough and blistered, and great pain is produced at its root on swallowing; profuse salivation, redness and soreness of the throat, followed by a collection of thick white or yellowish mucus about the fauces; the throat feels full and constricted, almost to suffocation, associated with a sense of suffocation also in the chest; every attempt to swallow attended with terrible shooting pains through the ears; nausea, cramps, and violent vomiting, followed by epigastric tenderness; griping pains in the abdomen, with flatulence; violent purging, continuing until the passages become mucus and blood, and the desire constant; dryness of the larynx, dry hacking cough, and shallow breathing; feeble pulse; stiffness of the neck, and in general, where lymphatic glands abound; constant dull, heavy aching in the lumbar region and sacrum, with painful weakness and stiffness of both the upper and lower limbs; general sense of soreness and prostration, with drowsiness and coldness, followed by profuse cool perspiration.

As Homœopathists, this account of the action of Phytolacca at once impresses us with its certain value in diphtheria, when a like condition exists, as it often does. Its numerous secondary symptoms in various organs noted in the provings, make it a valuable remedy in many forms of disease. On the whole, this remedy is one of the most important of the purely American plants.

DESCRIPTION OF PLATE 139.

1. End of a flowering branch, Pamrapo, N. J., August 2d, 1879.
    2. Root.
    3. Horizontal section of root.
    4. Fruit.
    5. Flower.
    6. Section of ovary.
       (1·4 once reduced.)

1

4

2

6

3

5

ℭℳ. ad nat del. et pinxt. PHYTOLÁCCA DECÁNDRA Linn.

140

CHENOPODIUM ANTHELMINTICUM.

WORMSEED.

SYN.—CHENOPODIUM AMBROSIOIDES, VAR. ANTHELMINTICUM, GRAY;
C. ANTHELMINTICUM, LINN.; C. SUFFRUTICOSUM, WILLD.; AMBRINA
AMBROSIOIDES, SPACH; ORTHOSPORUM ANTHELMINTICUM, R. BR.
COM. NAMES.—AMERICAN WORMSEED, JERUSALEM OAK,† STINK-
WEED; (FR.) CHÉNOPODE ANTHELMINTIQUE, L'ANSERINE VER-
MIFUGE; (GER.) WURMSAAMEN GANSEFUSS, AMERICANISCHER
WURMSAAMEN.

A TINCTURE OF THE SEEDS OF CHENOPODIUM AMBROSIOIDES, VAR. ANTHEL-
MINTICUM, GRAY.

Description.—This smoothish, more or less viscid-glandular, and pleasantly-aromatic annual, grows to a height of about 2 feet. *Stem* erect, stout, angular, and grooved. *Leaves* slightly petioled, oblong-lanceolate, repand-toothed or sometimes the lower almost lobed, the upper entire and tapering at both ends. *Inflorescence* in numerous simple, slender, elongated, more or less leafy or leafless spike-like racemes; *flowers* sessile, glomerulate, perfect, and bractless. *Calyx* 5-cleft; *lobes* ovate, pointed, not appendaged nor keeled. *Stamens* 5; *filaments* filiform; *anthers* globular, 2-celled. *Ovary* covered on the top with small oblong stalked glands; *styles* 2 to 3, stigmatic by a fringed inner surface. *Fruit* perfectly enclosed in the calyx, obtusely angled; *seed* lenticular, smooth and shining; *testa* crustaceous. *Embryo* forming about three-fourths of a ring around the mealy *albumen.*

Chenopodiaceæ.—This large family of homely and more or less succulent herbs furnishes to North American Botany 15 genera, comprising 90 species and 15 varieties. *Leaves* mostly alternate, exstipulate, and bractless. *Flowers* minute, greenish; *calyx* free, imbricated in the bud. *Stamens* as many as the lobes of the calyx or sometimes fewer; *filaments* inserted opposite the calyx-lobes or upon their base. *Ovary* 1-celled; *styles* or *stigmas* 2, rarely 3 or 5. *Fruit* a 1-celled utricle or rarely an achenium. *Embryo* coiled into a ring, conduplicate or spiral; *albumen* mealy or sometimes wanting.

---

* Χήν, *chen*, a goose; ποῦς, *pous*, a foot; from a fancied resemblance in the leaves.
† This name belongs to *C. Botrys*, Linn.

The only other proven plant in this order is the European Stinking Goosefoot (*Chenopodium vulvaria*, Linn.), which in general practice is considered antispasmodic and emmenagogue. General medical practice notices the following: The Egyptian *Chenopodium baryosmon*, Rom., a fetid emmenagogue; the European and Asiatic Jerusalem Oak (*C. Botrys*, Linn.), a French expectorant; and the American Mexican Tea (*C. ambrosioides*, Linn.), which is considered nervine, anthelmintic, and emmenagogue, and used in chorea. The seeds of the European *Atriplex angustifolia*, Smith, are emetic, as are also those of the Tartarian Garden Orache (*A. hortensis*, Linn.). The European and Asiatic *Salsola Kali*, Linn.; the Spanish *S. sativa*, Löft.; the Mediterranean *S. Soda*, Linn.; and the Mediterranean and Caspian *S. tragus*, Linn., yield the finest Alicant Soda. The European Saltwort (*Salicornia annua*, Smith) is another source of salsoda.

Among the esculent plants of this order the most prominent are: The common Garden Spinach of the Levant (*Spinacia oleracea*, Linn.) and the Beet (*Beta vulgaris*, Linn.). The young and tender plants of the Lamb's Quarter (*Chenopodium album*, Linn.) "are collected by the Navajoes, the Pueblo Indians of New Mexico, all the tribes of Arizona, the Diggers of California, and the Utahs, and boiled as herbs alone, or with other food. Large quantities also are eaten in the raw state. The seeds of this plant are gathered by many tribes, ground into flour after drying, and made into bread or mush. They are very small, of a gray color, and not unpleasant when eaten raw. The peculiar color of the flour imparts to the bread a very dirty look, and when baked in ashes it is not improved in appearance. It resembles buckwheat in color and taste, and is regarded as equally nutritious. The plant abounds in the Navajo country."*

History and Habitat.—American Wormseed is indigenous to Mexico and South America, but has become quite thoroughly naturalized as far north as Missouri and New England, where it grows in waste places about dwellings and in manured soils, and blossoms from July to September. It was introduced into England in 1732. The American Aborigines used the whole herb in decoction in painful menstruation, especially of the older women, but its principal use has been the leaves and seeds as a vermifuge; as such it was noticed by Kalm, Clayton, and Schoepf, and is to-day considered one of the best expellants of lumbricoids known. The principal method of administration is doses of from three to ten drops of the oil on sugar, three times a day for several days, the last dose being followed by a cathartic. The plant is also considered antispasmodic, antihysteric, emmenagogue, and a useful remedy in chorea.

The fruit and *Oleum chenopodii* are officinal in the U. S. Phar., and in the Eclectic Materia Medica, where it is also a compound of *Mistura Chenopodii Composita*† and *Mistura Olei Composita*.‡

PART USED AND PREPARATION.—The fresh seeds are ground to a pulp and weighed. Then two parts by weight of alcohol are taken, the pulp mixed with

---

* J. R. Dodge, in *U. S. Agric. Rep.*, 1870, 419.
† Castor Oil, Wormseed Oil, Anise Oil, and Tincture of Myrrh.
‡ In this preparation Oil of Turpentine is used in place of the Myrrh.

one-sixth part of it, and the rest of the alcohol added. The whole is then poured into a well-stoppered bottle, and allowed to stand eight days in a dark, cool place.

The tincture, separated from this mass by filtration, has a reddish-brown color by transmitted light; a characteristic repugnant odor; a bitter, astringent taste; and an acid reaction.

CHEMICAL CONSTITUENTS.—*Volatile Oil of Wormseed.* This light yellow oil has a peculiar, strong, and quite offensive odor, and a pungent, bitterish, disagreeable but aromatic taste. Its sp. gr. when fresh is 0.908. It is freely soluble in alcohol, and boils at 190° (374° F.).*

No analysis has yet been made to determine other principles in this species.

PHYSIOLOGICAL ACTION.—The symptoms in a man who took about half an ounce of the drug were those of a narcotico-acrid poison, affecting the brain, spinal cord and stomach. He was insensible, convulsed, and foamed at the mouth.† A man aged thirty took an ounce and a half of the oil and thirty drops of turpentine; the following symptoms came on: Nausea; vertigo; deafness to human voice, hearing acute for louder and more distant noises; aphasia; inability to control the muscles as desired for any continued effort, and fatigue from attempting so to do; hilarity at his futile attempts at talking; repeats his actions like a drunken man; convulsions and finally paralysis of right side; involuntary urination; apoplectic breathing; frothing at the mouth; drenching sweat; opisthotonos; icterus; and death during a comatose state followed; this on the fifth day from the ingestion of the drug.‡

DESCRIPTION OF PLATE 140.

1. Top of plant, Rawlinsville, Pa., Aug. 18th, 1885.
2. Leaf.
3. Portion of leaf, showing glands.
4. Male flower.
5. Sepal.
6. Stamen.
7. Pistil.
8. Fruit and calyx.
9. Seed.
10. Longitudinal section of seed.
11. Female flower.

(3–11 enlarged.)

* Garrigues, in *Am. Jour. Phar.*, xxvi, 405.
† *Phar. Jour.*, 1862, 330.
‡ T. R. Brown, M.D., in *Maryland Med. Jour.*, Nov. 1878, 20; Allen, *Encyc. Mat. Med.*, x, 457.

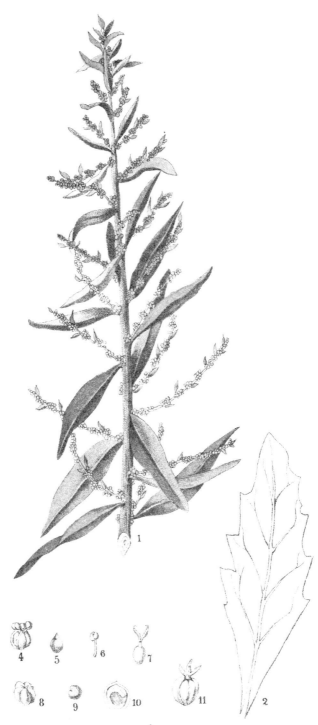

140.

.ad nat.del.et pinxt.   CHENOPÒDIUM ANTHELMÍNTICUM, Linn.

141

POLYGONUM.

WATER SMARTWEED.

SYN.—POLYGONUM ACRE, H. B. K.; P. HYDROPIPEROIDES, PURSH. (NOT
MICHX.); P. PUNCTATUM, ELL.
COM. NAMES.—WATER PEPPER, SMARTWEED, BITING KNOTWEED;
(GER.) KNÖTERICH.

A TINCTURE OF THE WHOLE FRESH PLANT POLYGONUM ACRE, H. B. K.

Description.—This pungently acrid, perennial herb grows to a height of from
2 to 5 feet. *Rootstock* creeping, ligneous; *roots* fibrous. *Stem* simple, smooth, or
nearly so, rooting at its decumbent base; *sheaths* cylindrical, bristly fringed. *Leaves*
larger and longer than those of *P. hydropiper*, L., taper-pointed. *Inflorescence* in
axillary and terminal, erect, slender, filiform, loosely-flowered, spike-like racemes.
Stamens 8. *Style* mostly 3-parted; *stigmas* capitate. *Achenia* sharply triangular,
smooth and shining. *Cotyledons* acumbent, slender; *embryo* in a groove on the
outside of the albumen, and curved half-way around it; *albumen* hard and horny.

Polygonaceæ.—This large family of herbs, furnished with watery acid or acrid
juice, is represented in North America by 15 genera, comprising 165 species, the
truly western genus, Erigonium, alone having 112 species and 10 varieties. The
order is characterized as follows: *Leaves* alternate, entire; *stipules* in the form of
sheaths (*Ochreæ*), and placed above the usually swollen joints of the stem. *Flowers*
mostly perfect; *calyx* more or less persistent, 3- to 6-parted. *Stamens* 4 to 12.
Ovary 1-celled; *styles* or *stigmas* 2 or 3. *Fruit* dry and grain-like; *seed* single,
erect, and orthropous; *embryo* curved or straightish, on the outside of the albumen, rarely in its centre; *radicle* pointing from the base to the apex.

The only proven plant of this family, beside the four treated of in this work,
is the Thibetan Rhubarb (*Rheum officinale*, Baill.). The rhubarbs used in general
practice, either in lieu of the above species or individually, are: Chinese or Russian Rhubarb (*R. palmatum*, Linn.); English Rhubarb (*R. raponticum*, Linn.);
R. Webbianum, Royle, *R. emodi*, Wallich, from China; *R. spiciforme* and *R. moorcroftianum*, Royle, from the West Indies; *R. leucorrhizum*, Pal., from the mountains
of Dolenkara; *R. undulatum*, Linn., from China and Siberia; *R. capsicum*, Fisch.,

---

* Πολύ, *poly*, many; γονυ, *gonu*, knees; from the jointed stems of many species.

from the Altaic Mountains; *R. compactum*, Linn., from Chinese-Tartary; and *R. crassinervium*, Fisch., whose nativity is doubtful.

Other medicinal plants of the order are: The Seaside Grape of the West Indies (*Coccoloba uvifera*, Linn.), a powerful astringent, whose decoction, evaporated, is known as Jamaica Kino; the fruit of this plant is edible and pleasant, forming an article of commerce in the native markets. Of the genus *Polygonum* many species are astringent, particularly, however, Bistort, the rhizome of *P. Bistorta*, Linn., which is highly esteemed in diarrhœa, leucorrhœa, gleet, and kindred affections; the European *P. amphibium*, Linn., is said to resemble sarsaparilla in its qualities, and has been substituted for it; *P. barbatum*, Linn., of the Cape of Good Hope, is considered diuretic; the fruit of the Knob Grass (*P. aviculare*, Linn.) is said to be emetic and cathartic; while *P. hydropiper*, Linn., is a vesicant and powerful diuretic when fresh.

The Western Indians, and especially those of Alaska, use the leaves of the Round-leaved Sorrel (*Oxyria digynia*, Campd.), chopped with those of the Water-cress and fermented, as a salad; the Indians along the Colorado River gather the abundant seeds of a species of *Rumex*, which they call Yerba Colorado, which they grind and make into bread;* while the domestic use of Buckwheat (*Fagopyrum esculentum*, Mœn.) as a flour for breakfast cakes is truly national.

History and Habitat.—Water Smartweed is indigenous to the United States, where it is common, especially southward; it habits ditches and waste places where the soil is wet and rich, and flowers from July to September. The use of Smart-weed among the laity, who include *P. hydropiper*, Linn., is very general and extended, especially as a fomentation in ammenorrhœa, dysmenorrhœa, enteritis, and mastitis, and internally in the same troubles and in coryza. The fresh leaves, bruised with those of the Mayweed (*Maruta Cotula*, Compositæ), and moistened with a few drops of oil of turpentine, make a speedy vesicant, and, as such, are highly esteemed; so quick is the action of Smartweed in this direction that it has received among boys the merited but unpleasant name, Ass-smart. A cold infusion has been found very serviceable in nursing sore-mouth, mercurial ptyalism, gout, and dysentery, and externally as a wash for indolent ulcers and painful hemorrhoids. In Mexico the infusion is used as a diuretic, and put into the baths of persons afflicted with rheumatism.

The Eclectic Materia Medica recommends its use in the following forms: *Infusum Polygoni, Extractum Polygoni Fluidum, Extractum Polygoni, Tinctura Polygoni*, and makes it a component of *Pilulæ Polygoni Compositæ*,† and *Tinctura Caulophylli Composita*.‡

PART USED AND PREPARATION.—The whole fresh plant is chopped and pounded to a pulp and weighed. Then two parts by weight of alcohol are taken, the pulp thoroughly mixed with one-sixth part of it, and the rest of the alcohol added. After having stirred the whole well, it is poured into a well-stoppered

* J. R. Dodge, in *U. S. Agric. Rept.*, 1870, 422.
† Sulphate of Iron, Resin of Cimicifuga, Oleo-resin of Iris, and Extractum Polygoni.
‡ Caulophyllum, Ergot, Polygonum, and Sabina.

bottle, and allowed to stand eight days in a dark, cool place. The tincture, prepared from this mass by pressure and filtration, has a beautiful carmine color by transmitted light; no characteristic odor or taste; and an acid reaction. A penetrating biting sensation is noticed upon the tongue a short time after tasting this tincture.

CHEMICAL CONSTITUENTS.—*Polygonic Acid.** This doubtful body is said to form in green, deliquescent crystals, having a bitter and acrid taste, and a strong acid reaction, and to be soluble in alcohol, choloroform, and ether. Messrs. Trimble and Schuchard decide† that this body is simply a mixture of impure tannic and gallic acids, together with chlorophyll; and failed in their analysis of this plant to isolate a stable active principle; a volatile principle was, however, appreciable, which gave the pungency of the plant to all preparations made without the application of heat.

PHYSIOLOGICAL ACTION.—The following essentially enumerate the symptoms noted from ingestion of doses of from 10 to 60 drops of the tincture: Dizziness, fullness of the head, and pulsating pain; itching and burning of the eyes; irritation of the pituitary membrane and frequent sneezing; heat in the mouth and throat, with burning and dryness of the fauces; increased appetite and great thirst; nausea and burning of the stomach; rumbling of the abdomen attended by colic; great and ineffectual urging to stool; diarrhœa; urging to urinate; smarting of the urethra, and greatly increased pale urine; sharp stitching or pulsating pains throughout the body; a general feeling of weakness and debility; alternate heat and coldness; and profuse perspiration from moderate exercise. These symptoms point to an irritant to the mucous membranes of high value in the treatment of enteritis, gastritis, cystitis, and other inflammatory diseases of these tissues.

DESCRIPTION OF PLATE 141.

1. Stem in fruit, from Rawlinsville, Pa., Aug. 27th, 1885.
   2. A portion of the base of the plant.
   3. Seed.
   4. Longitudinal section of seed.
   5. Horizontal section of same.
   (3-5 enlarged.)

---

* Dr. C. J. Rademaker, *Am. Jour. Phar.*, 1871, 490.   † *Ibid.*, 1885, 21.

141.

1

2

3

4

5

℄.𝔪. ad nat del. et pinxt.

POLÝGONUM ÀCRE, H.B.K.

142

FAGOPYRUM.

BUCKWHEAT.

SYN.—FAGOPYRUM ESCULENTUM, MOENCH.; POLYOGNUM FAGOPY-
RUM, LINN.
COM. NAMES.—BUCKWHEAT,† BEECH-WHEAT; (FR.) LE BLÉ NOIR, LE
BLÉ SARRASIN; (GER.) BUCHWEIZEN, HEIDEKORN.

A TINCTURE OF THE MATURE PLANT, FAGOPYRUM ESCULENTUM, MOENCH.

Description.—This annual herb grows to a height of from eighteen inches to
three feet. The *stem* is sub-cylindrical, delicate, smoothish, juicy, erect, and
branched. The *leaves* are triangular-cordate, cordate-sagittate, or halberd-shaped,
acute at the tip; the *sheaths* or *ochreæ* semi-cylindrical. *Inflorescence* terminal,
and axillary, corymbose racemes, or panicles; *flowers* octandrous, white, pinkish,
or greenish. *Calyx* petaloid, equally 5-parted, persistent, withering in fruit. *Stamens* 8; *filaments* filiform, arising from between the 8 honey-bearing glands;
anthers innate, introrse, composed of 2 nearly separate cells. *Styles* 3, short, more
or less persistent; *stigmas* 3, capitate. *Seed* acute, entire, triquetrous, longer than,
and situated in, the cup of the calyx; *albumen* copious; *embryo* large, dividing the
albumen into two equal parts; *cotyledons* broad, foliaceous, plicate, and twisted.
Read description of the N. Ord. under Polygonum, 141.

History and Habitat.—The buckwheat plant is a native of Northern or Central Asia; it was introduced into Europe about the year 1440, and cultivated in
England—according to Gerarde—in 1597. In the United States it is largely cultivated for fattening poultry, and for use as flour in breakfast-cakes; the production in 1880 was estimated at 14,617,535 bushels, fully one-third of which was
raised in New York State alone. Although buckwheat is far removed from the
cereals, yet in the composition of its seed it is strikingly similar to them. Its
nutritive value, however, is low as compared to the more important of the cereals,
not quite half its weight being fecula, while wheat yields nearly three-fourths its
weight. The seed is said to be employed in some parts of Germany in the manufacture of beer.

* Φηγός, *Phegos*, the beech; πυρός, *pyros*, wheat; the seed being shaped similarly to the nut of the beech (*Fagus
ferruginea, Ait.*).
† From the Scottish word "buck," the beech; and the English "wheat."

A field of buckwheat at the prime of its flowering season is very odorous, and attractive to bees, who gather a large store of honey from the glands at the bases of the stamens ; this honey, though very dark in color, and not as fine in grain and taste as that from clover, is greatly esteemed. Again, buckwheat is very valuable to the farmer as a reclaimer of soil, both on account of its "weeding" properties, and its value as a fertilizer when plowed under. A crop of this plant will thoroughly kill off weeds, even the Canada thistle, by its quick growth and ample shade. Escaping from cultivation it has become naturalized in many localities, flowering from June to September, and fruiting as it flowers.

The medical history of this plant is not extensive, the only previous uses of importance, as far as I can determine, are those of an infusion of the herb in erysipelas, and an application of the flour, made into a paste with buttermilk, as a poultice to bring back the flow of milk to the breasts of nurses.

The plant is official in none of the Pharmacopœias except the Homœopathic.

PART USED AND PREPARATION.—The fresh, mature plant and its seed is chopped and pounded to a pulp and weighed. Then two parts by weight of alcohol are taken, the pulp mixed thoroughly with one-sixth part of it, and the rest of the alcohol added. After having stirred the whole well, pour it into a well-stoppered bottle, and let it stand eight days in a dark, cool place. The tincture, separated from this mass by filtration, should have a deep crimson color by transmitted light, and a slightly acid reaction.

CHEMICAL CONSTITUENTS.—Many analyses of the ash of this herb have been made, but so far none to determine an active principle. The following analyses will serve to show the general constituents of the plant :

	Straw (Wolf).	Seed (Salisb'y).	Seed (Wolf).		Straw (Wolf).	Seed (Salisb'y).	Seed (Wolf).
Carbonic acid, . . .		trace		Magnesia, ...	3.6	15.84	13.4
Silica, ...	5.5	1.95	.0	Potash, ...	46.6	21.27	23.1
Sulphuric acid, . . .	5.3	1.55	2.1	Soda, ...	2.2	2.32	6.2
Phosphoric acid, . .	11.9	48.95	48.0	Chlorine, ...	7.7	.30	1.7
Lime, ...	18.4	3.01	3.3	Organic acids, . . .		2.75	

Mr. Salisbury's proximate analyses* of the seeds gave : Starch, 42.47, sugar and extractive matter, 6.16, gum, 1.60, a light-gray matter insoluble in water and hot alcohol, 10.10, a matter insoluble in water and soluble in alcohol, 2.66, and other common constituents of plants.

Indican.†—This glucoside has been determined in small percentage (Wittstein).

PHYSIOLOGICAL ACTION.—Although we have a good proving of this drug by Dr. Dexter Hitchcock, we have no record of the effects of the substance in

---

* Nat. Hist. State N. Y., Part V, Agric., p. 274.　　　　† See Baptisia tinctoria, 42.

quantity.   Many individuals cannot partake of breakfast-cakes made from the flour of the seeds without experiencing a severe itching, especially observed about the large joints ; a peculiarity of this itching is that it occurs particularly after removal of the clothing, and when first retiring at night.   The eruption incident to, and following this itching, takes the form of vesicles, which degenerate into dry, dark-colored, tedious scabs.   Another symptom arising, is a glutinous condition of the otherwise natural feces, making expulsion quite difficult.   Increased urinary discharge is also present in many cases.

Description of Plate 142.

1. Top of plant; Chemung, N. Y., Sept. 3d, 1879.
  2. Flower (enlarged).
  3. Fruit (slightly enlarged).
  4. Section of the seed (enlarged).

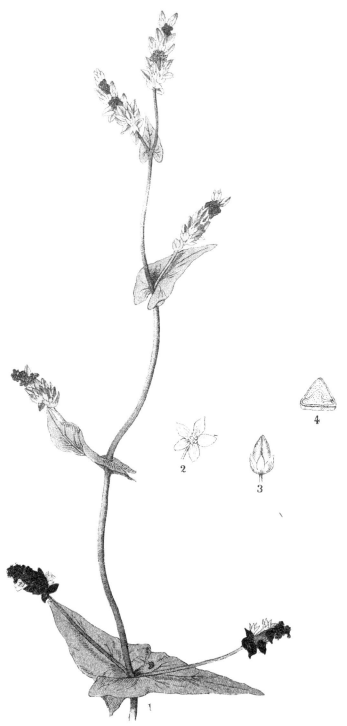

2

3

4

ℭℳ. ad nat.del.et pinxt.

FAGOPYRUM ESCULÉNTUM Moench.

143

RUMEX.

YELLOW DOCK.

SYN.—RUMEX CRISPUS, LINN.
COM. NAMES.—YELLOW DOCK, CURLED DOCK, GARDEN PATIENCE,
NARROW DOCK, SOUR DOCK; (FR.) PATIENCE FRISEÉ; (GER.) KRAU-
SER AMPFER.

A TINCTURE OF THE FRESH ROOT OF RUMEX CRISPUS, LINN.

Description.—This smooth, perennial herb, grows to a height of from 2 to 4 feet. *Root* deep, large, spindle-shaped, and yellow without and within; *stem* erect, sulcate, smooth, paniculately branching above. *Leaves* all lanceolate, acute, and wavy-curled on the margins, the lower large, tufted, and more truncate than cordate at the base, the upper lanceolate, acute at both ends; *petioles* present with all the leaves, but very long in the lower. *Inflorescence* in prolonged, wand-like racemes, somewhat leafy below; *flowers* crowded in whorls along the rachis; *pedicels* filiform. *Valves* prominently reticulate, rounded, cordate, obscurely denticulate or entire, mostly all of them grain-bearing. *Achenia* acuminate, brown, and shining.

Rumex.—This genus of coarse, homely herbs is characterized as follows: *Leaves* alternate, none of them halbred-shaped; *petioles* somewhat sheathing at the base. *Inflorescence* in crowded whorls, along panicled racemes; *flowers* small, greenish, perfect or monœciously polygamous; *pedicels* jointed near the base. *Calyx* of 6 herbaceous sepals, the 3 outer reflexed, sometimes united at the base, spreading in fruit, the 3 inner (*valves*) larger, veiny, somewhat colored, increasing after flowering, and converging over the fruit, often bearing a grain-like tubercle upon the dorsal surface of the midrib near its base. *Stamens* 6, inserted in pairs opposite the external sepals; *anthers* erect. *Ovary* triquetrous; *ovule* sessile; *styles* 3; *stigmas* tufted. *Fruit* a 3-angled achenium; embryo slender, slightly curved, and lying along one side of the farinaceous albumen; *cotyledons* narrow, incumbent; *radicle* pointing upward.

History and Habitat.—The Docks are some of our most troublesome weeds imported from Europe. The Yellow Dock grows in cultivated ground, and along roadsides, everywhere in the eastern section of the United States; where it flowers from May until August, and ripens its copious seeds from August to October. The root has been used in medicine from ancient times, as a mild astringent tonic, laxative, and depurant, its use being similar to that of rhubarb and of sarsaparilla. A decoction of the root has been found useful in dyspepsia, gouty tendencies,

---

* Derivation unknown.

143.

2

5

1

3   4

Ɠm.ad nat.del.et pinxt.   RÙMEX   CRÍSPUS, Linn.

hepatic congestion, scrofula, syphilis, leprosy, elephantiasis, and various forms of scabby eruptions. An ointment of the powdered root with lard, or a cataplasm with cream, has been considered a specific for the cure of itch, and a useful application to cancers, as well as a discutient for indolent glandular tumors. Whatever use the root may have in these latter troubles must reside in the peculiar acid contained in it. Rumex is also considered an excellent dentifrice, especially where the gums are spongy. As a pot-herb the young root-leaves of the Narrow Dock are well known in all country localities.

The officinal preparation in the U. S. Ph. is *Extractum Rumicis Fluidum ;* in the Eclectic Dispensatory the following are recommended: *Decoctum Rumicis ; Extractum Rumicis Alcoholicum ; Syrupus Rumicis Compositus ;* * *Tinctura Corydalis Compositus.*†

PART USED AND PREPARATION.—The fresh root, gathered after the fruit is ripe, but before frost has touched the plant, is treated as directed under the herb Polygonum.‡ The resulting tincture has a clear madder color by transmitted light; a peculiar sour, mousy odor, that I have also noted in Oxalis; a sourish, astringent, and slightly bitter taste; and a strong acid reaction.

CHEMICAL CONSTITUENTS.— *Chrysophanic Acid*, or *Rumicin*, $C_{14}H_{10}O_4$. This dioxyanthraquinone was discovered by Rochelder and Heldt (1843) in the yellow lichen (*Parmelia parietina*),§ and afterward recognized as such in rhubarb‖ by Schlossberger and Döpping (1844). It has since been found also in Rumex,¶ Cassia bijuga, and goa powder (*Andira Araroba*).** It crystalizes in tasteless, golden-yellow needles or tablets, fuses at 162° (323.6° F.), and sublimes with little change on careful heating. It is slightly soluble in hot water, also in alcohol, and dissolves quite readily in ether. This acid acts as a rubefacient and discutient, and is a valuable agent for destroying parasites of the skin.

The plant also contains sugar, gum, albumen, and tannin.

PHYSIOLOGICAL ACTION.—Rumex causes nausea; watery brown movements of the bowels, urging liquid passages; urging, copious urination; dry, spasmodic, irritating cough; sore, burning, aching, and sticking pains in the chest; increased heart's action; restlessness; itching of the skin; sleeplessness; chills, fever, and perspiration.

DESCRIPTION OF PLATE 143.

1. End of a fruiting branch, Binghamton, N. Y., Aug. 20th, 1886.
2. Outline of a lower leaf.
3. Fruit.
4. Valve.
5. Achenium.
(3–5 enlarged.)

---

* Yellow Dock, Celastrus, Ampelopsis, and Scrophularia.

† Corydalis, Podophyllum, Rumex, Scrophularia, and [Alnus rubra.

‡ Page 141–2.

§ Parietin, Parietinic Acid.

‖ Rhein, Rheic Acid, Rhabarbarin, Rhabarbaric Acid,

¶ Rumic Acid, Rumicin, Lapathin. [Rhaponticin.

** Chrysarobin, Chrysarobic Acid.

144

LAPATHUM.

BITTER DOCK.

SYN.—RUMEX OBTUSIFOLIUS, LINN.; R. DIVARICATUS, ELL.; LAPA-
THUM ACUTUM.
COM. NAMES.—BITTER DOCK, BLUNT-LEAVED DOCK; (GER.) GRIND-
WURZ.

A TINCTURE OF THE ROOT OF RUMEX OBTUSIFOLIUS, LINN.

Description.—This roughish perennial weed is of similar growth to the preceding species. *Root* brownish, thick, and branching; *stem* angular and sulcate.
Leaves rather downy upon the veins underneath and somewhat wavy margined;
the lower ovate, cordate, mostly obtuse; the upper lanceolate and acute at both
ends. *Flowers* in loose and distant whorls below, more crowded above; *pedicels*
recurved. *Valves* ovate-hastate, strongly reticulate, with a few sharp, awl-shaped
teeth at the base, one of them principally grain-bearing. (Read description of
Rumex, page 143.)

History and Habitat.—The Bitter Dock is in Europe a domestic weed of the
worst description—a trait that well characterizes its naturalized state here, where
it has rapidly spread wherever man has settled, defacing his fields, gardens, and
lawns. It is much harder to exterminate than *R. crispus*, on account of its branching roots, which, like the star-fish, will increase and multiply the faster if broken,
cut, or bruised. It flowers a month later than the yellow dock, and fruits at the
same period.

The use of this species in medicine is not so prominent as that of *R. crispus*,
though it is more bitter, and, if anything, more common. "A decoction of bitter
dock root is highly efficacious in obstinate cases of the kind of skin disease called
ichthyosis; and when taken in large quantity—as well, indeed, as the decoction
of any of the fusiform dock roots—it acts as a purgative, in the same manner as
the powder or tincture of Turkey rhubarb."*

The following European and American species of the genus manifest, with
R. obtusifolius, a certain line of generic usefulness: Water Dock (*R. aquaticus*);
Yellow Water Dock (*R. Britannica*); and Sharp Dock (*R. acutus*). The common
Horse Sorrel (*R. acetocella*) is refrigerant, diuretic, and antiscorbutic—characters
which also pervade *R. acetosa*, which yields, in Switzerland, part of the Oxalic Acid
of commerce. R. acetosa is also highly esteemed in many districts as an esculent,

---

* Wilson's *Rural Cyc.*

than which, however, *R. scutans* is much more delicate; both are unhealthy if used to excess. In France *R. patientia* is considered tonic, stomachic, and depurant; while the Alpine Dock, or Monk's Rhubarb (*R. alpinus*) is the most active of all species, possessing qualities very like those of *Rheum Rhaponticum*, for a variety of which, indeed, Linnæus mistook it, adding, however, to his observations, "*easdem esse species nullus quidem neget, qui structuram plantæ utriusque inspexerit.*"

PART USED AND PREPARATION.—The fresh root, gathered and prepared as in the preceding species, yields a tincture having a dark, reddish-brown color by transmitted light; a sourish odor; a bitterish astringent taste, and an acid reaction.

CHEMICAL CONSTITUENTS.—*Lapathin*, a body identical with Chrysophanic Acid, as described under R. crispus; a resin; albumen; sugar; gum; starch; and sulphur, have been determined in the root of this species.

PHYSIOLOGICAL ACTION.—The symptoms caused during the experiments of Dr. Widenhorn* are substantially as follows: Pressive headache; epistaxis; distension and pressure in the stomach and abdomen, with flatulence; pain and pressure in the kidneys; weariness and bruised pains in the limbs; and excessive coldness of the feet.

DESCRIPTION OF PLATE 144.

1. End of a flowering branch, Binghamton, N. Y., Aug. 20th, 1886.
2. Outline of a lower leaf.
3. Flower, showing calyx.
4. Face of flower.
5. Stamen.
6. Pistil.
7. Fruit.
8. Grain-bearing valve.
9. Seed.
10. Horizontal section of seed.
(3–10 enlarged.)

* *Archiv. de la Med. Hom.*, 1835, 305.

144.

2

3

4

5

6

7

8

9

10

1

℃.m. ad nat del.et pinxt.

RÙMEX OBTUSIFÒLIUS , Linn.

GENUS.—LINDERA,* THUN.

SEX. SYST.—ENNEANDRIA MONOGYNIA.

145

BENZOIN.

SPICE-BUSH.

SYN.—LINDERA BENZOIN, MEIS.; LAURUS BENZOIN, LINN.; BENZOIN ODORIFERUM, NEES; LAURUS PSEUDO-BENZOIN, MICHX.

COM. NAMES.—COMMON SPICE-BUSH, ALLSPICE-BUSH, BENJAMIN-BUSH, WILD ALLSPICE, FEVER-BUSH, SPICE-BERRY; (FR.) LAURIER BENZOIN; (GER.) BENZOELORBEER.

A TINCTURE OF THE FRESH YOUNG TWIGS OF LINDERA BENZOIN, MEIS.

Description.—This aromatic shrub grows to a height of from 6 to 18 feet. *Branches* smooth and maculate. *Leaves* deciduous, nearly glabrous, thin, pale beneath, oblong-ovate and acute at both ends. *Inflorescence* lateral, nearly sessile, umbel-like clusters, composed of umbellets of 4 to 6 flowers; *involucre* formed of 4 deciduous scales surrounding the flowers; *flowers* numerous, polygamous-diœcious, prefolial. *Calyx* open, honey-yellow, 6-parted, membraneous. *Stamens:* sterile flowers 9, in 3 rows; *filaments* of the *inner row* dilated and 1 to 2 lobed, bearing at the base a reniform and more or less peltate gland (Fig. 4); the external 6 simple; *anthers* 2-celled and -valved, opening upward to the apex; *fertile flowers: stamens* 15 to 18 rudimentary, some filiform and pointed, others more or less spatulate. *Ovary* globular or globose-ovoid; *style* short; *stigma* capitellate. *Fruit* a scarlet, ovoid drupe.

Lauraceæ.—A family of aromatic trees or shrubs widely distributed over the temperate and tropical portions of the globe. *Leaves* alternate, simple, entire or sometimes lobed, mostly having pellucid dots. *Flowers* clustered; *æstivation* imbricate in 2 rows; *calyx* regular, free from the ovary; *sepals* 4 to 6, petaloid, mostly fewer than the stamens. *Anthers* opening by 2 to 4 uplifting valves. *Ovary* 1-celled, 1-ovuled; *style* single. *Fruit* a 1-seeded berry or drupe; *seed* anatropous, suspended; *albumen* wanting; *embryo* large amygdalaceous.

We derive but two other remedies from this order, viz.: Camphor, the Chinese and Japanese *Laurus camphorifera* (*Cinnamomum Camphora, Camphora officinarum*); and Cinnamon, the Ceylon *Cinnamomum Zeylandicum* (*Laurus Cinnamomum*). The other products of this order are: Cassia buds, the dried, undeveloped flower buds of the cinnamon tree; Cassia bark (*Cinnamomum aroma-*

---

* John Linder, a Swedish botanist of the 18th century.

ticum) ; Sassafras (*Sassafras officinale, Laurus Sassafras*) ; and Sweet bay (*Laurus nobilis*), so celebrated by poets for its fragrance and beauty. The genus *Oreodaphne* yields : Jamaica sweetwood (*O. exaltata*) ; Canary Island *Til* (*O. fœtens*) ; Isle of France Cinnamon (*O. cupularis*) ; a Brazilian discutient (*O. opifera*) ; and a native species much used by the Californian Indians in cephalalgia, and destined to become one of our valuable remedies (*O. Californica*). The genus *Nectandra* affords the much-vaunted substitute for Quinia, sulphate of Berberia, a product of *N. rodiai*, now falling into disuse ; Santa Fe Cinnamon (*N. cinnamonoides*) ; Orinoko Sassafras (*N. cymborum*) ; the Brazilian Pichurim bean (*N. puchury*) ; and the Sassafras nuts of the London markets (*N. puchury minor*). Among all the products of this varied family one only is really edible, viz.: the West Indian *Avocado Pear* (*Persea gratissima*).

History and Habitat.—The spice-bush, so well known among the laity on account of its aromatic buds, bark, and berries, inhabits low marsh spots upon the banks of streams from Canada southward to Florida. It blossoms in March or April, before the leaves appear.

The economical use of this shrub has given it many of its vulgar names. During the war of the Revolution the Americans used the powdered berries as a substitute for allspice (Barton). During the war of the Rebellion the people of northern South Carolina used the leaves as a substitute for tea, they affording a pleasant antipyretic and aromatic drink (Porcher) ; and the berries as before mentioned. In domestic practice the bark, leaves, and berries have been used in decoction to produce diaphoresis and act as a febrifuge ; they were considered also as tonic, stimulant, antiperiodic, and anthelmintic. The oil of the berries was often used as an embrocation in neuralgic and rheumatic pains.

There are now no preparations in use officinally except the Homœopathic tincture.

PART USED AND PREPARATION.—The fresh, young twigs gathered before the buds have burst in the spring, are chopped and pounded to a pulp and weighed. Then two parts by weight of alcohol are taken, the pulp mixed thoroughly with one-sixth part of it, and the rest of the alcohol added. After stirring the whole well, pour it into a well-stoppered vial, and allow it stand for eight days in a dark, cool place.

The tincture separated from the above mass by filtration has a light-brown color by transmitted light, an aromatic odor and taste, and a slight acid reaction.

CHEMICAL CONSTITUENTS.—Three analyses have been made of this plant* to determine its active principle, resulting in the separation of a volatile oil, tannin, an essential oil, a tasteless resin, together with other unimportant and general plant constituents. Its medicinal properties, in all probability, lie in the oils, one being cinnamyl compound, the other a substitution product of benzene.

---

* A. Brockenbrough, Jun., "An Experimental Botanico-chemical essay on Two Native Species of Laurus," 1804; *American Journal of Pharmacy*, 1873, J. M. Jones; 1875, P. M. Gleim.

DESCRIPTION OF PLATE 145.

1. Flowering branch from Binghamton, N. Y., May 3d, 1884.
    2. End of branch in leaf.
    3. A flower in section.
    4. A stamen of the outer row.
    5. Pistil.
    6. Pollen x 380.
        (3-5 enlarged.)

Œm.ad nat.del.et pinxt.

LÍNDERA BENZÒIN, Meisner.

146

DIRCA PALUSTRIS.

LEATHERWOOD.

SYN.—DIRCA PALUSTRIS, LINN.
COM. NAMES.—LEATHERWOOD, MOOSEWOOD, WICOPY, ROPE BARK, SWAMPWOOD, THONG BARK, AMERICAN MEZEREON; (FR.) BOIS DE PLOMB;† (GER.) LEDERHOLZ.

A TINCTURE OF THE FRESH INNER BARK OF DIRCA PALUSTRIS, LINN.

Description.—This yellowish, largely-branching shrub, attains a height of from 3 to 6 feet. *Stem* erect; *wood* white, soft and brittle; *bark* remarkably tough and fibrous; *branchlets* jointed; *buds* made up of 3 or 4 large, oval, sometimes persistent, dark hairy scales, from which spring the flowers, leaves, and shoots of the season. *Leaves* alternate, oval-obovate or ovate-lanceolate, deciduous, short petioled, villous when young and smooth when old. *Inflorescence* terminal ternate clusters, those not terminal at the flowering season become so by the extension of the young shoots; *flowers* pendent, honey-yellow, slightly sweet-scented, preceding the leaves. *Calyx* petaloid, funnel-form; *limb* truncate, crenate or nearly 4-toothed. *Stamens* 8, exserted, alternately longer, inserted upon the edge of a disk that encircles the calyx-tube at its point of inflation, and furnished with alternate, small, subulate appendages at their insertion; *filaments* long and slender. *Ovary* ovoid; *style* lateral, filiform, more than twice the length of the stamens; *stigma* capitate. *Fruit* a cluster of three, reddish, ovoid, mucronate, baccate drupes; *seeds* large; *albumen* papyraceous.

Thymeleaceæ.—This small family consists of shrubs having an acrid, tough and fibrous bark. *Leaves* entire; *stipules* wanting. *Flowers* perfect. *Calyx* regular, petaloid, free from the ovary; *limb* 4- rarely 5-lobed, imbricate in æstivation. *Stamens* usually twice as many as the lobes of the calyx. *Ovary* 1-celled; *style* single, lateral, rarely terminal. *Fruit* a baccate, 1-seeded drupe; *seed* suspended, anatropous; *embryo* large; *albumen* thin or wanting.

The only genus of this family that is of special interest to us, besides the one under consideration, is Daphne, of which we use: mezereon (*Daphne mezereum, Linn.*), and the sweet-scented spurge laurel (*Daphne Indica, Linn.*). The economical history of this order is nevertheless interesting, from the varied uses of the species, principally on account of their tough bark. They are mostly indigenous to northern India, South America, and the Cape of Good Hope. The family fur-

---

* Δίρκη, *Dirke;* the name of a Thebian fountain; probably on account of the habitat of the plant.
† Lead wood, on account of its flexibility.

nishes a yellow dye for woolens (*Passerina tinctoria*), a pulp for manufacture into paper (*Dais Madagascariensis*), a lace-like material for ropes in the West Indies (*Lagetta lintearia*), and in Madagascar (*Gnidia daphnoides*). Medically it furnishes a Javanese purgative (*Dais octandria*), a Cayenne laxative (*Hernandia Guianensis*), an Indian purgative, depilatory, and antidote to poisons (*Hernandia sonora*), and an edible nut (*Inocarpus edulis*) in the South Sea Islands, said to be similar in taste to the chestnut; this latter is an exception, as the fruits of the thymeleaceæ are generally deleterious. In general the fresh bark is possessed of a caustic acridity, and when applied to the skin acts as a painful vesicant.

History and Habitat.—The Leatherwood is indigenous to North America, growing in swampy or springy woods from Canada to Georgia, east of the Alleghany Mountains; it flowers with the maples in April, before the appearance of the leaves. The fibrous bark afforded material for ropes, thongs, cordage, and baskets, to the American aborigines.

The medical history of this drug is slight, the only reference to its use is that of the Indians as a masticatory for aching, carious teeth.

PART USED AND PREPARATION.—The fresh inner bark of the twigs is chopped and pounded to a pulp and weighed. Then two parts by weight of alcohol are taken, the pulp thoroughly mixed with one-sixth part of it, and the rest of the alcohol added. After careful mixture the whole is poured into a well-stoppered bottle and allowed to stand eight days in a dark, cool place.

The tincture, separated from the above mass by filtration, has a clear, greenish, orange-brown color by transmitted light, retains the peculiar odor of the bark, has a sourish then burning taste, and a neutral reaction.

CHEMICAL CONSTITUENTS.—The only attempt at an analysis of this plant, as far as I am able to determine, is that of Dr. Bigelow and his pupil, Dr. Locke. They found that the acridity of the fresh bark was not retained in a distillate or decoction, and determined the presence of:

A bitter resinoid, soluble in alcohol; and an

Acrid principle. This body is apparently fully retained in the tincture prepared as above.

PHYSIOLOGICAL ACTION.—Dr. Locke observes that the powdered root causes emesis and catharsis, and that the bark causes vesication; other observers, who have carried this application farther, find that sores follow that are difficult to heal. Dr. Perkins notes a case of poisoning with the fruit in which vertigo, nausea, stupor, insensibility, and dilatation of the pupils occurred.* The bark when chewed produces ptyalism, burning in the fauces and stomach, and sometimes paresis of the tongue. Dr. Spooner's proving of the drug† substantiates the above, and leads us to the conclusion that Dirca acts as an irritant to the

---

* Bigelow, *Med. Bot.*, vol. ii, p. 157.
† Allen, *Ency. Pure Mat. Med.*, vol. iv, pp. 161-7.

mucous membranes of the gastro-intestinal tract and bladder, as well as to the nerves. This proves the drug to be quite similar to mezereum. It is to be deplored that the unripe fruits are not included in the preparation of the tincture; farther provings with a tincture thus prepared would add a valuable remedy to our store.

DESCRIPTION OF PLATE 146.

1. Flowering branch, Ithaca, N. Y., April 20, 1880.
2. A flower cluster (enlarged).
3. Half of flower (enlarged).
4. Bract.
5. Branch in leaf and fruit.
6. Section of seed (enlarged).
7. Seed.

1 2 3 4 5 6 7

⅊ℳ.ad nat.del.et pinxt.

DÍRCA PALÚSTRIS , Linn.

147

EUPHORBIA HYPERICIFOLIA.

COMMON SPURGE.

SYN.—EUPHORBIA HYPERICIFOLIA, LINN.
COM. NAMES.—LARGE SPOTTED SPURGE, BLACK OR MILK PARSLEY
OR PURSLANE, SPOTTED EYEBRIGHT; (GER.) JOHANNESKRAUT-
BLATTRIGE WOLFSMILCH.

A TINCTURE OF THE WHOLE PLANT EUPHORBIA HYPERICIFOLIA, LINN.

Description.—This inconspicuous annual herb, attains a growth of from 8 to
18 inches. *Stem* ascending or erect, smooth or with scattered hairs, divergently
branching and forking. *Leaves* ovate-oblong or linear-oblong, sometimes falcate,
oblique, or slightly cordate at the base, acute, serrate, and short-petioled; *stipules*
triangular, dentate. *Inflorescence* in loose, leafy, terminal cymes; *peduncles* longer
than the petioles; *flowers* numerous. *Involucral appendages* 4, large and white or
small and red. *Ovary* 3-celled, each cell 1-seeded. *Fruit* a glabrous, obtusely-
angled pod; *seeds* blackish, ovate, obtusely 4-angled, wrinkled, and tuberculated;
caruncle none.

Euphorbia.—This genus consists of herbs or shrubs with a milky juice. *Leaves*
alternate, or in a few cases opposite or scattered, the floral usually verticillate.
Peduncles terminal, often umbellate-clustered. *Flowers* monœcious, included in a
cup-shaped, 4- to 5-lobed involucre, resembling a calyx or corolla, and generally
having large thick glands at its sinuses; *glands* with or without petaloid margins;
sterile flowers numerous, lining the base of the involucre, each from the axil of a
little bract, and consisting of a single stamen jointed on a pedicel-like filament;
anthers with globular cells; *fertile flowers* solitary, in the centre of the involucre,
soon, however, protruded upon a long stipe, and consisting of a 3-lobed, 3-celled
ovary with no calyx; *styles* 3, each 2-cleft; *stigmas* 6. *Fruit* a compound capsule
of 3 carpels, each of which splits elastically into 2 valves. *Seeds* often caruncled,
and closely invested in a membraneous axil.

Euphorbiaceæ.—This vast family of mostly tropical plants is represented in
North America by 18 genera, 171 species, and 15 varieties, and is characterized

---

* Euphorbus, physician to Juba, king of Mauritania.

5   6   1   3   4

℃m.ad nat.del.et pinxt.   EUPHÓRBIA HYPERICIFÒLIA, Linn.

as follows: Herbs, shrubs, or trees, with milky, acrid, and mostly poisonous juice. *Leaves* commonly simple; *stipules* present. *Inflorescence* various; *flowers* monœcious or diœcious, sometimes achlamydeous, often with scaly or gland-like appendages. *Calyx* 3-several cleft or wanting. *Petals* mostly wanting. *Stamens* one or many, distinct or monadelphous; *anthers* 2-celled. *Ovary* free, usually 3-celled; *ovules* usually single, sometimes two, hanging from the summit of each cell; *stigmas* as many or twice as many as the cells of the ovary. *Fruit* generally a 3-lobed capsule; *carpels* separating elastically from the persistent axis, and elastically splitting into two valves. *Seeds* anatropous; *embryo* straight, axial; *albumen* fleshy and oily.

Beside the five species treated of in this work, we have provings of sixteen other plants of this order, viz.: The Indian *Cupameni* (*Acalypha Indica*, Linn.); the European and Asiatic Box (*Buxus sempervirens*, Linn.); the Spanish Cascarilla, the bark of *Croton Eleuteria*, Bennett; Cassada, the root of the Brazilian *Jatropha manihot*, Linn.; Croton Oil, a product of the seeds of the India and Ceylon *Croton Tiglium*, Lam.; the English Spurge (*Euphorbia amygdaloides*, Linn.); the Cypress Spurge of England, *E. cyparissias*, Linn.; the British Petty Spurge (*E. Peplus*, Linn.); Euphorbium, the resinous exudation of the North African *E. resinifera*, Berg.; Assacu, the juice of the Brazilian *Hura Braziliensis*, Willd.; the Cuban Physic Nut (*Jatropha Curcas*, Linn.); the Brazilian Stinging Physic Nut (*J. urens*), considered to be the most poisonous plant known; the European Dog's Mercury (*Mercurialis perennis*, Linn.); the West Indian *Manzanillo* (*Hippomanes Manzinella*, Linn.), under the shade of which men are said to die; and Castor Oil, the expressed oil of the seeds of *Ricinus communis*, Linn.

Among the numerous other plants of the order used in general practice, the following will prove of special interest: The Oriental Kamela (*Mallotus philippensis*, Müll.), a purgative noted as a tænicide; the Indian sudorific and cathartic, *Cicca disticha*, Willd.; and *Emblica officinalis*, Gaertn. The root and leaves of the Indian and South American *Phyllanthus Niruri*, Linn., are considered deobstruent and diuretic, a decoction of the leaves and seeds is said by Martius to be considered a specific cure for diabetes in Brazil; the Indian *P. urinaria*, Linn., is also a powerful diuretic; while *P. virosus*, Willd., of the same country, is used to intoxicate fish. The seed-coat of the Indian *Cluytia collina*, Roxb., is claimed to be powerfully toxic; and the bark of *C. spinosa*, Roxb., is astringent and vermifugal. Turnsole is a purple dye procured from the Mediterranean acrid and corrosive drastic *Croton tinctorium*, Linn.; Mexican Cascarilla, or Copalchi, is the bark of *Croton Pseudo-China*, Schl.; the Indian *C. Pavana*, Hamilt., is used as a producer of Croton Oil, and is supposed to be the original Tilly-seed; one of the finest kinds of Dragon's blood, is derived from the Mexican *C. Draco*, Schl.; this substance is also obtained from the New Granadian *C. hibiscifolius*, H. B. K., and *C. sanguifolius*, H. B. K., of New Andalusia; several other cathartics, or, more properly, purgatives, are derived from this genus, of which the Ceylon *C. lacciferum*, Linn., and *C. suberosum*, H. B. K., of Peru, are prominent; in Brazil *C. campestris*, *C. antisyphiliticum*, and *C. pardicipes*, St. Heil., are used in syphilis; and *C. origanifolius* is said to yield a balsam that greatly resembles Copaiva.

The seeds of the Tropical American *Jatropha multifida*, Linn., are an excellent emetic and purgative; the juice of the Indian *J. glandulifera*, Roxb., is said to be used by the Hindoos as an escharotic to remove films from the eye; and the oil of the seeds of *J. glauca*, Vahl., is used as an application in rheumatism.

The flowers of the East Indian *Caturus spiciflorus*, Linn., are said to be a specific in diarrhœa. The seeds of the Brazilian *Anda-açu* (*Anda Gomesii*, A. de J.) act as a very powerful but safe purgative. The Guayanian *Hovea Guianensis*, Aubl., furnishes Demerara and Surinam Caoutchouc. The roots of the Indian *Traga involucrata*, Linn., are said by Ainslie to be used by the Hindoo doctors to remove old syphilitic cachexias. The juice of the Ganges *Sapium Indicum*, Willd., is highly poisonous; while that of *S. acuparium*, Willd., is really venomous, its exhalations causing erysipelatous inflammation. The Tropical American Sandbox (*Hura crepitans*, Linn.) yields a juice that is exceedingly posionous; it is said to produce blindness in a few days after application to the eyes; the seeds are a dangerous purgative. Another plant, similar in its action, is the Indian *Excœcaria Ayallocha*, Linn., of which Rumphius says that sailors who were sent ashore in Amboyna to cut wood, sometimes became furiously mad from pain produced when the juice of this plant spattered in their eyes, and that some cases of blindness resulted. The Cochin-China *Commia Cochinchinensis*, Lour., yields an emetic and purgative gum; and the West-Indian Jew-bush (*Pedilanthus tithymaloides*, Poit.) is used in venereal complaints, amenorrhœa, and in lieu of Ipecacuanha.

The genus Euphorbia, the type of this order, is one of the largest purgative genera known, many of its species being dangerous, and all more or less active. The Indian *E. Tirucalli*, Linn., is a violent and dangerous cathartic, used also, in small doses, as an antisyphilitic; the Cape *E. heptagona*, Linn., is said by Virey to be used by the Ethiopians as an arrow-poison; *E. tribuloides*, Linn., of the Canary Islands, is said to be sudorific, and *E. Canariensis*, Linn., to act much like Gum Euphorbium; the Indian *E. ligularia*, Roxb., is claimed to be alexiteric, and *E. nereifolia*, Linn., diuretic; the European *E. esula*, Linn., is a dangerous poison, *E. Gerardiana*, Lacq., emetic and cathartic, *E. falcata*, Linn., purgative, and *E. Peplis*, Linn., of like action; the Indian *E. thymifolia*, Linn., is anthelmintic, while the juice of the Brazilian *E. linearis*, Retz., is said to cure wounds of the cornea directly it is applied.

Although we have found this order so highly active and so many of its species veritably toxic, especially the seeds, still it produces one of the finest of all edible nuts—the Tropical American *Omphalea triandria*, Linn.

History and Habitat.—The Common Spurge is indigenous to North America, its typical form being found in the West Indian Islands. It grows generally throughout the country in dry fields, cultivated grounds, and on hillsides, where it flowers from July to September.

This species was probably first introduced in medicine by Dr. Zollickoffer, who spoke of it as astringent and slightly narcotic, and recommended its use in menorrhagia, leucorrhœa, cholera infantum, diarrhœa, and dysentery; Rafinesque adds to this that the plant is also purgative. Martius claims that the plant is valuable in syphilis and ulcerations of the cornea.

PART USED AND PREPARATION.—The whole fresh plant is chopped and pounded to a pulp and weighed. Then two parts by weight of alcohol are taken, the pulp thoroughly mixed with one-sixth part of it, and the rest of the alcohol added. After having stirred the whole well, it is poured into a well-stoppered bottle, and allowed to stand eight days in a dark, cool place.

The tincture, separated from this mass by filtration, has a deep orange-red color by transmitted light; a sweetish vinous odor; an acrid, astringent, and slightly bitter taste; and an acid reaction.

CHEMICAL CONSTITUENTS.—No analysis of this species has been made that identified a special principle. The constituents of the Euphorbias of this country are probably much alike in all species, and, therefore, refer to *E. Ipecacuanhæ*, page 149–2.

PHYSIOLOGICAL ACTION.—Dr. True,* who took a half-pint of an infusion of one-half an ounce of the dried herb in a pint of water, experienced the following effects: Headache with frontal fulness and heat; heat about the eyes; languor and drowsiness; oppression of the stomach; and constipation. The juice applied to the eyes causes severe irritation, with smarting and burning, lachrymation, and momentary blindness; this we have experienced twice while gathering the plant. It is supposed that this species causes the affection in horses called "slabbers."

The Euphorbias in general are severe irritants of mucous membranes, upon which they act as acrid poisons.

DESCRIPTION OF PLATE 147.

1. Portion of a branch in fruit, Binghamton, N. Y., Sept. 6th, 1885.
2. A portion of the stem, showing method of branching, stipules, and petioles.
3. A leaf, showing obliquity.
4. A falcate leaf.
5. Fruit.
6. Horizontal section of fruit.
7. Seed.

(5–7 enlarged.)

* *Ec. Med. Jour.*, 1875, 260.

GENUS.—**EUPHORBIA**,* LINN.

SEX. SYST.—MONŒCIA MONADELPHIA.

148
EUPHORBIA COROLLATA.

FLOWERING SPURGE.

SYN.--EUPHORBIA COROLLATA, LINN.; TITHYMALUS MARINUS, PLUK.

COM. NAMES.—FLOWERING SPURGE, BOWMAN'S ROOT, BLOOMING SPURGE, WANDERING MILKWEED, SNAKE'S-MILK, INDIAN PHYSIC, LARGE FLOWERED SPURGE, WILD HIPPO, WILD IPECAC; (FR.) EUPHORBE À GARNDES FLEURS; (GER.) GROSSBLÜTHIGE WOLFSMILCH.

TINCTURE OF THE FRESH ROOT OF EUPHORBIA COROLLATA, LINN.

Description.—This erect perennial herb attains a growth of from 2 to 4 feet, appearing to an observer at a distance to be a member of the umbelliferæ. The *root* is large and branching, sending up a number of simple rounded *stems* glabrous or sometimes sparingly hairy. *Leaves* ascending, those of the stem alternate, of the pedicels opposite, and whorled only at the base of the inflorescence; all ovate-lanceolate or linear, entire, obtuse, equal at the base, sessile or nearly so, smooth above, slightly hairy beneath, from one-half to two inches long, and one-quarter to one-half inch wide. There are always as many leaves to the inflorescence as there are peduncles or pedicels, and situated at their bases. *Stipules* none. *Peduncles* generally 5, sometimes fewer; pedicels and their branches many, all forming a compound umbel-like bi-sexual inflorescence. *Involucres* (floral) numerous, each with 5 showy, obovate, petal-like false lobes; the true lobes minute, inflexed, alternate with the false, and cut into 2 deep, narrow, lanceolate laciniæ. *Fertile flowers* solitary, one to each umbellet, at length protruding beyond its corolla-like involucre. *Ovary* stalked, 3-lobed, 3-celled, each cell 1-seeded. *Style* 3-branched. *Stigmas* 6, a pair to each branch of the style. *Sterile flowers* numerous, their many *stamens* successively developing singly, or in pairs or trios. *Filaments* stalk-like, surmounted by twin *anthers* with globular cells. *Fruit* a smooth 3-carpelled, 6-valved pod. *Seeds* thick, ashen, with a nearly even surface. The natural order is described under E. hypericifolia, 147.

History and Habitat.—The flowering spurge is a favorite medicine among the aborigines of America, being used as a purgative; its action as such

---

* Euphorbus (physician to King Juba), who introduced Euphorbia.

fully warranting the favor it has received. The milky juice that flows freely from the wounded plant is an active irritant, causing vesication soon after its application to the skin. The plant grows rather sparsely in dry meadows and open woods in Canada and central United States, blossoming from June to September. E. corollata has been dismissed from the U. S. Ph. (1882); in Eclectic practice use is made of the powdered bark of the root, in doses of from 4 to 30 grains.

PART USED AND PREPARATION.—The fresh root gathered in the fall, is chopped and pounded into a pulp and weighed, then two parts by weight of alcohol are taken and the pulp thoroughly mixed with one-sixth part of it and the rest of the alcohol added. After having stirred the whole well, pour it into a well-stoppered bottle and allow it to stand eight days in a dark, cool place. The tincture is then separated by decanting, straining and filtering.

Thus prepared it has a clear, light-yellow color by transmitted light, no distinguishing odor, a sweetish or mawkish taste, leaving a sensation of fuzziness upon the tongue, and a decided acid reaction.

CHEMICAL CONSTITUENTS.—At the present we can do no better than to refer to E. hypericifolia, 147, for the chemistry of this plant, for so far only the generic qualities have been determined, no distinct and specific analysis having been made.

PHYSIOLOGICAL ACTION.—The action of the Euphorbias generically will be found under 147, the specific physiological action of E. corollata is so far little investigated. The minute effects can best be determined by consulting the provings contained in the Encyclopædia of Materia Medica, by Dr. T. F. Allen, vol. iv., p. 244.

DESCRIPTION OF PLATE 148.

1.—1a. Whole plant from the banks of the Chemung River, its principal habitat east.   Elmira, N. Y.,
   July 19, 1879.
2. Stamen (enlarged).
3. Sterile flower (enlarged).
4. Pistil (enlarged).
5. Fruit (enlarged).

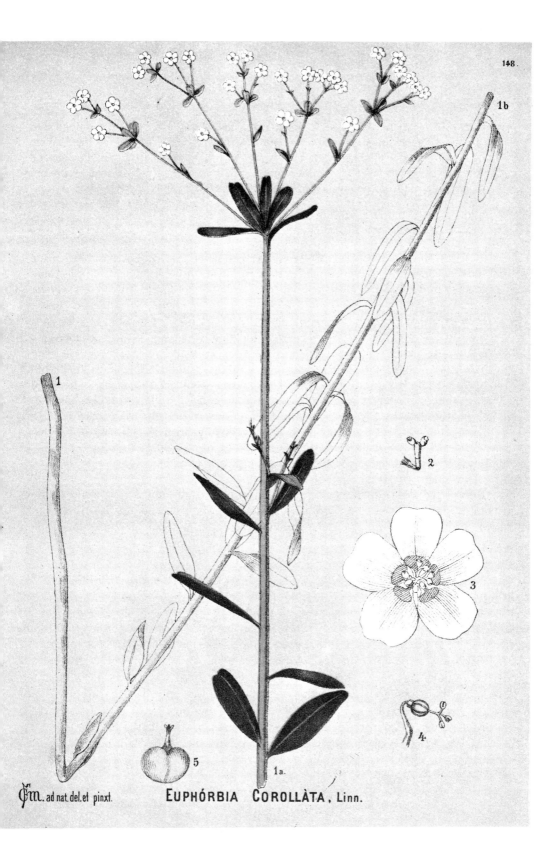

148.

1b

1

2

3

4

5

1a.

Cm. ad nat. del. et pinxt. EUPHÓRBIA COROLLÀTA, Linn.

GENUS.—**EUPHORBIA**, LINN.
SEX. SYST.—DODECANDRIA TRIGYNIA.

149

EUPHORBIA IPECACUANHÆ.

AMERICAN IPECAC.

SYN.—EUPHORBIA IPECACUANHÆ, LINN.
COM. NAMES.—AMERICAN IPECAC,* WILD IPECAC,† CAROLINA IPECAC, IPECACUANHA SPURGE, CAROLINA HIPPO; (FR.) EUPHORBE VOMI-TIVE; (GER.) BRECHWOLFSMILCH.

A TINCTURE OF THE WHOLE FRESH ROOT OF EUPHORBIA IPECACUANHÆ, L.

Description.—This tufted, shrub-like perennial grows to a height of from 6 to 12 inches. *Root* long, perpendicular, thick, subcylindrical, branching; *stems* many from the same root, erect or more frequently diffusely spreading, diver-gently forking throughout; *leaves* opposite, entire, glabrous, varying from obovate-oblong to narrowly-lanceolate, all very short petioled, and varying in color from shining green to brilliant red. *Inflorescence* on long peduncles arising from the forks; *involucres* 4 to 5 lobed; *lobes* ovoid; *glands* 5, obtuse, somewhat reniform, exappendiculate. *Fruit* a long pedicelled, obtusely angled, nearly smooth pod; *seeds* ovate, white, sparsely pitted with impressed dots; *caruncle* none. Read the description of Euphorbia and Euphorbiaceæ under E. hypericifolia, 147.

History and Habitat.—The Ipecac Spurge is indigenous to the low sandy soils of the Atlantic seaboard from Florida to Mississippi, and northward to Long Island. This very singular and extremely amorphous plant represents in itself seven "Rafinesquian species," so greatly does it vary in form, color, inflorescence, and leaf.

The emetic property of this root was well known to the Aborigines, but the first experiments with it in practice were those of Prof. Hewson and Dr. J. R. Bar-ton, though the first mention of its emetic properties is that by Dr. Puihn. Shoepf adds nothing to what was already known; nor does Prof. Barton in his Collections. Prof. W. C. P. Barton considered it equal if not superior to imported Ipecacuanha.‡ Dr. Bigelow observes,§ from his own experiments and those of Dr. McKeen at his instigation, that the species is an active emetic, safe when prudently adminis-tered, but injurious to the nervous system, and wanting in the mildness that characterizes officinal Ipecacuanha. The dose of the powdered root is from 10 to 20 grains for its emetic action, which also at times proves cathartic, thus making it more active than Ipecacuanha in proportion to the amounts used. The American

---

* A name also applied to *Gillenia stipulacea*, Nutt. (Rosaceæ.)
† Also applied to *Gillenia trifoliata*, Moen. (Rosaceæ.)
‡ *Am. Med. Bot.*, 3, 117.
§ *Veg. Mat. Med.*, 1, 217.

149.

ℭ.m. . ad nat del. et pinxt.   EUPHÓRBIA IPECACUÁNHÆ, Linn.

Ipecac acts as a hydragogue, expectorant, diaphoretic or emetic, according to the size of the dose.

PART USED AND PREPARATION.—The fresh root, treated as directed under *E. hypericifolia*, yields a tincture having a clear, light lemon-yellow color by transmitted light, a sweetish odor, an acrid taste, and an acid reaction.

CHEMICAL CONSTITUENTS.—No analysis yet made of this species has resulted in the separation of the glucoside it seems to contain. Dr. Bigelow's analysis separated caoutchouc, resin, and mucus; to which Mr. Cullen adds, by analysis, coloring-matter and starch.

Euphorbon, $C_{26}H_{44}O_2$.*—By evaporating the tincture to an extractive mass, dissolving in alcohol containing caustic potash, evaporating, and neutralizing the residue with dilute acetic acid, a brown body was precipitated (Euphorbic acid). On digesting the menstruum, separated from this precipitate, in ether, and evaporating spontaneously, crystals were obtained; these recrystallized frequently, and, boiled in a slightly-colored solution of permanganate of potash, resulted as tasteless, colorless, imperfect crystals, insoluble in water, slightly soluble in alcohol, readily soluble in ether, benzol and chloroform; melting at 241° (116.1° C.); and answering to the tests for the Euphorbon of Flückiger.

Euphorbic Acid.†—This amorphous, brown body, obtained as above, was slightly acrid, very bitter, soluble in water and alcohol, and capable of neutralizing slightly alkaline solutions.

The two bodies resulting as above were too small in quantity for experimentation in this analysis, as I had but little of the root in my possession. They are without a doubt identical with the bodies under which names I have described them, as given by experiments upon Gum Euphorbium from *Euphorbia resinifera*, Berg.

PHYSIOLOGICAL ACTION.—Euphorbia acts as an irritant to the mucous membranes throughout the alimentary tract, not only by its presence, but after the powder taken is all evacuated; vomiting once commenced is associated with vertigo, dimness of vision, flashes of heat and thirst; when the vomiting ceases, purging commences and lasts some time, often followed by prostration and cold sweat.‡

DESCRIPTION OF PLATE 149.

1 and 2. Flowering stems, Landisville, N. J., June 8th, 1885.
3. Flower and involucre.
4. Styles and stigmas.
5. Stamen.
6. Disk and fruit.
7. A portion of the root.
(3–6 enlarged.)

* Flückiger.   † Buchheim.   ‡ Bigelow, *Am. Med. Bot., loc. cit.*

N. ORD.—EUPHORBIACEÆ.
GENUS.—**EUPHORBIA**.
SEX. SYST.—DODECANDRIA MONOGYNIA.

150

EUPHORBIA LATHYRIS.

CAPER SPURGE.

SYN.—EUPHORBIA LATHYRIS, LINN.; TITHYMALUS LATHYRIS, KL. &
GAR.
COM. NAMES.—GARDEN SPURGE, CAPER SPURGE, MOLE PLANT OR
TREE; (GER.) PURGIENKÖRNER.

A TINCTURE OF THE WHOLE PLANT EUPHORBIA LATHYRIS, LINN.

Description.—This glabrous annual or biennial plant attains a growth of from
2 to 3 feet. *Stem* erect, stout, and cylindrical. *Leaves* entire, opposite, decussate
or strongly sessile, thick, linear- or oblong-lanceolate, pale. *Inflorescence* umbelli-
form; *umbels* 4-rayed, then forking; *leaves* ovate, long pointed, and somewhat cordate at the base; *involucral lobes* deeply cleft into two pointed divisions; *glands*
lunate, 2-horned; *horns* orange colored, obtuse. *Filamental peduncles* hairy: *abortive stamens* ligulate, hairy at the base. *Stigmas* recurved. *Fruit* a large, 3-car-
pelled capsule, red in the sulci when immature, black throughout when ripe;
carpels obtusely 3-angled; *seeds* carunculate.

History and Habitat.—The nativity of the Caper Spurge is doubtful; it is,
however, probably indigenous to Eastern Europe and Great Britian. It is adventive in this country, especially in New Jersey and Eastern Pennsylvania, where it
grows in dry, sterile places, and blossoms from July to September. Several of the
European Spurges, brought to this country as garden-plants on account of their
use as purges and their peculiar foliage, have run wild in many places. Three
years ago we discovered in Vestal, N. Y., two large patches of the Mediterranean
E. Nicænsis (not before reported in this country); it still grows there, and is
spreading luxuriantly as if thoroughly satisfied with its new home. *E. cyparissias*
has escaped in many places in Broome County, N. Y., and flourishes finely wherever
it grows.

The Caper Spurge is the *Cataputia minor* of old pharmacopœias, and is one
of the plants that Charlemagne ordered grown in every garden in France. The
laity in England are said to use one capsule to cause catharsis, and the women,
several to produce abortion. The oil of the seeds was probably first used by
Calderini, in doses of from six to eight drops, as a cathartic; he was followed by
Gounaud, and later by Bally; Frank suggested* its employment in ascites, hys-
teralgia, and tænia. Mr. Scattergood† tells us that the manufacturer of the oil

---

* *Jour. de Phar.*, xi, 273.   † *Phil. Jour. Phar.*, 1833, 124.

at Crosswick, N. J., claimed small doses, repeated if necessary at hourly intervals, act as a pleasant cathartic; but says that in his own experiments doses of from six to twelve drops invariably produced nausea and vomiting. The bark of the root has been found to produce emesis and catharsis. Rafinesque states that the pickling of the capsules as a substitute for capers in England was due to mistaking them for *Capparis spinosa*, the true caper; other authors, however, claim that the use of the fruit in this manner is intentional, and that the substitution is a passable one.

PART USED AND PREPARATION.—The whole plant, when half is in fruit, is treated as in the preceding species. The resulting tincture is bistre by transmitted light; it has an odor somewhat resembling spoiled oysters; a sweetish then bitterish, nauseous taste; and an acid reaction.

CHEMICAL CONSTITUENTS.—No analysis has yet been made of this species that isolated an active principle. The seeds are said to yield about 44 per cent. of a clear, yellowish, heavy oil, that deposits a crystalline mass on standing. The activity of the oil seems to vary much with the locality in which the plant grows, it being far more active from seeds produced in this country than from those of England or France.

PHYSIOLOGICAL ACTION.—The following symptoms occur after ingestion of a number of the seeds: Brilliant, staring, wide-open eyes, dilated pupils; death-like pallor of the countenance; retching and vomiting; violent purgation, stools frequent, copious, and in some cases bloody; irregular pulse; whole body cold and rigid,* followed by heat and perspiration. MM. E. Sudour and A. Caraven-Cachin state† that emesis always precedes purgation, and that the seeds have an irritating action upon the mucous membrane of the intestinal canal, principally in the larger intestines. They divide the effects into three stages: α, the cold stage, including vomiting and diarrhœa; β, the stage of excitation, including nervousness, vertigo, and delirium; γ, the stage of reaction, including heat and copious sweat.

DESCRIPTION OF PLATE 150.

1. A portion of the inflorescence in flower and fruit, from near a garden, Sept. 27th, 1885.
2. Summit of stem at the base of the inflorescence.
3. Involucre and contents.
4. Outer view of an involucral lobe.
5. Inner view of same.
6. Abortive stamen.
7. Sterile floret.
8. A stamen.
9. Fruit.
10. Under surface of a capsule separated from the axis.
11. A carpel.
12. Longitudinal section of a seed.
13. Horizontal section of a seed.

* Bennewitz, *A. H. Z.*, 7, 257: Jacob, *Am. J. Med. Sc.*, Jan., 1845; *Phar. Jour.*, 1861, 435; from Allen, *Ency. Mat. Med.*
† *Rep. de Phar.*, 1881, pp. 526–7; Maisch, in *A. J. Phar.*, 1882, p. 72.

150.

Ⓔ.m.ad nat del.et pinxt.

EUPHÓRBIA LÁTHYRIS, Linn.

151
STILLINGIA.

QUEEN'S DELIGHT.

SYN.—STILLINGIA SYLVATICA, LINN.; SAPIUM SYLVATICUM, TORREY.
COM. NAMES.—QUEEN'S DELIGHT, YAW-ROOT, MARCORY, COCKUP-
HAT, QUEEN'S ROOT; (FR., GER.) STILLINGIE.

A TINCTURE OF THE ROOT OF STILLINGIA SYLVATICA, LINN.

Description.—This herbaceous perennial grows to a height of from 1 to 3
feet. *Stems* clustered, glabrous, upright, and umbellately branched; *juice* milky;
root cylindraceous, thick and ligneous, extensively creeping. *Leaves* alternate,
crowded, almost sessile, varying in form, from ovate and obovate, to oblong and
lanceolate, all thick and fleshy, and acute at the tip; *margin* crenate-serrulate, with
a gland in each serrature; *stipules* minute, setaceous. *Inflorescence* a dense, terminal, monœcious spike; *flowers* destitute of petals or disk-glands. *Sterile flowers*
in dense clusters of 5 to 10, arranged about the spike for nearly its whole extent,
each cluster in the axil of a deltoid, scarious-margined, acute bract, and laterally
enclosed by two peculiar scutellate glands attached to the rachis by their centres;
calyx cup-shaped, membranaceous, with a 2-cleft margin, the divisions imbricated
in the bud; *stamens* 2, greatly exserted; *filaments* filiform, attached for nearly
half their length below; *anthers* erect, 2-lobed, adnate and extrorse. *Fertile flowers*
few, situated at the base of the spike in the axils of bracts similar to those of the
sterile flowers; *calyx* 3-lobed; *style* thick, articulated below, *stigmas* 3, simple,
diverging. *Fruit* a roundish, roughish capsule, composed of 3 1-celled, 1-seeded,
2-valved, carpels; *seeds* globose, roughish, carunculate.

History and Habitat.—Stillingia is indigenous to the United States, where it
grows in light, sandy and dry soil, from East Virginia southward to Florida, and
westward to Louisiana and Texas, flowering from April to September.

For many years before its introduction in medicine, by Dr. T. Y. Symons,† as
an alterative in syphilis, it had been used in the South, by the laity, as an emetic,
cathartic, and alterative; indeed it was and is still considered, in Southern States,
an absolute specific in syphilis, entirely superseding the use of mercury. It was
also used as an expectorant in pulmonary disorders; a purgative in hepatic troubles; an alterative in scrofulosis; and was said to greatly add to the usefulness of
sarsaparilla. Dr. Porcher says:‡ "This plant exudes a milky juice, very pungent

---

* In honor of Benjamin Stillingfleet, M.D.   † *Am. Med. Rec.,* 1828, 312.   ‡ *Resources Southern Field and Forest,* :21

to the taste, and flowing in great abundance from the bruised surface. It is used to some extent in this State (South Carolina) as an alterative in scrofula, in syphilis, in cutaneous diseases, in chronic hepatic affections, and in the composition of diet drinks. We are informed by a physician residing in this State that he has treated syphilis successfully with it. It is believed to be possessed of valuable properties, and greater attention should be paid to it by those living in the country, where it is easily obtained. A tincture is made with the root two ounces, diluted alcohol a pint. Dose, a fluid drachm. A decoction is made of the bruised root one ounce, water one and one-quarter pints; boil to one pint. Dose, one or two fluid ounces several times a day." The use of the drug in the North has not been as successful as it might have been, as the active properties of the plant deteriorate in aged roots or preparations. It is said that a drop of the oil of the plant placed upon the tongue, four times a day, has proved successful in severe croup.

The officinal preparation in the U. S. Ph., is *Extractum Stillingiæ Fluidum* from the root; in the Eclectic Materia Medica the following preparations are recommended: *Extractum Stillingiæ Alcoholicum, Extractum Stillingiæ Fluidum; Linimentum Stillingiæ Compositum;* Pilulæ Phytolaccæ Compositæ;† Syrupus Stillingiæ; Tinctura Stillingiæ; Syrupus Stillingiæ Compositus.‡*

PART USED AND PREPARATION. — The fresh root, gathered after the fruiting season, is treated as all Euphorbiaceous roots.§ The resulting tincture is nearly opaque; by transmitted light, in thin layers, it has a brilliant crimson color. It retains the odor and taste of the root; is quite astringent; and has an acid reaction.

CHEMICAL CONSTITUENTS.—*Stillingine.*—Harmanson‖ (1882) procured the sulphate of an alkaloid, for which, after special isolation, Bichy (1885) proposed the above name; very little, however, is known of the body. Bichy describes it as follows: "An amorphous powder, entirely volatilizing by heat, whose sulphate exists as fine scale-like crystals."¶

Oil of Stillingia.—The only product that I have examined, claimed to be this body, was certainly not a pure oil, but appeared like a resinous oily mixture; it had a burning, acrid, slightly bitter, and astringent taste, and the odor of the root; it was of a deep brown color, and contained brownish particles insoluble in water and alcohol. On adding it to water a resin was precipitated. Alcohol dissolved all but the particles mentioned. The root, however, does contain both a fixed and a volatile oil, as shown by Harmanson and Bichy.

The root also contains gum, starch, and coloring-matter.

PHYSIOLOGICAL ACTION.—Stillingia, in generous doses, causes the following disturbances in the system: Depression of spirits; vertigo; burning, smarting, and stinging in the mouth, fauces, and stomach; nausea and vomiting; diarrhœa

---

* Page 99-2.   † Page 139-2.

‡ Stillingia Root, Corydalis Root, Iris Root, Sambucus Flowers, Chimaphila Leaves, Coriander Seeds, and Xanthoxylum Berries.

§ Page 147-2.   ‖ *Am. Jour. Phar.*, 1882, 386.   ¶ *Am. Jour. Phar.*,1885, 530.

attended with colic and burning tenesmus; bilious and dysenteric stools; increased urine attended with burning along the urethra; short, hacking, dry, and spasmodic cough; weak, irregular pulse; aching and sharp pains of a rheumatoid character in the arms and legs; burning itching of the skin, followed by a general herpetic eruption; languor; sleepiness; perspiration; and a general feeling of malaise.

DESCRIPTION OF PLATE 151.

1. End of a fruiting branch, from which most of the ripe fruits have fallen. St. Augustine, Fla., Aug. 21st, 1886.

2, 3, 4 and 5. Leaf-forms.

6. A portion of the male inflorescence.

7. A male flower.

8. A fruiting calyx.

9. Fruit.

10. Horizontal section of fruit.

11 and 12. Seeds.

(6-12 enlarged.)

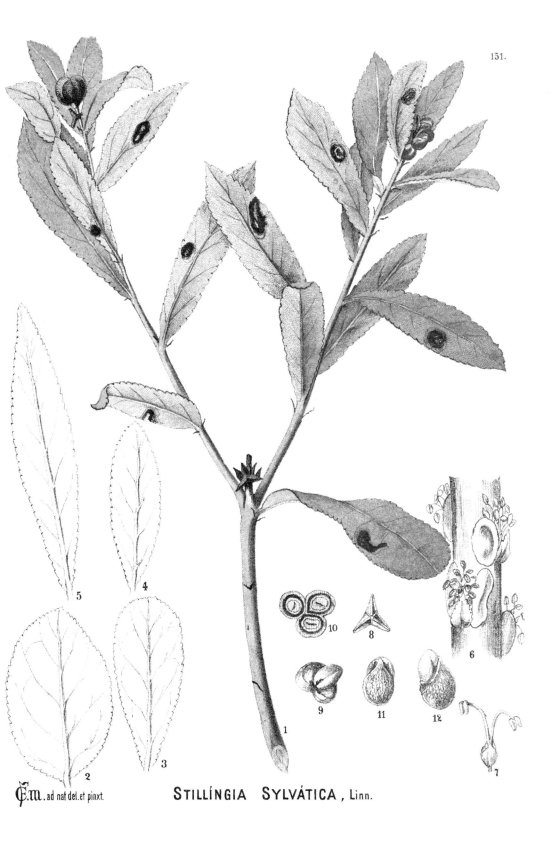

151.

5 4

2 3

1

10 8

9 11 12

6

7

STILLÍNGIA SYLVÁTICA , Linn.

𝕮.𝔪. ad nat del.et pinxt.

S. ORD.—ULMACEÆ.

GENUS.—**CELTIS**,* LINN.

SEX. SYST.—POLYGAMIA MONŒCIA.

152

CELTIS.

HACKBERRY.

SYN.—CELTIS OCCIDENTALIS, LINN.; C. AUDIBERTIANA, SPACH.

COM. NAMES.—HACKBERRY TREE, AMERICAN NETTLE TREE, SUGARBERRY, BEAVER-WOOD; (FR.) SUCRÉ BAIE; (GER.) ZUCKERBEERE.

A TINCTURE OF THE FRESH INNER BARK OF CELTIS OCCIDENTALIS, L.

Description.—This medium-sized tree grows to a height of 30 to 50 feet. *Trunk* very straight, about 8 or 10 inches in diameter; *wood* soft; *bark* very rough and corky, easily detached. *Leaves* petiolate, reticulated, ovate or ovate-lanceolate, smooth and scabrous above, downy pubescent beneath; *base* oblique or sometimes cordate; *margin* sharply, and plentifully or sparingly serrate, especially toward the tip, at the base often entire; *stipules*, caducous. *Inflorescence* monœciously polygamous, somewhat racemose along the upper shoots of the season. *Flowers* appearing with the leaves and before they are developed; *sterile* flowers grouped in twos and threes along the lower and leafless portion of the young shoots; *fertile* or polygamous flowers racemosely arranged at the leafy end of the shoot, the peduncles in the axils. *Calyx* 5-6 parted, persistent in the female; *lobes* more or less ovate-lanceolate, acute. *Stamens*, as many as the lobes of the calyx and opposite them; *filaments* curved inward and downward, inserted at the base of the calyx lobes; *anthers* large, sagittate, versatile and introrse, two-celled, with a longitudinal dehiscence. *Ovary* 1-celled; *ovule* anatropous; *stigmas* 2, sessile or nearly so, being in fact merely two lobes of the style divergently spreading and stigmatose upon the inner (now upper) surface. *Fruit* a dark purple, sweet and edible, globular drupe, of about the same appearance and size as a wild cherry; *peduncles* about twice the length of the petioles; *exocarp* coriaceous, divided into two equal parts by a prominent, circumvallating ridge. *Nutlet* spherical, about the size of a cherry-stone, pointed at the end and divided into four equal, rugose, portions by as many prominent ribs; *embryo* curved, almost completely enclosing the gelatinous albumen.

Urticaceæ.—This large family, now including the Ulmaceæ, Artocarpeæ and Cannabineæ, consists of trees furnished with a milky juice, and shrubs and herbs

---

* The ancient Greek name for the *Lotus-berry*, the fruit of the *Lote* (*C. australis*, Linn.), supposed to have been the food of the *Lotophagi*. (See, however, under Leguminosæ, p. 4–62.)

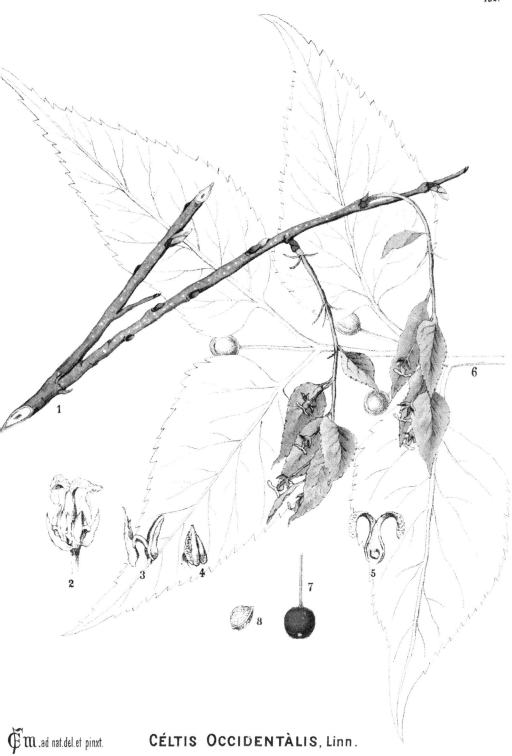

1

2

3

4

5

6

7

8

ℭℳ.ad nat.del.et pinxt.

CÉLTIS OCCIDENTÀLIS, Linn.

having a watery juice, inhabiting principally the warmer portions of the globe. *Stems* and *leaves* various, many furnished either with stings or rigid hairs; *stipules* persistent, caducous or wanting. *Inflorescence* spicate, amentaceous, racemose or capitate; flowers monœcious, diœcious or polygamous. *Calyx* regular. *Corolla* none. *Stamens* definite, as many as the calyx lobes, and opposite them, or fewer. *Ovary* simple, free from the calyx, 1-celled, rarely 2-celled; *ovules* 1 to each cell, anatropous or orthotropous; *styles* single, or two-lobed at the apex, the lobes stigmatose. *Fruit* an achenium, samara, urticle, or often rendered baccate by the persistent and now fleshy calyx. *Albumen* not always present; *radicle* pointing upward.

The sub-order ULMACEÆ, or Elm Family, furnishes us this remedy only; the other species used in medicine are: The East Indian *Celtis orientalis*, formerly used in epilepsy; and the European Lote Berry Tree (*C. australis*, Linn.), the bark of which is astringent, and is used in gonorrhœa and dysentery. The European *Ulmus campestris*, Linn., is considered to be diuretic as well as an astringent tonic; *U. effusa*, Willd., was at one time used as a substitute for sarsaparilla; and the American Slippery Elm (*U. fulva*, Michx.) is a well-known demulcent, and anti-herpetic, and is considered by many anti-syphilitic.

The sub-order ARTOCARPEÆ or Bread Fruit Family, yields several esculent fruits, while many of its members afford highly poisonous juices, and some a nourishing milk. The South Sea Island Bread Fruit is a product of *Artocarpus incisa*, and the Jack Fruit of *A. integrifolia*. The South American Cow Tree, so aptly named on account of the nourishing milky juice that freely exhudes from the wounded trunk, is a species of *Bromisum*, and the Jamaica Bread Nuts are the fruits of *B. alicastrum*. The Asiatic Fig, the fruit of *Ficus carica*, Linn., of this sub-order, highly esteemed in all countries as a laxative dessert fruit, is also useful, when roasted, as an application to hasten suppuration in small circumscribed formations of pus; the bark of the East Indian Banyan Tree (*F. Indica*, Linn.), whose immense growth is famous, is used by the Hindoos as a tonic and anti-diabetic; it also yields a gum known as Gum Lac, and a juice useful as an application for aching teeth; the Indian India-rubber Tree (*F. elastica*, Roxb.) and the South American *F. radula*, *elliptica*, and *prinoides*, yield a fine quality of caoutchouc; the East Indian *F. racemosa*, Linn., yields a bark that is a powerful tonic, useful in hematuria and menorrhagia; the wood of the African *F. sycamorus* is imperishable, and was used by the ancient Egyptians for mummy cases; *F. septica* is emetic, and the Indian *F. dæmona*, Vahl., and *toxicaria*, Linn., yield extremely virulent juices. The Brazilian *Caapeba*, or *Caa-apia*, a product of *Dorstenia Braziliensis*, Linn., the Mexican *D. contrayerva*, Linn., and *D. Houstoni*, Miller, are all supposed to contribute more or less to the commercial *Contrayerva*, which is a gentle stimulant, diaphoretic, and nervine, as well as an alexipharmic, and has, in a great measure, supplanted serpentaria. *Cecropia peltata* is astringent and was once much valued in the treatment of chronic intestinal catarrh, and *Musanga cecropioides*, a powerful emmenagogue. The Mulberries, including the Levantine Morus Nigra, the American *M. rubra*, and the Chinese *M. alba*, yield edible fruits, while their barks are considered cathartic and anthelmintic; Fustic is the bark of *M.* tinctoria. In concluding this varied sub-order, we are brought to that terrible Javanese tree, the deadly Upas (*Antiaris toxicaria*, Lesch.), under which most animals die; the toxic properties of this tree are, without doubt, greatly exaggerated, as all are not effected by its effluvia, still it is justly dreaded.

The sub-order URTICEÆ, or Nettle Family, contains many plants that are furnished with more or less toxic stings. Of this order we have provings of three species, viz.: The European Stinging Nettle, *Urtica Urens*, Linn.; the Bengalese *U. crenulata*, Roxb., whose sting is said to be as poisonous as the bite of a venomous serpent; and the Australian Stinging-Tree (*U. gigas*). The Timoor *U. urentissa* is probably the most virulent, its effects are said to last a year, and in some cases to have been followed by death; the Javanese *U. stimulans* is also very venomous. Our common nettle *U. dioica* is diuretic and astringent; the Egyptian *U. membranacea* emmenagogue and aphrodisiac; and it is claimed that the smooth species *U. pumila* relieves inflammation, erysipelas, and is a soothing application to the skin after Rhus poisoning. The Brazilian *Boehmeria caudata*, Swartz, is useful for the relief of hemorrhoidal tumors; and *Pilea muscosa*, of the same country, is found to be an excellent remedy in dysuria. *Parietaria officinalis* is considered diuretic and anti-arthritic; and *P. erecta* and *diffusa* are said to contain more sulphur than any other known plants.

The sub-order CANNABINEÆ, or Hemp Family, contains our proven species, *Cannabis sativa* and *Humulus Lupulus*.

History and Habitat.—The hackberry tree is indigenous to the Canadas and United States, as far south as the Carolinas. It habits more or less rich but rocky woods along the borders of streams, where it flowers just as the leaves appear in spring. It is often transplanted as a lawn shade, in such open situations it is much shorter in its growth and more umbrageous.

The only previous use of this species is that credited to the Aborigines, who are said to have given a decoction of the bark with good effect in syphilis. This decoction being astringent, was sufficient for its employment by the laity and Botanics as a "tonic" in various forms of alimentary and hematic trouble, though success in its use was of doubtful occurrence.

PART USED AND PREPARATION.—The fresh inner bark should be gathered when the tree is in full foliage, chopped and pounded to a pulp, and weighed. Then two parts by weight of alcohol should be taken, the pulp thoroughly mixed with one-sixth part of it, and the rest of the alcohol added. The whole is then to be poured into a well-stoppered bottle, and allowed to stand for eight days in a dark, cool place. The tincture, separated from this mass by decanting, pressing, and filtering, will have a deep, seal-brown color by transmitted light, and a strong acid reaction. This preparation has neither a distinctive odor nor taste.

PHYSIOLOGICAL ACTION.—Dr. J. S. Wright, in his experiments with this drug,* found it capable of causing a soreness of the muscles on pressure; sharp

* *U. S. Med. Invest.*, 1879, 339.

pains through the lungs; aching in the bones; swelling of the face, and afterwards of the whole body, with turgid blood-vessels; and sharp stitching pains generally throughout the system.

DESCRIPTION OF PLATE 152.

1. End of flowering branch, the fruiting female flowers alone showing, Binghamton, N.Y., May 17, 1885.

    2. A polygamous flower.

    3. Stamen and calyx lobe.

    4. Anther, showing dehiscence.

    5. Section of pistil.

    6. End of branch in fruit.

    7. A fruit.

    8. Seed.

       (2–5 enlarged.)

153

URTICA URENS.

STINGING NETTLE.

SYN.—URTICA URENS, LINN.; U. DIOICA, HUDS. (NOT LINN.).
COM. NAMES.—STINGING NETTLE, DWARF NETTLE,; (FR.) L'ORTIE; (GER.)
BRENN-NESSEL.

A TINCTURE OF THE WHOLE PLANT URTICA URENS, LINN.

Description.—This stinging annual, grows to a height of from 1 to 2 feet. *Stem* erect, 4-angled and branching; *bark* tough and fibrous; *stings* sparse but very virulent. *Leaves* opposite, elliptical or ovate, petiolate, 5-nerved, and furnished with a few scattered stings; *margin* deeply serrate, with long, spreading, and more or less blunt teeth; *base* truncate or sometimes slightly cordate; *stipules,* distinct, lanceolate, reflexed. *Inflorescence* in loose, axillary, drooping, racemose spikes, 2 in each axil; *flowers* androgynous. *Sterile flowers:* sepals 4; *stamens* 4, inserted around the rudimentary pistil; *filaments* transversely wrinkled and inflexed in the bud, spreading elastically when the flower opens. *Fertile flowers:* sepals 4, in pairs; the two outer small and spreading, the two inner concave, in fruit membranaceous and enclosing the akenium; *stigma* sessile, capitate, and penicillate; *ovary* 1-celled; *ovule* erect, orthotropous. *Fruit* a straight, erect, ovate, flattened, shining akene; *embryo* straight, axial; *albumen* present.

History and Habitat. — This European immigrant has established itself in many places eastward and southward near the coast, in damp, waste grounds, where it flowers in July and August.

The most ancient use of the Nettle is flagellation or urtication, a practice of whipping paralyzed limbs, to bring the muscles into action. This practice extended also to a stimulation of impotent organs, and to bring into action dormant energies. It was also resorted to in apoplexy, general cerebral and portal congestion, to bring the blood to the surface and thus relieve the more vital organs; in exanthematous fevers, to bring out the eruption; and for various affections where a powerful rubefacient was considered necessary.

The Nettle was afterward found to be styptic and anti-hemorrhagic, both topically and internally, and proved itself very beneficial in menorrhagic, epistaxic, and post-partum hemorrhage, hematemesis, and hematuria. Their decoction was found to be diuretic, and thus beneficial, in urinary calculus, scurvy, dropsy, gout, jaundice, etc.

---

* Latin, *uro*, to burn.

The seeds were given in goitre, corpulence, glandular enlargements and scrofulosis, and were also considered anthelmintic and hypnotic; while verrucæ were said to entirely disappear in a fortnight, under daily application of the juice.

The young shoots are considered excellent "greens," on their appearance in spring; and in Russia and Siberia, the stalks afford a tough fiber, not inferior to hemp for the manufacture of cloth, paper, nets, and ropes. A strong decoction of the plant, salted, is said to coagulate milk very quickly, and the product to prove devoid of any unpleasant taste.

PART USED AND PREPARATION.—The whole fresh plant is treated as in the preceding drug (page 152–3). The resulting tincture has a deep brown color by transmitted light; an odor resembling chocolate; an astringent herbaceous taste; and an acid reaction.

CHEMICAL CONSTITUENTS.—*Formic Acid*, H_2CO_2. This volatile acid is found in a free state in the stings of this species; it is also found in the poison-bags of the red ant, the hairs of a species of caterpillar (*Bombyx processionea*), in pine needles, turpentine, and in many plants. Formic Acid was first obtained by Samuel Fisher, by distilling red ants, since which time it has been proven quite widely distributed. When pure, this acid is a colorless liquid, solidifying at $+1°$ (33.8° F.), in the form of shining plates, and boiling at 100° (212° F.). It possesses a sour, pungent odor, something like acetic acid, a very acid taste, and is so corrosive to the skin that its blisters are very like those resulting from burns. It is freely soluble in both water and alcohol, as are also its salts.

As the effect of Nettle stinging differs considerably from that of Formic Acid, and as the distillate of the plant savors of ammonia, as well as of carbonic dioxide, another principle, alkaloidal in its nature, will probably be found in the species.

PHYSIOLOGICAL ACTION.—The following case of poisoning, by two cupfuls of a hot infusion of two ounces of the herb,* shows well the action of this drug; The skin of the face, arms, shoulders, and chest, was affected with extremely distressing, burning heat, with formication, numbness, and violent itching. The lips, nose, and ears were swollen, and the lids swollen and œdematous, so that they could scarcely be opened. After a while all the upper parts of the body, down to the navel, were frightfully swollen, pale and œdematous, rather than inflamed. A large number of small transparent blisters, filled with serum and looking like sudamina, developed and became confluent; on account of these the skin assumed a peculiar wrinkled appearance. There was no other remarkable disturbance, either of circulation or respiration. The patient complained neither of headache, nor of sensitiveness of the stomach and abdomen. The look of the patient was monstrous, the lids completely closed, forming transparent, and here and there bluish swellings, as large as hen's eggs. The upper lip, nose, and both ears were frightfully swollen. On the third day the face became free, but the chest and arms remained affected with an eruption, which itched so violently that the patient

---

* Dr. Fiard, Acad. de Med., Paris, *A. H. Z.*, 8, 81, Allen, *Ency. Mat. Med.*, x, 49.

153.

1

2   3   4   5   7   6

℃m. ad nat del et pinxt.   URTÌCA ÙRENS, Linn.

scratched off the blisters, which exuded a large amount of serum. The woman, who had had no children for three years and a half, and had nursed none of her children, had at first excessive swellings of the breasts, which discharged at first serum, afterwards perfect milk; a very copious secretion of milk lasted for eight days. The secretion of urine was at first suppressed, and in spite of all diuretics and other remedies, not a single drop was secreted for eight days. During the whole illness there was a constant distressing itching. On the sixth day everything disappeared, with desquamation.

DESCRIPTION OF PLATE 153.

1 Top of a flowering plant, Salem, Mass., July 8th, 1885.
    2. Male flower.
    3. Stamen.
    4. Female flower.
    5. Fruit, with calyx.
    6. Seed.
    7. Sting.
    (2–7 enlarged.)

154

CANNABIS.

HEMP.

SYN.—CANNABIS SATIVA, LINN.; CANNABIS INDICA, LAM.
COM. NAMES.—INDIAN HEMP; (FR.) CHANVRE; (GER.) HANF.

A TINCTURE OF THE TOPS OF AMERICAN-GROWN CANNABIS SATIVA, LINN.

Description.—This tall, roughish annual, usually grows from 3 to 10 feet high. *Stem* erect, striate, roughish, ligneous at the base, simple or sparingly branched; *inner bark* tough and fibrous. *Leaves* digitately-compound, the lower opposite, the upper alternate; *leaflets* 3-5-7, linear-lanceolate, coarsely and sharply serrate, attenuate at both ends; finely scabrous, and dark-green above, pale and downy beneath; *petioles* long, slender, and scabrous; *stipules* linear, acute. *Inflorescence* diœcious. *Sterile flowers* in axillary compound racemes, or panicles; *sepals* 5, nearly separate, reflexed-spreading, nearly equal, oblong and downy; *stamens* 5, opposite the segments of the calyx; *filaments* short, drooping, not inflexed in the bud; *anthers* large, pendulous, 2-celled. *Fertile flowers* in axillary, spiked clusters, leafy below; *flowers* 1-bracted and sessile; *calyx* of a single, 5-veined, hirsute sepal, enlarging and cordate at the base, acute at the apex; *ovary* 1-celled; *ovule* single, erect, orthotropous; *style* not evident; *stigmas* 2, elongated, hairy, protruding far beyond the perianth. *Fruit* a glandular achenium, enwrapped by the persistent sepal; *pericarp* membranaceous, indehiscent, but easily separable by pressure into two valves. *Seed* ovoid, smooth, brown, and veiny; *embryo* simply curved; *albumen* slight, oleaginous.

History and Habitat.—This native of the temperate portions of Asia—a plant of ancient cultivation—grows readily in this country, in waste places and cultivated grounds, where the cleanings of bird cages have found their way. It thrives well,† blossoming in July and August.

The plant in its travels westward is supposed to have reached Italy during the Roman period, from whence it has spread in all temperate regions of the globe. It does not seem to have been known to the ancient Egyptians as having

---

* Κάνναβις, *Kannabis;* an Oriental name of unknown meaning, probably, however, derived from the Arabian name of the plant *ganeb*.

† A thrifty female plant, nine feet high, grew last year in a farm-house yard near Binghamton; and several of both sexes, fully seven feet, at Union, N. Y.

narcotic properties. Herodotus terms the plant Κάνναβις ημερος, stating that the Thracians made a kind of cloth of it. The seeds were also thrown upon red-hot stones, and their perfumed vapor, so obtained, used for a fume bath, which excited from those enjoying it, cries of exultation. Dr. Royle considers it the Nepenthes of Homer, "the assuager of grief," given by Helen to Telemachus in honor of Menelaus; she is said to have received the plant from an Egyptian woman of Thebes. Dioscorides recommends the herb in the form of a cataplasm for inflammations, and to discuss tumors. Paulus Ægineta says the seeds are carminative and desiccative, and the juice of the fresh plant useful for pain and obstructions of the ears. In India, the plant is known by names which translated mean, "Grass of Fakirs," "Leaf of Delusion," "Increaser of Pleasure," "Exciter of Desire," "Laughter Mover," and "Cementer of Friendship."

The true Indian Hemp, *i. e.*, that which contains to the fullest extent the narcotic properties of the herb, grows at altitudes of 6000 feet and over, principally in the Himalayas above Calcutta, and in Thibet. These plants differ in nowise botanically from those that grow at lower levels, but medically the variation is wide. It is certainly admissible here to mention the products of the more active form which, for convenience, we will retain as *Cannabis Indica*. The principal commercial form of the Indian plant is called *Gunjah, Ganja*, or in England *Guaza*. It is this form that reaches the American markets through London, and from which our tincture of *C. Indica* should be made. It consists, according to a fine specimen kindly given us by Shifflein & Co., of New York, of the dried, flowering tops, compressed into small, ovoid masses, cohering by the natural resin contained, and composed of small floral leaves, female flowers, and undeveloped seed. Each separate mass exhales a small portion of the stemlet upon which it grew, and exhales to a high degree the odor peculiar to the plant. This *Gunja* yields an excellent extract, which, when at a temperature of 65° F., is thick, and only runs when held a long time at a sharp angle; it is of so dark a green color as to appear jet black; has a strongly narcotic, peculiar, and not unpleasant odor; is very adhesive, insoluble in water, and fully soluble in alcohol, its solution having a brilliant green color. When placed upon the tongue no taste is at first noticed on account of its very slow solubility in the natural secretions of the mouth, but after a few moments the taste is a counterpart of the odor, and when the solution reaches the base of the tongue an agreeable bitter is notable. This extract was formerly used for our tincture. Other forms of the plant sold in India and Arabia are, α. Bhang, Subjee, or Sidhee, which consists of the dried leaves broken into coarse powder with which are intermixed a few seeds. This form is used for smoking, and is the narcotic ingredient of the confection called *Majun*. β. *Charas*, or *Churrus*, consisting of the natural resin of the tops and leaves, mixed with bits of the plant and much dirt. This form is usually procured by natives who pass among the plants, wearing a leathern apron to which the resin adheres; in the mean time the plant tops are rubbed with their hands, and afterward the hands and aprons scraped to gather the product. γ. *Hashisch, Hashish*, or *Hashash*. These are the Arabian names for hemp. The product consists of the dried flowering tops gathered before the fruits are formed. The famous heretical sect of Mohammedans, who, by murderous attacks upon the Crusaders, struck their hearts with terror, derived their name *Hashashin* from the drug, and from that our word *assassin* is derived. δ. *Hemp.* This textile is produced principally by those plants whose narcotic powers are least marked; those that grow in the lower altitudes producing the best article. This product is made into ropes and coarse cloths. ε. *Hemp Seed.* The seeds of this plant are considered fattening, and egg-producing when fed to birds. Cage-birds are particularly fond of them, but on account of their limited chances for exercise only a few *per diem* are usually allowed them. ζ. *Oil of Hemp Seed.* The seeds yield about 25 per cent. of their weight of a limpid, almost colorless oil, that makes a fine burning-fluid, and is used in the arts for mixing colors, and as a varnish.

In general practice the drug is used wherever an anodyne, hypnotic, or antispasmodic is judged necessary; the various diseases where it proves effectual are hardly mentionable, as the benefit is almost always homœopathic, therefore, each disease should be individualized. Surgical tetanus, gonorrhœa, leucorrhœa, inflammation of the mucous membranes of the bladder and urethra, dysuria, delirium, and melancholia may be, however, mentioned as the diseases in which our Old School brothers usually get the most decided effects from this drug.

Cannabis Americana, i. e. the tops of American-grown plants, are officinal in the U. S. Ph. The plant is mentioned in the Eclectic Dispensatory, but no preparation is given.

PART USED AND PREPARATION.—The fresh flowering tops of the American-grown plants, both male and female, are treated as directed under Celtis.[*] The tincture, after straining and filtering, is opaque; has an herbaceous odor; a sweetish mucoid taste, followed by slight bitterness; and an acid reaction. The two tinctures of this plant may be compared as follows :

CANNABIS SATIVA.

Americana.	*Indica.*
Domestic Growth.	Indian Growth at 6000 Feet.
Tincture.	*Tincture.*
Appearance, in bulk, deep opaque brown.	Deep opaque greenish-brown.
Twenty drops in a drachm of alcohol give an orange-brown color by transmitted light.	A slight greenish tinge only is noticeable; the two solutions nearly correspond.
Ten drops in two drachms of water quickly show the difference in the amount of resin.	
This tincture shows only slight opalescence; while	this gives a completely opaque, heavy, dirty cream-colored mass.
In this tincture the peculiar pungent and heavy narcotic odor of *Gunja* is faintly, if at all, noticeable.	In this the odor is plainly distinguishable.

As the narcotic power of the drug lies mostly in the resin of the plant, the activity of the two states of the plant is readily understood by the above comparison, simple as it is.

---

[*] Page 152-3.

CHEMICAL CONSTITUENTS.—As far as I can determine, the American plant has not been analyzed, but as it at least contains a small amount of the resinoid principle of the Indian plant, it may be well to glance at the chemistry of *Gunja*, as it stands at this date. There is great uncertainty concerning the active principle of this drug, as the *Cannabin* of the Smiths fails, so far, to answer, at the hands of other chemists, to the characteristics claimed for it by them. Worden and Waddle find the nicotia-like alkaloid of Preobraschersky, but in their hands it proves inert; and, though Siebold and Bradbury found a volatile alkaloid (*Cannabinine*), they claim that it is unlike nicotia, though they have not tested its action upon animals. Merck isolated a glucoside, which he combines with tannin and calls *Cannabin Tannin*, and from which Bombelon obtained a body he terms *Cannabinum;* this tannin compound often proves inert. Matthew Hay reports an alkaloid, forming in acicular crystals, and having a tetanic action upon frogs, which he calls *Tetano-Cannabin*, and considers as a secondary principle.* This is about the condition of the chemistry of this drug to-day; which the following digest will farther explain:

Cannabin.—This body, extracted from Gunja, by Messrs. T. and H. Smith,† and considered much purer than Gastinel's *Hashascin*, results as a brown, amorphous, solid resin, which burns with a bright flame, leaving no ash, and is soluble in alcohol and ether. It is claimed, by its discoverers, to be very potent, two-thirds of a grain proving decidedly narcotic, and one grain causing complete intoxication. Personne claims that the activity of this body is due to the volatile oil, but his method of extracting the body was sufficient to render it inert, rendering his claim, therefore, inadmissible. Bolas and Francis‡ obtained from this body:

Oxycannabin, $C_{20}H_{20}N_2O_7$, which resulted in large, neutral prisms, from its solution in methylic alcohol. These crystals melt at 176° (348.8° F.), and evaporate without decomposition. Flückiger failed to obtain this body from purified resin of Charas.§

Oil of Cannabis.—This volatile, pale yellow oil, was discovered in the tops by Personne,‖ who claimed it to be the active principle of the plant, and to cause, in those who inhaled its effluvium, shuddering, and desire for locomotion, followed by prostration and sometimes syncope. Bolig obtained this oil from the fresh tops of the Arabian plant, and found its effects to be similar to those claimed for it by Personne, and further stated that it contained oxygen. Personne succeeded in separating the oil into two hydrocarbons: *Cannabine*, $C_{18}H_{20}$, and *Cannabine Hydride*, $C_{18}H_{22}$, the latter being a solid composed of platy crystals.

Other unessential bodies have been determined, to none of which the activity of the drug can be assigned.

---

* *Am. Jour. Phar.*, 1885, 264; from *Phar. Jour. and Trans.*, 1885, 574.
† *Phar. Jour.*, 1847, 171.
‡ *Chem. News*, 1871, 77.
§ *Pharmacographia*, 549.
‖ *Jour. de Phar.*, 1857, 48; Canstatt's *Jahres.*, 1857, 28.

PHYSIOLOGICAL ACTION.—Carefully excluding, as far as possible, symptoms that may have arisen from the Indian product, the following will give some idea of the action of the herb of low altitudes, collated from the experiments of Drs. Schreter, Knorre, Wibmer, Wirk, and Lembke with the tincture, in doses of from 5 to 70 drops, and the infusion :* Depression and absent-mindedness ; confusion, vertigo, and congestion, followed by cephalalgia ; earache ; toothache ; dryness of the mouth, throat, and lips ; loss of appetite ; nausea, and vomiting after coffee ; slight inflammation of the meatus urinarius, and diminished urine ; sexual excitement without desire ; oppression of the chest, and palpitation of the heart ; weakness of the limbs ; itching of the skin ; and dreaminess during sleep.

DESCRIPTION OF PLATE 154.

Drawn from plants growing at Union, N. Y., July 26th, 1886.
1. A portion of male inflorescence.
2. Sterile flower.
3. A portion of female inflorescence.
4. Female flowers.
5. Male flower-bud.
6, 7, 8. Stamens.
9. Female flower.
10. Calyx of female flower.
11. Ovary.
12. Section of ovary.
13. Styles.
14, 15, 16. Fruit.
17, 18, 19. Seed.
20. Longitudinal section ⎫ of a seed.
21. Horizontal section ⎭
22. Embryo.
(2 and 4–22 enlarged.)

* Allen, *Ency.*, 2, 492, *et seq.*

Ɛ.m. ad nat del.et pinxt.

CÁNNABIS.

SATÌVA, Linn.

155

LUPULUS.

HOP.†

SYN.—HUMULUS LUPULUS, LINN.; H. AMERICANUS, NUTT.
COM. NAMES.—COMMON HOP, NORTHERN VINE; (FR.) HOUBLON; (GER.)
HOPFEN.

A TINCTURE OF THE STROBILES OF HUMULUS LUPULUS, LINN.

Description.—This rough, twining perennial, grows to a height of 20 feet or
more. *Rootstalk* large, thick, and branching; *stems* several from the same root,
slender, solarly voluble, almost prickly downward. *Leaves* longer than the petioles,
mostly opposite, and cordate, the upper neither lobed nor cleft, the lower palmately 3- to 5-lobed, all coarsely serrate, sharply pointed, and very rough, the
roughness most resistant from the periphery inward; *stipules* at first erect, then
reflexed, ovate, persistent, interpetiolar, the adjacent ones of each opposite pair
confluent at their bases. *Flowers* diœcious. *Fertile flowers* in short axillary and
solitary, sessile catkins; *bracts* ovate, acute, smoothish, foliaceous, and imbricated,
each 2-flowered; *calyx* of a single sepal embracing the ovary; *ovary* ovoid, smooth,
1-celled; *ovules* solitary, pendulous; *styles* 2, very hairy, much longer than the ovary.
Sterile flowers in lax, divaricate, axillary panicles; *sepals* 5, oblong, obtuse; *stamens* 5,
opposite the sepals; *filaments* very short; *anthers* erect, oblong, linear, and apiculate, opening by two terminal slits. *Fruit* (!) a membranaceous, cone-like catkin
or strobile, consisting of the whole female inflorescence now enlarged and scale-
like; *achenium*, or true fruit, seed-like, subglobular, invested with a large scalaceous
calyx (the enlarged bractlet); the true fruits and calices sprinkled with yellow,
resinous, globular, and top-shaped grains (Lupulin). *Seeds* solitary, pendulous;
testa thin; *embryo* coiled in a flat spiral.

History and Habitat.—The Hop is found wild, and is indigenous throughout
Europe, except its most northern country, from whence it extends eastward
through Central Asia to the Altai Mountains. In North America it is without
doubt indigenous northward and westward, where it grows in alluvial soils, blossoming in July, and fruiting in September.

---

* From *humus*, damp, the habitat being alluvial soils.
† Anglo-Saxon, *hoppan*, to climb.

ℭℳ. ad nat del.et pinxt.

HÙMULUS LÙPULUS, Linn.

The cultivation of Hops in Central Europe—where their economic growth undoubtedly began—dates from about the middle of the eighth century. Their culture was introduced into England from Flanders in 1524, but they were not used in brewing until 1530, during the reign of Henry VIII, though they were indigenous to the British Islands at that time. The use of Hops in brewing is to add a wholesome bitterness, as well as to preserve the resulting product; this is the principal object of its culture, although the young shoots are often cooked and eaten in lieu of asparagus, and were once an article of hucksterage for that purpose. In keeping, Hops often become brown and acquire an unpleasant odor from the formation of valerianic acid; this is removed by bleaching them with sulphuric oxide. The use of the bleached hop caused an edict to be issued by Henry VIII that in his household no hops nor brimstone must be put into the ale. Gerarde, in speaking of the hop as used "to season" the ale, says that they "rather make it a physical drinke to keepe the body in health, than an ordinary drinke for the quenching of our thirst."

The medical use of hops was at first confined to their tonic, stomachic, and sedative properties; the latter was often doubted, but proved itself in many ways. During the illness of George III, in 1787, a pillow filled with hops was used instead of opiates to promote sleep; this practice is held to the present day. The principal use now is as a fomentation in painful swellings and suppurations, though their internal use in tincture, infusion, and powder, as an alterative, tonic, stomachic, diuretic, antirheumatic, antilithic, febrifuge, and anthelmintic is quite extensive. Hops are said to be not only a nerve sedative, but also to have the same influence upon the heart's action.

The use of Lupulin—i. e., the grains naturally found in the strobile—is principally due to the experiments of Dr. A. W. Ives, who first brought into notice the economy in bulk attainable by its use; and who, after naming the product as above, proved that most, if not all, the virtues of the hop lay in this product.

The strobiles are officinal in the U. S. Phar., as well as Lupulin, the first under the name *Humulus*, the second, *Lupulinum;* the preparations are: *Tinctura Humuli; Extractum Lupulini Fluidum;* and *Oleoresina Lupulini*. In the Eclectic Materia Medica the preparations are: *Extractum Lupulini; Infusum Humuli; Tinctura Lupulini;* and *Unguentum Humuli*.

PART USED AND PREPARATION.—The fresh ripe strobiles are treated like all the drugs of this order, as described under Celtis, page 152–3. The resulting tincture has a clear orange color by transmitted light; retains the odor of the strobiles to a high degree; is very bitter; and has an acid reaction.

CHEMICAL CONSTITUENTS.—*Lupulic Acid,*[*] $C_{32}H_{50}O_7$. This body was first determined by Payen,[†] and afterward more or less purified by Lermer,[‡] who called it *Bitter Acid of Hops*, and isolated it as large, odorless, brilliant, rhombic prisms,

---

[*] Lupulin, Lupulite, Humulin, Lupulina.
[†] *Ann. de Chim. et de Phys.*, 1822, 311.
[‡] $C_{32}H_{50}O_7$.

of extremely bitter taste, soluble in water; in this view he was corroborated by Etti.* Bungener,† however, disclaims the solubility and purity of the product on account of the potash used in its isolation, and describes the body as follows: *Hop Bitter Acid*, $C_{25}H_{35}O_4$. This "acid aldehyde" results in beautiful prismatic crystals, melting at 92°–93° (197.6°–199.4° F.), soluble in alcohol and chloroform, not soluble in water, and having a bitter, acid taste. On exposure to air it turns yellow and oxidizes like the oil, forming valerianic acid in part.

[Lupuline.—This body, claimed as a liquid, volatile alkaloid, having the odor of Conia, was isolated by Griessmayer;‡ no other analyst seems to have met with the product.]

Choline, $C_5H_{15}NO_2$.—This principle, found in the bile, brain, and yolk of eggs, was discovered in the hop by Griessmayer and Harrow.§

Trimethylamine, C_3H_9N.—This nitrogen base of methyl was discovered in the hop by Griessmayer. It boils at $+9.3°$ ($+48.5°$ F.), has a nauseous odor, resembling that of herring brine, in which in fact it is found, and is soluble in water and in alcohol.||

Humulo-Tannic Acid,¶ $C_{25}H_{24}O_{13}$.—This body forms in a whitish amorphous mass, soluble in water and alcohol, but not possessing the power—general in tannic acids—of precipitating gelatine; however, on heating the mass at 130° (266° F.), it parts with one molecule of water, and is transposed as follows:

Humulo-Tannic Acid.   Water.   Phlobaphine.
$$(C_{25}H_{24}O_{13})_2 = H_2O + C_{50}H_{46}O_{25}.$$

This *phlobaphine* results in a red amorphous substance which readily precipitates gelatine.**

Oil of Humulus, $C_{10}H_{16} + C_{10}H_{16}O$ (Wittstein).—This oil, obtained from the strobiles, results as a greenish- or reddish-brown body, according to the ripeness of the cones. It is thin, neutral, hot tasting, and slightly bitter, has a density of 0.910, distills at 125°–175° (257°–347° F.), and hydrates at 210° (410° F.). It resinifies when exposed to the air, and develops *valerianol* ($C_5H_{10}O$), which afterward passes into

Valerianic Acid, $C_5H_{10}O_2$.—This body, obtained from the roots of *Valeriana officinalis*, was determined by Méhu†† to also exist in Lupulin in the proportion

---

* *Am. Jour. Phar.*, 1879, 27; from *Jour. Chem. Socy.*, 1878: from *Ding. Polyt. Jour.*, 227, pp. 354-7.
† *Am. Jour. Phar.*, 1884, p. 427; from *Phar. Jour. and Trans.*, 1884, 1008.
‡ *Am. Jour. Phar.*, 1874, 360.
§ *Chem. News*, 1885, 149.
|| Griessmayer, *ibid.*
¶ Lupulo-Tannic Acid; but this name is not appropriate, as Dr. Bigelow appears to prove that there is no tannin in Lupulin, unless some other portion of the hop dusts into this product.
** Etti, 1826-8, and *Am. Jour. Phar.*, 1879, 27; before quoted.
†† *Thesé, Montpelier*, 1867, in Flück. and Han., *Pharmacographia*.

of 0.1 to 0.17 per cent., though other analysts claim that only in stale and spoiled hops, oxidized Lupulic Acid, and the resinified oil on account of an admixture of that acid, can the body be found. Valerianic Acid is a thin oily liquid, having a sour smell of rotten cheese, and boiling at 175° (347° F.).

Resins.—Etti determined two resins—α, white and crystallizable; β, brown and amorphous.

["**Hopeine.**"—This so-called narcotic alkaloid, claimed to be extracted from hops by Williamson and Springmuehl, of London, is proven by Dujardin-Beaumetz to be a commercial fraud. The product claimed a high price, as it was said to be only obtainable at great expense from American Wild Hops, and consisted of morphine and some aromatic oil.]

PHYSIOLOGICAL ACTION.—Hops are truly sedative in many nervous troubles, and to the heart's action, though probably not at all narcotic. In large doses they cause colic and constipation. The following symptoms, compiled from various doses of the drug, show it to be an irritant to the vaso-motor system and the inhibitory nerves. The symptoms were: Vertigo and confusion of the head; cerebral and arterial congestion; dilation of the pupils; thirst, nausea, loss of appetite and vomiting; diarrhœic stools with great urging; burning pain along the urethra with increased urine; respirations deep, almost stertorous, and rapid; decrease of the pulses; with high temperature and profuse perspiration.*

DESCRIPTION OF PLATE 155.

1. End of a fruiting branch, Binghamton, N. Y., Aug. 27th, 1885.†
2. A medium-sized leaf.
3. Male flower.
4. Female catkin.
5. A female bract.
6. Enlarged fruiting bract.
7. Achenium enveloped in its persistent calyx.
8. Achenium, with calyx removed.
9. Vertical ⎫ section of the seed.
10. Horizontal ⎭

(3–10 enlarged.)

* Allen, *Ency. Mat. Med.*, v, 625.
† By an error, the prickly points on the stem were omitted below the fruits in the drawing.

156
JUGLANS CINEREA.

BUTTERNUT.

SYN.—JUGLANS CINEREA, LINN.; JUGLANS CATHARTICA, MICHX.; JUGLANS OBLONGA, MILL.

COM. NAMES.—BUTTERNUT, OIL-NUT, WHITE WALNUT; (FR.) NOYER GRIS; (GER.) WALLNUSS.

A TINCTURE OF THE FRESH YOUNG INNER BARK OF JUGLANS CINEREA, LINN.

Description.—This oblate tree usually attains a height and breadth of from 25 to 40 feet. *Stem* early branching, deliquescent; *bark* strongly aromatic and resinous, smoothish when young, and of a grayish color; *wood* brown, somewhat lighter in color and texture than that of the black walnut, its specific gravity varies from .376 to .487, and its weight from 22 to 30 lbs. per cubic foot. *Leaves* alternate, compound, odd-pinnate, about one foot long when mature; *petioles* long, densely clammy-pubescent; *leaflets* opposite, or nearly so, in from 7 to 10 pairs, and the terminal one, each oblong-lanceolate, sharply serrate, rounded at the base, pointed, and downy beneath. *Inflorescence* terminal on the branches; *flowers* monœcious, the *fertile* ones in a cluster of from 3 to 5, amid the new leaves of the season; the *sterile* many, hanging in catkins (*aments*) from the leaf scars of the previous year. *Fertile flowers:* calyx regular, 4-toothed, clammy-pubescent; *corolla* consisting of 4 minute *petals* in the sinuses of the calyx. *Style* very short and comparatively thick; *stigmas* 2, long, and densely fringed with blunt papillæ upon their inner surfaces. *Sterile flowers: stamens* projecting from the rachis of the ament in sufficient numbers to cover it throughout its entire length; *calyx* an irregular, horizontal, flat, bracted scale, furnished with a terminal and from 3 to 5 lateral teeth; *stamens* 8 to 14 or more, irregularly suspended from the under surface of the bract; *filaments* very short and thick; *anthers* ovate-oblong, 2-celled, furnished with a short abrupt point. *Fruit* oblong, pointed, 2 to 3 inches long and 1 to 1½ inches in diameter when green; *epicarp* fleshy, fibrous, and densely covered with a sticky pubescence; when dry, coriaceous, indehiscent; *endocarp* thick, bony, sculptured with deep rough-edged sinuses; *nut* 1-celled above, 2-celled below.

---

* The classical name of the walnut, *Juglans regia;* a contraction from *Jovis glans,* Jupiter's nut.

JUGLANDACEÆ.—A small family of very useful trees. *Wood* hard and dense. *Leaves* alternate, pinnate, astipulate. *Flowers* monœcious, the fertile ones single or in a small cluster or spike; *calyx* adherent to the ovary, regular, 3 to 5 lobed; *petals* sometimes present; the sterile flowers in long catkins; *calyx* bracted and irregular, overlapping the stamens like a hood. *Ovary* somewhat more than 1-celled, containing a single orthotropous ovule, the walls become thick and fleshy, affording thus a covering (*epicarp*) for the nut. *Fruit* a dry drupe, furnished with a bony endocarp, splitting into 2 valves in germination, and enclosing a large 4-lobed seed; *albumen* none; *embryo* 2 large, lobed, corrugated, sarcous, oily cotyledons.

The following fruits or nuts of this family are greatly esteemed on account of their rich oily "meats": The black walnut (*Juglans nigra, Linn.*), the butternut (*Juglans cinerea, Linn.*), the Maderia nut or English walnut (*Juglans regia, Linn.*), a native of Persia and the Himalaya, and cultivated in England and along the Mediterranean, the hickory or mocker-nut (*Carya tomentosa, Nutt.*, and *var. maxima, Nutt.*), the shell-bark or shag-bark hickory (*Carya alba, Nutt.*), the western shag-bark hickory (*Carya sulcata, Nutt.*), and the pecan-nut (*Carya olivæformis, Nutt.*).

History and Habitat.—The butternut is a common tree throughout the Eastern, Middle, and Western States, and from the Canadas southward along the mountains, growing in rich woods along river banks, flowering from April to May, and ripening its fruit in September. The wood, as before mentioned, is valuable on account of its lightness, durability, and freedom from worm infestations; the fruit, when half formed, makes a fine pickle, and when ripe an article of hucksterage; the sap, gathered in its season, forms on boiling a fine sugar equal if not superior to that of the maple; the leaves, bark, and unripe fruit afford a dye of a chocolate-brown color for woollen goods, which, with that of the black walnut, was used in the South to great extent during the rebellion as a dye for the uniforms of the soldiers. The use of a decoction of the inner bark in medicine has been of some importance, especially as a mild cathartic; it acts thus without colic, and is said to leave none of the constipating effects so frequently following general cathartics; in diarrhœa and even dysentery it receives many encomiums from botanic physicians. The powdered leaves act as a rubefacient and vesicant, and have been used as a substitute for cantharides.

The inner bark of the root is officinal in the U. S. Ph. as *Extractum Juglandis;* in the Eclectic Materia Medica the same preparation is recommended.

PART USED AND PREPARATION.—The inner bark of young stems and roots, collected in May or June, is chopped and pounded to a pulp and weighed. Then two parts by weight of alcohol is taken, the pulp thoroughly mixed with one-sixth part of it, and the rest of the alcohol added. After having stirred the whole well, it is poured into a well-stoppered bottle and allowed to stand eight days in a dark, cool place.

The tincture, procured by straining and filtering, should be opaque in layers of any quantity; in thin layers it should have a deep, rich, reddish-brown color by

156.

ℭm. ad nat. del. et pinxt.   JÙGLANS CINÈREA, Linn.

transmitted light. It has an astringent, bitter taste, and an exceedingly acid reaction.

CHEMICAL CONSTITUENTS.—*Juglandin.* This body, extracted by Merrell, is spoken of as an impure resin; it probably contains the following principle, to which its action is doubtless due.

Nucin:[*] this acid, acrid body, was first discovered in the green epicarps of Juglans regia. Wittstein represents it as forming reddish-yellow, glossy, brittle needles, dissolving copiously in alkalies and ether, less soluble in alcohol, and but slightly in water. Nucin gives a beautiful purple color with the borates and phosphates of alkalies, and with subacetate of lead. Tannin,[†§] resin,[‡§] volatile oil,[†§] fixed oil,[‡] glucose,[‡] and a volatile acid,[§] have also been determined.

PHYSIOLOGICAL ACTION.—Juglandin, the extract of butternut, acts, according to Paine, as a drastic purge, producing irritation and inflammation of the mucous lining of the intestines, and if continued, its exhibition is followed by an exanthematous eruption much resembling the flush of scarlatina. It causes also a congestion of the portal circulation, and subsequent watery evacuations of the bowels.

DESCRIPTION OF PLATE 156.

1. End of flowering branch, with larger leaves removed; Binghamton, N. Y., June 2d, 1884.
2. Female flower (enlarged).
3. Male flower (enlarged).
4. Stamen (enlarged).
5. Section of ovary (enlarged).
6. Hair of pubescence (x 50).
7. Pollen (x 200).
8. Half-grown leaf.
9. Fruit.

---

[*] *Juglandic acid* (Thiebaud).   [†] Thiebaud.   [‡] S. Witherill.   [§] E. S. Dawson.

157

CARYA ALBA.

HICKORY.

SYN.—CARYA ALBA, NUTT.; CARYA SQUAMOSA, BART.; JUGLANS SQUAMOSA, MICHX.; JUGLANS ALBA, LINN.; JUGLANS COM-PRESSA, WILLD.

COM. NAMES.—SHAG-BARK OR SHELL-BARK HICKORY, WHITE HICK-ORY, KISKYTOM.

A TINCTURE OF THE RIPE "MEATS" OF THE NUTS, CARYA ALBA, NUTT.

Description.—This valuable, rapid-growing tree, furnishing the best hickory nuts of the markets, attains a height of from 30 to 80 feet, and a breadth of from 20 to 50 feet. *Stem* erect, deliquescent, from 9 to 20 inches in diameter; *bark* smooth when young, but after the twelfth to fifteenth year it exfoliates in strips or wide laminæ from 1 to 4 feet long, and one-eighth to a quarter inch thick; this without injury to the life of the tree. The *bark* is brownish-gray externally, cin-namon color internally, very oily and inflammable, producing on combustion a great heat. *Wood* white internally, yellow near the bark, very valuable in the arts, and as firewood; it is dense, tough, and elastic, its specific gravity .760, and weight 47½ lbs. per cubic foot. Notwithstanding its hardness it rots easily when sub-jected to moisture. *Leaves* 3 or 4 compound, odd-pinnate, appearing with the flowers; *leaflets* 5, taper-pointed, sessile, or nearly so, finely serrate, the three ter-minal obovate or obovate-lanceolate, the two nearest the short petiole much smaller, oblong-lanceolate. *Sterile flowers* in pendent catkins, branched to the form of a trident, situate on a common peduncle arising from the base of the shoot of the season, in the axis of the large, conspicuous, tardily deciduous, scaly, leaf buds; *calyx* naked, clinging to its bract, irregularly 2 to 3 parted. *Stamens* 3 to 8 or more, suspended from the bract-like calyx; *filaments* short and inconspicuous or wanting; *anthers* 4, downy pubescent. *Fertile flowers* 2 to 3 or more in a pedunculated cluster or spike amid the young leaves, and terminal on the growth of the season; *calyx* with a 4-toothed limb; *petals* wanting; *stigmas* 2 to 4, large, sessile, papillose, and persistent. *Fruit* a globular or depressed-globose, some-what four-sided nut; *epicarp* thick, fleshy, and fibrous, splitting into 4 equal valves when dry; *endocarp* bony, smooth between the rounded ridges, and tipped with a sharp point, somewhat 2-celled above and 4-celled below; *cotyledons* corrugated, rich, and sweet. Read description of Natural Order under Juglans cinerea, 156.

---

* An ancient name of the walnut, καρύα, *karya*.

History and Habitat.—The shag-bark hickory is indigenous to the Atlantic States of North America from Maine to the Carolinas, growing in rich woods and along streams. It blossoms in May and ripens its fruit in October.

The bark of the hickory affords with copperas an olive, and with alum a green, dye for woolens; the ash yields a very fine lye, and the "meats" an excellent oil for burning. The wood is valuable for the handles of most light and heavy implements, for barrel-hoops, sail-rings, hand-spikes, and pins, but is useless for any purpose in which it would be subjected to alternate wettings and dryings. In medicine I can find no account of its use prior to the provings, which so far are slight. Carya is not mentioned in the U. S. Ph. nor the Eclectic Materia Medica.

PART USED AND PREPARATION.—The ripe cotyledons are finely powdered, covered with five parts by weight of alcohol, and kept for eight days in a tightly-stoppered bottle, in a dark, cool place.

The tincture obtained by decanting and filtering, has a light-canary color by transmitted light, an odor and taste of the nut, and a neutral reaction.

CHEMICAL CONSTITUENTS.—I am unable to find record of any analysis of this plant or its seed. On evaporating the tincture under the addition of water until the alcohol entirely passed off, a light and a heavy oil separated, both liquid at ordinary temperatures. The heavy oil separated in greater quantity, and solidified at 7° (44.6° F.); both retained the peculiar odor and taste of the nut. No specific principle was yielded by farther analysis.

DESCRIPTION OF PLATE 157.

1. End of flowering branch; Binghamton, N. Y., June 3d, 1884.
   2. Female flower (enlarged).
   3. Male flower (enlarged).
   4. Nut.
   5. Longitudinal section of the nut.
   6. Horizontal section of the nut.
   7. Section of the ovary (enlarged).
   8. Trunk of tree (diminished).
   9. Pollen (3 views x 200).

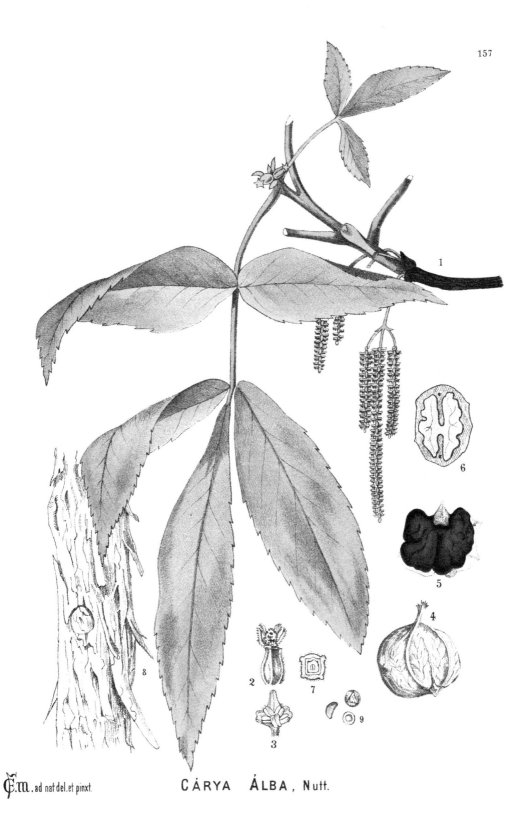

8

2

3

7

9

6

5

4

1

Ꝡꝛ.ꝥ.ad nat del.et pinxt.

CÁRYA ÁLBA, Nutt.

158
CASTANEA VESCA.

CHESTNUT.

SYN.—CASTANEA VESCA, LINN.; CASTANEA VESCA, VAR. AMERICANA. MICHX.; CASTANEA EDULIS, GAERTN.

COM. NAMES.—CHESTNUT; (FR.) CHATAIGNIER; (GER.) KASTANIE.

A TINCTURE OF THE FRESH LEAVES OF CASTANEA VESCA, VAR. AMERICANA, MICHX.

Description.—This forest tree, highly esteemed for its timber and edible nuts, attains a growth of from 40 to 80 feet in height. The *stem* is deliquescent, from 2 to 4 feet in diameter, and covered with a thick, corrugated bark, smoothish upon the corrugations; *branches* thick, very irregular, and contorted. The wood commercially, is light and porous, having a sp. gr. of 404, and weighing but 25 lbs., 4 oz. per cubic foot; on account of its durability it is valued principally for fencing. The *leaves* are petiolate, oblong-lanceolate, coarsely serrate, pointed at the tip and acute at the base, from 4 to 9 inches long, and from 2 to 4 inches wide; they are particularly noticeable on account of their straight pinnate veins. *Inflorescence* cream-colored, monœcious, axillary upon the ends of the branches, and appearing after the leaves. *Sterile flowers* in irregularly placed clusters upon naked, subcylindrical aments, that vary from 3 to 6 inches in length. *Calyx* generally 6-parted. *Stamens* 8 to 20; *filaments* slender; *anthers* 2-celled. *Fertile flowers* few, usually from 2 to 3 closely crowded in an involucre. *Involucres* in a cluster at the base of the aments, ovoid, thickly covered with spines. *Calyx* tubular with a bell-shaped 6-lobed border, encircling the ovary in the form of a crown. *Ovary* 3 to 6-celled; *ovules* 6 to 14; *stigmas* awned, equal in number to the cells of the ovary. *Stamens* 5 or more, rudimentary, rarely perfect, longer than the calyx. *Fruit*, a large hard, thick, echinate, 4-valved bur, enclosing from 1 to 3 or more nuts, laterally flattened by compression, in shapes depending upon the number in the bur.

Cupuliferæ.—Trees or shrubs with white, and generally firm, hard wood. *Stipules* caducous; *leaves* alternate, pinnately veined. *Inflorescence* upon the ends of the branches; *flowers* monœcious; *sterile flowers* in catkins (except Fagus); *fertile flowers* solitary, grouped or spiked, furnished with a scaly or echinate cup or bur forming a receptacle for the nuts; *calyx* adherent to the ovary, the border

---

* Κάσνανα or Κασθαναια, a city of Pontus, noted for its chestnut trees.

CASTÀNEA VÉSCA, var. Americana, Michx.

CM. ad nat. del. et pinxt.

forming a ring or crown about its summit. *Stamens* of sterile flowers either equal in number to the calyx lobes or two or three times as many, usually exserted; rudimentary stamens often present in the fertile flowers. *Ovary* generally more or less 2- to 7-celled; *ovules* anatropous, one or more in each cell; all of the ovules and cells except one aborting, to form a 1-seeded nut. *Seeds* mostly edible, forming among others the following nuts: Sweet-acorn (*Quercus alba*), Chestnut (*Castanea vesca* and *var. America*), Chinquapin (*Castanea pumila*), Beech-nut (*Fagus ferruginea*), Hazel-nut (*Corylus Americana, C. rostrata*), and Filbert (*Corylus avellana*). *Albumen* none; *embryo* formed of two thick, sarcous cotyledons and a short or retracted radicle, filling the whole nut.

History and Habitat.—This variety is indigenous to the United States from southern and middle parts of Maine to Michigan and southwards, especially along the hills and mountains; flowering in June and July, fruiting in October. The chestnut tree is remarkable both for its size and longevity; there is a specimen on the Neversink Highlands, New York Harbor, called the "elephant," which is said to be fully five hundred years old; Case's *Bot. Index*, April, 1880, mentions an individual near Seymour, Ind., measuring 22 feet in diameter two feet from its base, and 70 feet to the first branch. The nuts when dry are sweet and wholesome, forming an article of merchandise. The best chestnuts of France, the *marrons*, a large variety of *C. vesca*, are much esteemed when boiled, and form almost as prominent an article of hucksterage as the common roasted peanut does here. In the south of France and north of Italy the harvest is very large; here the nuts are largely used as a substitute for wheat flour and potatoes. The leaves are official in the U. S. Ph. as *Extractum Castaneæ Fluidum*.

PART USED AND PREPARATION.—The fresh leaves, gathered in September while still green, are chopped and pounded to a pulp and weighed. Then two parts by weight of alcohol are taken, the pulp mixed with one-sixth part of it and the rest of the alcohol added. After stirring the whole well and pouring it into a well-stoppered bottle, it is allowed to stand eight days in a dark, cool place. The tincture is then separated by decanting, straining and filtering. Thus prepared, it has a deep-brown color by transmitted light, an odor like that of the leaves, an astringent taste, and highly acid reaction.

CHEMICAL CONSTITUENTS.—The only analysis of this plant is one of the leaves, conducted by L. J. Steltzer (Am. Jour. Phar., 1880, p. 292). He determines the constituents to be: tannin 9 per cent, gum, albumen, a soft yellowish resin, fat and extractive; together with salts of K, Ca, Mg, and Iron. When assaying for an alkaloid, he obtained negative results.

PHYSIOLOGICAL ACTION.—I am unable to find any data upon this. The leaves in decoction have been used for whooping-cough. The provings by Dr. Houghton show no particular action upon the air-passages. Castanea is claimed to have a sedative action upon the nerves of respiration.

DESCRIPTION OF PLATE 158.

1. End of branch in flower, Binghamton, N. Y., July 26th, 1882.
2. A nut, representing the form when two are enclosed in the bur.

N. ORD.—CUPULIFERÆ.

Tribe.—CARPINEÆ.

GENUS.—**OSTRYA**,* MICHELI.

SEX. SYST.—MONŒCIA POLYANDRIA.

159

OSTRYA.

HOP-HORNBEAM.

SYN.—OSTRYA VIRGINICA, WILLD.; CARPINUS OSTRYA-AMERICANA; MICHX.; C. OSTRYA, MICHX. f.

COM. NAMES.—AMERICAN HOP-HORNBEAM, IRON-WOOD,† LEVER-WOOD; (GER.) HOPFENHAINBUSCHE.

A TINCTURE OF THE HEART-WOOD OF OSTRYA VIRGINICA, WILLD.

Description.—This small forest-tree seldom attains a growth of over 30 feet in height and a diameter of 8 inches. *Bark* of the younger trees birch-like, of the older ones, much resembling that of the white oak, although its furrows are narrower. *Buds* acute, their leaves plaited upon the veins. *Leaves* ovate-oblong, taper-pointed, pinnately-veined, smooth above, and downy beneath especially upon the veins; *margin* sharply, doubly or irregularly serrate. *Inflorescence* diœcious, the flowers appearing with the leaves; *sterile flowers* in drooping, cylindrical aments, consisting of several stamens in the axil of each bract, and terminating the branches of the previous year's growth; *fertile flowers* in short catkins, a pair under each deciduous bract, and terminating the short shoot of the season; *involucral sacs* bristly hairy at the base. *Calyx* of the fertile flowers adherent to the ovary; *limb* bearded. *Stamens* 8 to 10 or more; *filaments* short, once irregularly forked; *anthers* 1-celled, one on each branch of the fork (a single, divided, 2-celled anther?), hairy at the apex. *Ovary* incompletely 2-celled and 2-ovuled, enclosed in a tubular bractlet; *style* short; *stigmas* 2, long and linear. *Fruit* an oblong-ovoid, pendulous, strobile-like cluster of several membraneous involucral sacs, each enclosing a smooth, achenious nutlet. Read the description of the natural order, page 158.

History and Habitat.—The Hop-Hornbeam is indigenous to Eastern North America from Florida northward. It is commonly found in rich woods anywhere within its limit, and flowers in April, its peculiar fruit being fully ripe in August. The other American Iron-wood, *Carpinus Americana,* need never be confounded with this species, as it is much more like a beech.

---

* The classical name, from οστρεον, *ostreon,* a scale, alluding to the peculiar fruit.

† Also applied to the hornbeam, *Carpinus Americana,* Michx.

A decoction of the heart-wood of this tree has long been used by the laity as an antiperiodic in intermittent fever, and as a tonic and alterative in scrofulous dyscrasias and dyspepsia.

The wood is very hard, dense and tough, weighing 48 lbs. 11 oz. per cubic foot, and of .779 sp. gr. It is very valuable to the farmer as a "binder" for heavy loads, and for use as levers. In the manufactories it has often furnished fine cog-wheels and excellent handles for tools.

PART USED AND PREPARATION.—The fresh heart-wood, in coarse powder, is covered with five parts by weight of alcohol, and allowed to remain eight days in a well-stoppered bottle in a dark, cool place. The tincture then separated by filtration should have a clear, brilliant orange-red color by transmitted light, a slightly aromatic odor, a peculiar astringent and bitterish taste, and an acid reaction.

PHYSIOLOGICAL ACTION.—The heart-wood in powder or decoction causes headache, loss of appetite, nausea, flatulent colic, bilious defecation with great tenesmus, aching extremities, general debilitated condition, and diaphoresis.

DESCRIPTION OF PLATE 159.

1. End of sterile flowering branch, Binghamton, N. Y., May 16th, 1885.
2. Superior view of staminate bract.
3. Under view of same.
4. Stamen.
5. End of fruiting branch.
6. An involucrate scale of fruit.
7. Under view of same.

(2-4 and 6-7 enlarged.)

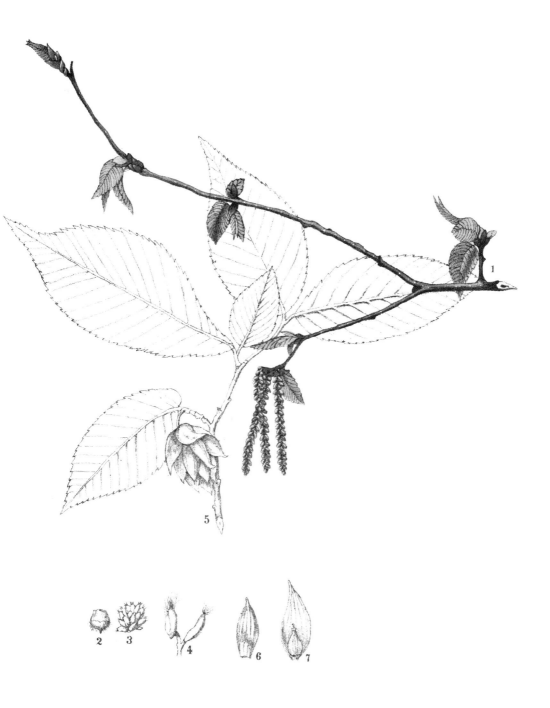

 . ad nat del.et pinxt.

ÓSTRYA VIRGÍNICA, Willd.

GENUS.—**MYRICA,*** LINN.

SEX. SYST.—DIŒCIA TETRANDRIA.

160

MYRICA.

BAYBERRY.

SYN.—MYRICA CERIFERA, LINN.

COM. NAMES.—BAYBERRY, WAX MYRTLE, CANDLE-BERRY, TALLOW
SHRUB; (FR.) ARBRE À SUIF; (GER.) WACHSBUSCH, WACHSGAGLE.

A TINCTURE OF THE FRESH ROOT BARK OF MYRICA CERIFERA, LINN.

Description.—This somewhat fragrant shrub attains a growth of from 3 to 8
feet. *Branches* numerous, especially at the summit of the plant; *branchlets* pubescent. *Leaves* somewhat preceding the flowers; they are oblong- or cuneate-
lanceolate, narrowing at the base, shining or resinous dotted on both sides and
pubescent underneath; *apex* obtuse; *margin* entire, or with a few wavy or short,
sharp serratures near the apex. *Inflorescence* diœcious, amentaceous, solitary, from
under the axillary scale-buds of the previous years' leaves; *flowers* destitute of calyx
or corolla, and furnished with a pair of wedge-shaped naked bractlets. *Sterile catkins* oblong or cylindrical; *bracts* rhombic; stamens 2 to 8, usually 4, longer than the
bracts; *filaments* somewhat united below; *anthers* large, 2-celled. *Fertile catkins*
ovoid, smaller than the sterile; *ovary* furnished with 2 to 4, usually 3, ciliate,
rounded, obscurely 3-lobed scales at its base; *stigmas* 2, thread like. *Fruit*
scattered groups of small, globular, bony, and naked nutlets, having numerous
minute black grains upon its surface that are incrusted with wax.

Myricaceæ.—A small family of monœcious or diœcious shrubs or small trees,
found in both Americas, India, Cape of Good Hope, and one species in Europe.
Leaves alternate, simple, resinous dotted, and often fragrant; *stipules* present or
absent. *Inflorescence*, both kinds in short scaly aments; *involucre* none. *Flowers*
destitute of both calyx and corolla; *fertile catkins* in an ovoid or cylindrical head;
ovary 1-celled, situated in the axil of a bract, and surrounded at the base by several
hypogynous scales; *ovule* single, erect, orthotropous; *styles* 2, filiform, subulate,
or dilated and petaloid. *Sterile catkins* with 2 to 10 stamens in the axil of a
squamous bract; *filaments* free or partly united; *anthers* 2- to 4-celled; *dehiscence*
longitudinal. *Fruit* a dry, drupaceous, indehiscent nut; *albumen* none; *cotyledons*
sarcous; *radicle* short, superior.

---

* Μυρω, *myro*, to flow, as the plant grows near water. The ancient name of the Tamarisk, μυρικη, *myrike*, from
μυριζω, *myrizo*, to perfume, does not apply.

2 3

4

1

.ad nat.del.et pinxt.   MYRÌCA CERÍFERA , Linn.

The plant under consideration is the only one of the family represented in our Materia Medica; several other species, however, are sometimes used as remedies, especially in domestic practice, viz.: The American and European Sweet Gale (*Myrica Gale*, Linn.), whose berries in infusion are said to be an efficient remedy for itch, and a vermifuge; the leaves are said to be substituted for hops in Sweden, in the manufacture of beer. The other six American species of the genus *Myrica* are often substituted for the species *cerifera* in domestic practice. The fruit of the Nepaul *M. sapida* is said to be pleasantly acid and edible; while the Cape of Good Hope *M. cordifolia* yields a wax, said by Thunberg to be eaten by the natives. The American Sweet Fern (*Comptonia asplenifolia*, Ait.) is in constant domestic use in some localities for checking diarrhœa, and as a fomentation in rheumatism and bruises.

History and Habitat.—The Wax Myrtle grows in thickets near swamps and marshes in the sand-belt along the Atlantic coast from Florida northward, also on the shores of Lake Erie; it is, however, rare in the interior. It flowers from April to May, according to locality. In the South it is a small evergreen tree; in Delaware and Southern New Jersey, a tall, semideciduous shrub; and in the North, dwarfed and deciduous.

Both the wax and root-bark have been used in medicine, the action of each being quite different, though both are astringent and stimulant to weakened mucous membranes.

The Bark.—Dr. Charles A. Lee* sums up the uses of the bark of the root: " Bayberry bark possesses tonico-astringent properties which entitle it to a very respectable rank among our indigenous astringents. Reduced to a powder, it is acrid and styptic to the taste, and in doses of one drachm causes a sensation of heat in the stomach, followed by vomiting and purging, and sometimes by diuresis. A decoction has been long used in diarrhœa, dysentery, uterine hemorrhage, dropsies succeeding fevers, and as a gargle in affections of the throat and fauces." When chewed it acts as a sialagogue, useful in toothache and to stimulate tender, spongy, or bleeding gums. In the Eclectic practice bayberry bark is a noted remedy in scrofulous sores and ulcers, used as a poultice; and for jaundice, especially the form termed black jaundice. In the Botanic practice bayberry bark and lobelia constituted almost a complete materia medica.

Myrica Wax.—The use of this substance in medicine was first published by Alexandre (1722), who mentions a wax which he describes and says is used in Louisiana by the colonists in the manufacture of candles; and farther adds that the water in which the wax has been "tried," when boiled to an extract, is a certain cure for the most violent cases of dysentery. Dr. Wm. Fahnestock considered the wax to be, in direct proportion to its viridity, astringent and plainly narcotic, and claims to have been eminently successful in treating with this substance many severe cases of typhoid dysentery. In Eclectic practice this wax (" Myricin ") is

---

* *Jour. Mat. Med.*, N. S., vol. i, 257.

held to be serviceable in aphthous affections of the mucous surfaces, such as stomatitis, nursing sore mouth, ulcerated fauces, bowels and stomach; also in leucorrhœa, etc., etc.

Production and Chemistry.—Vegetable wax is a compound substance furnished by many plants either naturally or from their juices through the agency of insects. The following table, including all those that are produced in a sufficient quantity to be available, will be of interest:

NAME.	SOURCE.	MELTING POINT.	
		Cent.	Fahr.
Cacao, Chocolate Butter,	*Theobroma cacao*, L.,	30°–33°	86–91.4°
Koya Wax,	*Cinnamomum pedunculatum*, N. ab E.,	38°–40°	100.4°–104.0°
Chinese Vegetable Tallow,	*Stillingia sebifera*, Mart.,	37°–45°	98.6°–113.0°
Myrica Wax,	*Myrica cerifera*, L.,	47°–49°	116.6°–120.2°
Japan Wax,	*Rhus succedeanea*, L.,	52°–53°	125.6°–127.4°
Cow Tree Wax,	*Galactodendron utile*, Humb.,	58°	136.4°
Bees' Wax	*Apis mellifica*, etc.,	62°–63°	143.6°–145.4°
Chinese Wax,	*Coccus ceriferus*,	79°	174.2°
Ibota Wax,	*Lingustrum Ibota*, Sieb.,	80°–82°	176°–179.6°
Sela Wax,	*Fraxinus Chinensis*, Roxb.,	82.5°	180.5°
Carramba Wax,	*Copernicia cerefera*, Mart.,	83.5°–84°	182.3°–183.2°
Brazil Wax,	Unknown,	97°	206.6°
Palm Wax,	*Ceroxylon andicola*, Humb.,	100°	212.0°

The production of myrica wax, or bayberry tallow, has been carried on to a somewhat large extent, mostly for the manufacture of candles and soap, generally as described by Toscan in a work entitled *L'Ami de la Nature*. This describes the method employed in an early day.* Candles made from this wax, though quite brittle, are less greasy in warm weather, of fine appearance, slightly aromatic, and smokeless after snuffing, rendering them much more pleasant to use than those made of either wax or tallow. Soap from this wax makes an aromatic and very softening shaving lather, and a fine body for surgeons' soap plasters.

Myrica wax, $C_6H_{12}O$,† is harder and more brittle than beeswax. Its specific gravity varies from 1.004 to 1.006, and its melting point from 47°-49° (116.6°–120.2° F.). Four-fifths of the wax is soluble in hot alcohol, leaving a residue not soluble; boiling ether dissolves more than one-quarter of its weight, of which,

---

* "Towards the end of autumn, when the berries are ripe, a man leaves his house, together with his family, to go to some island or bank near the seashore where the wax-trees grow in abundance. He carries with him vessels to boil the berries, and a hatchet to build a cottage where he may find shelter during his residence in this place, which is usually three or four weeks. While he cuts down trees his children gather the berries. A very fertile shrub will afford nearly seven pounds. When these are gathered the whole family employ themselves in procuring the wax. They throw a certain quantity of the berries into the kettle, and then pour a sufficient quantity of water on them so as to cover them to a depth of about half a foot. They then boil the whole, stirring the grains about and rubbing them against the sides of the vessel in order that the wax may more easily come off. In a short time it floats on the water like fat, and is collected with a spoon and strained through a coarse cloth to separate it from any impurities which might be mixed with it. When no more wax can be obtained they take the berries out with a skimmer and put others into the same water, but it must be entirely changed the second or third time, and in the meantime boiling water must be added as it evaporates, in order to avoid retarding the operation. When a considerable quantity of wax has been obtained by this means, it is laid on a cloth to drain off the water with which it is still mixed. It is then melted a second time, and it is then formed into masses. Four pounds of berries yield about one of wax; that which is first obtained is generally yellow; but in later boilings it assumes a green color from the pellicle with which the kernel of the berry is covered.'

† Levy, *Handwörterbuch der Chemie*, v, 413.

however, nearly all is deposited on cooling; at a moderate heat turpentine dissolves about six per cent.* The wax saponifies readily with a solution of caustic potash, yielding a fragrant soap, fully soluble in water, and breaking down under the action of sulphuric acid into a mixture of fatty acids. Myrica wax, according to G. E. Moore,† is composed of about one-fifth *palmitin*, the remaining four-fifths being free *palmitic* and *lauric* (myristic?) *acids*.

Myrica has no place in the U. S. Ph.; in the Eclectic Materia Medica its preparations are: *Cataplasma Myricæ, Decoctum Myricæ, Extractum Myricæ, Lotio Lobeliæ Composita,‡ Pulvis Asclepiæ Compositus,§* and *Pulvis Myricæ Compositus.*‖

PART USED AND PREPARATION.—The fresh bark of the root is chopped and pounded to a pulp and weighed. Then two parts by weight of alcohol are taken, the pulp mixed with one-sixth part of it, and the rest of the alcohol added. After having stirred the whole well, pour it into a well-stoppered bottle, and let it stand eight days in a dark, cool place.

The tincture separated from this mass by pressure and filtration should have a deep crimson color by transmitted light, a peculiar vinous odor, a very astringent taste, and strong acid reaction.

CHEMICAL CONSTITUENTS.—*Myricinic Acid.* This body, of unknown composition (bearing, however, great resemblance to myristic acid, $C_{14}H_{28}O_2$, from *Myristica fragrans*, Houtt.), may be obtained from the alcoholic extract of the root-bark by extracting with ether and washing in hot absolute alcohol. The acid then deposits as a granular, acrid mass, producing a dense froth on agitation with water. It fuses at 53.6° (128.4° F.), and is soluble in absolute alcohol.[1]

An acrid resin soluble in alcohol and ether;[1,2] an astringent resin soluble in alcohol;[1,2] volatile oil;[1,3] tannic,[1,2,3] and gallic acids;[1,2,3] starch;[1,2] gum;[1,2,3] and a red coloring-matter,[1,2] have also been determined in the bark of the root.

PHYSIOLOGICAL ACTION.—Myrica, in frequent doses of the extract, causes dizziness; headache; smarting, burning, and soreness of the eyes; burning catarrhal condition of the nostrils; yellowness of the countenance; heat and dryness of the throat; hunger; heat and nausea; distension of the stomach and abdomen, with griping and passage of very offensive flatus; diarrhœa, followed by total absence of stool; incresed secretion of urine, followed by diminished secretion, and even to scantiness; increased heart's action; general languor and depression; sleepiness; chilliness and sensations as of fever.

DESCRIPTION OF PLATE 160.

1. End of female branch, retaining one of the previous year's leaves, Landisville, N. J., May 29th, 1885.
2. Female flower.
3. Male catkin.
4. Portion of a fruiting branch.
(2 and 3 enlarged.)

---

* Bostock, *Nicholson's Jour.*, vol. iv, 130. † *Am. Jour. Sci. and Arts*, vol. xxxiii, 313.
‡ Bayberry bark, Lobelia leaves and seed, Yellow-dock root, and vinegar.
§ Pleurisy root, Spearmint, Sumach berries, Bayberry bark, Skunk Cabbage root, and Ginger.
‖ Bayberry bark and Bloodroot. [1] G M. Hambright, *Am. Jour. Phar.*, 1863, 193.
[2] Tilden's Analysis, *Jour. Mat. Med.*, N. S., vol. i, 260. [3] Bigelow, *Am. Med. Bot*, vol. iii, 34.

161

SALIX PURPUREA.

PURPLE WILLOW.

SYN.—SALIX PURPUREA, LINN.; S. HELIX, LINN.; S. MONANDRA, EHR.;
S. LAMBERTIANA, PURSH.
COM. NAMES.—BITTER PURPLE WILLOW, RED WILLOW; (GER.) PUR-
PURISHE WEIDE.

A TINCTURE OF THE BARK OF SALIX PURPUREA, L.

Description.—This species only attains a growth of from 6 to 10 feet. *Branches* terete and lithe; *twigs* olivaceous or reddish; *bark* very smooth and bitter. *Leaves* partly opposite on some branches, alternate on others, all oblanceolate, pointed, smooth, minutely and sparingly toothed. *Inflorescence* in lateral, sessile aments appearing before the leaves; *catkins* cylindrical, bracted at the base; *scales* entire, round and concave, very black, more or less hairy, and persistent. *Sterile flowers:* *stamens* 2; *filaments* united into one, and having a little gland at their base; *anthers* double, 4-celled, reddish. *Fertile flowers: ovary* sessile or nearly so, downy, with a little flat gland on the inner side of the base; *stigmas* 2, nearly sessile, or more properly 1, and emarginate.

Salicaceæ.—This small order is composed of but 2 genera, both of which are represented in North America by a total of 51 species and 29 varieties. Its species are all of the temperate and frigid zones, (*Salix arctica*, Pal.) being found farther north than any other known woody plant. The order is characterized as follows: Trees or shrubs with a bitter bark. *Leaves* alternate, undivided; *stipules* scale-like and deciduous, or leaf-like and persistent. *Inflorescence* amentaceous, the aments from under each bract; *flowers* diœcious; *perianth* wanting. *Sterile flowers* with from 2 to 12 or more stamens, sometimes monadelphous. *Fertile flowers* of a single 1- or imperfectly 2-celled ovary; *style* very short or none. *Fruit* a 2-valved pod; *placentæ* 2. *Seeds* numerous, ascending, provided with a long silky down; *cotyledons* flattened; *albumen* none.
Beside the two species here represented, there are a few others used in medicine, viz.: The European *Salix Russelliana*, Smith, which was considered by Sir James Smith to be the most highly therapeutic of the genus; the European *S. alba*, Linn., is the usual pharmacopœial species; the Sweet Willow of Europe

---

* Celtic, *sal*, near; *lis*, water.

(*S. pentandria*, Linn.) is sometimes preferred in decoction on account of its inherent aroma; while *S. Caprea*, Linn., is officinal in the Dublin Pharmacopœia. The leaf-buds of the European Black Poplar (*Populus nigra*, Linn.) are frequently used in the form of *Unguentum Populeum* as a vulnerary; the Lombardy Poplar (*P. dilatata*) is sometimes used as a substitute; and the buds of the Tacmahac Poplar (*P. balsamifera*, Linn.) are considered diuretic and antiscorbutic.

History and Habitat.—The Purple Willow is adventive in this country from Europe. It has become scattered here in many places, on wet meadows, probably by basket-makers, and blossoms in April and May. If the amount of salicin in the willows depends upon the bitterness of the bark, this species should probably furnish more than any other; we will, therefore, give the general action and history of willow under this species, in default of specific literature.

As a bitter tonic and astringent this genus has been used from the time of Dioscorides, but has attracted more attention among medical men since the year 1763, when it was brought forward as a remedy for fevers of an intermittent character. The bitterness of the bark makes it an excellent stomachic tonic, but its control over fever was never very satisfactory. Its principal utility has been found to be as an astringent tonic in convalescence from protracted diseases, atony of the digestive tract, chlorosis, chronic diarrhœa, dysentery, leucorrhœa, and kindred affections. Salicin itself appears to have a more thorough and effective action than the bark, but still cannot cover the generality of cases like quinine; it is, however, very useful in such cases of hectic fever and of diarrhœa where irritation and inflammation precludes the use of quinine.

The bark of Salix (various species) is officinal in the U. S. Ph., as is also Salicin.

PART USED AND PREPARATION.—The fresh bark, gathered during the budding season, is chopped and pounded to a pulp and weighed. Then two parts by weight of alcohol are taken, the pulp thoroughly mixed with one-sixth part of it, and the rest of the alcohol added. The whole is then poured into a well-stoppered bottle, and allowed to macerate for eight days in a dark, cool place.

The tincture thus prepared is, after straining and filtering, opaque. In thin layers it has a deep crimson color; its odor is sweet and balsamic; its taste extremely astringent, snuff-like, and bitter; and its reaction acid.

CHEMICAL CONSTITUENTS.—*Salicin*, $C_{13}H_{18}O_7$. This glucoside of the aromatic group, is found in the young bark of all species of this order, as well as in *Castoreum*, the preputial follicles of the beaver (*Castor Fiber*, Linn.). It was discovered by M. Buchner in 1828,[*] and two years afterward detected by M. Leroux,[†] though its first isolation from this species was by M. Becker.[‡] Pure salicin crystallizes in colorless prisms melting at 198° (388.4° F.), and decomposes at higher temperatures, yielding a resin, water, and salicylous acid. It possesses a bitter taste, and is soluble in 28 parts of cold water and in 30 parts of alcohol.

* *Jour. de Phar.*, xvi, 242.   † *Ann. de Chim. et de Phys.*, xliii, 440.   ‡ *Ann. der Phar.*, iv, 33.

Œm. ad nat del. et pinxt.

SÀLIX PURPÙREA, Linn.

Saligenin, or *Oxybenzyl Alcohol*, $C_7H_8O_2$, is obtained by acting upon an aqueous solution of salicin at 80° (176.0° F.) with saliva or emulsion:

Salicin.   Water.   Glucose.   Saligenin.

$$C_{13}H_{18}O_7 + H_2O = C_6H_{12}O_6 + C_7H_8O_2.$$

Saligenin results in small, brilliant rhombic plates, that melt at 82° (179.6° F.) and sublime above 100° (212° F.). It is soluble in alcohol and in hot water.

Saliretin, $C_{14}H_{14}O_3$, one of the oxybenzyl compounds, is formed by heating salicin with hydrochloric acid. It results as a yellowish amorphous powder.

Helecin, $C_{10}H_{16}O_7$.—This glucoside may be obtained by oxidizing salicin or saligenin with dilute nitric acid. It results as crystals, having a slightly bitter taste.

Salicylous Acid, or *Salicylaldehyde*, $C_7H_6O_2$, exists naturally in the leaves of the Meadow-sweet (*Spirea Ulmaria*). It can be obtained from salicin by distillation with dilute sulphuric acid and potassium dichromate. It results as a fragrant, colorless, oily liquid, having an odor similar to that of almond oil, and a burning aromatic taste; it boils at 196° (384.8° F.); congeals at 20° (−4° F.) into a translucent crystalline mass; has an acid reaction to litmus; and is soluble in water and alcohol.

[**Salicylic acid**, $C_7H_6O_3$, is a by-product of the above distillation, and only differs chemically from salicylous acid in having one atom more of oxygen in its composition.] (*Et supra*, Schorlemmer, Wittstein, Thomson.)

Tannin, resin, gum, sugar, and other general plant constituents are also present.

PHYSIOLOGICAL ACTION.—The symptoms caused in Dr. Duncan's experiments with the drug are concisely as follows:[*] Nervousness and irritability; giddiness; swelling of right parotid gland; painful flatulence; diarrhœa; pain in right hip; feeble pulse; sleeplessness; and alternate heat and coldness followed by morning perspiration.

DESCRIPTION OF PLATE 161.

1. End of a leafing branch.
2. A twig in flower, Ithaca, N. Y., May 10th, 1886.
3. Scale and stamen.
4. Stamen.
5. Double anther.

(3–5 enlarged.)

---

[*] *Trans. Hom. Med. Socy.*, N. Y., 1870, 328.

162

POPULUS.

AMERICAN ASPEN.

SYN.—POPULUS TREMULOIDES, MICHX.

COM. NAMES.—AMERICAN ASPEN† OR POPLAR;‡ UPLAND OR WHITE POPLAR;§ POPLE; (GER.) PAPPEL.

A TINCTURE OF THE FRESH INNER BARK OF POPULUS TREMULOIDES, MICHX.

Description.—This upland tree seldom reaches a height of over 40 feet. *Bark* smooth and greenish-white, except that of the old trunks; *branches* somewhat angular; *buds* large, scaly, and covered with a reddish-brown resinous varnish. *Leaves* orbicular-cordate, mostly broader than long, smooth and dark-green on both sides, and tipped with a short, sharp point; *serrations* small, nearly regular; *margin* downy; *petiole* long and slender, laterally compressed to such extent as to make it nearly ancipital. This position of the flattened petiole at right angles to the leaf-blade accounts for the agitation of the leaf during the slightest zephyr. *Inflorescence* diœcious, the male and female flowers in long, axillary, drooping, loosely imbricated aments, appearing before the leaves; *scales* oblong, cuneate, laciniate-lobed; *lobes* 3 to 4 linear, pointed, the margins fringed with long cilia; *flowers* one to each scale, springing from a calyx-like urceolate torus, which is obliquely truncated anteriorly. *Stamens* about 12; *filaments* distinct, capillary; *anthers* large and drooping, more or less quadrangular in form. *Style* none; *stigmas* 2, elongated, sessile, each bifurcating into linear lobes. *Fruit* an oblong or oblong-ovoid, pointed, 1-celled capsule, distinctly raised upon a peduncle; *seeds* ovate, numerous, minute, covered with a copious wool.

History and Habitat.—This beautiful white-trunked forest-tree, whose leaves have become the synonym of trembling, is indigenous to most parts of North America, where it is common on hillsides and in open forests. It blossoms in March or April, and fruits before the leaves are developed in May. Its wood is light and of an inferior quality, except for the lighter household utensils and the manufacture of certain chip hats. The Cree Indians—according to Mr. Walter Haydon, who has resided for some time in the Hudson Bay territory—esteem the

---

* The ancient name, *Arbor Populi,* from its having been planted to shade the public walks; or, according to Bullet, because the constant motion of the leaves resembles that of the populace.

† Or *asp,* from the German *espe,* a generic vulgarism.

‡ Sometimes applied to the Yellow Poplar or Tulip tree, *Liriodendron tulipifera* (Magnoliaceæ).

§ The white poplar is properly the British Abele, *Populus alba,* Linn.

inner bark (which they call *Metoos*) for food in early spring, considering it also as a gentle laxative and remedy for coughs. Mr. Haydon says he has eaten pounds of it without ill effects. It is very tender and sweet, and has a pleasant flavor.* The leaves and young shoots of Poplar are said to be gathered in Sweden and kept for sheep fodder in winter—a practice as old as the time of the Romans. In Kamtchatka the inner bark is used for making into bread in times of scarcity.

The previous uses of Poplar bark in medicine are all embodied in the following paragraph from Dr. C. A. Lee's article on "Indigenous Tonics :"† " The therapeutical properties of the Poplar are supposed to be nearly, if not quite, identical with those of the willow. As an anti-periodic, it has been used successfully in the treatment of intermittents, and also as an ordinary tonic, where such remedies are indicated. We have good reason for believing that its tonic properties are considerably superior to those of salix ; especially its anti-periodic power, and that there are few indigenous tonics superior to it in a certain class of cases, especially intermittents. As a stomachic tonic, the tincture has been extensively used in domestic practice, and with satisfactory effects ; also, as a vermifuge. It is thought by many to possess decided alterative properties, and those who have watched its effects closely, consider it diuretic, diaphoretic and a general depurant. It has been strongly recommended in jaundice, and in suppression and retention of urine."

PART USED AND PREPARATION.—The fresh inner bark, gathered as the leaves are falling, is treated as in the preceding drug. The resulting tincture is opaque in layers of an inch or more. In thin layers it is of a beautiful, deep, brownish-crimson color by transmitted light ; its odor is rich and woody ; its taste extremely bitter and astringent, the sensation lasting a long time without losing its intensity ; and its reaction acid.

CHEMICAL CONSTITUENTS.—*Populin*, $C_{20}H_{22}O_8(H_2O)$. This aromatic glucoside was determined by Braconnot in 1830.‡ It exists in company with *salicin* in the bark and especially the leaves, from which it may be separated by precipitating it with the carbonate of potassium from the aqueous solution. Populin crystallizes in very light, white, satiny, voluminous needles, having a bitterish-sweet licorice-like taste. It loses all its water of crystallization at 100° (212° F.), fuses at 180° (356° F.), and decomposes at higher temperatures, yielding benzoic acid. The crystals are only slightly soluble in water, more so in alcohol, and readily in dilute mineral, and acetic acids. Upon boiling with baryta water it breaks down into *salicin* and benzoic acid, and in dilute sulphuric acid into benzoic acid, glucose, and *saliretin*. This body is very similar in its properties and reactions to *salicin*, from which it seems to differ only in being in intimate combination with benzoic acid.

$$\text{Salicin.} \quad \text{Benzoic Acid.} \quad \text{Populin.}$$
$$C_{13}H_{18}O_7 + C_7H_6O_2 = C_{20}H_{22}O_8(H_2O).$$

---

* Holmes, in *Am. Jour. Phar.*, 1884, p. 619.   † *The Jour. of Mat. Med.*, Vol. II, N. S., 1860, p. 364.
‡ *Ann. de Chim. et de Phys.*, Vol. XLIV, 296.

Cm. ad nat.del.et pinxt.

PÓPULUS TREMULOÌDES , Michx .

Oil of Populus.—This body, obtained by aqueous distillation of the leaf buds, is colorless, lighter than water, and has a pleasant balsamic odor. The name *Tacamahaca* has been improperly applied to this product, to which, however, it bears no resemblance except, mayhap, in its odor.* The name was probably applied here on account of the oil having been extracted from the buds of the Balsam Poplar or Tacamahac (*Populus balsamifera*, Linn.).

Salicin,† starch, resin, and gum have also been determined.

PHYSIOLOGICAL ACTION.—Very few symptoms have as yet been credited to this drug, our experience with it being mostly clinical. Poplar bark, however, causes increased secretion of urine, nausea and vomiting, slight purging of bilious matters, and burning in the stomach.‡

DESCRIPTION OF PLATE 162.

1. A branchlet with half-ripe fruits, from Binghamton, N. Y., May 5, 1885.
2. A scale.
3. Pistil.
4. Fruit.
5. End of leafy branch.
6. A leaf.
   (2–4 enlarged.)

---

* *Tacamahaca* is a solid resinous product of the South American *Elaphrium tomentosum*, Jacq. (Burceraceæ.)
† See preceding plant, 161.   ‡ Dr. Hale, *N. Am. Jour. Hom.*, 1867, p. 391.

163

ABIES NIGRA.

BLACK SPRUCE.

SYN.—ABIES NIGRA, POIR.; PINUS NIGRA, AIT.; ABIES DENTICULATA, MICHX.; PINUS RUBRA, LAMB.

COM. NAMES.—BLACK SPRUCE, DOUBLE SPRUCE; (GER.) SCHWARTZ-TANNE.

A TINCTURE OF THE GUM EXUDATION OF THE TRUNK OF ABIES NIGRA, POIR.

Description.—This beautiful evergreen tree attains a growth varying between 30 and 70 feet in height, and 15 to 50 feet in breadth at the base. *Leaves* acerose, short, quadrilateral, very dark green, and projecting in all directions. *Anthers* tipped with a rounded, recurved appendage; *pollen* similar to that of *Pinus*—i. e., of three united grains.† *Cones* ¾ to 1½ inch long, ovate or ovate-oblong, mostly recurved, persistent, hanging from or near the ends of the branches especially at the summit of the tree; *scales* thin, rigid, persistent on the axis; *edges* generally eroded; *seeds* and their wings about two-thirds the length of the scale.

Abies.—This, the genus Abies of Linnæus, Tournefort and others, is synonymous with Picea of Link, but not with the genus Picea of Linnæus. It is characterized as follows: *Buds* scaly; *leaves* short, persistent, all of one form and foliaceous, scattered, or more or less 2-ranked, never fascicled. *Flowers* monœcious. *Fertile catkins* lateral or terminal on the branches of the preceding year; *sterile catkins* scattered, or sometimes clustered, in the axils of the leaves of the previous year's growth. *Cones* pendent, at the base of the new growth of the season; *scales* or flat open *carpels* imbricate, thin and even (not prickly-tipped nor thickened), situated in the axil of a bract; *bracts* subtending the scales, very small. *Seeds* 2, inverted, adhering to the base of each scale; *foramen* looking downward; *testa* smooth, coriaceous or ligneous; *wing* membranaceous. *Embryo* in the axis of the albumen; *albumen* sarcous or oleaceous; *cotyledons* 2 to 15.

Coniferæ.—This superb and wide-spread family is composed of evergreen (Ex. Larix) trees or shrubs, with branching, generally excurrent, trunks, rich in

---

* The classical Latin name.

† Or a single grain with bulged extremities, sometimes described as two grains with a curved connective.

gummy or resinous juice. *Wood* somewhat intermediate between woody fibre and vessels, and marked in circular disks. *Leaves* scattered or fascicled, sometimes opposite, linear, awl-shaped or acerose, rigid, and generally evergreen. *Inflorescence* amentaceous; *flowers* monœcious or diœcious, destitute of calyx or corolla. *Fertile flowers: pistils* absent, or represented by an open scale or metamorphosed leaf; *sterile flowers* consisting of one or more stamens; *stamens* generally monadelphous, situated upon an axis, thus forming a loose, deciduous catkin or spike. *Fruit* varying greatly in the different tribes, from a hard, bony nut with an edible "meat," to a soft, edible drupe. *Carpels* either wanting or represented by an open scale; *ovules* orthotropous, naked, not enclosed in an ovary; *embryo* consisting of a pair of opposite, or several whorled cotyledons.

This family of plants is one producing many valuable drugs, useful exudations, varied woods, and ornamental trees. Of the drugs, exudations, and constituents, the turpentines, balsams, and pitches rank highest. They are in general as follows: The common European and Russian turpentines, *Terebinthina vulgaris*, are derived from *Pinus sylvestris*, Linn.; the common American turpentine, *Terebinthina vulgaris*, together with common frankincense, *Thus Americana*, a concrete oleo-resin, and *Oleum Terebinthinæ*, from *Pinus australis*, Michx. (*P. palustris*, Mill.), and *Pinus Tæda*, Linn.; Canada balsam and *Terebinthina Canadensis*, from *Abies balsamea*, Marsh. (*A. balsamifera*, Michx.; *Pinus balsamea*, Linn.; *Picea balsamea*, Loud.), and from *Pinus Frazeri;* while Canada pitch, *Pix Canadensis*, is yielded by *Abies Canadensis*, Michx. Austrian turpentine is derived from *Pinus Laricio*, Poir.; Bordeaux turpentine, or galipot, from *Pinus pinaster*, Ait. (*P. maritima*, DC.); Strasburgh turpentine, *Terebinthina argentoratensis*, from *Pinus Picea*, Linn. (*Abies Picea*, Lindl.; *Abies pectinata*, DC.); Venice turpentine, *Terebinthina Veneta* or *laricinia*, from the European *Abies Larix*, Lam. (*Pinus Larix*, Linn., *Larix Europæa*, DC.); Pacific coast turpentine from *Abies Menziesii*, Lindl.; Damarra turpentine from *Damarra australis;* and the Chilian Dombeya turpentine from *Dombeya excelsa*. Hungarian balsam, *Balsamum Hungaricum*, is a product of *Pinus Pumilio*, Willd.; and Carpathian balsam of *Pinus Cembra*, Linn., and *Pinus pinea*. Burgundy pitch, *Pix Burgundica*, is derived from *Abies excelsa*, DC. (*Pinus Abies*, Linn.); while *Pix Nigra* or *Arida*, together with *Pix Liquida*, otherwise known as Archangel or Stockholm tar, are obtained upon destructive distillation of various coniferous roots, but especially those of *Pinus sylvestris*, Linn., and *Pinus Ledebourii*, Endl. (*Larix Sibirica*, Ledeb.). Rosin, *Resin* or *Colophony*, is the residue after the distillation of volatile oil from the turpentine of *Pinus palustris*, Mill., and other species. Juniper tar, *Pyroleum Oxycedri* or *Oleum Cadinum*, is a product of the Cade (*Juniperus oxycedrus*, Linn.). Morocco, or Barbarian Sandarach, is obtained from *Callitris quadrivalvis*, Vent. Rich. (*Thuja articulata*, Desf.); *Gummi Orenburgense* and Manna of Briançon from *Abies Larix*, Lam.; Oil of Sayin from *Juniperus Sabina*, Linn.; and *Fructus Juniperi* from *Juniperus Virginiana*, Linn. Edible nuts are produced by *Pinus pinea*, *Pinus Cembra*, and *Pinus Lambertiana;* edible drupes by *Taxus baccata*, and beverages by *Abies nigra*, in America, and *Dacydium taxifolium*, in New Zealand.

We have provings in the Homœopathic Materia Medica of the Scotch fir, *Pinus sylvestris ;* the sugar-pine, *Pinus Lambertiana ;* savin, *Juniperus Sabina,* and of *Cupressus australis,* besides those members of the order treated of in this work.

History and Habitat.—Abies nigra is a native of the Northern States of America, as far west as Wisconsin, and of the Canadas and British America, where it flowers in early spring and matures its fruit in autumn. The black spruce greatly resembles the Norway spruce (*Abies excelsa,* Lindl.) in its growth, and is judged by many prominent arborists and arboriculturists to be much more graceful in the drooping curves of its branches and the luxuriance of its foliage ; its twin species, the white spruce (*Abies alba,* Michx.), is certainly one of the very finest of all evergreens.

Concerning the uses of this tree, and other American spruces, Rafinesque says,* "The bark of spruce trees is sudorific, and in extensive use for tanning leather,† also to dye of a brick-red color. The inner bark is used by empirics, in powder and tea, for bowel and stomach complaints, rheumatism and gravel. The timber is valuable for masts and spars," in fact the most valuable we have for use in this direction. "The resin exuding from the trees is nearly like frankincense. Josselin says that it is very good in powder over wounds to reproduce the flesh. Spruce beer is an American beverage, made by the Indians with twigs and cones of spruces, boiled in maple syrup. Now it is chiefly made with molasses and yeast ; when no spruce is put in, it is only molasses beer. The proper spruce beer is a palatable and healthy drink, powerfully antiscorbutic. The discoverers of Canada were cured of the scurvy by it, since which it has become in common use in Canada, the Northern States, and even in Europe. The essence of spruce‡ is an article of exportation, used as naval stores ; spruce beer may be made by it in a short time, and anywhere."§

Abies nigra has no officinal recognizance in the Pharmacopœias.

PART USED AND PREPARATION.—Take two parts by weight of the gum, dissolve in nine parts of 95 per cent. alcohol, and filter. This tincture has a beautiful orange color by transmitted light, the full odor and taste of raw spruce gum, and an acid reaction.

CHEMICAL CONSTITUENTS.—The resin of this species is scanty and insufficient to produce pitch or turpentine in marketable quantity. The "essence of spruce," before mentioned, probably contains an essential oil. The tincture contains a large quantity of resin ; more in fact than that of Abies Canadensis. The specific chemical bodies and properties are unknown.

---

* *Medical Flora,* vol. 2, p. 183.

† *Abies Canadensis,* Michx., Hemlock spruce.

‡ A concentrated aqueous decoction of the young twigs.

§ Spruce beer may be made from the extract as follows : Take one part of essence of spruce and seventy-six parts of water, boil, strain, allow to cool, and add ninety-six parts warm water, seven parts molasses and one part of yeast. Allow the mixture to ferment, and bottle strongly while fermenting.

PHYSIOLOGICAL ACTION.—Our proving of this drug by Dr. Leaman,* though exhibiting a few quite specific symptoms, does not afford an insight into the primary action upon the system.

DESCRIPTION OF PLATE 163.

1. Distant view of tree, Binghamton, N. Y.
2. Branch-tip, with winter cones.
3. Seed.
4. Outer aspect of scale.
5. Inner aspect of scale, one seed gone.
6. End of branch, with female catkin.
7. Male catkin.
8. Fertile flower from female catkin.
9. Face view of ruptured anther-cell, with its scale (enlarged).
10. Profile of same (enlarged).
11. Pollen x 150.

* *Ohio Med. and Surg. Rep.*, 1.

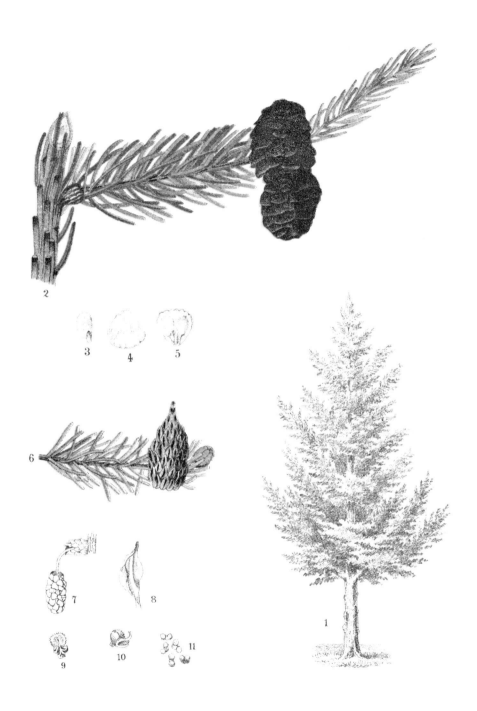

Œm.ad nat.del.et pinxt.

ÀBIES NÌGRA, Poir.

164

ABIES CANADENSIS.

HEMLOCK.

SYN.—ABIES CANADENSIS, MICHX.; PINUS CANADENSIS, WILLD., LINN.; PINUS-ABIES CANADENSIS, MARSH.
COM. NAMES.—HEMLOCK, HEMLOCK-SPRUCE, HEMLOCK-FIR; (GER.) CANADISCHE EDELTANNE.

A TINCTURE OF THE FRESH BARK AND YOUNG BUDS OF ABIES CANADENSIS, MICHX.

Description.—This evergreen forest tree attains a height of from 60 to 80 feet, and a width of 40 to 60. *Trunk* 2 to 3 or more feet in diameter, excurrent but tending to deliquescence; *wood* coarse and poor, it weighs 23 lbs. per cubic foot and has a sp. gr. of .384;* *branches* horizontal,* the uppermost pendulous at their apices. *Leaves* stiff, short, flat, linear, obtuse, irregularly crowded, but mostly spreading in two directions, thus appearing 2-ranked; they are dark, rich, glossy green above, and whitish by a single silvery line each side of the midrib underneath, making a branch upturned by the wind appear silvery-white; *petioles* short and slender. *Sterile aments* small, globose, composed of a few stamens, and surrounded at the base of the column by a few erect, brownish scales; *filaments* short; *anthers* capitate, with an apiculate crest; *cells* 2, confluent; *dehiscence* transverse; *pollen* simple, saucer-shaped. *Cones* ovoid, persistent, small, ½ to 1 inch long, pendent on the ends of the declined branchlets of the preceding year; *scales* few, thin, markedly imbricate, obtuse, ligneous, with a coriaceous edge; longer than the bracts and persistent on the axis; *bracts* broadly ovate, truncate. *Seeds* with a long, thin, membranaceous *wing*, greatly resembling in outline that of the fly. Read Abies and Coniferæ, under the preceding drug.

History and Habitat.—This common native tree is, when young, the most graceful of our evergreens. It is hardy, yet delicate in its outline, its feathery-tipped branches reminding one of the plumose ends of a bouquet of pampas grasses. When old it grows more rugged and sombre, but increases in the picturesque. Its foliage is soft to the hand, beautiful in sunshine and shadow, and rests the snow-blinded eye with that peace that verdure resplendent in light and

---

* My father, an excellent artist and etcher, kindly sketched, at my instigation, the trees in Plates 164 and 165. In this figure he unfortunately allowed his ideas of the picturesque, to somewhat supersede mine of the horizontality, of the branches.

shade alone can give. Hemlock-spruce abounds in the northern United States, the Canadas and British America, extending a little farther south than the black-spruce, with which it forms immense forests in the north. It flowers in May and ripens its cones in autumn.

Hemlock bark is largely used in tanning; though inferior to oak, its greater abundance predominates in its favor in this country. The timber, as before hinted, is very coarse-grained and poor, yet in thoroughly-protected places it is very durable; in carpentry it is used extensively for joists, scantling, girders and sub-flooring.

The stimulating effect of hemlock is well known and greatly utilized. A tired hunter arises fresh and invigorated from his bed of hemlock boughs, and the patient of the city physician, seeking health in our northern interiors, finds supreme comfort in a bath, in which hemlock leaves have been slowly steeping for some hours before his ablution, and quiet, refreshing slumber awaits him upon his couch of soft branches. A strong decoction of hemlock bark has received the praise of empirics and the laity as an astringent enema in diarrhœa and injection for leucorrhœa, prolapsus uteri, etc.; the oil as a liniment in croup, rheumatismus and other disorders requiring its stimulant action; and the essence as a diuretic and a remedy to allay gastric irritation and colic, and to correct acidity of the stomach. A decoction of the bark has been used to produce abortion with dangerous effects, tending toward serious peritonitis. Pregnant ewes are said to lose their lambs from gnawing the bark of the hemlock.

The officinal part of this species in the U. S. Ph. is *Pix Canadensis;* its preparation *Emplastrum Picis Canadensis.*

PART USED AND PREPARATION.—The fresh bark and young buds are pounded to a pulp and weighed. Then two parts by weight of alcohol are taken, and after mixing the pulp thoroughly with one-sixth part of it, the rest of the alcohol is added. After stirring the whole well, it is poured into a well-stoppered bottle and allowed to stand eight days in a dark, cool place. The tincture, separated by filtering, should be opaque in quantity, and show a deep, reddish, orange-brown color in thin layers; it should retain the exact odor and taste of the bruised leaves and branches, and exhibit a strongly acid reaction.

CHEMICAL CONSTITUENTS.—*Pix Canadensis* (Hemlock pitch, Hemlock gum, Canada pitch). This substance, the prepared resinous exudation from the trunk of the hemlock, is hard and brittle in cold weather, soft and conforming in the warmer seasons, and melts at 198° (388.4° F.). It is of a dark yellow-brown color when fresh, but oxidizes and becomes almost black on exposure. It contains a resin, and a volatile oil, uninvestigated, but supposed to be similar to the turpentine obtained from *Abies balsamea.*

Oil of Hemlock* (oil of spruce). This essential oil is obtained on distillation of the leaves, a process carried on to a large extent in some portions of the State of New York.

---

* *Ut supra*, Flück. & Han. Pharmacographia.

660 [164–3]

As far as I can determine, this tree has not been specifically examined as to its constituents.

PHYSIOLOGICAL ACTION. — Abies Canadensis causes, according to Gatchell,* vertigo and weakness; great hunger, with burning and distention of the abdomen; thirst; increased heart's action; restlessness and chilliness; the urine is increased and of a straw-color. The drug appears to cause a torpor of the liver, resulting in a diminished secretion of bile, pain in the right shoulder-blade, and constipation.

DESCRIPTION OF PLATE 164.

1. Tree, Binghamton, N. Y.
2. A winter spray in fruit.
3. Leaf, under surface.
4. Seed (slightly enlarged).
5. Inner face of a scale, with one seed removed.
6. Outer view of a scale.
7. Male catkin (enlarged).
8. Stamen (enlarged), showing the dehiscence of the anther-cell.
9. Pollen, two views, x 200.

* Hale, *New Rem.*, 4th ed., pp. 17 and 18.

164.

. ad nat del. et pinxt.

ÀBIES CANADÉNSIS, Michx.

165

THUJA.

AMERICAN ARBOR VITÆ.

SYN.—THUJA OCCIDENTALIS, LINN.; CEDRUS LYCEA, GER.
COM. NAMES.—AMERICAN ARBOR VITÆ, WESTERN ARBOR VITÆ, TREE
OF LIFE, WHITE CEDAR,† HACKMATACK,‡ THUJA; (FR.) THUIA
DU CANADA; (GER.) LEBENSBAUM.

A TINCTURE OF THE FRESH YOUNG TWIGS, LEAVES, AND BLOSSOMS OF THUJA
OCCIDENTALIS, LINN.

Description.—This spiry evergreen attains a height of from 20 to 50 feet,
though generally not above 40, and a diameter of about 10 to 20 feet through
the greatest breadth of foliage. *Sprays* or *branchlets* very flat, spreading, and
ancipital. *Leaves* small, appressed, tightly imbricated in 4 rows, persistent. They
are of two kinds on alternate or separated branchlets; one form is awl-shaped;
the other short, squamose, and obtuse; both forms have a small flattened dorsal
gland, filled with a thin aromatic turpentine. *Inflorescence* minute, terminal, ovoid
aments; *flowers* monœcious on different branchlets; *fertile aments* composed of
a few imbricated scales. *Filaments* forming scale-like connectives, bearing 4 concave anther-cells. *Cones* nodding, ovoid before ripening, spreading or gaping
when mature; *scales* blunt, arranged in three rows of two scales each, attached
to the rhachis by their bases, the outer pair seedless; *rhachis* composed of three
nearly separate metamorphosed scales, each tipped with a rounded stigma-form
body (Fig. 7). *Seeds* 6, double-winged, 2 in each of the second pair of scales,

* Concerning the etymology of Thuja, Dr. Mayrhoffer says (Essay on Thuja occidentalis, *Metcalf's Provings*,
N. Y., 1853): "In the time of Francis I, king of France, this tree was imported into France from Canada. The first
specimen was seen by Clusius in the royal garden of Fontainebleau, and a tolerably correct figure and description of it
were furnished by him under the name of *arbor vitæ*. (Caroli Clusii Rarior. Plantar. Histor., 1601.) The Greek name
ϑύα, also ϑύεια or ϑύια, from ϑύειν, *suffre*, to fumigate, points to a resinous tree, and is first seen in Theophrastus Lesbius, a
disciple of Aristotle. In his work, ' περι φυτων ἱστορια;,' he describes a tree resembling the cypress, and called ϑύον (δένδρον)
or ϑύα (ἰδέα, *species*). Roman authors Latinized the word ϑύα, changing it to Thya, Thuya, Thuia, Thuja, as ϑύς, gen.
ϑύεος, was changed to *thus*, gen. *thuris*, and the word κυπαρισσος, to *cupressus*. The native region of the Thuja of Theophrastus, according to his account, is the territory of Cyrene, in Africa, and especially the region in which the temple of
Jupiter Ammon was situated; whereas our Thuja is a native of North America." It would seem by this that the Thuja
of Theophrastus is *Thuja articulata*, Vahl., a native of Barbary.
† The true white cedar is *Cupressus thyoides*, Linn.
‡ The hackmatack is *Larix Americana*, Michx.

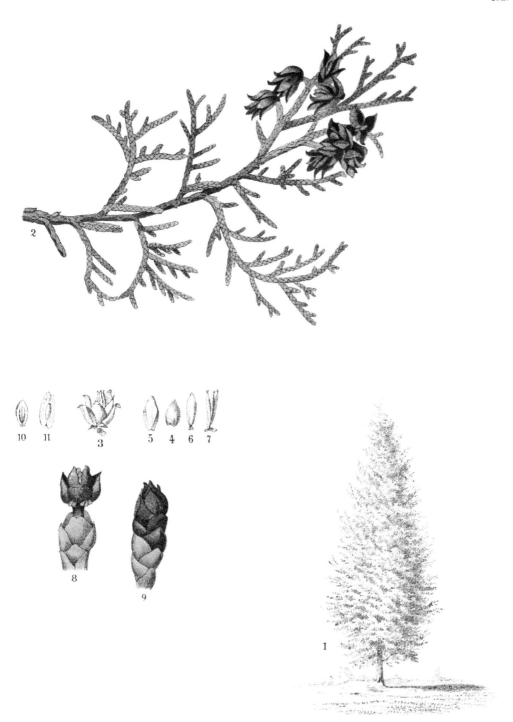

℮m.ad nat.del.et pinxt.

THÙJA OCCIDENTÀLIS, Linn.

1 in each of the inner pair;* *wings* lateral, equal; apparently emarginate, but on close inspection it will be seen that one wing is attached to the seed on a higher plane than the other (Fig. 11). *Cotyledons* 2. Read description of Coniferæ, under Abies nigra, 163.

History and Habitat.—This beautiful native tree abounds in the upper zones of North America, from the State of Pennsylvania northward, where it often forms what are commonly known as cedar-swamps. It grows upon the rocky banks of rivers and in low, swampy spots, blossoming from May until June, and maturing its fruit in autumn. The Arbor Vitæ assumes a conical form with such true lines as to appear "clipped," thus forming one of our most valued high-hedge trees. Its use in this direction is enhanced by the fact that it bears the shears well, and remains in full foliage, and beautiful, in any form to which it may be cut. The wood is light and soft, but extremely durable; it is seldom used, however, on account of the smallness of the trunk affording lumber of no useful size. There are four other species of this genus out of cultivation, viz.: the Chinese *Thuja orientalis*, the Javanese *Thuja dolabrata*, the Barbarian *Thuja articulata*, and the *Thuja cupressoides* of the Cape of Good Hope.

Concerning the previous medical uses of this plant, Rafinesque covers it almost fully in stating:† "Ointment of fresh leaves with bear's fat, excellent for rheumatism; decoction useful in coughs, fevers, cacœhyma, scurvy, gout, etc.; distilled water for dropsy; poultices of the cones and *polypodium*,‡ in powder with milk, remove the worst rheumatic pains." Farther uses are given in later works. The most striking to us as homœopaths is that of an application of the tincture to venereal warts (condylomata), which it removes in from three to four weeks. This is especially proven by Hahnemann, who says:§ "The following list of the pure symptoms‖ caused by this powerful plant furnishes to the homœopathic physician the means of applying it with advantage in the treatment of certain serious diseases for which no remedy has hitherto been found. He will see, for example, that the juice of the Thuja should cure specifically 'condylomes vénériens,' when not combined (or complicated) with other diseases; and experience proves that it is the only effectual means to employ against this affection."

Thuja was added to the U. S. Ph. at the last revision.¶

PART USED AND PREPARATION.—The fresh branchlets, leaves, and flowers are chopped and pounded to a pulp and weighed. Then two-thirds by weight of alcohol are taken, the pulp thoroughly mixed with it, and the whole strained through a piece of new linen, and allowed to stand eight days, in a well-stoppered

---

* Dr. Torrey, in his *Flora of the State of New York*, says, "Seeds 2 (or by abortion 1) under each scale." Prof. Asa Gray says, in his *Lessons in Botany*, 1874, . . . "each bearing 2 erect ovules." I examined, upon this point, from twenty to thirty cones, taken separately and carefully from different branchlets on each of a dozen or more trees, to corroborate the statement made as above. All cones examined answered the description I have given.

† *Medical Flora*, vol. 2, p. 268.

‡ *Polypodium vulgare*, the common polypody or female fern. Dr. John King, in his *American Dispensatory*, makes this read *Podophyllum*. It matters little.

§ *Mat. Med. Pura*, article Thuja.

‖ *Loc. cit.*　　　　¶ That great process, which added *Sapo Viridis*, while it dismissed *Arsenicum*.

bottle, in a dark, cool place. The tincture, separated from this mixture by filtration, has a deep orange-brown color by transmitted light, an odor of the bruised leaves, a bitter and astringent taste, and an acid reaction.

CHEMICAL CONSTITUENTS.—*Thujin*, $C_{20} H_{22} O_{12}$. This glucoside occurs in the green parts of the plant. It forms glistening, lemon-yellow, minute crystals, having an astringent taste, and soluble in both water and alcohol.

Thujetin.[*]—$C_{28} H_{28} O_{16}$. When thujin is heated with a dilute mineral acid, it breaks down into glucose, and this new crystalline body, soluble in alcohol, insoluble in water:

$$\underset{\text{Thujin.}}{(C_{20} H_{22} O_{12})_2} + \underset{\text{Water.}}{(H_2 O)_4} = \underset{\text{Glucose.}}{(C_6 H_{12} O_6)_2} + \underset{\text{Thujetin.}}{(C_{14} H_{14} O_8)_2}.$$

Thujenin, $C_{28} H_{24} O_{14}$. If, however, hydrochloric acid is used and the heating less prolonged, another crystalline body is yielded, having the composition above given, and differing chemically from thujetin by its containing $(H_2 O)_2$ less. Its solubility is the same:

$$\underset{\text{Thujin.}}{(C_{20} H_{22} O_{12})_2} + \underset{\text{Water.}}{(H_2 O)_2} = \underset{\text{Glucose.}}{(C_6 H_{12} O_6)_2} + \underset{\text{Thujetin.}}{(C_{14} H_{12} O_7)_2}.$$

Thujetic acid, $C_{28} H_{22} O_{13}$. When thujin is dissolved in baryta water, it takes up one molecule of water, leaves its glucose in the menstruum, and forms a yellow solution, which, on boiling, deposits orange-yellow crystals of this acid, having the same solubility as the preceding resultants:[†]

$$\underset{\text{Thujin.}}{(C_{20} H_{22} O_{12})_2} + \underset{\text{Water.}}{H_2 O} = \underset{\text{Glucose.}}{(C_6 H_{12} O_6)_2} + \underset{\text{Thujetic acid.}}{C_{28} H_{22} O_{13}}.$$

Pinipicrin, $C_{22} H_{36} O_{11}$. This glucoside has been extracted from the young leafy branchlets of this tree as well as from the needles of *Pinus sylvestris*. It forms a yellow, bitter, amorphous, hygroscopic powder, soluble in both water and alcohol, and becoming liquid at 100° (212° F.). Like all glucosides, it breaks down under the addition of water, when heated with dilute mineral acids. In this instance, boiling with dilute sulphuric acid converts this body into glucose and *ericinol*:[‡]

$$\underset{\text{Pinipicrin.}}{C_{22} H_{36} O_{11}} + \underset{\text{Water.}}{(H_2 O)_2} = \underset{\text{Glucose.}}{(C_6 H_{12} O_6)_2} + \underset{\text{Ericinol.}}{C_{10} H_{16} O}.$$

Oil of Thuja.—This colorless or greenish-yellow volatile oil, has a camphoraceous odor and taste, is soluble in alcohol, has a density of 0.925, boils at 190° (374° F.), and for the greater part at 193° to 197° (379.4° to 386.6° F.). It is a mixture of two oxygenized oils. (Wittstein.)

---

[*] *Thujogenin, Thujigenin.*
[†] Fownes's *Elementary Chemistry*, p. 582.
[‡] See under Ericaceæ, 100.

Pino-tannic acid,* $C_7 H_8 O_4$. This acid may be extracted from the green portions of the tree. It results as a brownish-yellow powder, becomes soft and glutinous at 100° (212° F.), and dissolves readily in both water and alcohol. (Wittstein.)

Kawalier† determined, beside the oil, thujin, pino-tannic acid, and pinipicrin, a gelatinous compound, sugar, tannin, and two uninvestigated resins.

PHYSIOLOGICAL ACTION.—" The pathogenesis of Thuja was published by Hahnemann in the fifth volume of the *Reine Arzneimittellehre*.

" The Austrian provings, which are entirely confirmatory of Hahemann's, show that the main action of Thuja is on the genito-urinary organs, with the anus, and on the skin. It causes copious and frequent urination; burning in several parts of the mucous tract; pains of various kinds in the penis; inflammation of the pre-puce and glans; ulcers, tubercles, and other excrescences on the sexual organs, with itching and profuse sweating; and, in the female, leucorrhœa. The sexual appetite was depressed, and the catamenia retarded. Burning, itching, swelling, and mucous discharge occurred at the anus; and on the skin generally, but espe-cially in the ano-genital region, tubercles and warts were developed. In the neigh-boring mucous membranes similar phenomena appeared, but naturally of moister character." ‡

The action of the drug in causing great flatulence and distension of the abdo-men, with rumbling and colic, leads us back to Bocclerus, who says,§ *"Folia (thujæ) resolvunt, exsiccant, flatus pellunt,"* etc.; while the excessive chilliness, heat, and profuse sweat, point to a remedy often indicated in intermittent fevers. The peculiar action of this drug is one difficult of explanation.

DESCRIPTION OF PLATE 165.

1. Distant view of tree; Binghamton, N. Y.
2. A winter branch in fruit.
3. A cone.
4. Scale of outer row.
5. Scale of 2d row.
6. Scale of inner row.
7. Centre scales or rhachis.
8. Male catkin (enlarged).
9. Female catkin (enlarged).
10. Inner view of outer scale.
11. Seed (enlarged).

---

* Pini-tannic acid.
† *Chem. Gaz.*, 1859, pp. 61 and 88.

‡ Hughes, *Pharmacodynamics*, 1876, p. 745.
§ *Cynosura Materiæ Medicæ Pauli Herrmanii*, editio ii, 1747.

166
JUNIPERUS VIRGINIANA.

RED CEDAR.

SYN.—JUNIPERUS VIRGINIANA, LINN.; JUNIPERUS SABINA, HOOK. (NOT LINN.).
COM. NAMES.—RED CEDAR, JUNIPER, OR SAVIN; PENCIL CEDAR; (FR.) CÉDRE DE VIRGINIE; (GER.) VIRGINISCHE CEDER, ROTH CEDER.

A TINCTURE OF THE FRESH TWIGS OF JUNIPERUS VIRGINIANA, LINN.

Description.—This evergreen species often attains a growth of from 60 to 90 feet in the East, though in the West it seldom grows much larger than a full-sized shrub. *Wood* very durable and compact, odorous, and of a reddish color. *Branches* more or less horizontal. *Leaves* small, usually opposite in pairs, not articulated, connate-decurrent upon the stems, awl-shaped, flattish, and scalaceous; upon the young branches acute, flattish, appressed imbricate, and often furnished with a dorsal resin-gland; *midrib* or *nerve* none. *Inflorescence* small catkins terminating lateral branchlets; *flowers* diœcious, or in some cases monœcious. *Fertile catkins* ovoid, scales 3 to 6, scarious, coalescent, each ovuled, and all uniting in fruit to form a berry. *Sterile catkins* formed of 3 to 6 peltate scales; *anther-cells* at the base of the scales. *Fruit* a small, roundish-ovoid, berry-like drupe, erect upon its pedicel-like branchlet and covered with a bluish bloom. *Seeds* 1 to 3, bony, wingless; the lower portion covered with a scarious membrane, smooth; the upper traversed by a smooth ridge, dividing it into two verrucose parts; *cotyledons* two.

History and Habitat.—The Red Cedar is common in sterile, dry soils in nearly all portions of North America, Japan, and the West Indies, flowering in May.

This tree is noted, above all others in this country, for the durability of its wood, no matter how exposed to changes of weather; many of the houses along the Jersey shore of New York Bay, built in the early days of the present century and shingled with cedar, have roofs still in excellent condition, and many posts for the support of outbuildings still stand stanch and firm. The highly-colored and fragrant heart-wood is largely used in the manufacture of lead-pencils, pails, tubs, and various household utensils subjected to wettings. Boxes made of the wood

---

* Celtic, *Jeneprus*, rough, from the scaly foliage.

are useful for the preservation of woollens and furs, it being an excellent insectifuge; for this purpose, also, many people scatter the chips in their closets, trunks, etc.

Sir W. Hooker considers Juniperus Virginiana identical with the European J. Sabina, the only true point of distinction being in the fruit (Figs. 6 and 8); that of J. Virginiana being erect and somewhat ovate, while that of J. Sabina is pendent or at least pendulous, larger, and more spherical. The leaves of J. Virginiana are much less rich in oil, the yield being nearly eighteen times less from this species than from Sabina.

The leaves of the Cedar are used by the Cree Indians as a diuretic;* they also form a good epispastic when made into a cerate; the berries, in decoction, are diaphoretic and emmenagogue; the oil is largely used as an application in arthritic and podagric affections, rheumatic, rheumatoid, traumatic; and the excrescences (cedar apples), often found upon the branchlets, are quite extensively used in domestic practice, in doses of from ten to thirty grains every four hours, as an anthelmintic.

In reference to the Western Juniper, *J. occidentalis*, Mr. J. R. Dodge says:† "The fruit of this tree is a large and tuberculated berry, sweet and nutritious, especially when it is first ripe; nevertheless it has a resinous taste, similar to that of all Junipers. It is largely consumed by the Indians of Arizona and New Mexico, who gather great quantities for winter store. When dried and ground into flour, mixed with water, kneaded into a hard mass, and dried in the sun, it has a chaffy look, a brownish-yellow color, is very light, easily digested, and not offensive. . . . . . Mexicans consume this fruit in large quantities, and it constitutes an article of trade among them."

Juniperus Virginiana is not officinal in the U. S. Ph. In the Eclectic Materia Medica the preparations are: *Oleum Juniperi Virginianeæ* and *Linamentum Olei*.‡

PART USED AND PREPARATION.—The fresh young twigs, gathered in May, are dealt with as in the preceding drug. The resulting tincture has a deep reddish-brown color by transmitted light, a strong balsamic odor, a bitterish, astringent and pleasant terebinthic taste, and an acid reaction.

CHEMICAL CONSTITUENTS.—*Cedren*, $C_{15}H_{24}$.§ This aromatic body, having no camphoraceous odor, a specific gravity of .948, and boiling at 237° (458.6° F.), may be obtained from the liquid portion of the oil that distils over at 264°–268° (507.3°–514.4° F.), by redistillation over metallic potash.

Oil of Cedar.—This aromatic oil is obtained from the wood by distillation, one bushel of chips yielding about a half pint. When extracted, it results as a soft white crystalline mass at 27° (80.6° F.), having a peculiar aromatic odor; when dry it distils almost entirely at 282° (539.6° F.). Cedar oil has a more feeble odor than that of Sabina, and a different polarity.

---

* Haydon, E. M. Holmes, *Am. Jour. Phar.*, 1884, 619.
† *Food-products of the N. A. Indians, U. S. Ag. Rep.*, 1870, 411.
‡ Oils of Cedar, Cajeput, Cloves, and Sassafras.
§ Gerhardt (Wittstein).

166.

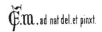 .ad nat del.et pinxt.

JUNÍPERUS VIRGINIÀNA, Linn.

Cedren-Camphor, $C_{15}H_{26}O$.—This aromatic, almost tasteless body, may be extracted from the oil from which it results as satiny needles, soluble in alcohol, and fusing at 79° (174.2° F.).

A bitter extractive, gum, fatty matter, resin, and tannic acid, have also been separated from the plant.*

PHYSIOLOGICAL ACTION.—Dr. C. A. Lee records a case of a woman who took an ounce of the oil to produce an abortion. Her symptoms were: Rigors; fever; thirst; raving while in fever, exhausted when out; vomiting of black then green matter; griping pain in the bowels; great difficulty in passing urine; uterine hemorrhage, accompanied with labor-like pains; great purging, with stupor without being able to regain consciousness, and death. Many other cases of poisoning by the oil taken in doses of from one drachm to an ounce, for the purpose of abortion or as an emmenagogue, show Juniperus Virginiana to cause severe venous congestion throughout the body. The class of symptoms are in general as follows: Raving or quiet delirium, followed by stupor; pupils dilated; veins of face, head, and neck fully distended; face swollen and livid, or lurid; great thirst, nausea, and vomiting; abdomen swollen, hot, and very painful; great heaving of the chest in effort at inspiration, with stertor and a general appearance of impending apoplexy; slow pulse; and violent convulsions.

DESCRIPTION OF PLATE 166.

1. End of fruiting branch, Ithaca, N. Y.
2. End of fertile branchlet.
3. Sterile flower head.
4. Scale of staminate rachis, showing unopened anthers.
5. Same, with anthers open.
6. Fruit.
7. Seed.
8. Fruit of *Juniperus Sabina*.
9. Distant view of tree.

(2–5 and 7 enlarged.)

---

* Jenks, *Am. Jour. Phar.*, xiv., 235.

SERIES

PHÆNOGAMIA.

Plants producing true flowers and seeds.

CLASS

MONOCOTYLEDONS.

Plants whose stems exhibit no distinction as to bark, wood
and pith; the woody fibre and vessels being in bundles
and scattered in the cellular tissue. Leaves generally parallel-veined and entire. Embryo containing a solitary cotyledon.

167
ARUM TRIPHYLLUM.

INDIAN TURNIP.

SYN.—ARISÆMA TRIPHYLLUM, TORR.; ARUM TRIPHYLLUM, LINN.; ARISÆMA ATRORUBENS, BLUME.

COM. NAMES.—INDIAN TURNIP, JACK-IN-THE-PULPIT, MEMORY-ROOT; (FR.) GOUET À TROIS FEUILLES; (GER.) DREIBLÄTTIGER ARON.

A TINCTURE OF THE FRESH CORM OF ARISÆMA TRIPHYLLUM, TORR.

Description.—This excessively acrid, almost caustic, erect herb, grows to a height of from 8 to 20 inches. *Root* a coarsely reticulated or wrinkled corm, giving off numerous branched rootlets from its juncture with the stalk. *Stalk* composed of the united petioles and scape, sheathed below by a few long membraneous scales. *Leaves* one or two, on long petioles, ternately divided; *leaflets* elliptical-ovate, pointed. *Scape* central, smooth, surmounted by a single spadiceous flower. *Spathe* convoluted below, expanded and forming an incurved arch above, covering the opening of the tube, green externally and brownish-purple within (*A. atrorubens?*); or green without and within (*A. triphyllum?*). *Spadix* elongated, club-shaped, obtuse and naked above, longer than the tube of the spathe, constricted below and bearing the flowers at its insertion in the base of the spathe. *Flowers* monœcious or sometimes androgynous by abortion. (Out of over five hundred specimens, green and purple, examined this spring (1884) only one androgynous spadix was found. In this the sterile flowers were, as usual, above the fertile.) *Sterile flowers* composed of a cluster of closely-appressed anthers; *filament* very short and comparatively thick; *anthers* 2-4 celled, opening at their summits by a pore or chink; *pollen* globular, transparent, the outer coat closely and regularly beset with minute knobs. *Fertile flowers* densely crowded in rows upon the lower portion of the spadix, like corn upon its cob, each flower consisting of a single pistil; *ovary* globular, 1-celled; *style* just apparent; *stigma* capitate, fringed; *ovules* orthotropal, standing erect from the base of the ovary. *Fruit* after the decay of the spathe and extremity of the spadix, composed of few or many 4- to 6-seeded scarlet berries; *embryo* in the centre of the albumen.

---

* Ἄρον, *aron*, and σημα, *sema*; marked arum, in allusion to the marked spathe. *Arisarum*, Tourn.

Araceæ.—This order is composed of plants having fleshy corms or rhizomes, or, in the tropics, sometimes woody climbers, an acrid or pungent volatile juice, and monœcious flowers situated upon the same spadix, destitute of floral envelopes, their place being generally filled by a spathe; their fruit is a berry, the seeds of which abound in mealy albumen, or the embryo large and fleshy. The leaves are generally compound, with sheathing petioles, and more or less reticulate veined. The genera are mostly tropical. Besides the genera Arisæma and Symplocarpus, finding representation in this work, the following members of this family are of interest to us: *Caladium seguinum* and *esculentum, Dieffenbachia seguina,* one of the most virulent of vegetable poisons, and *Arum dracunculus, Italicum,* and *maculatum.*

History and Habitat.—The Indian Turnip grows plentifully about boggy spots in deep, rich woods. It is indigenous to most portions of the United States and Canadas, flowering in May and fruiting in September. The corms, when fresh, especially, and all parts of the plant, have a severely acrid juice, imparting an almost caustic sensation to the mucous membranes, and swelling of the parts when chewed. This action upon the mouths of school-boys, who often play the trick of inviting bites of the corm upon each other, gave rise to the common name, "memory-root," as they never forget its effects. This acridity, however, is dissipated by heat or drying, the roots then becoming very nutrient and palatable, the fecula of the corm forming an excellent "arrow-root." The yield of nutrient matter is said to be about one-fourth the whole substance of the corm. This point is fully appreciated by the Indians of this country, who consider the roots a delicacy, either roasted or boiled. I have roasted them myself, when a boy, and enjoyed a repast very pleasing to an empty stomach. Slices of the fresh root, frequently laid upon the skin, are said to cause vescication.

Arum triphyllum is not officinally recognized in either the U. S. Ph. or Eclectic Materia Medica.

PART USED AND PREPARATION.—The fresh root, gathered before the expansion of the leaves, should be carefully bruised in a covered mortar and weighed. Then two parts by weight of alcohol are taken, the pulp mixed with one-sixth part of it, and the rest of the alcohol added. After stirring the whole well it should be placed in a well-stoppered bottle and allowed to stand at least eight days in a dark, cool place. The tincture, separated by straining and filtering, should have a pale-brownish-yellow color by transmitted light, a slightly sweetish taste, entirely devoid of acrimony, and a neutral reaction to test-paper.

In order to preserve the acrimony of the root, Dr. E. M. Hale recommends rapid trituration in ten parts by weight of coarse sugar-of-milk, and keeping the preparation in hermetically-sealed jars, protected against heat and light. The provings were made with dilutions.

CHEMICAL CONSTITUENTS.—The acrid principle of this plant, as before intimated, is rapidly dispersed by heat. Dr. Bigelow states that this body escapes as an inflammable gas, slightly explosive when mixed with air. The extreme volatility of this body has precluded the determination of its chemical characteristics. No other active body has been determined, though some principle other than the acrid body seems to reside in the corms. Starch, gum, and sugar have been isolated.

PHYSIOLOGICAL ACTION.—From personal observations and the literature upon this plant, its action, when fresh, seems to be quite similar to that of strong liquor ammonia, causing as it does an irritation and burning of mucous membranes and acceleration of secretions. The provings have developed a train of symptoms very characteristic, and therefore useful, but not belonging under this rubric.

DESCRIPTION OF PLATE 167.

1. Young plant, from Binghamton, N. Y., May 27, 1884.
    2. Corm.
    3. Female spadix.
    4. Fertile flower—*i. e.*, pistil (enlarged).
    5. Sterile flower—*i. e.*, stamen (enlarged).
    6. Pollen x 200.

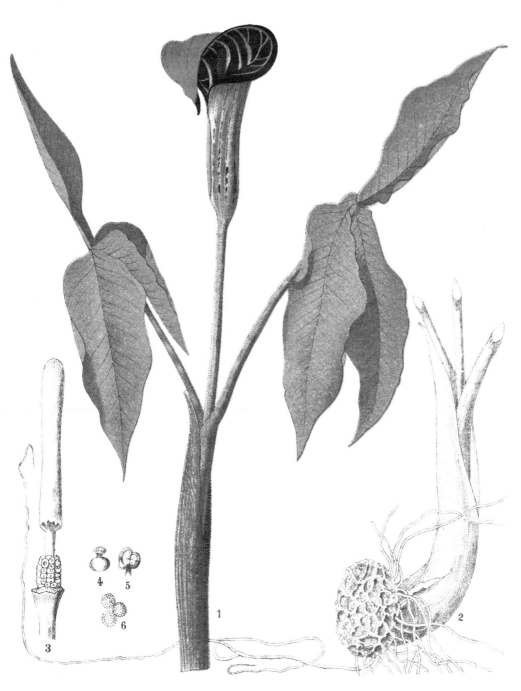

ℰ.m. ad nat del.et pinxt.

ARISÆMA TRIPHÝLLUM, Torr.

GENUS.—**ARISÆMA**, MART.

SEX. SYST.—MONŒCIA POLYANDRIA.

168
ARUM DRACONTIUM.

GREEN DRAGON.

SYN.—ARISÆMA DRACONTIUM, SCHOTT; ARUM DRACONTIUM, LINN.
COM. NAMES.—GREEN DRAGON, DRAGON ROOT; (FR.) GOUET À DRAGON;
(GER.) DRACHEN ARON.

A TINCTURE OF THE CORM OF ARISÆMA DRACONTIUM, SCHOTT.

Description.—This peculiar herb usually attains a growth of from 1 to 2 feet. *Corms* clustered, wrinkled, but not so markedly reticulate as in the preceding species; *stems* (if so they may be called) numerous from the same fascicle of corms. *Leaf* usually solitary, pedately compounded of from 7 to 13 oblong-lanceolate, pointed, and entire leaflets. *Inflorescence* in a mostly androgynous but sometimes polygamous spadix that tapers to a long, exserted, and more or less contra-curved point; *spathe* green, scaphoid, open along the inferior surface, and more or less convolute, especially about the apex of the floral portion of the spadix. *Fertile flowers* numerous, inferior, each composed of a single turbinate or quadrangularly compressed pistil; *style* peltate over the summit of the ovary; *stigma* a nipple-like projection at the summit of the style; *ovules* 6 to 8, erect. *Sterile flowers* superior, each composed of a single 4-celled stamen; *filament* short and thick. *Fruit* a globular head of orange-red berries; *rachis* flat; *seeds* 1 to 3 in each berry. Read description of Araceæ, under the preceding plant.

History and Habitat.—The Green Dragon is indigenous to the United States from Florida northward. It grows along the banks of rivers, where it flowers in May and ripens its brilliant fruit in September.

This plant was introduced into English gardens in 1749. It has gained no medical history whatever, its little employment having been in connection with *A. triphyllum* without distinction.

PART USED AND PREPARATION.—The fresh corms, gathered before flowering or after the fruit has fallen, are treated as in the preceding species. The resulting tincture has a slight straw tint by transmitted light, no distinguishing odor, a cold, biting taste, and an acid reaction.

PHYSIOLOGICAL ACTION.—The symptoms caused in the prover, Dr. C. P. Hart,* by doses of from fifteen grains to one drachm of a mixture of one oz. of the

---

* *Am. Hom. Obs.*, 1875, p. 537.

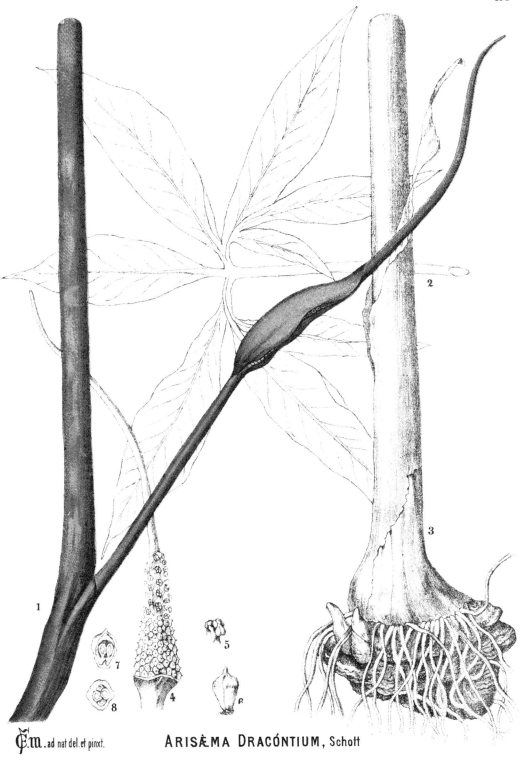

Ƶm. ad nat del.et pinxt.

ARISÈMA DRACÓNTIUM, Schott

expressed juice of the corms with nine ounces of sugar of milk, were quite similar to those caused by *A. tryphillum:* Prickling pains, dryness, then catarrhal secretion from the larynx and bronchial tubes, hoarseness; great prostration; increased heart's action; dyspnœa; rattling of mucus on expiration; muco-purulent expectoration, composed mostly of thick, heavy, yellowish pus; and increased urination.

DESCRIPTION OF PLATE 168.

1, 2, and 3. Whole plant, Pittsburgh, Pa.. June 10th, 1875.
>   2. Leaf (four times reduced).
>   4. Spadix.
>   5. Sterile flower.
>   6. Fertile flower.
>   7 and 8. Sections of the pistil.
>   (4–8 enlarged.)

POTHOS.†

SKUNK CABBAGE.

SYN.—POTHOS FŒTIDA, MICH.; ICTODES FŒTIDUS, BIGEL.; DRACON-
TIUM FŒTIDUM, L.; SYMPLOCARPUS FŒTIDA, SALISB.; (?) ARUM
AMERICANUM, CATESBY.

COM. NAMES.—SKUNK CABBAGE, SKUNK WEED, POLECAT WEED,
MEADOW CABBAGE, FŒTID HELLEBORE, (FR.) POTHOS FETIDE,
(GER.) STINKENDE DRACHENWURZEL.

TINCTURE OF THE FRESH ROOT OF DRACONTIUM FŒTIDUM,‡ L.

Description.—A low-spreading ill-favored weed; growing profusely in swamps
and on bottom lands. *Root* perennial, from 3 to 5 inches long, and about 2 inches
thick, of a reddish-brown color externally, terminating abruptly where it gives off
numerous crowded rootlets, which penetrate the boggy earth, its habitat, to a
depth of from 6 inches to 2 feet or more. *Stem* none. *Leaves* numerous, not
appearing until the ovules are fertilized; they are large, ovate, entire, smooth,
longitudinally furrowed by the thick pale ribs, cordate at the base, with an acute
tip, and spring from the root on long petioles, deeply grooved on their upper aspect,
and sheathed at their lower juncture. The flowers are enclosed by the *spathe*, a
fleshy, ovate, shell-form, swelling body, generally about 4 inches long, by from 2
to 3 inches in the greatest diameter; this hood has an auriculate base, an acute tip
and infolding edges, which are at length coalescent. The *spadix*, fully sheltered
in the basal cup of the spathe, is ovoid-globose, about 1 inch long by one-half to
three-quarters of an inch in diameter, situated upon a short peduncle, and completely invested by the perfect tetrandrous, purplish flowers. *Calyx* composed of
four fleshy, wedge-shaped sepals, whose inflected tips and edges match so perfectly
those of the neighboring flowers as to completely cover the spadix, making a
solid body of perianths. *Stamens* four, situated opposite the sepals, which, with
their subulate filaments, they fully equal in length. *Anthers* oblong, extrorse,
with two parallel cells. *Pollen* grains quite small considering the size of the
plant, and greatly resembling, under the microscope, pointed grains of wheat.
Ovary one-celled, with a single suspended anatropous ovule. *Style* four-angled,
pyramidal. *Stigma* minute, pubescent. *Fruit* compound, consisting of the
enlarged fleshy spadix together with the perianths, making in all a spongy, soft,
glutinous, uncanny, ill-smelling mass, inclosing near the surface the ovoid, bullet-

---

* From συμπλοκή, connection, and καρπός, fruit, alluding to the coalescence of the ovaries into a compound fruit.
† The name under which the plant was proven, see first synonym.
‡ Using the name as applied by the " Am. Hom. Phar.," see third synonym.

like *seeds;* destitute of albumen, but containing a large, fleshy, globular *embryo*, several *plumules* and a *radicle*. A general description of the class and order will be found under Arum triphyllum.

History and Habitat.—This is our only species of the genus; still it is regarded by the laity as one too many, on account of its very offensive and penetrating odor, which, though individualizing this plant, is still not peculiar to it alone, as the fruit of some of our wild currants, especially Ribes rigens, when crushed, emit a scent very similar to it.

In earliest spring, by carefully examining boggy grounds, one may notice the points of many spathes just appearing above the soil, from which they soon arise and mature before the leaves expand. The fruit ripens in September, usually after the leaves have all decayed. The rapidity with which this plant matures is so great that in some seasons a second appearance of the spathes is made in November.

This is one of the plants often wrongly classified, being a kind of broken link in the chain of Araceæ. The genera Pothos; Arum; Dracontium; Symplocarpus (without affinity) and Orontium, to which it has been successively assigned, will not admit it; we, therefore, must agree with Dr. Bigelow's observations and accept his expressive name, Ictodes fœtidus.* Concerning the cross-fertilization of this plant I have noted the following: the pollen when mature falls from the anthers in such large quantities that the cup-like base of the spathe is covered to a depth of a line or more; wallowing about in this fertilizing element may be found numerous carrion beetles attracted hither by the odor of the plant, which undoubtedly misleads them in their search for food. In this way, through their wanderings to and fro, fertilization is produced by their apparently aimless crawling about over the spadix and base of the spathe. They are prevented from spending valuable time upon the inner walls of the spathe, by its varnished smoothness and perplexing curves, which keep them up to their work. Those that visit the interior of a spathe before the pollen is discharged, are compelled to remain until the anthers are ripe, for it is not until then that the trap-like formation opens sufficiently at the base to permit easy exit. Much pollen is lost by being devoured by the numerous slugs that crawl into the spathe.

The skunk cabbage is not official in the U. S. Ph., having been dismissed. In the Eclectic Materia Medica the use of this drug, especially compounded with others, is considerable.

Tinctura Symplocarpi, Pulvis Lobeliæ Compositus, Pulvis Asclepiæ Compositus, Tinctura Lobeliæ Composita, Tinctura Lobeliæ et Capsici, Tinctura Sanguinariæ Compositus and Acetata, Tinctura Viburnii Composita.

The fresh or dried fleshy fruits, divested of the seeds, and mashed with an equal portion of Indian meal, have been used in this neighborhood (Central New York) to great extent, and with excellent success, as a poultice for caking mammæ, promptly, in many instances coming under my notice, dissipating the hardness and restoring the glands to health.

---

* ἰχτιζ, *viverra*, οςω, o'eo, Skunk oil.

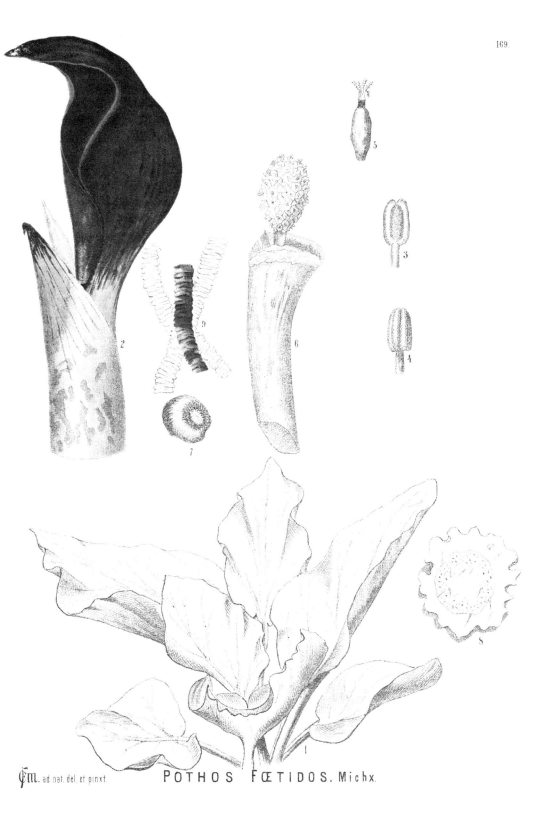

169

℄M. ad nat. del. et pinxt.

POTHOS FŒTIDOS. Michx.

PART USED AND PREPARATION.—The fresh root and rootlets gathered in the spring are chopped and pounded to a pulp and weighed. Then two parts by weight of alcohol are taken, and after thoroughly mixing the pulp with one-sixth part of it, the rest of the alcohol is added. After having stirred the whole, pour into a well-stoppered bottle and let it stand eight days in a dark, cool place. The tincture is then separated by decanting, straining and filtering. Thus prepared it is of a light brown color by transmitted light, a slightly acrid taste, and neutral to litmus papers.

CHEMICAL CONSTITUENTS.—The properties of this plant have not as yet been determined by analysis, but may doubtless be referred to a principle volatile in its nature, as drying for any length of time dissipates both the odor and acridity, and heat applied rapidly removes all its active properties. An analysis reported by Mr. J. M. Turner in "American Journal of Pharmacy," vol. 2, p. 1, seems to prove the above to be the case. He, however, obtained from his assay a *volatile fatty body*, a small amount of *volatile oil, resin, fixed oil, wax, starch, sugar* and *gum*.

PHYSIOLOGICAL ACTION.—The root when chewed produces irritation of the mouth and fauces, acting also as a stimulant to the secretory glands of the mucous membrane. Taken into the stomach it causes vertigo, nausea, sometimes vomiting and temporary blindness. Its volatile properties probably suggested to palliative practice its use in hysteria and spasmodic asthma, though the provings do not show it curative yet in those disorders.

DESCRIPTION OF PLATE 169.

1. Whole plant four times reduced.
2. Spathe ; Bergen, Jersey City, N. J., March 1st, 1880.
3. Stamen (enlarged), inner view.
4. Ditto, outer view.
5. Pistil (enlarged).
6. Spadix.
7. Seed.
8. Section of Rootstock.
9. Roots.
10. Pollen grains x 380.

N. ORD.—ORCHIDACEÆ.

GENUS.—**CYPRIPEDIUM**,* LINN.

SEX. SYST.—GYNANDRIA DIANDRIA.

170

CYPRIPEDIUM PUBESCENS.

YELLOW LADY'S SLIPPER.

SYN.—CYPRIPEDIUM PUBESCENS, WILLD.; CYPRIPEDIUM LUTEUM, AIT.(?)

COM. NAMES.—LARGER YELLOW LADY'S SLIPPER, MOCCASIN FLOWER, AMERICAN VALERIAN, YELLOWS, NOAH'S ARK, YELLOW UMBIL, NERVE-ROOT; (FR.) SABOT DE VENUS JAUNE, CYPERIPEDE JAUNE; (GER.) GELBFRAUENSCHUH.

A TINCTURE OF THE FRESH ROOT OF CYPRIPEDIUM PUBESCENS, WILLD.

Description.—This beautiful, pubescent herb, grows to a height of from 1 to 2 feet. *Root* horizontal, cylindrical, thickly beset with fibrous rootlets. *Stem* simple, erect, leafy to the top. *Leaves* large, ovate, or ovate-lanceolate, pointed, prominently many-nerved, plicate, and sheathing at the base. *Inflorescence* terminal; *flowers* single or in pairs, scentless. *Sepals* 3, two of which are united under the lip, elongated lanceolate, brownish or purplish, pointed, and spreading. *Petals* lanceolate, undulate and twisted, brownish or purplish, pointed, narrower than the sepals; *sac, lip,* or *labellum* roundish, shorter than the sepals and petals, much inflated above, horizontal, laterally compressed, convex, pale yellow. *Column* short, declined; *stamens* 3, the two fertile ones situated each side of the column. The body that answers to the stamen in other orchids is but rudimentary in this genus; and situated on the upper side of the column, covering the whole style. It is dilated-triangular or heart-shaped and pointed; *filaments* short; *anthers* 2-celled, opening by the face of the cells becoming filmy and glutinous, causing it to be ruptured when touched; *pollen* mealy-pulverent, adhering to the detached portions of the cell-face. *Style* a broad, terminal, obscurely 3-lobed, roughish, moist disk.

Orchidaceæ.—This vast order of striking and strangely beautiful plants is characterized as follows: *Herbs* of varied aspect, often epiphytes. *Roots* often tuberous or tuber-bearing. *Leaves* alternate, parallel veined. *Flowers* irregular, each subtended by a bract, and assuming such varied forms as to often resemble birds, insects, etc.: *perianth* of 6 parts (*calyx* 3, *corolla* 3); one of the petals, the upper one, is termed the *labellum* or *saccate lip;* this, by the twisting of the ovary or axis, becomes generally anterior. A *column,* composed of the united filament and style, renders the essential organs gynandrous. *Stamen* single (Ex. Cypripe-

---

* Κύπρις, *Kypris,* Venus; πόδιον, *podion,* a sock or buskin; Venus's slipper.

dium), fertile; *filament* combined in the column; *anther* 2-celled, sometimes deciduous; *dehiscence* sometimes opercular, sometimes accomplished by a disintegration of the face of the cell; *pollinia* composed of one or two masses of pollen-grains in each anther-cell; *pollen* waxy or mealy-pulverent. *Ovary* inferior, 1-celled, 6-ribbed, sometimes twisted; *placentæ* 3, parietal; *style* forming a part of the column; *stigma* a viscid, concave disk in front of the column. *Seeds* minute, innumerable; *testa* reticulate.

It would seem an almost essential feature of Orchidaceæ that some part or organ of each plant should be twisted.

Our materia medica contains but one drug from the family, besides the one under consideration, viz., the European lady's tresses (*Spiranthes autumnalis*, Rich.).

Two other members are well known—vanilla (*Vanilla planifolia, Andrews*), and the mucilaginous nutritive Salep, a preparation of the tubers of several species of the genera *Orchis* and *Eulophia*. A few other species are sometimes referred to in medicine—a West Indian stomachic (*Bletia verecunda, R. Br.*), a Guinean purgative and Tortolan anthelmintic (*Epidendrum bifidum, Aubl.*), an Indian vermifuge and diuretic (*Epidendrum auriculatum*), a reputed American remedy for scrofula (*Goodyera pubescens, R. Br.*), and a masticatory in toothache (*Arethusa bulbosa, Linn.*). There are also three genera whose tubers yield an excellent glue: the South American *Catasetum* and *Cyrtopodium*, and our *Aplectrum*. Rafinesque says:* "The orchidaceous plants which have long roots, like the cypripedium, appear to have different properties from those which have round or oval tubercles."

History and Habitat.—The Larger Yellow Lady's Slipper is indigenous to the lower parts of Canada, and the northern and western United States, growing in bogs and wet, shady woods, where it blossoms from May until June. This plant was introduced into medical literature by Rafinesque, who says:† "Of this beautiful genus, all the species are equally medical; they have been long known to the Indians. . . . The most efficient is the C. luteum. . . . They are sedative, nervine, antispasmodic, etc., and the best American substitute for valerian in almost all cases. They produce beneficial effects in all nervous diseases and hysterical affections, by allaying pain, quieting the nerves and promoting sleep. They are also used in hemicrania, epilepsy, tremors, nervous fever, etc., . . . having no baneful nor narcotic effects. The dose is a teaspoonful of the powder, diluted in sugar-water, or any other convenient form." The above uses of the powdered root have been corroborated fully in domestic practice.

Cypripedium is officinal in the U. S. Ph. as *Extractum Cypripedii Fluidum*, from both Cypripedium pubescens, Willd., and C. parviflorum, Salisb. The preparations in the Eclectic Materia Medica are: *Extractum Cypripedii Alchoholicum, Extractum Cypripedii Fluidum*, and *Tinctura Serpentariæ Composita.*‡

---

* *Med. Flora*, vol. i, p. 145.
† Ibid., pp. 143–4.
‡ Aristolochia, Ipecacuanha, Crocus, Camphora, and Cypripedium or Opium.

170.

Œm..ad nat.del.et pinxt.

CYPRIPÈDIUM PUBÉSCENS, Willd.

PART USED AND PREPARATION.—The fresh root, gathered in early spring, or in autumn, is chopped and pounded to a fine pulp and weighed. Then two parts by weight of alcohol are taken, the pulp mixed with one-sixth part of it, and the rest of the alcohol added. After a thorough mixture is made, pour it into a well-stoppered bottle, and let it stand eight days in a dark, cool place.

The tincture, separated from this mass by filtration, should have a beautiful crimson color by transmitted light, a nauseous fecal odor, a taste somewhat similar to that of the black walnut, and an acid reaction.

CHEMICAL CONSTITUENTS.—An analysis of the root by H. C. Blair* resulted in the separation of a volatile oil and acid, tannic and gallic acids, two resins, and the usual plant constituents.

Cypripedin.† The body sold under this name is simply a mixed mass of all the constituents of the root not soluble in water.

PHYSIOLOGICAL ACTION.—Cypripedium acts as a sedative to the nerves in general, causing a sense of mental quiet and lassitude, and subduing nervous and mental irritation. It seems also to quiet spasms of voluntary muscles, and hysterical attacks, especially in women. This is one of our drugs that has not been sufficiently thought of by provers. It merits a full proving, and would, without doubt, prove more useful if the preparation be made of the whole plant, thus bringing in its action upon the skin, which as yet seems to be little known.‡

DESCRIPTION OF PLATE 170.

1. Upper part of plant in flower, Binghamton, N. Y., June 2d, 1884.
2. Lower portion and root.
3. Bird's-eye view of flower (somewhat reduced), showing the third or abortive stamen.
4. Column (enlarged), inner view.
5. Column, outer view, after removal of the abortive stamen.

---

* *Am. Jour. Phar.*, 1866, p. 494.
† *Oleoresina Cypripedii.*
‡ See Hale's " New Remedies," art. Cypripedium.

GENUS.—**LACHNANTHES,**[*] LINN:

SEX. SYST.—TRIANDRIA MONOGYNIA.

171

LACHNANTHES.

RED ROOT.

SYN.—LACHNANTHES TINCTORIA, ELL.; HERITIERA GMELINI, MICHX.; DILATRIS TINCTORIA, PURSH.; D. HERITIERA, PERS.

COM. NAMES.—RED ROOT, SPIRIT WEED, DYERS' DILATRIS.

A TINCTURE OF THE WHOLE PLANT LACHNANTHES TINCTORIA, ELL.

Description.—This perennial herb grows to a height of from 1 to 2 feet. *Rhizome* more or less horizontal, cylindrical, ligneous; *rootlets* fibrous, deep orange-red, mostly springing from the head of the rootstock. *Stem* erect, simple, hairy above the last leaf. *Leaves* equitant, sword-shaped, mostly clustered at the base of the stem, those evident on the stem remote, small, and sheathing at the base. *Inflorescence* a dense, terminal, compound, leafy-bracted cyme; *flowers* dingy yellow; *perianth* woolly externally, 6-parted, the three inner divisions larger, the outer three linear. *Stamens* 3, opposite the larger lobes; *filaments* dilated below; *anthers* exserted, linear, versatile, 2-celled, opening longitudinally. *Ovary* globular, 3-celled, wholly adherent to the calyx-tube; *ovules* amphitropous; *style* filiform, exserted, declined, deciduous; *stigma* evident, capitate. *Fruit* a globular, 3-angled capsule; *placentæ* fleshy; *seeds* few in each cell, discoid, concave, fixed by the middle.

Hæmodraceæ.—This small family of herbaceous plants belongs chiefly to South Africa and Australia, only 3 genera and 4 species being found in the United States. The order is characterized as follows: *Roots* fibrous, spreading; *stem* scape-like, leafy; *leaves* mostly equitant, sword-shaped. *Flowers* regular and perfect, 3 to 6 androus; *perianth* tubular, woolly, or mealy outside, 6-lobed, and coherent with a portion or all of the ovary; *sepals* and *petals* undistinguishable. *Stamens* inserted upon the tube of the perianth; *anthers* introrse. *Ovary* 3-celled; *ovules* anatropous or amphitropous, and attached to central placentæ; *style* single and deciduous or 3-partible and persistent; *stigma* single, or, when 3, then alternate with the cells of the ovary. *Fruit* a 3-celled, loculicidal capsule, crowned by or enclosed within the persistent perianth; *seeds* 3–many; *embryo* small; *albumen* hard or fleshy, surrounding the embryo.

The only proven plants of this order are those treated of in this work. The roots of several south-tropical species are tonic, bitter, and astringent, while several

---

[*] Λάχνη, *lachne*, wool; ἄνθος, *anthos*, flower: from the resemblance.

Australian species have roots that, though acrid when in a recent state, form a nutritious food for the natives when roasted.

History and Habitat.—Lachnanthes is indigenous to the United States, growing in sandy swamps from Florida to New Jersey and Rhode Island along the coast, where it blossoms from June to September, according to locality. It was introduced into England as a green-house perennial in 1812, and then propagated from seed.

The root was esteemed as an invigorating tonic by the Aborigines, especially the Seminoles, in whom it is said to cause brilliancy and fearless expression of the eye and countenance, a boldness and fluency of speech, and other symptoms of heroic bearing, with, of course, the natural opposite after-effects. A tincture of the root has been recommended in typhus and typhoid fevers, pneumonia, various severe forms of brain disease, rheumatic wry-neck, and laryngeal cough.

PART USED AND PREPARATION.—The whole fresh plant, while flowering, is chopped and pounded to a pulp and weighed. Then two parts by weight of alcohol are taken, the pulp mixed with one-sixth part of it, and the rest of the alcohol added. After thorough stirring the whole is poured into a well-stoppered bottle, and allowed to macerate for eight days in a dark, cool place.

The tincture, separated from this mass by pressure and filtration, has a brilliant carmine color by transmitted light; no distinguishing odor; a slightly bitter and ligneous taste; and an acid reaction.

CHEMICAL CONSTITUENTS.—The roots yield a fine red dye and a bitter resin, but no analysis has yet been made of the plant that determines the nature of its specific constituents.

PHYSIOLOGICAL ACTION.—Lachnanthes, in doses varying from a few drops to a drachm of the tincture, causes: Mental exhilaration followed by ill-humor; vertigo and headache; brightness of the eye with dilation of the pupil followed by dullness, pressive pains, and impaired vision; tearing in the ears; hectic redness of the cheeks; dryness of the throat; rumbling of flatus in the abdomen; fullness and heat in the chest; increased heart's action; pain and stiffness of the neck and shoulders;* restlessness; sleeplessness; and coldness and fever followed by sticky sweat. The action of this drug appears, as far as proven, to be quite similar to that of Pulsatilla.

DESCRIPTION OF PLATE 171.

1 and 2. Whole plant, Landisville, N. J., July 18th, 1885.
3. Section of flower.
4 and 5. Anther.
(3–5 enlarged.)

---

* I have found Lachnanthes an excellent remedy for rheumatic stiffness of the neck and shoulders, with inability tto turn the head without severe pain, especially where the trouble seemed to be first a neuralgia of the fifth nerve then ransferred to the neck and shoulder.

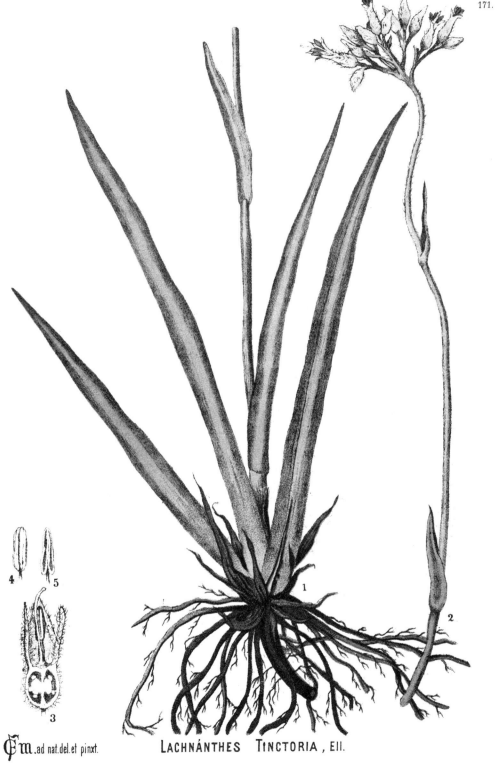

171.

4   5

3

Ⓕᶆ.ad nat.del.et pinxt.   LACHNÁNTHES TINCTORIA , Ell.

172

ALETRIS.

STAR WORT.

SYN.—ALETRIS FARINOSA, LINN.; A. ALBA, MICH.

COM. NAMES.—STAR WORT, STAR ROOT, AGUE ROOT, AGUE GRASS, ALOE ROOT, BITTER GRASS, BLACK ROOT, BETTIE GRASS, COLE ROOT, CROW CORN, FALSE UNICORN ROOT, UNICORN ROOT,† DEVIL'S BIT,‡ COLIC ROOT,§ STAR GRASS,‖ BLAZING STAR;¶ (FR.) ALÉTRIS FARINEUX; (GER.) MEHLIGE ALETRIS.

A TINCTURE OF THE FRESH ROOT OF ALETRIS FARINOSA, LINN.

Description.—This prostrate, perennial, spreading herb is characterized as follows: *Root* cylindrical-tuberous, more or less horizontal, giving off numerous fibres from its lower surface. *Stem* none; *leaves* stellate-rosulate, all smooth, flat, thin, coriaceous, pale, sessile and lanceolate acute. *Inflorescence* in a wand-like, crowded raceme terminating a long, nearly naked, terete and rigid scape, that arises from the axis of the leaf-cluster; *flowers* nearly sessile, creamy white; *perianth* tubular-cylindrical, somewhat campanulate, persistent, and cohering below with the base of the ovary; *limb* 6 cleft; *lobes* lanceolate-triangular, somewhat spreading. *Stamens* 6, equal; *filaments* short, inserted at the base of the lobes of the perianth; *anthers* included, sagittate, introrse. *Ovary* globular, 2-celled; *ovules* anatropous; *style* subulate, 3-cleft at the apex; *stigmas* small, minutely 2-lobed. *Fruit* an ovate-tapering, coriaceous capsule, enclosed in the persistent floral envelope; *dehiscence* loculicidal; *carpels* 3. *Seeds* numerous, ovate, ribbed; *embryo* minute, roundish, situated near the hilum; *albumen* fleshy and oily.

History and Habitat.—Aletris is indigenous to North America, where it frequents the borders of wet, sandy or swampy woods from Florida northward, especially at the seaboard.

This plant furnishes one of the many examples of the uncertainty attending the use of vulgarisms in reference to plants, no less than half its common names being also used to designate another plant, our Helonias (*Chamælirium luteum*), which it no more resembles than a cucumber does a pumpkin, except mayhap in the root when separate from the rest of the plant; the root of Helonias, however,

---

* Ἀλετρίς, *Aletris,* a female slave, who grinds corn; from the mealy appearance of the perianth.

† The Unicorn is *Martynia proboscidea,* Glox. (Bignoniaceæ).

‡ The name usually designates *Chamælirium luteum,* Gray (Liliaceæ).

§ More properly a vulgarism of *Dioscorea villosa,* Linn. (Dioscoreaceæ).

‖ This name should only indicate *Hypoxys erecta,* Linn. (Amyrillidaceæ).

¶ The true Blazing Star is *Liatris squarrosa,* Willd. (Compositæ).

172.

Œm. ad nat del.et pinxt.

ÁLETRIS FARINÒSA, Linn.

always shows, on section, holes in its cortex, through which the fibrous rootlets pass (see figure, Plate 177); this is not so in Aletris root, and will always serve as a distinguishing point between them.

Aletris was held in high repute by the Aborigines as a stomachic, bitter tonic, and emmenagogue; from them it passed into the hands of the laity and herbalists. Probably the first printed notice of the plant appeared, unnamed, in 1730.* It was introduced into England in 1768, but received little attention except for its extreme bitterness. Pursh speaks of the benefits obtained from this drug in colic; Dr. Cullen recommends it in rheumatism, and Dr. Thacher in anasarca. Dr. Bigelow judges that it probably will prove a tonic bitter of value, remarking at the same time that he knows of no plant which surpasses it in genuine, intense, and permanent bitterness. Rafinesque claims that it relieves flatulent and hysteric colic, speedily avails in fevers, is too powerful for bitters, and in large doses is narcotic. The first notice given of its action upon the female organs of reproduction is in Eclectic practice, where it receives consideration in chlorosis, dysmenorrhœa, engorged uteri, amenorrhœa, and prolapsus.

The officinal preparation in the Eclectic Materia Medica is *Extractum Aletridis Alcoholicum.*

PART USED AND PREPARATION.—The fresh root is chopped and pounded to a pulp, and treated as in the preceding drug. The resulting tincture has a clear orange color by transmitted light, no characteristic odor, a very bitter taste, and an acid reaction.

CHEMICAL CONSTITUENTS.—No analysis has yet been made to determine the properties of the bitter principle of this species, which, however, proves more soluble in alcohol than in water. The Tilden's analysis† determines a large proportion of a bitter extractive, resin, and coloring-matter, besides the usual constituents of plants.

PHYSIOLOGICAL ACTION.—Aletris proves, when used in the fresh state, emetic, cathartic, and somewhat narcotic; this mostly disappears on drying. In smaller doses it produces vertigo, stupefaction, colic in the hypogastrium, and heaviness in the uterine region. The drug deserves a very thorough proving, as, from clinical results, it seems especially adapted to many forms of uterine trouble that appeal to our utmost care.

DESCRIPTION OF PLATE 172.

1. Whole plant, Landisville, N. J., July 3d, 1885.
 2. Flower.
 3. Perianth, opened.
 4. Stamen.
 5. Pistil.
 6. Horizontal section of ovary.
     (2–6 enlarged.)

* Clayton, *Lond. Philosoph. Trans.*, 333.   † *Journ. Mat. Med.*, N. S., 2, 231.

173

IRIS VERSICOLOR.

LARGER BLUE FLAG.

SYN.—IRIS VERSICOLOR, L., IRIS AMERICANA VERSICOLOR, DILL.

COM. NAMES.—BLUE FLAG, FLOWER-DE-LUCE, FLAG LILY, LIVER LILY; (FR.) GLAIEUL BLEU; (GER.) VERSCHIEDENFARBIGE SCHWERT-LILIE.

TINCTURE OF THE FRESH ROOT OF IRIS VERSICOLOR, LINN.

Description.—This beautiful perennial bog plant attains a height of from 2 to over 3 feet. *Root* fleshy, thickened, horizontally creeping, giving off from two to four lateral branches, the under surface especially about the annual joints is thickly beset with simple fibrous rootlets. The joints vary from 1 to 4 inches in length, are flattened upon the upper surface, and from three-quarters to one and a quarter inches in breadth. The root is annulated by the scars of previous leaves. The *stem* is terete, angled on one side, rounded on the other, flexuous, simple or sometimes branched. *Leaves* sword-shaped, striate, erect, clasping at the base, one to one and one-half feet long, and one-half to one inch wide. *Flowers* 2 to 6 on each plant, spathacious, large and attractive, peduncles short, flattened on the inner side. *Calyx* tube funnel-form, prolonged more or less beyond the ovary, shorter than the three divisions (*sepals*) which are reflexed or spreading and destitute of beard or crest; the three inner divisions of the perianth (*petals*) are erect, and shorter than the sepals. *Stamens* 3, distinct, their *anthers* oblong-linear, hidden under the petaloid branches of the style. *Ovary* obtusely triangular with flattened sides, 3-celled, each containing numerous anatropous ovules. *Pollen* grains large, much resembling date stones in form. *Style* mostly connate with the tube of the perianth, its three branches petal-like, crenate, and more or less reflexed at the tip, each branch bearing a true *stigma* as a thin lip or plate, on the under surface of its apex. *Pod* leathery, 3 to 6 angled, 3-valved. *Seeds* triangularly depressed-flattened. *Embryo* straight in the hard fleshy albumen. IRIDACEÆ is represented in gardens by the *Crocus*, *Gladiolus* and tiger-flower (*Tigridia*), and wild in the United States by *Iris*, *Pardanthus* and *Sisyrinchium*.

---

* Ἴρυς, *rainbow deified*, applied by the ancients on account of the bright and diversified colors in the blossoms of this genus.

History and Habitat.—This beautiful flower abounds throughout the United States in wet places, blossoming from May to June. Iris was highly esteemed by the Aborigines of this country, as a remedy for gastric disturbances, and also by laymen as a domestic remedy, when ptyalism was considered necessary.

The fresh root pounded to a pulp is considered, and justly, one of the best poultices that can be applied to a felon, often quickly relieving the pain, even when suppuration is far advanced. It will generally too discuss the affection, if applied early in its development.

Iris is officinal in the U. S. Ph. as *Extractum Iridis* and *Extractum Iridis Fluidum.* In the Eclectic Materia Medica it is used as above, and as *Tinctura Iridis.* It is also a component of *Syrupus Stillingiæ Compositus.*

PART USED AND PREPARATION.—The fresh root. The rhizome of Iris is so often confounded by laymen with that of calamus, that a comparison might be considered in place.

Iris (*Blue-flag*).	Calamus (*Sweet-flag*).
Root horizontal, its sections flattened above. Annular by the scars of leaf-sheaths. The scars of the rootlets crowded mostly near the larger end, on the rounded side. When dry it is grayish brown externally, and grayish or brownish internally, having a nucleus sheath enclosing a number of scattering bundles of woody fibres. No specific odor, acrid and nauseous to the taste.	Root horizontal, nearly cylindrical. Leaf-sheath scars obliquely transverse. The scars of the rootlets upon the under surface are quite regularly arranged in single or double lines that branch alternately, first to one side then to the other. Pinkish or pale-red internally, wood bundles scattered irregularly. An agreeable aroma and a pleasant taste characterize it.

The fresh root, gathered late in autumn or early in spring, is chopped and pounded to a pulp and weighed. Two parts by weight of alcohol are taken, and after thoroughly mixing the pulp with one-sixth part of it, the rest of the alcohol is added. After having stirred the whole, pour it into a well-stoppered bottle, and let it stand eight days in a dark, cool place. The tincture is then separated by decanting, straining and filtering.

Thus prepared it has a light straw-color by transmitted light, at first a stinging, soon followed by a decided bitter taste, and a very slight acid reaction.

CHEMICAL CONSTITUENTS.—Several analyses of the root of Iris have been made, and all without success as regards the true and specific active principle. D. W. Cressler (Jour. Phar., 1881, 601) arrives at the conclusion that very probably an alkaloid exists in the roots; he also succeeds in extracting a volatile matter, starch, gum, tannin, and fixed oil.

Irisin or *Iridin*, an acrid resinoid body, results as a constant factor in all the analyses so far made. It occurs as a dark red-brown, viscid liquid, with an odor and taste resembling that of the root.

PHYSIOLOGICAL ACTION.—Iris acts powerfully upon the gastro-intestinal tract, the liver, and especially the pancreas; causing burning sensations and a high state of congestion, as proven by post-mortem examinations of animals after the exhibition of the drug.

It is an excitant of the salivary and biliary secretions, being therefore an excellent remedy to be thought of in ptyalism and obstinate constipation.

173.

7

1

2   3   5

6

4

C.M. ad nat del.et pinxt.   IRIS VERSICOLOR, Linn.

The gastro-intestinal effects are: profuse acid vomitings, and frequent watery evacuations, the latter accompanied by severe colic and burning. Upon the nervous system its action is marked, as shown by the severe toxic neuralgias of the head, face, and limbs.

DESCRIPTION OF PLATE 173.

1. Flowers.
2. A branch of the style.
3. Stamen.
4. Whole plant three times reduced, Ithaca, N. Y., May 31st, 1880.
5. Fruit.
6. Seed.
7. Pollen grains x 200.

GENUS.—**DIOSCOREA**,* PLUM.

SEX. SYST.—DIŒCIA HEXANDRIA.

174

DIOSCOREA.

WILD YAM.

SYN.—DIOSCOREA VILLOSA, LINN.; D. QUATERNATA, WALT.; D. PANI-
CULATA, JACQ.

COM. NAMES.—WILD-YAM ROOT, COLIC ROOT, RHEUMATISM ROOT,†
DEVIL'S BONES; (FR.) IGUAME INDIGENÉ; (GER.) WILDE YAM.

A TINCTURE OF THE ROOT OF DIOSCOREA VILLOSA, LINN.

Description.—This herbaceous, never villous twiner, usually attains a growth of from 5 to 15 feet over fences, bushes, and undershrubs. *Root* horizontal; *stems* solarly voluble, slender. *Leaves* variously arranged, those at the base of the plant sometimes in fours, those of the middle section nearly opposite, while the upper are alternate; *blade* ovate, 7- to 11-ribbed, more or less downy and grayish beneath; *base* cordate; *margin* entire or wavy; *apex* conspicuously pointed; *petioles* nearly the length of the blade and dilated at the base. *Inflorescence* in drooping, axillary racemes and panicles; *flowers* very small, diœcious, pale green-ish-yellow. *Sterile flowers* in elongated panicles; *perianth* 6-parted; *lobes* oval; *stamens* 6, situated at the base of the lobes, included; *ovary* abortive, minute; *filaments* terete; *anthers* introrse; *cells* roundish, distinct. *Fertile flowers* in simple racemes; *perianth* tubular; *limb* cut into 6 rounded segments; *stamens* 6, abor-tive; *ovary* oblong, sharply triangular, 3-celled; *ovules* 1 to 2 in each cell, pen-dulous, anatropous; *styles* very short, bifid. *Fruit* an oval, 3-celled, 3-winged, membranaceous pod; *dehiscence* loculicidal into 3 valves by splitting through the winged angles. *Seeds* winged, plane, semi-conoid, 2 in each cell; *embryo* somewhat pyriform, compressed.

Dioscoreæ.—This small natural order is represented in North America by this species only, 7 genera and about 150 species being all the representatives known upon the globe, and those are mostly tropical. The plants in general are known by the following characters: *Stems* twining; *roots* usually tuberous, large, or sometimes horizontal and knotted. *Leaves* with a few conspicuous, parallel ribs, otherwise closely-netted, veined; *petioles* always present. *Inflorescence* usually in axillary racemes or racemose panicles. *Flowers* regular. *Male flowers: peri-*

---

* Dedicated to Pedacius Dioscorides, the Greek physician and naturalist.
† Rheumatism Root generally alludes to *Jeffersonia diphylla* (Berberidaceæ).

anth 6-cleft and calyx-like ; *stamens* 3 or 6, perigynous ; *filaments* subulate ; *anthers* globose, introrse, 2-celled. *Female flowers: perianth* tubular, 3-margined, 6-cleft, adherent to the ovary ; *ovary* 3-celled ; *ovules* anatropous, 1 to 2 in each cell ; *styles* 3, segregate or nearly so ; *stigmas* linear, spreading. *Fruit* sometimes baccate, but usually a membranaceous, 3-angled or margined pod. *Embryo* minute ; *albumen* cartilaginous.

No other species are used in medicine, but a few are worthy of mention here on account of their roots, which, when fresh, are juicy, irritant, and vesicating, but after prolonged boiling are rendered more or less pleasant, and always nutritious, from an abundance of starch. Of all the Yams yielded by this order, the pleasantest is the East Indian Sweet Yam (*Dioscorea sativa*, Linn.), next to which ranks the White Negro-Yam of India (*D. alata*, Linn.), which often reaches a weight of 30 pounds, and the Prickly Yam (*D. aculeata*, Linn.), which is the most generally cultivated form. The Ceylon White Yam (*D. bulbifera*, Linn.) ; the Japanese Yam (*D. Japonica*, Linn.) ; and the Indian Yam (*D. trifida*, Linn.), are also pleasant and edible. The East Indian Buck Yam (*D. triphylla*, Linn.), and the Tropical Devil's Yam (*D. dæmona*) remain nauseous, even after prolonged boiling, yet are eaten by the natives in times of need. The Yam is largely cultivated for food in Africa, East and West Indies, and the Southern United States, especially for, and by, the negroes. The roots grow often to a large size, are farinaceous, and considered to be easily digested ; they are in general palatable, and are considered not inferior to any root at present in use. They are eaten in lieu of bread, boiled or baked, or dried and ground into flour for bread and puddings.

The Cape Hottentots' Bread (*Testudinaria elephantipes*, Burch) is often, in times of scarcity, eaten in lieu of Yams, but is a poor substitute. The root of the European Black Bryony (*Tamus communis*, Linn.), is used as a stimulating poultice ; internally it is an acrid purgative, an emetic and diuretic, yet the young shoots are used in lieu of asparagus ; and the Candian (*T. Cretica*, Linn.), is very similar in its properties.

History and Habitat.—Dioscorea is indigenous to North America, where it ranges from Canada and New England, to Wisconsin and southward ; it is common, however, only in the South.

The root of Dioscorea Villosa, as it appears in commerce, is of two kinds, so obviously different that, for many years, one sort was thrown out by druggists as spurious. This discrimination so affected the gathering of the roots that what was considered the true root could no longer be procured in sufficient quantity. Diggers finally, on their side, protested and claimed that the two roots came from almost identical plants, and, in order to supply the trade, the wholesale druggists were compelled to accept, although under protest, the product as sent by the gatherers. Mr. C. G. Lloyd finally examined carefully into what made the difference in the rhizoma, and his decision created a new variety of the species which he called *var. glabra*. The differentiation is as follows :[*]

---

[*] *Am. Disp., Suppl.*, 82, plate vii.

DIOSCOREA VILLOSA, LINN.	DIOSCOREA VILLOSA, VAR. GLABRA, LLOYD.
True Wild-Yam Root.	*False Wild-Yam Root.*

Plant, under general inspection, smaller than the next; isolated.

Larger; growing in dense clumps.

Leaves more sharply pointed, almost aristate; densely short pubescent beneath.

Sharply pointed; absolutely glabrous.

Rhizome horizontal, about ½ inch in diameter, oval, flattened above and below, seldom branched, but decidedly tubercled by small protuberances that appear like abortive attempts to branch; the upper surface is marked at intervals of about an inch with the scars of previous years' stems.

This rhizome resembles greatly that of Collinsonia Canadensis. It is found in thick, matted, rough clumps, the main portion contorted by the procession of branches, which are in themselves knotty and of the full diameter of the rhizome-axis itself; these branchings issue at an acute angle forward, and themselves bear for the most part the cup-shaped scars of former stem-growths.

My herbarium contains three female and four male plants in flower, and one fruiting specimen, representing the States of New York, Pennsylvania, Ohio, Virginia, and Georgia,—all sent to me by botanists, who designated each as *D. villosa;* according to the above differentiation, two of the females and one male, as well as the fruiting specimen, are *var. glabra,* Lloyd.

Dioscorea has held a place in domestic and general practice for a long period as almost specific in certain forms of bilious colic, in which it is promptly efficacious; it is also considered diaphoretic, emetic, and expectorant. As a visceral antispasmodic, and remedy for intestinal irritations, it has proved itself a valuable remedy in cholera morbus, spasm of the diaphragm, spasmodic asthma, dysmenorrhœa, and kindred afflictions.

Although the leaves of the chestnut are official in the U. S. Ph., the root of this valuable plant is not. In Eclectic Practice, the following preparations are used: *Decoctum Dioscoreæ,* and *Extractum Dioscoreæ.*

PART USED AND PREPARATION.—The fresh root of either form, that of the first year preferred, is gathered in September, and chopped and pounded to a pulp and weighed. Then two parts by weight of alcohol are taken, the pulp thoroughly mixed with one-sixth part of it and the rest of the alcohol added. After stirring the whole well, it is poured into a well-stoppered bottle, and allowed to stand for eight days in a dark, cool, place.

The tincture separated from this mass by straining and filtering, should have a deep amber color by transmitted light; a cherry-like odor; a taste at first woody, then bitter, and an acid reaction.

CHEMICAL CONSTITUENTS.—Dioscorea roots contain, without doubt, an acrid principle, resin, and starch, but as yet they have not been isolated. *Dioscorein* is not a principle, it being simply an extract embodying the solid constituents of the fluid extract of the root.

PHYSIOLOGICAL ACTION.—The experiments of Drs. Cushing and Burt, with doses of from 5 drops of the tincture to 200 drops of the fluid extract, gave essentially the following symptoms of disturbance: Vertigo and dizziness; heaviness and aching of the head; smarting and soreness of the eyes; irritation and congestion of the mucous membrane of the nostrils; tongue brown-coated, dry, and stiff; dryness of the mouth, followed by salivation; throat dry and sore; bitter and sour eructations and belchings; nausea, with burning distress, bloating, and cramps of the stomach, which becomes sore and feels raw; hard, dull, or sharp pains in the hepatic region; severe, dull, cutting, and griping pains in the umbilical region; severe abdominal pain, with much flatulent distention; very severe colic, with passage of large quantities of flatulence; itching of the rectum, with prolapsed hemorrhoids; profuse yellow diarrhœic stools; great sexual excitement, followed by loss of desire and nocturnal emissions; irritation of the bronchi and lungs; great lumbar pain and weakness; weakness of the extremities; general tired, weak, and faint feelings; itching of the skin; sleeplessness and chilliness.

Dioscorea proves itself an irritant of the mucous membranes in general, but especially those of the intestinal tract, and causes congestion and inflammation of those tissues if persisted in.

DESCRIPTION OF PLATE 174.

1. Portion of a fruiting stem, Pittsburgh, Pa., Aug. 20th, 1885.
2. Female flower.
3. Male flower.
4. Seed.
(2-3 enlarged.)

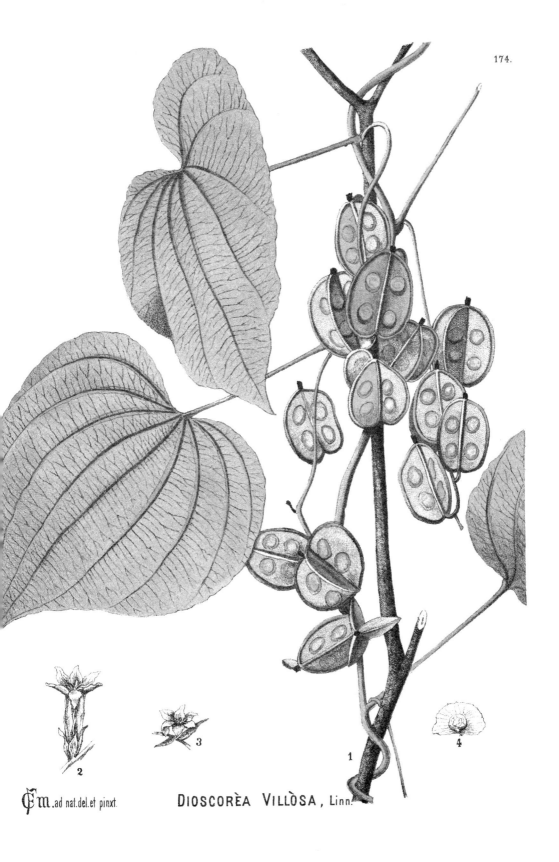

174.

2

3

1

4

Œ M.ad nat.del.et pinxt.   DIOSCORÈA VILLÒSA, Linn.

175

TRILLIUM.

BETHROOT.

TRILLIUM ERECTUM, LINN.

> SYN.—TRILLIUM RHOMBOIDEUM, VAR. ATROPURPUREUM, MICHX.; TRILLIUM ATROPURPUREUM, BOT. MAG., TORREY; TRILLIUM ERECTUM, VAR. ATROPURPUREUM, PURSH.; TRILLIUM FŒTIDUM, SALISB.

> COM. NAMES.—PURPLE TRILLIUM, BETHROOT, BIRTHROOT, LAMB'S QUARTER, GROUND LILY, RATTLESNAKE ROOT, WAKEROBIN, INDIAN BALM, THREE-LEAVED NIGHTSHADE, INDIAN SHAMROCK; (FR., GER.) TRILLIUM.

TRILLIUM ERECTUM, VAR. ALBUM, PURSH.

> SYN.—TRILLIUM PENDULUM, AIT., WILLD.; TRILLIUM RHOMBOIDEUM, VAR. ALBUM, MICHX.

> COM. NAMES.—(NOT SPECIFIC.)

A TINCTURE OF THE FRESH ROOT OF TRILLIUM ERECTUM, LINN.

Description.—**Trillium erectum.**—This common species of the genus is characterized as follows: *Leaves* just sessile, rhomboid, dilated, nearly as broad as long; *base* cuneiform or acute. *Flower* nodding, dull purple, raised upon a peduncle, and having a disgustingly fishy odor; *peduncle* 1 to 3 inches long, inclined. *Petals* plane, ovate, acutish, spreading, and caducous. *Sepals* acute, a little shorter than the petals.

Var. **Album.**—*Leaves* not so abruptly taper-pointed as in the species, broader and more fully sessile. *Flower* odorless, and averaging smaller; *peduncle* strongly curved. (The flower in the plate is constrainedly elevated to show the markings upon the petals and the color of the ovary); *petals* plane, greenish- or creamy-white, the veins and veinlets either green or purple.† *Ovary* deep, dull purple. *Stigmas* yellow.

Trillium.—This genus is composed of low, perennial herbs. *Roots* præmorse, tuber-like, circularly wrinkled, and giving off numerous long, primarily wrinkled, then smooth and branching, fibrous rootlets. *Stems* simple, smooth, stout, naked below, enlarged at the base, and furnished with several large, membranaceous, lanceolate, acute scales. *Leaves 3*, in a single whorl at the summits of the stems,

---

* *Trilix, triple,* the parts of the plant being in threes.

† In *Trillium erythrocarpum*, Michx., the purple markings upon the petals are situated at their bases, and are broad, gradually narrowing, to cease in the middle. *Petals* wavy-edged.

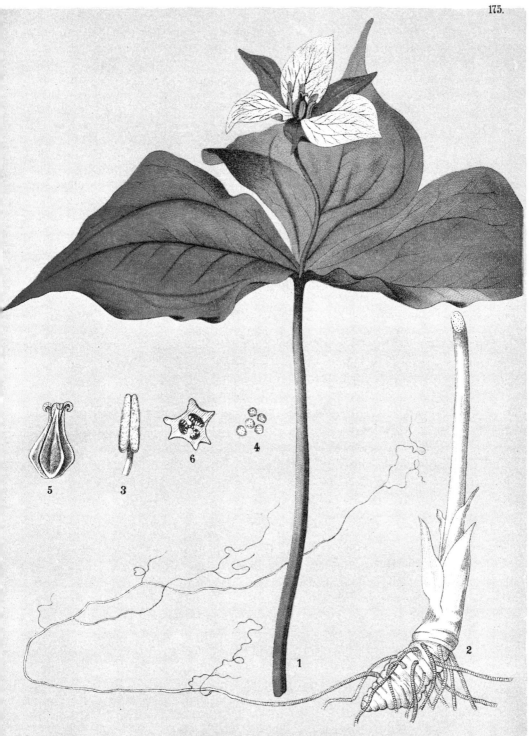

5   3   6   4

1   2

C.m.. ad nat del.et pinxt.   TRÍLLIUM ERÉCTUM Var ÁLBUM Pursh.

broad and netted veined! *Inflorescence* single, terminal, sessile, or pedunculated; *flowers* large, white or purple, sometimes marked. *Petals* 3, larger than the sepals, withering; *sepals* 3, foliaceous, lanceolate, and spreading, persistent. *Stamens* 6; *filaments* short; *anthers* elongated, linear, adnate and introrse; *cells* 2, opening by a lateral, longitudinal fissure; *pollen* more or less globular, echinated. *Ovary* pyriform, 3–6 angled; *styles* 3, distinct down to the ovary, awl-shaped, recurved or spreading, persistent, stigmatic upon their faces. *Fruit* baccate, 3-celled. *Seeds* horizontal, a number in each cell, ovoid, with a tumid raphe; *embryo* minute; *albumen* dense, sarcous.

Rafinesque, in his *Medical Flora*, made a grand revision of this genus, naming no less than 19 species, and 68 varieties, including 14 other species, and constituting 3 sub-genera; but Prof. Gray, in his *Lessons and Manual*, allows but 8 species and 2 varieties in the Northern States.

LILIACEÆ.—This large order of beautiful plants has representatives in all portions of the globe. It consists of herbs or sometimes woody plants springing from bulbs, tubers, or a fascicle of fibrous roots. *Leaves* simple, clasping at the base. *Perianth* not glumaceous, free from the ovary; *flowers* 6-androus, regular, and symmetrical; *sepals* and *petals* generally colored alike (Exc. Trillium); *stamens* 6, one at each division of the perianth; *anthers* 2-celled, introrse. *Ovary* 3-celled, free; *styles* united (Exc. Trillium); *stigmas* generally 3-lobed; *ovules* anatropous or amphitropous. *Fruit* a capsule or berry; *seeds* few or many in each cell; *embryo* minute; *albumen* sarcous.

This important family has been divided by botanists generally, into three, viz., *Melanthaceæ, Liliaceæ*, and *Smilaceæ*; other divisions have also been made. It will, however, answer best for us to speak of the drugs and useful plants here, under the headings as tribes or suborders, to agree with the general plan of the work as begun—*i. e.*, according to Prof. Gray's *North American Botany*. The useful plants of the *Melanthaceæ* are: The European white hellebore, *Veratrum album*, Linn.; the Mexican and West Indian Sabadilla, *Veratrum Sabadilla*, Retz. (*Asa Græ officinalis*, Lindl., *Schœnocaulon officinale*, Gray); the Mexican *Helonias officinalis*, Don (*Veratrum officinale*, Schl.), spoken of as a plant also furnishing cebadilla seeds, is accounted by Flückiger and Hanbury to be synonymous with *V. Sabadilla*. The root of the poisonous *savœja* of the Mexicans, *Helonias frigida*, Lindl. (*Veratrum frigida*, Schl.), appears to exactly resemble that of *V. album*;* the rhizomes of *Veratrum nigrum*, Linn., an Austrian species, are said to be substituted for white hellebore.† The narcotic poison *Helonias erythrosperma*, Michx. (*Melanthium muscætoxicum*, Walt.), is said to be used in the Southern States as an insecticide. Concerning this property, Porcher says,‡ the insects are only stupefied, and are generally burned in that state by housewives. The Indian cucumber, *Medeola Virginica*, Linn., has been used as a diuretic; *Melanthium Virginicum*, W., is an irritant poison, formerly used as an application in itch. The meadow

---

* Flück. & Han. *Pharmacographia*, p. 695.
† *Ibid.*
‡ *Resourc. South. Field and For.*, p. 527.

saffron, *Colchicum autumnale*, Linn., is also a member of this section. Veratrum viride, Helonias dioica and Trillium are represented in this work. *Liliaceæ* proper. Under this head are classed the Aloë, Squillæ, Allia, etc. Squills, *Squilla* and *Scilla maritima*, Stein., Linn., come to us from the Mediterranean coasts; a milder form, *Squilla Pancration*, Stein., thought to be the Pancration of Dioscorides, is found, with the previous form, especially at Malta. Other forms of squills are the South African *Urginea altissima*, Baker, the North African *Scilla Indica*, Roxb., and the Abyssinian *Scilla Indica*, Baker. Nearly allied forms, with varied properties, are the Cape Itch-bulb, *Drimia ciliaris*, Jacq., and the Indian emetic, *Crinum toxicarium*, Roxb. The common or Barbados Aloe is the North African *Aloe vulgaris*, Lam. (*A. Barbadensis*, Mill.). The Socotrine Aloe is a product of *Aloe Socotrina*, Lam. (*A. vera*, Miller), growing upon the southern shores of the Indian Ocean, Red Sea, and Island of Socotra. Cape Aloes are said to be derived from *Aloe ferox*, Linn., *Aloe Africana*, Mill., *Aloe spicata*, Thun., *Aloe linguæformis*, *Aloe arborescens*, Mill., *Aloe Commelini*, Willd., and *Aloe purpurascens*, Haw. *Allium sativum*, Linn., the common garlic, is of uncertain nativity; *Allium cepa*, Linn., the common onion, is a native of Egypt; other allied species are the Leek, *Allium porrum;* the Echalotte, *Allium ascalonicum;* Chives, *Allium schænoprasum;* Rocambole, *Allium scodoprasum;* the Southern Wild Garlic, *Allium Carolinianum;* and the Meadow Garlic, *Allium Canadense*. The dog's-tooth violet, *Erythronium Americanum*, Ker., was offered by Bigelow as a substitute for Colchicum; the Indian *Erythronium Indicum* is used against equine strangury (Ainslie); and the bulbs of the European *Erythronium Dens canis* as a food in Siberia (Pallas). The Lily of the Valley (*Convallaria majalis*, Linn.), a plant whose reputed value in some forms of cardiac diseases is at present before the profession, belongs to this section. The bulbs of *Tulipa gesneriana*, like many other liliaceous bulbs, are used for cataplasms; those of *Tulipa sylvestris* are emetic (Poiret); those of *Fritillaria imperialis*, and *Gloriosa superba*, are violent poisons; while those of *Calochortus elegans* and various species of the genus *Lilium*, form nutritious foods. The North American Indians use as foods the following species under this order: Kamass root (*Cammassia esculenta*) is eaten raw or cooked; in the latter form it is said to resemble the potato. These roots also yield a very good molasses when boiled in water, and are greatly esteemed by the Nez Perces, Pitt River, and Cape Flattery Indians. Spanish bayonet (*Yucca baccata*): This spinous-leaved plant yields a fruit that nearly resembles in size and shape the West Indian banana. The Indians of Arizona, Utah, and New Mexico are very fond of these fruits, which they either eat fresh, or dry and preserve when ripe, and roast when green together with the young flower buds.* African hemp is a product of several species of *Sanseviera* (Griffith), and New Zealand hemp of *Phorimum tenax*. Dragon's-blood, an astringent resin, long used, is a product of that famous East Indian tree, *Dracæna Draco*. Various pot-herbs are found in this family, the principal ones being *Asparagus officinalis*, *Asparagus acutifolius*, and the South Sea Island Ti-plant, *Cordyline terminalis*. The *Smilaceæ* yield Jamaica sarsaparilla, *Smilax offici-*

---

* J. R. Dodge, in *U. S. Agric. Rep.*, 1870, pp. 408, 418.

nalis, Kunth.; Vera Cruz or Honduras sarsaparilla, *Smilax medica,* Schl. & Cham.; and Brazilian sarsaparilla, *Smilax syphilitica,* Willd. (Pereira). Many other so-called sarsaparillas are derived from various species scattered throughout the more tropical regions of the world. The Javanese China-root, *Smilax China,* Linn., is a noted alterative; its substitutes and supposed analogues are: the Brazilian *China branca e rubra, Japicanga* or *Ihapecanga, Smilax glauca,* Mart.; the Sylhetian *Smilax glabra,* Roxb.; the Indian *Smilax, lanceæfolia,* Roxb.; the sweet-tea of New Holland, *Smilax glycyphylla,* Smith; and the American China-root, *Smilax Pseudo-China.*

History and Habitat.—Trillium erectum is one of our common indigenous plants, ranging from North Carolina northward. It grows in damp, rich, well-shaded woods, and flowers in the month of May. The variety *album* is not common eastward; it habits the same localities, and flowers a little later.

Concerning the properties of this genus, Rafinesque, who claims to introduce it into Materia Medica, says:* "Almost all the species may be used indifferently, although the Indians have a notion that those with red blossoms (which they call male) are the best, and those with white blossoms (called female) are best for women's complaints. The species most commonly used, because most common, are the *T. nutans (i. e. T. erectum), T. pictum (T. erythrocarpum), T. grandiflorum, T. medium, (T. cernuum),* etc. They are all astringent, restringent, pectoral, tonic, antiseptic, alterative, etc. They are employed internally in hematuria, uterine hemorrhage, metrorrhagia, hematemesis, etc. The Indians of Canada and Missouri value the roots much in leucorrhœa, menorrhœa, and as a restringent after parturition." The use of the tubers as an external application in ulcers, inflamed swellings, sores, etc., is similar to that of the liliaceæ in general. On account of the acridity of the roots they have been used to promote ptyalism, and are claimed to check epistaxis when a newly-cut root is held to the nose and the acridity inspired.

Trillium is not officinal in the Pharmacopœias.

Pharmacy.—Considerable doubt exists among our authors and pharmacists concerning which species of this genus should be used for our tincture. I therefore consider it full time, and this the place, to settle upon the most proper source of the drug. Dr. Minton, the original prover—whose MS. is printed in the *Encyclopedia,* under Trillium cernuum †—informs me that he procured his tincture for proving "from a botanic physician, long since dead;" the species used and the mode of preparation are uncertain. The *American Homœopathic Pharmacopœia* ‡ directs the use of *T. pendulum,* Ait., and describes no distinct species, but approaches nearer *T. cernuum* than any other. Dr. E. M. Hale says:§ "From the remarks of Dr. John King, in the *Eclectic Dispensatory,* we learn that it is a matter of indifference which, or how many, species of Trillium go to make up the preparations

---

* *Medical Flora,* 1830, pp. 102-3.
† *Encyclopedia of Pure Mat. Med.,* Allen, vol. x, p. 637.
‡ Second edition, p. 442.
§ *Hale's New Remedies,* 4th ed., vol. i, p. 629.

in use in that school. It is my conviction that no reliable knowledge can be gained by using a preparation made in this loose manner. For use in disease, some definite, reliable tincture, made from a single species should be used. I am satisfied, however, from my inquiries, that none of the tinctures or triturations now in use by homœopathists is prepared from the Trillium pendulum alone. We must adopt one of two methods—either one species exclusively, or several combined in exact proportions."

On account of its wide range, prolific growth, acridity and evident strength, I deem *Trillium erectum, Linn.*, the common purple Trillium, the proper species for homœopathic use. In this I am upheld by Dr. T. F. Allen and others of our most thorough botanically educated physicians. I am assured also that our most important pharmacies in the East use this species, under the label *T. pendulum ; one pharmacy only* using *T. pendulum*, Ait.

In regard to the frequency of the species of Trillium in this State (New York), taking *T. grandiflorum* to be the most common, and giving it the value 10, the value in occurrence of the other species in proportion—according to my personal observations—would be :

T. erectum 9, *T. cernuum* 6, *T. pendulum*, Ait., 3, *T. erythrocarpum* 2, and *T. sessile* 1.

PART USED AND PREPARATION.—The fresh tubers should be chopped and pounded to a pulp and weighed. Then two parts by weight of alcohol are taken, the pulp mixed thoroughly with one-sixth part of it, and the rest of the alcohol added. After having stirred the whole well, pour it into a well-stoppered bottle, and allow it to stand eight days in a dark, cool place.

The tincture, separated from this mass by filtration, should have a light, slightly brownish-orange color, by transmitted light, no distinguishing odor nor taste, an acid reaction, and should raise a soap-like foam on shaking. This tincture will deposit a heavy cream-colored sediment on standing, which can be filtered off without detriment to it. This sediment, when dried, forms an amorphous mass, without odor or taste, and answers to none of the starch tests. It is insoluble in water, alcohol, ether, alkalies, or acids to any extent; melts at 249° (480.2° F.), and burns at a higher temperature with a bright yellow flame, leaving no ash.

CHEMICAL CONSTITUENTS.—*Trilline.* Prof. E. S. Wayne* separated from a tincture of Trillium, a dry, whitish, amphorous, pulverable, powerfully acrid mass, soluble in alcohol, and forming, when shaken with water, a permanent, opaline, frothing, soap-like mixture. A tincture of this body, spread thinly on glass, formed a bright glistening scale.

He also separated a volatile oil, gum, resin, extractive, tannic acid and starch.

I have followed his line of procedure and corroborated his analysis in full, having, however, too small quantities of the resultants to further experiment upon. I shall, next season, analyze the tubers of Trillium erectum and other species, to

---

* *Am. Jour. Phar.*, 1856, p. 512.

better settle upon the qualities of this genus, and determine, if possible, its most representative species.

PHYSIOLOGICAL ACTION.—We have a careful proving of Trillium by Prof. Henry Minton, as before mentioned, and some excellent clinical experience; the full action, however, is not yet determinable from these. This certainly is a drug deserving full and careful study and proving, and I promise the fraternity to do my share as fully and promptly as time and material shall render possible.

DESCRIPTION OF PLATE 175.

Trillium erectum, var. album.

TRILLIUM PENDULUM, AIT.

1. Upper portion of plant, Binghamton, N. Y., May 12th, 1884.
    2. Lower portion and root.
    3. Stamen (enlarged).
    4. Pollen x 280.
    5. Pistil (enlarged).
    6. Ovary in horizontal section (enlarged).

N. ORD.—LILIACEÆ.
Tribe.—MELANTHIEÆ.
GENUS.—**VERATRUM**,* TOURN.
SEX. SYST.—POLYGAMIA MONŒCIA.

176

VERATRUM VIRIDE.

AMERICAN WHITE HELLEBORE.

SYN.—VERATRUM VIRIDE, AIT.; V. ALBUM, MICHX. (NOT LINN.); V. ALBUM, VAR. (?) REGEL; V. PARVIFLORUM, BONG. (NOT MICHX.); V. ESCHSCHOLTZII, GRAY; HELONIAS VIRIDIS, BOT. MAG. 1096.

COM. NAMES.—AMERICAN WHITE HELLEBORE, FALSE HELLEBORE, INDIAN POKE, MEADOW POKE, SWAMP HELLEBORE, ITCH WEED, INDIAN UNCUS, PUPPET ROOT, EARTHGALL, CROW POISON; (FR.) VÉRATRE VERT; (GER.) GRÜNER GERMER.

A TINCTURE OF THE FRESH ROOT OF VERATRUM VIRIDE, AIT.

Description.—This pubescent perennial grows to a height of from 2 to 5 feet. *Root* coarse, thick, fleshy, and more or less horizontal; the lower part throwing off numerous white fibres. *Stem* erect, simple, stout, and leafy to the top. *Leaves* 3-ranked, broadly oval, and strongly pointed, plaited, clasping by a sheathed base, and gradually decreasing in size upward to mere lanceolate bracts. *Inflorescence* a terminal pyramidal panicle, 8 to 18 inches long, composed of dense, spike-like, spreading, loosely floral racemes; *flowers* monœciously polygamous, greenish or olivaceous green. *Sepals* 6, ovate-oblong, moderately spreading, separate, contracted at the base, clawless and glandless, and entirely free from the ovary. *Stamens* 6; *filaments* free from, and shorter than, the sepals, recurving; *anthers* extrorse, reniform, confluently 1-celled at the apex. *Ovules* ascending, anatropous; *styles* none; *stigmas* 3, ligulate, separate down to the ovary, recurved. *Fruit* a 3-horned and carpelled, septicidal capsule; *seeds* 8 to 10 in each carpel, flattish-oblong, with a broad membranaceous margin and an acute apex; *embryo* oval; *albumen* sarcous.

Although much like the *V. album* of Europe in its minor points, yet our species is strikingly different in general appearance. The American species has a much more pointed leaf and its panicle looser and more compound; the racemes of *V. album* being compact, and, as a whole, cylindrical; while those of *V. viride* are scattered, compounded, and scraggly.

History and Habitat.—Veratrum viride is indigenous to North America, where it habits low grounds from Canada southward to the mountain meadows of Georgia, flowering in the north in July, and in the south in April or May.

---

* *Vere,* truly; *atrum,* black.

There are four other North American species of Veratrum, all of which may be compared with the species under consideration.

The first account we have of the use of this plant is that of Josselyn* (1638), who speaks of the use of the root as an ordeal by the young Aborigines in the selection of their tribal chiefs—"he whose stomach withstood its action the longest was decided to be the strongest of the party, and entitled to command the rest." Kalm (1749) states† that at the time of his visit here the people used a decoction of this plant externally in the cure of scorbutic affections, and to destroy vermin. He also states that corn was soaked in a strong decoction of the root before planting, to protect it against birds, and observed that birds, after eating of this corn, became attacked with vertigo, and in their blind struggling frightened away the balance of the flock ; those who ate of the grain, however, recovering from its effects. The first prescriber of the drug in regular practice was probably Dr. John Ware,‡ who used it in the Boston Almshouse in cases of tinea capitis. Dr. Bigelow states§ that during the Revolutionary War, when *V. album* could not be procured, various gouty patients used the American plant with success, not finding a point of difference. It is doubtless right to give Dr. Norwood, of South Carolina, the credit of establishing the proper method of administering the drug,|| and it was through his use in part that its employment began in England in 1862. Although Dr. Ware was probably the first to experiment with this drug to gain an idea of its physiological action, Drs. Tully and Ives (1830) were the first to investigate its therapeutic action as well. Dr. Charles Osgood, who studied under Professor Tully—modestly giving the professor most of the honor of learning its properties —wrote an excellent essay upon the drug in 1835.¶ Little attention, however, seemed to follow this essay until Dr. Norwood's paper appeared in 1851, from which time the drug gained gradually the prominence it now holds, principally through the efforts of Prof. Samuel Percy in 1856, Drs. Miller, Belden, Cutter, Richard (1858), Ingalls, and Prof. M'Gugin of Iowa (1861).

The principal uses of the drug were as a depressor of the heart's action wherever it was deemed necessary, and an application and internal remedy in arthritic troubles of all kinds; its officinal preparations in the U. S. Ph. being *Extractum Veratri Viridis Fluidum* and *Tinctura Veratri Viridis.*

PART USED AND PREPARATION.—The fresh root, gathered after the leaves have fallen in autumn, is treated as in the preceding drug, excepting that *dilute* alcohol is used.

The resulting tincture has a brilliant, slightly orange, madder color by transmitted light; a peculiar rich odor and taste; and an acid reaction.

CHEMICAL CONSTITUENTS.—Dr. Chas. Osgood** and Thos. A. Mitchell†† were the first to suspect by analysis that the alkaloid commonly known as Veratrine existed in the species viride, and H. W. Worthington‡‡ the first to assert the

---

* *New England Rarities Discovered*, Lond., 1672, p. 46 ; *Account of Two Voyages to New England*, 1674, pp. 60–76.
† *Travels in North America*, vol. ii.   ‡ Communication to Dr. Bigelow.   § *Am. Med. Bot., loc. cit.*
| 5 to 8 drops of the tincture, as advised in this work.   ¶ *Am. Jour. Med. Sci.*
** *Am. Jour. Phar.*, vol. i, series 2.   †† Ibid., vol. ix.   ‡‡ Ibid., vol. x, p. 110.

fact. From this time the chemistry of the plant became a great study by many, principally G. J. Scattergood (1862),* Chas. Bullock (1865† and 1879),‡ Prof. G. B. Wood, E. Peugenet (1872), C. L. Mitchell (1874), Robbins (1877),§ and Wright and Luff (1879).‖ The results of these studies show a similarity in this species to *V. album* of Europe; tabulated from the observations of Wright and Luff, as follows. One kilogramme of the roots of each species yielded:

	V. album.	*V. viride.*
Jervia,	1.30	0.20
Pseudojervia,	0.40	0.15
Rubijervia,	0.25	0.02
Veratralbia,	2.20	traces
Veratria,	0.05	0.004
Cevadina,	(?)	0.43
	4.20	0.804

Jervia, $C_{26}H_{37}NO_3$.—This amorphous alkaloid (the *viridia* of G. B. Wood) forms an almost insoluble sulphate, crystallizing with two molecules of water, melting at 239° (462.2°, F.), and giving with sulphuric acid almost the same coloration as the next.

Pseudojervia, $C_{29}H_{43}NO_7$.—A snow-white base, crystallizing anhydrous from alcohol, melting at 299° (570.2°, F.), and giving a yellow solution with sulphuric acid, gradually turning green.

Rubijervia, $C_{26}H_{43}NO_2$—A base forming a readily-soluble sulphate and well-crystallized salts in general. It melts at 237° (458.6°, F.), and resembles in many ways the preceding; it, however, gives with sulphuric acid a red coloration.

Veratralbia, $C_{28}H_{43}NO_5$.—This base gives a red coloration with sulphuric acid, and greatly resembles cevadina and the veratria of other authors.

Cevadina, $C_{32}H_{49}NO_9$.—An amorphous mass, greatly resembling the vera-tralbia of *V. album*, and termed the sternutatory property of V. viride.

The above digest of Wright and Luff's analysis is anything but satisfactory, and is open to much criticism as regards its solution of the problem still before us. The following latest analysis of the Veratrine of *V. album*, by Dr. Emil Bossetti,¶ will serve to throw some light upon the complex nature of the principles of this genus. First: he claims that veratrine is a homogeneous mixture of two isomeric alkaloids; these he designates as insoluble

Veratrine, $C_{32}H_{49}NO_9$.—A crystallizable alkaloid (the cevadina of Wright and Luff), insoluble in water, which decomposes on boiling with an alcoholic solution of barium hydrate,** into angelic acid, $C_5H_8O_2$, and

Cevadine, $C_{27}H_{45}NO_9$.—An amorphous, yellowish-white powder, having an alkaline reaction and a peculiar sweetish taste.

The other isomer soluble veratrine, or

* *Am. Phar. Assoc.*, Aug., 1862, p. 226.   † *Am. Jour. Phar.*, 1865, p. 321.   ‡ Ibid., 1879, p. 337.
§ *Am. Phar. Assoc.*, 1877, pp. 439, 523.   ‖ *Phar. Jour. and Trans.*, May 31, 1879.   ¶ *Arch. der Pharm.*, 21, p. 81.

         Veratrine.   Water. Angelic Acid. Cevadine.
** $C_{32}H_{49}NO_9 + (H_2O)_2 = C_5H_8O_2 + C_{27}H_{45}NO_9$.

Veratridine, $C_{32}H_{49}NO_9$.—An uncrystallizable alkaloid (the soluble veratrine of Weigelin and E. Schmit), soluble in water, and decomposing when boiled with an alcoholic solution of baryta water* into veratric acid, and

Veratroine, $C_{55}H_{92}N_2O_{16}$.—A body forming, after dehydration and trituration, a yellowish-white powder, the dust of which causes coughing and sneezing. It is sparingly soluble in water, but readily soluble in chloroform, ether, amylic alcohol. benzol, and carbon bisulphide; therefore answering fully to C. L. Mitchell's *veratroidia* as obtained from *V. viride*, to which Tobien gave the formula $C_{51}H_{78}N_2O_{16}$.

Veratric Acid, $C_9H_{10}O_4$, crystallizes in colorless needles, losing their water of crystallization on heating. and sublimes completely at high temperatures. This body is soluble in water and alcohol, and insoluble in ether.

PHYSIOLOGICAL ACTION.—*On Animals.*—Dr. Percy's experiments upon dogs and frogs show finely the action of the drug. From his prize essay from the *Am. Med. Assoc.*, 1863, I have selected two of the more prominent cases:

"EXPERIMENT VII.—Into the cellular tissue of the right lumbar region of a mongrel dog weighing sixteen pounds was passed, by Wade and Ford's hypodermic syringe, ten minims of the concentrated tincture. The pulse at the time was 110. The movements soon became uneasy and unsteady. In eighteen minutes the dog vomited, and the pulse was reduced to 63. In thirty-four minutes the dog staggered, lay down, and was unable to rise, the retching continuing frequent. In thirty minutes the dog lay completely on its side, and the saliva flowed very freely from his mouth. The eye was dull, the pupils widely dilated, but fixed; but the eye closed if the cornea was touched. The limbs were very flaccid, the pulse 32. Ten minims more of the same tincture were now injected into the left lumbar region. In forty-five minutes from the first injection, the heart was beating 14 in the minute, and very irregular; the saliva continued to flow freely from the mouth, being almost as limpid as water. *The dog was perfectly insensible to pain.* The respirations were slow but full. At one hour from the first injection, the heart merely fluttered; the dog could be moved in any way without the slightest *voluntary* motion. The urine and feces were passed involuntarily.

"EXPERIMENT I.—Ten minims of a solution containing ⅓ gr. of the alkaloid veratria made from veratrum viride, by Mr. George Scattergood, of Philadelphia, were given to a large dog weighing about thirty pounds, in gelatine capsules; great care was taken that none of it escaped into the mouth.

3.35 P.M.		Pulse	150
4 "	salivation very profuse.	"	148
4.05 "	vomited.	"	——
4.20 "	vomiting very frequently.	"	140
4.45 "	vomiting viscid mucus and bile.	"	128
5.20 "	prostration very great, unable to stand.	"	122
5.45 "	pupils widely dilated, eyes fixed.	"	122
6 "	prostration great, profuse salivation.	Intermittent	
9 "	walking about, but sober and dejected.	"	112

Veratridine.   Water.   Veratric Acid. Veratroine.

$$* (C_{32}H_{49}NO_2)_2 + (H_2O)_2 = C_9H_{10}O_4 + C_{55}H_{92}N_2O_{16}.$$

" Three days afterward the same dose was again given to the same dog, with very similar results. With this animal, the pulse was not much depressed, the prostration was very great, and there was almost total loss of power of the voluntary muscles.

"During the months of July and August, 1857, I tried thirty-one experiments upon dogs with the alkaloid, made by myself from veratrum viride, and with the commercial veratria made by Merck, for the purpose of ascertaining if they were alike in their therapeutic action.

" From these experiments I learned that the alkaloid from the viride was more sedative in its effects upon the pulse than the commercial veratria ; that it was less irritant, seldom causing an increase in the number of pulsations, which the commercial veratria frequently did ; that it produced vomiting and prostration in about an equal degree ; that when a large dose was given, and prostration induced, there was most generally a dilatation of the pupils, but this effect was not produced by small doses ; that purging was but seldom produced by either when given by the mouth, but nearly always when given by hypodermic injection ; that large doses of either, amounting to two grains at a time, might be given, producing alarming prostration, and most painful and protracted vomiting, without causing death, if brandy, brandy and morphia, or tincture of cantharides was administered; and that in every instance the animal's life might be saved by proper attention.

" In those instances where death took place from these alkaloids, it was caused by repeating the dose, and not by a dose of two grains administered at one time. Upon post-mortem examination, the mucous membrane of the stomach was much inflamed, and in some instances the inflammation extended more or less through the whole intestinal tract, and was always seen at the rectum ; the kidneys were in a state of congestion, and the heart filled with dark blood.

" Both alkaloids produced a sedative effect upon the pulse, but the commercial veratria did not to the same extent as that from the viride, and neither of them to the same extent as the pure resinoid, or the tincture made from veratrum viride.

" The prostration was more complete, alarming, and prolonged, and the vomiting was more painful and continued from the effects of the alkaloid than from the other preparations named."

Dr. Percy's experiments upon frogs, meanwhile watching their circulation with the aid of a microscope, are very interesting. After the injection of the tincture, the course of the blood through the capillaries " may be watched until the circulation is so regular and sluggish that the blood-globules may be counted as they course through the smaller vessels, and the difference between the white and red disks, and their position in the larger capillaries, may be easily discerned. Sometimes the circulation would almost entirely cease in the web, but would return again in ten or fifteen minutes if the frog upon the plate was placed in fresh running water.

" It was always interesting to watch the cessation of the circulation and its recommencement.

" When large doses of the veratrum viride were given by the stomach, the cessation of the circulation never occurred suddenly. There would be intermissions of longer or shorter duration; after each one, the current of blood when re-established would be slower than before, and after a while would cease. After it had ceased there would be an occasional throb, which would cause a general movement, but upon the subsidence of the impetus, the blood-disks would be in about the same situation as before.

"The occurrence of this throb was the first notice given of the return of the circulation; it would be repeated at shorter intervals, sometimes a minute elapsing, and then several of such pulsations would occur in a minute. Then a short but general movement would take place of the blood-disks, at each pulsation, ceasing upon cessation of the *vis a tergo*, and again renewed, until the circulation was entirely established in a slow but steady current."

On Man.—Veratrum viride causes slight or temporary delirium; vertigo, especially when in an erect position; dimness and unsteadiness of vision, which compels a horizontal position; dry mouth and lips; tongue coated at base and sides, with a red streak down the centre; dryness of the throat and numbness of the fauces; excessive and painful singultus, profuse salivation, with severe spasms of the superior portion of the œsophagus, and great nausea, vomiting and cold sweat; vomit composed of mucus, bile, and dark-colored blood; pain and soreness of the lower abdomen; urine clear and scant; convulsive, suffocating breathing; pulse slow, weak, small, and soft, reduced even to almost imperceptibility; very profound prostration, the patient is unable to rise or to walk; profuse cold sweat, with chills and coldness of the surface of the body.

The action, then, is that of an arterial and nerve sedative; it paralyzes both the voluntary and involuntary muscles; it increases all secretions through its influence in paralyzing the vaso-motor system of nerves, allowing thus a great dilation of the capillaries.

DESCRIPTION OF PLATE 176.

1. Whole plant, 6 times reduced, Binghamton, N. Y., July 7th, 1885.
2. A small raceme, from the lower portion of the panicle.
3. Under surface of flower, showing bract.
4. Sepal.
5. Stamens.
6. Pistil.
7. Longitudinal section of ovary.
8. Horizontal section of ovary.

(3–8 enlarged.)

3

6 7 8

4

5

1

2

ℰ.𝔪. ad nat del. et pinxt.

VERATRUM VÍRIDE, Ait.

N. ORD.—LILIACEÆ.

Tribe.—MELANTHIEÆ.

GENUS.—**CHAMAELIRIUM,*** WILLD.

SEX. SYST.—HEXANDRIA TRIGYNIA.

177
HELONIAS.†

DEVIL'S BIT.

SYN.—CHAMAELIRIUM LUTEUM, GRAY; C. CAROLINIANUM, WILLD.; HELONIAS DIOICA, PURSH.; H. PUMILA, JACQ.; H. LUTEA, AIT.; VERATRUM LUTEUM, LINN.; MELANTHIUM DIOICUM, WALT.; M. DENSUM, LAM.; OPHIOSTACHYS VIRGINICA, DEL.; ABALON ALBIFLORUM, RAF.

COM. NAMES.—DEVIL'S BIT, BLAZING STAR, UNICORN PLANT, DROOPING STARWORT, FALSE UNICORN ROOT, STARWORT, COLIC ROOT.‡

A TINCTURE OF THE ROOT OF CHAMAELIRIUM LUTEUM, GRAY.

Description.—This smooth perennial herb attains a growth of from 1 to 3 feet. *Stem* wand-like, leafy. *Rootstock* thick, abrupt, light colored, and furnished with many long roots from the base of the stem, and a number of fibrous rootlets from its thickest portion. *Leaves* alternate, parallel veined, those of the upper stem small, lanceolate, and sessile, increasing in size toward the root, where they tend toward spatulate and are tapered into a petiole. *Inflorescence* diœcious, both kinds in long, terminal, virgate, spike-like racemes, the fertile nearly erect, the sterile more or less curved; *pedicels* spreading in the male, erect in the female, all bractless. *Perianth* in both sexes composed of 6, spatulate, spreading, marcescent sepals. *Stamens* 6, unequal, longer than the sepals in the male flower, short and rudimentary in the female; *filaments* thread-shaped; *anthers* yellow, 2-celled, roundish oval, and extrorse. *Ovary* green, usually wanting in the sterile flowers; *styles* 3, linear-clavate, spreading, separate down to, and nearly as long as, the ovary; *stigmas* simply the inner surfaces of the styles. *Fruit* an ovoid-oblong, 3-celled pod, loculicidally 3-valved from the apex. *Seeds* numerous, linear-oblong, winged at each end.

History and Habitat.—The Devil's Bit is indigenous to North America, where it ranges from Western New England westward to Illinois and southward; it habits rich woods, and flowers in June.

* χαμαί, *chamai*, on the ground; λειριον, *leirion*, lily.

† Ἑλος, *helos*, marsh; as some species frequent bogs.

‡ For analysis of the common names, see foot-note and history, under Aletris, 172.

On account more of the similarity of vulgarisms than aught else, this plant and Aletris are gathered as the same in various localities, or are interchanged. The root of Helonias, however, is too characteristic, even when thoroughly dried, to be mistaken for that of any other plant known to me. When this root is cut across it will be plainly noticeable that the fibrous rootlets pierce the cortex through ample foramina, in which they are found to be freely movable, like a thread in the eye of a needle (Fig. 9); this character is constant and specific. It is said that there is an aboriginal legend to the effect that the bad spirit, angered that this root should cure all disorders—as was then supposed—bit off a portion of it to curtail its usefulness, whence the name Devil's Bit.

The previous medical history of this plant dates from the aboriginal use against colic, worms, and fevers. In domestic and botanic practice it is considered tonic, diuretic, emetic, sialagogue, emmenagogue, vermifuge, and antiscorbutic. Rafinesque says that its mere application to the skin causes diuresis. Dr. B. S. Barton thought that its relief of colic was on account of some narcotic power. Dr. Ives used it as a tonic, and commends it for checking nausea and vomiting. Dr. Braman* had the utmost confidence in the root in the cure of leucorrhœa. The Indian squaws employed the root to check miscarriages, and chewed the root to relieve coughs. Helonias proves itself very useful in atony of the generative organs of both sexes, especially when associated with colic and severe lumbar pains.

PART USED AND PREPARATION.—The fresh root, gathered after the fruits have bursted, is treated as directed under Trillium.† The resulting tincture has a beautiful, clear orange color by transmitted light; no distinguishing odor; a pleasant, but very bitter, taste; and an acid reaction.

CHEMICAL CONSTITUENTS.— *Chamælirin.* Dr. Green succeeded in isolating this glucoside from the root, and suggests the name. Like many principles of the lily tribe, this body is saponaceous in its alcoholic and aqueous solutions, and insoluble in other general solvents. He describes the body as an amorphous, neutral, bitter powder, splitting, through the agency of dilute acids, into glucose and an uninvestigated body that is insoluble.

The Tildens' analysis‡ resulted in the determination of an oleo-resin, a bitter principle, extractive, gum, starch, and other bodies not essential.

PHYSIOLOGICAL ACTION.—The symptoms caused in several experimenters from the ingestion of varying doses of the tincture and of *helonin*, are in substance as follows: Mental depression; headache, fulness, and vertigo; dimness of vision; dryness of the mouth and fauces; irritation and burning of the stomach; colic; slight purging followed by scyballa; burning in the region of the kidneys "like two bags of hot water;" profuse urination followed by uncertainty of the sphincter vesicæ; uterine hemorrhage, and burning of the pudenda; lowering of the

---

* *Bost. Med. and Surg. Jour.*, xl, 416.   † Page 175-5.   ‡ *Jour. Mat. Med.*, N. S., ii, 122.

frequency of the pulse; severe lumbar pain; languor, chilliness, and flashes of heat.*

DESCRIPTION OF PLATE 177.

1 and 2. Whole male plant, Port Crane, N. Y., June 29th, 1885.
3. A male flower.
4. Sepal.
5. Stamen.
6. Anther.
7. Female flower.
8. A style.
9. Horizontal section of the rootstalk.
10. Fruit.
11. Horizontal section of the fruit.
(3–8 and 10–11 enlarged.)

* Allen, *Ency. Mat. Med.*, iv, 565–72; mostly from Dr. Samuel A. Jones' experiments.

℃m. ad nat. del. et pinxt.   CHAMÆLÌRIUM LÙTEUM, Gray.

178
LILIUM SUPERBUM.

TURK'S-CAP LILY.

SYN.—LILIUM SUPERBUM, LINN.; L. CAROLINIANUM, MICHX. (?)
COM. NAMES.—TURK'S-CAP LILY, SUPERB LILY, MEADOW LILY, WILD
TIGER LILY.

A TINCTURE OF THE FRESH BULB OF LILIUM SUPERBUM, LINN.

Description.—This beautiful perennial herb attains a growth of from 3 to 7 feet. *Bulb* scaly; *stems* simple, erect, glabrous, rounded. *Leaves* sessile, the lower in whorls of from 5 to 7, the upper scattered, all 3-nerved, lanceolate, pointed, and smooth. *Inflorescence* a terminal pyramidal raceme; *flowers* 3 to 40, nodding; *perianth* open campanulate, its divisions somewhat coherent at their bases. *Sepals* 6, sessile, strongly revolute, deciduous, bright orange with numerous dark purple spots inside, and a honey-bearing furrow at the base. *Stamens* 6, shorter than the style, hypogynous; *filaments* dilated and somewhat adherent at their bases, from which they taper to a very fine apex at the point of fixture of the anther; *anthers* linear, versatile, at first included then projecting, opening by a lateral or slightly introrse line. *Ovary* 3-celled; *ovules* anatropous. *Style* elongated club-shaped; *stigma* apical, 3-lobed, the receptive surface velvety. *Fruit* an oblong, subtriangular, 3-celled, loculicidal capsule, each cell containing two rows of seeds. *Seeds* numerous, horizontally flattened by compression; *testa* soft; *embryo* small, axial; *albumen* fleshy.

History and Habitat.—This beautiful lily is indigenous to North America from the Carolinas northward to Canada and westward to the Rocky Mountains, where it habits rich low grounds, and flowers from June through July.

This species has no medical history, its congener, *L. tigrinum*, of China, covering all that is known concerning this.

PART USED AND PREPARATION.—The fresh bulbs are treated in the same manner as those of Trillium (p. 175–5). The resulting tincture has a beautiful orange color by transmitted light; no distinguishing odor; a bitter and astringent taste, and an acid reaction.

---

* The classical Latin name, from the Celtic *li*, or the Greek λειριον, *leirion*, white.

Ⓔ.ɱ.. ad nat del.et pinxt.

LÍLIUM SUPÉRBUM, Linn.

In preparing the tincture in further provings, the flowers, when in full sexual power, should be included, thus extending its therapeutic usefulness.

PHYSIOLOGICAL ACTION.—The only account of the action of this drug is that of Dr. E. Reading,* who records the following effects: Mental exhaustion; headache; dullness of the eye; epistaxis; paleness and sickly expression of countenance; bitter taste in the mouth; burning of the mouth and œsophagus; increased appetite; splenic discomfort; constipation; oppression of chest; acceleration of the pulses; weakness of the extremities; languor; debility, prostration, and restlessness.

DESCRIPTION OF PLATE 178.

1. Upper portion of flowering plant, Elmira, N. Y., Aug. 11th, 1885.
2. Section of mid-stem.
3. Stamen.
4. Stigma.
5. Young fruit.
6. Section of ovary.
(3, 4, and 6 enlarged.)

---

* Allen, *Encyc. Mat. Med.*, X, 572.

SERIES

CRYPTOGAMIA.

Plants without flowers; *i. e.* destitute of the essential organs
stamens and pistils, and producing in lieu of
seeds, numerous microscopic bodies
capable of germination,
called spores.

CLASS

ACROGENS.

Cryptogams with distinct stems and branches, exhibiting
woody tissue and vessels, and generally with
some sort of foliage

GENUS.—**EQUISETUM**,* LINN.

SEX. SYST.—CRYPTOGAMIA FILICES.

179

EQUISETUM.

GREAT SCOURING RUSH.

SYN.—EQUISETUM HYEMALE, LINN.

COM. NAMES.— SCOURING RUSH, DUTCH RUSH, SCRUBBING RUSH, SHAVE-GRASS, WINTER HORSETAIL ; (FR.) PRÊLE ; (GER.) SCHACH-TELHALM.

A TINCTURE OF THE WHOLE FRESH PLANT EQUISETUM HYEMALE, LINN.

Description.—This erect, arrow-like plant grows to a height of from 1 to 3 or 4 feet. *Root* perennial, horizontal, jointed like the stem, putting off from the sections, at their middle, numerous moss-like rootlets. *Stem* simple, rarely inconspicuously branched, sub-cylindrical from root to spike, hollow, evergreen, surviving the winter; *ridges* 17 to 27, very rough; *tubercles* in two more or less distinct lines on the ridges, constituting the roughness of the stem. *Sheaths* elongated, closely appressed to the stem at each joint, and furnished with a black zone at their bases; *limb* black, composed of as many teeth as there are ridges upon the stems; *teeth* linear, narrow, each with a keel at its base, appearing as a prolongation of the ridge below ; the awned points deciduous. *Epidermis* abounding in silex; *stomata* disposed in two lines, one on each side of the groove. *Spike* apical, ovate, armed with a sharp, rigid, black tip; *scales* with a dark, brownish-black face.

Equisetaceæ and Equisetum.—This family of flowerless plants is very characteristically distinct, consisting of one genus only, the *Equiseta*, immediately recognized after once examined. They consist of fertile and sterile stems, often branched, and always jointed, hollow, and rough. The root, in its solid portion, is composed from centre to circumference of the following layers: strong cellular tissue ; a circle of air-canals, each surrounded by a zone of vascular bundles; a circle of vascular bundles composed of annular ducts; a parenchyma traversed by air-canals; a circlet of parenchymatous cells; and the cuticle. As the rhizome approaches the stems it becomes hollow through the loss of the central cellular tissue and the modification of the other layers. The jointed *stems* and *branches* are hollow and bridged by a thin membranous diaphragm at each joint. The

---

* *Equus*, a horse; *seta*, a hair or bristle.

fruiting head is somewhat cone-shaped, composed of a central axis as a prolongation of the last joint of the stem, upon which are situated, like growing toad-stools,
numerous groups of *thecæ* or *sporanges*, joined by their bases to a central axis, and
looking inward, so that only the somewhat hexagonal flattened cap is seen externally. These sporanges, as they ripen, separate from one another, and finally
burst longitudinally, allowing the escape of the spores. The *spores* are very strange
bodies, unlike any other form of vegetable matter. They are ovoid in shape, and
composed of two coats, the outer splitting spirally, thus forming four thread-like
bodies, thicker at their free ends, called *elaters*, which, from what follows, will be
seen to be very useful in scattering the seed. While the spores are crowded in
the sporangia, or when they are damp, these elaters are tightly coiled around the
spore; but, as soon as the theca bursts, or the spores become dry, the elaters un-
coil with force, causing the propulsion of the spore to quite an extent. This may
be seen by placing a few spores under the microscope and breathing upon them;
the exhaled moisture causes the elaters to coil up immediately; by quickly placing
the eye at the tube a curious sight is witnessed as drying commences. If the drying is slow, the spores roll and twist about like spiders in pain; while, if the drying
is quick, they will skip from the field of view like grasshoppers. The *germination*
of the spore is quite similar to the process of multiplication in the rod-bacteria.
A bud-like process puts out from the spore and soon becomes cut by a septum;
this grows on and multiplies in all directions until a tuft is formed, from the centre
of which arises *archegonia* and *antheridia*, in distinct bodies. After fertilization of
an archegonium, the germ-cell developes like an embryo. At the present day the
Equiseta are all comprised in one genus, but paleontology shows many species of
great size and more varied features.

History and Habitat.—The Scouring Rush grows on wet banks, in open
woods, especially northward, fruiting in early spring. From the abundance of
silex in the cuticle, the stems have been variously used for scouring purposes;
this use has contributed largely to its vocabulary of vulgarisms. It is gathered
into bundles by many housewives and used to brighten tins, floors, and wooden-
ware, and in the arts for polishing woods and metals. Rafinesque says: "This
plant, and allied species, furnish good food for cattle in winter." He speaks of a
tall species, called *Nebratah* by the Missouri Indians, used in the manufacture of
mats, and of a species which he names *E. tuberosum*, the roots of which are used
as food by the Indians.

This plant is not mentioned in the U. S. Ph., and not official in the Eclectic
Materia Medica.

PART USED AND PREPARATION.—The whole fresh plant is chopped and
pounded to a pulp and weighed. Then two parts by weight of alcohol are taken,
the pulp mixed well with one-sixth part of it, and the rest of the alcohol added.
After thorough mixture the whole is poured into a well-stoppered bottle and
allowed to stand eight days in a dark, cool place. The tincture thus formed, after
straining and filtering, should have a light greenish-brown color by transmitted
light, a woody taste, followed by a slight tobacco-like burning of the tongue, and
an acid reaction to litmus-paper.

CHEMICAL CONSTITUENTS, Silicia, SiO_2.—This oxide of silicium is present in the plant in large quantities, ranging, according to different authorities, from 7.5 to 41.2 per cent. of the whole herb.

Equisetic Acid, Aconitic Acid, $C_6H_6O_6$.—This acid was determined in *E. flu-viatile* as magnesium aconitate by Braconnot, who considers it present in the other species of the genus. It forms in highly acid klinorhombic prisms, fusing at about 130° (266° F.), and soluble in both water and alcohol. This acid has also been called "mallic," because it is formed upon the destructive distillation of mallic acid; but it fails to answer to the properties of that acid, as well as to its composition, $C_4H_4O_4$.

PHYSIOLOGICAL ACTION.—Dr. Hugh M. Smith states[*] the following symptoms arising in persons taking from 50 to 150 drops of the tincture: Greatly increased appetite; severe sharp pain, with soreness, in the lower abdomen; pain, tenderness, and distention of the bladder, with frequent urging to urinate; sharp pain along the urethra, burning and aching in the penis and testicles when urinating, with soreness of the testicles and spermatic cord; dull pain and soreness in the back, with prostration.

It is said that where cattle have been given too large quantities of an infusion as a diuretic, it has caused the voidance of blood.

DESCRIPTION OF PLATE 179.

1. Lower portion of stem.
2. Upper portion of stem.

(Two feet of stem between Nos. 1 and 2 left out.)

3. Fruiting head (enlarged.)
4. Sporangia, outer; 5. inner view.
6. Damp spore x 200.
7. Dry spore x 200.
8. Stoma x 200.

From Binghamton, N. Y., May 1, 1884.

---

[*] *Thesis*, N. Y. Hom. Med. Coll., 1876; Allen, *Ency. Pure Mat. Med.*, vol. iv., pp. 204–210.

179

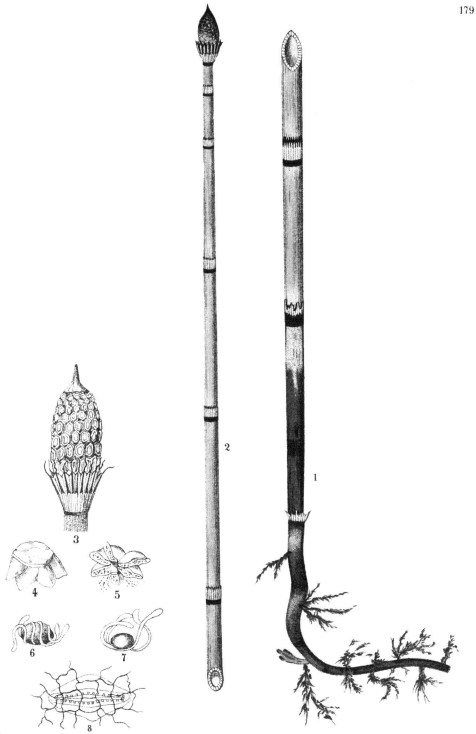

Ɛℳ. ad nat del. et pinxt.   EQUISÈTUM   HYEMÀLE , Linn.

180

LYCOPODIUM.

CLUB MOSS.

SYN.—LYCOPODIUM CLAVATUM, LINN.; L. TRISTACHYUM, PERS.; L. INTEGRIFOLIUM, HOOK.

COM. NAMES.—COMMON CLUB MOSS, GROUND PINE, HOG'S BED, SNAKE MOSS, STAG'S HORN, WOLF'S CLAW; (FR.) PIED DE LOUP; (GER.) KALBEN-MOOS, GEMEINES BÜRLAPP. THE SPORES: VEGETABLE SULPHUR; (FR.) LYCOPODE, SOUFRE VÉGÉTAL; (GER.) BÜRLAPP-SAMEN, BLITZ PULVER, WURM MEHL, HEXEN MEHL.

A TRITURATION OF THE SPORES OF LYCOPODIUM CLAVATUM, LINN.

Description.—This evergreen perennial extends to a length of 30 feet or more. *Stem* tough, flexible, terete, and very leafy, creeping extensively and striking root at varied intervals; *roots* light yellow, wiry, solitary and straight; *branches* ascending, similar to the stems, but short and subdivided, the fertile terminated by a fruiting peduncle. *Leaves* crowded, homogeneous, equal and many-ranked, all linear-awl-shaped, incurved, spreading, light green, and tipped by a long, incurved capillaceous bristle. *Peduncle* of the female branches erect, strict, 4 to 6 inches long, and bearing from 1 to 4, but usually 2, spikes; *bracts* sparse, somewhat appressed, tipped with a fine bristle; *spikes* linear, cylindrical, blunt, erect, mostly in pairs, each composed of an axis and many closely appressed scales; *scales* ovate-triangular, closely imbricated, membranaceous, erosely denticulate, pedicelled and tipped by a filiform point. *Spore-cases* (*theca*) all of one kind, situated in the axils of the scales, all more or less flattened-reniform, coriaceous, 1-celled, and opening by a trans-marginal line down through even the pedicel, leaving each valve an individual stalk. *Spores* copious, very minute, together forming a very mobile, sulphur-yellow powder, which is described further on.

Lycopodiaceæ.—This family of low, moss-like plants, is represented in North America by 2 genera and 13 species; its general characteristics are: *stems* herbaceous or ligneous, simple or branched, and usually prostrate and extensively creeping. *Leaves* usually crowded, linear, simple, sessile, persistent, 1-nerved, and more or less appressed. *Fructification* axillary or spiked; *spore cases* quite large, 2-valved; *spores* generally copious and minute.

---

* Λύκος, *lykos*, a wolf; ποὓς, ποδός, *pous, podos*, a foot; from a fancied resemblance.

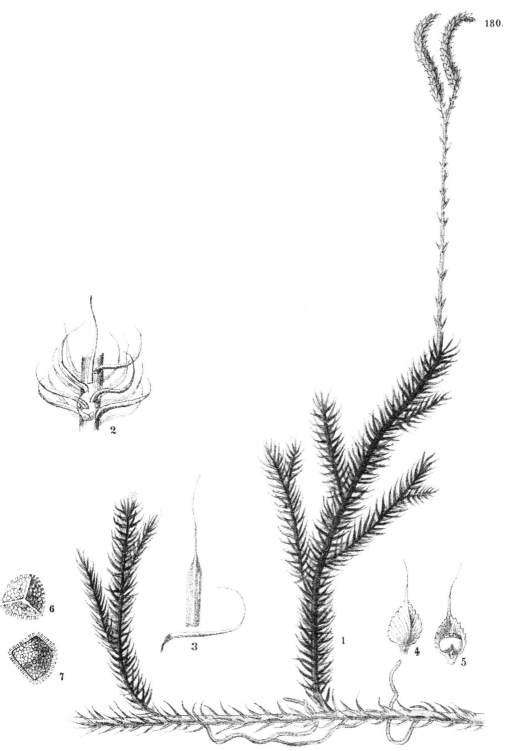

180.

2

6

7

3

1

4

5

𝕮𝖒.ad nat.del.et pinxt.　　LYCOPÒDIUM　CLAVÀTUM, Linn.

This peculiar order furnishes but few drugs, but, contrary to their general appearance, they have high medicinal qualities. The West Indian *Lycopodium cernuum*, Linn., is diuretic, and recommended as a specific for certain forms of dysentery; the Peruvian *L. catharticum*, Hook., is a violent purgative, valued by the natives in leprosy and elephantiasis; the East Indian *L. phlegmaria*, and *L. hygrometricum*, L., are considered aphrodisiac, especially the latter, which is noted for its qualities in this direction; and the European and American *L. Selago*, Linn., an active, narcotic poison; emetic and cathartic in small doses, but dangerous in large, bringing on violent purgation and convulsions; it is also strongly counter-irritant when applied to the skin, being used to keep blisters open, and to kill lice upon animals.

History and Habitat.—The common Club Moss is indigenous to North America, Northern Europe and Asia, as well as like countries of the Southern Hemisphere. It occurs in this country in dry woods, where it is common northward, fruiting in July and August.

Under the names *Muscus terrestris*, or *Muscus clavatus*, this plant was used as a whole, by ancient physicians, as a stomachic and diuretic, though the powder does not appear to be used alone, until about the 17th century. *L. Selago* was employed, by the Druids, as an active cathartic and deobstruent.

The spores have been used as a diuretic in dropsy; a drastic in diarrhœa, dysentery, and suppressions; a nervine in spasms and hydrophobia; an aperient in gout and scurvy; and a corroborant in rheumatism. Externally they are largely used as a dusting powder for various skin diseases, and in excoriations of infants, to prevent chafing; and are considered the most efficacious application to *plica polonica*. In pharmacy, they form the best powder for keeping pills and lozenges from cohering with each other. They are very inflammable, so much so as to flash with a hissing noise when ignited. This property has determined their use in pyrotechnics, and for imitating the lightning's flash in theatrical performances.

The spores are official in the U. S. Ph.; in the Eclectic Dispensatory the plant is not mentioned.

PART USED AND PREPARATION.—The *spores, en masse,* form a very fine, odorless, tasteless, mobile, light-yellow powder, adhering to the fingers, but exhibiting a repulsive force for water. If shaken with water a portion sinks, with alcohol it is readily miscible; it is tinged brown by iodine; and sulphuric acid, when hot, instantly penetrates the spores, rendering them transparent, but not rupturing their coat. *Individually*, under a strong lens, the spores are seen to be bluntly tetrahedral, one surface (the base) being convex, the others triangularly pyramidal, their apices not fully meeting, but leaving a three-armed space. They show a surface finely reticulated by minute ridges, that are more elevated at their junctions, and enclose pent- or hexagonal spaces, the floors of which are occupied by a transparent, but astonishingly tough membrane, which, when ruptured, allows the escape of globules of an oily nature.

Sophistication.—The pollen of some plants, such as the cat-tail (*Typha lati-folia*); pine (various species of *Pinus*); spruce (*Abies*), and hemlock (*Abies Canadensis*), are often mixed fraudulently with the powder, the microscope alone being able to detect the imposition.* Starch, when incorporated with the powder, may be detected by iodine; and talc, gypsum, and chalk may be discovered by throwing the powder into water, or bisulphide of carbon; boxwood powder may be separated by the use of a fine sieve that will allow the spores to pass and retain the wood. However, the Lycopodium of commerce, which is mostly gathered in Russia, Germany, and Switzerland, is usually quite pure.

To obtain an efficacious tincture of Lycopodium, a previous severe trituration for hours, first dry and then with the addition of sufficient alcohol to form a paste, is necessary; then five parts, by weight, of alcohol is added, the whole poured into a well-stoppered bottle, and allowed to stand for eight days in a dark, cool place, being thoroughly shaken twice a day. The tincture, separated by straining and filtering, has a clear straw-color by transmitted light; an oily odor and taste; and a neutral reaction.

CHEMICAL CONSTITUENTS.—Analyses made by Buchholtz and Cadet determined the presence of fat oil 6.0, sugar 3.0, gum 1.5, pollenin 89.5, this last being a mixed body. Stenhouse determined the presence of volatile bases, which were corroborated by Flückiger, who also determined that the ash was not alkaline, and contained alumina and phosphoric acid.

Oil of Lycopodium.—This bland liquid, of which Buchholtz found only 6 per cent., was determined by Flückiger to exist in large amount (47.0 per cent.) when the spores are ruptured. It does not solidify, even at $-15°$ ($+5°$ F.).

[*Lycopodine,* $C_{32}H_{52}N_2O_3$.—This alkaloid, isolated by K. Boedecker† from an aqueous solution of the alcoholic extract of *L. complanatum*, Linn., may prove to exist also in this species. He describes it as a bitter, crystalline body, melting at 114° (237.2° F.), and freely soluble in many liquids, including alcohol and water.]‡

PHYSIOLOGICAL ACTION.—The experiments with this drug by Dr. Arnold, of Heidelberg, with the tincture, and by Prof. Martin, of Jena, and six of his pupils, gave the following: The general symptoms were those of excitement, quickened circulation, headache, increased appetite, more frequent evacuations, and stronger sexual desire. The chief local affinity manifested was for the urinary organs. There was frequent and sometimes painful micturition; and the urine was cloudy and sedimentous, occasionally charged with mucus and even blood. This mostly covers the so-called physiological action, though, when long-continued doses of the more highly potentized drug are taken, the scope of this remedy is immeasurably enlarged.§

* See Fig. 11, Plate 163, and Fig. 9, Plate 164.
† *Ann. de Chim.*, 208, 363.
‡ *Am. Jour. Phar.*, 1882, 77.
§ Consult *Allen's Encyclopædia of Pure Materia Medica*, vol. 6, pp. 1–69.

DESCRIPTION OF PLATE 180.

1. A portion of a stem after fruition, from Wenham, Mass., Nov. 23d, 1886.
2. A section of a stem.
3. Leaf.
4. A bract, outer view.
5. A bract, inner view, showing theca.
6 and 7. Two views of a spore × 250.

(2–5 enlarged.)

APPENDIX.

GLOSSARY.

A, when beginning a Greek derivative, signifies a want of something, or a negative (*acau* lescent—without a stem).

Abnormal, contrary to the usual order of things.

Aboriginal, truly original.

Aborigine, in this work means the American Indian.

Abortion, an imperfect formation, or the non-formation, of some part.

Abortive, imperfect or rudimentary (the stamen, plate 113, fig. 5).

Abrupt, suddenly terminating ; as

Abruptly pinnate, without an odd leaflet at the end. (Plate 35, fig. 10.)

Acaulescent, apparently stemless. (Plate 19, fig. 1.)

Accumbent, lying against a thing.

Acetabuliform, saucer-shaped.

Achenium, pl. *achenia*, a one-seeded, seed-like fruit. (Plate 95, fig. 6.)

Achlamydeous, without floral envelopes.

Acicular, needle-shaped.

Acinaciform, scimitar-shaped.

Acrogenous, growing from the apex. (Plate 179, fig. 2.)

Acrogens, or *acrogenous plants*, the higher cryptogamous plants.

Aculeate, armed with prickles. (Plate 33, fig. 1.)

Aculeolate, slightly prickly (the stem of fig. 1, plate 155).

Acuminate, taper-pointed (the leaves of fig. 6, plate 152).

Acute, merely sharp pointed (the leaves of fig. 8, plate 156).

Adelphous, said of stamens when joined in a fraternity.

Adherent, sticking to, or growing fast to, another body (calyx to ovary, fig. 3, plate 70).

Adnate, said of an anther when fixed by its whole length to the filament. (Plate 80, fig. 8.)

Adventitious, out of the usual place.

Adventive, said of foreign plants when sparingly introduced—not really naturalized.

Æquilateral, equal sided.

Æstivation, the arrangement of the parts in the flower bud.

Akenium, or *akene*. See *achenium*.

Ala, pl. *alæ*, a wing ; the side petals of a papilionaceous corolla. (Plate 46, fig. 3, *b*.)

Alate, winged; as the seeds of the ash. (Plate 137, fig. 4.)

Albumen, a vegetable product stored with the embryo in the seed. (Plate 142, fig. 4.)

Albuminous, furnished with albumen.

Alexipharmic, that which obviates the effects of a poison.

Alexiteric, something that thwarts the action of venom.

Alternate, said of leaves when arranged one after the other. (Plate 81, fig. 1.)

Ament, a catkin. (Plate 156, fig. 1.)

Amorphous, without definite form.

Amphitropous, an ovule attached by the middle of one side, *i. e.* the raphe truly lateral. (Plate 9, fig. 4.)

Amplectant, embracing.

Amplexicaul, clasping the stem by the base (as the leaves of fig. 2, plate 68).

Amylaceous, starchy.

Anastomosing, forming a net-work, like the veins in a leaf.

Anatropous, an ovule bent back upon its stem. (Plate 22, fig. 6.)

Ancipital, two-edged (as the petioles, fig. 5, plate 162).

Andrœcium, the stamens collectively.

Androgynous, having both male and female flowers in the same cluster.

Angiospermous, plants with their seeds formed in an ovary.

Annual, said of a plant that flowers and fruits the year it is raised from the seed, then dies.

Annular, in the form of a ring.

Annulate, marked by rings. (Plate 139, fig. 3.)

Anther, the essential part of a stamen, which contains the pollen. (Plate 152, fig. 4.)

Antheriferous, having an anther. (Plate 113, stamen 4, in contradistinction to stamen 5.)

Anthesis, the act of expansion of a flower.

Anthrocarpous, multiple fruits, like the blackberry.

Apetalous, destitute of petals. (Plate 33, figs. 3 and 4.)

Apex, the terminal point of a body.

Aphyllous, destitute of leaves. (Plate 179, figs. 1 and 2.)

Apical, belonging to the apex.

Apiculate, tipped with an abrupt point. (Plate 5, fig. 5.)

Appendage, any superadded part (as seen on the sepals, plate 25, fig. 5).

Appendiculate, provided with appendages.

Appressed, brought into contact, but not united. (Plate 9, fig. 3.)

Aquatic, growing in water.

Arachnoid, cobwebby.

Arboreous, arborescent, tree-like, both in size and form.

Areola, the scar of attachment (seen on the root, plate 11, fig. 2).

Arillate, furnished with an

Aril, or *arillus*, a fleshy, false coat to a seed. (Plate 13, fig. 6.)

Aristate, see *Awned.*

Arrow-shaped, same as *Sagittate*, which see.

Articulated, furnished with joints.

Ascending, rising obliquely upwards.

Aspergilliform, shaped like the brush used to sprinkle holy water. (Plate 82, fig. 6.)

Assurgent, see *Ascending.*

Atropous, see *Orthotropous.*

Auriculate, ear-shaped (as the bases of the leaves, plate 138).

Awl-shaped, sharp pointed from a broader base. (Plate 1, fig. 5.)

Awn, a bristle-like appendage (as seen on anther, plate 100, fig. 7).

Axil, the angle on the upper side between a leaf and the stem.

Axile, belonging to the axis, or occupying the axis (the placenta in fig. 3, plate 70).

Axilary, occurring in an axil (the flowers of plate 130).

Axis, the central line of any body ; the organ around which others are attached (as that portion of the stem occupied by the flowers, plate 172).

Baccate, berry-like (fruit of plate 124).

Barbate, bearded in lines, spots, or tufts (fig. 4, plate 122); not when the whole surface is hairy—then the part is truly bearded.

Barbellate, beset with short, stiff hairs, as is often the case with the pappus bristles in *Compositœ.* (Plate 92, fig. 6.)

Bark, the outside covering of a woody stem.

Basal, attached or belonging to the

Base, that end of a body that is attached to its support.

Beaked, surmounted by a long and narrow tip. (Plate 4, fig. 5.)

Bearded, covered with a growth of fine hairs. (Plate 1, fig. 8.)

Bell-shaped, see *Campanulate*.

Berry, a fruit that is juicy or pulpy throughout, as a grape.

Bi, or *Bis*, twice; as

Biauriculate, two-eared (the leaves of plate 138).

Bicipital, two-headed.

Biconjugate, twice paired (stigmas, fig. 5, plate 130).

Bidentate, two-toothed (as the ligule, fig. 5, plate 80).

Biennial, of two years' existence, *i. e.* growing from the seed one season and from the root the next, then bearing fruit and dying entirely.

Bifid, cleft to about the middle, into two parts. (Plate 150, fig. 4.)

Bifoliate, a leaf composed of two leaflets.

Bifurcate, forked into two branches. (Plate 132, fig. 1.)

Bijugate, see *Biconjugate*.

Bilabiate, two-lipped (as the corolla, fig. 3, plate 121).

Bilamellate, of two plates—*lamellæ* (the style of fig. 2, plate 152).

Bilobed, two-lobed (as the gland, fig. 5, plate 150).

Bilocular, two-celled (as the anther, fig. 3, plate 125).

Bipinnate, twice pinnate.

Bipinnatifid, pinnatifid with the lobes again pinnatifid.

Biserrate, doubly serrate (the leaf margins, fig. 2, plate 69).

Biternate, the principal divisions three, each bearing three leaflets. (Plate 4, fig. 2.)

Bladdery, inflated and thin, like the pod of *Lobelia inflata*. (Plate 99, fig. 3.)

Blade of a leaf; the expanded portion.

Boat-shaped, see *Scaphoid*.

Bract, a small leaf or scale of the axil from which some other part of the plant grows. (Plate 146, fig. 1.)

Bractlet, a bract seated upon the pedicel of a flower. (Plate 172, fig. 2.)

Branch, a woody division of a stem or root.

Bristles, stiff, sharp hairs (on the leaves of plate 62).

Bud, a branch in its undeveloped state.

Bulbous, bulb-shaped.

Caducous, dropping off very early, like the sepals of *Podophyllum*, which fall as the flower expands.

Cæspitose, growing in tufts like turf.

Calceolate, slipper-shaped.

Callose, hardened, or having callosities (hardened spots).

Calyculate, having an accessory calyx outside of the true. (Plate 31, fig. 3.)

Calyx, the outer (usually green) set of floral leaves. (Plate 128, fig. 2.)

Campanulate, bell-shaped (said of a flower when like fig. 4, plate 102).

Campylotropous, said of an ovule or seed when bent upon itself, like that of fig. 8, plate 14.

Canaliculate, channeled with a longitudinal groove.

Cancellate, latticed. (Plate 99, fig. 4.)

Capillaceous, capillary, hair-like in shape.

Capitate, having a globular apex, like a pin's head (fig. 4, plate 1), or forming a head (as the inflorescence of plates 62 and 76).

Capitillate, diminutive of *capitate* (the apices of fig. 7, plate 122).

Capriolate, bearing tendrils. (Plate 40, fig. 2.)

Capsule, any dry, dehiscent pod. (Plate 104, fig. 4.)

Capsular, relating to a capsule.

Carina, a keel ; the two anterior petals of a papillionaceous flower. (Plate 56, fig. 3 *c*.)

Carinate, keeled; furnished with a ridge on one side. (Plate 61, fig. 6.)

Carneous, flesh-colored.

Carnose, for this work see *Sarcous*.

Carpel, a simple pistil. (Plate 57, fig. 5.)

Carpellary, having the appearance of a carpel, or pertaining to such.

Carpophore, the stalk of a fruit within the flower. (Plate 149, fig. 6.)

Cartilaginous, firm and tough ; cartilage-like.

Caruncle, a warty excrescence upon a seed. (Plate 151, fig. 12.)

Carunculate, having a caruncle.

Catkin, a scaly, deciduous spike of flowers. (Plate 162.)

Caudate, having a tail. (Plate 1, fig. 8.)

Caulescent, obviously stemmed. (Plate 81, fig. 1.)

Cauline, belonging, or pertaining, to the stem (In plate 171, fig. 1, the upper leaf is cauline; the lower, radical.)

Cell, a cavity more enclosed than a pit.

Centrifugal, said of anything that is produced, or extends, from the center outward.

Centripetal, the opposite of *Centrifugal*.

Cernuous, nodding at the summit (the flower of plate 19).

Chaff, small, membranous scales found upon the receptacle of some Compositæ.

Chaffy, having chaff, or a chaff-like texture.

Channeled, hollowed out like a gutter, like the petioles of the plantain. (Plate 107.)

Characteristic, a trait, or form, belonging to individuals.

Chartaceous, papery, or parchment-like in character.

Chlorophyl, the green coloring matter of plants.

Cicatrix, the scar left by the fall of some portion of a growth.

Ciliate, having a fringe like eye-lashes (*cilia*) upon the margin. (Plate 122, fig. 2.)

Cinereous, having an ashy hue.

Circinate, rolled inwards from the top. (Plate 51, fig. 5.)

Circumscissile, dividing by an equatorial line. (Plate 108, fig. 3.)

Clathrate, see *Cancellate*.

Clavate, club-shaped; narrower below than above. (Plate 167, fig. 3.)

Claw, the narrow, stalk-like base of some petals. (Plate 51, fig. 4.)

Climbing, rising by the help of some other object.

Club-shaped, see *Clavate*.

Clustered, aggregated in a bunch (as the leaves of plate 15).

Coalescent, growing together (as the filaments, fig. 2, plate 50).

Cochleariform, spoon-shaped.

Coherent, growing together from first to last, *i. e.*, their whole length (the styles, fig. 5, plate 69).

Columella, the axis to which the carpels of a compound fruit are attached. (Plate 32, fig. 5).

Column, the united stamens and pistils of an orchid. (Plate 170, fig. 4.)

Columnar, column-like (the style of fig. 4, plate 102).

Coma, a tuft.

Comose, bearing a tuft of hairs. (Plate 134, fig. 4.)

Commissure, a line of junction (as seen in fig. 7, plate 168; fig. 11, plate 150; fig. 8, plate 152, etc.).

Compound leaf, fig. 2, plate 69; *compound pistil*, fig. 5, plate 30; *compound umbel*, fig. 1, plate 63.

Compressed, flattened upon opposite sides (the seeds, fig. 12, plate 11).

Conduplicate, folded upon itself on its longest diameter, like a double sheet of note paper.

Cone, a dry, compound fruit, like that of the pine. (Plate 164, fig. 2.)

Confluent, blended together. See *Coherent.*

Conjugate, coupled in single pairs. (Plate 149, fig. 4.)

Connate, see *Coherent.*

Connective, that portion of the anther that connects its cells. (Plate 1, fig. 6.)

Connivent, brought close together (the styles, fig. 2, plate 13).

Contorted, twisted together.

Contracted, either narrowed or shortened (corolla, fig. 4, plate 138).

Convolute, rolled up lengthwise, one edge over the other.

Cordate, heart-shaped at the base. (Plate 109, fig. 2.)

Coriaceous, leathery.

Corm, a solid bulb. (Plate 168, fig. 3.)

Corneous, horny.

Corniculate, bearing a small horn-shaped appendage (the lateral lobe of fig. 4, plate 121).

Corolla, usually the inner flower leaves, generally showy in form or color. (Plate 128, fig. 2.)

Corona, a crown-like appendage, or group of the same. (Plate 134, fig. 3.)

Coronate, crowned (the achenium of fig. 4, plate 93).

Corymb, a flat, or convex, flower-cluster where the peduncles or pedicels do not all issue from the same point upon the stem.

Corymbose, like a corymb in form. (Plate 30, fig. 2.)

Cotyledons, the leaves of the embryo—as the oily meats of the butternut, which consist of the cotyledons only, joined by their connective.

Crateriform, shaped like a goblet.

Creeping, growing horizontally upon, or beneath, the ground. (Plate 104, fig. 1.)

Cremocarp, the double achenium of the Umbelliferæ. (Plate 68, fig. 7.)

Crenate, scalloped upon the edge with rounded teeth. (Plate 158, fig. 2.)

Crested, bearing an elevated appendage like a crest. (Plate 45, fig. 4.)

Crinite, furnished with long hairs (calyx and leaf bases of plate 31).

Crown, see *Corona.*

Cruciate, or *Cruciform*, shaped like a cross. (Plate 58, fig. 3.)

Crustaceous, hard and brittle.

Cryptogamous, said of plants that bear no flower—as mosses, ferns, and lichens.

Cucullate, hood-shaped (fig. 6, plate 45, the stigma).

Cuneate, *Cuneiform*, wedge-shaped (the leaflets of plate 48).

Cup-shaped, *Cupuliform*, wine-glass-shaped (the corolla, fig. 3, plate 79).

Cuspidate, tipped with a sharp, stiff point (the apex of fig. 2, plate 179).

Cut, see *Incised.*

Cyathiform, shaped like a wine-glass.

Cylindraceous, approaching to a

Cylindrical form, as stems that are round and gradually tapering. (Plate 179, fig. 2.)

Cyme, a centrifugal inflorescence. (Plate 75, fig. 1.)

Cymose, having a cyme-like character.

Deca, ten ; when preceding Greek derivatives.

Decagynous, ten-pistiled, or ten-styled.

Deciduous, falling later than caducous, *i. e.*, before the formation of fruit.

Declined, turned downwards, or to one side (as the stamens, fig. 3, plate 43).

Decompound, more than once compounded or divided (the leaves of fig. 1, plate 64).

Decumbent, reclined upon the ground, the summit tending to rise (the root-stock of plate 104).

Decurrent, said of leaves that are prolonged down the stem beyond their point of insertion upon it. (Plate 163, fig. 2.)

Decussate, a successive arrangement of pairs which cross each other (the leaves of plate 79).

Definite, of a uniform number.

Deflexed, bent downward at an angle (as some of the leaves in plate 140).

Deflorate, beyond the flowering state—as an anther after the pollen is discharged.

Dehiscence, the method of bursting or splitting open (as seen in fig. 4, plate 104).

Dehiscent, a regular mode of splitting.

Deliquescent, branching so that the stem is lost in the branches. (Plate 132, fig. 1.)

Deltoid, shaped like the Greek letter *Δ*.

Dentate, toothed (the leaf margins of plate 153).

Denticulate, the diminutive of *Dentate* (the leaf margins of plate 55).

Depauperate, starved or impoverished.

Depressed, flattened from above downward (as the seeds in fig. 12, plate 11).

Descending, bent gradually downward (as the fruiting axis of plate 69).

Dextrorse, turned to the right.

Di-, two ; in Greek compounds, as

Diadelphous, said of stamens when united in two sets by their filaments. (Plate 50, fig. 2.)

Diandrous, having but two stamens. (Plate 119, fig. 3.)

Dichogamous, said of the styles when protruding from the bud.

Dichotomous, two-forked.

Dicotyledonous, having a pair of cotyledons—as in the butternut.

Didynamous, having two pairs of stamens—the one shorter than the other. (Plate 109, fig. 4.)

Diffuse, widely and irregularly spreading.

Digitate, said of a compound leaf when the leaflets are given off from the apex of the petiole. (Plate 44, fig. 1.)

Digynous, having two pistils or styles. (Plate 68, fig. 6.)

Dimorphous, of two forms.

Diœcious, when the stamens are in separate flowers on different plants (as in plate 154).

Dipetalous, two-petaled ; *diphyllous*, two-leaved ; *dipterous*, two-winged.

Disciform, or *Disk-shaped*, flat and circular. (Plate 164, fig. 9.)

Disk, the face of any flat, circular body ; the central part of a head of flowers—as in the sunflower.

Disk-floret, the flower of a disk in *Compositæ*.

Dissected, cut deeply into many divisions (as the leaves of plate 86).

Dissepiments, the partitions of an ovary or a fruit (as seen in fig. 5, plate 173).

Distinct, not in combination with each other (as the styles, fig. 5, plate 30).

Divaricate, straddling widely apart (as the branches of plate 149).

Divided, cut into divisions that extend almost to the mid-rib (leaf 2, plate 4).

Dodeca, twelve.

Dorsal, pertaining to the back (*dorsum*).

Double - flowers, so-called ; when the petals are unduly multiplied.

Downy, clothed with a coat of soft hairs.

Drupe, a stone fruit—like the plum, peach, cherry, etc.

Drupaceous, partaking of the nature of a drupe.

Ducts, closed channels.

Dumose, bushy.

Dwarf, low in stature.

E or Ex, when beginning compound words, signifies an absence of; as, *edentate*, toothless; *exstipulate*, destitute of stipules.

Ebracteate, without bracts.

Echinate, armed with prickles (the pod of Æsculus Hippocastanum, plate 44). *Echinulate*, a diminutive of it. (Plate 93, fig. 7.)

Effete, past bearing (as the anther of fig. 4, plate 110).

Elaters, the erectile appendages of the spores of Equisetum. (Plate 179, fig. 6.)

Elliptical, oval or oblong, with the ends regularly rounded. (Plate 61, fig. 1.)

Emarginate, notched at the apex (the white, involucral lobes of plate 71).

Embryo, the rudimentary plantlet in the seed. (Plate 140, fig. 10.)

Endocarp, the inner layer of the walls of a fruit.

Endogenous, when the stem exhibits no distinction as to bark, wood and pith, the woody fibre and vessels being in bundles and scattered in the cellular tissue, *i. e.*, "inside growing."

Endosperm, the same as *Albumen*, which see.

Enneandrous, having nine stamens.

Ensiform, sword-shaped (as the leaves of plate 173).

Entire, when the margins of an organ are not at all toothed, cut, or divided, but perfectly even (as in the leaves of plate 170).

Ephemeral, lasting a day or less.

Epi-, upon ; as

Epicarp, the exterior layer of a fruit.

Epidermis, the covering of an organ—its external skin.

Epigæous, growing close upon the ground.

Epigynous, upon the ovary (as seen in fig. 2, plate 61).

Epipetalous, borne upon the petals (as the filaments in fig. 3, plate 172).

Epiphyllous, borne upon a leaf.

Equal, of the same number or length, as the case may be, of the body in comparison.

Equitant, riding astraddle (as the bases of the leaves, plate 171).

Erose, as if gnawed.

Essential Organs of the flower, those absolutely necessary to fertilization, *i. e.*, the stamens and pistils.

Estivation, see *Æstivation*.

Evergreen, keeping its leaves until replaced by others, or even longer.

Exalbuminous, without albumen.

Excurrent, said of a tree when the trunk is traceable to the very top. (Plate 163, fig. 1.)

Exogenous, plants with stems composed of bark, wood and pith, *i. e.*, "outside growing."

Explanate, spread, or flattened out. (Plate 25, fig. 9.)

Exserted, protruding out of; said of stamens and pistils when surpassing the floral envelope (see figs. 3 and 4, plate 33).

Exstipulate, destitute of stipules.

Extra - axillary, said of anything a little out of the axil (as the prickles on fig. 1, plate 33).

Extrorse, turned outward; said of an anther when it opens away from the pistil.   (Plate 72, fig. 2.)

Falcate, scythe - shaped.   (Plate 147, fig. 4.)

Family, a collection of closely related genera.

Farinaceous, mealy in texture.   (Plate 172, fig. 2.)

Fascicle, a close cluster.

Fascicled, growing in a bundle; *Fasciculate* (the leaves of plate 15).

Fastigiate, upright, close and parallel.   (Plate 69, fig. 5.)

Faveolate, honey-combed.

Feather-veined, see *Pinnate*.

Female flowers, those having pistils but no stamens.   (Plate 33, fig. 4.)

Fenestrate, pierced with one or more large holes.

Ferrugineous, resembling iron rust.

Fertile, capable of producing.

Fertilization, the process by which the pollen causes the embryo to become fertile.

Fibrous, composed of fibres.

Filament, the slender portion of a stamen supporting the anther (fig. 3, plate 34), or any thread-shaped appendage.

Filamentous, formed of threads.

Filiform, thread-shaped, long, slender and cylindrical.   (Plate 113, fig. 3.)

Fimbriate, fringed (as seen between the stamens of fig. 3, plate 119).

Fistulose, hollow and cylindrical.   (Plate 68, fig. 2.)

Flavescent, yellowish.

Fleshy, see *Sarcous*.

Fleshy Plants, those containing a great deal of substance (as that of plate 61).

Flexuous, gently bending in opposite directions.   (Plate 124, fig. 1.)

Floccose, bearing tufts of long, soft hair.

Flora, an aggregation of the plants of any certain district.

Floral, pertaining to the blossom.

Floral Envelope, the leaves of the flower; includes either calyx or corolla, or both.

Floret, a diminutive flower (only used when several flowers are in the same head).

Flower.   This word comprises the organs of reproduction and their envelope.   (Plate 128, fig. 2.)

Foliaceous, leaf-like.

Foliole, leaflet.

Follicle, a simple pod, opening down the inner suture.   (Plate 50, fig. 4.)

Follicular, like a follicle.

Foramen, a hole or orifice (as in the anther-cells of fig. 3, plate 104).

Fornicate, arching over (as in the upper lobe of the corolla, fig. 3, plate 121).

Foveate, or *Foveolate*, deeply pitted.   (Plate 105, fig. 6.)

Free, not united with any other parts of a different kind.

Fringed, having a margin beset with slender appendages.   (Plate 109, fig. 6.)

Fructification, the state of fruiting.

Fruit, the matured ovary and everything connected with it.   (Plate 104, fig. 4.)

Frutescent, somewhat shrubby.

Fruticose, shrubby.

Fugacious, quickly falling or perishing.

Fulvous, tawny.

Funiculus, the stalk of a seed or ovule.

Funnel-form, gradually expanding upwards (the corolla, plates 127 and 130).

Furcate, forked.

Furfuraceous, branny.

Furrowed, marked by longitudinal grooves. (Plate 63, fig. 2.)

Fusiform, shaped like a spindle (the pod of fig. 7, plate 22).

Galeate, helmet-shaped (the upper petal, fig. 3, plate 121).

Gamopetalous, see *Monopetalous*.

Gamosepalous, see *Monosepalous*.

Geminate, twin (the flowers of fig. 2, plate 77).

Gemmation, the budding state.

Geniculate, bent abruptly, like a knee. (Plate 54, fig. 7.)

Genus, a group of like species.

Germ, the point of beginning of a growth.

Germination, the development of an embryo into a plantlet.

Gibbous, swollen at one place or on one side (base of style, fig. 6, plate 117).

Glabrate, almost glabrous, or becoming so with age.

Glands, small organs which secrete some oily or nectariferous product of the part, or any small swelling, whether it secretes or not (see base of petal, fig. 5, plate 15).

Glandular, furnished with glands.

Glaucescent, slightly glaucous.

Glaucous, covered with a fine, white powder that rubs off; as the bloom of the grape.

Globose, spherical, or nearly so (ovary of fig. 4, plate 125).

Globular, nearly globose (base of style, fig. 6, plate 117).

Glomerate, closely aggregated into a dense cluster (the fruits of fig. 1, plate 143).

Glomerule, a dense, head-like cluster. (Plate 94, fig. 1.)

Granular, composed of grains.

Granule, a small grain.

Guttate, spotted as if by colored drops (the petals of Hypericum, as represented by fig. 8, plate 30).

Gymnospermous, naked-seeded (as seen in fig. 5, plate 163).

Gynandrous, where the stamens are borne on the pistil. (Plate 170, fig. 4.)

Gynæcium, name for the pistils when taken altogether.

Gynobase, a special support for the pistils (as seen in fig. 4, plate 146).

Habitat, a situation in which a wild plant grows.

Halberd-shaped, see *Hastate*.

Halved, when a body appears as if one half were taken away. (Plate 169, fig. 3.)

Hastate, shaped like a halberd (see leaves, plate 123).

Head, an aggregation of florets more or less globose (see plate 76).

Heart-shaped, of the shape a heart is commonly drawn. See *Cordate*.

Hemi-, half; in Greek derivatives, as

Hemicarp, half-fruit. See *Mericarp*.

Hemitropous, nearly the same as *Amphitropous*, which see.

Hepta-, seven; in Greek derivatives, as

Heptagynous, having seven pistils or styles.

Heptandrous, seven-stamened.

Herb, a plant that dies down to ground in autumn.

Herbaceous, like an herb.

Hermaphrodite, same as *Perfect,* which see.

Heterogamous, bearing two sorts of flowers as to their stamens and pistils, as in many Compositæ.

Heteromorphous, having more than one shape (the leaves, figs. 2, 3, 4, 5, plate 151).

Hexa-, six; in Greek derivatives; as, *hexagonal,* six-angled.

Hexagynous, having six pistils or styles.

Hexandrous, six-stamened.

Hilum, a scar of attachment of a seed. (Plate 43, fig. 5.)

Hirsute, hairy.

Hispid, beset with stiff hairs.

Hoary, greyish-white.

Homogamous, when the flowers are all of one kind in the head.

Homogeneous, all of one kind.

Homotropous, curved one way.

Hood, see *Galea.*

Horn, a spur or like appendage.

Hybrid, a cross between two allied species.

Hypocrateriform, salver-shaped (the corolla of plate 108).

Hypogynous, inserted under the pistil (as the stamens, fig. 3, plate 69).

Icosandrous, when twelve or more stamens are inserted upon the calyx.

Imbricate, -ed, or *-ive,* placed like shingles upon a roof (as the scales of the cones, plate 163).

Imparipinnate, pinnate, with a single leaflet at the apex of the common petiole (as in fig. 5, plate 50).

Imperfect flowers, wanting one or the other of the essential organs (as in figs. 3 and 4, plate 33).

Incised, deeply and irregularly cut (the leaves of plate 95).

Included, when of the parts in question some do not project beyond others.

Incomplete flowers, those in which the calyx or corolla is wanting.

Incumbent, leaning or resting upon, as anthers when looking inwards.

Incurved, curving inward. (Plate 67, fig. 5.)

Indefinite, too numerous to mention, or when the parts are not uniform in different individuals.

Indehiscent, said of a fruit that neither splits nor bursts. (Plate 37, fig. 6.)

Indigenous, a native of the country in which it is found.

Individual, different plants of the species.

Induplicate, with the edges turned inward (the top leaves of plate 74).

Inferior, grown below some other organ (as the ovary, fig. 3, plate 70).

Inflated, puffed out like a bladder. (Plate 99, fig. 3.)

Inflexed, bent inward at an angle.

Inflorescence, the arrangement of flowers on the stem.

Infra-axillary, beneath an axil.

Infundibuliform, see *Funnel-shaped.*

Innate, said of an anther when attached to the very tip of its filament. (Plate 58, figs. 4 and 5.)

Insertion, the point at which an organ or part of an organ is attached to another.

Introrse, facing inward.

Inverse, or *Inverted*, in a position opposed to an original direction. (Plate 104, fig. 3.)

Involucel, a small involucre.

Involucre, a set of bracts around a flower (plate 1), umbel (plate 148), or head (plate 62).

Involute, grown inwards from the edges (the upper leaves of plate 74).

Irregular flowers. This name is given when members of the same sort as, for instance, the petals are unlike in shape or size (fig. 3, plate 46).

Jointed, separate or separable at one or more places into pieces (the stamens, fig. 2, plate 148; the plant, plate 61).

Keel, see *Carina*.

Kidney-shaped, resembling a kidney in general outline. (Plate 61, fig. 6.)

Labiate, lipped. (Plate 97, fig. 7.)

Laciniate, slashed into deep narrow lobes (the leaves of plate 95).

Lactescent, milky, or producing a milky juice.

Lamellar, consisting of flat plates.

Lanate, woolly.

Lanceolate, lance-shaped (leaves of plate 114).

Lanuginous, cottony.

Lateral, pertaining to one side.

Lax, the opposite of crowded.

Leaflet, one of the divisions of a compound leaf.

Legume, a simple pod that splits into two pieces—like that of the pea.

Leguminous, pertaining to legumes, or the order *Leguminosæ*.

Lenticular, lens-shaped. (Plate 152, fig. 8.)

Ligneous, woody.

Ligulate, having a ligule.

Ligule, the strap-shaped limb of the corolla of many *Compositæ*. (Plate 81, fig. 5.)

Limb, the border of a monopetalous corolla.

Linear, flat and narrow, with parallel margins, as the leaves of the hemlock. (Plate 164, fig 3.)

Lineate, marked with parallel lines.

Lip, the principal lobes of a bilabiate corolla or calyx (plainly seen in the flowers of plate 113); also the peculiar petal of the orchids. (Plate 170, fig. 3.)

Lobe, any division of a leaf or other organ.

Loculicidal, splitting through the middle of the dorsum of each cell. (Plate 23, fig. 5.)

Lunate, crescent-shaped.

Lyrate, lyre-shaped. (Plate 24, fig. 2.)

Maculate, spotted or blotched. (Plate 68, fig. 2.)

Male flower, having stamens but no pistils. (Plate 33, fig. 3.)

Mammæ, teat-like projections. (Plate 103, fig. 2.)

Marcescent, withering without falling off (as the petals of plate 30).

Marginal, belonging to the edge.

Masked, see *Personate*.

Medium, pertaining to the middle.

Medullary, having the nature of pith.

Membranaceous, membrane-like (as the sheaths, fig. 2, plate 168).

Mericarp, one carpel of an umbilliferous fruit. (Plate 36, fig. 9.)

Midrib, the main rib of a leaf.

Monadelphous, said of stamens when united by their filaments into one set. (Plate 46, fig. 4.)

Monandrous, having only one stamen.

Moniliform, necklaced, *i. e.*, contracted at intervals. (Plate 23, fig. 5.)

Monocotyledonous, having only one cotyledon.

Monœcious, having stamens or pistils only. (Plate 33, figs. 3 and 4.)

Monogynous, having but one pistil or style. (Plate 102, fig. 4.)

Monopetalous, when the corolla is united into one piece. (Plate 102, fig. 3.)

Monosepalous, when the sepals are united into one body (as in the flower of plate 127).

Monospermous, one-seeded.

Mucronate, tipped with a short, abrupt point. (Plate 179, fig. 3.)

Multifarious, in many rows.

Multifid, many-cut.

Multilocular, many-celled.

Muricate, beset with short, hard points. (Plate 44, fig. 5.)

Napiform, shaped like a rounded turnip.

Naturalized, an introduced plant that has run thoroughly wild, and perfects its seed.

Nectar, honey, or honey-like secretions.

Nectariferous, bearing honey, or having a nectary.

Nectary, a cavity or gland that secretes nectar.

Needle-shaped, see *Acerose*.

Nerve, used to distinguish leaf-ribs or veins when parallel, and more or less straight.

Netted-veined, when the veins branch and anastomose, forming a net-work.

Nodding, said of an organ when the summit hangs downward.

Nodose, nubby.

Normal, in a usual way, according to rule.

Nuciform, nut-shaped.

Nut, a hard, bony, mostly one-seeded fruit. (Plate 43, fig. 5.)

Nutlet, diminutive of nut; the stone of a drupe.

Ob-, a prefix signifying inversion or opposition ; as

Obcordate, heart-shaped, with the notch upward, and the point of fixture or support at the apex. (Plate 25, fig. 9.)

Oblanceolate, lance-shaped, with the point downward (the leaves of plate 104).

Oblique, applied to organs having unequal sides. (Plate 147, fig. 3.)

Oblong, much longer than broad (as the brown leaf, plate 160).

Obovate, ovate, with the broadest end uppermost. (Plate 151, fig. 3.)

Obtuse, blunt-ended (the apex of leaf 3, plate 51).

Ochroleucous, dull cream-color.

Octo-, eight, in Greek derivatives; as

Octogynous, eight-pistiled.

Octandrous, eight-stamened.

Offset, a branch given off near the ground and taking root.

Opposite, said of leaves when their petioles are exactly opposite each other upon the stem. (Plate 132.)

Orbicular, circular in outline. (Plate 18, fig. 2.)

Organ, any member of a plant—as a petal, stamen, leaf, branch, etc., etc.

Orthotropous, said of an ovary when its point of attachment is at its base and the apex is in direct line with it. (Plate 28, fig. 6.)

-ose, as a suffix means like whatever root-word precedes it; as, *racemose*—like a raceme.

Osseous, bony.

Oval, broadly elliptical. (Plate 151, fig. 2.)

Ovary, that portion of the pistil that contains the ovules. (Plate 28, fig. 5.)

Ovoid, a solid oval. (Plate 28, fig. 6.)

Ovule, that organ that is destined to become a seed (plainly seen in fig. 5, plate 125).

Palea, pl. *Paleæ*, the chaff of composite receptacles.

Paleaceous, chaffy.

Palmate, when the organs in question radiate more or less from the point where some other organ is attached (the veins of the leaf, plate 18; the leaflets, plate 40 (digitate); and the lobes of the leaf, fig. 2, plate 8).

Palmately, in a palmate manner, as above.

Panicle, an open cluster (the arrangement of the flowers, fig. 1, plate 119).

Papery, see *Papyraceous*.

Papillionaceous, spreading like a butterfly. (Plate 50, fig. 1.)

Papilla, pl. *Papillæ*, small mammæ (as seen on the corolla, fig. 3, plate 79).

Pappus, thistle-down. (Plate 81, fig. 3.) In Compositæ this, with chaff, teeth, or scales, represents the calyx in this order.

Papyraceous, of the texture of writing paper.

Parenchyma, the pulp of plants.

Parietal, attached to the walls (as the ovules in fig. 5, plate 7).

Parted, cleft almost to the base. (Plate 4, fig. 4.)

Pauci-, means few when prefixed to root words. (*Pauciflorous*, few-flowered.)

Pear-shaped, solid obovate.

Pedate, palmately cleft, with the lobes again cleft. (Plate 1, fig. 2.)

Pedicel, the individual stalk of each flower in a cluster. (Plate 104, fig. 2.)

Peduncle, the main stalk of a flower cluster (fig. 2, plate 104), or the flower stalk when the plant is one-flowered (as seen above the leaves in plate 175); or when the flowers are single (as in plate 2). The same distinctions pertain to the stalk of heads and clusters (as in plates 62 and 70).

Peltate, shield-shaped (the style of fig. 3, plate 19); said of a leaf, no matter what its shape, when the petiole is attached anywhere within its margin (as in plate 18).

Pendent, hanging (the fruit of fig. 3, plate 15).

Pendulous, somewhat hanging (the flowers of plate 49).

Penicillate, like a painter's pencil. (Plate 97, fig. 6.)

Penta-, five, in Greek derivatives; as

Pentagynous, having five pistils or styles.

Pentandrous, five-stamened.

Perennial, growing on year after year.

Perfect, a flower having the essential organs.

Perfoliate, passing through a leaf, or appearing so (the leaves, plate 79).

Perforate, pierced with holes, or having transparent dots giving that appearance. (Plate 30, fig. 7.)

Perianth, the leaves of the flower, especially when they cannot be distinguished as to calyx or corolla.

Pericarp, a ripened ovary; or the fruit walls.

Perigynium, arranged around the pistil.

Perigynous, when the petals and stamens are borne on the calyx. (Plate 55, fig. 2.)

Periphery, the outside of an organ.

Persistent, remaining beyond the usual time.

Personate, the throat of a bilabiate corolla when masked by some projection (as seen in the flowers of plate 111).

Petal, a leaf of the corolla; usually bright-colored.

Petaloid, when any other organ is petal-like.

Petiole, the stem of a leaf.

Petioled, Petiolate, possessing a petiole.

Petiolulate, said of leaflets when having their own petioles.

Phænogamous, Phænogams, Phænerogams, plants bearing flowers and producing seeds.

Pilose, clothed with fine soft hairs.

Pinna, the petiole of a pinnate leaf.

Pinnule, a secondary pinna of a bipinnate leaf.

Pinnate, feather-form; said of a compound leaf when its leaflets are arranged along the main petiole (as in plate 50).

Pinnatifid, cut until partaking of the nature of a pinnate leaf. (Plate 96, fig. 4.)

Pistil, the female organs of a flower (usually central), taken as a whole (fig. 5, plate 130: the lowest portion is the receptacle; next above, the ovary; next, the style, and at the apex, the stigmas).

Pistillate, said of a flower having pistils and no stamens. (Plate 33, fig. 4.)

Pith, the central portion of exogenous stems.

Pitted, having small depressions upon the surface.

Placenta, that surface or part of an ovary to which the ovules are attached. (Plate 25, fig. 10.)

Placentiferous, having the nature of a placenta, or having placentæ.

Plaited, arranged like a fan that admits of closure.

Plane, flat.

Plicate, see *Plaited.*

Plumose, feathery. (Plate 1, fig. 9.)

Pluri-, in composition, several; as

Plurifoliate, many-leaved.

Pod, any kind of capsule. (Plate 11, fig. 11; plate 22, fig. 7; plate 24, fig. 3; plate 132, fig. 3.)

Pollen, the fertilizing agent of a plant, formed in the anther cells. It is varied in form, but usually granular. (Plate 107, fig. 5; plate 1, fig. 7; plate 16, fig. 8; plate 22, fig. 9; plate 27, fig. 5; plate 47, fig. 5; plate 68, fig. 8; plate 83, fig. 8; plate 93, fig. 7; plate 101, fig. 5; plate 163, fig. 11; plate 164, fig. 9; plate 167, fig. 6; plate 103, fig. 5; plate 105, fig. 6; plate 109, fig. 7; plate 169, fig. 10, and plate 175, fig. 4.)

Pollen-mass, applied when the grains cohere into a mass. (Plate 135, fig. 4.)

Poly-, many; in Greek derivatives; *multi* in Latin, as

Polyadelphous, when stamens are united by their filaments. (Plate 50, fig. 2.)

Polyandrous, many-stamened, more than twenty.

Polygamous, having perfect and separate flowers upon the same plant.

Polygonal, many-angled.

Polygynous, many-pistilled or -styled.

Polymorphous, of varying forms.

Polypetalous, when the petals are separate or distinct (whether few or many). Opposed to *Monopetalous.*

Polysepalous, same as the above when applied to the calyx. Opposed to *Monosepalous*.

Porous, full of holes.

Præfloration, same as *Æstivation*, which see.

Præfoliation, same as *Vernation*, which see.

Præmorse, ending abruptly (the root of plate 177).

Prickles, short, angular thorns. (Plate 33, fig. 1.)

Prismatic, having three or more angles bounding flat or hollowed sides.

Process, a superficial projection.

Procumbent, trailing upon the ground.

Prostrate, lying flat upon the ground.

Puberulent, covered with an almost invisible down.

Pubescent, downy.

Pulverent, see *Glaucous;* or if the powder is only such in appearance.

Punctatè, see *Perforate*.

Pyramidal, shaped like a pyramid.

Pyrene, Pyrena, the nutlet, especially said of a drupe when small.

Pyxis, Pyxidium, a pod opening by a circumscissile line; the top falling off like a lid, (Plate 108, fig. 3.)

Quadri-, four; in Latin derivatives.

Qudrangular, four-angled.

Quadrifid, four-cleft.

Quaternaie, in fours.

Quinate, in fives.

Raceme, where one-flowered pedicels are arranged in succession along a general peduncle. (Plate 11, fig. 1.)

Rachis, see *Rhachis*.

Radiate, pertaining to the ray.

Radicle, the stem part of the embryo.

Raphe, see *Rhaphe*.

Ray, the marginal flowers of a composite head, especially when different from the rest, and diverging. The pedicels of an umbel (seen in the flowers of plate 84, and the umbel, plate 68).

Receptacle, the support of a flower, *i. e.*, the thickened upper surface of the apex of the peduncle or pedicel (fig. 4, plate 1); particularly, however, the place of attachment of the flowers of a head.

Recurved, curved outward or backwards (the styles, fig. 5, plate 130.)

Reflexed, bent outward and downward. (Plate 134, fig. 3.)

Regular, when the parts are all similar.

Reniform, see *Kidney-shaped*.

Repand, wavy-margined. (Leaves of plate 39.)

Repandly-toothed, rounded-toothed (the margins of the leaves, plate 7).

Repent, creeping along the ground by successive rootings.

Reticulated, formed into a net-work, or rather appearing as if covered by a net. (Plate 99, fig. 4; plate 167, fig. 2.)

Retroflexed, same as *Reflexed*, which see.

Retuse, so blunt at the apex as to be slightly indented.

Revolute, rolled backward; usually said of margins of organs or their extremities (both phases are apparent in the petals, fig. 2, plate 71).

Rhachis, back-bone; the axis of a spike.

Rhaphe, the prolongation of a seed stalk along the side of an ovule.   (Plate 22, fig. 6.)

Rhizoma, the main root.

Rib, the main and largest pieces of the frame work of a leaf.

Ringent, gaping open (the flowers of plate 113).

Rootlets, small branches of a rhizome.   (Plate 138, fig. 2.)

Rootstock, that portion of the stem where it joins the root.   (Plates 20 and 167, fig. 2.)

Rostrate, bearing a beak.   (Plate 4, fig. 5.)

Rosulate, forming a rosette (as the leaves, fig. 1, plate 29).

Rotate, wheel-shaped (the corollas of plate 108).

Rotund, having a roundish outline (the leaves, fig. 1, plate 77).

Rudimentary, imperfectly developed.

Rugose, wrinkled (as the corm of plate 168).

Runner, a slender, postrate branch, rooting at the end or joints.   (Plate 17, fig. 2.)

Sac, a closed membrane.

Sagittate, shaped like an arrow-head.

Salver-form, when the limb of the corolla spreads at right angles from a slender tube.

Samara, a winged fruit.   (Plate 35, fig. 9.)

Sarcous, (in this work) fleshy.

Saw-toothed, see *Serrate*.

Scales, small bracteate rudiments of leaves, or bodies of that nature (as on the base of the stem, fig. 1, plate 105).

Scandent, climbing.

Scape, a peduncle when starting from near the ground (as in fig. 2, plate 19).

Scaphoid, boat-shaped.

Scarious, thin and dry.

Scorpioid, circinate at the end (as the unilateral racemes, plate 57).

Scurf, dandruff-like superficial scales.

Scutellate, platter-shaped (seen upon the *rachis*, fig. 6, plate 151).

Segment, one of the subdivisons of any cleft body.

Segregate, see *Separate*.

Semi-, half; in Latin derivatives.

Semiconoid, depressed-conoidal.

Sempervirent, see *Evergreen*.

Sepal, a lobe of the calyx.   (Plate 128, fig. 2.)

Sepaloid, having the appearance of a sepal.

Septa, partitions (seen in fig. 5, plate 173).

Septicidal, said of a pod that splits through its partitions.

Sericeous, silky.

Serrate, having teeth like a saw (leaf margins, plates 40, 69, 70, etc.).

Serrulate, diminutive of the last.

Sessile, said of organs that have no individual stem (as the leaves of plates 28 and 30; the anthers, fig. 5, plate 138, etc.).

Seta, a bristle.

Sheathing, wrapped around a stem (the bases of the leaves, plates 31 and 167; the stipules, plates 64, 68, etc.).

Shield shaped, see *Peltate.*

Silicle, a pouch, or short pod. (Plate 25, fig. 9.)

Silique, a long pod of the mustard family. (Plate 23, fig. 5.)

Simple, of one piece.

Sinistrorse, turned to the left.

Sinuate, said of a leaf when its margin waves out and in. (Plate 143, fig. 2 ; plate 19, fig 1.)

Sinus, the recess between two parts of an organ (as the re-entering angle in the fruits of plate 174).

Solitary, unassociated with its kind.

Solarly, with the sun ;—*solarly voluble*, turning daily to keep face to the sun.

Spadix, a fleshy spike of flowers. (Plate 167, fig. 3 ; plate 169, fig. 6.)

Spathe, a large bract covering an inflorescence. (Plate 169, fig. 2.)

Spatulate, shaped like a spatula. (Plate 105, fig. 3.)

Species, the individuals of a genus having special characters belonging to themselves and no other known plant.

Spicate, belonging to or disposed like a

Spike, an arrangement of flowers similar to a raceme, but the flowers are sessile (as in plate 107).

Spine, a thorn (as seen on fig. 1, plate 61).

Spindle-shaped, see *Fusiform.*

Spinescent, degenerating into a thorn (as the end of the branch, plate 41).

Spinose, thorny. (Plate 15, fig. 1.)

Spore, the reproducing grains of cryptogams.

Squamate, Squamose, scaly. (Plate 105, fig. 1.)

Squarrose, where scales, leaves, or other appendages, spread widely from the axis.

Stalk, a stem.

Stamen, the male organ of a flower (usually arranged around the pistil, and appearing generally like those seen in fig. 2, plate 10. In fig. 3, plate 34, an enlarged stamen is depicted ; the stem part is the filament; the head, the anther).

Standard, the upper petal of a papillionaceous corolla. (Plate 46, fig. 3 *a*.)

Stellate, disposed in a star-like manner.

Sterile, incapable of producing its kind.

Stigma, the highest point of a pistil (see *Pistil*); the receptive portion of the female organs of a plant. (Plate 178, fig. 4.)

Stigmatose, that portion of a style resembling a stigma in being capable of receiving the pollen.

Stipe, the stalk of a pistil, or ovule when present. (Plate 149, fig. 6)

Stipel, the stipule of a leaflet.

Stipitate, being possessed of a stipe (as the ovule, fig. 6, plate 28).

Stipulate, having stipules.

Stipules, the appendages at the base of certain leaves (seen in plate 151).

Stoloniferous, producing stolons or rooting shoots.

Stomata, the breathing pores of leaves. (Plate 179, fig. 8.)

Strap-shaped, long, flat and narrow.

Striate, marked with longitudinal, slender grooves.

Strict, straight.

Strobile, a multiple, cone-shaped fruit. (Plate 159, fig. 5 ; plate 155, fig. 1.)

Style, that portion of the pistil that unites the stigma to the ovary (see description of pistil).

Sub-, almost; as, subcordate, nearly heart-shaped.

Subulate,—Awl-shaped, which see.

Succulent, pulpy, or juicy.

Suffrutescent, slightly shrubby.

Sulcate, deeply channelled.

Supra-axillary, growing above an axil.

Suspended, hanging down (as the ovule, fig. 3, plate 12).

Suture, a line of junction when parts are grown together.

Sword-shaped, see *Ensiform*.

Symmetrical flower, one whose parts are equal in number, each kind with the other, or in multiples (flower of plate 175).

Syngenesious, said of stamens when united by their anthers.

Taper-pointed, tapering gradually to a point. See *Acuminate*.

Tap-root, a stout root with a tapering body.   (Plate 63, fig. 7.)

Tawny, dull brownish-yellow.

Terete, long and round; same as cylindrical, only may taper. (Plate 132, fig. 3.)

Terminal, belonging to the summit.

Ternate, arranged in threes.

Testa, the external seed coat.

Tetra-, four; in Greek composites; as,

Tetradynamous, when having six stamens, two of them shorter than the rest. (Plate 23, fig. 2.)

Tetragonal, four-angled.

Tetragynous, four-pistilled or -styled.

Tetrandrous, four-stamened.

Theca, a case.

Thorn, see *Spine*.

Thread-shaped, see *Filiform*.

Throat, the opening of a tubular corolla, a little below the ring where the limb joins the tube.

Thyrsus, a compact pyramidal panicle. (Plate 43, fig. 1.)

Tomentose, woolly.

Toothed, furnished with sharp projections on the margin that do not point forward.

Top-shaped, cone-shaped, the apex downward.

Torus, the receptacle of the flower.   (Plate 1, fig. 4.)

Tri-, three; as

Triadelphous, said of stamens when united by their filaments into three bundles.

Triandrous, three-stamened.

Trifid, three-cleft.

Trifoliate, three-leaved.

Trifoleolate, of three leaflets. (Plate 48.)

Trygynous, having three pistils or styles. (Plate 56, fig. 3.)

Trilobed, having three lobes (the leaves of plate 2).

Triquetrous, sharply three-angled—like a beechnut.

Triternate, three times ternate, *i. e.*, divided into threes three times.

Triticose, shaped like a grain of wheat. (Plate 110, fig. 6.)

Trumpet-shaped, tubular, enlarging toward the summit (the flowers of plate 130).

Truncate, as if cut off at the apex.

Tubercle, a small excrescence.

Tubercled, pimply.

Tubular, elongated and hollow.

Tumid, swollen at one portion.

Turbinate, top-shaped.

Turgid, swollen throughout.

Turnip-shaped, broader than high, *i. e.*, narrowed below.

Twin, see *Geminate*.

Twining, see *Voluble*.

Typical, embracing all the characteristics of a species, genus, or family.

Umbel, said of an arrangement of peduncles when like the ribs of an umbrella, bearing flowers in a flat or convex canopy (as in plate 63).

Umbellet, a small umbel, formed upon the apex of a division of an umbel (as in plate 67).

Umbilicate, depressed in the centre, like one end of an apple. (Plate 139, fig. 4.)

Unarmed, destitute of spines, prickles, or like appendages.

Uncinate, hooked. (Plate 92, fig. 4.)

Undulate, see *Wavy*.

Uni, one; as *unicellular*, one-celled.

Unisexual, having stamens or pistils only. (Plate 14, figs. 3 and 7.)

Urceolate, urn-shaped.

Urticle, a small, thin-walled, one-seeded fruit. (Plate 153, fig. 5.)

Valve, one of the pieces into which a pod splits. (Plate 173, fig. 5.)

Valvate, said when parts meet each other by their edges, without over-lapping.

Vascular, containing vessels.

Vaulted, see *Fornicate*.

Veins, the small ribs forming the frame-work of leaves, or other organs.

Veiny, said when the veins are evident.

Veinlets, diminutive of veins.

Venation, the method of arrangement of veins.

Ventral, the opposite of dorsal.

Vermicular, worm-like.

Vernation, the methodical arrangement of leaves in their buds.

Verrucose, warty. (Plate 72, fig. 6.)

Versatile, attached by one point, with ability to swing to and fro. (Plate 178, fig. 3.)

Vertex, the same as *Apex*, which see.

Vertical, perpendicular; at right angles to the plane of the ground.

Verticil, a *Whorl*, which see.

Verticillaster, a whorl of small flowers, as in many mints.

Verticillate, whorled.

Vesicle, a little bladder. (Plate 153, fig. 7.)

Vexillum, the standard of a papillionaceous flower. (Plate 46, fig. 3a.)

Villose, shaggy, with long, soft hairs.

Virgate, wand-like. (Plate 114, fig. 1.)

Viscid, having a glutinous surface.

Vittæ, the oil-tubes of Umbelliferous fruits.

Voluble, twining (as the stem of plate 130).

Wavy, when the margin is alternately convex and concave (as the leaves of plate 19).

Wedge-shaped, see *Cuneate*.

Wheel-shaped, see *Rotate*.

Whorl, Whorled, arranged in a circle around the stem (as the leaves of plates 78 and 114).

Winged, having a membranous expansion (see *Alate*).

Woolly, clothed with entangled, soft hair.

BIBLIOGRAPHY.

Allen, Encyc.—The Encyclopædia of pure Materia Medica. A Record of the positive Effects of Drugs, Etc. 10 vols. Timothy F. Allen, A.M., M.D. Phila., 1877–1879.

Am. Disp.—The American Dispensatory. John King, M.D. Cincinnati, 1870.

Am. Disp. Suppl.—Supplement to the American Dispensatory. John King, M.D., and J. U. Lloyd. Cincinnati, 1880.

Am. Hom. Phar.—The American Homœopathic Pharmacopœia, 2d Edition. Joseph T. O'Connor, M.D. Phila., 1883.

Am. Jour. Pharm.—The American Journal of Pharmacy, Philadelphia. 58 vols. to date.

Bart. Flora.—A Flora of North America. William P. C. Barton, M.D. Phila., 1820.

Bart. Med. Bot.—Vegetable Materia Medica of the United States; or Medical Botany. 2 vols. William P. C. Barton, M.D., 1817–1818.

Bent. and Trim.—Medicinal Plants. Descriptions and Original Figures of the Principal Plants Employed in Medicine. 4 vols. Robert Bentely, F.L.S., and Henry Trimen, M.B., F.L.S. London, 1880.

Berberidaceæ.—The Constituents of the Berberidaceæ. J. U. and C. G. Lloyd.

Bigel., Am. Med. Bot.—American Medical Botany. A collection of the Native Medicinal Plants of the United States. Jacob Bigelow, M.D. 3 vols. Boston, 1817–1820.

Bot. Gaz.—The Botanical Gazette; a paper of Botanical Notes. John M. Coulter (in part). Crawfordsville, Ind. 8 vols. 1878–1884.

Brock., Essay.—A Botanico-Chemical Essay on Two Native Species of Laurus. A. Brockenbrough. Phila., 1804.

Chap., Flora.—Flora of the Southern United States. A. W. Chapman, M.D. New York, 1860.

Chem. Carb. Comp.—A Manual of the Chemistry of the Carbon Compounds; or Organic Chemistry. C. Schorlemmer, F.R.S. London, 1874.

Church., Med. Bot.—Medical Botany. J. Churchill. London, 1827.

Clapp, Cat.—A Synopsis; or Systematic Catalogue of the Indigenous and Naturalized Medicinal Plants of the United States. A. Clapp, M.D. Transactions American Medical Association, 1852.

Darl., Ag. Bot.—Agricultural Botany. Useful Plants and Weeds. Wm. Darlington, M.D. Phila., 1847.

Darl., Am. Weeds.—American Weeds and Useful Plants, being a 2d Edition of the above. New York, 1859.

Drugs and Med. of N. A.—Drugs and Medicines of North America. Vol. 1, Ranunculaceæ; and to date. J. U. and C. G. Lloyd. Cincinnati, 1884–7.

Dungl., New Rem.—New Remedies, 3d Edition. Robley Dunglison, M.D. Phila., 1841.

Erig. Can., De Puy.—An Inquiry into the Botanical History, Chemical Properties, and Medicinal Qualities of the Erigeron Canadense. Cornelius E. De Puy, M.D. 1815.

Flor. Med.—Flora Medica. A Description, etc., of the Medicinal Plants Admitted into the London, Edinburgh and Dublin Pharmacopœias. G. Spratt, Surgeon. 2 vols. London, 1829.

Flück. and Han.—Pharmacographia. A History of the Principal Drugs of Vegetable Origin, Met with in Great Britain and British India. Friedrich A. Flückiger and David Hanbury, F.L.S. London, 1879.

Good, Bot.—A Materia Medica Botanica. Peter Good, M.D. New York, 1846.

Gray, Bot. Text.—The Botanical Text-Book, an Introduction to Scientific Botany. Asa Gray, M.D. New York, 1850.

Gray, Contrib.—A Contribution to the Flora of North America. American Academy of Arts and Sciences. Asa Gray, M.D., 1883.

Gray, Flora, N. A.—Synoptical Flora of North America. Asa Gray, LL.D. 2 vols. New York, 1878 and 1884.

Gray, Genera.—Genera of the Plants of the United States. Asa Gray, M.D. 2 vols. New York, 1848.

Gray, Man.—Manual and Lessons in Botany and Vegetable Physiology. Asa Gray. New York, 1874.

Griff., Med. Bot.—Medical Botany; or Descriptions of the more Important Plants used in Medicine, Etc. R. Griffith, M.D. Phila., 1847.

Hale, New Rem.—The Special Symptomatology of the New Remedies. Edwin M. Hale, M.D. Phila., 1877.

Hamilt., Flor. Hom.— The Flora Homœopathica; or Illustrations and Descriptions of the Medicinal Plants used as Homœopathic Remedies. Edward Hamilton, M.D., F.L.S., F.Z.S. 2 vols. London, 1852.

Hughes, Phar.—A Manual of Pharmacodynamics. Richard Hughes, L.R.C.P. 3d Edition. London, 1876.

J. and G. Phar.—New Homœopathic Pharmacopœia of Jahr, Buchner and Gruner. C. J. Hempel, M.D. New York, 1850.

Johnson, Med. Bot.—A Manual of the Medical Botany of North America. Laurence Johnson, A.M., M.D. New York, 1884.

King, Am. Disp.—The American Dispensatory. John King, M.D. Cincinnati, 1866.

Lindley, Flor. Med.—Flora Medica. A Botanical Account of all the more Important Plants used in Medicine. John Lindley, Ph.D., F.R.S. London, 1838.

Loudon, Encyc.—An Encyclopædia of Plants. J. C. Loudon, F.L.S., H.S. London, 1836.

Mich., Man. Weeds.—A Manual of Weeds; or the Weed Exterminator. E. Michener, M.D. Phila., 1872.

Park, Derm. Ven.—Dermatitis Venenata, or Rhus Toxicodendron and its Action. R. Park, 1879.

Peck, Blk. Spruce.—The Black Spruce. Albany Institute, 1875. Chas. H. Peck, A.M.

Percy, Verat. Vir.—An Inquiry into the Properties of Veratrum Viride. Transactions American Medical Association. S. R. Percy, M.D.

Plügge.—Die Wichtigstein Heilmittel in ihrer Wechselnden Chemischen Zusammensetzung und Pharmakodynamischen Wirkung, &c. Dr. P. C. Plügge. Jena, 1886.

Porch., Pl. S. C.—Report on the Indigenous Medicinal Plants of South Carolina. Francis P. Porcher, M.D. Transactions American Medical Association, 1849.

Porch., Resourc. South.—Resources of the Southern Fields and Forests. Francis Peyre Porcher, Surgeon P.A.C.S., Richmond, 1863.

Raf., Med. Flor.—Medical Flora; or Manual of the Medical Botany of the United States of North America. 2 vols. C. S. Rafinesque, A.M., Ph.D. Phila., 1828.

Read, Stram.—On the Use of Datura Stramonium in Certain Diseases. Alex. Read, M.D.,1816.

Smithson. Inst.—Smithsonian Institute Publications, especially No. 258. Washington, D. C., 1878.

Spratt, Tox.—A Compendium of Toxicology of the Principal Indigenous and Exotic Plants. G. Spratt, Surgeon. London (no date).

Strong, Am. Flor.—The American Flora. A. B. Strong, A.B. 2 vols. New York, 1848.

Taylor, Tox.—On Poisons in relation to Medical Jurisprudence and Medicine. Alfred Swaine Taylor, M.D., F.R.S. 3d Am. and Eng. Edition. Phila., 1875.

Thomp., Exp. Diss.—An Experimental Dissertation on the Spigelia Marilandica or Indian Pink. Hedge Thompson. Phila., 1802.

Thom., Org. Chem.—Chemistry of Organic Bodies. Thomas Thomson, M.D. London, 1838.

Torr., Bot. S. N. Y.—Natural History of the State of New York. Part 2, Botany. John Torrey. M.D., F.L.S. 2 vols. 1843.

Torr., Bull.—Bulletin of the Torrey Botanical Club. 7 vols. and to date. New York, 1887.

U. S. Ag. Rep.—United States Agricultural Reports, especially 1870.

U. S. Phar.—Pharmacopœia of the United States, 6th revision. New York, 1882..

Warder, West. Catalp.—The Western Catalpa; a Memoir of the Shavanon. John A. Warder, M.D. Journal American Agricultural Association, 1881.

Wats., Bib.—Bibliographical Index to North American Botany. Polypetalæ. Soreno Watson. Washington, 1878.

Wats., Contrib.—Contributions to American Botany. Soreno Watson. Proceedings American Academy of Arts and Sciences, XXI. 1886.

Wigand.—Lehrbuch der Pharmakognosie. Albert Wigand. Berlin, 1879.

Williams, Med. Bot. Mass.—Report on the Indigenous Medical Botany of Massachusetts. Stephen W. Williams, M.D. Transactions American Medical Association, 1849.

Wittstein.—The Organic Constituents of Plants and Vegetable Substances, and their Chemical Analysis. G. C. Wittstein, M.D. Melbourne, 1878.

Wood, Class Book.—Class Book of Botany. Alphonso Wood, A.M. New York, 1868.

Woodv., Med. Bot. — Medical Botany, 2nd edition. William Woodville, M.D. 4 vols. London, 1810.

And numerous Pamphlets, Brochures, Essays, Letters, Journals, and Works on Botany, Medicine, Travel, and Chemistry, acknowledged in the text.

BIBLIOGRAPHICAL INDEX

TO

THE WORKS CONSULTED IN GENERAL.

ABBREVIATIONS.

Pulsatilla Nuttalliana, 1.

Bot. Gaz., 1884, 77; Am. Hom. Phar., 382; Allen Ency., 8, 242; U. S. Phar., 271: Drugs and Med. of N. A., 1, **t. 4**, 25; Clapp Cat., 689; Am. Disp., 110; Hale New Rem., 539; Wood, 202; Gray Man., 36.

Anemone Hepatica, 2.

Griff. Med. Bot., **f. 48**, 81; Raf. Med. Flor, 1, **f. 48**, 231; Williams Med. Bot. Mass., 874; Darl. Am. Weeds, 26; Porch. Resourc. South., 17; Allen Ency., 4, 558; Am. Hom. Phar., 249; Gray Man., 38; Torr. Bot. S. N. Y., 1, 10; Clapp Cat., 717; Porch. Pl. S. C., 684; Aing. Am. Disp., 483; Loud. Ency., **f. 7935**, 480; U. S. Phar., 444; Drugs and Med. of N. A., **t. 5**, 37; Am. Disp., 421.

Ranunculus sceleratus, 3.

Spratt Tox., 32; Lindl. Med. Bot., **f. 212**, 148; Williams Med. Bot. Mass., 874; Porch. Resourc. South., 18; Raf. Med. Flor., 2, 74; Woodv. Med. Bot., 3, 483; Clapp Cat., 719; Lond. Ency., 486; Drugs and Med. of N. A., 1, **ff. 22**, 58; Hamilt. Flor. Hom., 2, 119; Allen Ency., 8, 270; Am. Hom. Phar., 387; U. S. Phar., 445; Torr. Bot. S. N. Y., 1, 13; Gray Man., 42.

Ranunculus repens, 4.

Darl. Am. Weeds, 39; Clapp Cat., 718; Porch. Pl. S. C., 686; Torr. Bot. S. N. Y., 1, 14; Porch. Resourc. South., 19; Am. Hom. Phar., 386; Allen Ency., 8, 270; Gray Man., 43.

Ranunculus bulbosus, 5.

Hamilt. Flor. Hom., 2, **ct. 49**, 109; Bigel Am. Med. Bot., 3, **ct. 47**, 61; Darl. Am. Weeds, **f. 1–2**, 25; Clapp Cat., 719; Torr. Bot. S. N. Y., 1, 16; King Am. Disp., 781; Am.

Hom. Phar., 385; Allen Ency., 8, 257; Loudon Ency., **f. 8055**, 486; Mich. Man. Weeds, 2; Drugs and Med. N. A., **t. 7**, 54.

Ranunculus acris, 6.

Spratt Tox., **cf. 4**, 16; Griff. Med. Bot. **f. 50**, 83; Raf. Med. Flor., 2, **f. 80**, 72; Woodv. Med. Bot., 3, **t. 172**, 482; Williams Med. Bot. Mass., 874; Darl. Am. Weeds, **t. 3–6**, 29; Lindl. Flor. Med., 5; Clapp Cat., 719; Porch. Pl. S. C., 685; Torr. Bot. S. N. Y., 1, 14; Am. Hom. Phar., 385; Allen Ency., 8, 256; Lindl. Med. Bot., 147; Gray Bot. Text., **f. 476 –9**, 376; Gray Man., 43; Ludon Ency., 486.

Caltha palustris, 7.

Wats. Bib., 8; Gray Man., 44; Clapp Cat., 720; Am. Hom. Phar., 144; Drugs and Med. N. A., **f. 26**, 74; Raf. Med. Flor., 2, 202; Allen Encyc., 2, 421; Bot. Gaz., 1883, 316; Williams Med. Bot. Mass., 874; Darl. Am. Weeds, 80; Porch. Resourc. South., 18; Torr. Bot. S. N. Y., 1, 17; Ludon Encyc., **f. 8089**, 490.

Helleborus viridis, 8.

Am. Journ. Phar., 1883, 367: 1882, 303; Raf. Med. Bot., 2, 227; Wigand, **rf.** 91; Loudon Ency., **f. 8081**, 488; Wood Bot., 209; Gray Man., 45; Torr. Bot. S. N. Y., 1, 19; Fluck. and Han., 2; Lindl. Flor. Med., 7; Griff. Med. Bot., 87; Allen Ency., 4, 565; Clapp Cat., 721; Plugge, 70; Chem. Carb. Comp., 465; Wittstein, 104–5.

Hydrastis Canadensis, 9.

New. Rem., 1879, 17, 109, 211; Am. Journ. Phar., 1879, 11; Griff. Med. Bot., **f. 49**, 82; Porch. Pl. S. C., 685; Clapp Cat., 722; Lindl. Flor. Med., 3; Raf. Med. Flor., 1, **f. 51**, 251;

Torr. Bot. S. N. Y., 1, 26; U. S. Phar., 181; Porch. Resourc. South., 18; King Am. Disp., 496: Wittstein, 26, 106; Chem. Carb. Comp., 480; Am. Hom. Phar., 250; Hale New. Rem., 355; Allen Ency., 4, 613; Gray Man., 47; Hughes Phar., 406; Williams' Med. Bot. Mass., 872; Wigand, 92; Bart. Veg. Mat. Med., 2, **ct. 26,** 17; Loudon Ency., **f. 8091,** 490; Drugs and Med. of N. A., 1, **t. 8,** 76.

Actæa alba, 10.

Raf. Med. Flor., 2, 186; Griff. Bot., 94; Wats. Bib., 2; Allen Encyc., 1, 45; Clapp Cat., 12; Wigand, **rf.** 92 ; Am. Homœopath, 1883, 289; Am. Journ. Phar., 1884, 619; Fluck. and Han., 3; Gray Man., 47; Loudon Ency., **f. 7650,** 460; Drugs and Meds. of N. A., 1, **t. 18,** 232.

Cimicifuga racemosa, 11.

New Rem., 1879, 19; Griff. Med. Bot., **f. 55,** 9; Raf., Med. Flor., 1, **f. 16,** 85 ; Bent. and Trim., **ct.,** 8 ; Torr. Bot. S. N. Y., 1, **ct. 4,** 22 ; Williams Med. Bot. Mass., 914; Darl. Am. Weeds, 33 ; Porch. Resourc. South., 19 ; Allen Encyc., 3, 296; Am. Hom. Phar., 175; Gray Man., 48; Porch. Pl. S. C., 686; Clapp Cat., 723; Am. Journ. Phar., 1884, 459 ; Am. Disp., 227 ; Wats. Bib., 9; U. S. Phar., 78; Fluck. and Han., 16; Dugl. New Rem., 144; Hale New Rem., 200; Hughes Phar., 60; Drugs and Meds. of N. A., 1, **t. 21,** 244.

Magnolia glauca, 12.

Torr. Bul., 1880, 101; Bigel. Am. Med. Bot., 2, **ct. 27,** 67; Torr. Bot. S. N. Y., 1, **ct. 5,** 27; Darl. Am. Weeds, 34; Porch. Resourc. South., 36; Gray Bot. Text., **f. 486-9,** 377 ; Bart. Med. Bot., **ct. 7,** 77 ; Journ. Mat. Med., 2, 369; Gray Man., 49; Allen Ency., 6, 142 ; U. S. Phar., 215; Lindl Med. Bot., 144; Griff. Med. Bot., **f. 56,** 97 ; Am. Disp., 507; Lindl. Flor. Med., 23 ; Am. Hom. Phar., 300.

Asimina triloba, 13.

Torr. Bot. S. N. Y., 1, 30; Darl. Am. Weeds, 36; Porch. Resourc. South., 41 ; Gray Bot. Text., **f. 490-4,** 378; Wats. Bib., 30; Gray Man., 50; Griff. Med. Bot., 101 ; Lindl. Flor. Med., 27; Clapp Cat., 727; Am. Hom. Phar., 106; Allen Ency., 1, 598; Am. Disp , 843; Loudon Ency., **f. 7930,** 480.

Menispermum Canadense, 14.

Raf. Med. Flor., 2, 242 ; Porch. Resourc. South., 376; Gray Bot. Text., **f. 495-502,** 379; Am. Jour. Phar., 1884, 401 ; Ludon Encyc., **f. 13,** 997, 844; Hale's Monograph, **ct. ;** Jour. Mat. Med., 2, 362; Allen Ency., 6, 177; Hale New Rem., 438; Am. Disp., 522; Am. Hom. Phar., 306; Gray Man., 51; Torr. Bot. S. N. Y., 1, 31.

Berberis vulgaris, 15.

Berberidaceæ; Griff. Med. Bot., **f. 64,** 212 ;

Hamilt. Flor. Hom., **ct. 10,** 88; Lindl. Med. Bot., **lf. 154,** 104; Torr. Bot. S. N. Y., 1, 32; Woodv. Med. Bot., 3, **t. 219,** 618; Gray Man., 52; Clapp Cat., 728; Lindl. Flor. Med , 63 ; Porch. Resourc. South., 51 ; King Am. Disp., 166; Wittstein, 26, 165 ; Chem. Carb. Comp., 480-1; Am. Hom. Phar., 119; Hale New Rem., 98; Gray Bot. Text., **f. 503-5,** 380; Fluck. & Han., 36; Allen Ency., 2, 139; Hughes Phar., 189; Williams Med. Bot. Mass., 878; Darl. Am. Weeds, **f** p. 37; Wigand, **rf.** 50; Loudon Ency., **f. 4922,** 286.

Caulophyllum thalictroides, 16.

Griff. Med. Bot., **f. 65,** 114; Raf. Med. Flor., **f. 19,** 97; Am. Hom. Phar., 157; Williams Med. Bot. Mass., 879; Berberidaceæ, 9; Gray Man., 53; Hughes Phar., 253; Hale New Rem., 163; Allen Ency., 3, 34; Am. Disp., 198; Clapp Cat., 729; Wats. Bib., 35; U. S. Phar., 68; Torr. Bot. S. N. Y., 1, 33; Loudon Ency., **f. 4914,** 286.

Podophyllum peltatum, 17.

New Rem., 1879, 43, 262: 1881, 47; Am. Jour. Phar., 1879, 543, 580: 1882, 108; Bot. Gaz., 1881, 178; Bull. Torr. Club, 1884, 62 ; Gray Bot., 54; Darl. Am. Weeds, 38 ; Raf. Med. Bot., 2, **t. 73,** 59 ; Porch. Resourc. South., 21, 77, 577; Griff. Med. Bot., **f. 66,** 115 ; Clapp Cat., 730; Lindl. Flor. Med., 13; Torr. Bot. S. N. Y., 1, 35 ; U. S. Phar., 260; Allen Ency., 8, 130; Bent. & Trim., **ct. 17;** Wittstein, 76; Am. Hom. Phar., 377; King Am. Disp., 731; Bigel. Am. Med. Bot., 2, **t. 23,** 34; Barton Med. Bot., 2, **ct. 25,** 9; Fluck. & Han., 36; Wigand, 384; Hughes Phar., 647; Loudon Ency., **f. 7652,** 460.

Nymphæa odorata, 18.

Am. Jour. Phar., 1883, 96; Bot. Gaz., 1881, 266; Raf. Med. Bot., 2, **f. 67,** 44; Bigel. Am. Med. Bot., 3, **ct. 55,** 134; Gray Man., 56; Griff. Med. Bot., 119; Lindl. Flor. Med., 20; Porch. Resourc. South., 35; King Am. Disp., 630; Porch. Pl. S. C., 693; Clapp Cat., 732; Am. Hom. Phar., 344; Hale New Rem., 445; Lindl. Med. Bot., **f. 453, 265-8,** 383; Torr. Bot. S. N. Y., 1, 39; Allen Encyc., 7, 127; Williams Med. Bot. Mass., 876; Loudon Ency., **f. 7678,** 462.

Sarracenia purpurea, 19.

New Rem., 1879, 146; Bot. Gaz., 1883, 192: 1881, 242; Torr. Bot. S. N. Y., 1, **ct. 6,** 41; Gray Bot., **lf. 224,** 383; Wigand, 93, 211 ; Therap. Gaz., vol. 5, 547; Loudon Ency., **f. 7676,** 462; Am. Disp., 752; Hale New Rem., 573; Watson Bib., 40; Hughes Phar., 683; Allen Ency., 8, 574; Am. Hom. Phar., 402; Gray Man., 58.

Argemone Mexicana, 20.

Griff. Med. Bot., 129; Lindl. Med. Bot., **f. 222,** 154; Darl. Am. Weeds, **sf. 19,** 41; Porch.

and Trim., **ct. 42**; Williams Med. Bot. Mass., 888; Darl. Am. Weeds, **f. 49–50**, 72; Porch. Resourc. South., 138; Gray Bot. Text., **f. 632–8**, 399; Watson Bib., 151; Allen Ency., 4, 407; Gray Man., 107; Good Bot., **ct. 22**; Lindl. Flor. Med., 221; Porch. Pl. S. C., 731; Clapp Cat., 748; Griff. Med. Bot., 209; Raf. Med. Flor., 1, **f. 42**, 215; U. S. Phar., 169; King Am. Disp., 1, 45; Am. Hom. Phar., 233; Wittstein, 90; Lindl. Med. Bot., 120; Bart. Med. Bot., **ct. 13**, 150; Loudon Ency., **f. 9656**, 580.

Xanthoxylum Americanum, 33.

Griff. Med. Bot., **f. 103**, 195; Raf. Med. Flor., 2, **f. 96**, 113; Bigel. Am. Med. Bot., 3, **ct. 59**, 156; Williams Med. Bot. Mass., 911; Porch. Resourc. South., 136; Darl. Am. Weeds, **f. 53–5**, 75; Gray Bot. Text., **f. 639–46**, 402; Loudon Ency., **f. 13896**, 834; Torr. Bot. S. N. Y., 1, 132; Gray Man., 110; Allen Ency., 10, 169; Watson Bib., 155; Lindl. Flor. Med., 216; Am. Hom. Phar., 458; Am. Disp., 871; U. S. Phar., 379.

Ptelea trifoliata, 34.

Jour. Mat. Med., 4, 290; Loudon Ency., **f. 1764**, 100; Am. Hom. Phar., 381; Gray Man., 110; Am. Disp., 680; Allen Ency., 8, 177; Hale New Rem., 526; Raf. Med. Flor., 2, 254; Hale's Monograph, 1869, **ct.**; Torr. Bot. S. N. Y., 1, 133; Clapp Cat., 753; Lindl. Flor. Med., 215.

Ailantus glandulosus, 35.

Darl. Am. Weeds, 76; Loudon Ency., **f. 14310**, 866; Am. Disp. Suppl., 20; Am. Jour. Phar., 1885, 600; Gray Man., 111; Hale New Rem., 28; Allen Ency., 1, 133; Am. Hom. Phar., 60.

Rhus glabra, 36.

Raf. Med. Flor., 2, 256; Strong Am. Flor., 1, **cf. 46**, 97; Williams Med. Bot. Mass., 911; Darl. Am. Weeds, **f. 56–8**, 78; New Remedies, 1880, 370; Jour. Mat. Med., 1, 195; Porch. Resourc. South., 202; Loudon Ency., 226; Mich. Man. Weeds, 15; Am. Hom. Phar., 390; Wats. Bib., 182; Torr. Bot. S. N. Y., 1, 129; U. S. Phar., 283; Am. Disp., 707; Allen Ency., 8, 329

Rhus venenata, 37.

Bigel. Am. Med. Bot., 1, **ct. 10**, 96; Porch. Resourc. South., 206; Loudon Ency., 226; Am. Disp., 709; Gray Man., 111; Lindl. Flor. Med., 284; Allen Ency., 8, 378; Hale New Rem., 546; Torr. Bot. S. N. Y., 1, 130; Am. Hom. Phar., 392.

Rhus Toxicodendron, 38.

New Rem., 1880, 370: 2, 208; Med. Counsellor, 516, 522; Bot. Gaz., 1880, 42: 1879, 211, 219: 1878, 53; Hamilt. Flor. Hom., 2, **ct. 51**, 130; Bigel. Am. Med. Bot., 3, **ct. 42** (Radi-

cans?), 19; Williams Med. Bot. Mass., 911; Darl. Am. Weeds, **f. 60**, 80; Porch. Resourc. South., 200, 201, 273; Wigand, 198; Park Derm. Ven.; Ludon Ency., **f. 3801**, 226; New Rem., 1879, 199, 240; Mich. Man. Weeds, 16; Griff. Med. Bot., 372; Hale New Rem., 506; Jour. Mat. Med., 3, 402; Am. Hom. Phar., 390; Wats. Bib., 183; Torr. Bot. S. N. Y., 1, 130; U. S. Phar., 283; Am. Disp., 709; Allen Ency., 8, 330.

Rhus aromatica, 39.

Am. Nat., 12, 597; Am. Jour. Phar., 1881, 209; Loudon Ency., 226; Am. Hom. Phar., 183; Wats. Bib., 181; Torr. Bot. S. N. Y., 1, 131.

Ampelopsis quinquefolia, 40.

Bot. Gaz., 1883, 201; Torr. Bot. S. N. Y., 1, 148; Darl. Am. Weeds, **ff. 65, lf. 64**, 85; Loudøn Ency., **f. 2868**, 176; Gray Man., 113; Am. Hom. Phar., 75; Allen Ency., 10, 290; Am. Disp., 100; Clapp Cat., 759.

Rhamnus catharticus, 41.

Am. Jour. Phar., 1885, 496; Torr. Bot. S. N. Y., 1, 143; Am. Disp., 697; Fluck. and Han., 157; Flora Med., **ct. 129**, 128; Bent. and Trim., 1, **ct. 64**; Lindl. Med. Bot., **f. 234**, 164; Woodv. Med. Bot., 3, **t. 210**, 593; Darl. Am. Weeds, 86; Loudon Ency., **f. 2874**, 176; Gray Man., 114; Allen Ency., 8, 301; Griff. Med. Bot., 216; Lindl. Flor. Med., 167; Clapp Cat., 758.

Euonymus atropurpureus, 42.

Torr. Bot. S. N. Y., 1, 141; Gray Man., 116; Am. Hom. Phar., 293, 214; Wats. Bib., 162; U. S. Phar., 99; Clapp Cat., 758; Am. Jour. Phar., 1883, 367; Therap. Gaz., 1885, 39; Griff. Med. Bot. **f. 112**, 219; Ludon Ency., 178; New Rem., 1880, 80; Raf. Med. Flor., 1, 195; Jour. Mat. Med., 2, 406.

Æsculus Hippocastanum, 43.

Griff. Med. Bot., **f. 109**, 212; Raf. Med. Flor., 2, 219; Flor. Med., 1, **ct. 44**, 113; Lindl. Med. Bot., **f. 152**, 102; Gray Man., 117; Woodv. Med. Bot., 3, **t. 217**, 614; Darl. Am. Weeds, 88; Torr. Bot. S. N. Y., 1, 138; Allen Ency., 1, 48; Am. Hom. Phar., 57; Lindl. Flor. Med., 124; Hale New Rem., 20; Fluck. and Han., 541; U. S. Ag. Rept., 1870, 405; Dugl. New Rem., 269; Ludon Ency., **f. 5057**, 296; Am. Disp., 69; Chem. Carb. Comp., 461, 465; Tomp. Org. Chem., 809; Wittstein, 6, 84, 201.

Æsculus glabra, 44.

Ludon Ency., 296; Am. Hom. Phar., 57; Allen Ency., 1, 48; Gray Man., 118; Wats. Bib., 178; Hale New Rem., 19.

Polygala Senega, 45.

Flor. Med., 2, **ct. 106**, 62; Hamilt. Flor. Hom., 2, **ct. 58**, 176; Bigel. Am. Med. Bot.,

2, **ct. 30**, 97 ; Bent. and Trim., 1, **ct. 29**; Lindl. Med. Bot., **f. 148**, 100 ; Woodv. Med. Bot., **t. 162**, 452 ; Darl. Am. Weeds, 92 ; Porch. Resourc. South., 85 ; Wiegand, **rf.** 43 ; Bart. Med. Bot., 2, **ct. 36**, 113 ; Loudon Ency., **f. 10005**, 602 ; Jour. Mat. Med., 1, 237 ; Gray Man., 122 ; Clapp. Cat., 760 ; Tomp. Org. Chem., 820 ; Am. Disp., 659 ; Raf. Med. Flor., 2, 64 ; Lindl. Flor. Med., 125 ; Griff. Med. Bot., **f. 114**, 225 ; Am. Hom. Phar., 409 ; Hughes Phar., 693 ; U. S. Phar., 291 ; Fluck. and Han., 77 ; Torr. Bot. S. N. Y., 1, 151 ; Allen Ency., 8, 586.

Genista tinctoria, 46.
Raf. Med. Flor., 2, 223 ; Darl. Am. Weeds, 96 ; Wigand, **ffol.**, 197 ; Loudon Ency., 610 ; Gray Man., 126 ; Lindl. Flor. Med., 238 ; Wats. Bib., 221 ; Torr. Bot. S. N. Y., 1, 185 ; Allen Ency., 4, 403.

Trifolium pratense, 47.
Am. Jour. Phar., 1883, 194 ; Darl. Am. Weeds, **ff. 74-5**, 97 ; U. S. Agric. Rept., 1864, 322 : 1880, 151 ; Porch. Resourc. South., 177 ; Loudon Ency., **f. 10802**, 642 ; Torr. Bot. S. N. Y., 1, 168 ; Am. Disp., 832 ; Gray Man., 127 ; Allen Ency., 10, 22 ; Am. Hom. Phar., 441 ; Wats. Bib., 265.

Trifolium repens, 48.
Williams Med. Bot. Mass., 886 ; Darl. Am. Weeds, 98 ; Porch. Resourc. South, 177 ; Ludon Ency., **f. 10787**, 640 ; Torr. Bot. S. N. Y., 1, 169 ; Gray Man., 127 ; Allen Ency., 10, 22 ; Wats. Bib., 266.

Melilotus officinalis, 49.
Williams Med. Bot. Mass., 886 ; Darl. Am. Weeds, 299 ; Porch. Resourc. South., 176 ; Ludon Ency., **f. 10771**, 640 ; Gray Man., 128 ; Allen Ency., 6, 176 ; Am. Disp., 832 ; Griff. Med. Bot., 231 ; Am. Hom. Phar., 304-5 ; Torr. Bot. S. N. Y., 1, 170.

Robinia Pseudacacia, 50.
Am. Nat., 12, 6 ; Raf. Med. Flor., 2, 258 ; Darl. Am. Weeds, 101 ; Porch. Resourc. South., 188 ; Loudon Ency., **f. 10460**, 626 ; Gray Man., 131 ; Allen Ency., 10, 628 ; Am. Disp., 712 ; Griff. Med. Bot., 238 ; Am. Hom. Phar., 392 ; Clapp Cat., 761 ; Torr. Bot. S. N. Y., 1, 165.

Phaseolus vulgaris, 51.
Bot. Gaz., 1883, 194 ; Raf. Med. Flor., 2, 251 ; Darl. Am. Weeds, 107 ; U. S. Agric. Rep., 1870, 422 ; Ludon Ency., 614 ; Thom. Org. Chem., 887 ; Allen Ency., 7, 334 ; Wittstein, 112, 171 ; Chem. Carb. Comp., 492 ; Allen Ency., 7, 334.

Baptisia tinctoria, 52.
Am. Jour. Phar., 1879, 577 ; Bot. Gaz., 1880, 94 ; New Rem., 1879, 143 ; Griff. Med. Bot., **f. 119**, 231 ; Raf. Med. Flor., **f. 14**, 79 ; Darl.

Am. Weeds, 108 ; Porch. Resourc. South., 175 ; Gray Man., 143 ; Torr. Bot. S. N. Y., 1, 187 ; Allen Ency., 2, 31 ; Am. Hom. Phar., 114 ; King Am. Disp., 160 ; Porch. Pl. S. C., 739 ; Clapp Cat., 761 ; Lindl. Flor. Med., 237 ; Bart. Med. Bot., 2, **ct. 29**, 53 ; Wats. Bib., 205 ; Am. Disp., 154 ; Ludon Ency., **f. 5691**, 342.

Gymnocladus Canadensis, 53.
Bull. Torr. Club., 1882, 130 ; Raf. Med. Flor., 2, 226 ; Darl. Am. Weeds, 110 ; Loudon Ency., **f. 13987**, 842 ; Am. Disp., 407 ; Gray Man., 145 ; Allen Ency., 4, 519 ; Am. Hom. Phar., 243 ; Wats. Bib., 222 ; Hale New Rem., 336 ; Torr. Bot. S. N. Y., 1, 191.

Geum Rivale, 54.
Darl. Am. Weeds, **f. 82**, 121 ; Torr. Bot. S. N. Y., 1, 203 ; Lindl. Med. Bot., 185 ; Raf. Med. Flor., 1, 221 ; Lindl. Flor. Med., 226 ; Gray Man., 152 ; Am. Disp., 387 ; Wats. Bib., 384 ; Loudon Ency., **f. 7626**, 454.

Fragaria vesca, 55.
Griff. Med. Bot., **f. 140**, 277 ; Raf. Med. Flor., 1, **f. 38**, 189 ; Williams Med. Bot. Mass., 884 ; Darl. Am. Weeds, **f. 83**, 123 ; Porch. Resourc. South., 144 ; Gray Man., 156 ; Torr. Bot. S. N. Y., 1, 212 ; Allen Ency., 4, 365 ; Wats. Bib., 282 ; Porch. Pl. S. C., 733 ; Am. Hom. Phar., 229 ; Lindl. Med. Bot., 184 ; Gray Bot. Text., **f. 677-9**, 412 ; Am. Disp., 365 ; U. S. Agric. Rept., 1870 ; Loudon Ency., **f. 7566**, 452.

Pirus Americana, 56.
Darl. Am. Weeds, 134 ; Porch. Resourc. South., 167 ; Torr. Bot. S. N Y, 1, 224 ; Gray Man., 161 ; Allen Ency., 10, 623 ; Am. Hom. Phar., 383 ; Raf. Med. Flor., 2, 265 ; Griff. Med. Bot., 293 ; Lindl. Flor. Med., 234 ; Clapp Cat., 769 ; Lindl. Med. Bot., 183.

Penthorum sedoides, 57.
Loudon Ency., **f. 6460**, 384 ; Torr. Bot. S. N. Y., 1, 253 ; Am. Hom. Phar., 361 ; Am. Disp. Suppl., 119 ; Allen Ency., 7, 301 ; Gray Man., 171.

Hamamelis Virginiana, 58.
Griff. Med. Bot., **f. 165**, 351 ; Raf. Med. Flor., 1, **f. 45**, 227 ; Williams Med. Bot. Mass., 882 ; Darl. Am. Weeds, 144 ; Porch. Resourc. South., 58 ; Ludon Ency., **f. 1814**, 104 ; Gray Man., 173 ; Torr. Bot. S. N. Y., 1, 270 ; Wats. Bib., 355 ; Am. Disp., 411 ; U. S. Phar., 124, 174 ; Am. Hom. Phar., 244 ; Allen Ency., 4, 528 ; Clapp Cat., 775.

Epilobium palustre, 59.
Wats. Bib., 366 ; Gray Man., 177 ; Am. Disp., 340 ; Loudon Ency., **f. 5487**, 320 ; Torr. Bot. S. N. Y., 1, 233 ; Chap. Bot., 140 ; Wood Bot., 35 ; Allen Ency., 4, 204.

Œnothera biennis, 60.

Raf. Med. Flor., 2, 247; Darl. Am. Weeds, 136; Porch. Resourc. South., 55; Gray Man., 178; Torr. Bot. S. N. Y., 1, 234; Allen Ency., 7, 137; Am. Hom. Phar., 346; Griff. Med. Bot., 304; Porch. Pl. S. C., 706; Clapp Cat., 771; King Am. Disp., 633; Hale New Rem., 446; Barton Flora, **t. 6**, 21; Am. Homœopath, 1883, 317; Wats. Bib., 377; Loudon Ency., 318.

Opuntia vulgaris, 61.

Am. Jour. Phar., 1884, 3; Bull. Torr. Club, 1883, 79; Raf. Med. Flor., 2, 247; Lindl. Med. Bot., **f. 237**, 244; Porch. Resourc. South., 66; Gray Man., 185; Allen Ency., 7, 237; Loudon Ency., **f. 6884**, 412; Am. Hom. Phar., 353; Torr. Bot. S. N. Y., 1, 245.

Eryngium yuccæfolium, 62.

Raf. Med. Flor., 2, 218; Porch. Resourc. South., 43; Allen Ency., 4, 213; Gray Man., 100; Hale New Rem., 290; Am. Hom. Phar., 212; Clapp Cat., 776; Am. Disp., 345; Wood Bot., 378; Griff. Med. Bot., 315; Chap. Bot., 160.

Pastinaca sativa, 63.

Raf. Med. Flor., 2, 251; Lindl. Med. Bot., **f. 348**, 254; Darl. Am. Weeds, 147; Loudon Ency., **f. 3724**, 222; Gray Man., 191; Allen Ency., 7, 291; Torr. Bot. S. N. Y., 1, 278.

Archangelica atropurpurea, 64.

Am. Jour. Phar., 1883, 469: 1882, 159: 1885, 339; Griff. Med. Bot., 322; Raf. Med. Flor., 2, 192; Torr. Bot. S. N. Y., 1, 276; Loudon Ency., 221; Man. Weeds, 26; Allen Ency., 1, 344; Gray Man., 193; Am. Disp., 111.

Æthusa Cynapium, 65.

Spratt Tox., 78; Church. Med. Bot., **ct. 8**; Hamilt. Flor. Hom., 1, **ct. 2**, 15; Bent. and Trim., 2, **ct. 125**; Lindl. Med. Bot., **f. 333**, 247; Torr. Bot. S. N. Y., 1, 274; Darl. Am. Weeds, **sf. 23–5**, 151; Loudon Ency., **f. 3666**, 218; Man. Weeds, 28; Am. Hom. Phar. 58; Clapp Cat., 778; Allen Ency., 1, 59; Wittstein, 63; Taylor Tox., 711; Lindl. Flor. Med., 40; Gray Man., 193; Wood Bot., 386.

Thaspium aureum, 66

Gray Man., 194; Allen Ency., 10, 234; Wats. Bib., 433; Torr .Bot. S. N. Y., 1, 271; Hale New Rem., 616; Raf. Med. Flor., 2, 267.

Cicuta maculata, 67.

Am. Jour. Phar., 1882, 491; Griff. Med. Bot., **f. 154**, 316; Raf. Med. Flor., 1, **f. 22**, 107: 2, 209; Bigel. Am. Med. Bot., 1, **ct. 12**, 125; Darl. Am. Weeds, **sf. 106–7**, 152; Porch. Resourc. South., 44; Loudon Ency., **f. 3608**, 216; Man. Weeds, 29; Biegl. Am. Med. Bot., 4, 181; Allen Ency., 3, 281; Gray Man., 196; Wats. Bib., 416; Clapp Cat., 778; Torr. Bot. S. N. Y., 1, 267.

Conium maculatum, 68.

Am. Journ. Phar., 1882, 359; 1885, 247; Bull. Torr. Club, 1881, 9; Griff. Med. Bot., **f. 160**, 339; Spratt, Tox., **cf. 24**, 44; Church. Med. Bot, **ct. 13**; Griff. Med. Bot., **f. 160**, 339; Raf. Med. Flor., 1, **f. 25**, 118; Flora Med., 1, **ct. 53**, 143; Hamilt. Flor. Hom., 1, **ct. 26**, 219; Bigel. Am. Med. Bot., 1, **ct. 11**, 113; Bent. and Trim., 2, **ct. 118**; Lindl. Med. Bot., **f. 232**, 247; Woodv. Med. Bot., 1, **t. 42**, 104; Darl. Am. Weeds, **f. 108–11**, 154; Wiegand, 211; Loudon Ency., **f. 3609**, 216; Am. Hom. Phar., 187; Clapp Cat., 779; U. S., Phar., 85; Lindl. Flor. Med., 57; Gray Man., 197; Chem. Carb. Comp., 470; Wittstein, 55–6; Am. Disp., 283; Fluck. and Han., 299; Taylor Tox., 698; Hughes Phar., 317; Man. Weeds, 29; Jour. Mat. Med., 4, 49; Allen Ency., 3, 519.

Aralia racemosa, 69.

Bot. Gaz., 1882, 122; Torr. Bot. S. N. Y., 1, 284; Gray Man., 198; Williams Med. Bot. Mass., 870; Porch. Resourc. South., 51; Griff. Med. Bot., 346; Gray Bot., 425; Loudon Ency., 230; Wats. Bib., 436; Hale New Rem., 53; Am. Disp., 124; Clapp Cat., 779; Raf. Med. Flor., 2, 195; Darl. Am. Weeds, 156; Am. Hom. Phar., 90; Allen Ency., 10, 323.

Aralia quinquefolia, 70.

Griff. Med. Bot., **f. 162**, 342, 344; Raf. Flor. Med., 2, **f. 71**, 52; Bigel. Am. Med. Bot., 2, **ct. 29**, 82; Bart. Med. Bot., 2, **ct. 45**, 191; Woodv. Med. Bot., 1, **t. 58**, 149; Williams Med. Bot. Mass., 870; Darl. Am. Weeds, 156; Porch. Resourc. South., 48; Loudon Ency., **f. 14391**, 872; New Rem., 1880, 227; Gray Man., 199; Allen Ency., 4, 415; Torr. Bot. S. N. Y., 1, 286; Clapp Cat., 781; Am. Disp., 596; Lindl. Flor. Med., 59; Wittstein, 166; Am. Hom. Phar., 234.

Cornus florida, 71.

Am. Jour. Phar., 1879, 390; Bull. Torr. Club, 1880, 121; Jour. Mat. Med., 3, 284: 1, 294: 4, 40; Griff. Med. Bot., **f. 164**, 347; Raf. Flor. Med., 1, **f. 28**, 131; Bigel. Am. Med. Bot., 2 **ct. 28**, 73; Bent. and Trim., 2, **ct. 126**; Williams Med. Bot. Mass., 910; Darl. Am. Weeds, **f. 112–13**, 158; Porch. Resourc. South., 59; Bart. Med., **ct. 3**, 43; Loudon Ency., **f. 1793**, 102; Am. Disp., 298; U. S. Phar., 87; Allen Ency., 10, 492; Hale New Rem., 242; Am. Hom. Phar., 191; Torr. Bot. S. N. Y., 1, 290; Wats. Bib., 439; Gray Man., 200; Lindl. Flor. Med., 81; Gray Bot., 425; Lindl. Med. Bot., 259; Wittstein, 59; Chap. Bot., 168.

Cornus circinata, 72.

Am. Journ. Phar., 1880, 433; Raf. Med. Flor., 1, 135; Griff. Med. Bot., 139; Loudon

Ency., **f. 1798,** 102 ; Wats. Bib., 438 ; Gray Man., 200 ; Torr. Bot. S. N. Y., 1, 289 ; Am. Hom. Phar., 191 ; Hale New Rem., 243 ; Am. Disp., 297 ; Allen Ency., 3, 565.

Cornus sericea, 73.
Raf. Med. Flor., 1, 135 : 2, 213 ; Griff. Med. Bot., 349 ; Porch. Resourc. South., 62 ; Bart. Med. Bot., **ct. 9,** 115 ; Am. Journ. Phar., 1884, 618 ; Good Bot., **ct. 19 ;** Loudon Ency., **f. 1797,** 102 ; Gray Man., 200 ; Am. Disp., 299 ; Torr. Bot. S. N. Y., 1, 290 ; Clapp Cat., 782 ; Allen Ency., 10, 493 ; Am. Hom. Phar., 192.

Triosteum perfoliatum, 74.
Raf. Med. Flor., 2, 269 ; Bigel. Am. Med. Bot., 1, **ct. 9,** 90 ; 4, 181 ; Williams Med. Bot. Mass., 911 ; Darl. Am. Weeds, 161 ; Porch. Resourc. South., 407 ; Bart. Med. Bot., **ct. 4,** 59 ; Loudon Ency., **f. 2802,** 170 ; Gray Man., 205 ; Gray Flor. N. A., 12 ; Torr. Bot. S. N. Y., 1, 301 ; Am. Disp., 834 ; Allen Ency., 10, 25 ; Griff. Med. Bot., 352 ; Lindl. Flor. Med., 445 ; U. S. Phar., 446 ; Am. Hom. Phar., 443.

Sambucus Canadensis, 75.
Am. Jour. Phar., 1881, 382, 553 ; Raf. Med. Flor., 2, 260 ; Bent. and Trim., 2, **ct. 138 ;** Darl. Am. Weeds, 162 ; Porch. Resourc. South., 408 ; Good Bot., **ct. 39 ;** Loudon Ency., **f. 3731,** 224 ; Gray Flor. N. A., 9 ; Allen Ency., 8, 476 ; Chap. Bot., 171 ; Gray Man., 205 ; Am. Disp., 740 ; Torr. Bot. S. N. Y., 1, 303 ; Fluck. and Han., 334 ; Am. Hom. Phar., 399 ; U. S. Phar., 787.

Cephalanthus occidentalis, 76.
Griff. Med. Bot., **f. 169,** 356 ; Raf. Med. Flor., 1, **f. 20,** 100 ; Williams Med. Bot. Mass., 910 ; Porch. Resourc. South., 405 ; Gray Bot. Text., **f. 751-3,** 430 ; Gray Man., 211 ; Allen Ency., 10, 456 ; Torr. Bot. S. N. Y., 1, 313 ; Porch. Pl. S. C., 788 ; Clapp Cat., 788 ; King Am. Disp., 214 ; Am. Hom. Phar., 159 ; Am. Disp., 205 ; Loudon Ency., **f. 1677,** 96.

Mitchella repens, 77.
Allen Ency., 6, 373 ; Am. Hom. Phar., 320 ; Porch. Pl. S. C., 788 ; Clapp Cat., 788 ; King Am. Disp., 600 ; Hale New Rem., 441 ; Raf. Med. Flor., 2, 243 ; Loudon Ency., **f. 1758,** 100 ; Bull. Torr. Club, 1883, 1 ; Williams Med. Bot. Mass., 910 ; Porch. Resourc. South., 405 ; Gray Man., 201 ; Torr. Bot. S. N. Y., 1, 314.

Eupatorium purpureum, 78.
Raf. Med. Flor., 1, 179 ; Williams Med. Bot. Mass., 874 ; Porch. Resourc. South., 412 ; Loudon Encyc., 688 ; Porch. Pl. S. C., 790 ; Am. Disp., 351 ; Gray Flora N. A., 95 ; Gray Man., 225 ; Am. Hom. Phar., 216 ; Torr. Bot. S. N. Y., 1, 326 ; Allen Ency., 4, 237.

Eupatorium perfoliatum, 79.
Torr. Bot. S. N. Y., 1, 329 ; Am. Disp., 350 ;

Gray Flora N. A., 99 ; Am. Hom. Phar., 215 ; Porch. Resourc. South., 410 ; Lindl. Flor. Med., 451 ; U. S. Phar., 99 ; Am. Jour. Phar., 1880, 392 : 1879, 342 ; Griff. Med. Bot., **f. 180,** 390 ; Raf. Med. Flor., 1, **f. 36,** 174 ; Bigel. Am. Med. Bot., 1, **t. 2,** 33 ; Bart. Med. Bot., 2, **ct. 37,** 125 ; Bent. and Trim., 3, **ct. 147 ;** Darl. Am. Weeds, 170 ; Loudon Ency., **f. 11536,** 688 ; Man. Weeds, 35 ; Jour. Mat. Med., 2, 243 ; 241 ; Hale New Rem., 294 ; Gray Man., 226 ; Torr. Bot. S. N. Y., 1, 329 ; Allen Ency., 4, 234.

Erigeron Canadense, 80.
Am. Jour. Phar., 1883, 372 ; Raf. Med. Flor., 2, 218 ; Bent. and Trim., 3, **ct. 149 ;** Darl. Am. Weeds, **f. 116-17,** 192 ; Porch. Resourc. South., 415-16 ; Am. Jour. Phar., 1884, 619 ; Loudon Ency., 704 ; Allen Ency., 4, 211 ; Gray Man, 236 ; Gray Flora N. A., 221 ; Torr. Bot. S. N. Y., 1, 353 ; Am. Disp., 343 ; Am. Hom. Phar., 211 ; U. S. Phar., 236.

Inula Helenium, 81.
Am. Jour. Phar., 1881, 469 ; Raf. Med. Flor., 2, 231 ; Flor. Med., 1, **ct. 40,** 106 ; Strong Am. Flor., 1, **ct. 19,** 43 ; Bent. and Trim., 3, **ct. 150 ;** Woodv. Med. Bot., 1, **t. 26,** 64 ; Williams Med. Bot. Mass., 896 ; Darl. Am. Weeds, 176 ; Porch. Resourc. South., 417 ; Wiegand, 68 ; Loudon Ency., **f. 12147,** 714 ; Allen Ency., 5, 112 ; Am. Disp., 444 ; Wittstein, 104, 112 ; Gray Man., 246 ; U. S. Phar., 185 ; Am. Hom. Phar., 255.

Ambrosia artemisiæfolia, 82.
Am. Jour. Phar., 1885, 341 ; Allen Ency., 10, 285 ; Gray Flor. N. A., 249 ; Gray Man., 251 ; Am. Hom. Phar., 470 ; Raf. Med. Flor., 2, 190 ; New Rem., 1879, 239 ; Torr. Bot. S. N. Y., 1, 376 ; Porch. Resourc. South., 419.

Helianthus annuus, 83.
Raf. Med. Flor., 2, 226 ; Darl. Am. Weeds, 181 ; Porch. Resourc. South., 422 ; Loudon Ency., 730 ; Am. Hom. Phar., 246 ; Gray Man., 255 ; Wittstein, 104 ; Am. Disp., 416 ; Allen Ency., 4, 545 ; Gray Flora N. A., 272.

Anthemis nobilis, 84.
Griff. Med. Bot., **f. 184,** 404 ; Flor. Med., 1, **ct. 28,** 73 ; Strong Am. Flor., 1, **cf. 55,** 119 ; Bent. and Trim., 3, **ct. 154 ;** Lindl. Med. Bot., **f. 310,** 231 ; Woodv. Med. Bot., 1, **t. 19,** 47 ; Loudon Ency., **f. 12324,** 724 ; Allen Ency., 1, 358 ; Am. Hom. Phar., 81 ; Lindl. Flor. Med., 59 ; Wood Bot., 457 ; Gray Man., 265 ; Gray Flora N. A., 363 ; Fluck. and Han., 384 ; Chem. Carb. Comp., 269 ; Wittstein, 141 ; U. S. Phar., 37 ; Am. Disp., 112.

Achillea Millefolium, 85.
Am. Nat., 12, 651 ; Griff. Med. Bot., 403 ; Raf. Med. Flor., 2, 185 ; Bent. and Trim., 3, **ct. 153 ;** Lindl. Med. Bot., **ff. 306,** 229 ; Torr.

Bot. S. N. Y., 1, 392; Woodv. Med. Bot., 1, **t. 15**, 36; Williams Med. Bot. Mass., 896; Darl. Am. Weeds, 187; Porch. Resourc. South., 424; Loudon Ency., 726; Am. Disp., 25; Wittstein, 3, 140; Chem. Carb. Comp., 487; Am. Hom. Phar., 319; Clapp Cat., 800; Allen Ency., 6, 366; Gray Flora N. A., 363; Gray Man., 265.

Tanacetum vulgare, 86.

Am. Jour. Phar., 1882, 288, 493; Am. Nat., 13, 572; Raf. Med. Flor., 2, 266; Flor. Med., 2, **ct. 131**, 132; Woodv. Med. Bot., 1, **t. 27**, 66; Williams Med. Bot. Mass., 896; Porch. Resourc. South., 425; London Ency., **f. 11680**, 696; Therap. Gaz., 1885, 215, 342; Allen Ency., 9, 503; Gray Man., 266; Clapp Cat., 800; Gray Flora N. A., 366; Torr. Bot. S. N. Y., 1, 393; Chap. Bot., 242; Wood Bot., 458; Lindl. Flor. Med., 464; Lindl. Med. Bot., 229; Thom. Org. Chem., 478; Am. Disp., 823; U. S. Phar., 331; Am. Hom. Phar., 432; Griff. Med. Bot., 406.

Artemisia vulgaris, 87.

Griff. Med. Bot., 406; Torr. Bot. S. N. Y., 1, 395; Woodv. Med. Bot., 1, **t. 23**, 57; Wiegand **rf.** 71; Loudon Ency., 698; Am. Hom. Phar., 101; Gray Man., 267; Allen Ency., 1, 558; Gray Flora N. A., 372.

Artemisia Absinthium, 88.

Griff. Med. Bot., 405; Raf. Med. Flor., 2, 183; Flor. Med., 1, **cf. 38**, 96; Bent. and Trim., 3, **ct. 156**; Lindl. Med. Bot., **f. 308**, 230; Woodv. Med. Bot., **t. 22**, 54; Am. Jour. Phar., 1882, 310; New Rem., 11, 64; Darl. Am. Weeds, 190; Williams Med. Bot. Mass., 895; Loudon Ency., 698; Therap. Gaz., 1886, 239; Taylor Tox., 651; Allen Ency., 1, 2; 10, 242; Clapp Cat., 802; Gray Man., 267; Am. Hom. Phar., 31; U. S. Phar., 1; Wittstein, 2; Chem. Carb. Comp., 218; Lindl. Flor. Med., 464; Am. Disp., 135; Thom. Org. Chem., 864; Gray Flora N. A., 370.

Gnaphalium polycephalum, 89.

Raf. Med. Flor., 2, 224; Williams Med. Bot. Mass., 894; Darl. Am. Weeds, 191; Porch. Resourc. South., 426; Therap. Gaz., 1884, 547; Am. Hom. Phar., 237; Gray Flora N. A., 234; Am. Disp., 399; Allen Ency., 4, 456; Torr. Bot. S. N. Y., 1, 396; Gray Man., 268; Wood Bot., 461; Chap. Bot., 243; Hale New Rem., 331; Clapp Cat., 802.

Erechthites hieracifolia, 90.

Am. Jour. Phar., 1883, 372; 1885, 107; Darl. Am. Weeds, 191; Man. Weeds, 50; Hale New Rem., 278; Allen Ency., 4, 210; Am. Hom. Phar., 211; Am. Disp., 342; Chap. Bot., 244; Wood Bot., 462; Gray Man., 270; Gray Flora N. A., 398; Torr. Bot. S. N. Y., 1, 400; Clapp Cat., 803.

Senecio aureus, 91.

Raf. Med. Flor., 2, 262; Darl. Am. Weeds, 193; Porch. Resourc. South., 427; Torr. Bot. S. N. Y., 1, 402; Gray Man., 271; Allen Ency., 8, 582; Gray Flora N. A., 391; Am. Disp., 767; Hale New Rem., 578; Hughes Phar., 692; Am. Hom. Phar., 408; Clapp Cat., 803; Loudon Ency., 706.

Lappa officinalis, 92.

Raf. Med. Flor., 2, 195; Griff. Med. Bot., 411; Flor. Med., 2, **ct. 138**, 152; Strong Am. Flora, 1, **ct. 14**, 33; Lindl. Med. Bot., **f. 313**, 233; Woodv. Med. Bot., 1, **t. 13**, 32; Williams Med. Bot. Mass., 893; Darl. Am. Weeds, 209; Wiegand, **rf.** 73; Therap. Gaz., 1884, 552; Good Bot., **ct. 11**; Am. Jour. Phar., 1885, 127; Loudon Ency., **f. 11345**, 680; Man. Weeds, 59; Allen Ency., 10, 571; Hale New Rem., 55; Gray Flora N. A., 397; Gray Man., 275; Am. Disp., 126; Torr. Bot. S. N. Y., 1, 408; Am. Hom. Phar., 91; U. S. Phar., 189.

Cichorium Intybus, 93.

Raf. Flor. Med., 2, 208; Griff. Med. Bot., **ff. 179**, 388; Strong Am. Flora, 1, **cf. 44**, 95; Lindl. Med. Bot., **r.** and **ff. 314**, 235; Woodv. Med. Bot., 1, **t. 29**, 70; Darl. Am. Weeds, **f. 135-6**, 201; Porch. Resourc. South., 431; Wiegand, **rf.** 76; Loudon Ency., **f. 11336**, 678; Torr. Bot. S. N. Y., 1, 411; Am. Disp., 226; Clapp Cat., 805; Gray Man., 275; Gray Flora N. A., 412; Allen Ency., 3, 181.

Prenanthes Serpentaria, 94.

Am. Jour. Phar., 1886, 117; Am. Hom. Phar., 327; Allen Ency., 6, 444; Gray Man., 278; Torr. Bot. S. N. Y., 1, 415; Raf. Med. Flor., 2, 253; Gray Flora N. A., 434; Clapp Cat., 806; Wood Bot., 472; Chap. Bot., 251; Am. Disp., 543.

Taraxacum Dens-Leonis, 95.

Church. Med. Bot., **ct. 5**; Raf. Med. Flor., 2, **f. 58**, 18; Griff. Med. Bot., **f. 186**, 414; Flor. Med., 1, **ct. 23**, 59; Strong Am. Flora, **ct. 3**, 9; Hamilt. Flor. Hom., 2, **ct. 62**, 198; Bent. and Trim., 3, **ct. 159**; Woodv. Med. Bot., 1, **t. 16**, 39; Williams Med. Bot. Mass., 893; Porch. Pl. S. C., 799; Darl. Am. Weeds, **f. 137-40**, 204; Porch. Resourc. South., 428; Wiegand, **rf.** 75; Clapp Cat., 806; Gray Flora N. A., 440; Wittstein, 112; Chem. Carb. Comp., 278; Fluck. and Han., 392; Lindl. Med. Bot., 234; Darl. Ag. Bot., 99; Hughes Phar., 738; Allen Ency., 9, 539; Lindl. Flor. Med., 469; King Am. Disp., 928; Am. Disp., 824; Torr. Bot. S. N. Y., 1, 417; Gray Man., 280; U. S. Phar., 331; Am. Hom. Phar., 432; Loudon Ency., **f. 11154**, 690.

Lactuca Canadensis, 96.

Am. Jour. Phar., 1883, 593; Raf. Med. Flor.,

1, **ct. 17**, 203; Good Bot., **ct. 14**; Loudon Ency., **f. 4916**, 286; Jour. Mat. Med., 1, 329; Allen Ency., 8, 155; Griff. Med. Bot., 434; Lindl. Flor. Med., 394; Lindl. Med. Bot., 193; U. S. Phar., 271; Am. Disp., 677; Torr. Bot. S. N. Y., 2, 3; Chap. Bot., 270; Wood Bot., 498; Gray Bot., 307; Brock. Essay, 160.

Plantago major, 107.

Sci. Am. Suppl., 1883, 6627; Woodv. Med. Bot., 1, **t. 33**, 81; Williams Med. Bot. Mass., 892; Darl. Am. Weeds, **f. 148**, 218; Porch. Resourc. South., 436; Loudon Ency., 96; Raf. Med. Flor., 2, 252; Am. Hom. Phar., 370; Hale New Rem., 497; Gray Bot. Text., 441; Lindl. Flor. Med., 473; Torr. Bot. S. N. Y., 2, 14; Gray Flora, 388; Am. Disp., 651; Fluck. and Han., 490; Clapp Cat., 820; Gray Man., 310.

Anagallis arvensis, 108.

Church Med. Bot., **ct. 16**; Lindl. Med. Bot., **f. 269**, 198; Torr. Bot., S. N. Y., 2, 12; Porch. Resourc. South., 384; Loudon Ency., 128; Gray Flora, 62; Gray Man., 316; Am. Disp., 106; Allen Ency., 329; Am. Hom. Phar., 78; Wittstein, 62; Chem. Carb. Comp., 466.

Catalpa Bignonioides, 109.

Bot. Gaz., 1880, 70; 1883, 191; Raf. Med. Flor., 2, 205; Porch. Resourc. South., 460, 45; Allen Ency., 10, 453; Clapp Cat., 823; Torr. Bot. S. N. Y., 2, 25; Gray Man., 321; Wood Bot, 513; Chap. Bot., 285.

Verbascum Thapsus, 110.

Am. Jour. Phar., 1883, 267; Sci. Am. Suppl., 1883, 6625; Raf. Med. Flor., 273; Hamilt. Flor. Hom., 2, **ct. 66**, 218; Lindl. Med. Bot., **f.** and **sf. 293**, 216; Woodv. Med. Bot., 2, **t. 75**, 202; Williams Med. Bot. Mass., 902; Darl. Am. Weeds, 224; Porch. Resourc. South., 463; Gray Man., 325; Gray Flora, 250; Allen Ency., 10, 114; Griff. Med. Bot., 517; Clapp Cat., 824; Lindl. Flor. Med., 507; Torr. Bot. S. N. Y., 2, 30; Am. Hom. Phar., 450; Loudon Ency., 132; Man. Weeds, 64; Hughes Phar., 766; Am. Disp., 855.

Linaria vulgaris, 111.

Lindl. Med. Bot., **ff. sf. 290**, 214; Woodv. Med. Bot., 2, **t. 136**, 371; Darl. Am. Weeds, **f. 150**, 225; Wiegand, 226; Torr. Bot. S. N. Y., 2, 32; Gray Bot., 326; Clapp Cat., 825; Lindl. Flor. Med., 505; Raf. Med. Flor., 2, 238; Gray Flora, 251; Loudon Ency., 526; Allen Ency., 5, 587.

Scrophularia nodosa, 112.

Bull. Torr. Club, 1881, 133; Raf. Med. Flor., 2, 262; Lindl. Med. Bot., **ff. 289**, 214; Porch. Resourc. South., 465; Am. Disp., 757; King Am. Disp., 854; Griff. Med. Bot., 518; Am. Hom. Phar., 405; Wittstein, 202; Lindl. Flor. Med., 503; Williams Med. Bot. Mass., 326; Torr. Bot. S. N. Y., 2, 31; Gray Flor.,

258; Gray Man., 327; Wood Bot., 520; Chap. Bot., 289; Allen Ency., 8, 546.

Chelone glabra, 113.

Griff. Med. Bot., **f. 224**, 519; Raf. Med. Flor., 2, **f. 97**, 117; Strong Am. Flora, 1, **cf. 54**, 111; Williams Med. Bot. Mass., 900; Porch. Resourc. South., 465; Loudon Ency., 516; Gray Man., 327; Hale New Rem., 198; Chap. Bot., 289; Wood Bot., 520; Torr. Bot. S. N. Y., 2, 34.

Veronica Virginica, 114.

Bent. and Trim., 3, **ct. 196**; Porch. Resourc. South., 467; Loudon Ency., 14; Jour. Mat. Med., 2, 155; Allen Ency., 5, 556; Am. Hom. Phar., 289; Gray Man., 332; Torr. Bot. S. N. Y., 2, 44; Gray Flora, 286; Am. Disp., 479; U. S. Phar., 199; Clapp Cat., 827; Hughes Phar., 500; Raf. Med. Flor., 2, **f. 57**, 20.

Euphrasia officinalis, 115.

Hamilt. Flor. Hom., 1, **ct. 33**, 275; Woodv. Med. Bot., 2, **t. 135**, 368; Loudon Ency., **f. 8753**, 526; Allen Ency., 4, 254; Am. Hom. Phar., 218; Am. Disp., 358; Gray Flora, 305; Wood Bot., 533; Lindl. Med. Bot., 215; Griff. Med. Bot., 617; Lindl. Flor. Med., 506; Gray Man., 336; Wittstein, 81.

Mentha piperita, 116.

Am. Jour. Phar., 1882, 70, 77, 83; 1885, 429, 484, 515, 600; Flor. Med., **ct. 61**, 164; Bent. and Trim., 3, **ct. 203**; Chap. Bot., 313; Woodv. Med. Bot., 2, **t. 120**, 336; Darl. Am. Weeds, 231; Porch. Resourc. South., 440; Wiegand, 217; Loudon Ency., **f. 8229**, 500; Gray Flora, 352; Allen Ency., 6, 180; Gray Man., 344; Torr. Bot. S. N. Y., 2, 56; Am. Disp., 523; Fluck. and Han., 481; Lindl. Flor. Med., 487; Griff. Med. Bot., 502; Am. Hom. Phar., 306; U. S. Phar., 221; Lindl. Med. Bot., 218; Wittstein, 152; Chem. Carb. Comp., 305.

Lycopus Virginicus, 117.

Griff. Med. Bot., **f. 219**, 505; Raf. Flor. Med., 2, **f. 61**, 26; Williams Med. Bot. Mass., 902; Porch. Resourc. South., 441; Loudon Ency., 20; Jour. Mat. Med., 1, 326; Allen Ency., 6, 69; Gray Man., 345; U. S. Phar., 444; Am. Hom. Phar., 295; Am. Disp., 494; Torr. Bot. S. N. Y., 2, 57; Clapp Cat., 829; Gray Flora, 353.

Hedeoma pulegioides, 118.

Griff. Med. Bot., **f. 220**, 508; Raf. Med. Flor., 1, **f. 46**, 231; Flor. Med., 1, **ct. 62**, 166; Bart. Med. Bot., 2, **ct. 41**, 165; Bent. and Trim., 3, **ct. 200**; Williams Med. Bot. Mass., 902; Darl. Am. Weeds, 232; Porch. Resourc. South., 446; Loudon Ency., 20; Wood Bot., 544; Allen Ency., 4, 543; Lindl. Flor. Med., 491; Torr. Bot. S. N. Y., 2, 66; Gray Man., 250; Clapp Cat., 801; Am. Hom. Phar., 245;

Taylor Tox., 766; U. S. Phar., 331; Gray Flora N. A., 1, 251; Chem. Carb. Comp., 138, 154; Allen Ency., 7, 1; 9, 467; Hughes Phar., 735; King Am. Disp., 626; Am. Hom. Phar., 431; Darl. Am. Weeds, **ff. 167**, 259; Wigand, 215; Bart. Flora, **ct. 25** (Rustica), 91; Loudon Encyc., **f. 2193**, 136.

Menyanthes trifoliata, 129.

Bot. Gaz., 1882, 147; Griff. Med. Bot., **f. 209**, 464; Raf. Med. Flor., 2, 33, 63 (M. Verna); Flora Med., 2, **ct. 85**, 5; Bigel. Am. Bot., 3, **ct. 46**, 55; Bent. and Trim., **ct. 184**; Lindl. Med. Bot., **f. 266**, 196; Woodv. Med. Bot., 2, **t. 97**, 277; Williams Med. Bot. Mass., 899; Wiegand, 213; Loudon Ency., **f. 2080**, 130; Therap. Gaz., 1885, 274; Jour. Mat. Med., 2, 90; Gray Man., 390; Thom. Org. Chem., 660, 861; Hughes Phar., 516; Chem. Carb. Comp., 466; Wittstein, 130; J. and G. Phar., 130; Am. Disp., 525; Lindl. Flor. Med., 523; Am. Hom. Phar., 307; Torr. Bot. S. N. Y., 2, 114; Allen Ency., 6, 182.

Gelsemium sempervirens, 130.

Am. Jour. Phar., 1882, 337; 1883, 256; Bent. and Trim., 3, **ct. 181**; Porch. Resourc. South., 461; Gray Man., 391; Porch. Pl. S. C., 812; Clapp Cat., 824; Raf. Med. Flor., 2, 223; U. S. Phar., 169; King Am. Disp., 436; Am. Hom. Phar., 232; Wittstein, 89; Allen Ency., 4, 385; Gray Flora N. A., 1, 107; Taylor Tox., 487–8; Fluck. and Han., 541; Hughes Phar., 61; Allen Ency., 19, 529; Smithson. Inst., 258, 662; Am. Disp., 378; Hale New Rem., 320; Hughes Phar., 372; Gray Bot. Text., 430; Therap. Gaz., 1884, 548; Loudon Ency., **f. 2451**, 154.

Spigelia Marilandica, 131.

Am. Jour. Phar., 1879, 398; 1883, 631; 1884, 570; Church. Med. Bot., **ct. 7**; Griff. Med. Bot., **f. 210**, 466; Raf. Med. Flor., **f. 87**, 89; Flor. Med., 1, **ct. 19**, 51; Hamilton Flor. Hom., 1, **cf. 45**, 93; Bigel. Am. Med. Bot., 1, **ct. 14**, 142; Bent. and Trim., 3, **ct. 180**; Thompson Exp. Disp.; Woodv. Med. Bot., 1, **t. 69**, 178; Darl. Am. Weeds. **f. 115**, 165; Porch. Resourc. South., 481; Bart. Med. Bot., 2, **ct. 31**, 75; Loudon Ency., **f. 2173**, 134; Jour. Mat. Med., 2, 373; Allen Ency., 9, 94; Gray Man., 392; Chap. Bot., 182; Wood Bot., 515; U. S. Phar., 304; Clapp Cat., 788; Lindl. Flor. Med., 524; Am. Disp., 799; Fluck. and Han., 433; Gray Flora, 108; Lindl. Med. Bot., 193.

Apocynum androsæmifolium, 132.

Griff. Med. Bot., **f. 200**, 449; Raf. Med. Flor., 1, **f. 7**, 49; Bigel. Am. Med. Bot., 2, **ct. 46**, 148; Torr. Bot. S. N. Y., 116; Williams Med. Bot. Mass., 898; Porch. Resourc. South., 454; Lindl. Flor. Med., 534; Clapp Cat., 845;

Porch. Cat. Pl. S. C., 827; Gray Bot. Text., **f. 950–4**, 455; Am. Hom. Phar., 87; Loudon Ency., **f. 3200**, 194; Gray Flora, 82; Gray Man., 393; Am. Disp., 113; Am. Disp. Suppl., **t. 3**, 39; Allen Ency., 1, 424.

Apocynum cannabinum, 133.

Griff. Med. Bot., **f. 201**, 450; Torr. Bot. S. N. Y., 2, 117; Williams Med. Bot. Mass., 898; Porch. Resourc. South., 483; Raf. Med. Flor., 1, 51; Gray Man., 394; Lindl. Flor. Med., 535; Clapp Cat., 846; Porch. Pl. S. C., 826; U. S. Phar., 40; King Am. Disp., 114; Hale New Rem., 45; Gray Bot. Text., 455; Am. Hom. Phar., 88; Allen Ency., 1, 425; Gray Flora, 83; Am. Disp., 114; Am. Disp. Suppl., **t. 4**, 40; Hughes Phar., 776; Loudon Ency., 194.

Asclepias cornuti, 134.

Am. Jour. Phar., 1881, 433; Torr. Bot. S. N. Y., 2, 119; Williams Med. Bot. Mass., 898; Darl. Am. Weeds, **f. 168–70**, 262; Loudon Ency., 196; Gray Flora, 91; Gray Man., 395; Am. Disp., 141; Porch. Resourc. South., 388; Am. Hom. Phar., 105; Allen Ency., 1, 590; Hale New Rem., 64.

Asclepias tuberosa, 135.

Am. Jour. Phar., 1882, 5; Therap. Gaz., 1885, 328; Loudon Ency., 198; Gray Man., 397; Gray Flora, 89; Torr. Bot. S. N. Y., 2, 123; Williams Med. Bot. Mass., 898; Darl. Am. Weeds, 263; Porch. Resourc. South., 487; Griff. Med. Bot., **f. 203**, 454; Raf. Med. Flor., **f. 13**, 74, 263; Bigel. Am. Med. Bot., 2, **ct. 26**, 59; Barton Mat. Med., **ct. 22**, 239; Am. Disp., 142; Hale New Rem., 59; Am. Hom. Phar., 105; Clapp Cat., 847; U. S. Phar., 49; Lindl. Med. Bot., **ff. 278**, 206; Lindl. Flor. Med., 539; Allen Ency., 1, 591.

Chionanthus Virginica, 136.

Raf. Med. Flor., 2, 208; Darl. Am. Weeds, 266; Porch. Resourc. South., 494; Loudon Ency., 12; Allen Ency., 10, 403; Gray Man., 401; Griff. Med. Bot., 441; Clapp Cat., 849; Am. Hom. Phar., 170; Hale New Rem., 209; Gray Flora, 77; Chap. Bot., 369.

Fraxinus Americana, 137.

Am. Jour. Phar., 1882, 99, 282; 1883, 371; 1886, 117, 370; Torr. Bot. S. N. Y., **t. 89**, 125; Darl. Am. Weeds, 266; Porch. Resourc. South., 494; Loudon Ency., **f. 14329**, 868; Gray Man., 401; Univ. Wis. Dept. Phar. F. B. Powers, 19; Allen Ency., 4, 368; Chap. Bot., 369; Am. Disp., 367; Gray Flora, 74; Wood Bot., 597.

Aristolochia Serpentaria, 138.

Griff. Med. Bot., **f. 228**, 529, 531; Raf. Med. Flor., 1, **f. 10**, 61; Flora Med., 2, **ct. 171**, 243; Bigel. Am. Med. Bot., 3, **ct. 49**, 82; Bent. and Trim., 4, **ct. 246**; Lindl. Med. Bot., **l. and ff.**

Stillingia sylvatica, 151.

Am. Jour. Phar., 1882, 386; 1885, 529; Raf. Med. Flor., 2, 266; Bent. and Trim., 4, **ct. 241**; Porch. Resourc. South., 121; Gray Man., 436; Chap. Bot.,404; Wood Bot., 629; Allen Ency., 9, 169; Am. Disp., 810; Clapp Cat., 863; U. S. Phar., 312; Am. Hom. Phar., 421.

Celtis occidentalis, 152.

Raf. Med. Flor., 2, 206; Darl. Am. Weeds, **f. 184–5**, 293; Porch. Resourc. South., 312; Loudon Ency., **f. 14297**, 864; Allen Ency., 10, 456; Gray Man., 443; Torr. Bot. S. N. Y., 2, 167.

Urtica urens, 153.

Am. Jour. Phar., 1883, 98; Woodv. Med. Bot., 4, **t. 241**, 708; Darl. Am. Weeds, **f. 187–9**, 298; Porch. Resourc. South., 269; Loudon Ency., **f. 13226**, 784; Gray Man., 444; Torr. Bot. S. N. Y., 2, 222; Chap. Bot., 412; Wood Bot., 636; Am. Hom. Phar., 445; Am. Disp. Suppl., 7; Am. Disp., 842; Allen Ency., 10, 47; Hale New Rem., 633.

Cannabis sativa, 154.

Raf. Med. Flor., 2, 203; Griff. Med. Bot., **f. 248**, 573; Hamilt. Flor. Hom., 1, **ct. 15**, 134; Bent. and Trim., 4, **ct. 231**; Lindl. Med. Bot., **ff. 116, a.b.**, 77; Porch. Resourc. South., 273; Loudon Ency., **f. 13908**, 834; Am. Jour. Phar., 1885, 264, 388; Therap. Gaz., 1885, 329; Taylor Tox., 651; Allen Ency., 2, 492; Am. Hom. Phar., 197; U. S. Phar., 64; Gray Man., 446; Lindl. Flor. Med., 279.

Humulus lupulus, 155.

Ag. Rep. U. S., 1864, 103; Am. Jour. Phar., 1879, 27; 1884, 427; 1885, 323; Jour. Mat. Med., 4, 310; Therap. Gaz., 1886, 233; Griff. Med. Bot., **f. 249**, 574; Raf. Med. Flor., 1, **f. 50**, 246; Flor. Med., 2, **ct. 112**, 80; Strong Am. Flor., 2, **ct. 47**, 167; Bigel. Am. Med. Bot., 3, **t. 60**, 163; Bent. and Trim., 4, **ct. 230**; Lindl. Med. Bot., **sf. 117**, 77; Williams Med., Bot. Mass., 887; Darl. Am. Weeds, **f. 190–94**, 300; Porch. Resourc. South., 275; Loudon Ency., **f. 13909**, 834; Allen Ency., 5, 625; Am. Hom. Phar., 293; Torr. Bot. S. N. Y., 2, 225; Am. Disp., 429; Thom. Org. Chem., 918; Wittstein, 123, 151, 219; Fluck. and Han., 551; U. S. Phar., 175, 211; Lindl. Flor. Med., 296; Gray Man., 446.

Juglans cinerea, 156.

Am. Jour. Phar., 1879, 456, 542; Raf. Med. Flor., 2, 23; Bigel. Am. Med. Bot., 2, **t. 32**, 115; Bent. and Trim., 4, **ct. 247**; Williams Med. Bot. Mass., 920; Darl. Am. Weeds, 303; Porch. Resourc. South., 317; Gray Man., 447; Torr. Bot. S. N. Y., 2, 180; Allen Ency., 5, 193; Am. Hom. Phar., 263; Porch. Pl. S. C., 760; Clapp Cat., 864; Lindl. Flor. Med., 307; Griff. Med. Bot., 589; U. S. Phar., 188; King

Am. Disp., 528; Gray Bot. Text., 471; Hale New Rem., 380; Darl. Ag. Bot., 155; Am. Disp., 460; Loudon Ency., **f. 13377**, 794.

Carya alba, 157.

Am. Jour. Phar., 1879, 542; Darl. Am. Weeds, 304; Porch. Resourc. South., 322; Allen Ency., 3, 17; Gray Man., 448; Torr. Bot. S. N. Y., 2, 181; Am. Hom. Phar., 154.

Castanea vesca, var. Americana, 158.

Am. Jour. Phar., 1880, 292; Bot. Gaz.,1880, 70; 1881, 159; Raf. Med. Flor., 2, 205; Lindl. Med. Bot., **f. 138**, 91; Torr. Bot. S. N. Y., 2, **t. 111**, 195; Williams Med. Bot. Mass., 918; Darl. Am. Weeds, 318; Porch. Resourc. South., 238; Loudon Ency., **f. 13361**, 792; Gray Man., 455; Allen Ency., 3, 21; Am. Hom. Phar., 153; U. S. Phar., 68.

Ostrya Virginica, 159.

Torr. Bot. S. N. Y., 2, **t. 102**, 185; Allen Ency., 7, 249; Gray Man., 456; Am. Hom. Phar., 356; Loudon Ency., 792; Am. Disp., 592; King Am. Disp., 675; Porch. Resourc. South., 233; Darl. Am. Weeds, 323.

Myrica cerifera, 160.

Bigel. Am. Med. Bot., 3, **ct. 43**, 32; Williams Med. Bot. Mass.,925; Darl. Am. Weeds, 324; Porch. Resourc. South., 312; Loudon Ency., 830; New Rem., 1879, 326; Jour. Mat. Med., 1, 259; Allen Ency., 6, 432; Gray Man., 457; Porch. Pl. S. C., 759; Clapp Cat., 868; Am. Disp., 535; Thom. Org. Chem., 446; Torr. Bot. S. N. Y., 2, 197; Am. Hom. Phar., 326; Lindl. Flor. Med., 305; Griff. Med. Bot., 583; Chap. Bot., 426; Wittstein, 134, 166; Hale New Rem., 445.

Salix purpurea, 161.

Am. Jour. Phar., 1883, 199; 1882, 22; Jour. Mat. Med.., 2, 166; Lindl. Med. Bot., **lf. 115**, 75; Porch. Resourc. South., 335; Loudon Ency., **f. 13727**, 822; Allen Ency., 8, 475; Thom. Org. Chem., 239; Chem. Carb. Comp., 460; Wittstein, 198; Am. Hom. Phar., 398; Lindl. Flor. Med., 318; U. S Phar., 286; Gray Man., 463.

Populus tremuloides, 162.

New Rem., 1879, 235; Williams Med. Bot. Mass., 910; Darl. Am. Weeds, 330; Loudon Ency., **f. 13961**, 840; Am. Jour. Phar., 1884, 618; Jour. Mat. Med., 2, 364; Gray Man., 466; Torr. Bot. S. N. Y., 2, 214; Am. Hom. Phar., 378; Hale New Rem., 524; Raf. Med. Flor., 2, 252; Griff. Med. Bot., 582; Am. Disp., 635; Thom. Org. Chem., 766, 810; Wittstein, 177, 156; Chem. Carb. Comp., 460; Lindl. Flor. Med., 320; Allen Ency., 8, 154.

Abies nigra, 163.

Griff. Med. Bot., 606; Torr. Bot. S. N. Y., 2, 230; Peck's Bl'k Spruce; Williams Med. Bot. Mass., 921; Darl. Am. Weeds, 338;

Porch. Resourc. South., 507; Am. Hom. Phar., 30; Gray Man., 471; Allen Ency., 1, 2; Raf. Med. Flor., 2, 182; King Am. Disp., 19; Lindl. Med. Bot., 67; Loudon Ency., **f. 13533**, 806.

Abies Canadensis, 164.

Griff. Med. Bot., 606; Bent. and Trim., 4, **ct. 264**; Torr. Bot. S. N. Y., 2, 230; Williams Med. Bot. Mass., 820; Darl. Am. Weeds, 237; Porch. Resourc. South., 506; Gray Man., 471; Clapp Cat., 874; Porch. Pl. S. C., 831; U. S. Phar., 258; Allen Ency., 1, 1; Am. Hom. Phar., 29; Hale New Rem., 17; Gray Bot. Text., **f. 395–401**, 307; Fluck. and Han., 612; King Am. Disp., 15; Loudon Ency., **f. 13527**, 804.

Thuja occidentalis, 165.

Am. Jour. Phar., 1883, 163; Hamilt. Flor. Hom., 2, **ct. 63**, 202; Williams Med. Bot. Mass., 922; Darl. Am. Weeds, 340; Porch. Resourc. South., 507; Torr. Bot. S. N. Y., 2, 233; Gray Man., 472; Raf. Med. Flor., 2, 263; Clapp Cat., 875; Griff. Med. Bot., 1, 609; U. S. Phar., 332; Allen Ency., 9, 596; Am. Hom. Phar., 439; Am. Disp., 830; Dougel. New Rem., 474; Loudon Ency., **f. 13548**, 806.

Juniperus Virginiana, 166.

Bigel. Am. Med. Bot., 3, **ct. 45**, 49; Darl. Am. Weeds, 342; Porch. Resourc. South., 510; Am. Jour. Phar., 1884, 619; Loudon Ency., **f. 14056**, 848; Allen Ency., 5, 507; Gray Man., 473; Torr. Bot. S. N. Y., 2, 235; Wittstein, 151; Fluck. and Han.; 628; Am. Disp., 464; Lindl. Flora Med., 609.

Arisæma triphyllum, 167.

Griff. Med. Bot., **f. 276**, 616; Raf. Med. Flor., 1, **f. 11**, 66; Strong Am. Flora, 2, **ct. 12**, figures *A. Maculatum*, 35; Bigel. Am. Med. Bot., 1, **ct. 4**, 52; Torr. Bot. S. N. Y., 2, 239; Williams Med. Bot. Mass., 909; Porch. Resourc. South., 540; Gray Man., 475; Allen Ency., 1, 561; Darl. Am. Weeds, 345; Lindl. Flor. Med., 601; Clapp Cat., 877; King Am. Disp. 140; Am. Hom. Phar., 102; Loudon Ency., **f. 13465**, 800.

Arisæma dracontium, 168.

Torr. Bot. S. N. Y., 2, **t. 123**, 240; Williams Med. Bot. Mass., 909; Loudon Ency., **f. 13463**, 800; Gray Man., 476; Allen Ency., 10, 363.

Symplocarpus fœtidus, 169.

Raf. Med. Flor., 230; Bigel. Am. Med. Bot., 2, **ct. 24**, 43; Williams Med. Bot. Mass., 909; Darl. Am. Weeds, 345; Porch. Resourc. South., 544; Barton Mat. Med., **ct. 10**, 123; Good Bot., **ct. 20**; Loudon Ency., **f. 1504**, 88; Allen Ency., 8, 154; Gray Man., 477; Am. Hom. Phar., 206; Am. Disp., 820.

Cypripedium pubescens, 170.

Gray Man., 512; Griff. Med. Bot., **f. 298**, 640; Raf. Med. Flor., 1, **f. 30**, 140; Williams Med. Bot. Mass., 906; Porcher. Resourc. South., 425; U. S. Phar., 90; Am. Hom. Phar., 201; Torr. Bot. S. N. Y., 2, 286; Fluck. and Han., 79; King Am. Disp., 375; Am. Disp., 319; Clapp Cat., 880; Loudon Ency., 766; Hale New Rem., 254.

Lachnanthes tinctoria, 171.

Porch. Resourc. South., 522; Allen Ency., 5, 471; Gray Man., 514; Am. Disp., 472; Clapp Cat., 882; Am. Hom. Phar., 284; Loudon Ency., **f. 751**, 44.

Aletris farinosa, 172.

Griff. Med. Bot., **f. 280**, 623; Raf. Med. Flor., 1, **f. 4**, 37; Strong Am. Flor., 1, **cf. 29** (a poor representation of *Helonias*), 67; Bigel. Am. Med. Bot., 3, **t. 50**, 92; Torr. Bot. S. N. Y., 2, 310; Porch. Resourc. South., 532; Loudon Ency., **f. 4533**, 268; Jour. Mat. Med., 2, 130; Allen Ency., 1, 146; Gray Man., 515; Am. Disp., 78; Am. Disp. Suppl., **t. 1**, 23; Hale New Rem., 39; Lindl. Flor. Med., 590; Am. Hom. Phar., 61.

Iris versicolor, 173.

Am. Jour. Phar., 1881, 601; Raf. Med. Flor., 2, 232; Bigel. Am. Med. Bot., 1, **ct. 16**, 155; Porch. Resourc. South., 523; Loudon Ency., **f. 778**, 44; Gray Man., 516; U. S. Phar., 187; Am. Disp., 456; Lindl. Flor. Med., 575; Griff. Med. Bot., 625; Am. Hom. Phar., 260; Allen Ency., 5, 153.

Dioscorea villosa, 174.

Raf. Med. Flor., 2, 217; Porch. Resourc. South., 539; Loudon Ency., **f. 13955**, 838; Allen Ency., 4, 123; Gray Man., 518; Chap. Bot., 474; Mood. Bot., 701; Am. Disp. Suppl., **t. 7**, 81; Am. Disp., 235; Griff. Med. Bot., 659; Am. Hom. Phar., 204; Torr. Bot. S. N. Y., 2, 293; Hughes Phar., 351; Hale New Rem., 258.

Trillium pendulum, 175.

Griff. Med. Bot., **f. 301**, 646; Raf. Med. Flor., 2, **f. 91**, 96; Williams Med. Bot. Mass., 908; Am. Disp., 833; Hale's New Rem., 628; Torr. Bot. S. N. Y., 2, 295; Am. Hom. Phar., 442; Gray Man., 523; Clapp Cat., 885; Allen Ency., 10, 637; King Am. Disp., 937; Loudon Ency., **f. 4974**, 290.

Veratrum viride, 176.

Am. Jour. Phar., 1879, 337, 368; 1882, 491; 1883, 262; New Rem., 1879, 302, 303; Raf. Med. Flor., 2, 273; Bigel. Am. Med. Bot., 2, **t. 33**, 121; Bent. and Trim., 4, **ct. 286**; Williams Med. Bot. Mass., 907; Porch. Resourc. South., 528; Loudon Ency., **f. 14204**, 858; Gray Man., 525; Percy Essay; Clapp Cat., 890; Griff. Med. Bot., 644; Torr. Bot. S. N. Y., 2,

317 ; Am. Hom. Phar., 449 ; Fluck. and Han., 695 ; U. S. Phar., 374 ; Am. Disp., 852 ; Allen Ency., 10, 95 ; Hughes Phar., 764.

Chamælirium luteum, 177.

Raf. Med. Flor., 2, 182 ; Williams Med. Bot. Mass., 907 ; Porcher Resourc. South., 527 ; Lindl. Flor. Med., 588 ; Jour. Mat. Med., 2, 122, 296 ; Allen Ency., 4, 565 ; Am. Disp., 418 ; Am. Disp. Suppl., **t. 6**, 63 ; Clapp Cat., 891 ; Torr. Bot. S. N. Y., 2, 318 ; Gray Man., 527 ; Am. Hom. Phar., 247.

Lilium superbum, 178.

Loudon Ency., 264 ; Allen Ency., 10, 572 ; Gray Man., 532 ; Torr. Bot. S. N. Y., 2, 305.

Equisetum hyemale, 179.

Raf. Med. Flor., 2, 217 ; Williams Med. Bot. Mass., 924 ; Porch. Resourc. South., 590 ; Gray Man., 655 ; Torr. Bot. S. N. Y., 2, 482 ; Allen Ency., 4, 204 ; Am. Hom. Phar., 210 ; Clapp Cat., 892 ; King Am. Disp., 397 ; Wiegand, 242 ; Lindl. Med. Bot., 22 ; Loudon Ency., **f. 14631**, 890.

Lycopodium clavatum, 180.

Am. Jour. Phar., 1882, 77 ; Raf. Med. Flor., 2, 240 ; Hamilt. Flor. Hom., 2, **ct. 41**, 28 ; Bent. and Trim., 4, **ct. 299;** Loudon Ency., **f. 14632**, 892 ; Gray Man., 674 ; Torr. Bot. S. N. Y., 2, 510 ; Wood Bot., 811 ; Lindl. Med. Bot., 23 ; Griff. Med. Bot., 671 ; Clapp Cat., 896 ; Fluck. and Han., 731 ; Lindl. Flor. Med., 621 ; U. S. Phar., 212 ; Allen Ency., 6, 1 ; Am. Hom. Phar., 294.

INDEX.

THERAPEUTIC INDEX

THE APPLICATION OF REMEDIES FOR THE CURE OF DISEASES

INDEX

FRENCH COMMON NAMES OF PLANTS

Absinthe 88
Actee à Grappé 11
Ailante 35
Alétris Farmeux 172
Ambrosie 82
Apalachine à Feuilles du
  Prunier 106
Arbre à Poison 38
Arbre a Suif 160
Argémone 20
Asclepiade a la Soie 134
  " Tubereuse 135
Asimmier 13
Aunee 81

B

Bardane 92
Baume de Cheval 119
Bec de Grue 32
Benoite Aquatique 54
Bois de Plomb 76, 146
Bonnet de Pretre 42
Bouillon-Blanc 110
Bourquepine 41
Bourse de Pasteur 25
Busserolle 100

C

Cédre de Virginie 166
Cephalanthe de Amerique 76
Chamomile Romaine 84
Chanvre 154
  " du Canada 133
Chasse Diable 30
Chataignier 158
Chélone 113
Chénopode Anthelmintique
  140
Chicorée Sauvage 93
Chionanthe 136
Cique d'Amerique 67
  " Ordinaire 68
Cohoche Bleu 16

Commune 26
Cornouile à Feuilles Ronde
  72
  " Soyeux 73
Cornuillier à Grandes Fleurs
  71
Couleuvrée de Virginie 138
Couronne de St. Jean 87
Cyperipede Jaune 170

D

Dent de Lion 95
Douce-Amere 124
Drosére à Feuilles Rondes 29

E

Ellébore Vert 8
Epine-Vinette 15
Erigéron de Canada 80
Eupatorie Perfoliée 79
Euphorbe à Grandes Fleurs
  148
  " Vomative 149
Euphrasie 115

F

Fusain 41

G

Genet des Teintuiers 46
Ginseng d'Amerique 70
Glaieul Bleu 173
Glouteron 92
Gouet à Dragon 168
  " à Trois Feuilles 167
Grande Cique 68
Grande Kalmie 103

H

Haricot 51
Helianthéme du Canada 28.
Hépatique 2
Herbe a Fièvre 79
  " a la Ouate 134
  " à l' Hirondelle 21

Herbe de Feu 90
  " de la Laque 139
  " de St. Antoine 59
  " de Ste. Christophe
    Blanc 10
  " Parfaite 79
  " St. Jean 30
Houblon 155
Hydrastis 9

I

Iguame Indigené 174
Immortelle le Cotonnière 89
Indigo Sauvage 52
  " Trèfle 52

J

Jasmin Jaune 130
Jusquiame Noir 126

L

Laitue Blanc 94
  " du Canada 96
La Nielle des Blés l' Ivraie 31
L'Anserine Vermifuge 140
La Petite Cique 65
Laurier Benzoin 145
Le Blé Noir 142
  " " Sarrasin 142
L'Endorme 127
L'Ortie 153
  " Blanche 121
Le Fraisier 55
Le Frene Blanc 137
Le Lisseron 123
Le Magnolier Glauque 12
Le Tourne Sol 83
Linaire Commune 111
Lobelie Cardinale 97
  " Enflée 99
  " Syphilitique 98
Lycope de Virginie 117
Lycopode Soufre Végétal 180

INDEX

OF

GERMAN COMMON NAMES OF PLANTS